Historical Dictionary
of the
1970s

Historical Dictionary
of the
1 9 7 0s

EDITED BY JAMES S. OLSON

Greenwood Press
Westport, Connecticut • London

Library of Congress Cataloging-in-Publication Data

Historical dictionary of the 1970s / edited by James S. Olson.
    p.   cm.
    Includes bibliographical references (p.   ) and index.
    ISBN 0–313–30543–9 (alk. paper)
    1. United States—History—1969– —Dictionaries. 2. Nineteen
seventies—Dictionaries. I. Olson, James Stuart, 1946– .
    E839.H57   1999
    973.924—dc21   98–46818

British Library Cataloguing in Publication Data is available.

Library of Congress Catalog Card Number: 98–46818
ISBN: 0–313–30543–9

First published in 1999

Greenwood Press, 88 Post Road West, Westport, CT 06881
An imprint of Greenwood Publishing Group, Inc.
www.greenwood.com

Printed in the United States of America

The paper used in this book complies with the
Permanent Paper Standard issued by the National
Information Standards Organization (Z39.48–1984).

10 9 8 7 6 5 4 3 2

Contents

Preface

Scholars will soon begin to write histories about the twentieth century. They will not find it difficult to identify the years of the Great Depression during the 1930s as the most trying in recent American history, and they will also probably identify the decade of the 1970s as a close second. The 1970s, when the country experienced a collective identity crisis, were difficult years for the United States. Not since the Civil War has the bedrock of American political culture been so shaken.

Traditionally, the American self-identity has revolved around four distinct but highly interrelated convictions. First, Americans have long been confident that their political system provides freedom and equality to every individual. Second, we have been equally convinced that the Founding Fathers created a political system that made the abuse of power extremely difficult. Third, we have long taken pride in the American economy and capitalism's ability to sustain permanent growth and prosperity. Finally, fourth, during the first half of the twentieth century, American policymakers assumed responsibility for maintaining freedom and prosperity around the world. Collectively, historians have characterized these four convictions as "Mission and Manifest Destiny."

The events of the 1970s sorely tested all these convictions. Women and minority groups called into question the belief that freedom and equality were the birthright of every American, and the civil rights movements of the 1970s argued that American history had been full of racism and violence against women and people of color. Watergate and the related scandals of Richard Nixon's administration badly damaged the country's faith in politicians and the political system. The Arab oil boycott, the energy crisis, the environmental movement, and years of stagflation raised unprecedented doubts about the future of the American economy. And in the jungles of Vietnam, many Americans began to doubt their responsibility, and even their ability, to police the world.

The Historical Dictionary of the 1970s provides brief essays about the prominent people, events, issues, and controversies of the decade, as well as the culture of the era. All unsigned entries are my own. Asterisks in the text indicate a cross-reference to another entry.

I wish to express appreciation to my contributing scholars and to the staff of the Newton Gresham Library at Sam Houston State University in Huntsville, Texas. I remain ever grateful to Cynthia Harris, my editor at Greenwood Publishing Group.

A

AARON, HENRY. On April 8, 1974, baseball player Henry Aaron broke what had been considered an unbreakable record in professional sports. The longtime right fielder for the Atlanta Braves, who had played his entire career with the team, swung at a pitch thrown by Los Angeles Dodgers' pitcher Al Downing and hit it over the left-field fence for his 715th career home run, breaking Babe Ruth's 714 career home run total. Tens of millions of Americans had tuned into the nationally televised game, hoping to watch history being made. They were not disappointed. On the negative side, Aaron's race for the record inspired a considerable amount of hate mail from racist fans, who did not want an African American to supplant Ruth. Surpassing Babe Ruth's record was a defining moment in Aaron's life because he learned just how deep racism runs in American society.

Aaron, who had started his career in the Negro Leagues, followed Jackie Robinson into the majors, where he soon established a reputation as being one of the game's greatest long-ball hitters. Aaron eventually raised his career total to 755 home runs before he retired in 1976. He also holds the lifetime record for runs batted in at 2,297, extra-base hits at 1,477, and total bases at 6,856.

After retiring, he took a front office job with the Braves as director of player development. He was later promoted to vice president of the organization. Since then, Aaron has campaigned actively for the hiring of more black managers and more black corporate officials in major league baseball.

SUGGESTED READINGS: Hank Aaron, *I Had a Hammer: The Hank Aaron Story*, 1991; *New York Times*, April 9–10, 1974; Richard Rennert, *Henry Aaron*, 1993.

ABBA. Abba, a Swedish rock group formed in 1971, included Benny Andersson, Bjorn Ulvaeus, Agnetha Faltskog, and Anni-Frid Synni-Lyngstad-Fredriksson-Andersson. They became stars on the European rock-and-roll circuit in the early 1970s with such hits as ''Fernando,'' ''Waterloo,'' ''Money-Money-

Money,'' and ''Knowing Me, Knowing You.'' Their first American tour in 1977 was a smash hit. ''Dancing Queen'' became the number one single on the pop charts in 1977, and ''Take a Chance on Me'' rose to number three in 1978. By 1982, when the group broke up because of death and kidnapping threats, Abba had sold nearly 100 million records, making them the most commercially successful rock group of the 1970s. They were also the most popular rock-and-roll band of the disco* era.

SUGGESTED READING: John Tobler, *ABBA Gold: The Complete Story*, 1993.

ABDUL-JABBAR, KAREEM. Kareem Abdul-Jabbar, the only child of Lewis and Cora Alcindor, was born in New York City on April 16, 1947. The Alcindors named their son Lewis Ferdinand Alcindor. Although the father had a degree in musicology from Juilliard, he made a living as a transit cop in New York City. Alcindor was raised in a middle-class housing project in the Inwood neighborhood of Manhattan. As a child he attended Saint Jude's, a Roman Catholic parochial school, and then Power Memorial Academy, a Catholic high school. Although Alcindor excelled at music and other academic subjects, basketball became the early focus in his life. Not only was he six feet, eight inches tall in the ninth grade, he was athletic and exhibited good judgment. Power Memorial became one of the country's premier high school basketball powers during Alcindor's years there.

In 1965 Coach John Wooden* recruited Alcindor to UCLA, where he became the backbone of one of the dynasties in U.S. collegiate sports history. With Alcindor playing center, UCLA won three consecutive NCAA basketball championships. Alcindor's patented ''skyhook'' shot was unblockable, and his slam dunks so threatened to change the game of basketball that the NCAA outlawed the dunk shot. The so-called Alcindor Rule lasted for ten years. Alcindor was voted All-American every year of his three years on the UCLA varsity.

At UCLA, Alcindor's political and religious thought, already stimulated by the civil rights movement* and the race riots of the 1960s, developed further. In 1968 he supported Professor Harry Edwards's boycott of the Olympic Games and refused to participate as a member of the American basketball team. That same year, he gave up his Roman Catholic faith and, like Muhammed Ali,* became a Muslim, changing his name in the process to Kareem Abdul-Jabbar.

After graduating from UCLA, Jabbar signed a professional basketball contract with the Milwaukee Bucks, and in 1971 the Bucks won the NBA championship. During his six seasons with the Bucks, Jabbar won three NBA Most Valuable Player awards. He began to study Arabic in order to read the Koran, the Muslim sacred text, in its original language. He also purchased a house in Washington, D.C., for the extended family of Hamaas, the man who had taught him the Islamic faith. Jabbar's name appeared on the front pages of U.S. newspapers in January 1973 when a rival Muslim faction attacked the Hamaas home and slaughtered several inhabitants. Hamaas was later imprisoned for engaging in illegal activities designed to stop the broadcast of a movie that negatively portrayed the Prophet Mohammed.

In 1975 the Bucks traded Jabbar to the Los Angeles Lakers, where he spent the next fourteen years. During thirteen of those years, he led the Lakers to the NBA playoffs and three NBA championships. With a career average of 24.6 points a game, Jabbar retired in 1989, at which time he held lifetime NBA records for most games played, most shots blocked, and most points scored. Since then Jabbar has attended to his business interests and has dabbled in the film industry.

SUGGESTED READINGS: Kareem Abdul-Jabbar, *Giant Steps: The Autobiography of Kareem Abdul-Jabbar*, 1983, and *Kareem*, 1990.

ABM TREATY (1972). *See* ANTI-BALLISTIC MISSILE TREATY.

ABORTION. By the end of the decade of the 1970s, abortion had become the most volatile issue in American politics. Although it had long been a matter of debate in the United States, ever since the nineteenth century when state after state passed antiabortion ordinances, the thalidomide controversy of the 1960s reintroduced abortion as a political issue. The sedative and hypnotic drug thalidomide caused severe birth defects among infants whose mothers had taken the drug during pregnancy. The Food and Drug Administration (FDA) had never approved thalidomide for use in the United States, but many well-to-do Americans managed to acquire it abroad. Sherri Finkbine, an Arizona woman, had access to thalidomide through her husband's regular business trips to Germany. In 1962 the FDA issued a warning about the drug's dangerous side effects, and Finkbine worried that the baby she was carrying might have been deformed by the drug. She decided to have an abortion, which required her to travel to Sweden, where abortion was legal. Her Swedish gynecologist confirmed that her baby was deformed and would have been born with no arms or legs. Between 1958 and 1962 more than 10,000 babies around the world were born with similar defects. Only twelve such babies were born in the United States, but Finkbine's decision to have an abortion ignited a firestorm of debate between pro-choice and pro-life groups.

The pro-choice groups argued that the decision to have an abortion must be exclusively private, completely within the domain of an individual woman to decide what happens to her own body and to her own life. They turned to the Fourth Amendment to the Constitution to support that demand for privacy and to the Fifth Amendment, which guaranteed a woman the right to "liberty." In 1967 the newly founded National Organization for Women* placed "reproductive rights" at the top of its political agenda, and in 1969 the National Abortion and Reproductive Rights Action League (NARAL), the country's first national pro-choice group, was founded. The leading figures in the formation of NARAL were Lawrence Lader, Ruth Proskauer Smith, Betty Friedan, and Bernard Nathanson.

Abortion became a huge controversy on January 22, 1973, when the U.S. Supreme Court rendered its decision, by a 7 to 2 vote, in the *Roe v. Wade** case. At the time, Texas law prohibited abortions except in instances where the procedure was necessary to save the life of the mother. Most other states in the United States had similar statutes on the books. Upholding personal privacy as a right protected by the Fourteenth Amendment to the Constitution, the court proclaimed that during the first three months of pregnancy, the state has no "compelling" interest to limit a women's right to have an abortion for any reason. During the last six months of pregnancy, the state may "regulate the abortion procedure in ways that are reasonably related to maternal health," which included licensing and regulating abortion providers. The court allowed states to ban abortions during the last ten weeks of pregnancy because, at that point in the pregnancy process, the fetus was capable of surviving outside the womb.

The decision triggered a ferocious debate over abortion that continues today. Alan Guttmacher of Planned Parenthood hailed *Roe v. Wade* as a "wise and courageous stroke for the right to privacy, and for the protection of a woman's physical and emotional health." John Cardinal Krol, the Roman Catholic archbishop of Philadelphia, remarked, "The Supreme Court's decision today is an unspeakable tragedy for this nation." The National Organization for Women praised the decision as a "great victory for individual rights and privacy."

After *Roe v. Wade* legalized most abortions in 1973, the issue became even more intense. The case of *Bigelow v. Virginia** was a perfect example of how the abortion debate could affect other issues. The dispute involved a newspaper editor in Virginia who had published an advertisement from a New York abortion clinic. Virginia had outlawed abortion and even passed legislation making it a felony to "encourage" the practice. Local prosecutors went after the editor for publishing the advertisement, which, in their minds, "encouraged" abortion. Convinced that the right to freedom of the press was at stake, the editor filed a suit of his own. The U.S. Supreme Court decided the case on June 16, 1975, by a vote of 7 to 2. The Court agreed with the editor, arguing that such state attempts to control what people read was a violation of the First Amendment.

By the end of the decade, abortion had begun to fracture American politics, and there seemed little ground for compromise. Pro-choice advocates claimed that the Fourth Amendment extended to women the right to privacy and that the Fifth Amendment gave them the right to liberty. On the basis of those two amendments and *Roe v. Wade*, pro-choicers said women enjoyed a civil right to have an abortion. Anti-abortion advocates, on the other hand, also cited the Fifth Amendment to the Constitution, claiming that abortion procedures violated the right of the fetus "to life." The two sides could find no way to come together on the issue.

By the end of the decade, the abortion issue had also begun to work its way into the two-party political structure. Liberal and urban Democrats tended to side with abortion supporters on the grounds that abortion was a civil rights issue. More conservative southern and rural Democrats, closely linked with the Bible Belt, viewed abortion as a horrible sin. During the late 1970s, 1980s, and 1990s, many of these Democrats drifted into the Republican party, where they found a more positive reception for their views. But abortion was about to cause Republicans difficulty as well. Upper and upper middle-class Republican women grew increasingly sympathetic with the pro-choice groups, perhaps because they had always been able to afford foreign travel to secure abortions even when their own states outlawed it. As Bible Belters flowed into the party and demanded strict antiabortion party policies, more liberal women became more outspoken in support of abortion rights. The Republican party soon became divided over the issue of abortion.

Complicating the issue during the 1970s were major advances in neonatology. The *Roe v. Wade* decision essentially allowed abortion during the first three months of pregnancy because babies born prematurely could not survive. No sooner had *Roe v. Wade* been handed down than neonatologists were able to save a few infants born before the second trimester of pregnancy. By the late 1980s and 1990s, they were saving thousands of such infants, undermining in the process some of the logic on which *Roe v. Wade* had been based.

SUGGESTED READINGS: Leonard Stevens, *The Case of Roe v. Wade*, 1996; Susan Gold, *Roe v. Wade: Abortion*, 1994; *New York Times*, January 23, 1973.

ABRAMS, CREIGHTON. Creighton Abrams was born on September 16, 1914, in Springfield, Massachusetts. He graduated from West Point in 1936 after earning a reputation for toughness and dedication. During World War II, he served in the Third Army, which was commanded by the legendary General George Patton and won its place in military history by relieving Bastogne in the Battle of the Bulge. By the end of the war, Abrams had also become widely known in the military as one of the army's leading combat officers. He could stand toe to toe with anyone on earth as a consumer of hard liquor, and he was rarely seen without a large cigar sticking out from his mouth. Oddly enough, however, Abrams loved classical music and was a devotee of eighteenth- and nineteenth-century sonatas.

In July 1968, after the disastrous Tet Offensive, Abrams replaced General William Westmoreland as commander of Military Assistance Command, Vietnam. By that time the war in Vietnam had changed dramatically. The Tet Offensive had been a political and strategic disaster for the United States, even though it had been a tactical victory. The antiwar movement* had grown so strong in the United States that large U.S. casualties were no longer acceptable. Abrams abandoned large-unit search-and-destroy combat operations for small-unit missions designed to keep pressure on Vietcong and North Vietnamese Army (NVA) forces while avoiding heavy American losses. Explaining his approach to journalists, Abrams remarked, "We work in small patrols because that's how the enemy moves—in groups of four or five. When he fights in squad size, so do we. When he cuts to half squad, so do we.'' The Abrams approach had a dramatic impact on U.S. combat operations. While Westmoreland had typically launched 1,200 to 1,500 battalion-size combat operations a year, Abrams reduced the total to 700.

As commander of the Military Assistance Command, Vietnam, Abrams had the responsibility of presiding over the staged withdrawal of U.S. combat troops from Vietnam and handing over combat operations to the Army of the Republic of Vietnam. Although he did the best he could with the mission, he privately harbored serious doubts about whether the South Vietnamese were capable of carrying on the war without U.S. assistance. President Richard Nixon* dubbed the program ''Vietnamization.''* Abrams found himself in an extremely difficult position as a commanding officer. The withdrawal of U.S. troops signaled to everyone around the world that the United States would soon be out of Vietnam, and tens of thousands of soldiers decided that the war was not worth dying for. Desertion rates skyrocketed, as did drug abuse among American troops and incidents of fragging* officers.

Abrams did manage to oversee the withdrawal of U.S. troops from South Vietnam. When Abrams assumed command, more than 543,000 American soldiers were in Vietnam. That number dropped to 536,000 at the end of 1968, to 475,200 in 1969, 334,600 in 1970, 156,800 in 1971, and 24,000 in 1972. Abrams was in command when the last U.S. combat troop left Vietnam in August 1972. Shortly thereafter, Nixon promoted Abrams to chief of staff of the United States Army. He remained at that position even after he had been diagnosed with cancer. Creighton Abrams died of the disease on September 4, 1974.

SUGGESTED READINGS: R. E. Dupuy, *The Compact History of the U.S. Army*, 1973; David Halberstam, *The Best and the Brightest*, 1972; George C. Herring, *America's Longest War: The United States in Vietnam, 1950–1975*, 1986; Lewis Sorley, *Thunderbolt: General Creighton Abrams and the Army of His Times*, 1992; *New York Times*, September 5, 1974.

Sean A. Kelleher

AC/DC. AC/DC, an Australian rock group formed in 1973, included Angus Young, Malcolm Young, Bon Scott, Phillip Rudd, and Mark Evans. They were among the most popular of the so-called hard-rock bands, and in such songs as ''Big Balls'' and ''The Jack'' they projected an image of raucous sexuality and rebellion. They were very popular in Australia, but in 1979, with their album *Highway to Hell*, they went platinum and became extraordinarily popular in the United States. Conservatives accused AC/DC of glorifying drug abuse, mindless rebellion, and uninhibited sexuality, and their behavior on stage and off frequently confirmed those criticisms. Soon after their American tour, Bon Scott choked to death on his own vomit in an alcoholic stupor. Brian Johnson replaced him. Their success continued in the 1980s, with such popular albums as *Back* *in the Black* (1980), *Dirty Deeds Done Cheap* (1981), *For Those About to Rock We Salute You* (1981), *A Flick of the Switch* (1983), and *Fly on the Wall* (1985). Their 1990 album *Who Made Who* was a multiplatinum success.

SUGGESTED READING: Martin Huxley, *AC/DC: The World's Heaviest Rock Band*, 1996.

ACCURACY IN MEDIA. The consumer interest group Accuracy in Media was organized in 1969 by people who were convinced that the mass media reporting of the Vietnam War* was hopelessly biased by antiwar liberals. Ever since the early 1960s, when journalists such as David Halberstam and Neil Sheehan began reporting negative news from Indochina, conservatives had begun to sense a liberal bias in the eastern media. The boom of television network news broadcasts in the 1960s and 1970s only confirmed, in the minds of political conservatives, the existence of such a bias. The goal of Accuracy in Media was to counter that bias.

During the early 1970s, Accuracy in Media came to the defense of the Richard Nixon* administration. Convinced that the Watergate scandal* was a minor political offense that was being used by liberal Democrats to expel Nixon from the White House, they defended Nixon to the end, backing away only when the U.S. Supreme Court ordered the release of all the White House taped conversations and it became clear from those tapes that the president had ordered a cover-up.

By the late 1970s, Accuracy in Media began playing a central role in the political events that led to the election of Ronald Reagan* as president. Major media institutions, including the television networks and such newspapers as the *New York Times* and the *Washington Post*, Accuracy in Media argued, consistently adopted antiwar, anti-business, and pro-environmentalist stands on every major issue. Not surprisingly, Accuracy in Media criticized the Carter administration (*see* Carter, James) for relying on the federal government, not the market, to address the energy crisis,* unemployment, and inflation. They also criticized Carter for not adopting a more activist U.S. foreign policy around the world.

Perhaps Accuracy in Media's greatest impact on the relationship between media insitutions and political attitudes in the United States has been their role in promoting the establishment of conservative talk radio shows throughout the country, which have evolved into powerful institutions that counter the political opinions of the major television networks.

SUGGESTED READING: Loree Bykerk and Ardith Maney, *U.S. Consumer Interest Groups: Institutional Profiles*, 1995.

ACTION FOR CHILDREN'S TELEVISION. Action for Children's Television, a children's advocacy group, was founded in 1968 by Peggy Charren in Boston, Massachusetts. Charren was concerned about the overcommercialization of children's television, deceptive advertising targeting juvenile viewers, and the lack of variety in children's television programming, as well as the general dearth of high-quality productions. The group protested the fact that on Saturday mornings nearly fifteen minutes of every sixty minutes of airtime was devoted to commercials. Action for Children's Television lobbyists began to work the corridors of the Federal Communications Commission (FCC), trying to get new guidelines and regulations passed for children's television programming. The group has campaigned actively in the advertising industry to improve the advertising of children's toys. In addition, Action for Children's Television has worked to secure more diversity in children's programming, not only in terms of the racial and ethnic backgrounds of the featured actors but also in the balance between cartoons and educational programming.

In 1974 Action for Children's Television won its first major battle with the FCC. The FCC adopted a Children's Television Report and Policy Statement that required broadcasters to limit the amount of advertising during children's programming to 9.5 minutes per hour on weekends and 12 minutes on weekdays. In response, the National Association of Broadcasters voluntarily designated one hour of prime time each evening for "family viewing" and launched a series of scientific, cultural, and historic specials and news shows. During the late 1970s, the FCC began to engage in a campaign to get the major networks, through voluntary compliance initiatives, to improve programming balance and to reduce the time devoted to commercials in children's television.

SUGGESTED READING: Loree Bykerk and Ardith Maney, *U.S. Consumer Interest Groups: Institutional Profiles*, 1995.

ADAM 12. *Adam 12* was one of the more popular television dramatic series of the 1970s. Produced by Jack Webb of *Dragnet* fame and broadcast by NBC, it featured the exploits of two uniformed police officers in Los Angeles. Martin Milner starred as Officer Pete Malloy and Kent McCord as Officer Jim Reed. First aired on September 21, 1968, *Adam 12* was canceled on August 26, 1975. Television historians explain the success of the weekly series as part of a conservative backlash that occurred in America during the late 1960s and early 1970s. The cops of *Adam 12* were squeaky-clean public servants committed to law, order, and patriotism. In their weekly trials, they had to deal with an endless variety of criminals, radicals, and protesters. In every case, they were tough, patient, and understanding. They also became icons to political conservatives who believed that the television media in the United States was hopelessly biased in favor of left-wing interests. *Adam 12* helped spawn other similar television dramas, such as *CHiPS*,* which featured California highway patrolmen on motorcycles. The popularity of *Adam 12* provided pop culture proof that the tide had turned in the United States on many of the liberal values of the 1960s.

SUGGESTED READING: Tim Brooks and Earle Marsh, *The Complete Directory to Prime Time Network and Cable TV Shows, 1946–Present*, 1995.

ADAMS-WESTMORELAND CONTROVERSY. During the course of the Vietnam War,* one of the most closely guarded and controversial military issues revolved around the troop strength of the North Vietnamese and the Vietcong. It was a critical problem because of the U.S. strategy of attrition, which gradually evolved as U.S. officials realized that neither diplomatic negotiations nor strategic bombing was going to force the enemy to settle the war. Once that decision had been made, the United States gradually relied more and more on its massive military firepower to stop enemy troops. The U.S. military began massive bombings in Communist-controlled territory in South Vietnam and eventually carried the bombing into Laos and North Vietnam. The American military attempted to approach the conflict on the same terms under which the nation had fought in World War I, World War II, and the Korean War: crush the enemy with massive military firepower. Between 1964 and 1973, the United States detonated more than seven million tons of explosives on North Vietnam and South Vietnam, a greater volume of firepower than was employed during all of World War II. Even then, the tactical initiative remained with the enemy. The only way to win the war was to kill so many enemy troops that they could no longer field combat-ready military units.

The strategy of attrition ultimately became a numbers game in which the United States was obsessed with body counts,* but the arithmetic of attrition was flawed. By any estimate, the United States would have had to kill as many as 250,000 enemy troops a year to limit North Vietnam's ability to field proper combat units. In order to inflict those kinds of losses, however, the United States would have had to have more than one million combat troops in Vietnam and have been willing to accept as many as 35,000 dead troops of its own each year. While North Vietnam was prepared politically to make that kind of commitment, the United States was not, and North Vietnam knew it. It was only a matter of time before the United States withdrew its forces.

The final collapse of South Vietnam came in 1975, the same year that Sam Adams wrote an explosive article for *Harper's*. In 1965 Sam Adams was an intelligence officer with the Central Intelligence Agency* (CIA). Using captured enemy documents and interrogations of enemy personnel, he concluded that Pentagon estimates of enemy killed, wounded, captured, and deserted were inflated. Adams also found support for a far higher estimate of the number of enemy soldiers in South Vietnam, for the infiltration rate of regular troops from North Vietnam to the south, and a higher capability for supplying those larger numbers than the U.S. Army intelligence estimates coming out of Military Assistance Command, Vietnam headquarters in Saigon.

Adams gradually became the center of a growing controversy. Inside the official beltway of Washington, D.C., a huge, though secret, political struggle emerged. Adams tried to get his estimates of enemy strength incorporated into official policy, but the Pentagon resisted and apparently managed to put enough pressure on the CIA to squelch Adams's data. Although both sides tried to reach a political compromise on the arithmatic of death, a settlement could not be reached. General William Westmoreland was unwilling to change enemy totals, although he was willing to reallocate figures within various categories. Such a change, of course, would have undermined much of his strategic position. If indeed there were tens of thousands or hundreds of thousands more enemy troops fighting in the war, any successful U.S. military policy would require at least hundreds of thousands more American troops, a reality that would have required either a massive escalation of the war or a U.S. withdrawal.

The issue, at least as a military controversy, became moot after Tet. General Creighton Abrams* replaced Westmoreland as MACV commander, and Richard Nixon's* decision to deescalate made it only a matter of time before the United States withdrew from Indochina. As a political issue, however, the controversy continued to consume a great deal of energy during the late 1970s after Adams published his article in *Harper's*. In his article, Adams accused Westmoreland of knowingly underestimating enemy strength in South Vietnam by not counting irregular Vietcong troops. The Vietcong were divided into main force conventional military units that were always deployed in the field, as well as irregular Vietcong troops who fought or acted as logistical support on a part-time basis, something like U.S. National Guard forces. By not counting those soldiers, Adams claimed, Westmoreland knowingly and vastly underestimated enemy troop strength.

For his part, Westmoreland denied knowingly making such an underestimate. He claimed that he simply employed the data supplied by the CIA, the National Security Agency, and army intelligence units, and that from that data he had developed a strategy for fighting the war. The issue festered in the press for a few months and then died out, only to be resurrected in January 1982 when *CBS News* broadcast a documentary based on Sam Adams's data. The documentary charged General Westmoreland with a conspiracy to report low figures for the enemy. The documentary enraged Westmoreland, who believed that CBS had used innuendo, not hard data, in producing the program, and who felt that the charges indirectly accused him of unnecessarily sending tens of thousands of U.S. soldiers to their deaths.

Westmoreland filed a lawsuit against CBS, accusing them of libel and slander. CBS then fell back on the First Amendment to the Constitution, arguing that freedom of the press should protect the network from Westmoreland's suit. The case went to trial in 1985, and evidence submitted lent credibility to Adams's claims. Proving that Westmoreland, however, had knowingly conspired to disregard the data was another matter altogether. Westmoreland and CBS settled the case out of court.

SUGGESTED READINGS: Renata Adler, *Reckless Disregard: Westmoreland vs. CBS*, 1987; Larry Berman, *Planning a Tragedy: The Americanization of the War in Vietnam*, 1982, and *Lyndon Johnson's War: The Road to Stalemate in Vietnam*, 1989; Bob Brewin and Sydney Shaw, *Vietnam on Trial: Westmoreland v. CBS*, 1986; Robert L. Gallucci, *Neither Peace nor Honor: The Politics of American Military Policy in Vietnam*, 1989; Don Kowet, *A Matter of Honor*, 1984.

AEROBICS. During the 1970s, aerobics acquired a new twist. Kenneth Cooper's regimen for fitness involved a series of solitary activities, like brisk walking, jogging, running, rowing, cycling, and swimming. Individuals who engaged in such activities, Cooper promised, would enjoy higher metabolic rates, weight loss, stronger cardiovascular systems, and longer life spans. The problem, of course, was that many Americans did not enjoy spending large amounts of time by themselves in solitary activities. Although many people committed themselves to aerobic exercises, they could not sustain the commitment.

In 1971 Jackie Sorensen, a dancer in Malibu, California, started an aerobics dance class at her local church, and six students signed up for the class. This form of aerobics had all of the benefits of Ken Cooper's regimen without the social disincentives. Sorensen taught the students how to dance aerobically as a group to popular, fast tunes. The fad spread quickly throughout the country. Aerobic dancing was a popular activity—a way to exercise and meet people and interact socially. Eventually, various aerobics video tapes were released by such popular stars as Jane Fonda,* Victoria Principal, and Racquel Welch. By the 1990s, aerobics had become a huge business in the United States, and it spawn a tremendous demand for aerobic exercise equipment.

SUGGESTED READINGS: Randy Roberts and James S. Olson, *Winning Is the Only Thing: Sports in America Since 1945*, 1989; Jeff Savage, *Aerobics*, 1995.

AEROSMITH. Aerosmith, a prominent American rock group formed in 1970, still performs today. Critics charged that Aerosmith was a pale imitation of the Rolling Stones and that lead singer Steven Tyler was little more than a Mick Jagger look-alike. In addition to Tyler, the group included Joe Perry, Brad Whitford, Tom Hamilton, and Joey Kramer. They became the number one hard-rock band of the 1970s. Among their most successful albums were *Aerosmith* (1973), *Get Your Wings* (1974), and *Toys in the Attic* (1975). Their concert tours were sellouts, but life on the road took its toll. Serious drug problems, including full-fledged heroin addictions, and infighting sent the band into a steep decline. Their 1977 album *Draw the Line* was a bust. Aerosmith tried to hype their bad-boy image, but it did not help.

In 1984, however, they resurrected themselves. The bad-boy image was still part of the act, but band members were strictly sober and more in control of their lives. The advent of rock videos, combined with such successful releases as *Done with Mirrors* (1984) and *Permanent Vacation* (1987), introduced Aerosmith to a new generation, and they rocketed to success. Their 1989 album *Pump*, which went multiplatinum, included three top ten hits: "Love in an Elevator," "Janie's Got a Gun," and "What It Takes." Their 1993 album *Get a Grip* included three hit singles. The 1998 film *Armageddon* gave the band another boost because they provided the soundtrack for the movie.

SUGGESTED READINGS: Mark Putterford, *Aerosmith Live!*, 1994, and *The Fall and Rise of Aerosmith*, 1993.

AFFIRMATIVE ACTION. "Affirmative action" first emerged in the 1970s as an explosive political issue around which bitter political controversy still rages. The term itself comes from President Lyndon B. Johnson, who, on September 24, 1965, issued an executive order that required all federal contractors to use "affirmative action" in ensuring that minority workers were hired in numbers consistent with their ratio in the population. In doing so, the president was responding to a deep concern among civil rights activists that the movement to end racial discrimination was stalling. With the Civil Rights Act of 1964, most forms of formal, legal discrimination had been eliminated, but civil rights advocates soon realized that there were a host of other practices and traditions, such as seniority rights and aptitude tests, which continued to militate against hiring and promoting minority workers. Critics called these practices forms of "institutional racism." Since the president's 1965 executive order, affirmative action has referred to a series of rules and regulations designed to counteract the effects of historical discrimination against certain designated minority groups.

During the mid-1960s, affirmative action attracted relatively little political attention and appeared to have become a linchpin of the civil rights movement.* A number of congressional laws and federal court decisions upheld affirmative action in principle. In *Griggs v. Duke Power Company** in 1971, for example, the U.S. Supreme Court invalidated the use of intelligence tests that had the effect of limiting minority hiring and promotion. The court agreed that such tests could be culturally biased in favor of middle-class whites, making it difficult for blacks, Hispanics, and Native Americans to compete successfully. The Court further ordered that companies begin using a variety of criteria, not just intelligence tests, to recruit and promote employees.

The Supreme Court's decision in *Morton v. Mancari* in 1974 was another example of affirmative action. Ever since the 1930s, the Bureau of Indian Affairs, a federal government agency, had given hiring and promotion preferences to American Indian employees. In the early 1970s, several non-Indian employees claimed racial discrimination based on the Civil Rights Act of 1964, which required equal treatment in federal employment. They filed a lawsuit that charged civil rights violations. Tribal governments, however, did not want to be forced to establish racially blind hiring policies, since they wanted to give as many jobs as possible to their own members. To accommodate their wishes, Congress had exempted them from those provisions of the Civil Rights Act of 1964. In *Morton v. Mancari*, the Court held that Congress could give preference to Native Americans in hiring. The Court determined that federal statutes were not race based but were, instead, the result of the "special relationship" existing between the U.S. government and the Indians.

Affirmative action also received a boost from the strengthening of the Equal Employment Opportunity Commission (EEOC), which had been created on July 2, 1965, as directed by Title VII of the Civil Rights Act of 1964. Its charge was to prohibit employment discrimination on the basis of race, color, religion, sex, or national origin. As a result of the Equal Employment Opportunity Act of 1972,* the provisions apply also to state and local governments as well as federal agencies and private employers. At first its authority was limited to persuasion and conciliation, but amendments in 1972 empowered the EEOC to bring suit when necessary, and amendments in 1974 gave the EEOC power to file pattern and practice lawsuits as well. Affirmative action almost immediately became central to the culture of the EEOC.

Affirmative action also caught the attention of the women's movement.* The Civil Rights Act of 1964 had prohibited employment discrimination on the basis of sex, and women's rights advocates made affirmative action in the hiring and promotion of women one of their major goals. By the early 1970s, affirmative action had become one of the central policy goals of the National Organization for Women.*

No sooner had affirmative action become the law of the land than a political backlash set in. Whites had always been an important element in the political coalition that promoted the civil rights movement.* Blacks, Hispanics, and Native Americans constituted less than 20 percent of the American population, and they tended to vote in smaller percentages than their white counterparts. Political success for the civil rights movement in general and affirmative action in particular depended upon substantial support from white voters.

In the early 1970s, that support began to evaporate. The black power movement was partly responsible. Unity, peace, non-violence, and brotherhood had always characterized the political rhetoric of Martin Luther King, Jr., and other prominent early civil rights crusaders, and large numbers of whites rallied to such a philosophy. But in the late 1960s, the black power rhetoric of people like Stokely Carmichael and H. Rap Brown alienated large numbers of whites who had previously sympathized with the hopes and dreams of the civil rights movement. The racial rebellions in dozens of American cities between 1965 and 1968 only confirmed the fears of many whites that the civil rights movement was turning violent.

The dismal economy of the 1970s, together with the impact of affirmative action legislation and court orders, alienated large numbers of working-class whites, who had been since the 1930s a key element in the Democratic party's advocacy of racial equality. The Arab oil boycott of 1973–1974* and the subsequent energy crisis* created an unprecedented economic problem known as ''stagflation,''* in which high inflation coexisted with high unemployment. Many blue-collar workers lost their jobs or were threatened with the loss of jobs just when it appeared to them that minorities were receiving preferences in hiring and promotion. That scenario violated a tried-and-true principle of union policy. Ever since the nineteenth century, seniority had been a basis of labor unions. Unions insisted that companies recognize seniority as a worker right in promotion and firing decisions. ''Last hired, first fired'' was almost religious dogma to union officials. Minorities, of course, countered with the telling argument that since they had been discriminated against for years, and not since the late 1960s had they been protected in hiring and promotion decisions, seniority rules in a declining economy would guarantee the protection of white jobs and the promotion of white workers as well as the wholesale firing of minorities.

Critics claimed that affirmative action had spun out of control, that what had begun as a well-meaning attempt to right wrongs in American society had actually rigidified into admission, hiring, and promotion quotas that amounted to little more than reverse discrimination against white males. The Fourteenth Amendment to the Constitution, they argued, guaranteed to every individual the right to equal protection under the law. Opponents of affirmative action even appealed for support to the words of deceased Martin Luther King, Jr., who once said that he yearned for the day in America when every person would be judged ''not by the color of his skin but by the content of his character.'' The chorus of protests from whites became louder and louder, and the number of whites filing ''reverse discrimination'' lawsuits with the Equal Employment Opportunity Commission skyrocketed.

In 1978 the U.S. Supreme Court heard the *University of California Board of Regents v. Bakke** case. Allan Bakke had been denied admission to the medical school at the University of California at Davis. Because of the university's quota system for admission, several minority students with lower grade point averages and lower test scores had been admitted. Bakke claimed that the practice constituted reverse discrimination. The only reason he had not been admitted, he claimed, was the fact that he was a white man. That constituted, his attorneys argued, a violation of his Fifth and Fourteenth Amendments to due process and equal protection under the law. The Supreme Court agreed with Bakke, proclaiming that rigid, special preference admission programs were unconstitutional. After the Bakke decision, rigid quotas were dead, although affirmative action programs that actively sought to hire or admit minority workers were still legal. With the *Bakke* decision, the political tide in America had turned against affirmative action, and the 1980s and 1990s witnessed a steady retreat from its principles.

SUGGESTED READINGS: Susan Banfield, *The Bakke Case: Quotas in College Admissions*, 1998; Nathan Glazer, *Affirmative Discrimination: Ethnic Inequality and Public Policy*, 1987; Katharine Greene, *Affirmative Action and Principles of Justice*, 1990; Stephen L. Pevar, *The Rights of Indians and Tribes: The Basic ACLU Guide to Indian and Tribal Rights*, 1992; Bernard Schwartz, *Behind Bakke: Affirmative Action and the Supreme Court*, 1988.

AFGHANISTAN. The Soviet Union's 1979 invasion of Afghanistan became a Cold War* issue in superpower relations. In 1978 Marxist Nur Mohammad Taraki seized power in Afghanistan and tried to build a centralized, dictatorial Communist state. Muslim clerics viewed the palace coup as an attempt by godless communism to destroy their religion, and they declared a holy war on the Taraki regime. Within months his political rivals had assassinated Taraki, and Hafizullah Amin, another Communist, came to power. Illegitimate to its very roots, the Amin government found itself fighting a losing war against Muslim rebel troops known as the Mujahadin. The guerrillas soon controlled 75 percent of the Afghan countryside.

Soviet officials worried about the collapse of the Communist regime in Afghanistan and the possibility of Islamic fundamentalism spreading into the Soviet Union's Islamic republics. Religious fundamentalism, with the Ayatollah Khomeini in Iran* as the best example, was gaining credibility in the Muslim world, especially in regions where Western technology, industrialism, and secularism were having their greatest impact. Since Muslims hated communism because of its official atheism, Soviet authorities feared the eruption of political revolutions in such places as Kazakhstan, Kirghizia, Uzbekistan, Georgia, and Azerbaijan.

To prevent the spread of revolution and fundamentalism from Afghanistan to the Soviet Union, Soviet officials invaded Afghanistan on December 26, 1979. It was a miscalculation of enormous proportions. They overthrew the Amin government and installed a Soviet puppet regime under Babrak Karmal, but the war quickly degenerated into a bloody guerrilla conflict fought in the inhospitable Afghan highlands. The war, which dragged on for nine years, cost the Soviet Union 15,000 dead soldiers and more than 30,000 wounded soldiers. And they were never able to conquer the Mujahadin, who received money and weapons from the United States and Great Britain. Analysts around the world began referring to the Afghan war as "the Soviet Union's Vietnam."

The United States and Western European nations viewed the Soviet invasion of Afghanistan with alarm. They worried that the Soviets were actually making a move on oil resources in the Persian Gulf. President Jimmy Carter* demanded a Soviet withdrawal from Afghanistan, and when the Soviets refused, he imposed trade sanctions on them and launched a boycott of the 1988 Olympic Games in Moscow. Eventually fifty-nine other countries joined the boycott. In May 1988 Soviet Premier Mikhail Gorbachev began withdrawing Soviet troops from Afghanistan, and the pullout was complete by February 1989.

SUGGESTED READINGS: Anthony Hyman, *Afghanistan Under Soviet Domination, 1964–1991*, 1992; Edgar O'Ballance, *Afghan Wars, 1839–1992: What Britain Gave Up and the Soviet Union Lost*, 1993.

AGENT ORANGE. "Agent Orange" was a nickname used during and after the Vietnam War* for a chemical agent employed by U.S. military forces. Use of the chemical, which began in 1962 and continued unabated until 1970, was part of Operation Ranch Hand. Agent Orange was composed of equal amounts of 2,4-dichlorophenoxyacetic acid (2,4-D) and 2,4,5-trichlorophenoxyacetic acid, as well as small amounts of 2,3,7,8-tetrachlorodibenzo-**p**-dioxin (TCDD). This chemical herbicide was used to defoliate heavily forested regions near the Demilitarized Zone in South Vietnam and near the borders between Cambodia, Laos, and South Vietnam. During the course of Operation Ranch Hand, U.S. military pilots sprayed 11.22 million gallons of Agent Orange in the area.

The decision to defoliate millions of acres of Indochinese jungles grew out of the nature of the war. Vietcong and North Vietnamese used the dense foliage of tropical jungles to hide from American troops and, even worse as far as the Pentagon was concerned, exploited that cover to ambush GIs. U.S. military planners found the situation extremely frustrating. The tactical initiative remained with enemy troops, who almost always started firefights, and when it came time to disengage, the Vietcong and North Vietnamese escaped by melting into the thick jungle cover. Also, the jungle cover made it more difficult for U.S. infantry to receive effective tactical air support. The solution seemed obvious: destroy the jungles so that the enemy would be visible. Fixed-wing aircraft and helicopters were used for the job. By the time Operation Ranch Hand was brought to a conclusion, nearly seven million acres of South Vietnam, Laos, and Cambodia had been sprayed.

The strategic logic of Operation Ranch Hand proved to be badly flawed. It essentially assumed that Vietcong and North Vietnamese troops were static constants and that enemy soldiers would always use the same transportation routes, even if the jungle cover were removed. Enemy commanding officers were hardly that stupid. When defoliation occurred in one area, they simply moved their military operations to another region where the topography gave them the tactical advantages they needed.

By the late 1960s, the use of Agent Orange also attracted the opposition of the antiwar movement* and the environmental movement.* For years the Department of Defense and Dow Chemical, the principal manufacturer of the defoliant, insisted that Agent Orange had no short-term or long-term effects on human beings. For precautionary reasons, however, Agent Orange was rarely sprayed directly on American troops. Environmentalists disagreed. Any product capable of killing all of the trees and plants in a jungle would surely have long-term effects on other species coming into contact with it. Antiwar activists also protested the frequency with which South Vietnamese civilians found themselves being sprayed with Agent Orange. They claimed that Operation Ranch Hand was blatant proof that the United States had absolutely no regard for the health and well-being of the civilian population. Also, U.S. troops who moved into an area that had been sprayed with Agent Orange inevitably came into contact with the toxic substance. In 1970, as a result of pressure from the environmental and antiwar movements, and because of disturbing results from their own laboratory studies into the toxicity of Agent Orange, the Pentagon ordered an end to Operation Ranch Hand.

But the controversy did not end. After the war, many Americans and South Vietnamese exposed to the dioxin developed health problems ranging from cancer to chronic skin rashes. Critics also reported high numbers of birth defects among children born to Vietnam veteran fathers who had been exposed to Agent Orange. Similar problems appeared among the children of South Vietnamese civilians exposed to the dioxin. The Department of Defense and Dow Chemical, however, continued to deny any statistically significant links between health problems and exposure to the herbicide. They were able to produce dozens of medical studies that had examined the possibility of such a correlation, but none of them had been able to confirm it. Thousands of veterans and dozens of veterans advocacy groups disagreed and began seeking financial compensation for themselves and their families. They brought a class-action suit against Dow Chemical and other manufacturers.

By the 1980s, as sympathy in the United States for Vietnam veterans began to grow, both the Defense Department and Dow Chemical and the other manufacturers of Operation Ranch Hand herbicides found themselves on the wrong side of a very unpopular issue. Critics even accused the Department of Defense of engaging in a gigantic conspiracy to cover up the environmental disaster that had occurred. Without ever agreeing to culpability, the chemical companies voluntarily established a $180 million fund to compensate alleged victims. The issue remains in litigation today.

SUGGESTED READINGS: Paul Cecil, *Herbicidal Warfare: The Ranch Hand Project in Vietnam*, 1986; Clifford Linedecker, *Kerry, Agent Orange and an American Family*, 1982; Peter Shuck, *Agent Orange on Trial*, 1987; Carol Van Strum, *A Bitter Fog: Herbicides and Human Rights*, 1983.

Carol Nguyen

AGNEW, SPIRO. Spiro Theodore Agnew was born to Greek immigrant parents on November 9, 1918, in Baltimore, Maryland. He attended Johns Hopkins University and spent one year at the Baltimore Law School. When World War II broke out, he joined the army. After the war, Agnew returned to law school and graduated in 1947. He began practicing law and working in local Republican politics, and in 1957 he was appointed to the Baltimore County Zoning Board of Appeals. He won election to the position of county executive in 1962, and in 1966 he won the governorship of Maryland, defeating a segregationist Democrat and earning liberal credentials. During his two terms as governor, however, Agnew became increasingly conservative and strident in his rhetoric. In 1968 he supported the candidacy of Richard Nixon* for president, and Nixon rewarded him with the spot of running mate. They won the election over Democrats Hubert H. Humphrey and Senator Edmund Muskie of Maine, and Agnew became the vice president of the United States in 1969.

As vice president, Agnew carried the battle to the opponents and critics of the Nixon administration. Opponents of the Vietnam War,* whether in Congress or on campus, were the special targets of his alliterative verbal assaults. The baiting and buzzwords of the 1950s were dusted off for reuse, together with many new ones of Agnew's invention. But while Agnew carried the cudgels for the Nixon administration, serving as an unofficial verbal hit man, his excesses often inflamed an already overheated national debate, and the vice president himself was severely criticized for exacerbating the situation.

Thus, when Agnew's past caught up with him, those who had been the victims of his denunciation could hardly conceal their delight. During his years as county

executive and governor in Maryland, Agnew had accepted kickbacks on government contracts. Investigators brought those crimes to light during his term
as vice president. Faced with the threat of prosecution and impeachment for
violation of bribery, conspiracy, and tax laws, on October 10, 1973, Agnew
entered into a plea bargaining agreement, pleading no contest (*nolo contendere*)
to one count of income tax evasion. He also resigned from the vice presidency.
For the remainder of his life, Spiro Agnew kept a very low profile. He died on
September 17, 1996.

SUGGESTED READINGS: Spiro T. Agnew, *Go Quietly . . . Or Else*, 1980; *New York
Times*, September 18–19, 1996.

Joseph M. Rowe, Jr.

AIR SUPPLY. Air Supply, an Australian rock-and-roll band formed in Melbourne in 1976, went to the top of the American pop charts in 1979 with the
hit song "Lost in Love." Air Supply then put together several more top-ten
hits, including "Every Woman to Me" (1980), "The One That You Love"
(1981), "Even the Nights Are Better" (1982), and "Making Love Out of Nothing At All" (1983). Critics accused Air Supply of producing nothing more than
lightweight, fluffy soft rock, but record buyers purchased more than fifteen million of their records. The original group disbanded in 1988.

SUGGESTED READING: Patricia Romanowski and Holly George-Warren, eds., *The
New Encyclopedia of Rock & Roll*, 1985.

AIRLINE DEREGULATION ACT OF 1978. Long before Ronald Reagan*
was victorious in the presidential election of 1980, which put modern conservatism in the White House and set the stage for the Republican congressional
triumphs of 1994, deregulation had become a prominent political issue. In the
context of the 1970s, deregulation meant withdrawal of some federal regulatory
agencies from the economy and restoration of market economics. Many critics
charged that the federal agencies once designed to prevent monopoly and price
gouging of consumers had actually become impediments to real competition and
the source of high prices and poor levels of service.

One key industry targeted for deregulation was passenger air service. Since
the late 1930s, the federal government, through the Civil Aeronautics Board
(CAB), had regulated the airline industry. Over the years, to prevent monopolistic powers in the industry, Congress had awarded the CAB the authority to
determine the rates that airlines could charge and the routes they could fly. It
also had the power to limit the access of new carriers to the skies, which tended
to reinforce monopolistic practices. The existing carriers also exerted great political pressure through lobbyists to preserve the existing system.

By the 1970s, however, critics charged that the the regulations were simply
producing high fares for customers and high profits for carriers. Early in the
decade, a number of intrastate carriers in such states as California and Texas
entered the business. Since they did not fly across state lines, they did not come

under the interstate commerce laws; the CAB had no authority over them. Those intrastate carriers soon showed just how cheap air travel could be. As they competed with one another, prices fell and service improved. Demands for deregulation of the industry began to grow more intense.

In 1977 President Jimmy Carter* appointed Alfred Kahn as head of the CAB and charged him with bringing about deregulation. Kahn promoted deregulation, although both the airline companies and the airline unions opposed the move. Nonetheless, in 1978, Congress passed the Airline Deregulation Act, which allowed airlines to compete in fare rates and allowed new carriers to enter the market. The results were dramatic. During the 1980s the number of Americans flying at least once a year doubled and then doubled again. The competition also hurt a number of airline carriers, including TWA and Pan-American, which were no longer competitive, and drove them into bankruptcy. Economic historians today identify the Airline Deregulation Act as the birthdate for the modern airline business.

SUGGESTED READING: Barry Friedman, *Regulation in the Reagan-Bush Era*, 1995.

AIRPORT. Based on Arthur Hailey's novel of the same name, *Airport*, a disaster film with a star-studded ensemble cast, was released in 1970. *Airport* took its cue from *The High and the Mighty*, a 1953 film starring John Wayne about a commercial airliner in crisis. While the pilot tries to cope with a series of technical problems, other cast members are trying to work out a variety of problems in their personal lives. Burt Lancaster, Dean Martin, Jean Seberg, Jacqueline Bissett, George Kennedy, Helen Hayes, Van Heflin, and Lloyd Nolan all starred in *Airport*. Set aboard a Boeing 707, the film concerns a commercial airliner threatened by a crazed, bomb-carrying passenger. In the midst of the crisis, the airport manager must deal with demonstrators and a blizzard; the pilot is worrying about a stewardess he has impregnated; and an elderly woman stowaway is trying to avoid capture. The film proved to be prophetic, since terrorist hijacking plagued the airline industry in the 1970s.

SUGGESTED READING: *New York Times*, March 6, 1970.

ALASKA NATIVE CLAIMS SETTLEMENT ACT OF 1971. The nature of Indian culture in Alaska had posed a difficult challenge to federal Indian officials ever since the United States purchased Alaska from Russia in 1867. Unlike Native Americans in the lower forty-eight states, whose lives revolved politically around a variety of tribal governments, Indian politics in Alaska functioned at the level of isolated, individual villages. In 1946 Congress had passed the Indian Compensation Act to compensate Native American tribes for the loss of their land, but the legislation did not apply to Alaskan natives because Native Americans there did not have tribal governments that could apply for compensation and approve the settlements.

During the mid-twentieth century, however, the issue of Native American land in Alaska became even more controversial because of the discovery of vast oil reserves and untapped mineral wealth there. Economic development accelerated the alienation of Alaska native land. Soon, the quest for profit produced a steady influx of whites, which increased the population to such an extent that Alaska attained statehood in 1959. With their ancient way of life in peril, the indigenous peoples banded together to form the Alaska Federation of Natives. The federation was formed in 1966 by more than four hundred representatives of Alaskan native groups from throughout the state. Their original purpose was to organize to promote the settlement of their land claims against the state and federal governments. By mounting an effective lobbying campaign in Congress, the Alaska Federation of Natives stimulated passage of the Alaska Claims Settlement Act of 1971, which affected nearly 50,000 Indian, Eskimo, and Aleut tribesmen.

The act constituted a signal victory for Indian rights advocates. In exchange for 40 million acres in federal land grants, an immediate $462 million cash settlement, and another $500 million in future payments for mineral rights, Alaska's indigenous peoples relinquished all outstanding land claims and acquiesced in the elimination of existing reserves. Four million acres were set aside for Native American corporations in cities, cemeteries, historic sites, and reserves. To develop economically, Alaskan natives, it was presumed, needed to be organized at the village level. Under the provisions of the new law, Alaska natives were awarded shares in newly created regional economic corporations that were divided into twelve distinct geographical regions. Nonresident natives received shares in a thirteenth region set aside for their benefit. On the local level, the village corporations held surface rights and dispensed federal benefits. The regional corporations wielded authority over subsurface or mineral rights, parceled out dividends, and invested much of the remainder of the proceeds in various economic ventures.

However, despite the favorable terms of the agreement, its half-hearted implementation by the Department of the Interior worried many Indian rights advocates who voiced their concern that the measure merely supplanted traditional tribal authority with money-oriented corporations. Joe Upickson of the Arctic Slope Native Association charged that the legislation would destroy indigenous cultures. The legislation resulted in the loss of millions of acres of land, as well as hunting and fishing rights, and greatly stimulated the economic development of the region. Millions of acres also ended up in national parks and forest reserves.

Actually, that criticism was hardly new to Native American affairs. In the process of securing justice for past fraudulent treatment by the federal government, Alaskan natives actually accelerated the acculturation process that was already driving them closer to white culture. The Alaskan Native Claims Settlement Act provided a monetary solution to a historical, political, and cultural problem, and in doing so actually moved Alaskan natives farther away from their traditional ways and closer to a commercial, consumer culture.

SUGGESTED READINGS: Robert D. Arnold, *Alaska Native Land Claims*, 1978; David S. Case, *Alaska Natives and American Laws*, 1984; Arthur Lazarus, Jr., and W.

Richard West, Jr., "The Alaska Native Claims Settlement Act: A Flawed Victory," *Law and Contemporary Problems* 11 (Winter 1976), 132–65; James S. Olson and Raymond Wilson, *Native Americans in the Twentieth Century*, 1984.

Mark Baxter

ALASKA PIPELINE. During the first half of the twentieth century, the United States produced enough oil for all of its domestic needs and was able to export surpluses to foreign markets. Beginning in 1953, however, that pattern changed. The easiest and cheapest fields to tap had already been discovered in the United States, and production costs began to rise, increasing the price per barrel of domestic crude. Rich, abundant fields in the Middle East came on line, and the United States had to begin importing oil to meet domestic needs. Ever since then that trend has continued.

U.S. policymakers realized that economic and strategic needs required development of new fields, so the 1968 announcement of the huge oilfield at Prudhoe Bay, Alaska, was welcome news. The major problem was how to transport that crude oil to market because of weather and ice problems. Prudhoe Bay was located on Alaska's north slope, and ocean access to the bay was seasonal because of winter ice. It became clear that a pipeline was the best answer. In another era, that would simply have been a matter of economics, but the environmental movement* had gained momentum in the 1960s, and construction of hundreds of miles of pipeline across virgin wilderness seemed a conservationist's nightmare. Environmentalists worried about disrupting animal migration routes and melting tundra ice. They were also concerned, of course, about the possibility of a break in the pipeline and a massive oil spill.

Construction of the pipeline pitted environmentalists against economists, who argued that the U.S. need for petroleum justified the project. Debate raged in Congress for five years, but when the energy crisis* hit in 1973, and gasoline prices skyrocketed, environmentalists lost their political clout. Environmentalists still had influence, however. When Congress passed the Alaska Pipeline Act of 1973 to finance construction, the legislation made sure that the pipeline was the most environmentally sensitive project in the history of the world. The legislation provided for the construction of a huge pipeline capable of transporting 2 million barrels of crude oil a day, from Prudhoe Bay to the port of Valdez on the Gulf of Alaska. A consortium of oil and construction companies, known as Aleyeska, completed the job in 1977. Today, the project is looked back upon as one of the greatest engineering achievements of the era.

SUGGESTED READING: Robert Mead, *Journey Down the Line: Building the Trans-Alaska Pipeline*, 1978.

ALCATRAZ ISLAND. On November 9, 1969, a group of American Indian college students and urban Indian people from the San Francisco Bay area set out in a chartered boat to circle Alcatraz Island and symbolically claim the island for Indian people. On November 20, 1969, this symbolic occupation of Alcatraz

Island turned into a full-scale occupation when Indian students from San Francisco State University, the University of California at Berkeley, the University of California at Santa Cruz, and the University of California at Los Angeles joined with urban Indian people from the greater San Francisco Bay area and reoccupied the island, claiming title by "right of discovery."

The newly formed Alcatraz organization, Indians of All Tribes,* demanded clear title to Alcatraz Island, the establishment of an American Indian University, an American Indian Cultural Center, and an American Indian Museum. The Indian occupiers on Alcatraz Island kept Americans aware of the occupation and their demands by publishing a newsletter, *Rock Talk*, and by starting their own radio program, "Radio Free Alcatraz." As a result, letters and telegrams began to pour in to government officials, including President Richard Nixon.* The mood of the public could be summed up in a telegram sent to Nixon on November 26, 1969 that read, "For once in this country's history let the Indians have something. Let them have Alcatraz."

The Indian occupiers successfully held the island until June 11, 1971, and Alcatraz soon became a rallying cry for the new American Indian activism that would continue into the mid-1970s under the names of red power* and the American Indian Movement.* This activism included the 1972 occupation of the headquarters of the Bureau of Indian Affairs in Washington, D.C. which lasted for seven days, and the occupation of Wounded Knee* in 1973, which lasted for seventy-one days. The occupation of Alcatraz Island represents the longest continuous occupation of a federal facility by a minority group in the history of the United States, and it is on Alcatraz that modern activism finds its roots. Alcatraz set in motion a wave of overtly nationalist Indian militancy that ultimately resulted in abandonment of the termination program and the adoption of a policy of Indian self-determination.*

The nineteen-month occupation of Alcatraz Island is a watershed event in the American Indian protest and activist movement. The Alcatraz occupation brought together hundreds of Indian people who came to live on the island and thousands more who identified with the call for self-determination, autonomy, and respect for Indian culture. The Indian people who organized the occupation and those who participated either by living on the island or working to solicit donations of money, water, food, clothing, or electrical generators, came from all walks of life. As the occupation gained international attention, Indian people came from Canada, South America, and from Indian reservations across the United States to show support for those who had taken a stand against the federal government. Thousands came, some stayed, and others carried the message home to their reservations that Alcatraz was a clarion call for the rise of Indian activism.

Today Alcatraz Island remains a strong symbol of Indian activism and self-determination, as well as a rallying point for unified Indian political activities. On February 11, 1978, Indian participants began the Longest Walk,* to Washington, D.C., to protest the government's ill treatment of Indian people. That walk began on Alcatraz Island. On February 11, 1994, American Indian Movement leaders Dennis Banks,* Clyde Bellecourt,* and Mary Wilson met with Indian people to begin the nationwide "Walk for Justice," a walk that also began on Alcatraz Island. On Thanksgiving Day of each year since 1969, Indian people have gathered on Alcatraz Island to honor those who participated in the occupation and those who share in the continuing struggle for Indian self-determination. The 1969 occupation of Alcatraz Island stands out as the most symbolic, the most significant, the most successful Indian protest action of the modern era.

SUGGESTED READINGS: Peter Blue Cloud, *Alcatraz Is Not an Island*, 1972; Troy R. Johnson, *The Occupation of Alcatraz Island: Indian Self-Determination and the Rise of Indian Activism*, 1996.

Troy Johnson

ALCINDOR, LOU. See ABDUL-JABBAR, KAREEM.

ALI, MUHAMMAD. Muhammad Ali was born Cassius Marcellus Clay on January 18, 1942, in Louisville, Kentucky. He grew up in a poor, black neighborhood where he struggled to find his own identity. Although quite bright and articulate, he suffered from dyslexia and had a difficult time academically at school. A gifted athlete blessed with strength, speed, and extraordinary agility, he found a home away from home in a local gymnasium, where he took up boxing at the age of twelve. Ring experts soon saw his great potential—the body of a heavyweight or light heavyweight with the speed and agility of a featherweight. No other boxer in the history of the world combined those talents: a 6-foot, 3-inch, 200-pound body and lightning speed. Clay won two Golden Glove championships and, when he was only eighteen years old, won the gold medal at the 1960 Olympic Games in Rome. He returned to Louisville a national hero, and a consortium of local businessmen decided to finance his run for the heavyweight championship. Angelo Dundee, a gifted trainer, took Clay under his wing, and they began preparing to fight for the heavyweight championship of the world.

Brash, outspoken, and a marketing genius, Clay fancied himself another "Gorgeous" George, the outlandish professional wrestler who preened before the press in elaborate outfits and bragged incessantly about his abilities. Clay bragged as well. He also took the ghetto practice of the "dozens"—a game of verbal one-upmanship—and elevated it to a pop culture art form, poetically praising his own talents ("float like a butterfly, sting like a bee") and ridiculing those of his opponents. Clay irritated many American whites, who expected the politeness of Jackie Robinson and Joe Louis from black athletic heroes. Most sportswriters, sportscasters, referees, boxing promoters, and trainers secretly waited for the day when Clay would meet his match in the ring. What they did not realize at the time, of course, was that Cassius Clay was among the best boxers, perhaps the very best, to step into a ring.

Under Angelo Dundee's careful tutelage, Clay rose through the ranks and finally got a shot at the heavyweight title in 1964. The reigning champion was Sonny Liston, a man of few words whose reputation for ferocity was unmatched. Liston had a criminal record and a resumé that included some time in jail. He was also highly regarded in the ring as the man who had taken the heavyweight belt from Floyd Patterson. Most boxing experts felt that Clay was badly over-matched and that Liston would make short work of him. Clay then made reams of copy for sportswriters by denigrating Liston's abilities and predicting an easy victory for himself. He was a promoter's dream. Clay bragged about humiliating Liston in the ring, and the world waited for the young challenger to get what was coming to him. He did. Clay delivered an unmerciful beating to Liston and won the heavyweight championship.

The next day, Clay stunned the sports world by announcing his conversion to the Nation of Islam and the change of his name from Cassius Clay to Muhammad Ali. Up to that time, Americans had seen only a talented athlete with a big mouth in Clay. What they did not realize was that underneath that loud-mouthed exterior was a man who deeply resented the racism, poverty, and discrimination faced for so long by African Americans in the United States. At the time, the so-called Black Muslims, led by Elijah Muhammad, * were considered a radical, subversive force in the United States because they preached a racist doctrine of their own—that whites were literally "devils" and the source of all evil and suffering in the world. America for the first time had a heavyweight champion who actually appeared to be anti-American.

In the rematch with Sonny Liston, Ali dispatched the former champion in the first round. During the course of the next several years, Ali defended his title against all comers and was rarely even challenged by his opponents. He kept up the poetic banter with his opponents and soon won a following among whites who considered him to be talented, outrageous, and arrogant—pure American. Outside the ring, he had to defend constantly his religious beliefs, which were genuinely sincere, against the criticisms of non-Muslims.

The Vietnam War* then intervened in Ali's career, transforming him from superathlete to icon among African Americans, civil rights and antiwar move-ment* activists, and political liberals. The escalation of the Vietnam War in 1965 had created enormous personnel demands for the U.S. military, and draft calls increased dramatically. Because of his dyslexia, Ali failed an army intel-ligence test and was at first classified as unfit for duty, but he was reclassified late in 1966. He then appealed for deferment as a religious conscientious ob-jector, arguing that his Muslim faith would not allow him to go abroad and fight a war against people of color, especially since his own people still faced racism and discrimination in the United States. The selective service rejected the re-quest, and he was classified 1-A, which meant he could be drafted immediately in the armed forces. Early in 1967, Ali announced that he would not go to war against the Vietnamese. "I ain't got no quarrel with those Vietcong, anyway," he said. "They never called me nigger." On April 18, 1967, he refused to take the oath and enter the U.S. Army. The World Boxing Association immediately stripped him of his title, and in June 1967 a federal jury convicted him of draft evasion. Ali was sentenced to five years in prison and fined $10,000.

To African Americans and antiwar activists, Ali became an overnight sensation and then a hero. Although he had appealed his conviction and the case was winding its way through the federal courts, he could not pursue his livelihood, even though, as a twenty-five-year-old athlete, he was at the peak of his athletic skills. State boxing commissions refused to issue him a license, and the State Department would not issue him a passport to travel abroad. Unable to fight, Ali traveled widely throughout the country, denouncing the Vietnam War and promoting the Nation of Islam. He appealed his case, and in June 1970 the U.S. Supreme Court overturned the conviction, agreeing with his contention that his religious beliefs precluded him from joining the military and fighting in a war.

After a few tune-up bouts, Ali won the right to challenge Joe Frazier, who had taken the title during Ali's hiatus from the ring, for the heavyweight championship of the world. The 1971 fight at Madison Square Garden in New York City was one of the greatest spectacles in the history of American sports. Frazier and Ali fought a maximum fifteen rounds, delivering ferocious beatings to one another. Both men had to be hospitalized after the fight. Frazier was able to knock Ali down once during the fight, and he retained his title by decision. Frazier did not, however, enjoy an undisputed heavyweight title. Several boxing organizations existed at the time, and one of them, the North American Boxing Federation (NABF), recognized Jimmy Ellis as the champion. In July 1971, Ali defeated Ellis and won that portion of the heavyweight crown. Ken Norton challenged and defeated Ali for the NABF title in July 1973. Six months later, Ali regained the title.

By 1974 Joe Frazier had lost his share of the heavyweight crown to George Foreman, and on October 30, 1974, in what Ali dubbed the "rumble in the jungle" in Kinshasa, Zaire, Ali won the fight and united the two heavyweight championship titles into one. Joe Frazier then challenged Ali for the title in 1975. The match was fought in Manila, Philippines, which Ali called the "Thrilla in Manila."* In another bout remarkable for the punishment both men delivered and received, Ali retained the title.

By then, Ali was also on his way to becoming a pop culture icon around the world. He had long enjoyed that status among African Americans, who wholeheartedly approved of his black pride and his willingness to speak his mind in front of white audiences, but other Americans began to appreciate him too. The Vietnam War had turned out so badly that many people concluded that Ali had been correct in his decision not to serve. Also, the war was over, and when South Vietnam fell so quickly to North Vietnamese forces in 1975, millions of Americans realized what a complete folly the war had been.

There were other reasons for the dramatic elevation in Muhammad Ali's status. The urban violence of the 1960s, which had so frightened millions of whites, subsided in the 1970s, and Elijah Muhammad died on February 27, 1975. At the time of his death, the Nation of Islam enjoyed a membership of more than 100,000 people in seventy temples. Elijah Muhammad's son—Warith Deen Muhammad—assumed his father's mantle and soon abandoned the anti-white theology and steered the Nation of Islam into the mainstream Sunni Muslim community. Many Americans came to see Muhammad Ali simply as a Muslim, not a Black Muslim, and they no longer feared or resented his religious beliefs.

Finally, Ali's boxing career in the late 1970s thrilled sports-minded Americans, who came to see the courage, resiliency, and determination in Ali's character. Although his physical skills had deteriorated, he was still able to win boxing matches, now because he fought with mental toughness and strategic skill. On February 15, 1978, Ali lost the title to Leon Spinks, and seven months later, he became the first individual to win the heavyweight championship for a third time when he defeated Spinks in a rematch. He then retired from the ring. Like too many other old fighters, he tried a comeback in 1980 but lost two matches in quick succession and retired permanently.

Since then, Ali has become a beloved figure all around the world. A gentle man who has remained faithful to his religion, Ali has come to epitomize the best combination of pride and humility. Although suffering from Parkinson's syndrome, a neurological disorder caused by too many blows to the head over the years, Ali thrilled global television audiences in July 1996 when he lighted the torch at the summer Olympic Games in Atlanta, Georgia.

SUGGESTED READINGS: Thomas Hauser, *Muhammad Ali*, 1991; Muhammad Ali, *The Greatest*, 1975; Wilfred Sheen, *Muhammad Ali*, 1975; Jose Torres, *Sting Like a Bee: The Muhammad Ali Story*, 1971.

ALICE. *Alice* was one of the most popular television situation comedies of the 1970s and 1980s. First broadcast on CBS television on August 31, 1976, the show starred Linda Lavin as Alice Hyatt, Philip McKeon as Tommy Hyatt, Vic Tayback as Mel Sharples, and Polly Holliday as "Flo" Castleberry. Alice was a recently divorced single mother with a twelve-year-old son. She hoped to become a singer, but in the meantime she paid the bills by working as a waitress at Mel's Diner in Phoenix, Arizona. The television series was based on the successful film *Alice Doesn't Live Here Anymore*, which starred Ellen Burstyn. Many television historians consider *Alice* to be historically significant because it was the first situation comedy in American television with a working-class woman as its lead star. Until then, most women featured in situation comedies were middle- and upper middle-class married women.

SUGGESTED READING: Tim Brooks and Earle Marsh, *The Complete Directory to Prime Time Network and Cable TV Shows, 1946–Present*, 1995.

ALIEN. *Alien*, film director Ridley Scott's 1979 science fiction thriller, set aboard the spaceship *Nostromo* hundreds of years in the future, stars Tom Skerritt as Dallas, commander of the *Nostromo*; Sigourney Weaver as Ripley, the ship's executive officer; and Veronica Cartwright, Harry Dean Stanton, John Hurt, and Ian Holm as members of the crew. On its return voyage to earth after an extended stay at the edge of the galaxy, the *Nostromo* receives orders to investigate strange signals from an alien craft that has crash-landed on a nearby planet. During its investigation, the *Nostromo* inadvertently takes on board a malignant, pathological alien creature that needs human bodies to reproduce. *Alien*, a throwback to an earlier, 1950s genre of horror films, was not at all like the benign *Stars Wars** or *Close Encounters of the Third Kind.** One by one, the alien kills the crew members, leaving only one alive—executive officer Ripley. Eventually, through her own wits, she manages to kill the beast before it kills her. Ripley then settles in for the rest of her return voyage to Earth. Feminists loved the film because it provided an action heroine who prevailed over danger and evil. *Alien* eventually spawned three successful sequels.

SUGGESTED READING: *New York Times*, May 25, 1979.

ALL IN THE FAMILY. *All in the Family* was one of the most popular and controversial prime-time programs in television history. The show, which premiered on CBS in January 1971, starred Carroll O'Connor as Archie Bunker, Maureen Stapleton as Edith Bunker, Sally Struthers as Gloria Bunker Stivic, and Rob Reiner as Mike Stivic. The family lived in a working-class row house in Queens, New York. Archie was an unabashed blue-collar bigot ready to condemn ethnic and gender minorities at the drop of a hat. His politics ranged from populist to fascist to conservative. Predictably, his son-in-law Mike, who happened to be living in the Bunker home with his wife Gloria while he attended college, was a long-haired former hippie who was a politically correct, antiwar liberal. The extremism of Archie's bigotry was matched only by the superficial, predictable liberalism of Mike.

On each episode, Archie offered up his bufoonish, narrow-minded, and occasionally vulgar observations about women, politics, minorities, sexuality, race, ethnicity, and crime, and Michael and Gloria argued with him. Critics charged that the show made a hero out of a bigot, but most viewers saw Archie for what the writers and producers made him out to be—a well-meaning, hardworking, uneducated man whose attitudes were outrageously unacceptable. The character of Archie Bunker was not very different from Jackie Gleason's Ralph Kramden of *The Honeymooners* or Bill Bendix's Riley in the *Life of Riley* during the 1960s, but he voiced real prejudices and feelings about real issues. *All in the Family* was the number-one television program in America for five years, and combined with its transformation into *Archie Bunker's Place*, it remained on the air in prime time until 1983. *All in the Family* can still be seen in reruns in every major media market in the United States.

SUGGESTED READING: Donna McCrohan, *Archie & Edith, Mike & Gloria: The Tumultuous Years of All in the Family*, 1997.

THE ALLMAN BROTHERS BAND. The Allman Brothers Band, which still performs today, was formed in Macon, Georgia, in 1968 and became the model for subsequent groups like Lynryd Skynryd* and the Marshall Tucker Band,* which fused blues, rock and roll, and gospel music into a new genre. The original band included Duane Allman, Gregg Allman, Berry Oakley, Dickey Betts, Johnny Johanson, and Butch Trucks. Their debut album, *The Allman Brothers Band*, released in 1969, was a modest success; it sold well in the South but poorly elsewhere. *At Fillmore East* did better in 1971, reaching number ten on the charts. Shortly after its release, Duane Allman was killed in a motorcycle accident. *Eat a Peach* reached number four in 1972. In 1973 *Brothers and Sisters* went all the way to the top. Internal dissension disintegrated the band in the mid-1970s. They regrouped in 1978, and their 1979 album *Enlightened Rogues* sold enough copies to become a gold record.

SUGGESTED READING: Scott Freeman, *Midnight Riders: The Story of the Allman Brothers Band*, 1995.

ALL-VOLUNTEER MILITARY. By the last stages of the Vietnam War,* the U.S. military was approaching a point of collapse in terms of its morale. One reason in Vietnam was the obvious fact that the killing continued even though everybody was aware that President Richard Nixon * was gradually withdrawing U.S. troops from the theater. The war would soon be over, and little doubt existed in the minds of most Americans fighting there that North Vietnam would make short work of the South Vietnamese. Soldiers did not want to die for nothing, and their attitudes toward their military superiors reflected that attitude. Desertion rates and absent-without-leave (AWOL) cases had reached unprecedented levels. The fragging * (murder) of unpopular officers in Vietnam had become an increasingly serious problem by the early 1970s. Opposition to the Vietnam War had also made the military one of the country's most unpopular institutions. More than two million men had been inducted under the draft laws during the war. The selective service system administered the program, and critics charged that it was biased against minorities and working-class Americans; educated, middle-class whites were the least likely to be drafted during the Vietnam era.

The Nixon administration decided to address the problem by abandoning the draft and moving toward an all-volunteer military. With the war winding down in the early 1970s, military manpower needs no longer depended on the draft, and the president hoped to create a professional military establishment, one that would attract and keep good recruits and officers. General Creighton Abrams,* commander of U.S. forces in Vietnam in the early 1970s, supported the idea. He had grown tired of the problems of desertion, AWOLs, fragging of officers, and the horrendous drug abuse among his troops. One solution was obvious: scuttle the draft and enlist only volunteers who wanted military careers.

President Nixon did just that. Between 1968 and 1971, the president ordered a careful study be made of military manpower needs, and in December 1972, with the Paris Peace Talks* reaching their conclusion and the end of the Vietnam War in sight, Nixon announced the end of all draft calls and the beginning of an exclusively professional, all-volunteer military. Congress authorized better pay and more realistic benefits packages to make the recruitment of voluntary soldiers easier. By all accounts, the all-volunteer armed forces has been a resounding success.

SUGGESTED READINGS: Lawrence M. Baskir and William A. Strauss, *Chance and Circumstance: The Draft, the War, and the Vietnam Generation,* 1978; Stephen M. Kohn, *Jailed for Peace: The History of American Draft Law Violators,* 1986.

AMERICAN AGRICULTURAL MOVEMENT. During the 1970s, American farmers, especially small family farmers, found themselves caught between falling commodity prices and rising costs. The Arab oil boycott of 1973–1974,* along with geometric increases in the price of oil throughout the decade, imposed crushing costs for fuel, fertilizers, and chemicals. In 1977 Eugene and Derral Schroder, Alvin Jenkins, and Jerry Wright established the American Agricultural Movement (AAM) in Springfield, Colorado, to address the problems faced by the farming community. In June 1978 the AAM held a convention in Washington, D.C., and asked the Jimmy Carter* administration to raise the parity ratio on farm commodities to 100 percent, which would have guaranteed farmers an income equal to the cost of production, plus a reasonable profit. President Carter refused to support their demand, arguing that such massive government subsidies would be inflationary. In the 1980s, tens of thousands of farmers went bankrupt when they could not support the high-interest working capital loans that they had taken out to maximize production. The AAM then gained some more ground. By 1983 there were more than 600 AAM chapters in forty states.

To dramatize the plight of farmers and AAM demands, AAM leaders tried to sponsor production strikes and massive farm boycotts of livestock, grain, and equipment purchases, but they were unsuccessful. More spectacular and visible were the AAM "tractorcades" of the late 1970s and early 1980s, when farmers participated in long parades of slow-moving tractors through major American cities. It was difficult for farmers to wield much political power in the United States because, by the late 1980s, farmers constituted only 4 percent of the population, and production was increasingly dominated by large, corporate concerns. Nevertheless, the American Agricultural Movement was probably the most politically visible of all farm interest groups in the 1970s and 1980s.

SUGGESTED READING: Aruna Michie, *Why Farmers Protest,* 1980.

AN AMERICAN FAMILY. In 1973 the Public Broadcasting System broadcast in twelve episodes *An American Family,* one of the most unique television programs, up to its time, in American history. From May 1, 1971, to January 1, 1972, William and Patricia Loud of Santa Barbara, California, allowed a television crew complete access to their home and family. At the time, Bill Loud was fifty years old and Pat nearly forty-six; they had five children: Lance, twenty; Kevin, eighteen; Grant, seventeen; Delilah, fifteen; and Michele, thirteen. The series, produced by Craig Gilbert, was one of American television's first experiments with cinema verité, in which the medium explores reality, with all of its warts.

At the beginning of the series, the Louds appear to be a typical American, upper middle-class family. They are well-to-do, non-practicing Roman Catholics living the good life in one of California's loveliest cities. Their large Spanish-style stucco home is equipped with a pool, recording studio, and all of the latest amenities, including a four-car garage filled with foreign automobiles. Broadcast in twelve programs beginning in January 1973, *An American Family* became one of the major television events of the 1970s.

The supposedly idyllic suburban family was not quite so idyllic. During the course of the year, the Loud family disintegrated. Bill Loud had a drinking problem and was not faithful to Pat, and she gave the appearance of being emotionally tightly wound and ready to burst. Their son Lance came out of the closet and announced his homosexuality and his excitement with the gay life-style in New York City. In September 1971 Bill and Pat filed for divorce. At a time of the Watergate scandal, * the Vietnam War, * and escalating economic problems, *An American Family* convinced many Americans that a serious malaise blanketed the country.

SUGGESTED READING: *New York Times*, January 22–23, 1973.

AMERICAN GRAFFITI. *American Graffiti*, produced and directed by George Lucas,* was one of the most popular films of the 1970s and is today considered to be a classic by film historians. Lucas shot *American Graffiti* in twenty-eight days on a shoestring budget of $700,000. The film takes place in Modesto, California, in 1962—before the Vietnam War,* the assassination of John F. Kennedy, and the urban riots. It was an innocent time in American history, and the film evokes a profound sense of nostalgia. How much America had changed between the idyllic days of 1962 and the self-doubts of 1973. Two high school graduates—Steve (Ronnie Howard) and Curt (Richard Dreyfuss)—are on the eve of leaving for college. On their last night at home, they cruise Main Street in automobiles, drinking spiked Cokes, eating french fries, listening to rock and roll, and racing their cars. They realize that, in the morning, their lives will change; nothing will ever be the same again. The specter of change frightens them, and they both reconsider their plans. By the next morning, Curt is ready to leave for an eastern college, and Steve decides to stay home, marry his girlfriend (Cindy Williams), and go to junior college. *American Graffiti* reminded millions of Americans of a time when moral lines were more clearly drawn and right and wrong were easily distinguished from one another.

SUGGESTED READING: *New York Times*, August 5, 1973.

AMERICAN INDIAN MOVEMENT. During the decade of the 1970s, the American Indian Movement (AIM) became the most visible ethnic protest and advocacy group in the United States. After the assassination of Martin Luther

King, Jr., in 1968, the civil rights movement* lost some of its steam, and the urban rioting and rise of black power alienated many whites who had formerly supported the crusade for African-American rights. The rise of affirmative action* programs deepened white alienation. Just as the black civil rights movement was waning, the movement for Native American rights was accelerating.

Native American civil rights militancy had two primary sources. First, the termination program of the 1950s and 1960s, which ended the special legal status of many tribes and removed them from federal guardianship to state sovereignty, generated intense opposition among American Indians. Feeling exploited and deceived by the federal government, many Indians decided to take their cue from black militants and protest what was happening to them. Second, a new generation of well-educated, urban Indians was just coming of age in the late 1960s, and they were prepared to adopt militant political tactics to achieve their goals.

Many of the objectives of Indian militants were similar to those of black militants. They hoped to end racism, discrimination, negative stereotyping, and police brutality, and they wanted to secure full civil rights before the law. But Indian militancy also had different objectives from those of African-American activists. Indian militants felt that the whites had, over the centuries, robbed them of their landed estates. They began to campaign for the return of the stolen land or for monetary compensation under the Fifth Amendment, which awarded every American compensation for private property taken for public use under eminent domain proceedings. Many Indian activists also demanded exemption from state fish and game laws, which subjected them to the restrictions of seasonal hunting and fishing and catch limits. They argued that such laws were designed to prevent white people from hunting and fishing various species to extinction.

The most militant of the Native American advocacy groups in the 1970s was the American Indian Movement, which was established in Minneapolis, Minnesota, in 1968 by a group of Anishinabes (Chippewas) protesting police brutality. Among its founders were Dennis Banks,* Mary Jane Williams, and George Mitchell. They used the Black Panthers* as a model for their organization. In urban areas of the United States, where police forces were composed overwhelmingly of whites who lived in the suburbs, relationships between policemen and minority communities were usually tense and hostile. In such western cities as Oklahoma City, Albuquerque, Salt Lake City, Phoenix, Denver, Minneapolis, Milwaukee, and Los Angeles, Indian people received similar treatment, according to AIM leaders. Harassment and being beaten by police, AIM leaders claimed, had become commonplace. Like the Black Panthers in Oakland, California, AIM leaders organized patrols to follow police cars during patrols through towns. The process of monitoring police activities through ''Indian patrols'' brought about dramatic decreases in the arrests of Indian people, as well as complaints about police brutality. Those Indian patrols became the standard operating procedure for AIM chapters throughout urban America. Using insurgent political tactics, AIM soon established chapters in major American cities. In April 1972, AIM convened a protest demonstration at the Fort Totten Indian Reservation in North Dakota to demand an end to police brutality.

AIM did not come to the attention of national leaders, however, until 1969, when they participated in the occupation of Alcatraz Island* by Indians of All Tribes.* According to federal law, abandoned U.S. government property should revert to its previous owners, and they claimed that Alcatraz, an abandoned federal penitentiary, therefore belonged to Indians. A swarm of media descended on Alacatraz, and the occupation became the most publicized event in American Indian history. The occupation also became a model for the activities of AIM leaders in other areas of the country. Whites even found the occupation tactic intriguing, because they knew instinctively that Indians had lost their land through fraudulent white tactics, and the image of Indians reoccupying such land captured the public eye.

AIM leaders also wanted to end the negative stereotyping of Native Americans in the media, a demand that required protest demonstration to secure public attention. In April 1970, various AIM local chapters throughout the country staged protest demonstrations outside movie theaters showing the film *A Man Called Horse*, which was considered stereotypical by the Indians. Similar protests accompanied the release of other films about Indians in the 1970s.

AIM leaders continued to occupy territory that they deemed had been illegally seized from Indian tribes. Russell Means,* an Oglala Sioux raised in Oakland, California, became the most prominent AIM leader. Following the lead of Indians of All Tribes and the occupation of Alcatraz, Means, on July 4, 1971, led a protest at Mount Rushmore in South Dakota. In August 1971, AIM protestors seized an abandoned Coast Guard lifeboat station in Milwaukee, Wisconsin. Later in the year, on Thanksgiving Day, an AIM group occupied Plymouth Rock in Massachusets and painted it red in symbolic protest. In February 1972, Means led a "caravan" of more than 1,000 Indians into Gordon, Nebraska, to protest the murder of Raymond Yellowthunder, an Oglala, and the community's refusal to indict the killers. The protest succeeded in securing the indictments and eventual convictions of the white men involved in the crime. In February 1975, AIM activists occupied the Fairchild Camera factory in Shiprock, New Mexico, after the company decided to lay off 140 Navajo workers.

AIM leaders actively participated in "fish-ins" in the Pacific Northwest to protest state fish and game laws, and in 1972 they organized the Trail of Broken Treaties* caravan to Washington, D.C. In cars, buses, and vans, they left in October, stopping at reservations across the country to pick up more protesters. At Minneapolis, the caravan leaders issued their Twenty Points, a series of political demands. When they arrived in Washington, D.C., AIM leaders learned that their advance people had not made enough room arrangements. Most of the caravan went over to the Bureau of Indian Affairs (BIA) building. When federal guards in the building tried to push some of the demonstrators outside, the affair quickly became violent. The Native Americans seized the BIA building and blockaded all the doors and windows with office furniture. For six days they occupied the building, demanding amnesty and a government pledge to recognize the Twenty Points.

The Twenty Points constituted the minimum terms for their surrender to federal authorities. Foremost among them was the immediate rectification of treaty violations, the reestablishment of the treaty relationship formerly in operation between the U.S. government and the various tribes, the repeal of termination laws, the reversal of Public Law 280 and any laws executed under its auspices, the timely release of some 110 million acres of land for Indian use, tribal jurisdiction over crimes committed by non-Indians on the reservation, the substitution of an Office of Federal Indian Relations and Community Reconstruction directly in place of the BIA, and a variety of measures designed to foster cultural and economic development. Even though the protesters had ransacked the bureau offices, destroying BIA files and damaging considerable property, the Richard Nixon* administration wanted a negotiated settlement. On November 8, Nixon offered the protestors immunity from prosecution and transportation money to return home. The impasse was resolved.

Soon after the occupation of the BIA building, several hundred AIM members traveled to Rapid City, South Dakota, to protest the murder of Wesley Bad Heart Bull, an Oglala. Darold Schmitz, a white man, was charged with manslaughter in the case, but AIM protestors demanded an indictment for first-degree murder. On February 6, 1973, more than two hundred AIM protestors fought with police in Custer, South Dakota, over the incident. It soon escalated into AIM's most spectacular, most controversial protest demonstration: the occupation of Wounded Knee,* South Dakota, on the Pine Ridge Reservation.

The occupation began as a symbolic protest of Oglala Sioux politics, but when the Federal Bureau of Investigation (FBI) appeared on the scene, it became a broad-based protest of the plight of American Indians. Oglala traditionalists resented the leadership of Richard Wilson, who headed the federally backed tribal government. When they protested his leadership, the government dispatched sixty federal marshals to Pine Ridge. The traditionalists asked AIM for support. AIM protestors arrived at Pine Ridge, and on February 28, 1973, an armed confrontation began in the village of Wounded Knee. The FBI assigned 250 federal agents to the Pine Ridge Reservation to protect local property, enforce security, and establish ongoing surveillance of "radicals." On February 28, 1973, to protest the FBI's presence, Means led an AIM demonstration to Wounded Knee, where he claimed the establishment of a sovereign nation and demanded recognition. FBI agents and federal marshals soon surrounded them and set in motion a long-term siege. The standoff lasted for seventy-one days, with AIM committed to the notion of tribal sovereignty and the federal government committed to the destruction of AIM. When it was over, two Indians were dead and a federal marshal was permanently paralyzed.

The federal government then brought hundreds of charges against AIM leaders for their participation in the standoff, but of the 562 indictments, only fifteen convictions resulted, and these were for minor offenses. In the election for tribal president on the Pine Ridge Reservation in 1974, AIM nominated Russell Means for the office. In the election, Wilson won by a narrow margin, and although the Civil Rights Commission recommended decertification of the election because of irregularities, the BIA let it stand.

In 1975 AIM established a protest encampment at Jumping Bull near the Oglala village. Federal agents joined forces with the GOONS (Richard Wilson's Guardians of the Oglala Nation) and attacked the encampment. During the confrontation, a firefight took place. One AIM member and two federal agents were killed. Three AIM members—Bob Robideau, Darrel Butler, and Leonard Peltier—were brought to trial. Robideau and Butler were acquitted by an all-white jury, but Peltier was convicted of murder and given two life sentences.

After Wounded Knee, AIM membership gradually declined. AIM tended to be overrepresented by Sioux and Chippewas and failed to broaden its tribal representation significantly. The end of the Vietnam War* took a great deal of steam out of protest movements in general, and the civil rights movement entered a long period of decline in the 1970s. With the passage of the Indian Self-Determination Act of 1975, many Indian peoples felt they had succeeded, at least temporarily, in reversing the direction of government Indian policy. In 1974 Russell Means emerged as national chairperson of AIM. He promoted the International Indian Treaty Council* movement in the late 1970s. In 1978 Dennis Banks organized the Longest Walk* demonstration, which memorialized the Caravan of Broken Treaties protest of 1972. Since then, AIM has functioned more at the local than the national level in promoting Indian civil rights.

SUGGESTED READINGS: Ward Churchill and Jim Vander Wall, *Agents of Repression: The FBI's Secret War Against the Black Panther Party and the American Indian Movement*, 1988; Rex Weyler, *Blood of the Land: The Government and Corporate War Against the American Indian Movement*, 1982.

AMERICAN INDIAN RELIGIOUS FREEDOM ACT OF 1978. Religious freedom is and has been an important element of Indian culture. Natives, however, were excluded from constitutional guarantees of freedom of religion, an exclusion reinforced by a federal court in the decision *Native American Church v. Navajo Tribal Council*, 272 F. 2d 131 (10th Cir. 1959). Only Congress can protect Indians in the free expression of their religious beliefs. The American Indian Religious Freedom Act of 1978 prescribed that Native Americans should come under the "free exercise" clause of the First Amendment to the U.S. Constitution. No earlier legislation provided such protection, including the Indian Reorganization Act. That act confirmed and protected Indians' right to freedom of religion but did not place that protection under the First Amendment clause. The California Supreme Court, in *People v. Woody* (1964), gave constitutional freedom of religion only to California Native Americans.

However, as Robert S. Michaelson pointed out in 1985, the American Indian Religious Freedom Act was toothless; it stated only what should be done. Because it was in the form of a joint resolution of Congress, it possessed no provisions. A survey of cases revealed that the most important decisions had come when Indians sued to protect sacred sites from development or federal encroachment.

Indian religion is often more about place than a person. For many Indian peoples, religion revolves around notions of sacred geography. Those places are frequently located where developers or recreationists wish to build. The American Indian Religious Freedom Act does not specifically address that issue, but the courts since 1978 have protected many sacred places from development. That protection, however, has not been universal; courts have occasionally refused to protect a site. Courts seem to be reluctant to provide tests of protection for sites. The effects of the act have been mixed for Indians.

SUGGESTED READINGS: Vine Deloria, Jr., and Clifford M. Lytle, *American Indians, American Justice*, 1984; Arrell Morgan Gibson, *The American Indian: Prehistory to the Present*, 1980; Robert S. Michaelson, "Civil Rights, Indian Rites," in *The American Indian: Past and Present*, ed. Roger L. Nichols, 1985.

Timothy Morgan

AMERICAN TELEPHONE AND TELEGRAPH. The case of *U.S. v. American Telephone and Telegraph* during the 1970s constituted the largest federal antitrust suit in American history. At the time, American Telephone and Telegraph (AT&T) was the global leader in telecommunications. When the company was founded in 1885, by Theodore N. Vail, it was a subsidiary of the American Bell Telephone Company with responsibility for running the long-line operations of telephones. In 1900 the entire corporate structure was reorganized, and AT&T took control of the parent company. From that time until the early 1970s, AT&T expanded steadily, both in geography and in technology, creating the world's most sophisticated telephone system but also branching out into weapons technology and space and satellite communication systems and developing global radio and transoceanic cable communications systems. At the same time, AT&T began to develop a place for itself in the new world of computer technology. As a result of its extraordinary growth and the nature of communications technology at the time, when huge capital investments, in the form of transmission lines, were required for the distribution of information, AT&T became a horizontally and vertically integrated corporation, dominating the industry from top to bottom. Not only did AT&T maintain its own research corporation—Bell Telephone Laboratories—but it had its own product manufacturing unit in the Western Electric Company. In addition, AT&T maintained twenty-two local companies, known as "Baby Bells," which had regional monopolies of telephone service all over the United States.

Attorneys in the antitrust division of the Department of Justice became concerned that given the dominance of AT&T, it had become impossible for new communications companies to enter the market. The Department of Justice also concluded that a monopoly existed at the local and national level, which enabled

AT&T and its subsidiaries to charge whatever the market would bear. Although rates at the state level were often controlled by governmental commissions, critics charged that AT&T had essentially co-opted those state political bodies.

In 1974 the U.S. government sued AT&T for monopolizing the telephone industry. Company officials lobbied with the Richard Nixon* administration to drop the suit, but at the time, the president was in the midst of the Watergate scandal* and did not have the political clout to stall the case. President Gerald Ford* was little more than a caretaker at the White House, and in 1977, when Democrat Jimmy Carter* won the presidential election, the lawsuit against AT&T had a strong supporter. The suit wound its way through federal courts until 1982–1983 when AT&T agreed to divest its twenty-two local companies as of January 1, 1984. Those twenty-two local companies were consolidated into seven holding companies: Nynex, Bell, Atlantic, Ameritech, BellSouth, Southwestern Bell, US West, and Pacific Telesis. AT&T retained Western Electric and Bell Telephone Laboratories. The effect of the decision was to open the way for more competition in telephone service, especially for the long-distance markets. By the 1980s, AT&T was also the leader in linking up communications systems with computer technologies. The company strengthened its position in the computer field in 1991 by purchasing the NCR Corporation for $7.4 billion.

SUGGESTED READING: Sonny Kleinfeld, *The Biggest Company on Earth: A Profile of AT&T*, 1981.

AMOCO CADIZ. During the 1970s, the environmental movement* took on great political momentum among the developed nations, where citizens became interested in quality of life issues and the possibility that unbridled economic growth might compromise the future of the world. In March 1978, an oil spill off the French coast highlighted those concerns. The supertanker *Amoco Cadiz* ran aground off the Brittany coast. It was the world's third major oil spill in eighteen months, and more than 1.3 million barrels (546,000,000 gallons) of crude oil carpeted beaches and wetlands in a thick ooze, destroying bird and marine life, badly damaging the local fishing industry, and all but eliminating tourism.

While journalists examined just exactly what had happened, the *Cadiz* spill assumed bizarre proportions. A local tugboat appeared on the scene soon after the *Cadiz* ran aground, but the *Cadiz* captain felt that the tugboat skipper was asking too much money to tow the *Cadiz* back to deeper waters. With crude oil pouring into the North Sea, the two dickered over a few dollars, turning what might have been a serious but not devastating event into a national disaster— the worst oil spill, up to its time, in world history. While French volunteers spent months cleaning up the coast, the French government banned the travel of oil tankers within seven miles of the national coastline.

SUGGESTED READINGS: David Fairhall, *The Wreck of the Amoco Cadiz*, 1980; Rudolph Chelminski, *Superwreck: Amoco Cadiz; The Shipwreck That Had to Happen*, 1987.

AMTRAK. Amtrak is the trade name for the National Railroad Passenger Corporation, which provides noncommuter intercity rail passenger service throughout the United States. Although the U.S. government owns controlling amounts of Amtrak stock, there is also a minority of private stockholders. Because of the automobile boom in the United States and the huge volumes of capital put into road and highway construction, railroad passenger service steadily declined after World War II. The major railroads of the United States, long burdened by heavy debt structures and high capital costs, could not deliver passenger rail service profitably. By the 1960s, it was becoming clear that the economic viability of passenger rail service was threatened and that the United States was about to become the only major country in the world without such service.

To avoid that possibility and guarantee the future of railroad passenger service, Congress passed the National Railroad Passenger Act of 1970. Amtrak eventually purchased more than 24,000 miles of routes, which critics claimed was a huge "boondoggle," a "multibillion dollar welfare payment for railroads." When the energy crisis* struck the United States in 1973, the decision to launch Amtrak seemed even more timely, since fully utilized railroads could deliver passengers at a fraction of the energy cost of automobiles. The problem, of course, was full utilization, which rarely occurred. Travelers vastly preferred the convenience of automobiles, and Amtrak earned a bad initial reputation for late departures and late arrivals. The other convenience problem revolved around the fact that Amtrak delivered passengers to downtown locations, and if cities had poor public transportation systems, it was difficult for passengers to get to their final destinations. Throughout the 1970s, Amtrak operated at huge losses, and critics began calling for the end of federal subsidies.

For a while during the 1970s, Amtrak enjoyed an improving reputation. Modernization of equipment and increased ridership had improved its outlook. By the late 1980s, nearly two-thirds of its operating budget came from fares and one-third from federal subsidies. The good times were short lived, however. By the late 1980s, revenues began falling again, and in the 1990s Amtrak began drastically cutting back on unprofitable routes, to the point that some critics wondered whether it would ever really be economically viable. The government efforts to provide reliable rail service were successful in terms of passenger convenience, but they never managed to operate the road in the black. With the resurgence of conservative political values in the 1980s, Americans became less enamored with the role of government in providing services, and Amtrak lost considerable political support.

SUGGESTED READING: Harold A. Edtnonson, *Journey to Amtrak*, 1972.

ANIMAL HOUSE. Animal House was the epic fraternity party film of the 1970s. At upscale Faber College (actually Dartmouth) in 1962, Animal House is a euphemism for Delta House, the worst fraternity on campus, a decrepit shambles inhabited by a band of fun-loving, idiotic, scatalogical young men more interested in partying than studying and completely unable to exit their adolescence. Naturally, they must confront the combined forces of elite houses, ROTC, and narrow-minded deans bent on decertifying Delta House and expelling the fraternity from campus. The film is a sequence of uproarious pranks played out by Larry Kroger (Tom Hulce), Kent Dorfman (Stephen Furst), and John Blutarsky (John Belushi). The college eventually succeeds in suspending Delta House, but the "animals" get even in the end by ruining the college's annual downtown parade. A production of *National Lampoon* magazine, the film was a huge hit among students and young adults, who returned again and again to theaters to see the movie. *Animal House*'s popularity emerged from its ability to evoke images of a simpler time and nostalgia for American innocence before the Vietnam War,* the Manson family, and the assassinations of the Kennedys and Martin Luther King, Jr.

SUGGESTED READING: *New York Times*, July 28, 1978.

ANNIE HALL. Woody Allen's brilliant comedy and love story *Annie Hall* was released in 1977. The film, which stars Woody Allen as Alvy, a neurotic New York Jew, and Diane Keaton as Annie, a ditsy WASP, tells the story of their falling in and out of love as both try to come to terms with the conjunction of the sexual revolution, the women's movement,* and emerging Yuppiedom. *Annie Hall* won Oscars for Best Picture, Best Director, Best Actress, and Best Screenplay.

SUGGESTED READING: *New York Times*, September 17, 1977.

ANTI-BALLISTIC MISSILE TREATY (1972). When the Nuclear Non-Proliferation Treaty was signed in 1968, American and Soviet officials agreed that the next item in nuclear weapons diplomacy would revolve around the need for mutual reductions in the stockpiles of strategic nuclear weapons. Not only was the race for nuclear superiority increasing the risk of global thermonuclear war, the expense of developing increasingly sophisticated, and destructive, nuclear technologies posed financial problems to both the United States and the Soviet Union. What became known as the Strategic Arms Limitation Talks* (SALT) between the United States and the Soviet Union began in 1969.

Soviet diplomats, however, proved quite reluctant to cooperate in any serious negotiations until President Richard Nixon* proposed to Congress the need for the development of an anti-ballistic missile shield to protect the United States from a Soviet nuclear first strike. Nixon took heat from congressional Democrats, who argued that the defensive system would be too expensive, and from scientists, who doubted the feasibility of the proposal. But the president's proposal was more a diplomatic ploy than a nuclear arms issue. The nuclear arms race placed more pressure on the Soviet economy than on the American, and the Soviets did not want to find themselves in an expensive race to develop an anti-ballistic missile system. The SALT negotiations then began to progress. Talks continued until early 1972 when the two sides agreed to the Anti-Ballistic Missile (ABM) Treaty, in which they mutually pledged to disengage from the development of anti-ballistic missile shields. Without the possibility of anti-ballistic systems becoming part of each side's defensive infrastructure, the ABM Treaty jumpstarted negotiations to freeze nuclear missile deployments. The Anti-Ballistic Missile Treaty was signed by President Nixon and Soviet Premier Leonid Brezhnev on May 26, 1972.

SUGGESTED READING: Richard L. Garwin, Kurt Gottfried, and Henry Kendall, eds., *The Fallacy of Star Wars*, 1984.

ANTIWAR MOVEMENT. By 1970 the antiwar movement protesting the Vietnam War* had largely run out of steam. During the presidential election campaign of 1968, Republican candidate Richard Nixon* had hinted to voters that he would be able to bring the war to an honorable conclusion, but after his inauguration in January 1969, he waited several months before initiating any policy changes, and the delay galvanized the antiwar movement. On March 26, Women Strike for Peace pickets carried out the first large-scale antiwar demonstration since the inauguration. Nixon soon announced his plan of Vietnamization,* which would turn the war gradually over to the South Vietnamese. In June 1969, he informed the country that he was planning to withdraw 25,000 of the 543,000 soldiers from Vietnam. Nevertheless, two antiwar groups—the Vietnam Moratorium Committee and the reconstituted New Mobilization Committee to End the War in Vietnam—decided to sponsor a series of nationwide protests on a monthly basis beginning in October 1969. Millions of people participated in the demonstrations on October 15, 1969. Thousands of soldiers in South Vietnam wore black armbands to support the demonstrations. Another nationwide demonstration took place in November.

By that time, however, it had become clear to most Americans that the president was trying to live up to his campaign promises to wind down the war. When he took office in January 1969, the number of troops exceeded 543,000, and one year later they had fallen to below 475,000. During the previous four years, the antiwar movement had escalated from a small group of left-wing pacifists to millions of Americans who opposed the war. Antiwar liberals condemned the Vietnam War because they believed it was an immoral war fought for the wrong reasons. Antiwar conservatives condemned the war effort because they believed that it was a badly managed conflict that asked soldiers to do the impossible. As Nixon implemented his staged troop withdrawals, the antiwar movement all but disappeared from public life.

In April 1970, however, the president galvanized the antiwar movement into frenetic activity. The withdrawal of U.S. troops from Vietnam posed difficult strategic issues for the president. Like Dwight Eisenhower, John Kennedy, and Lyndon Johnson before him, Richard Nixon did not want to become the first U.S. president "to lose a war," but that was a distinct possibility because the South Vietnamese forces were so inept. In order to keep on top of the conflict militarily even while U.S. troops levels were declining, the president decided to increase U.S. bombing campaigns and expand the war into previously neutral areas. In April 1970, President Nixon ordered U.S. troops into Cambodia to eliminate the Vietcong and North Vietnamese sanctuaries there.

Almost overnight, the antiwar movement kicked into gear again. Protests on college campuses attracted millions of demonstrators, and hundreds of thousands of antiwar activists descended on Washington, D.C., and camped out on the mall area. The ferocity of the demonstrations caught the Nixon administration off guard. None of the administration's rhetoric—such as using the term "incursion" instead of "invasion" to describe the Cambodian operation—satisfied critics, who feared that Nixon was actually escalating the war. Only when the president withdrew U.S. troops from Cambodia in June 1970 did the antiwar demonstrations subside. As Nixon incrementally but steadily reduced the number of U.S. combat troops in Vietnam, the number of American casualties declined, as did the expense of the war. His policy of Vietnamization seemed a reasonable approach to most Americans. As U.S. troop levels declined toward zero in 1972, the antiwar movement became all but moribund, except for brief outbursts during Nixon's Christmas bombing campaigns in 1972.

SUGGESTED READINGS: Charles DeBenedetti and Charles Chatfield, *An American Ordeal: The Antiwar Movement of the Vietnam Era*, 1990; David W. Levy, *The Debate over Vietnam*, 1991; Melvin Small, *Johnson, Nixon, and the Doves*, 1988; Nancy Zaroulis and Gerald Sullivan, *Who Spoke Up? American Protest Against the War in Vietnam, 1963–1975*, 1984.

APOCALYPSE NOW. *Apocalypse Now* is the title of Francis Ford Coppola's 1979 antiwar film. Hollywood had been slow to put Vietnam stories in film, and it was not until 1978 that movies like *The Boys in Company C,* The Deer Hunter,** and *Coming Home** made their way into commercial distribution. *Apocalypse Now* was by far the most ambitious of those films. Filming it was a nightmare for Coppola. The hot, humid weather on location in the Philippines sapped the energies of the actors and often fouled up the equipment. The movie was a labor of love for Coppola, however, and he spared no expense. In the end, *Apocalypse Now* became the most expensive film in Hollywood history.

Based loosely on Joseph Conrad's novel *Heart of Darkness*, the film stars Marlon Brando as Colonel Kurtz, Robert Duvall as Lieutenant Colonel Kilgore, and Martin Sheen as Captain Willard. Colonel Kurtz is a rogue Green Beret who has deserted the army and has headed up into the highlands, where he rules a Montagnard kingdom of his own. Colonel Kilgore, a firepower-happy American military robot, sees violence and combat as ends in themselves. Captain Willard is charged with the task of going upriver into the highlands to find Kurtz and exterminate him before he becomes more of an embarrassment to the United States or, worse, a military force of his own. Willard eventually succeeds in his mission, but, in the process, the Vietnam conflict is shown to be a hopelessly contradictory, unwinnable war that built nothing and destroyed everything.

SUGGESTED READINGS: Linda Dittmar and Gene Michaud, eds., *From Hanoi to Hollywood: The Vietnam War in American Film*, 1990; *New York Times*, August 15, 1979.

APPLE. Late in the 1960s, engineers revolutionized the computer industry with the invention of the integrated circuit (IC)—an extremely tiny silicon chip used as a stage for hundreds of transistors, diodes, and resistors. The huge mainframes, such as IBM's 360, soon gave way to smaller hardware systems capable of processing just as much information. In 1971 computer sizes became even smaller because of the invention of the microprocessor. The microprocessor represented a giant technological leap forward, since it contained a large-scale integrated (LSI) circuit. Each LSI on a single chip contained hundreds of thousands of electronic components. Improvements soon made it possible for information to be processed by a mouse, optical scanners, and keyboards. The LSI soon led to random access memory (RAM) chips, which enabled the permanent storage and constant updating of information.

In 1976 two college dropouts in California took commercial advantage of the new computer technologies by inventing the Apple I, and easy-to-use personal computer (PC) designed for individual home and office use. Steven Wozniak was the engineering genius behind Apple, and Steven Jobs provided the entrepreneurial skills. Apple quickly became the fastest growing company in American history, making Jobs and Wozniak two of the richest individuals in the United States.

SUGGESTED READINGS: Lee Butcher, *Accidental Millionaire: The Rise and Fall of Steven Jobs and Apple Computer*, 1988; Keith Elliot Greenberg, *Steven Jobs and Stephen Wozniak: Creating the Apple Computer*, 1994.

ARAB OIL BOYCOTT OF 1973–1974. The long-simmering problems in the Middle East erupted into war in the 1970s and posed unprecedented economic problems to the United States. On October 6, 1973, Egyptian and Syrian troops launched a simultaneous invasion of the Sinai Desert and the Golan Heights, both Israeli-occupied territories. Journalists dubbed it the Yom Kippur War* because the invasion began on the sacred Jewish holiday. Egypt claimed sovereignty over the Sinai; Syria over the Golan Heights. The Soviet Union airlifted massive supplies to the Arab armies, and the United States then agreed to resupply Israel with all the military equipment it needed to survive. Bloody, armored warfare ensued on Middle Eastern desert battlefields, but Israel soon prevailed, laying siege to the Egyptian city of Suez and trapping the Egyptian Third Army up against the canal.

When the Israelis threatened to annihilate an entire Egyptian army, Secretary of State Henry Kissinger* began his so-called shuttle diplomacy between Cairo, Tel Aviv, and Damascus, trying to forge a settlement. On October 22, he managed to establish a cease-fire between Israel and Egypt, and two days later Syria joined as well. In mid-November, Israel lifted the siege of Suez and allowed the safe withdrawal of the Egyptian army, and the belligerents began the mutual exchange of prisoners of war. A United Nations peacekeeping force deployed to the Middle East to preserve the cease-fire. Late in December, peace talks were undertaken in Geneva, Switzerland, to work out a more permanent settlement. One month later, Egypt and Israel agreed to mutual troop withdrawals. Final peace documents were not signed until May 31, 1974.

The war itself may have been over, but its impact on the world economy was just beginning. Frustrated with the transparent willinginess of the United States to side so consistently with Israel, oil-rich Arab nations decided to retaliate. In mid-October, eleven Arab oil-producing states announced a 5 percent reduction in oil exports and an outright boycott of crude oil to the United States and any other country friendly to Israel.

The economic consequences were immediate. The boycott inspired a scramble for oil in Western Europe, Japan, and the United States. The Organization of Petroleum Exporting Countries* (OPEC) took quick advantage of the boycott and jacked up crude oil prices from four to twelve dollars a barrel. Gasoline shortages soon appeared in the United States, and pump prices skyrocketed. In Houston, Texas, regular gasoline, which sold for $0.19 a gallon on October 1, hit $0.60 a gallon three months later. Farmers, shippers, and manufacturers passed the costs on to consumers, and the retail price index ballooned.

Although the Arab nations called off the boycott on March 18, 1974, the decision had little impact on prices. After years of importing cheap foreign oil, American production, which was more expensive, had declined dramatically. For the first time in its history, the United States was dependent on foreign oil producers and had to accept world market prices. The boycott ended but inflation did not. In 1974 the consumer price index went up 7 percent.

An unusual twist complicated the inflation. In the past—during the Civil War, World War I, World War II, the Korean War, and early in the Vietnam War*— rising prices had always occurred in the context of full employment. Consumers may have been paying more for goods, but their jobs were secure and their wallets full. This ''war'' was different. With so much disposable income going to the purchase of petroleum and natural gas, consumers reduced their demand for other industrial goods, causing declines in production and pink slips for workers. Economists soon described the new economic reality as stagflation*— unemployment and rapidly escalating prices in a stagnant, shrinking economy, the worst of both worlds.

SUGGESTED READINGS: Chaim Herzog, *The War of Atonement, October 1973*, 1975; Fesheraki Fereidun, *OPEC, the Gulf, and the World Petroleum Market*, 1982.

ATTICA. The word ''Attica'' became a euphemism for prison brutality in the 1970s. Attica State Prison, located east of Buffalo, New York, was badly over-crowded on September 9, 1970, when 1,200 prisoners rioted and seized control of the facility. Most of the prisoners who rebelled were African Americans and Puerto Ricans. In recent years, the prison had become a civil rights battleground between minority inmates who felt mistreated and white correctional officers who had no intention of ''coddling'' criminals. A significant number of the leaders of the rebellion were members of the Black Panthers* and the Nation of Islam. The death in December 1969 of Black Panther leader Fred Hampton at the hands of Chicago police had produced demands for better treatment from inmate leaders.

The rioters took thirty prison employees hostage, many of them correctional officers, and issued their demands to the press. The rioters requested a variety of penal reforms—better food, improved libraries, pay for work, less crowding, and less guard brutality—as well as amnesty for crimes committed during the riot itself. Inmate leaders entered into negotiations with representatives of Governor Nelson Rockefeller* of New York, but after several days, the talks broke down. The governor ordered state police to retake Attica.

On September 13, hundreds of National Guardsmen, state police, correctional officers, and other law enforcement officials opened fire and launched a military assault on Attica State Prison. It was a bloody confrontation that resulted in the shooting deaths of twenty-eight prisoners and twelve guards. State police insisted that the inmates had killed the guards, but a subsequent investigation proved that police gunfire was responsible for every one of the forty deaths at Attica. Although sixty-two indictments were returned against various inmates, by 1976 most of the cases had been dismissed.

SUGGESTED READINGS: Malcolm Bell, *The Turkey Shoot: Tracking the Attica Cover-Up*, 1985; Tom Wicker, *A Time to Die: The Attica Prison Revolt*, 1994.

B

B-1 BOMBER. Early in the 1970s, the U.S. Air Force proposed to build, at a cost of approximately $25 billion, a total of 244 B-1 bombers, a new generation of swept-wing, supersonic bombers designed to replace the aging B-52 bombers. North American Rockwell Corporation was awarded the contract for the aircraft. Supporters of the new weapons system claimed that the B-52 fleet was rapidly becoming obsolete and losing its technological superiority over high-altitude Soviet bombers. They also claimed that the B-52 was becoming more and more vulnerable to Soviet defense systems, and that if that process continued, the Russians might be inclined to launch a first strike. At the time, the Soviet Union's nuclear delivery systems relied more heavily on intercontinental ballistic missiles than on high-altitude bombers, while the B-52s constituted the heart of the U.S. nuclear capability. If those B-52s were becoming obsolete and vulnerable to Soviet defense systems, Russian leaders might conclude that a first strike was worth the risk.

Inside Congress, critics led by Senator William Proxmire questioned the Pentagon's logic. Proxmire claimed that the B-1 was not really cost effective. Total costs, he predicted, would eventually spin completely out of control, doubling or tripling the final bill for the 244 bombers. He also claimed that the B-52 could be re-equipped with state-of-the-art U.S. radar systems, which, far superior to their Soviet equivalents, would dramatically reduce their vulnerability to surface-to-air missile attack. Proxmire also claimed that the B-52s could be refitted with cruise missiles and achieve the same strategic gains at a fraction of the cost. North American Rockwell and the Pentagon launched an unprecedented media campaign to drum up support for the project, claiming that cancellation would cost the defense industry 35,000 jobs.

The whole controversy became a high-stakes political football game, with President Jimmy Carter* acting as referee. Although Carter agreed with Proxmire that the B-1 was unnecessary and that B-52s could be suitably refitted, he also worried about the jobs issue. The country was caught in the midst of the energy crisis* and stagflation,* and unemployment was running high. Cutting the B-1 would be unpopular, especially in California, where North American Rockwell was headquartered. Carter hoped to be reelected in 1980, and he would need California's electoral votes. In the end, however, the president put politics aside, and in July 1977 he canceled the B-1 program. Predictably, he received enormous political criticism for the decision in California and was not reelected.

SUGGESTED READINGS: William G. Holder, *The B-1 Bomber*, 1988; Jeffrey A. Merkley, *The B-1B Bomber and Options for Enhancement*, 1988; *Newsweek*, July 11, 1977; Wayne Wachsmuth, *The B-1 Lance: In Detail and Scale*, 1990.

BAD COMPANY. Bad Company, a rock-and-roll band formed in England in 1973, included Paul Rodgers, Mick Ralphs, Simon Kirke, and Boz Burrell. Their debut album, *Bad Company* (1974), became number one around the world, largely because of its hit single "Can't Get Enough." In the next two years, their albums *Straight Shooter* and *Run with the Pack* went platinum. Five years later, *Desolation Angels* was another hit. The group broke up in 1982.

SUGGESTED READING: Patricia Romanowski and Holly George-Warren, eds., *The New Encyclopedia of Rock & Roll*, 1985.

BANKS, DENNIS. Dennis Banks, an Anishnabe Native American, was born in 1930 on the Leech Lake Indian Reservation in northern Minnesota. In 1968, with Clyde Bellecourt* and other Indian community members, Banks organized the American Indian Movement* (AIM) to protect the traditional ways of Indian people, improve government-funded social services, and prevent the harassment of local Native Americans by police. On Thanksgiving Day, 1970, while attempting to extend its activism to a national audience, Banks and other members of AIM seized the *Mayflower II*,* a replica of the original ship that had carried the Pilgrims to the North American continent. AIM members proclaimed Thanksgiving Day a national day of mourning in protest against the seizure of Indian lands by the early white colonists.

In February 1973, Banks and other AIM members led a protest in Custer, South Dakota, after the mother of murder victim Wesley Bad Heart Bull was pushed down a flight of stairs following a meeting with officials. Banks was arrested as a result of his involvement in the seventy-one day occupation of Wounded Knee,* South Dakota, in 1973. Acquitted of charges related to the occupation at Wounded Knee, Banks was convicted of assault with a deadly weapon without intent to kill and rioting while armed, charges stemming from the Custer incident. After jumping bail, he fled to California. Governor Jerry Brown* refused to honor extradition requests from South Dakota, citing the strong hostility there against AIM members in general and Banks in particular. In March 1983, the Onondaga Nation, located south of Syracuse, New York, granted Banks asylum. Later in the year, after nine years as a fugitive, Banks surrendered to state authorities in Rapid City, South Dakota. He served approximately one year of a three-year sentence.

In the late 1980s, Banks actively protested the disturbance of Native American ancestral burial grounds by collectors and archaeologists. Due in part to Bank's efforts, the Smithsonian Museum agreed to return 25,000 Indian bones and other artifacts for reburial. Banks organized ceremonies for over twelve hundred of these reinternment efforts. In 1988 Banks published his autobiography, *Sacred Soul*, in Japanese rather than English, citing English as the language of the conquerors. Banks played important roles in the movies *The Last of the Mohicans* (1992) and *Thunderheart* (1992).

SUGGESTED READINGS: Arlene Ehrlich, "The Right to Rest in Peace," *The Sun*, Baltimore, Maryland, October 22, 1989; David Holmstrom, "Oglala Sioux: Up from Wounded Knee, Parts 1–3," *Christian Science Monitor*, October 16–18, 1989; Stanley David Lyman, *Wounded Knee, 1973: A Personal Account*, 1991; Kenneth Stern, *Loud Hawk. The United States Versus the American Indian Movement*, 1994; Rex Weyler, *Blood of the Land: The Government and Corporate War Against the American Indian Movement*, 1984; Theodore W. Taylor, *American Indian Policy*, 1983.

David Ritchey

BARBIE. "Barbie" was the brainchild of Ruth Handler, one of the founders of the Mattel Toy Company. By 1954, one decade after the company's founding—on the backs of such toys as Chuck Wagon, Lullabye Crib, Peek-A-Boo Egg, Jack-in-the-Box, and Musical Merry-Go-Round—Mattel sales had reached $14 million a year. Ten years later, the annual gross exceeded $100 million, making the company the top toymaker in the country.

Barbie explained Mattel's phenomenal success. In the late 1940s and early 1950s, research and development at Mattel were quite simple: the Handlers watched children play. Ruth became fascinated with her daughter Barbie's affection for paper dolls. Although Barbie and her little girlfriends spent some time with traditional baby dolls, they pretended to be adults when they played with paper dolls, dressing and undressing the cardboard figures for hours on end, creating a make-believe world of dates, proms, weddings, and outings. When Handler broached the idea of creating an adult plastic doll, complete with different outfits, the men at Mattel brushed her off, claiming that the doll would require an Asian manufacturer to keep costs down. "That was the *official* reason," she later wrote. "But I really think that the squeamishness of those designers—every last one of them male—stemmed mostly from the fact that the doll would have *breasts* . . . Elliott [her husband] claimed that 'no mother will ever buy her daughter a doll with a chest'."

She promoted her idea unsuccessfully until 1956, when she returned home from a family vacation in Lucerne, Switzerland. During an afternoon of shopping, Ruth and Barbara noticed Lilli—an eleven-inch adult doll dressed in a European ski outfit—adorning the window of a Lucerne shop. Six versions of Lilli in the window each had a different outfit. Handler purchased one of the

Lilli dolls for Barbara and then asked about buying just the outfits from the other dolls. When the clerk informed her that each doll and each outfit were a single unit, Handler had a brainstorm. Millions of little girls in America, she was convinced, would want one of the dolls and dozens of outfits—wedding gowns, nightgowns, prom dresses, sports ensembles, casual fashions, school clothes. There was a fortune to be made, and Handler made it.

It took several years for the Handlers to structure a manufacturing system, which required overseas factory production of the doll and its accessories. By the mid-1960s, however, Barbie had become one of the most successful toys in American manufacturing history. Tens of millions of American girls received the doll as birthday and Christmas gifts, and the accessories proved to be a cash cow for Mattel.

During the 1970s, the popularity and profitability of Barbie continued for Mattel, but the doll also became part of the culture wars affecting the United States during the decade. As the women's movement* strengthened, the Barbie doll was targeted for criticism by feminists, who felt the doll created stereotypical images of womanhood. With her tiny waist, long, slim legs, and pointed, uplifted breasts, the doll became a pop culture icon in the United States and around the world, with tens of millions of prepubescent girls expecting and hoping that their own bodies would develop that way. The bodies of real women, of course, come in infinite variety, with very few fitting the Barbie mold. Feminists also claimed that Barbie only intensified the way in which American culture treated women as sexual objects, even creating in the minds of little girls the expectation that they should be treated that way.

Mattel responded with Ruth Handler's typical marketing genius. She wanted to blunt the criticism but also wanted to continue to make money from the sale of the toy. Mattel broadened the range of accessories to accompany the doll. In the past the accessories had fit into what feminists called a sexist mode—bathing suits, bikinis, prom dresses, wedding dresses, and a variety of recreational clothing. Late in the 1970s, Mattel added a line of occupational clothing, so that Barbie could be dressed up as a lawyer, doctor, businesswoman, and engineer, making the doll less objectionable to some feminists. Ruth Handler was right too. Sales of the doll and the accessories accelerated. By the mid-1990s, Barbie sales around the world had a total of $1.1 billion annually.

SUGGESTED READING: Ruth Handler, *Dream Doll*, 1994.

BARNABY JONES. *Barnaby Jones* was an extraordinarily popular television dramatic series of the 1970s. CBS broadcast the first episode on January 28, 1973. The private detective series starred Buddy Ebsen (of Jed Clampett of *Beverly Hillbillies* fame) as Barnaby Jones. Jones had retired from a career in private investigation and had turned his business over to his son. When his son was murdered, however, Jones came out of retirement to find the killer. His widowed daughter-in-law, Betty Jones (Lee Meriwether), assisted him in the business. Barnaby Jones was an unassuming, homespun character who was generally underestimated by his targets. In the 1970s, when Americans were re-bounding from the traumas of the 1960s, *Barnaby Jones* offered a conservative, gentle law-and-order escapist theater every week. Its last episode was broadcast on September 4, 1980.

SUGGESTED READINGS: Buddy Ebsen, *The Other Side of Oz*, 1993.

"BATTLE OF THE SEXES." The term "battle of the sexes" served as the billing for the superhyped 1973 tennis match between Bobby Riggs and Billie Jean King. At the time, Billie Jean King was the most well-known female athlete in the world. She had won twenty Wimbledon singles and doubles titles, and she was campaigning for gender equity in tennis. King wanted women's purses to be equal to those of men. Bobby Riggs, a retired tennis professional in his fifties, claimed that there should be no gender equity in tennis because the men's game was so superior to the women's game. He then claimed that he could beat Billie Jean King, even though he was thirty years her senior. Actually, Riggs knew that he could make a nice paycheck from the event. King took him up on the challenge. The two met in the Astrodome in Houston, Texas, on September 20, 1973, before 30,000 spectators and a national television audience. King made short work of Riggs, whose game was no match for hers. Although the so-called battle of the sexes was more hype than anything else, it does stand as a bench-mark of sorts in the rise of the women's movement* in the 1970s.

SUGGESTED READING: *New York Times*, September 20–22, 1973.

THE BEE GEES. The Bee Gees, one of the most commercially popular bands of the 1970s, was formed in Brisbane, Australia, in 1958. The original group included brothers Maurice Gibb, Barry Gibb, and Robin Gibb. They played small-town events in Australia during the early 1960s and had several American hits later in the decade, including "To Love Somebody" (1967), "Holiday" (1967), "Words" (1968), "I've Got to Get a Message to You" (1968), and "I Started a Joke" (1969). Two more hits followed in 1970 and 1971: "Lone Days" and "How Can You Mend a Broken Heart."

Their luck changed, however, in 1971, and the Bee Gees put together several flops. In an attempt to recover their popularity, they moved to Miami in 1975 and started playing rhythm and blues. In 1976 they had two megahits: "You Should Be Dancing" and "Love So Right." But their real success came in 1977 when they supplied five songs for the soundtrack of the film *Saturday Night Fever*.* The soundtrack included their hit singles "Stayin' Alive," "Night Fe-ver," and "How Deep Is Your Love." By the end of the decade, the Bee Gees had accumulated a total of five platinum albums and twenty hit singles. They had been the perfect pop culture act for the 1970s. At a time when Americans had tired of 1960s-like protest and were more worried about just getting by on a day-to-day basis, the Bee Gees delivered non-threatening, non-political escapist music, and Americans made them one of the most successful musical groups of the decade.

SUGGESTED READINGS: Barry Gibb, *The Bee Gees: The Official Autobiography*, 1979; Paul Sahner, *The Bee Gees*, 1979; Craig Schumacher, *The Bee Gees*, 1979.

BELLECOURT, CLYDE. Clyde Bellecourt, an Ojibway Native American, was born in 1939 on the White Earth Reservation in Minnesota. Bellecourt, with Dennis Banks* and other Native American community leaders, cofounded the American Indian Movement* in Minneapolis, Minnesota, in July 1968. The American Indian Movement (AIM) was originally formed to improve government-funded social services to urban neighborhoods and to prevent the harassment of local Native Americans by police. Increasingly confrontational, Bellecourt and other AIM leaders implemented an armed occupation of the tiny South Dakota hamlet of Wounded Knee* on February 27, 1973. Bellecourt was elected to the council of the AIM-declared "Nation of Wounded Knee" and eventually cosigned the peace agreement that ended the confrontation. Not long after Wounded Knee, Bellecourt was wounded when he was shot in the stomach by Carter Camp, another occupation leader.

During the 1972 occupation of the Bureau of Indian Affairs building in Washington, D.C., Bellecourt helped draft the Twenty Points, a document presented to the government. Although AIM demands were ignored, the government did establish a task force that met with movement leaders and promised to make no arrests in connection with the occupation. Bellecourt also worked extensively to raise funds for AIM-sponsored projects, and he was briefly associated with militant black activist Stokely Carmichael.

In the 1990s, Bellecourt lobbied energetically on behalf of the Mille Lac Chippewa during their struggle to maintain traditional walleye pike harvests along the shores of Flathead Lake in Minnesota. Earlier successes in Wisconsin allowed Native Americans to continue their treaty-guaranteed right to maintain their traditional subsistence fishing economy. Powerful opposition in Minnesota, led by former Minnesota Viking football coach Bud Grant, persuaded the state legislature to reject an agreement that would have allowed the tribe to harvest about half of the walleye pike in Flathead Lake.

SUGGESTED READINGS: Margaret L. Knox, "The New Indian Wars: A Growing Movement is Gunning," *Los Angeles Times*, November 7, 1993; Edward Lazarus, *Black Hills, White Justice: The Sioux Nation Versus the United States, 1775 to the Present*, 1991; Stanley David Lyman, *Wounded Knee, 1973: A Personal Account*, 1991; Kenneth Stern, *The United States Versus the American Indian Movement*, 1994; Rex Weyler, *Blood of the Land: The Government and Corporate War Against the American Indian Movement*, 1984.

David Ritchey

BERLIN TREATY (QUADRIPARTITE AGREEMENT ON BERLIN, 1971). Ever since the Berlin Airlift of 1947–1948, controversy had raged over access to the city of Berlin. The city was located inside East Germany, but at the end of World War II it had been divided into two zones—West Berlin and East Berlin. To stop the movement of refugees from Communist-controlled East Germany into West Berlin, a wall dividing the city had been constructed by Communists in 1961. Formal diplomatic discussions over access to West Berlin commenced in 1969 when Willy Brandt became chancellor of West Germany.

In 1971 the negotiations reached fruition with the Quadripartite Agreement on Berlin, in which the Soviet Union guaranteed open access through East Germany to West Berlin and agreed to allow West Berliners to visit relatives in East Berlin and East Germany during a thirty-day period each year. In return, West Germany promised to stop holding parliamentary sessions in West Berlin, and the Western powers agreed to no longer refer to West Berlin as a ''constituent part'' of West Germany. Between September and December 1971, the following entities signed the treaty: the Soviet Union, the United States, Great Britain, France, East Germany, West Germany, East Berlin, and West Berlin.

SUGGESTED READING: *New York Times*, September 4–6, 1971.

THE BERRIGAN BROTHERS. Daniel and Philip Berrigan were born in Minnesota in 1921 and 1923, respectively. After completing college, both became Jesuit priests who committed their lives to liberal social and political activism. Daniel founded the Catholic Peace Fellowship in 1964 and Clergy and Laity Concerned About Vietnam in 1965. In 1964 Philip founded the Emergency Citizens Group Concerned About Vietnam and helped establish the Catholic Peace Fellowship. The two brothers actively opposed the Vietnam War* during the 1960s and early 1970s. On October 27, 1967, Philip Berrigan broke into the Baltimore Customs House and poured blood on selective service files there. The act earned him a felony conviction, but while he was waiting for trial, he joined Daniel and several others in breaking into another selective service facility— this one in Catonsville, Maryland—and destroying more files. The ''Catonsville Nine'' were charged with conspiracy and destruction of government property, found guilty, and sentenced to three years in federal prison. Daniel jumped bail in April 1970 and spent eight months underground until the Federal Bureau of Investigation (FBI) caught him. He then began serving his prison sentence. During the rest of the decade, after being paroled in January 1972, Berrigan continued to protest the war. Philip was sentenced to six years in prison, but he jumped bail on April 9, 1970, and began planning to blow up heating systems in government buildings in Washington, D.C. Federal authorities accused him of conspiring to kidnap national security advisor Henry Kissinger.* He was arrested late in April 1970 and began serving his prison sentence. Berrigan was paroled in December 1972.

After the Vietnam War ended, the Berrigan brothers changed their activist agenda and began to campaign against nuclear power and nuclear weapons and for the protection of the environment. In 1975 the two brothers were arrested for digging a hole on the White House lawn to protest nuclear weapons, and in

1980, as two of the "Plowshares Eight," they broke into a General Electric plant and sprinkled fake blood on nuclear warhead cones. Since then, they have added abortion* to their protest agenda, labeling it mass murder.

SUGGESTED READINGS: Daniel Berrigan, *No Bars to Manhood*, 1970; John Kinkaid, "Daniel Berrigan," in *Dictionary of the Vietnam War*, ed. James S. Olson, 1988; Charles Meconis, *With Clumsy Grace: The American Catholic Left, 1961–1975*, 1979.

BIGELOW V. VIRGINIA (1975). During the 1970s, spurred on by the growing power of the women's movement,* abortion* became an inflammatory political issue in the United States. After *Roe v. Wade** legalized most abortions in 1973, the issue became even more intense, and groups of every political persuasion began to debate the issue and organize to promote their own point of view. *Bigelow v. Virginia*, an early post-*Roe* case, was designed to test the U.S. Supreme Court's continuing commitment to reproductive rights. The case involved a newspaper editor in Virginia who had published an advertisement from a New York abortion clinic. Abortion clinics in northeastern states, where abortion was legal at the time, regularly solicited business from states where the practice was illegal. Virginia state law prohibited individuals from "encouraging" abortion, and the editor was prosecuted under the law for printing the advertisement. The newspaper filed suit, claiming that the First Amendment protections of freedom of speech of the press had been violated. Although the case was not about the legality of abortion per se, it certainly had an impact on the issue. The U.S. Supreme Court decided the case on June 16, 1975, by a vote of 7 to 2. The Court, which agreed with the editor, argued that such state attempts to control what people read was a violation of the First Amendment.

SUGGESTED READING: 421 U.S. 809 (1975).

BILLY JACK. *Billy Jack* was a cult film of 1973, an ode to the rapidly disappearing hippies and counterculture in the United States. The film is set in a small southwestern town where Jean Roberts (Delores Taylor) has established a rural home for troubled teens and runaways. Her hope is to build a commune where interracial harmony, nonviolence, peace, and love are the dominant values. The commune's culture supposedly revolves around benign American Indian values—respect for the environment, lack of materialism and consumerism, and complete internal unity. The commune's leaders also display a fundamental pacifism.

The local townspeople, on the other hand, are a different breed. Led by Sheriff Cole (Clark Howat), they are portrayed as a sadistic bunch of ignorant rednecks whose only reason for being appears to be the destruction of the little desert utopia. The townspeople are racist, fascist, and prone to gratuitous violence. They are symbols of the materialism, anti-environmentalism, and consumerism that, according to the counterculture of the 1960s, had ruined America.

Only the presence of Billy Jack (Tom Laughlin), a karate-kicking cowboy loner willing to mete out violence for violence, saves the peace-and-love people from annihilation. The irony, of course, is that Ms. Robert's village of love can be redeemed only by Billy Jack's butt-kicking violence against the townies. If anything, *Billy Jack* was a countercultural western but a western nonetheless, in which a near-mystical cowboy revenges evil in old-fashioned ways.

SUGGESTED READINGS: *New York Times*, March 11, 1973; Richard Slotkin, *Gunfighter Nation: The Myth of the Frontier in Twentieth-Century America*, 1992.

BLACK PANTHERS. The Black Panthers, a militant African-American civil rights organization of the 1960s and 1970s, was founded in Oakland, California, in 1966 by Huey Newton and Bobbie Seale. Rejecting the middle-class values of white society and the nonviolent, civil disobedience tactics of mainstream civil rights organizations, the Black Panthers appealed to unemployed black young men living in urban ghettoes. They asserted the right to defend themselves against racist attacks by the white power structure, especially the police, imposed a militaristic discipline on members, advocated arming the black community, and espoused a militant machismo philosophy. During the 1960s Bobby Seale, Huey Newton, and Eldridge Cleaver* came to symbolize, for blacks and whites, the new assertiveness of urban African-American culture. By 1969 their newspaper, *Black Panther*, had a circulation of 140,000. The Panthers espoused a philosophy of black nationalism and tried to maintain breakfast programs for poor children in the ghettoes.

In the 1970s, however, Black Panther rhetoric no longer matched reality. They had preached an eye-for-an-eye philosophy in stark contrast to Martin Luther King, Jr's., message of nonviolence, but all too often in the 1970s Black Panther violence was gratuitous, directed at one another as well as at police. Drug abuse within many Black Panther chapters reached epidemic proportions in the early 1970s, and many leaders were arrested on drug-related charges. The children's breakfast program, launched with such fanfare in the 1960s, had deteriorated by the early 1970s into extortion and racketeering, in which businesses not participating in the contribution program were targeted for firebombing. And large amounts of the money received never found its way into the food program but disappeared within the Black Panther organization.

Legal problems and personal rivalries also diminished Black Panther influence. In 1971 Huey Newton formally split with Eldridge Cleaver, arguing that Cleaver was guilty of overemphasizing armed rebellion as the best vehicle to achieve black equality in the United States. Faced with criminal charges for drug abuse, Newton fled the United States in 1974 and took up residence in Cuba. Newton returned from Cuba in 1977, but by that time the organization was only a shell of its former self.

The rise of the women's movement* as the premier civil rights crusade of the 1970s also undermined Black Panther influence. Black Panther culture had a decidedly anti-feminist, anti-woman streak to it, one that offended feminists and brought their wrath down upon Black Panther leaders. Many Black Panther leaders had been convicted on assault charges against women, and former political supporters of the organization began backing away. The Panthers began losing monetary support and members. Early in the 1970s, the Panthers rejected their emphasis on violence and tried to focus on political organization. By then, however, the group was in an advanced state of decline. Today, the Black Panthers continue to exist only in Oakland, California, where they are merely a shadow of their former selves.

SUGGESTED READINGS: David Burner, *Making Peace with the Sixties*, 1996; G. Louis Heath, ed., *Off the Pigs! The History and Literature of the Black Panther Party*, 1976; David Hilliard, *Side of Glory: Autobiography of David Hilliard and the Story of the Black Panthers*, 1993; Gene Marine, *The Black Panthers*, 1969; Huey Newton, *Revolutionary Suicide*, 1973.

BLACK POWER. See AFFIRMATIVE ACTION and CIVIL RIGHTS MOVEMENT.

BLACK SABBATH. Formed in Birmingham, England, in 1967, Black Sabbath was the most influential heavy metal rock-and-roll group of the 1970s. Their lead singer, Ozzie Osbourne, was joined by Terry Butler, Tony Iommi, and Bill Ward. When they began a continuous concert of the United States, Black Sabbath trafficked in the dark themes of death, depression, and apocalypse, but they generated a huge following and produced five successive gold albums, including *Black Sabbath* (1970) and *Sabbath, Bloody Sabbath* (1973). Black Sabbath did not survive Osbourne's drug use and decision to go solo in 1979. During their time in the pop culture spotlight, Black Sabbath drew attention from conservatives and moralists concerned that the group represented the dark side of contemporary society.

SUGGESTED READINGS: Chris Welch, *Black Sabbath*, 1988.

BLAXPLOITATION. The term "blaxploitation," which emerged in the 1970s, describes a short-lived film genre that was targeted at black audiences. The term itself was first employed on June 12, 1972, by the *New York* magazine to describe the film *Superfly*, although film historians generally recognize Melvin Van Peebles's 1971 *Sweet Sweetback's Baadasss Song* as the first of the blaxploitation films. Throughout the twentieth century, film roles for black actors had been highly stylized, fulfilling white stereotypes of childlike, obsequious behavior. The civil rights movement* helped overthrow some of those stereotypes, and on the big screen, a number of films were released portraying black people as strong, courageous, violent, and proud. White critics charged that blaxploitation films glorified the drug culture and urban violence, but to black moviegoers, the actors became new icons. Included in a list of the most memorable of these films are *Cotton Comes to Harlem* (1970), *Sweet Sweetback's Baadasss Song* (1971), *Shaft* (1972), *Superfly* (1972), *Blacula* (1972), *The Legend of Nigger Charlie* (1972), *Melinda* (1972), *Cleopatra Jones* (1973), *Coffy* (1973), *Black Ceasar* (1973), and *The Mack* (1973). Eventually, a total of 150 films were produced in the genre. The highly profitable blaxploitation films made stars out of such actors as Richard Roundtree, Fred "The Hammer" Williamson, and Pam Grier.

SUGGESTED READINGS: Thomas Cripps, *Black Film as Genre*, 1979; Chris Vognar, "Back in Blax," *Dallas Morning News*, December 21, 1997.

BLONDIE. The rock group Blondie was formed in New York City in 1975. The lead singer was Deborah Harry, a former *Playboy* bunny who found fame in trash punk rock* and disco.* The group also included Chris Stein, Frank Infante, Nigel Harrison, Jimmy Destri, and Clem Burke. Harry was characterized by her bleached-blonde hair and deadpan vocal deliveries, and the group became one of the most commercially successful musical groups of the 1970s. Their 1978 album *Parallel Lines* reached the top five in sales, highlighted by the number-one hit single "Heart of Glass." *Eat to the Beat* (1979) and *Autoamerican* (1980) were also successful albums. The group disbanded in 1982.

SUGGESTED READINGS: Lester Bangs, *Blondie*, 1980; Debbie Harry, *Making Tracks: The Rise of Blondie*, 1982.

BLUE LAKE. During the 1960s, Native American activists, the so-called advocates of red power,* began rejecting the idea of monetary compensation from the federal government as payment for land taken illegally from them. Instead, many red power advocates began insisting on the return of the land itself, a demand that posed serious political and economic problems to government officials. In the decades, or even centuries, since the taking of the land, white settlers and developers had completely incorporated it into their own economy. Returning it to Native Americans would cost hundreds of trillions of dollars, making red power demands impossible to fulfill.

In 1970 President Richard Nixon* found an opportunity to acquiesce in at least one tribal demand for the return of ancestral lands. The president was grateful for the opportunity. His standing among other minority groups, particularly blacks and Hispanics, was not good, and he relished the chance of appearing on the popular side of a minority issue.

The case in point was Blue Lake in northwest New Mexico. Blue Lake is an ancient holy place to the Taos Indians who consider it a religious shrine, the source of life and a manifestation of the great spirit of the universe. Blue Lake, economically and spiritually, was the center of their lives. In 1906, the federal government had incorporated Blue Lake and the surrounding 48,000 acres into the Kit Carson National Forest. Later, the U.S. Forest Service opened the area to non-Indian hunters, fishermen, and campers. Taos Indian leaders began to demand the return of the lake, and in 1965 the Indians Claims Commission offered the tribe $10 million and 3,000 acres near the lake. Paul Bernal, a Taos leader, rejected the offer, telling the Indian Claims Commission, "My people will not sell our Blue Lake that is our church, for $10 million, and accept three thousand acres, when we know that fifty thousand acres is ours. We cannot sell what is sacred. It is not ours to sell." Blue Lake became a symbol of Indian land claims and a rejection of the notion that cash settlements could make up for assaults on Indian culture.

In 1970 President Nixon decided to throw his support behind the Taos Indians demand for the return of Blue Lake. At his insistence, Congress passed the Taos Blue Lake Act in 1970, which returned the lake and 48,000 surrounding acres to the tribe.

SUGGESTED READINGS: R. C. Gordon-McCutchen, *The Taos Indians and the Battle for Blue Lake*, 1991; Marcia Keegan, *The Taos Pueblo and Its Sacred Blue Lake*, 1991; Nancy Wood, *Shaman's Circle*, 1996.

BOAT PEOPLE. The term "boat people" was used to describe the initial group of Vietnamese immigrants to the United States. Eventually, the term "boat people" became a euphemism for all Vietnamese refugees fleeing South Vietnam after the North Vietnamese and Vietcong military triumph, but its actual meaning is more specific. Although some of the refugees made their way to freedom overland through Laos and Cambodia into Thailand, most of them left in small boats, hoping to make it to Indonesia, Malaysia, or the Philippines. Demographers now estimate that more than a million people fled Vietnam by boat, earning the title of 'boat people.' Their voyages were beset with danger. Pirates in the South China Sea regularly victimized the Indochinese immigrants,* and Indonesia and Malaysia frequently rejected them even when they did make landfall. Tens of thousands drowned at sea. Although exact statistics are difficult to obtain, perhaps 250,000 Vietnamese boat people died on the South China Sea from various causes.

SUGGESTED READING: Bruce Grant, *The Boat People,* 1979.

THE BOB NEWHART SHOW. Bob Newhart was a popular stand-up comedian during the 1960s, and in 1972 he brought his deadpan delivery style to the small screen. *The Bob Newhart Show* first aired on CBS television on September 16, 1972, and it proved to be one of the most successful situation comedies of the 1970s. The series starred Bob Newhart as psychologist Robert Hartley; Suzanne Pleshette as his schoolteacher wife, Emily; Bill Daily as their neighbor, Howard Borden; Peter Bonerz as dentist Jerry Robinson; and Marcia Wallace as receptionist Carol Bondurant. The comedy was provided by Dr. Hartley's patients and their grab bag of hang-ups and neuroses. The group therapy exchanges among the patients were hilarious. *The Bob Newhart Show*, a Nielsen's rated top-ten program during its heyday, remained on the air until August 26, 1978, when Newhart decided to pursue other career interests. The show's popularity was, no doubt, a function of the times. As a result of high unemployment, high inflation, the Watergate scandal,* and the Vietnam War,* the country as a whole was caught in a gigantic neurotic crisis. On the small screen, the neuroses of Dr. Hartley's patients reflected that general malaise, and as Dr. Hartley reassured them about their self-worth and ability to cope, tens of millions of Americans took the advice too.

SUGGESTED READINGS: Jeff Sorensen, *Bob Newhart*, 1995.

BODY COUNT. Because the Vietnam War* was a guerrilla conflict without front lines and territorial objectives, as well as shifting defensive positions, it became impossible to use geography as a reliable index of progress. Instead, Secretary of Defense Robert McNamara and General William Westmoreland came to rely on the body count—the number of Vietcong and North Vietnamese soldiers killed—to evaluate the progress of the war. The body count figures were unreliable, however, owing to several factors. Combat conditions required estimates of enemy killed, often from aerial observation or memory. It was also very difficult to distinguish between Vietcong and civilian Vietnamese casualties. Counts were often duplicated. Also, American officers, desperate for good efficiency reports, were known to exaggerate the body counts of civilian casualties in Vietnam.*

SUGGESTED READING: James S. Olson and Randy Roberts, *Where the Domino Fell: America and Vietnam, 1945–1995,* 1997.

BOOBY TRAPS. During the course of the Vietnam War,* one of the most unique, frustrating, and tragic dimensions of the conflict was the number of casualties caused to U.S. soldiers by booby traps. The devices were planted by Vietcong troops; North Vietnamese soldiers, and anti-American Vietnamese civilians. The most dangerous of the makeshift weapons included a bullet buried straight up with its firing pin on a bamboo stub, activated when someone stepped on the bullet's tip; hollowed-out coconuts filled with gunpowder and triggered by a trip wire; walk bridges with ropes almost cut away so they would collapse when someone tried to cross them; bamboo stakes connected to grenades and planted at helicopter landing sites; and the "Malay whip" log, attached to two trees by a rope studded with iron barbs and buried in streambeds and rice paddies.

The most memorable and infamous of the booby traps were so-called punji stakes, which consisted of bamboo cut into strips, sharpened to points, and then stiffened and hardened over a fire. The Vietcong then dipped the points into feces or infectious agents and concealed them so that U.S. troops would unexpectedly step on them or run into them. Thousands of U.S. soldiers died in Vietnam after being wounded by punji stakes.

The widespread employment of booby traps created more distance and distrust between American troops and Vietnamese civilians. Nearly 70 percent of American battlefield casualties during the war were caused by booby traps, which became extremely frustrating to U.S. soldiers, since they had been wounded or killed without ever engaging the enemy. They often blamed Vietnamese civilians for placing the booby traps or for not warning patrolling U.S. soldiers of the dangers nearby.

SUGGESTED READINGS: Christian Appy, *Working-Class War*, 1993; Edgar C. Doleman, Jr., *The Vietnam Experience: Tools of War*, 1984; Peter Goldman and Tony Fuller, *Charlie Company: What Vietnam Did to Us*, 1983.

BOSTON. Boston, a rock-and-roll band formed in Boston, Massachusetts, in 1975, included Tom Scholz, Brad Delp, Barry Goudreau, Fran Sheehan, and Sib Hashian. Their debut album in 1976, *Boston*, was a megahit, the fastest-selling album release in the history of rock and roll. With such hit singles as "More Than a Feeling," "Long Time," and "Peace of Mind," Boston sold eleven million copies. Two years later, their album *Don't Look Back* reached number one and sold six million copies.

SUGGESTED READING: C. T. Crowe, "Boston," *Rolling Stone* (August 10, 1978), 37–42.

BOWIE, DAVID. Born David Robert Jones in London, England, on January 8, 1947, David Bowie became one of the era's most successful rock-and-roll performers. Able to continuously reinvent himself, and moving through folk, soul, and punk genres, Bowie burst on the rock scene in 1967 with his album *The World of David Bowie*. During the early 1970s, Bowie pioneered "glitter rock," a musical genre that essentially assaulted traditional gender roles. Glitter rock's real debut came in 1972 when Bowie went on a world tour to promote his new album *The Rise and Fall of Ziggy Stardust and the Spiders from Mars*.

Bowie was far more popular in Europe than in the United States until 1975, when the single "Fame," which he had written with John Lennon, reached number one. Bowie moved to Los Angeles that year. In 1975 his album *Young Americans* was a success, led by the top-ten single "Golden Years." Bowie's concerts changed in the mid-1970s when he abandoned the elaborate sets and costumes for a sparse, lean look. He concluded a very successful world tour in 1978 with the release of the album *Stage*. His *Scary Monsters* album in 1980 was one of the first to take advantage of the rise of rock videos. He stopped recording then in favor of writing and production, and he launched a stage career. In 1983 Bowie returned to recording with the album *Let's Dance*. Its three hit singles—"Let's Dance," "China Girl," and "Modern Love"—took it to number three on the pop charts. Since then Bowie has maintained his influential position in popular music.

SUGGESTED READINGS: Angela Bowie, *Backstage Passes: Life on the Wild Side with David Bowie*, 1993; George Tremlett, *David Bowie: Living on the Brink*, 1997.

THE BOYS IN COMPANY C. *The Boys in Company C* was one of Hollywood's first attempts at commercial exploitation of the Vietnam War.* The film trafficks in the stereotypes of a traditional World War II movie. Five young marines go off to war. Tyrone Washington (Stan Shaw) is a street-smart African American from some urban ghetto; David Bisbee (Craig Wasson) is a hippie drafted into the war; Vinnie Fazio (Michael Lembeck), who hails from Brooklyn, fancies himself a ladies man; Billy Ray Pike (Andrew Stevens) leaves a pregnant sweetheart behind and comes home with a heroin addiction; and Alvin Foster (James Canning) is the intellectual who keeps the proverbial war journal. But the similarities with World War II stop with the characters. *The Boys in*

Company C exposes the corruption of the South Vietnamese, the misguided vanity and ambition of the American officer corps, the ludicrous nature of body counts,* and the extent of drug use among U.S. troops. The film ends with a symbolic soccer game between American and South Vietnamese soldiers; like the war itself, the Americans are not supposed to win. They are expected to make the South Vietnamese look good.

SUGGESTED READING: *New York Times*, February 2, 1978.

THE BRADY BUNCH. *The Brady Bunch* was a popular television situation comedy that aired on ABC in 1969. Set in an upper-middle-class California suburb, *The Brady Bunch* revolved around the escapades of a "mine, yours, and our" family. Mike Brady, a widower played by Robert Reed, had three sons: Greg (Barry Williams), Peter (Christopher Williams), and Bobby (Michael Lookinland). Carol Brady, a widow played by Florence Henderson, had three daughters: Marcia (Maureen McCormick), Jan (Eve Plumb), and Cindy (Susan Olsen). When Mike and Carol got married, they fused their two families, and the whole bunch was presided over by housekeeper Alice (Ann B. Davis). In an age of rebellion and the counterculture, the Bradys were squeaky clean and conventional. Most of the humor emerged from typical sibling and parent-child rivalries. During the 1970s, when Americans were plagued by so much self-doubt and political and economic problems, *The Brady Bunch* was pure escapist fare—tens of millions of Americans needed an escape, and the show provided it. Critics considered it terminally bland and vacuous, but the show survived in prime time for five years and became an icon of the 1970s.

SUGGESTED READINGS: Andrew Edelstein, *The Brady Bunch Book*, 1990; Barry Williams, *Growing Up Brady: I Was a Teenage Greg*, 1992.

BRANCH V. TEXAS. See *FURMAN V. GEORGIA: JACKSON V. GEORGIA: BRANCH V. TEXAS.*

BRANDO, MARLON. Marlon Brando was born in Omaha, Nebraska, on April 3, 1924. Fascinated by the stage, Brando went to New York as a young man and enrolled in Lee Strasburg's Actors' studio, where he studied "method" acting. He had a number of roles in summer stock before landing a role in 1944 in the Broadway production of "I Remember Mama." He came to the attention of a variety of producers in 1947 when he played Stanley Kowalski in the Broadway production of Tennessee Williams' "A Streetcar Named Desire." His screen debut came in 1950, when he portrayed a crippled veteran in *The Men*. One year later, he reprised the role of Kowalski in the film version of *A Streetcar Named Desire*, which garnered him a best actor Academy Award nomination. He starred in *Viva Zapata!* in 1952 and *Julius Caeser* in 1953. But what cemented Brando's reputation as one of America's most versatile actors came with his smoldering performance in *On the Waterfront* (1954), which won him an Oscar for best actor. That same year, in *The Wild One*, he epitomized a budding sense of rebellion against the social conformity demanded in the 1950s.

During the late 1950s and 1960s, Brando starred in a number of films which demonstrated his skills, but which did not have near the impact of *On the Waterfront* or *The Wild One*. Included in this group are *Guys and Dolls* (1955), *The Teahouse of the August Moon* (1956), *Sayonara* (1957), *Mutiny on the Bounty* (1962), *Bedtime Story* (1964), *Reflections in a Golden Eye* (1967), *Burn!* (1969).

In the 1970s, he once again rocketed to the top of his craft. His performance as Don Corleone in *The Godfather* (1972) won him another Oscar, which he refused to accept, sending a Native American woman to the Academy Awards ceremonies in his place. On behalf of Marlon Brando, she denounced Hollywood's treatment of American Indians. In 1973, Brando appeared in *Last Tango in Paris*, and he starred in *Apocalypse Now*, an anti–Vietnam War film, in 1979. He remains today one of Hollywood's most enigmatic figures. Included in his most recent films are *A Dry White Season* (1989) and *The Freshman* (1990).

SUGGESTED READING: Peter Manso, *Brando: A Biography*, 1994.

BREAKDANCING. The phenomenon of breakdancing emerged in the African-American community in the early 1970s, starting out in New York City's South Bronx and then spreading from there to other cities. The physical expression of rap music had its origins in *capoeira*, a Brazilian martial arts form. Breakdancers, also known as ''B-Boys,'' performed at parties and discotheques when disk jockeys took breaks. Breakdancing was one dimension of youthful black urban culture, along with hip-hop music, graffiti, and such fashions as unlaced sneakers and hooded sweatshirts. The dance involved extraordinary feats of agility and athleticism—flips, rotating spins while balanced on one's shoulders, robot-like movements, floating walks, ''moonwalks,'' and freezes. It was not until 1983, with the release of the film *Flashdance*, that breakdancing became part of the larger popular culture of the United States.

SUGGESTED READINGS: Peter J. Rosenwald, ''Breaking Away 80s Style,'' *Dance* 58 (April 1984), 70–74.

BREAST CANCER. During the 1970s the American people, having succeeded in placing a man on the moon in July 1969, turned their commitment toward more practical purposes. In the forefront was the war against cancer. More than 40,000 Americans died of the disease each year, and the public began to demand that something be done. Jumping on the bandwagon, President Richard Nixon* took on the cancer issue. He declared in his State of the Union Address in January 1971, ''The time has come when the same kind of concentrated effort that split the atom and took man to the moon should be turned toward conquering this dread disease. Let us make a total commitment to achieve this goal.'' However, few people, including the president, realized just how formidable cancer would prove to be.

Breast cancer had always been of great concern to American women, and because the disease carried a sexual stigma, it was shrouded in secrecy. In the 1970s, however, the disease came out of its so-called closet. One key to a new public consciousness revolved around the prominent women who were attacked by the disease during the decade. Early in 1970 Marvella Bayh, wife of Senator Birch Bayh of Indiana, was diagnosed with breast cancer and underwent a radical mastectomy causing her husband to withdraw from his recently announced presidential candidacy. At the end of 1972 Shirley Temple, who had been one of America's most beloved child film stars, discovered a lump in one of her breasts. She agreed to a simple mastectomy which involved the removal of the breast rather than the more conventional modified radical mastectomy which removed the breast, axilla lymph nodes, and some chest muscle. The media picked up both stories. Until then, many Americans had looked upon breast removal as a form of female castration. Temple, who attacked the taboo, insisting that her womanhood was still intact, received more than 50,000 letters praising her courage for going public with the news. The process of demystifying breast cancer was under way.

In 1974 First Lady Betty Ford* and Happy Rochefeller, the wife of Vice President Nelson Rockefeller* were almost simultaneously diagnosed with breast cancer. All of America was on alert. Obviously no one was safe. The dreaded disease did not stop there but continued to maintain a high profile throughout the 1970s. Betty Rollin, the *NBC News* correspondent who had reported the Ford and Rockefeller stories, was diagnosed with breast cancer in the spring of 1976. The book she wrote about her ordeal, *At First You Cry*, soon made its way on to the bestseller lists. Breast cancer was no longer a disease women had to hide.

The decade also witnessed important intellectual advances in treating breast cancer. In the forefront of discovery was Bernard Fisher, an associate professor at the University of Pittsburgh. In 1966 he had turned the world of scientific oncology upside down when he published several articles contradicting the long-held consensus that breast cancer spread along major tissue lines and the lymphatic system and not through the bloodstream. His research showed that breast cancer was a systematic disease. Lymph nodes did not "trap" cancer cells, and the cancerous cells that often escaped into the lymph system and bloodstream were either overcome by the body's immune system or took root somewhere else in the body. If cancer cells had spread throughout the body then no amount of surgery would save the patient. Fisher's research soon led to less radical surgeries, a trend that was already under way. In 1967 the National Cancer Institute appointed Fisher to head its new National Surgical Adjuvant Breast Project, which included thirty-five medical schools and cancer centers cooperating on a long-term study of breast cancer treatment. By 1979, Fisher had collected enough data to not only justify less radical surgeries, but to put an end to the Halsted radical mastectomy.

Though the surgical methods for dealing with breast cancer improved in the 1970s, Fisher emphatically believed that, in the future, surgery would "play a subsidiary role in the management of solid tumors." One of the methods used in managing cancerous growths was chemotherapy, but in the 1960s and 1970s researchers learned that only a fifth to a third of the women responded to this technique by showing some regression in their tumors. This percentage was increased to 50 percent and later to nearly 70 percent when Richard Cooper of the University of Rochester suggested combination chemotherapy. Although breast cancer still claimed more than 40,000 women a year at the end of the 1970s, the progress made had been immeasurable.

SUGGESTED READINGS: James Patterson, *The Dread Disease: Cancer and Modern American Culture,* 1987; Richard A. Rettig, *Cancer Crusade: The Story of the National Cancer Act of 1971,* 1977.

Daniel Harris

BRENNAN, WILLIAM (JOSEPH JR.). William Joseph Brennan, Jr., was born in Newark, New Jersey, on April 25, 1906. He received his undergraduate degree from the University of Pennsylvania and his law degree from Harvard. After leaving Harvard, Brennan moved to Newark, New Jersey, where he concentrated his energy and intellect in the field of labor law, a specialty that was in a state of rapid development because Congress had just passed and President Franklin D. Roosevelt had just signed the National Labor Relations Act, or Wagner Act, guaranteeing the right of labor unions to bargain collectively with management. Those early years in labor law had a dramatic impact on Brennan's political views, balancing his normally conservative nature with an appreciation for the problems and concerns of blue-collar Americans.

During World War II, he joined the U.S. Army and served in a staff position to Undersecretary of War Robert Patterson. For a few years after the war, Brennan practiced law privately, but in 1949 he accepted an appointment as a judge in the New Jersey Superior Court system. He became a judge in the appellate division in 1950 and a justice on the New Jersey Supreme Court in 1952. Brennan was still serving in that position when President Dwight Eisenhower named him to the U.S. Supreme Court in 1956.

As an associate justice of the U.S. Supreme Court, Brennan quickly became part of the liberal majority headed by Chief Justice Earl Warren. In fact, many Supreme Court historians consider Brennan to have been the "heart" of the Warren Court, a moderate who believed passionately in individual rights. As such, he was part of the court majority that essentially revolutionized American jurisprudence during the 1960s. Brennan worked over the decades to broaden the meaning of the Fourteenth Amendment to the Constitution to, in his own words, "guarantee the essential dignity and worth of each individual." During his tenure as an associate justice, Brennan wrote a total of 1,360 formal opinions. One constitutional historian wrote, "If we look at Justices in terms of their role in the decision process, [Brennan] was actually the most influential Associate Justice in Supreme Court history."

During the 1970s and 1980s, however, Brennan found himself filing more and more minority opinions. When Chief Justice Earl Warren retired in 1969, President Richard Nixon* replaced him with Warren E. Burger,* a conservative.

Although the Burger court did not dismantle the civil rights decisions of the Warren years, it did take a more conservative approach to those rights, and Brennan often found himself in the minority and more than once was forced to observe his majority opinions of earlier years being overturned. That trend continued when Burger stepped down and was replaced as chief justice by William Renquist, who was even more conservative. Still, Brennan made his mark on the Supreme Court in the 1970s. In two important cases, *Frontiero v. Richardson* and *Craig v. Boren*, he made sure that gender disputes stood up to scrutiny of the Fourteenth Amendment, and he fought valiantly to protect affirmative action* programs. In the 1972 case of *Eisenstadt v. Baird*, he upheld, on the grounds of privacy, the right of unmarried people to receive information about birth control. Not surprisingly, he often found himself in dissent. Brennan retired in 1990. He died on July 24, 1997.

SUGGESTED READINGS: Hunter Clark, *Justice Brennan: The Great Conciliator*, 1995; Roger L. Goldman, *Justice William J. Brennan, Jr.: Freedom First*, 1994; *New York Times*, July 25, 1997.

BROOKE, EDWARD. Edward William Brooke was born into a middle-class Washington, D.C., family on October 26, 1919. During World War II, he served in an all-black army regiment and then returned to Washington, D.C., to attend Howard University. He graduated at the top of his class at the Boston University Law School, where he edited the *Law Review* and earned a reputation for wit, intelligence, and political savvy. He then practiced law and became active in Republican party politics. In 1962 Brooke defeated Elliot Richardson in the Republican primary and went on to win election as the attorney general of Massachusetts. He had already tried and failed on three previous occasions to win that office. In the post of attorney general, Brooke increased his public profile by vigorously prosecuting political corruption. At the Republican presidential nominating convention held in San Francisco in 1964, Brooke opposed the candidacy of Senator Barry Goldwater of Arizona and, in doing so, established his credentials as a liberal Republican. Brooke was elected to the U.S. Senate in 1966, the first African American to be afforded that honor since Reconstruction.

Brooke was convinced that the welfare state had gone too far, that it had robbed many poor men and women of their dignity. "You don't help a man," he often said, "by constantly giving him more handouts." In 1966 President Lyndon Johnson appointed Brooke to serve as one of the members of the President's Commission on Civil Disorders, an investigation into the rioting afflicting American cities in the mid-1960s. After the investigation, Brooke became the leading sponsor of what became the Civil Rights Act of 1968.

Brooke supported the political candidacy of Richard Nixon* in 1968 and in 1972, but he increasingly found himself estranged from the president. Senator Brooke believed that Nixon was disengaging too slowly from the Vietnam War,* that he was not pushing racial integration vigorously enough, and that his social and economic policies only made life worse for minorities and the poor. The final wedge between Brooke and Nixon came in 1969 and 1970 when the senator opposed two successive Nixon appointees to the U.S. Supreme Court: Clement F. Haynesworth and G. Harrold Carswell. Brooke was convinced that both individuals had been appointed to appease racist southern senators. When both men failed to receive confirmation in the Senate, Nixon blamed Brooke. At home, of course, Brooke's opposition to Nixon only endeared him more to Massachusetts voters. He won reelection in 1972 by a landslide.

By the time Brooke began his second term, the nation was in the midst of the Watergate scandal,* and the senator became the first Republican to call for the president's resignation. Within the next eighteen months, most other Republican senators decided to make the same request. Brooke took no satisfaction in Nixon's August 1974 resignation. He considered the entire Watergate scandal a tragedy for the country. Brooke failed in his 1978 bid to win a third term in the Senate, and he returned to private life, practicing law in Boston and Washington, D.C.

SUGGESTED READING: John Henry Cutler, *Ed Brooke: Biography of a Senator*, 1972.

BROWN, JAMES (JOE, JR.). James Joe Brown, Jr., was born near Barnwell, South Carolina, on May 3, 1933. Raised in poverty, Brown shined shoes and picked cotton as a child to make money. He was convicted of armed robbery in 1949 and spent three years in juvenile detention. After his term in prison, Brown tried his hand at semiprofessional boxing and minor league baseball. He also began to sing gospel music with a group known as the Flames. In 1956 they had their first hit, "Please, Please, Please." Brown's music was influenced by gospel sounds, but it gradually acquired a sharper, rougher edge. In 1958 his song "Try Me" went to number one on the rhythm and blues charts. Later that year, he formed the James Brown Band.

The James Brown Band received bigger and bigger bookings. Bedecked in his characteristic cape, Brown put on a stage show as well as a concert, with his trademark pumping hips, twisting feet, and floor splits. Raw and powerful, Brown's music became the most important in black rhythm and blues, and included such hits as "Bewildered" (1961), "I Don't Mind" (1961), "Lost Someone" (1961), "Live at the Apollo" (1962), and "Out of Sight" (1963). In the mid-1960s, a number of Brown's rhythm and blues hits made their way into the top twenty of the pop charts. By that time, he had become recognized as the godfather of soul music—"Soul Brother Number One." He was also an icon in the black community, a man who had overcome poverty and established an unparalleled reputation for independence and pride. His 1968 song "Say It Loud—I'm Black and I'm Proud" became an anthem for the black pride movement. Other songs reflected his sense of independence, such as "I Don't Want Nobody to Give Me Nothing." Brown's fame was significant enough that political candidates began to seek his endorsement.

During the 1970s, Brown's career began to change. He made the transition to polyrhythmic funk* music in the early 1970s with such albums as *Sex Machine* (1970) and *Super Bad* (1971), but he also faced mounting personal problems. The failure of his second marriage brought him a great deal of personal turmoil, as did the death of his oldest son. He also faced serious tax problems and the bankruptcies of most of his personal businesses. Although he recorded such albums as *Hot* (1976) and *Bodyheat* (1976), he went into semiretirement.

James Brown came roaring back in the 1980s. Such albums as the *Federal Years* (1984) and *Dead on the Heavy Funk* (1985) were commercial successes, and his 1986 performance of "Living in America" for the film *Rocky IV* was a runaway hit. That year, however, he was arrested for assaulting a police officer and sentenced to six years in prison. He had exhausted his appeals in 1989, when he began to serve his prison term. Paroled in 1991, Brown resumed his concert career and released the album *Star Time*. In 1998 Brown received treatment for a recurrence of his substance abuse illness.

SUGGESTED READINGS: James Brown, with Bruce Tucker, *James Brown: The Godfather of Soul*, 1986; Gerri Hirshey, *Nowhere to Run: The Story of Soul Music*, 1984.

BROWN, JERRY (EDMUND GERALD, JR.). Jerry Brown was born in San Francisco, California, on April 7, 1938. After studying for several years to become a Jesuit priest, Brown left the Sacred Heart Novitiate in Los Gatos, California, and enrolled at the University of California at Berkeley and graduated in 1964 and then earned a law degree at Yale. After several years of travel, he joined a private California law firm and became active in Democratic party politics, following his father who was governor of the state. Brown openly opposed U.S. involvement in the Vietnam War* and was an early proponent of the environmental movement.* He won election as California secretary of state in 1970, and in 1970 he surprised most observers by winning the Democratic gubernatorial primary election. Voters swept him into office in the general election. Committed to political reform and the inclusion of women and minorities into state politics, Brown won reelection in 1978.

For a time in the 1970s, Brown enjoyed almost celebrity status in California politics and popular culture. His political positions—women's rights, minority rights, affirmative action,* limited economic growth, aid to higher education, and assertive environmentalism—were extremely popular among California liberals, and he regularly socialized with the "beautiful" people of Hollywood and the music industry. As a bachelor, he dated starlets and performers and was never shy to have his picture appear in the tabloids. Jerry Brown perfectly symbolized California glitz during the 1970s.

Later in the decade, his political star was beginning to set. He opposed capital punishment and nuclear power, which California voters generally approved of, and his opposition to Proposition 13* tax relief, which succeeded overwhelmingly, tarnished his luster. Some also perceived him as a bit "flaky" because of his ascetic lifestyle and dalliances with rock star Linda Ronstadt.*

Brown's bid for the 1980 Democratic presidential nomination failed badly, and in 1984 he failed to win a seat in the U.S. Senate. He practiced law for several years and then came out of political retirement in June 1998 when he won the mayoral election in Oakland, California.

SUGGESTED READINGS: J. D. Lorenz, *Jerry Brown: The Man on the White Horse*, 1978; *New York Times*, June 3–4, 1998.

BROWNE, JACKSON. Jackson Browne was born on October 9, 1948, in Heidelberg, West Germany. He was raised in southern California, and by the late 1960s he had written successful songs for Linda Ronstadt,* the Eagles,* and the Byrds. His first performing hit came in 1972 with the single release "Doctor My Eyes," which reached number eight on the pop charts. Browne then released several increasingly successful albums: *Jackson Browne* (1972), *For Everyman* (1973), *Late for the Sky* (1974), and *The Pretender* (1976), which went platinum. In 1977 he enjoyed a very successful concert tour, and much of the music, recorded live, went into his highly successful *Running on Empty* (1978). Although he has continued to write, record, and perform since then, Browne has not enjoyed the same success he did in the 1970s.

SUGGESTED READINGS: Alberto Manzano Lizandro, *Jackson Browne*, 1982; Rich Wiseman, *Jackson Browne: The Story of a Hold Out*, 1982.

BRZEZINSKI, ZBIGNIEW (KAZIMIERZ). Zbigniew Brzezinski was born in Warsaw, Poland, on March 28, 1928. He left Poland in 1946 to study at McGill University in Canada, from which he graduated in 1949. Brzezinksi then took a master's degree in political science at McGill and went on to Harvard for doctoral work. He received his Ph.D. there in 1953. That same year he took up permanent residence in the United States and became a naturalized citizen in 1958. After spending three years (1953–1956) as a fellow at Harvard's Russian Research Center, Brzezinski accepted an assistant professorship there and remained in Cambridge until 1960, when he became associate professor of political science at Columbia. By that time he had written two well-received books: *The Permanent Purge: Politics in Soviet Totalitarianism* (1956) and *The Soviet Bloc—Unity and Conflict* (1960).

In 1962 Brzezinski published *Ideology and Power in Soviet Politics* and became director of research for the Institute for International Change. He was also a faculty member at Columbia's Russian Institute. Among his other books published at this stage in his career are *Alternative to Partition* (1965), *Between Two Ages* (1970), and *The Fragile Blossom* (1971). From 1973 to 1976, he served as director of the Trilateral Commission. Known for his hard-line approach to Soviet-American relations, Brzezinski was a critic of the detente* policy of Henry Kissinger.* Brzezinski's intellect had been shaped by Cold War* politics, in which his native Poland suffered under the heavy hand of Soviet and Communist dictatorship. As far as Brzezinski was concerned, the Soviets understood power, nothing more and nothing less. In 1977 President

Jimmy Carter* named Brzezinski special assistant for national security affairs. Brzezinski returned to Columbia University in 1981 and retired in 1989.

SUGGESTED READING: Zbigniew Brzezinski, *Power and Principle: Memoirs of the National Security Advisor, 1977–1981*, 1985.

BUCKLEY, WILLIAM F(RANK), JR. William F. Buckley, Jr., was born on November 24, 1925, in New York City to a well-to-do family. After serving a stint in the U.S. Army during World War II, Buckley attended Yale University, where he served as editor of the *Yale Daily News*. He graduated in 1950. In 1951 Buckley came to national attention when his book *God and Man at Yale*, a powerful attack on the liberal biases in the curriculum at Yale, was published. Buckley did not endear himself to the Yale faculty when he arranged to have the book distributed at the university's commencement ceremonies.

Buckley worked for the Central Intelligence Agency* from 1951 to 1952, and in 1954 he wrote his second book, *McCarthy and His Enemies*, a defense of the anti-Communist movement. Buckley saw nothing wrong with a society defending itself from alien ideas. In 1955 he cemented his reputation as one of America's leading conservatives when he launched the *National Review*, a weekly conservative political journal. In 1959 he wrote *Up from Liberalism*, a book that demanded an uncompromising, tough foreign policy toward the Soviet Union, which he considered to be the twentieth century's most evil force. In 1962 Buckley began writing "On the Right," a syndicated weekly newspaper column. First broadcast over the Public Broadcasting System (PBS), his weekly television interview program *Firing Line* eventually became the longest continuing series in PBS history.

During the 1970s, as Americans became increasingly disenchanted with liberalism, Buckley emerged as the intellectual godfather of modern conservatism. During the stagflation* years of the 1970s, during which unemployment and inflation undermined economic strength, Buckley spoke constantly and eloquently about the need to let market forces, not federal government programs, address the problem. *Firing Line* and *National Review* promoted the political career of Ronald Reagan,* and during Reagan's presidency from 1981 to 1989, Buckley attributed American prosperity and the revival of America's world reputation to conservative political decisions in the White House. When the Soviet Union collapsed in 1991, Buckley took great pleasure in the demise of his archenemy—communism. Today Buckley writes fiction and continues his political commentary.

SUGGESTED READINGS: John B. Judis, *William F. Buckley, Jr.: Patron Saint of the Conservatives*, 1988; Mark Royden Winchell, *William F. Buckley, Jr.*, 1984.

BURGER, WARREN E(ARL). Warren Earl Burger was born on September 17, 1907, in Saint Paul, Minnesota. He attended the University of Minnesota for two years and then earned his law degree at the Saint Paul College of Law in 1931. He then practiced for a Minneapolis firm for the next twenty-two years.

While practicing law, Burger became active in state Republican politics. He became well acquainted with Herbert Brownell, Thomas E. Dewey's presidential campaign advisor, and in 1953, when Brownell became Dwight D. Eisenhower's attorney general, Burger was appointed assistant attorney general, at which he headed the Department of Justice's civil division. His reputation as a conservative grew quickly there, especially in civil liberties and loyalty issues. In 1956 President Eisenhower appointed him to the U.S. Court of Appeals for the District of Columbia. There, his conservative reputation grew, particularly in his handling of criminal justice cases.

President Richard Nixon* agreed with Burger's view that the U.S. Constitution should be interpreted narrowly, and in 1969 he appointed Burger to replace Earl Warren as chief justice of the Supreme Court. Burger served until his retirement in 1986. He surprised conservatives by not stepping back from the decisions of the Warren years. The Warren decisions on school desegregation, one person one vote, the right to privacy, and the *Miranda* description of defendants' rights all survived. His court also upheld the constitutionality of busing* to achieve racial desegregation of public schools and affirmative action,* as well as the right of a woman to have an abortion.*

During the Watergate scandal,* critics of the Nixon administration worried that Burger would be politically sympathetic to the president and not pursue the relevant legal issues to their logical conclusions. But Burger proved to be a man of integrity who worried about the independence of the judicial system and his own historical reputation, and he was not about to compromise either one in order to keep Nixon in the White House. The Supreme Court under Burger denied Nixon's claims to executive privilege and eventually ordered the president to deliver taped White House recordings to Congress. The tapes revealed Nixon's complicity in the Watergate cover-up and his many lies to the American people about the extent of the scandal. He resigned from the presidency in August 1974. Burger continued to serve as chief justice until his retirement in 1986. He died on June 24, 1995.

SUGGESTED READINGS: Nancy Maveety, *Representation Rights: The Burger Years*, 1991; *New York Times*, June 25, 1995; Bernard Schwartz, *The Ascent of Pragmatism: The Burger Court in Action*, 1992.

BURNS, ARTHUR (FRANK). Arthur Frank Burns was born in Stanislau, Austria, on April 27, 1904. The family immigrated to the United States when Burns was still a child, and he earned a number of degrees, including a Ph.D. in economics in 1934. Burn's economic ideas were decidedly conservative, as were his Republican politics, but he was no ideologue. He served as chairman of the Council of Economic Advisers during the Dwight D. Eisenhower administration and was later president of the National Bureau of Economic Research. In 1969 he came back into government service as an economic adviser to President Richard Nixon,* who appointed him head of the Federal Reserve Board in 1970. An expert on the business cycle, Burns argued that the violent swings in the

American economy were things of the past, and he opposed business monopolies, wage-price controls, or social spending to stimulate an ailing economy. At
the Federal Reserve Board, he argued that the board should concentrate more
on managing the total supply of money in the economy rather than worrying
about how monetary policy would affect credit market conditions.

The economic theories of Arthur Burns, however, collided head on with the
problem of stagflation* in the 1970s. Because of the international energy crisis*
and skyrocketing petroleum prices, the world entered a long period of severe
inflation, and in the United States price increases reached levels unknown since
World War II. Burns reacted by requiring the Federal Reserve Board to raise
interest rates, a policy which drove the prime rate through the roof and dis-
couraged business investment. High petroleum prices also cut into consumer
demand and resulted in higher unemployment rates. Nothing in Burns's academic experience had prepared him for such an economic scenario. During the
Jimmy Carter* administration, his appointment on the Federal Reserve Board
was not renewed. Burns retired to private life and died on June 26, 1987.

SUGGESTED READINGS: *New York Times*, June 27, 1987; "Spotlight on Arthur
Frank Burns," *Banking* 62 (1970), 47, 110.

BUSING. The busing of schoolchildren to achieve racial integration was one
of the most controversial and bitterly contested political issues of the 1970s.
Although *Brown v. Board of Education* (1954) outlawed the de jure, or by law,
racial segregation of children in public schools, it did not end segregation.
Southern schools that had practiced legally mandated racial segregation were
quite slow in accommodating themselves to *Brown*, but even when they did
racial segregation continued throughout much of the United States. The de facto
segregation of schools was common everywhere because blacks and whites lived
in segregated neighborhoods. In most instances, neighborhood segregation was
an economic rather than legal phenomenon, a consequence of the rise of white
suburban neighborhoods and the white flight from urban centers after World
War II. But the results were nevertheless the same: black and white children
tended to attend different schools.

To overcome the de facto segregation of schools, civil rights advocates in the
early 1970s began calling for the mandatory busing of children across school
district lines. A percentage of inner-city children would be bused daily to suburban schools, and an equal percentage of suburban children would be transported daily to downtown schools. The U.S. Supreme Court endorsed the
practice in its 1971 *Swann v. Charlotte-Mecklenburg County Board of Education** case. More than 24,000 black children in the Charlotte, North Carolina,
school district attended all-black schools, and the court ordered that no fewer
than 14,000 of them be bused to schools outside their neighborhoods.

School busing generated enormous resentment among whites. Many whites
who had supported the civil rights movement* and opposed de jure segregation
broke ranks over busing, which they considered social engineering at its worst.

Many suburban parents opposed busing also because they did not want their children attending inner-city schools, which they considered inferior. They argued that busing destroyed the idea of the neighborhood school and was certain to remove parents from school-based activities. Busing also was harmful to children, they claimed, because it forced them to spend hours each day on a crowded school bus. Many racist whites also opposed busing because they did not want black children in their neighborhoods. The most virulent example of such racism occurred in South Boston, Massachusetts, in 1974 and 1975 when whites rioted in protest of black children attending their schools. Politicians were quick to exploit white fears and resentments. In the elections of 1968 and 1972, Richard Nixon* and George Wallace* both condemned busing as a warping of the civil rights dream. Not until the late 1980s, however, would the practice begin to disintegrate.

SUGGESTED READINGS: Mary Frances Berry, *The Politics of Parenthood*, 1993; James P. Comer, *School Power*, 1980; Marian Edelman, *Families in Peril*, 1987; Edward M. Jackson, *Black Education in Contemporary America*, 1986; Jonathan Kozol, *Savage Inequities*, 1992; Gary Orfield, *Public School Desegregation in the United States, 1968–1980*, 1983; Diane Ravitch, *The Troubled Crusade*, 1983.

C

CALLEY, WILLIAM (LAWS, JR.). In December 1969, when *Life* magazine published its grisly photographs of the My Lai massacre, William Calley became the most infamous individual in the United States, a symbol of all that had gone wrong in Vietnam. Born on June 8, 1943, he grew up in Miami, Florida. After graduating from high school he worked at a number of odd jobs and finally joined the army in 1966 to avoid being drafted. The few community college classes he had completed put him on a fast track to Officer Candidate School (OCS). At the time, the Vietnam War* required such large increases in junior officers that standards were relaxed, and William Calley was one of many who should never have qualified for OCS.

After completing OCS, he was assigned to Company C of the 1st Battalion of the 20th Infantry. At the time, the unit was stationed in Hawaii. Company commander Captain Ernest Medina put Calley in charge of the 1st Platoon. They arrived in South Vietnam in December 1967 and deployed to Quang Ngai Province, where they were assigned to the 11th Infantry Brigade. Quang Ngai Province was well known among U.S. soldiers for the number of Vietcong soldiers who operated there and for the general hostility of the civilian population toward Americans.

On March 16, 1968, during an operation in the village of My Lai, Company C slaughtered nearly five hundred Vietnamese civilians without encountering any Vietcong resistance. Hugh Thompson, a helicopter pilot observing the operation, reported large-scale civilian casualties, but officers of the 11th Infantry Brigade and the American Division, Colonel Oran K. Henderson and Major Gen. Samuel W. Foster, conducted only a cursory investigation and concluded that nothing out of the ordinary had taken place at My Lai. The fact that only two weapons were recovered from the nearly five hundred bodies apparently did not seem incongruous to those responsible for the investigation.

Over the course of the next year, rumors about the massacre circulated within the 11th Brigade, but the story did not make it into the media until April 1969 when Ronald L. Ridenhour, a Vietnam veteran who had heard about the incident, wrote a letter to President Richard Nixon* and thirty U.S. congressmen and requested an investigation. In November 1969, Lieutenant General William Peers launched a special investigation of the massacre. Calley was soon charged with war crimes. In his defense, he claimed that he was acting under orders received from Captain Medina, who allegedly instructed him to destroy every living thing in the hamlet. Members of Calley's platoon, who had been present at Medina's briefing, gave contradictory testimony. Some claimed that Medina had indeed given such orders, and others emphatically denied such accusations. In his own defense, Calley was also completely unapologetic about the fact that so many civilian noncombatants had been killed. They were "all Communists," he said and even claimed that the dead children "would just have grown up to be Communists." On March 29, 1971, William Calley was convicted of the first-degree murder of at least twenty-two Vietnamese noncombatants. The military judge sentenced him to life imprisonment at hard labor.

The conviction provoked a firestorm of political controversy. Many Americans felt that Calley was taking the entire blame for the incident, that his military superiors were making him the scapegoat. Veterans groups, especially the American Legion and the Veterans of Foreign Wars, rallied to Calley's defense, raising hundreds of thousands of dollars for a legal defense fund to provide him with high-quality legal assistance. President Nixon, in tune with public opinion, ordered Calley released from the military stockade and placed under confinement in Calley's own base apartment. The president then implemented a formal review of the conviction and sentence.

The controversy did not subside. Large numbers of Americans did not believe Calley should spend a day in jail, especially when no superior officers had been convicted of war crimes. Henderson and Koster were eventually forced to resign from the army over the case, but there were no other criminal convictions. In August 1971, President Nixon reduced Calley's sentence to twenty years, and then, in April 1974, to ten years. William Calley was released on parole in November 1975.

The controversy over My Lai raised larger questions than just William Calley's guilt or innocence. The case of William Calley and the massacre at My Lai was the most intense example, but the press regularly circulated stories about civilian casualties in Vietnam,* the torture and execution of Vietcong prisoners, the throwing of Vietcong prisoners of war out of helicopters, and cutting off the ears of the Vietcong and North Vietnamese dead. Americans were forced to debate, throughout the 1970s, the question of whether My Lai had been a horrible aberration or whether such atrocities had become commonplace in Vietnam.

As a guerrilla war without fronts, fought in a distant land against a different ethnic group, the Vietnam War was ripe for atrocities. Cultural attitudes also played a huge role in the issue. Many American soldiers, tired and frustrated about the environment and the nature of the conflict, and angry about losing comrades and being unable to separate the Vietcong from civilians, came to look upon all Vietnamese as combatants. Approximately 70 percent of all American casualties resulted from booby traps,* and during lulls in formal military engagements that rate was even higher. American soldiers often developed feelings of deep hostility toward the Vietnamese. Between 1965 and 1973, 278 army and marine soldiers were convicted of serious offenses—murder, rape, and negligent homicide—against Vietnamese civilians, but civilian casualties in the field, from accident and atrocities, were far higher. The press, which was more active in the Vietnam War than in any earlier conflict in American history, was able, more than ever before, to send the story of the war home.

The debate was so intense in 1971 that the Vietnam Veterans Against the War* (VVAW) decided to hold special hearings on the issue of atrocities. Between January 31 and February 2, 1971, the VVAW convened the Winter Soldier Investigation* in Detroit, Michigan. For three days 116 veterans testified about war crimes they had either committed in Vietnam or had witnessed. There were also panel discussions on weaponry, medical care, prisoners, racism, ecological devastation, and the psychological effects of the war on American soldiers. Although no definitive answer has yet appeared for the question about the extent of U.S. atrocities in Vietnam, this investigation showed that such brutalities were commonplace.

SUGGESTED READINGS: Philip Caputo, *A Rumor of War*, 1977; Joseph Goldstein, Burke Marshall, and Jack Schwartz, *The My Lai Massacre and Its Cover-Up: Beyond the Reach of the Law?* 1976; Richard Hammer, *The Court-Martial of Lieutenant Calley*, 1971; Guenter Lewy, *America in Vietnam*, 1978; James S. Olson and Randy Roberts, *My Lai: A Documentary History*, 1997; W. R. Peers, *The My Lai Inquiry*, 1979; John Sack, *Lieutenant Calley: His Own Story*, 1971; Peter D. Trooboff, ed., *Law and Responsibility in Warfare: The Vietnam Experience*, 1975; Vietnam Veterans Against the War, *The Winter Soldier Investigation*, 1972.

CAMBODIA. During the course of the Vietnam War,* Cambodia gradually became drawn into the conflict and eventually experienced a national catastrophe unique in the twentieth century. At the close of the Geneva Accords of 1954, Cambodia received its independence, after spending nearly a century under French imperial rule. Since the 1850s, Cambodia had been one of the five colonies, along with Laos, Tonkin, Annam, and Cochin China, of French Indochina. Independence pulled Cambodia out of the French orbit, but it did not solve another of the country's historical dilemmas. For centuries, Cambodians, known to themselves as Khmer people, had also worried about Vietnamese expansionism, and when the Vietnam War erupted in the 1950s and 1960s, they found themselves walking a political tightrope, hoping to maintain their independence. Prince Norodom Sihanouk,* who had become head of state in Cambodia in 1954, proclaimed neutrality in the Indochinese War, not wanting to offend either the powerful Americans or his longtime nemesis, the Vietnamese.

Under international law, however, Cambodia's claim to neutrality was undermined by the fact that Vietcong and North Vietnamese used the country as a sanctuary. From bases in Cambodia, they regularly staged military actions on U.S. and South Vietnamese troops, and they just as regularly fled across the border of South Vietnam into Cambodia when U.S. forces pursued them. Both the Johnson and Nixon administrations pressured Prince Sihanouk to expel the Vietcong and North Vietnamese forces from Cambodia, but Sihanouk actually feared the North Vietnamese more than he feared the Americans. He also had a fight of his own to conduct. Communist forces known as the Khmer Rouge* were conducting a guerrilla war against his own government, and Sihanouk feared angering the North Vietnamese, who might then come to the assistance of the Communists.

Walking that neutralist tightrope between the Vietnamese-backed Khmer Rouge Communists and the American-backed South Vietnamese eventually proved impossible. Sihanouk's prime minister, a man named Lon Nol, was bitterly anti-Communist and resented the willingness of Sihanouk to allow Vietcong and North Vietnamese Army (NVA) troops to occupy sanctuaries in eastern Cambodia and infiltrate supplies and personnel into South Vietnam via the Ho Chi Minh Trail. Sihanouk tolerated their presence only because he feared a North Vietnamese invasion and the triumph of the Khmer Rouge if he tried to drive out the Vietcong and NVA soldiers. Beginning in 1969 he secretly allowed the United States to begin bombing enemy targets inside Cambodia. The bombing campaign was designated Operation Menu. Even so, the Nixon administration was anxious to see that Sihanouk's government fell so that more widespread U.S. military operations could be conducted in Cambodia.

U.S. embassy officials secretly informed Lon Nol and his political supporters that in the event of a coup d'état against Sihanouk, they would enjoy the support and quick recognition of the United States. Lon Nol was not about to let such an opportunity slip through his grasp. In March 1970 Sihanouk traveled to France, and while he was gone Lon Nol engineered a coup d'état. The National Assembly displaced Sihanouk, and Lon Nol became the new head of state. Prince Sihanouk fled to the People's Republic of China where he announced his support for the Khmer Rouge.

One month later, President Richard Nixon* and Henry Kissinger* took advantage of the coup d'état, and, with Lon Nol's active encouragement and consent, launched the infamous invasion of Cambodia. Combined U.S. and South Vietnamese forces hoped to capture the Central Office for South Vietnam* (COSVN), ostensibly North Vietnam's headquarters for directing military operations in South Vietnam. The plan was to capture the Vietcong headquarters and disrupt North Vietnamese and Vietcong command and control effectiveness. Actually, the COSVN was not a large bureaucracy but a highly mobile group of two dozen military officials and staff aides. The U.S. forces never located them.

The U.S. invasion of Cambodia, which President Nixon euphemistically termed an "incursion," reignited the antiwar movement* at home and subjected the president to severe criticism. Within two months the invasion was over. Its effects, however, eventually destroyed Cambodia. The massive bombing campaigns and artillery bombardment, directed at Communist forces there, accidentally killed hundreds of thousands of Cambodian civilians. The Khmer Rouge, who took political advantage of those deaths, blamed Lon Nol for the widespread deaths. Lon Nol's government lost political influence, and the Khmer Rouge assumed a heroic stance among millions of Cambodians. The invasion also drove the North Vietnamese far deeper into western Cambodia than they had ever been before, a political and military reality which greatly strengthened the Khmer Rouge. By the time U.S. troops were withdrawn several months later, the Khmer Rouge had become a much stronger political force in Cambodia.

In October 1970 Lon Nol abolished the monarchy and proclaimed a republic, but in effect he had become the dictator of Cambodia. His administration was marked by extraordinary corruption and ineptitude, and his 1971 stroke left him unable to maintain control of the government. Pol Pot* and the Khmer Rouge made steady gains in the countryside. In the spring of 1975, the Khmer Rouge surrounded the Cambodian capital of Phnom Penh. Lon Nol fled to Hawaii early in April 1975, and the Khmer Rouge overran the capital later in the month. They then renamed the country Kampuchea, its ancient name.

Pol Pot, the leader of the Khmer Rouge, then declared "Year Zero" and began forcibly to depopulate all Kampuchean cities, massing everyone into rural labor camps and murdering anyone and everyone with ties to the French, Norodom Sihanouk, or Lon Nol. The killings assumed genocidal dimensions; as many as two million people died between 1975 and 1979. Astonished by the brutality of Pol Pot, worried about the political stability of the regime, and still interested in their ancient quest for dominance of the Khmer people, the Vietnamese, went on the march again in 1979 when soldiers of the Socialist Republic of Vietnam invaded Kampuchea. They drove to the capital, and Pol Pot fled back into the jungles, where he organized the remnants of the Khmer Rouge into a new guerrilla force to fight against the Vietnamese occupation force.

Pol Pot and the Khmer Rouge continued their political and guerrilla struggle throughout the 1970s and 1980s, even though they were only shadows of their former strength. Pol Pot was finally captured in 1997 and placed under house arrest; all the time he denied that he had had anything to do with the holocaust in Cambodia. Although many people in the world community wanted Pol Pot put on trial for crimes against humanity, the political situation in Cambodia remains delicate and unpredictable, and Cambodian authorities were moving very slowly in any efforts to punish him. Pol Pot died on April 15, 1998.

SUGGESTED READINGS: Ben Kiernan, *How Pol Pot Came to Power*, Ph.D. diss., 1986; William Shawcross, *Sideshow: Kissinger, Nixon, and the Destruction of Cambodia*, 1979; Michael Vickery, *Cambodia, 1975–1982*, 1984; William Shawcross, *The Quality of Mercy. Cambodia, Holocaust, and the Modern Conscience*, 1984; François Ponchaud, *Cambodia: Year Zero*, 1978.

CAMBODIAN INVASION OF 1970. *See* CAMBODIA.

CAMP DAVID. During the 1970s, political unrest in the Middle East exerted a direct impact on American political, economic, and social life. The Yom Kippur War* of 1973, in which an Arab military coalition had attacked Israel, only to suffer a humiliating defeat, produced a bitter backlash among Arab nations toward the United States. Arab leaders felt that even though they sold millions of barrels of oil a day to the United States, Americans had sided with Israel in the war. Their resentment led to the Arab oil boycott of 1973–1974,* which produced a dramatic increase in petroleum and then consumer prices. Unemployment rose with inflation, and the U.S. economy went into a tailspin. On the foreign policy front, the Yom Kippur War had produced a superpower confrontation, with the United States backing the Israelis and the Soviet Union supporting the Arab states. It had also left a military and diplomatic residue of bitterness in the Middle East. As part of their successful military operations during the war, the Israelis had invaded the Egyptian Sinai, a vast desert region south and west of Israel, but when the cease-fire had been signed, Israel had not withdrawn its forces. Israeli Prime Minister Menachem Begin claimed that to prevent a future Egyptian attack on Israel from the Sinai, Israeli troops would have to remain in the region on military alert. Restoring peace and stability to the Middle East became a priority of the Carter administration.

In September 1978 President Jimmy Carter* invited President Anwar el-Sadat of Egypt and Israeli Prime Minister Begin to meet with him at the presidential retreat at Camp David, Maryland. Carter insisted that the two leaders come to terms, and in subsequent discussions a final agreement was worked out. In a well-publicized White House ceremony on March 26, 1979, both men signed a peace treaty. Begin agreed to withdraw Israeli troops from the Egyptian Sinai, where they had been since the end of the Yom Kippur War, and Egypt agreed to normalize its diplomatic relations with Israel. The so-called Camp David accords proved to be the high-water mark of the Carter presidency.

SUGGESTED READING: William B. Quando, *Camp David: Peacemaking and Politics*, 1986.

THE CANDIDATE. *The Candidate*, one of the most successful political comedies in American film history, was released ironically in June 1972, just when President Richard Nixon's* political minions set about to cover up the Watergate scandal.* *The Candidate* is a cold comedy that savages the American political system. Bill McKaw (Robert Redford) is a decent, liberal California Democrat concerned with the civil rights movement* and the environmental movement.* Young, handsome, and charismatic, he is a publicist's and photographer's dream, and the Democratic party nominates him to run for a U.S. Senate seat. But in the big time of media intensive, national politics, where honest politicians with well-developed political philosophies are ambushed by the press and fall by the wayside, McKaw must compromise his principles to avoid controversy.

The political campaign becomes not an opportunity to debate real issues but a long, expensive, drawn-out ordeal to prevent mistakes.

In the end, McKaw wins the election, but he pays the terrible price of all successful American politicians. By the time he has survived the election campaign and the unrealistic expectations of voters and the press, he has compromised himself, neutralizing his positions on most issues to the point that he stands for nothing. With the election won, McKaw asks his advisors, "What do we do now?" He knows a great deal about campaigning but nothing about being a senator.

SUGGESTED READING: *New York Times*, June 30, 1972.

CAPTAIN AND TENNILLE. Captain and Tennille were a successful husband-and-wife pop act of the 1970s. Daryl Dragon, "The Captain" was accompanied on keyboards by his vocalist wife Toni Tennille. Between 1975 and 1977, they released a string of top-ten hit singles, including "Love Will Keep Us Together," "The Way I Want to Touch You," "Lonely Night," "Muskrat Love," "Shop Around," "Can't Stop Dancin'," "You Never Done It Like That," and "Do That to Me One More Time." By 1977, however, audiences began losing interest, and the Captain and Tennille disappeared from the big time of American rock and roll.

SUGGESTED READING: James Spada, *Captain and Tennille*, 1978.

CARNAL KNOWLEDGE. Released in 1976, the film *Carnal Knowledge* was directed by Mike Nichols and written by Jules Feifer, the same team who produced *Little Murders, The Graduate*, and *Catch-22*. The film is made up of a series of conversations between Jonathan (Jack Nicholson*) and Sandy (Art Garfunkel) about their sexual relationships over a period of about thirty years, from their days as Amherst roommates in the 1940s to their desperation at middle-age in the 1970s. It is slightly more about the complete and crippling stubbornness of Jonathan to avoid being "castrated" than it is about the flaky intellectualism and general weakness of Sandy.

Both of them go from one dysfunctional relationship to another, and the first major one for each of them is the same woman—Susan (Candice Bergen), a Smith student who eventually gives them (separately) their first sexual encounter. And with her and several others, Nichols captures many major life stages of sexual experimentation: the awkward tentativeness of youthful encounters, the self-deceptive smug confidence which accompanies a new partner, and the exploitative cynicism of middle-aged desperation. The only other major character in the film is Bobbie (Ann-Margret), who is the most serious relationship of Jonathan's life, and the one he calls "the greatest ball-buster of 'em all." Much like the prevailing pessimism of America in the mid-1970s, the film ends hopelessly, with Sandy in a serious relationship with an eighteen-year-old who he claims has saved his life, and Jonathan's impotence, which can be cured only if a prostitute (Rita Moreno) cites a mysogynistic appraisal of masculinity from memory, which really mocks Jonathan's pathetic desperation.

All four of the major actors gave accurate and complicated performances. Nicholson created a Don Juan for whom women were at best a pleasure and worst an alimony payment, but he made him mean and stubborn enough so as not to evoke any sympathy in the end. Garfunkel and Bergen each succeeded in making their characters vulnerable and without direction. And Ann-Margret was nominated for an Academy Award for the complexity of Bobbie, who perfectly balanced desperation, aggressiveness, and simplicity.

Carnal Knowledge came at a critical time in the 1970s, when Americans first began to call into question traditional stereotypes of masculinity; the film also makes the entire game of American sexual politics seem silly, contrived, and even tragic. It was also a time when the women's movement* was coming into its own, and although *Carnal Knowledge* criticizes masculinity to cartoonish extremes, it also makes fun of the naiveté of women.

SUGGESTED READING: *New York Times*, July 1, 1971.

Bradley A. Olson

THE CAROL BURNETT SHOW. *The Carol Burnett Show* was a staple of American Saturday night television from 1967 to 1979. The comedy variety show starred Carol Burnett, Harvey Korman, Lyle Waggoner, Vicki Lawrence, and Tim Conway. Carol Burnett was a one-of-a-kind comedienne, a woman of enormous talent who could sing, dance, act, mime, and clown with equal skill, all the while retaining a homey comraderie with her audience. Each episode of *The Carol Burnett Show* began with her characteristic question-and-answer session with the studio audience and then went into a series of sketches that spoofed various films, television shows, and mass entertainment forms. "As the Stomach Turns," for example, was a spoof of daytime television soap operas. The program was generally apolitical, perhaps because so much of American life had been politicized in the late 1960s and 1970s that audiences were ready for a weekly respite. The program also established a group of regular characters— such as "Mr. Tudball and Mrs. Wiggins" and "Ed & Eunice"—who became quite popular. The last episode of *The Carol Burnett Show* was telecast on September 8, 1979.

SUGGESTED READING: J. Randy Taraborelli, *Laughing till It Hurts: The Complete Life and Career of Carol Burnett*, 1988.

THE CARPENTERS. The Carpenters were a commercially successful rock-and-roll group of the early 1970s. Richard Carpenter was the songwriter and pianist, and his sister Karen was the vocalist. Her deep, lyrical voice became the group's trademark. *Ticket to Ride* in 1969 was their first album, but their first number-one hit, "Close to You," came on the album of the same name in 1970. They followed it up with a series of top-ten hits, including "We've Only Just Begun" (1970), "For All We Know" (1971), "Rainy Days and Monday"

(1971), "Superstar" (1971), "It's Going to Take Some Time" (1972), "Hurting Each Other" (1972), "Goodbye to Love" (1972), "Sing" (1973), "Yesterday Once More" (1973), "Top of the World" (1973), "I Won't Last a Day Without You" (1974), "Please Mr. Postman" (1975), and "Only Yesterday" (1975). They traveled around the world giving concerts in the 1970s and hosted several television specials. They did not have another hit song, however, until 1981, when "Touch Me When We're Dancing" reached number twenty on the charts. By that time, Karen Carpenter was suffering from the anorexia nervosa that eventually killed her in 1983.

SUGGESTED READING: Ronald Garcia, *Close to You: The Story of Richard and Karen Carpenter*, 1994.

CARRIE. This 1976 cult classic was one of the first Stephen King novels to be made into a movie. Directed by auteur Brian DePalma, who in the 1970s, according to Guy Flatley, was praised "both for technical virtuosity and his quirky—some might say perverse—point of view." This perverseness is evident in DePalma's explanation of the film. He claimed that *"Carrie* is a parapsychological horror story set in an *American Graffiti* milieu. . . . The film deals with the strong religious morality we have in the West, the juxtaposition of sexuality and guilt, and the concept of corruption and evil being engendered by women."

The movie begins when ugly duckling Carrie White, played by Sissy Spacek, has her first menstrual period in the school shower, and because of severe repression, she is completely unprepared. She reacts hysterically, and the other girls respond to that hysteria by throwing tampons at her and chanting, "Plug it up!" The haunting realism of this first scene sets the tone for the rest of the film. During this traumatic experience, Carrie discovers that she has telekinesis—the power to move objects by simple concentration.

Carrie hardly uses the power until her maniacally religious mother, Margaret, played by Piper Laurie, tries to prevent her from attending her senior prom, warning her repeatedly, "They're all gonna laugh at you." Carrie throws her to the bed twice and orders to stay there and not speak. But when she goes to the prom, the students elect her prom queen as a joke, and one vicious girl pours a bucket of pig blood on her head in her moment of triumph. Carrie then gets revenge by destroying the gym and everyone in it with her telekinetic powers. And when she goes home to apologize to her mother, she stabs her in the back instead; the scene climaxes with Margaret White hanging like a crucifix.

Carrie is important because it is completely unlike any horror movie that came before it. The story fits into the genre easily, with a very short, unrealistic screenplay. But because of DePalma's artsy direction and the powerful performances by Spacek and Laurie, the characters were not reduced to simple dichotomies of "good" and "bad." Additionally, the protagonist dies in the end at the mercy of her own fury. Spacek and Laurie each earned Academy Award nominations, the first horror film to be so honored since *The Exorcist.** And until *The Silence of the Lambs* won Best Picture in 1992, there had never been an equal.

SUGGESTED READING: *New York Times*, November 17 and December 5, 1976.

Bradley A. Olson

THE CARS. The Cars, a rock-and-roll band formed in Boston, Massachusetts, in 1976, included Ric Ocasek, Benn Orr, Eliot Easton, and Greg Hawkes. They were the most successful of the new wave bands of the decade. Their first album, *The Cars* (1978), included three songs that made it into the top forty on the pop charts, but the album was a much bigger success, going platinum and remaining on the pop charts until well into 1979. Their 1979 album *Candy-O*, with such hit singles as "Let's Go" and "It's All We Can Do," went platinum in only two months, as did their 1980 album *Panorama* and *Shake It Up* in 1981. Before the group disintegrated in the late 1980s, they had also recorded the hit albums *Heartbreak City* and *Door to Door*.

SUGGESTED READING: Philip Kamin, *The Cars*, 1986.

CARTER, JIMMY (JAMES EARL). James Earl "Jimmy" Carter was born on October 1, 1924, in Plains, Sumter County, Georgia. His father was a peanut farmer and small businessman. In 1942, after spending a year at Georgia Southwestern College in Americus, Georgia, Carter accepted an appointment to the U.S. Naval Academy at Annapolis. He did not start at the academy, however, until 1943 because he needed to improve his analytical and mathematical skills, which he did at the Georgia Institute of Technology in Atlanta. Carter graduated from the Naval Academy in 1946, was commissioned as a second lieutenant, and was assigned to the submarine corps. He completed submarine training in 1948 and spent the next four years aboard the USS *Pomfret* and the USS *K-1*. In 1952 Carter became part of the navy's new nuclear-powered submarine program. He served under Captain Hyman Rickover on the USS *Sea Wolf*.

After his father's death in 1953, Carter resigned his commission in order to return to Georgia and manage the family businesses. He also became interested in local politics and served for seven years on the Sumter County Board of Education. In 1962 Carter won election to the state senate, where he spent two terms before making an unsuccessful campaign for the governorship. Out of elective office in 1966, Carter returned to full-time work in the family business, but he continued to speak about political issues throughout the state. In 1970 Carter made another bid for the governor's mansion, and this time he won. His four years as governor were successful ones for Carter and for Georgia. He implemented reforms in the state budgetary process, passed important environmental protection legislation, and put in place an affirmative action* program that dramatically increased minority employment in state government. Ambitious and successful, Carter announced in 1975 his candidacy for president of the United States.

Few political pros gave him a chance of gaining the nomination. He was all but unknown around the country and did not bring much strength to the Democratic ticket, at least according to political observers who thought that candidates from states with large electoral votes had an advantage. But what many assumed was Carter's greatest liability—that he was a Washington outsider with few political IOUs to collect—proved to be his greatest strength. In the aftermath of the Watergate scandal* and the Vietnam War,* voters had grown decidedly suspicious and cynical about career politicians, and Carter made the most of the fact that he was not part of the Washington establishment.

The country's economic situation was also miserable. Inflation and unemployment, dubbed "stagflation"* by many economists, resulted in the worst economy since the Great Depression. Combined with public cynicism toward Republicans over Watergate and the backlash from the North Vietnamese victory over South Vietnam, incumbent Gerald Ford* had an uphill battle to win election in his own right.

The election itself was relatively uneventful. Democrats charged Republicans with presiding over the most corrupt presidential administration in U.S. history and letting the economy degenerate precipitously. Republicans tried to blame the big-spending Democratic Congress for America's plight, but not many voters bought the accusation. Still, given the problems in which the country was mired, the election proved surprisingly close. Some analysts believe that President Ford actually lost the election during a televised debate when he said, "The Soviet Union does not dominate eastern Europe." He meant to say, "The Soviet Union does not dominate the spirit of eastern Europe." The controversy cost Ford votes in the white ethnic communities of the Midwest. Jimmy Carter won by a narrow margin in the popular vote—40,828,587 (50.1 percent of the total) to Ford's 39,147,613 (48.0 percent). The Electoral College margin was somewhat broader: 297 to 240.

It was a different story, however, in the congressional elections. There the voters overwhelmingly expressed their dissatisfaction with the Republican party. When Jimmy Carter entered the White House on January 20, 1977, the Democrats enjoyed a 291 to 142 margin in the House of Representatives and a 62 to 38 majority in the Senate. Not since the Great Depression had one political party so dominated the federal government.

But President Carter could not take advantage of his victory or his congressional margins. He had some successes. He negotiated the Panama Canal Treaties* providing for the return of the canal to Panamanian sovereignty, brought about full diplomatic relations with the People's Republic of China, achieved the Camp David* accords providing for peace between Egypt and Israel, and became the most powerful advocate for human rights in the world.

But his presidency floundered on the sense of impotence that afflicted America in the late 1970s. Inflation and the prime rate skyrocketed during Carter's administration, driving up the cost of capital goods and housing to the point that average Americans could no longer afford them. He scuttled the B-1 bomber* and neutron bomb* programs, and critics charged him with being soft on defense. On November 4, 1979, militant Iranians seized control of the U.S. embassy in Teheran and took hostage the fifty Americans inside. Carter's attempts to negotiate for their release failed, as did a botched military rescue attempt. Under Jimmy Carter, many Americans concluded, the United States had lost its status in the world. Duing the presidential election campaign of 1980, Republican candidate Ronald Reagan* repeatedly asked the American public if they were "better off in 1980 than in 1976." Most answered "no" and swept Carter out of office.

In political retirement, Jimmy Carter's reputation with the American public has vastly improved. He has been active as a diplomatic troubleshooter in Europe, the Caribbean, and Africa, and his support of Habitat for Humanity has helped construct homes for thousands of poor families.

SUGGESTED READINGS: Betty Glad, *Jimmy Carter: In Search of the Great White House*, 1980; Laurence H. Shoup, *The Carter Presidency, and Beyond: Power and Politics in the 1980s*, 1980; James Wooten, *Dasher: The Roots and the Rising of Jimmy Carter*, 1978.

CASSIDY, DAVID. David Cassidy, who became a teen heartthrob in the 1970s, was born in New York City on April 12, 1950. His father, actor Jack Cassidy, introduced his son to the entertainment business. In 1970, David Cassidy won the role of Keith Partridge in *The Partridge Family*, a television sitcom about a white, middle-class, suburban, musically talented family. On the show, the Partridge family were regular concert performers, and Keith was the lead singer. In real life, the Partridge Family's first single, "I Think I Love You," sold more than six million copies, and the television program spawned a veritable gold mine of Partridge Family merchandise—clothes, lunch boxes, T-shirts, comic books, books, magazines, and dolls. In the process, David Cassidy became a superstar to teens and preteens. He left the show after its 1974 season, but the program was popular as a rerun throughout the 1970s and early 1980s. Cassidy's solo recording career was not as successful, and he never really succeeded in appealing to mature audiences, at least not until the 1990s, when his teenager fans of the 1970s were adults. Cassidy developed a highly successful Las Vegas act then.

SUGGESTED READING: David Cassidy with Chip Deffaa, *C'mon—Get Happy*, 1994.

CATCH-22. Catch-22, an important antiwar movement* film released in 1970, is based on Joseph Heller's 1961 novel of the same name. A brilliant satire set on the imaginary island of Pianosa during World War II, the film centers around bomber pilot Captain John Yosarian's (Alan Arkin) efforts to survive. Flying bombers in World War II was deadly business, and Yosarian's commanding officers kept raising the number of missions a pilot must complete before earning a leave. When Yosarian tries to get out of the service by feigning insanity, he collides head-on with "Catch-22," a military regulation claiming that since a man must be insane to agree in the first place to go on bombing missions, his request for a mustering out of the military is proof positive that he is sane. Yosarian is just numbly trying to understand and maybe survive what has become an insane situation. He tries to escape the insanity by pretending to be insane. That then becomes the Catch-22 because it is normal—sane—to want to escape from insane situations. Yosarian's squadron is asked to bomb towns so that they can produce nice "tight" bombing patterns that look very efficient in aerial photographs.

The film became a cultural icon of the 1960s because it spoofed large bureaucracies and their naive convictions about their ability to bring order to a chaotic world. By the mid-1960s, the phrase "Catch-22" had entered the American vocabulary as a synonym for bureaucratic rules that possess no logic or sense and whose consequences are counterproductive. Many Americans came to view the U.S. military effort in Indochina as one enormous example of Catch-22. The film demonstrated how far from victory the United States was and how contradictory were the goals of winning the "hearts and minds" (see *Heart and Minds*) of the Vietnamese people by destroying their country.

SUGGESTED READING: Joseph Heller, *Catch-22*, 1961.

CB RADIO. One of the communications fads of the 1970s was the citizens band, or CB radio, which allowed people to communicate with other CBers within a ten-mile radius. For several years in the mid-1970s, CB radios were the fastest-growing sector of the communications industry. People purchased CB radios for their cars, boats, trucks, homes, and recreational vehicles. Developing a catchy "moniker" or "CB name" became part of the fad. In 1976 singer-songwriter C. W. McCall's song "Convoy," an ode celebrating CB radios and life on the highway, reached number one on *Billboard* magazine's hit parade. Late in the 1970s, computers replaced CB radios as new communications fads, and cellular phones made CBs an anachronism in the 1990s.

SUGGESTED READING: Larry Adcock, *Not for Truckers Only*, 1977.

CENTER FOR THE STUDY OF RESPONSIVE LAW. The Center for the Study of Responsive Law was founded in 1969 by consumer advocate Ralph Nader. The law students he hired became known as "Nader's raiders" for the crusading zeal they brought to the task of consumer protection. They subjected a variety of consumer products to safety studies and then published their results widely, lobbying actively for federal, state, and local consumer protection legislation. Nader's efforts also inspired the establishment of Public Interest Research Groups (PIRGs) to investigate consumer issues and promote consumer interests. Brilliant, articulate, and indefatigable, Ralph Nader became one of the decade's most influential people. In subsequent years, he has continued his liberal activism and expanded his reach to the concerns of the environmental movement* where he again argues that big business is more concerned with the bottom line than with environmental protection. The nuclear power industry, he argues, is one of the best examples. During the 1996 presidential elections, Rader placed himself on the California ballot as a third-party environmental candidate. Although he had no chance of winning, he used the election to promote his environmentalist agenda.

SUGGESTED READINGS: Hays Gorey, *Nader and the Power of Every Man*, 1975; Charles McCarry, *Citizen Nader*, 1972; Ralph Nader, *No Contest: Corporate Lawyers and the Perversion of Justice in America*, 1996.

CENTRAL INTELLIGENCE AGENCY. The Central Intelligence Agency (CIA) was established by Congress in 1947 to serve as a clearinghouse for all foreign intelligence operations. Subsequent legislation in 1949 allowed the CIA to use secret administrative procedures and even insulated it from the congressional budget process. During the hearings over creation of the CIA, Federal Bureau of Investigation (FBI) director J. Edgar Hoover expressed concern that the new agency might compete with the FBI. To prevent that possibility, Congress confined CIA jurisdiction to intelligence gathering outside the United States.

For the first twenty years of its existence, the CIA enjoyed widespread political support. At a time when the United States was fighting the Cold War* against the Soviet Union, most Americans regarded the Central Intelligence Agency as critically important to national survival. After all, the Soviet Union's intelligence arm, known as the KGB, had agents all over the world, as well as in the United States, and common sense dictated that the United States possess an appropriate response. The CIA was that response.

But late in the 1960s and throughout the 1970s, the CIA became the target of intense political criticism. Part of the problem was the so-called credibility gap.* Americans had grown extremely suspicious of political leaders—Republican as well as Democrat—who lied to them, and the fact that the CIA was a supersecret agency with an all but independent budget made many people extremely suspicious. As the American public soured on the Vietnam War,* they also soured on the CIA, which had been heavily involved since the 1950s in the Indochinese conflict. The CIA had conducted secret bombing campaigns over Laos, had recruited and trained anti-Communist armies among Montagnard tribesmen, and had conducted the Phoenix program in Vietnam responsible for thousands of political assassinations. The ostensible objective of the Phoenix program had been to destroy the Vietcong infrastructure, but in the convoluted political climate of South Vietnam in the late 1960s and early 1970s, Phoenix had actually led to the assassinations of hundreds of South Vietnamese who were not Communists, just political enemies of the local regime. Finally, the CIA had actively interfered with the internal political affairs of Cuba, Chile, Iran, Laos, and many other countries and had plotted the assassination of anti-U.S. political operatives in those countries.

When all of these problems came to light in the 1970s, it precipitated a vigorous debate about the role of the Central Intelligence Agency. First, CIA political assassinations around the world raised eyebrows about the agency's mission. There had long been suspicion about political assassinations, but President Gerald Ford* unwittingly let the news out officially in a White House press conference in 1974. Worse, during the Watergate scandal* of the Richard Nixon* administration, the public learned about Operation CHAOS, a secret, government-sponsored program of CIA surveillance of Vietnam War critics. Such a program was a clear violation of the CIA's charter, which confined CIA jurisdiction to areas outside the United States. President Nixon's decision in 1973 to appoint William Colby as director of the CIA only added fuel to the political fire. A longtime CIA operative, Colby had headed up the bloody Phoenix program in South Vietnam. He found himself the target of very personal political assaults and had to defend the agency during its most difficult years.

In 1974 Congress amended the Foreign Assistance Act of 1974 and clearly delineated CIA powers—especially that the CIA be used only for intelligence operations outside the United States. The so-called Hughes-Ryan amendment required the president to inform Congress before the CIA engaged in covert operations abroad. It fell to William Colby to help the CIA adjust to the increased political scrutiny of Congress. To blunt criticism of the CIA, President Ford appointed George Bush to head the agency.

In the presidential election of 1976,* Democratic candidate Jimmy Carter* called for reform of the Central Intelligence Agency, and when Carter won the election, both houses of Congress established permanent oversight committees to monitor CIA activities. Senator Frank Church* of Idaho headed the Senate committee, and Congressman Otis Pike of New York supervised the House committee. By an executive order issued in 1978, President Carter established guidelines and restrictions on CIA investigations of U.S. citizens abroad. In 1980 Congress formalized the process by passing the Intelligence Accountability Act, which created the House Intelligence Committee and the Senate Intelligence committee to oversee CIA operations.

SUGGESTED READINGS: William E. Colby and Peter Forbath, *Honorable Men: My Life in the CIA*, 1978; Morton Halperin et al., *The Lawless State: The Crimes of the U.S. Intelligence Agencies*, 1976; Harry Howe Ransom, *The Intelligence Establishment*, 1970; John Prados, *Presidents' Secret Wars: CIA and Pentagon Covert Operations Since World War II*, 1986; Peer da Silva, *Sub Rosa: The CIA and the Uses of Intelligence*, 1978.

CENTRAL OFFICE FOR SOUTH VIETNAM. During the 1970s, the acronym COSVN, which stands for Central Office for South Vietnam, the name of the headquarters for North Vietnam's Military command of Vietcong forces, became a symbol of American frustration in South Vietnam. When U.S. military officials heard the words "command headquarters," however, they developed an extraordinary misguided image, based on comparing it to their own Military Assistance Command Vietnam (MACV), a huge bureaucracy located in Saigon. COSVN was nothing of the sort. Although COSVN was nominally located in Tay Ninh Province, it was highly mobile and quite different from what most

American military officials thought of as a command headquarters. COSVN consisted of a small number of senior officers and staff assistants, but it was not a fixed installation. The North Vietnamese had the ability to relocate COSVN on a moment's notice, which rendered the office highly elusive.

U.S. military strategists longed for the day when they could "capture" COSVN and, as they supposed, completely disrupt North Vietnamese and Vietcong command and control operations. Such a success, they assumed, would cripple the Vietcong and North Vietnamese Army (NVA). General Creighton Abrams* in 1970 remarked that the "successful destruction of COSVN headquarters in a single blow would, I believe, have a very significant impact on enemy operations throughout South Vietnam." After all, if North Vietnam and the Vietcong managed to capture MACV in Saigon, U.S. military operations in South Vietnam would be badly disrupted.

Late in 1969, U.S. military intelligence informed General Abrams, who then informed President Richard Nixon,* that North Vietnam had relocated the COSVN across the border in Cambodia.* The desire to strike at the COSVN became the rationale for the bombing of Cambodia in 1969 and the invasion of Cambodia in 1970. Supposedly it had been located and was vulnerable to B-52 strikes. Because Cambodia was a neutral nation, elaborate steps were taken to maintain secrecy, including falsification of military records. In the invasion of Cambodia, American and South Vietnamese soldiers captured large amounts of Vietcong supplies, but they never located the COSVN. The primary results of the invasion were to push the Vietcong and North Vietnamese Army deeper into Cambodia, increase the flood of refugees into Phnom Penh, strengthen the Khmer Rouge,* hasten the collapse of the Cambodian military, and undermine the Cambodian government. The American pursuit of COSVN became a symbol of the difficulties of fighting a guerilla war.

SUGGESTED READINGS: William Shawcross, *Sideshow: Kissinger, Nixon, and the Destruction of Cambodia*, 1979; Malcolm Caldwell and Tan Lek, *Cambodia in the Southeast Asia War*, 1973; Jonathan Grant et al., *The Widening War in Indochina*, 1971.

Samuel Freeman

CHÁVEZ, CÉSAR. César Estrada Chávez was born on March 31, 1927, outside Yuma, Arizona. His parents were migrant farm laborers, and Chavez spent his early years in the fields. During World War II, he served in the U.S. Navy. A bright, articulate young man, he had always chaffed at the poverty and discrimination his family had faced, and he decided that only labor union organization could guarantee farm laborers a decent life. In 1946 Chávez joined the National Agricultural Workers Union, and between 1952 and 1962, he worked for the Community Service Organization, the last two years as its general director. He finally resigned from the Community Service Organization because of its refusal to organize farm workers.

During the early 1960s, he was impressed with the effectiveness of Martin Luther King, Jr.'s, nonviolent civil rights movement,* and Chávez decided to adopt similar tactics as a means of organizing farm workers into labor unions. He relocated to Delano, California, and in 1962 he established the National Farm Workers Association (NFW). He gained national attention when the NFW joined with Filipino workers in their strike against Coachella Valley grape growers. He secured the support of a number of liberal politicians, including Senator Robert Kennedy of New York. Although he encountered opposition from the International Brotherhood of Teamsters, which was also trying to organize farm workers, Chávez was successful. In 1966 the NFW merged with the Agricultural Workers Organizing Committee to form the United Farm Workers Organizing Committee (UFWOC), with Chávez as president.

The growers proved to be every bit as intransigent as Chávez had expected, refusing to sign a contract with the union, and in 1967, after affiliating the UFWOC with the AFL-CIO, Chávez launched a national boycott of all California-grown table grapes. Liberals throughout the United States rallied to the boycott, and sales of California grapes plummeted. The growers decided that they had no choice but to recognize the union and sign contracts to raise wages and improve working conditions. In 1970 California's three largest growers gave in and signed the contracts. In an instant, César Chávez became the most prominent Mexican American in the country, a man whose influence among his own people rivaled that of the deceased Martin Luther King, Jr.

Chávez then turned his attention to the problems of migrant workers in Texas, but he encountered intense hostility there from the growers and even from the Mexican-American farm workers, who were decidedly more conservative than their California counterparts. He also found himself tied up in fierce jurisdictional disputes with the Teamsters Union, and with the Teamsters and the UFWOC fighting one another, the growers never had to deal with a single political opponent. The drive to organize Texas workers did not succeed.

During the 1980s and 1990s, although Chávez's stature among most Mexican Americans remained quite high, he opened himself to serious political criticism. Blessed with a mystical nature, Chávez began promoting psychological encounter groups and holistic medicine among union members, which many found silly at best and, at their worst, detrimental to the union movement. Still, Chávez kept the faith and urged Mexican Americans to take pride in their religion, heritage, and language. César Chávez died on April 23, 1993.

SUGGESTED READINGS: David Goodwin, *Cesar Chavez*, 1991; Richard Griswold del Castillo, *Cesar Chavez*, 1995; Joan London and Henry Anderson, *So Shall Ye Reap: The Story of Cesar Chavez and the Farm Workers Movement*, 1970; *New York Times*, April 24, 1993.

CHEAP TRICK. Cheap Trick, a rock-and-roll band formed in Rockford, Illinois, in 1974, included Robin Zander, Tom Petersson, Rick Nielsen, and Bun Carlos. Their popularity grew slowly in the United States. The albums *Cheap Trick* (1977), *In Color* (1978), and *Heaven Tonight* (1979) were only moderately successful, but they were huge hits in Japan. The group toured Japan in 1979 and were received as superstars. During the tour, they recorded the album *Live at Budokan*. Its lead single, ''I Want You to Want Me,'' helped the album reach triple platinum in sales. They peaked in 1979 with the album *Dream Police*. They then came on hard times, recording a string of disappointments until 1988, when the album *Lap of Luxury* and its number-one single ''The Flame'' put them back on top. They went into another long dry spell until 1994, when their album *Woke Up with a Monster* was a hit.

SUGGESTED READING: M. M. Barackman, ''Cheap Trick on Tour: Rook Rock and Perverse Roll?'' *Crawdaddy* (January 1978), 24.

CHICAGO. The rock-and-roll group Chicago, formed in Chicago, Illinois, in 1967, included Peter Cetera, Terry Kath, Robert Lamm, Walter Parazaider, Danny Seraphine, James Pankow, and Lee Loughnane. The group started out as brass horn players and made the transition to rock and roll. Known at first as the Chicago Transit Authority, they released an album of the same name in 1969. They shortened their name to Chicago in 1970 and had a string of top-twenty hit singles, including ''Does Anybody Really Know What Time It Is'' (1970), ''Saturday in the Park'' (1972), ''Feeling Stronger Every Day'' (1973), and ''Wishing You Were Here'' (1974).

Their popularity then began to flag. Kath died of a self-inflicted gunshot wound in 1978 and was replaced by Donald Dacus. In the 1980s, Chicago underwent a revival, which included eight top-ten hits: ''Hard to Say I'm Sorry'' (1982), ''Hard Habit to Break'' (1984), ''You're the Inspiration'' (1984), ''Will You Still Love Me'' (1986), ''I Don't Wanna Live Without Your Love'' (1988), ''Look Away'' (1988), ''You're Not Alone'' (1989), and ''What Kind of Man Would I Be'' (1989). Cetera then began his own solo career, and Chicago entered a long period of decline.

SUGGESTED READING: Mary Jo O'Shea, *Chicago*, 1975.

CHICO AND THE MAN. *Chico and the Man*, a pathbreaking situation comedy of the 1970s, starred comedian Freddie Prinze as Chico Rodriguez and Jack Albertson as Ed Brown. Brown ran a small, mom-and-pop garage in East Los Angeles, and Chico wanted in on a piece of the business. Eventually, Brown brought Chico in as a partner. The humor came from the contrast in the two personalities. Brown was an old, cranky Anglo; Chico, a young, enthusiastic Hispanic. While Brown was universally pessimistic about human nature and the outlook of the world, Chico was just the opposite, seeing only good in people and always anticipating good outcomes in every situation. In 1976 Della Reese joined the cast as Della Rogers, owner of a diner across the street from the garage as well as the property on which Brown's business was located. She was a sassy, in-charge woman who could take as well as she gave, and the rumbles among Brown, Chico, and Della provide much of the humor. *Chico and the Man* was the first situation comedy in American history to feature a Hispanic lead, and it was highly popular until Freddie Prinze committed suicide in 1977.

SUGGESTED READING: Maria Pruetzel, *The Freddie Prinze Story*, 1978.

THE CHINA SYNDROME. The old adage of "life imitates art" was never more compelling than in 1979, when Columbia Pictures released *The China Syndrome*, starring Jack Lemmon as Jack Godell, chief operator of a nuclear power plant in California; Jane Fonda* as Kimberley Wells, a reporter for a local television station; and Michael Douglas as Richard Adams, her cameraman. On a routine "light" news assignment, Wells and Adams are in the plant when an accident occurs and radioactive material is released into the environment. They have the commotion in the control room on camera, and the plot revolves around their attempt to investigate and broadcast the story while the power company tries to cover up the incident.

Several days after the nationwide release of *The China Syndrome*, a hauntingly similar nuclear accident occurred at the Three Mile Island* power complex in Pennsylvania. No film could have asked for better, free publicity. News stories and headlines for weeks discussed the accident, and the antinuclear energy movement was galvanized by the event and the film.

SUGGESTED READING: *New York Times*, March 16, 1979.

CHINATOWN. Roman Polanski, assisted by John Towne's Oscar-winning screenplay, changed the face of film noir forever. Set in the Great Depression in the 1930s, *Chinatown* is a classic tale of divided loyalties, overwhelming greed, and the futility of honor in a corrupt world.

The film begins when Jake Gittes (Jack Nicholson*), a Los Angeles private eye, is called in on what appears to be a routine investigation of marital infidelity, except for the fact that the husband is Hollis Mulwray, the head water commissioner of Los Angeles. Water was the lifeblood of the Southern California economy in the 1930s, the stuff of which real estate fortunes were made and lost. Gittes takes incriminating photos of the commissioner, which are stolen and published, tainting Mulwray's impeccable image before he supposedly commits suicide.

But nothing is as it appears—not the wife, not the affair, not the suicide. The real Mrs. Mulwray, Evelyn (Faye Dunaway), introduces herself to Gittes, threatens to sue, and suspiciously withdraws as soon as he begins to look deeper for the truth. Nevertheless, he continues, and his investigation leads him to an affair with Evelyn and an ominous discussion with Evelyn's father and Hollis's former business partner, Noah Cross (John Huston). Cross gives him a classic warning that he is not ready to find what he is looking for, but Gittes presses on and uncovers a horrifying mystery involving murder, real estate fraud, an artificial water shortage, terrible family secrets, and powerful, untouchable corruption. In *Chinatown*, evil prevails completely, and Gittes is left in Chinatown once again to mourn losing everything he tried to protect.

Nicholson gave one of the best performances of his career as the savvy Gittes, copying Humphrey Bogart's cool toughness and adding a flawed naiveté to complete Polanski's vision. Similarly, Dunaway displays unwillingness and discomfort with trusting Gittes enough to tell him the truth, but she adds originality by generating sympathy from her helpless situation. And finally, John Huston creates a chilling villain, a man who accepts no limits to his power and position, whether in business or family life.

Chinatown was released at a telling time in the 1970s. Because of the Watergate scandal* and other political scandals, the credibility gap* was widening, and the distrust of persons in power caused widespread paranoia. *Chinatown* was a perfect metaphor for those suspicions because it emphasized the powerful and untouchable people and interests who controlled depression-era Los Angeles.

SUGGESTED READING: *New York Times*, August 11, 1974.

Bradley A. Olson

CHiPs. *CHiPs*, an acronym for the California Highway Patrol, was a popular police drama of the 1970s. While *Dragnet* had been about Los Angeles detectives and *Adam 12* about street cops in a patrol car, *CHiPs* focused on motorcycle cops. First broadcast on NBC on September 15, 1977, *CHiPs* starred Larry Wilcox as Officer Jon Baker and Erik Estrada as Officer Frank Poncherello. Each episode included four or five instances of the officers assisting citizens and capturing criminals. Since Baker and Poncherello were bachelors, the program also focused on their social lives. Like *Adam 12, CHiPs* placed a high value on law and order, patriotism, service, and discipline, values that were returning to vogue in America during the 1970s. The last broadcast of *CHiPs* took place on July 17, 1983.

SUGGESTED READING: Tim Brooks and Earle Marsh, *The Complete Directory to Prime Time Network and Cable TV Shows, 1946–Present*, 1995.

A CHORUS LINE. *A Chorus Line* was one of the most successful musicals in Broadway history. A brilliant cooperative effort by writer James Kirkwood, dancer and choreographer Michael Bennett, writer and dancer Nicholas Dante, composer Marvin Hamlisch, and lyricist Ed Kleban, *A Chorus Line* debuted at the Shubert Theater on Broadway in the spring of 1975, after a run at New York Shakespeare Festival's Public Theater. The set was simple—a black background, large rehearsal mirror, and a white line stretching across the floor—and the play focused on the hopes, dreams, and neuroses of eighteen dancers auditioning for a Broadway musical. *A Chorus Line* had a run of 6,137 performances, won a Pulitzer prize and nine Tonys, and had a final gross of more than $50 million. It also produced one pop musical hit: "What I Did for Love."

SUGGESTED READING: *New York Times*, February 25, 1976.

CHURCH, FRANK. Frank Forrester Church was born in Boise, Idaho, on July 25, 1924. During World War II, he served as a military intelligence officer in China, India, and Burma, and in 1947 he graduated from Stanford University. After attending Harvard Law School for one year, a bout with cancer sent him west again, and in 1950 he graduated from the Stanford University Law School.

Between 1950 and 1956, Church practiced law in Idaho and was active in Democratic politics, serving as chairman of the statewide Young Democrats organization. He won the party's nomination for the U.S. Senate in 1956 and went on to upset the Republican incumbent, Herman Welker. At thirty-two, Church was the youngest member of the Senate. He quickly earned a reputation as an outspoken liberal, and by supporting majority leader Lyndon B. Johnson on civil rights movement* legislation, Church gained favor and was appointed to the prestigious Senate Foreign Relations Committee in 1959. In 1960 he supported John F. Kennedy for the presidential nomination, and in 1962 he won reelection.

After 1965 Senator Church became increasingly apprehensive about U.S. involvement in Southeast Asia. He warned against American support for repressive regimes such as that in Vietnam unless substantial progress was made toward reform. In 1965 he repeated this warning, contending that the rift in the Communist world between the People's Republic of China and the Soviet Union had diminished the threat of "monolithic communism." In 1966 Church broke with the Johnson administration over Vietnam policy by calling for an end to the bombing. In 1970 he cosponsored the Cooper-Church Amendment* to prohibit American deployment of ground forces in Cambodia,* setting off a six-month debate in the Senate. In 1972, in reaction to the Richard Nixon* administration's bombing of Hanoi and Haiphong and the mining of Haiphong Harbor,* Church joined with Senator Clifford Case of New Jersey in sponsoring a resolution seeking an end to all U.S. military activity in Southeast Asia. The proposal was considered the first step in the eventual adoption of the War Powers Resolution of 1973.

On the domestic front, Church chaired the Senate Select Committee on Intelligence, which investigated excesses and violations of law by the Central Intelligence Agency,* Federal Bureau of Investigation, and National Security Agency under the Nixon administration. In 1976 Church made a bid for the Democratic presidential nomination, but he lost to Governor Jimmy Carter* of Georgia. In 1980 Church was defeated for reelection to the Senate. He continued to live in Washington, D.C., where he practiced international law until his death from cancer on April 7, 1984.

SUGGESTED READINGS: Mark Bill, *Frank Church, D.C., and Me*, 1995; *New York Times*, April 8, 1984.

Joseph M. Rowe, Jr.

CINQUE. "Cinque" was the alias for Donald David DeFreeze, an African American who founded the Symbionese Liberation Army (SLA) and engineered the kidnapping of Patricia Hearst.* DeFreeze was born in Cleveland, Ohio, in 1943. A habitual criminal, DeFreeze was serving a six-to-fourteen-year sentence in California's Soledad Prison in 1973. Prison education programs awakened in him a political consciousness, and he founded the Symbionese Liberation Army with several convict friends. DeFreeze escaped from Soledad in March 1973. Hoping to pull off a social justice and public relations coup, DeFreeze kidnapped Patricia Hearst, heir to the Hearst publishing fortune. He claimed that Hearst headed a fascist economic empire that oppressed millions of poor people around the world. In a ransom tape, DeFreeze ordered the Hearsts to hand over, in a four-week period, $70 in high-quality meat, dairy products, and vegetables to each of the 5.9 million Californians who were disabled veterans, welfare recipients, probated convicts, and social security recipients.

The Hearsts implemented such a program, but the SLA went on to commit a series of robberies, all in the name of social justice. In a bizarre twist, Patty Hearst was converted to the SLA cause and took the name of "Tanya." De-Freeze's life came to a violent end. He was killed in a bloody shoot-out with Los Angeles police on May 17, 1974. Other members of the SLA died with him that day.

SUGGESTED READINGS: William L. Van Deburg, *New Day in Babylon: The Black Power Movement and American Culture, 1965–1975*, 1992; Herbert Haines, *Black Radicals and the Civil Rights Mainstream, 1954–1970*, 1988; *Los Angeles Times*, May 18, 1974.

CIVIL RIGHTS MOVEMENT. If the 1960s was the decade in which the civil rights movement succeeded in putting together a political coalition that destroyed legal, de jure segregation, then the 1970s was the decade that witnessed the disintegration of that coalition and the decline of the civil rights movement. A series of Supreme Court decisions, as well as the Civil Rights acts of 1964, 1965, and 1968, ended legal segregation in public facilities throughout the United States.

But those court decisions and laws did not put an end to segregation. As whites fled to the suburbs, businesses relocated outside the city, making it more difficult for African Americans to find work. At the same time the whole American economy was shifting from a manufacturing to a service base; blue-collar jobs were steadily decreasing as white-collar ones became more plentiful. But white-collar jobs required educational and technical skills, and large numbers of underprivileged African Americans were unable to qualify. While earlier immigrants had used unskilled urban jobs as the bootstrap out of the ghettos, blacks no longer had those choices. They were trapped in a changing economy and a deteriorating physical environment, and their poverty became endemic and permanent, passing from one generation to the next.

In 1970 more than one in three African-American families functioned below the poverty line, and the median black income was only about 60 percent that of whites. During the course of the decade, the situation only deteriorated. The energy crisis* sent shock waves through the U.S. economy, exacerbating unemployment and sending prices and interest rates higher and higher. Unemployment for blacks was twice as high as for white workers, and joblessness for African-American teenagers exceeded 40 percent in some cities during the 1970s. A terribly poor African-American "underclass" emerged, made up of people who had never had jobs or lived in decent homes.

In the face of such debilitating economic problems, the end of formal seg-regation no longer seemed so important to civil rights advocates. For people worrying about how to pay their rent, utility, and food bills, whether or not their community was integrated was less important than how to support themselves.

During the 1970s, African-American leaders turned their attention to poverty, de facto segregation, and institutional racism as the focus of their civil rights efforts. The Civil Rights Act of 1968 had eliminated many forms of housing discrimination, but African-American leaders concluded that if school integra-tion were to wait for integrated neighborhoods, it would probably never happen. They believed that busing* children was the only way to overcome segregation in schools and second-class education for African-American children. In 1971 the U.S. Supreme Court heard the case of *Swann v. Charlotte-Mecklenburg County Board of Education*,* which involved the busing of children in the Char-lotte metropolitan region of North Carolina. Civil rights advocates claimed the busing would improve educational opportunities for black children and improve the racial atmosphere of the community. Opponents claimed that such a busing program would only disrupt the lives of children and their families. In its de-cision, the Supreme Court sided with pro-busing forces, claiming that since earlier plans for desegregation had not significantly improved black educational opportunities, school busing was a legitimate approach to the problem.

To deal with black economic problems, black advocacy groups demanded economic assistance and job training for educationally disadvantaged and low-income blacks and affirmative action* admissions, hirings, and promotions of African Americans by business, government, and universities. Congress passed the antipoverty program in 1965 to assist lower-class blacks and other poor people, and in the 1970s the Equal Employment Opportunity Commission or-dered government agencies, corporations, and universities to establish hiring, promotion, and admission policies favoring African Americans until the racial mix in American institutions, from the lowest service positions through the ad-ministrative hierarchy, reflected the racial composition of the whole society. Mexican-American and Puerto Rican leaders made similar demands.

But school busing and affirmative action drove a wedge into the original civil rights coalition and robbed it of much of its influence. During the late 1950s and early 1960s, the civil rights movement coalesced around several prominent constituencies in the Democratic party, including African Americans, Jews, in-tellectuals, blue-collar workers, and labor union leadership. Since blacks con-stituted only 12 percent of the American population, their chances of securing federal civil rights legislation depended largely on their ability to win the loy-alties of large numbers of whites. They managed to do so under the leadership of Martin Luther King, Jr., whose nonviolent civil disobedience did not seem so threatening and whose condemnation of legal segregation gave civil rights advocates the moral high ground. Fair-minded people of every ethnic group instinctively knew that keeping an individual from the right to vote, hold public office, or go to school on the basis of race was inherently wrong.

But as the court-ordered school busing programs went into effect and sent millions of schoolchildren on long rides across urban areas everyday, all in the name of integration, many whites refused to accept such social engineering as necessary to civil rights and equality. Large numbers of white males also felt victimized by affirmative action programs, which they perceived as anti-white, anti-male, and anti-Fourteenth Amendment. In the presidential election of 1968 and the election of 1972,* President Richard Nixon* took advantage of white resentments and made significant inroads into traditionally Democratic constituencies in the urban Northeast and the Midwest. By the late 1970s, civil rights activists no longer had any real hope of extending the reach of their political influence and instead tried to protect the gains they had already made.

SUGGESTED READINGS: David Burner, *Making Peace with the Sixties*, 1996; Donald L. Burnett, "An Historical Analysis of the 1968 'Indian Civil Rights Act,' " *Harvard Journal of Legislation* 9 (1972); David J. Garrow, *Bearing the Cross: Martin Luther King, Jr. and the Southern Christian Leadership Conference*, 1986; Hugh Davis Graham, *The Civil Rights Era: Origins and Development of a National Policy, 1960–1965*, 1990; Hurst Hannum, *Autonomy, Self-Determination and Sovereignty: The Accommodation of Conflicting Rights*, 1990; Roxanne Dunbar Ortiz, *Indians of the Americas: Human Rights and Self-Determination*, 1984.

CIVILIAN CASUALTIES IN VIETNAM. During the course of the Vietnam War,* Americans of every political persuasion debated the nature of the war, and one key element of the discussion was the casualty rate among South Vietnamese civilians. U.S. soldiers often complained that it was often impossible to distinguish enemy troops from South Vietnamese civilians, since the war was fought without fronts and because it was often a guerrilla conflict. The fact that the war was fought almost exclusively on the soil of America's ally, South Vietnam, guaranteed large numbers of civilian casualties. So did the American decision to Americanize the conflict and to employ massive amounts of firepower to kill enemy troops. Antiwar critics charged that U.S. military policy in South Vietnam killed so many civilians that it became impossible for Americans to win the "hearts and minds" (see *Hearts and Minds*) of the civilian population and build any loyalty whatsoever toward the South Vietnamese government or the United States. Because of excessive civilian casualties, they claimed, the United States stood no chance of ever achieving its political goals in Indochina.

The actual number of civilian casualties is difficult to gauge accurately because of the nature of the war, but during the 1970s a fierce intellectual battle raged over just how damaging the U.S. military had been in Vietnam. In 1974 Senator Edward Kennedy* of Massachusetts launched a Senate investigation of the casualty issue, and he concluded that between 1965 and 1974, American, Vietcong, and North Vietnamese forces had killed nearly 500,000 South Vietnamese civilians and wounded more than one million others. Most of the deaths had been caused by U.S. aerial bombing and artillery fire. Kennedy supported his claim that large numbers of civilians had been killed and wounded by citing Pentagon figures indicating that for every one Vietcong or North Vietnamese weapon captured, six soldiers had been killed. According to the senator, the discrepancy could be explained by factoring in civilian deaths; U.S. and South Vietnamese forces had actually killed large numbers of noncombatants. Actually, the discrepancy meant that either large numbers of civilians were killed along with the Vietcong, or that the body count figures were seriously inflated, or both.

The Pentagon and the Lyndon Johnson and Richard Nixon* administrations contested those figures, terming them "exceedingly exaggerated." They came up with different figures, ones that were, in the minds of critics of the war, just as damning. One Department of Defense study claimed that "only" 250,000 civilians had been killed and 800,000 wounded. The debate over civilian casualties in the Vietnam War, which first erupted on a major scale in the 1970s, continues today.

SUGGESTED READINGS: Edward S. Herman, *Atrocities in Vietnam: Myths and Realities*, 1970; John E. Mueller, "The Search for the 'Breaking Point' in Vietnam: The Statistics of a Deadly Quarrel," *International Studies Quarterly* 24 (December 1980), 497–519; Telford Taylor, *Nuremberg and Vietnam: An American Tragedy*, 1971; Guenter Lewy, *America in Vietnam*, 1978; Harry G. Summers, Jr., *Vietnam War Almanac*, 1985.

CLAPTON, ERIC. Eric Clapton was born in Ripley, England, on March 30, 1945. During the early 1960s, he played guitar with several British groups, including the Yardbirds, Casey Jones and the Engineers, and the Bluesbreakers. Clapton, who was perfecting his technique, was well on the road to becoming the individual many consider to be the greatest blues guitarist in history. He formed the group Cream in 1966, by which time concert audiences looked forward to his virtuoso guitar solos. He released his first solo album in 1970. Then, as part of Derek and the Dominoes, he recorded the album *Layla*, which made it into the top twenty. A heroin addiction sidelined Clapton in 1971 and 1972, but he returned to business in 1974 with *461 Ocean Boulevard*, an album that went to the top of the charts.

During the 1970s, Clapton became one of the most popular acts in rock and roll. He added vocals to his guitar solos and enjoyed several megahit singles, including "I Shot the Sheriff" (1974), "Lay Down Sally" (1978), and "Promises" (1979). In the 1980s, Clapton moved somewhat away from blues toward a rock-and-roll balladry, and his hits continued, such as "I Can't Stand It" (1981), "I've Got a Rock-and-Roll Heart" (1983), and "Forever Man" (1985). A bout with alcoholism hurt him in the mid-1980s, but he dealt successfully with the problem and was recording and touring again by 1990. His four-year-old son Conor died in a fifty-story fall in 1991. The song "Tears in Heaven," written and recorded in Conor's memory, went to number two on the pop charts. Clapton's album *From the Cradle* topped the charts in 1994.

SUGGESTED READING: Christopher Sandford, *Clapton, Edge of Darkness*, 1994.

CLEAN AIR ACT OF 1970. The Clean Air Act of 1970 was a landmark piece of legislation in the budding environmental movement.* Increasingly large numbers of Americans had been growing concerned about the quality of air and water in the United States, and the source of pollution was hotly debated. Liberals blamed private corporations for dumping chemical wastes into water supplies and for inefficient automobile engines that spewed pollutants into the air, but the companies countered that any federal program to eliminate pollution would hurt economic growth and eliminate jobs from the economy. In March 1970 Senator Edmund Muskie, Democrat of Maine, sponsored the Clean Air Act, a unique piece of legislation because of what Muskie termed "forced technology." The law ordered the automobile industry to reduce automobile emissions by 90 percent or risk federal sanctions and monetary punishment. The law constituted a $1.1 billion program that required that 1975 automobiles reduce carbon monoxide and hydrocarbon emissions by 90 percent, and that 1976 automobiles emit 90 percent less of the nitrogen oxides. The Clean Air Act also provided tax incentives to electric utilities to switch from coal to oil and natural gas as the fuels used to generate electricity. Oil and natural gas burn more cleanly. The Environmental Protection Agency (EPA) was eventually assigned the responsibility of enforcing the legislation.

The Clean Air Act inadvertently contributed to the country's economic problems in the 1970s. In response to the legislation, electric utilities across the country began making, at great capital expense, the transition from coal-burning generators to oil and natural gas–burning generators. When the Arab oil boycott of 1973–1974* and the Organization of Petroleum Exporting Countries* (OPEC) caused oil price increases to sweep across the world in the 1970s, the cost of electricity jumped and added dramatically to inflationary pressures in the United States.

SUGGESTED READINGS: Elting E. Morison, *From Know-How To Nowhere: The Development of American Technology*, 1974; Richard Nixon, *RN: The Memoirs of Richard Nixon*, 1978.

CLEAVER, ELDRIDGE. Eldridge Cleaver, an icon of radicals during the 1960s, became a symbol in the 1970s of just how feeble radicalism's roots were in the United States. Cleaver, born in 1935 in Wabeseka, Arkansas, moved with his family to Oakland, California, when Cleaver was still a child. Before he finished high school he had been convicted of possessing marijuana. A series of convictions for drug offenses landed him prison terms at Soledad, Folsom, and San Quentin. During his confinement, Cleaver earned a high school diploma and converted to the Black Muslim faith, becoming a dedicated follower of Malcolm X. A gifted writer, Cleaver came out of prison in 1966 and began writing for publication. He was soon given a staff writer's position with *Ramparts* magazine.

After settling in Oakland, California, Cleaver became active in the Black Panthers* and wrote his most famous book, *Soul on Ice* (1969), which is part autobiography, part political philosophy. Raw in its expression of rage over American racism, *Soul on Ice* made Cleaver a household name in radical and student circles at the end of the 1960s. The book was a powerful indictment of racism and police brutality in American society, but it was also a veiled attempt by Cleaver to justify some of his own crimes, which included the intentional rape of white women as a political statement. Although radicals and some liberals found *Soul on Ice* to be a modern manifesto for the left, most Americans found the book inflammatory.

Cleaver's literary fame could not protect him from his own past or from the desire of Oakland police to get him off the streets. Cleaver fled the United States soon after the publication of *Soul on Ice* to avoid imprisonment for parole violations and trial on charges of assaulting Oakland police officers. Over the next decade, he lived in Cuba, the Soviet Union, and Algeria. During his stay abroad, Cleaver underwent a philosophical transformation. He abandoned the Marxism he had so carefully cultivated during the 1960s as well as his Black Muslim faith. He decided that real happiness could not come from political ideology, only from personal spiritual rebirth. Cleaver returned to the United States as a born-again Christian in 1976 and pleaded guilty to the assault charge. He was placed on probation and ordered to complete two thousand hours of community service.

Cleaver became a very popular speaker on the college lecture circuit, commanding fees of up to $5,000 per appearance in the 1970s and early 1980s. In 1978 he wrote *Soul on Fire*, a spiritual autobiography that put him in the vanguard of the rise of the Christian right, which would soon become a force in American politics. His own odyssey became symbolic of what had happened in the United States during the transition from the 1960s to the 1970s, when Americans abandoned social crusades for more personal goals. He became an ardent American patriot during the 1980s, regularly describing the United States as the "freest and most democratic country in the world."

But Cleaver never really did enjoy long-term stability in his personal life. He changed religious groups often, always trying to find the "answer" to his personal problems, and run-ins with the police continued. In 1979, 1983, and 1988 he was charged with cocaine possession. Eldridge Cleaver died on May 2, 1998.

SUGGESTED READINGS: Eldridge Cleaver, *Soul on Ice*, 1969; *New York Times*, May 3, 1998; Kathleen Rout, *Eldridge Cleaver*, 1991.

CLOSE ENCOUNTERS OF THE THIRD KIND. *Close Encounters of the Third Kind*, Steven Spielberg's phenomenally successful science fiction film of 1977, stars Richard Dreyfuss, François Truffaut, Teri Garr, and Melinda Dillon. The film has the look of a 1950s science fiction, alien invasion film, but writer and director Steven Spielberg had a surprise for his audiences. Instead of earth's being invaded by aliens bent on destruction, the space creatures of *Close Encounters*, though technologically far ahead of earthlings, are benign, loving creatures. Perhaps in the 1950s, when America was in the midst of the Red Scare and the National Aeronautic and Space Administration had not yet taken some of the mystery out of the galaxy, moviegoers expected sinister, outer space conspiracies on the silver screen. But in the late 1970s, with America still suffering from the Vietnam War,* the Watergate scandal,* and the Arab oil boycott of 1973–1974,* audiences yearned for warm, escapist fantasies, and Spielberg provided one of the best in Hollywood's history.

SUGGESTED READING: *New York Times*, November 17, 1977.

CLUB OF ROME. After Rachel Carson's enormously influential book *Silent Spring* (1962), the environmental movement* steadily gained political strength in the United States. It also gained influence around the world. In April 1968, a group of thirty scientists, educators, economists, humanists, industrialists, and national and international civil servants gathered in the Italian capital to consider the future of the world economy. Out of their meeting emerged the Club of Rome, a group committed to keeping the world informed about the state of the global economy and environment.

Between 1969 and 1972, the Club of Rome conducted what it called the Project on the Predicament of Mankind. Using computer models and assuming no change in population growth rates, the members of the Club of Rome predicted an ecological and economic disaster in the early decades of the twenty-first century. They warned that exponential population growth combined with continued industrialization would eventually send the world economy into a tailspin and lead to mass starvation and global suffering. The only answer, they argued, was to establish limits on world growth. During the late 1960s and early 1970s, when the environmental movement in the United States was especially strong, the apocalyptic predictions of the Club of Rome found a sympathetic audience.

By the late 1970s and early 1980s, however, critics were charging the Club of Rome with gross hyperbole. Its predictions of global disaster became more and more ludicrous and exaggerated, and Club of Rome defenders had to extend the time line of their predictions. Critics within the environmental movement even held the Club of Rome responsible for making the path to a clean environment more difficult. By erroneously predicting a collapse in the world economy, they argued, environmentalists lost credibility and in turn made Americans more critical and skeptical of the movement. In 1998, when the World Health Organization predicted that the quality of life and life span of peoples throughout the world, including the poor, would dramatically improve in the twenty-first century, the Club of Rome's predictions seemed even more ludicrous.

SUGGESTED READING: Peter Moll, *From Scarcity to Sustainability: The Role of the Club of Rome*, 1991.

COLD WAR. The term ''Cold War'' has been used for a half-century to describe the global struggle for influence among the United States, the Soviet Union, and the People's Republic of China after World War II. The three countries represented an ideological battleground between capitalism and communism, and by 1946 every side had concluded that the others were bent on its annihilation. During the 1940s, the Cold War included the Truman Doctrine of 1946, the Marshall Plan of 1947, the containment policy,* the Berlin airlift of 1948, and the fall of China in 1949. During the 1950s, the Cold War continued with the Korean War, the Vietnamese intervention of 1954, the Suez crisis of 1956, the Lebanon intervention of 1958, and the beginnings of the Berlin crisis in 1958.

The Cold War reached its peak in the early 1960s. President John F. Kennedy preached a rhetoric of toughness, competition, and resolve, and when the Soviet Union decided to introduce interregional ballistic missiles into Cuba in 1962, the world came to the brink of nuclear disaster. The Cold War could have become the global meltdown. Both sides stepped back from the brink and resolved the crisis, but the event scared some sense into world leaders. To enhance communications between the United States and the Soviet Union, Kennedy and Soviet Premier Nikita Khrushchev installed the "hot line" in 1963, linking the White House and the Kremlin with a direct telephone line. Later in the year, the two countries signed the Nuclear Test Ban Treaty outlawing the atmospheric testing of nuclear weapons. Many historians of the Cold War, therefore, look to 1963 as the year in which detente* between the two international rivals first began. During the remainder of the 1960s, in spite of the Vietnam War,* relations between the superpowers improved, and the Cold War thawed. The United States and the Soviet Union agreed to the Outer Space Treaty in 1967, which outlawed the introduction of nuclear weapons into space, and the Nuclear Non-Proliferation Treaty of 1968, which worked to stop the spread of nuclear weapons.

The Cold War continued to thaw during the presidential administration of Richard Nixon.* A spirit of detente, or mutual cooperation, began to characterize U.S.-Soviet and U.S.-Chinese relations. The fact that Nixon began withdrawing U.S. troops from South Vietnam in the summer of 1969 proved to the Soviets that he was serious about deescalation, and they even cooperated with him on a number of occasions in trying to convince the North Vietnamese to negotiate a settlement of the conflict. In 1972, for example, when Nixon announced the mining of Haiphong Harbor,* the Soviet Union issued only the weakest of diplomatic protests and did not turn the issue into an international controversy.

The real mastermind behind detente, however, was Henry Kissinger,* the president's national security advisor and later secretary of state. Kissinger possessed a well-developed, carefully conceived approach to foreign policy. His approach rested on two fundamental assumptions. First, one nation, except in the most unusual circumstances, should not interfere with the internal political or social affairs of an international rival, especially when that intervention was based on a belief in moral superiority. Much of the Cold War, Kissinger believed, could be traced to Soviet communism's sense of moral superiority to U.S. capitalism, and U.S. capitalism's sense of moral superiority to Soviet communism. The U.S. refusal, since 1949, to extend diplomatic recognition to the People's Republic of China was a good example of a high-minded bias that did not serve world peace. Second, world peace required a delicate balance between the superpowers. Kissinger firmly believed that absolute security for one nation automatically meant insecurity for all other nations. The nuclear arms race, Kissinger was convinced, had gotten completely out of hand and threatened the survival of humanity; it served as a perfect example of superpower competition run mad.

As a result of the combined efforts of Henry Kissinger and Richard Nixon, detente achieved several notable successes in the early 1970s. First, the president conducted summit conferences in Moscow and Beijing in 1972, heralding a new attempt at the cooperation of superpower affairs. The trip to Beijing was especially dramatic, since the Chinese Communists had been cut off for so long from U.S. diplomatic communication. Some historians believe that only Richard Nixon could have accomplished such a diplomatic coup. Because of his unimpeachable anticommunist credentials, Nixon enjoyed real credibility among right-wing Republicans, who would have been the most likely to scuttle detente with the Soviet Union and the People's Republic of China.

When the Nuclear Non-Proliferation Treaty had been signed in 1968, American and Soviet officials agreed that the next item in nuclear weapons diplomacy would revolve around the need for mutual reductions in the stockpiles of strategic nuclear weapons. Not only was the race for nuclear superiority increasing the risk of global thermonuclear war, the expense of developing increasingly sophisticated, and destructive, nuclear technologies posed financial problems to both the United States and the Soviet Union. What became known as the Strategic Arms Limitation Talks* (SALT) between the United States and the Soviet Union began in 1969.

Soviet diplomats, however, proved quite reluctant to cooperate in any serious negotiations until President Nixon proposed to Congress the need for the development of an anti-ballistic missile shield to protect the United States from a Soviet nuclear first strike. Nixon took heat from congressional Democrats, who argued that the defensive system would be too expensive, and from scientists, who doubted the feasibility of the proposal. But the president's proposal was more a diplomatic ploy than a nuclear arms issue. The nuclear arms race placed more pressure on the Soviet economy than on the American, and the Russians did not want to find themselves in an expensive race to develop an anti-ballistic missile system. The SALT negotiations finally began to progress.

Talks continued until early 1972 when the two sides agreed to the Anti-Ballistic Missile Treaty,* in which they mutually decided to disengage from the development of anti-ballistic missile shields. With the threat of an expensive new weapons system development removed, the two sides were then able to reach the Interim Agreement on Strategic Offensive Weapons, which froze deployment of intercontinental ballistic missiles (ICBMs) at current levels. That agreement was much less than it appeared to be because new technologies had already rendered it obsolete. Both the United States and the Soviet Union had developed multiple independent reentry vehicles (MIRVs), which allowed the placement of several nuclear warheads into one missile, each of which could be dropped on a separate target. Still, it was the first time the two superpowers had agreed to impose limits on their nuclear arsenals. These initial strategic arms limitations talks, which became known as SALT I, included an agreement on an improved hot-line communication system. During President Nixon's summit visit to Moscow in May 1972, the SALT I treaties were signed.

In November 1972, the SALT II discussions began with the hope of developing a quantitative limit on the number of MIRV warheads each side possessed. The Watergate scandal* in the United States stalled the SALT II talks, as did the short-term presidential administration of Gerald Ford.* When Jimmy Carter* defeated President Ford in the presidential election of 1976,* SALT II discussions were again delayed. The SALT II treaty was finally signed in June 1979, but by that time the spirit of detente was already dissipating in the United States, and the Senate did not ratify the treaty.

During the Carter administration, the United States again began to use human rights issues as a litmus test for cooperation with the Soviet Union and the People's Republic of China. Both of those countries had preferred Kissinger's willingness to not concern himself with internal political issues in other countries unless they had a direct bearing on U.S. national security. But what really ended detente in the 1970s was the Soviet Union's decision in 1979 to invade Afghanistan.* The Carter administration bitterly opposed the intervention, and Congress began supplying sophisticated weapons to the Afghan rebels fighting the Russians. In protest of the invasion, President Carter announced that the United States would boycott the 1980 Olympic Games, which were scheduled to take place in Moscow.

SUGGESTED READING: John Newhouse, *War and Peace in the Nuclear Age*, 1989.

COLSON, CHARLES. Charles Wendell Colson was born in Boston, Massachusetts, on October 16, 1931. He graduated from Brown University in 1953 and then earned a law degree at George Washington University. Colson was soon working as an administrative assistant to Republican U.S. Senator Leverett Saltonstall, a position he kept until 1961, when be began practicing law privately in Washington, D.C. Charles Colson served as special counsel to President Richard Nixon* from 1969 to 1973 and was deeply involved in Nixon's 1972 reelection campaign and the subsequent Watergate scandal.* During this period, he employed Watergate conspirator E. Howard Hunt* as a consultant. Colson was tried and convicted of obstruction of justice, and he spent nearly eight months in prison. His experiences in prison led Colson to found the Prison Fellowship, a Christian counseling program now found in hundreds of prisons.

Colson became a celebrity of sorts for his statement that he "would walk over his grandmother if necessary to assure the re-election of President Nixon."

SUGGESTED READINGS: Charles Colson, *Born Again*, 1995; Theodore H. White, *Breach of Faith*, 1975; Stella Wiseman, *Charles Colson*, 1995.

Sean A. Kelleher

COLUMBO. *Columbo*, a hit television police drama of the 1970s, was first broadcast by NBC on September 15, 1971, starring Peter Falk as Lieutenant Columbo, a Los Angeles detective whose shrewd ability to solve murders was masked by his disheveled hair, wrinkled coat, and beat-up old Peugot. In the series, the murderers were always well-to-do, successful people whose crimes had been intricately planned. Disarmingly polite and apparently incompetent, Columbo lulled his suspects into a false sense of safety. Some odd bit of evidence would always catch Columbo's attention, and he would use it to unravel the case. Although NBC produced several made-for-television *Columbo* movies in the 1980s and 1990s, the last episode of the regular series was broadcast on September 26, 1977.

SUGGESTED READING: Tim Brooks and Earle Marsh, *The Complete Directory to Prime Time Network and Cable TV Shows, 1946–Present*, 1995.

COMANECI, NADIA. Nadia Comaneci was born outside Bucharest, Romania, in 1962. Her innate artistic abilities and athleticism were evident when she was a small child, and Bela Karolyi, coach of the Romanian national gymnastics team, noticed her on a school playground in 1968. At the time, Communist bloc countries viewed international athletic events as forums for Cold War* demonstrations of Communist superiority. The government removed Comaneci from her family to be raised in a sports camp where training went on hour after hour, day after day. Under Karolyi's tutelage, Comaneci became a world-class gymnast.

The 1976 Olympic Games at Montreal became the international showcase for her considerable skills. At eighty-six pounds and at fourteen years of age, she had a pixie-like quality that masked iron nerves and steely determination. In all four events—the vault, floor exercises, balance beam, and uneven bars—she seemed to defy gravity, and in the process she received seven perfect scores of ten and three gold medals. For a time, Comaneci was the most recognized athlete, male or female, in the world. After the Montreal games, her coach Bela Karolyi defected to the United States, and Comaneci followed him in 1989.

SUGGESTED READING: Ion Grumeza, *Nadia*, 1977.

COMING HOME. *Coming Home*, a powerful anti-Vietnam War* film, was released in 1978. It stars Jane Fonda* as Sally Hyde, the sheltered wife of a military husband; Jon Voight as Luke Martin, a handsome young man who returns from Vietnam a paraplegic; and Bruce Dern as Captain Bob Hyde,

Sally's husband who goes enthusiastically to Vietnam but returns psychologically shattered, with all of his convictions about right and wrong turned upside down. During his absence, Sally evolves from a shy, obsequious homemaker to an assertive woman in her own right. Much of her transformation comes from a love affair with Luke, conducted during her husband's tour of duty on the other side of the world. Vietnam changes all of them. Luke, the golden boy athlete who could do no wrong, returns a cynical cripple who believes in nothing. Bob Hyde, the professional soldier out to protect the world from communism, eventually kills himself. Vietnam wrought chaos in all of their lives, as it did in the lives of everyone the United States.

SUGGESTED READINGS: Linda Dittmar and Gene Michaud, eds., *From Hanoi to Hollywood: The Vietnam War in American Film*, 1990; *New York Times*, February 16, 1978.

COMMITTEE FOR THE RE-ELECTION OF THE PRESIDENT. *See* CREEP.

CONCORDE. During the 1950s and early 1960s, when passenger service by jet aircraft became a technological and economic reality, American carriers came to dominate the international market. In a desire to regain a share of that market and to demonstrate their own technological prowess, the governments of France and Great Britain decided to develop a jet of their own. In 1961, with the financial backing of their governments, the British Aircraft Corporation and France's Aerospatiale formed a consortium to build the world's first supersonic transport, or SST. Their goal was to design a jet capable of carrying 100 passengers at speeds up to 1,200 miles per hour, more than twice as fast as regular passenger jets. The two companies promised to have the jet, to be known as the Concorde, ready to fly by February 1968.

But the project proved to be an economic nightmare. Serious technological problems consumed more time to solve then originally anticipated, and cost overruns were huge. Student riots in France in May 1968 further delayed the project. In December 1968, the Soviet Union put the first SST, the Tupelev Tu144, into the air. Environmentalists also turned their wrath on the very idea of SSTs. The aircraft were noisy because of the sonic booms they generated, and they flew at such high altitudes that they threatened to damage the earth's protective ozone layer in the upper atmosphere. The energy crisis* of the 1970s posed another challenge. At a time when world oil supplies were dwindling and fuel costs skyrocketing, the SST consumed jet fuel voraciously. Under such pressures, the United States canceled its contract with Boeing to develop an American SST. New York then banned SST service within the boundaries of the state.

Finally, in 1976, a total of nine Concordes went into service, with connections to London, Paris, Washington, D.C., Bahrain, and Caracas. Except for British Airways and Air France, no other major carriers put in orders for SSTs. It was not until October 1977 that a nineteen-month legal battle ended and overturned New York's ban on SST service. In October 1977 the Concorde took off from New York's Kennedy Airport and crossed the Atlantic in record time. Since then, regular passenger service has continued from Paris and London to Dulles Airport outside of Washington, D.C., but the service remains a luxury for the privileged few able to afford the ticket prices.

SUGGESTED READINGS: Phillip Birtles, *Concorde*, 1984; Kenneth Owen, *Concorde and the Americans: International Politics of the Supersonic Transport*, 1997.

CONGRESSIONAL BLACK CAUCUS. Establishment of the Congressional Black Caucus was tangible evidence of the impact of the civil rights movement* on American politics. Because of the Civil Rights Act of 1964 and the Voting Rights Act of 1965, black political activity increased dramatically in the late 1960s, and in 1969 Congressman Charles Diggs,* Democrat from Michigan, formed the Democratic Select Committee, a group of nine African-American members of Congress who decided to articulate black concerns. In 1970 the Democratic Select Committee boycotted President Richard Nixon's* State of the Union Address, demanding a more responsive attitude on the part of the president toward civil rights, welfare reform, the Vietnam War,* and antidrug legislation.

The Democratic Select Committee proved to be a forerunner of the Congressional Black Caucus (CBC). On June 18, 1971, Charles Diggs formed the Congressional Black Caucus. The caucus quickly drafted the Black Declaration of Independence and the Black Bill of Rights and demanded that the Democratic party commit itself to full employment, a guaranteed annual income, an end to U.S. military aggression in Vietnam and Africa, affirmative action,* and set aside programs to guarantee that 15 percent of all government contracts went to black-owned businesses. In 1973 Congressman Louis Stokes, Democrat from Ohio, succeeded Diggs as chairman of the CBC, and he was succeeded by Charles Rangel, Democrat from New York, in 1974. During the mid-1970s the CBC took on apartheid in South Africa as one of its causes, and it also focused its attention on urban housing issues, affirmative action, and narcotics control. By the early 1980s, CBC members chaired seven of the House of Representatives' twenty-seven committees. By 1992, when forty African Americans were elected to Congress, the CBC was one of Washington, D.C.'s most influential bodies.

SUGGESTED READINGS: Marguerite Ross Barnet, "The Congressional Black Caucus," in *Congress Against the President: Proceedings of the Academy of Political Science*, ed. Harvey C. Mansfield, 1975; William L. Clay, *Just Permanent Interests: Black Americans in Congress, 1870–1991*, 1992.

CONRACK. This 1974 film is based on the real life experiences of Pat Conroy, which he anthologized in a book entitled *The Water Is Wide*. The film concerns a teacher who is hired to teach a classroom of fifth to eighth graders on an island off the coast of South Carolina. Conroy, played by Jon Voight, enters the school and announces his name, which all of them pronounce as "Conrack." He goes on to introduce himself flamboyantly and then questions the class to see what they know. He finds that none of them know what country they live in, what ocean they swim in, or even how to count or read.

He enthusiastically teaches them about gravity, toothbrushing, flowers, genitals, pyramids, Babe Ruth, swimming, singing, Brahms, and Beethoven, and reads them Robert Herrick's "To the Young Virgins Who Make Much of Time." The children learn to trust him, and he eventually charms the whole town. He even teaches a depressed bootlegger how to read. Eventually, he is fired by a conservative superintendent who does not appreciate his style.

The film follows in the genre of other teacher-student inspirational films in several negative ways: Conroy's character is underdeveloped, the subplots seem incomplete, and the film lacks power because of its predictability. However, Conroy also strays from these films for several positive reasons. It is a true story based on life; Voight's teacher is flamboyant instead of reserved, and the students do not resist his efforts, but are eager to learn everything he shows them. *Conrack* made a touching real life story famous.

SUGGESTED READING: *New York Times*, March 28, 1974.

Bradley A. Olson

CONRAIL. In the late 1960s the railroad industry in the Northeast entered a catastrophic economic period. Dramatic improvements in highway construction, especially the new interstate highway system launched during the Eisenhower administration, made it increasingly efficient to ship industrial goods by truck. At the same time, the improved highway system only accelerated the decline of railroad passenger revenues. Traveling from city to city by automobile was much more convenient for most middle-class Americans than traveling by rail, and traveling by bus was much more convenient, and cheaper, than rail travel for poor and working-class Americans.

Railroads also had to face the challenge of declining shipments of coal, iron ore, and steel from American heavy industries, which had entered a period of decline. Old physical plants had rendered them vulnerable to foreign competition, and because of declines in freight volume, railroad revenues declined as well.

At the same time, however, the railroads were burdened with heavy debt structures—the economic residue of heavy capital investments made during boom times. Although revenues were down, railroads still had to make fixed payments on loans and bond issues. The huge Penn Central Railroad went bankrupt in 1970, and bankruptcy loomed on the horizon for many other railroads as well.

Because the services it provided were essential to the regional economy, however, the federal government kept the Penn Central running with large subsidies. To deal with the crisis, Congress passed the Regional Rail Reorganization Act of 1973, which authorized the establishment of the Consolidated Rail Corporation (Conrail) as a private company. Conrail took over six bankrupt railroads in 1976: the Penn Central, the Jersey Central, the Lehigh Valley, the Reading, the Erie Lackawanna, and the Lehigh & Hudson River. After huge losses in the 1970s, Congress passed the Northeast Rail Reorganization Act of 1981, which allowed Conrail to drop its unprofitable passenger service and renegotiate its labor contracts. Under the leadership of L. Stanley Crane, Conrail showed its first profit in 1981 and was sold to private investors in 1987.

SUGGESTED READING: Richard Saunders, *The Railroad Mergers and the Coming of Conrail*, 1978.

CONTAINMENT POLICY. First pronounced by George Kennan in a 1947 article in *Foreign Affairs*, "containment" was the most important postwar American foreign policy. At first it was designed to keep Soviet expansionism under control, preferably behind its 1945 military boundaries. In the beginning, containment was nonmilitary, focusing on economic and technical assistance, and it was embodied in such programs as the Marshall Plan in 1947 and 1948 to rebuild the European economies and the Truman Doctrine to provide the funds Greece and Turkey needed to fight Communist guerrillas. As the Cold War* escalated in the late 1940s, however, containment took on new global, military dimensions. After the fall of China in 1949, it came to imply the encirclement of the People's Republic of China and the Soviet Union with a network of military alliances: the North Atlantic Treaty Organization, the Baghdad Pact, the Southeast Asia Treaty Organization, and the enormous military buildup of the 1950s and 1960s. When the North Koreans invaded South Korea in 1950, the United States intervened in the conflict in the name of containment. Containment reached its peak during the Eisenhower years and the tenure of Secretary of State John Foster Dulles (1953 to 1959).

During the 1960s, American policymakers mistakenly applied the containment theory to Indochina, where Vietnamese leader Ho Chi Minh was staging a successful rebellion against the U.S.-backed forces of South Vietnam. The policy proved to be a disaster. In Europe, the containment doctrine had evolved against a backdrop of communism and the militaristic, heavy-handed occupation forces of the Soviet Union. Soviet troops invaded and occupied Latvia, Lithuania, Estonia, Poland, Czechoslovakia, Hungary, Bulgaria, and Yugoslavia, and in each of those countries nationalists identified communism as an alien, Soviet-imposed force. Behind the Iron Curtain, communism and patriotism were polar opposites.

In Southeast Asia, on the other hand, history had brought about a fusion of nationalism, communism, and patriotism. Ho Chi Minh, a dedicated Marxist, had also engineered the successful Vietnamese rebellion against the French empire, and he was widely considered the "George Washington of his country." For most Vietnamese, Ho Chi Minh's communism was a homegrown ideology, not a foreign imposition. U.S. policymakers did not begin to grasp that reality

until the early 1970s, when they finally began to realize the importance of colonialism and nationalism in the history of the anti-French and anti-American
movements in Vietnam. By that time as well, American policymakers realized
that communism was a polycentric movement that required creative, individual
responses.

Events later in the decade confirmed that new view of the relationship between
communism and nationalism. In 1979 the Soviet Union made a disastrous mistake in invading Afghanistan.* The invasion was part of an effort to quell the
spread of Islamic fundamentalism and to augment Soviet influence in Central
Asia and the Persian Gulf, but the Afghans wanted nothing to do with foreign,
communist occupation forces. They staged a bloody guerrilla war against Soviet
forces that drained the Soviet Union of billions of dollars and took the lives of
thousands of its troops. In Afghanistan, Soviet communism became the enemy
of religion, patriotism, and nationalism.

The containment policy enjoyed somewhat of a revival during the years of
the Jimmy Carter* administration. For his national security advisor, President
Carter selected Zbigniew Brzezinski,* a professor of political science at Columbia University. A native of Poland, Brzezinski loathed the Soviet Union and the
pain and suffering it had imposed on Poland and other eastern bloc countries.
During the years of the Carter administration, Brzezinski convinced the president
to halt exports of grain and high technology to the Soviet Union and to monitor
carefully Soviet activities in the Persian Gulf. When the Soviet Union invaded
Iran* in 1979, Brzezinski immediately interpreted the event as a first step in a
secret Soviet plan to secure a warm water port. He also urged and convinced
the president to stage a U.S. boycott of the 1980 Olympic Games, which were
held in Moscow.

SUGGESTED READINGS: Douglas S. Blaufarb, *The Counterinsurgency Era: U.S.
Doctrine and Performance 1950 to the Present*, 1977; Zbigniew Brzezinski, *Power and
Principle: Memoirs of the National Security Advisor, 1977–1981*, 1985; John L. Gaddis,
''Containment: A Reassessment,'' *Foreign Affairs* 55 (July 1977), 873–87; Alexander L.
George and Richard Smoke, *Deterrence in American Foreign Policy*, 1974; Nancy Pea-
body Newell and Richard S. Newell, *The Struggle for Afghanistan*, 1981.

COOPER, ALICE. Alice Cooper, born Vincent Furnier on February 4, 1948,
in Detroit, Michigan, formed the group Alice Cooper in Phoenix, Arizona, in
1965. Glen Buxton, Michael Bruce, Dennis Dunaway, and Neal Smith were the
other members of Alice Cooper. They pioneered the shock-rock phenomenon
of the 1970s, calling themselves, successively, the Earwigs, the Spiders, the
Nazz, and finally Alice Cooper, who allegedly had been a seventeenth-century
witch reincarnated as Furnier. Alice Cooper developed an outrageous concert,
complete with raw lyrics, simulated executions and black magic, and black eye
and lip makeup. Their first really successful album, *Love It to Death*, was released in 1971. Their next three albums, *Killer* (1971), *School's Out* (1972), and

Billion Dollar Babies (1973), all went platinum. The personnel in the group then changed, and Furnier came on hard times, trying to deal with alcoholism and depression. When he returned to the rock scene in the 1980s, he had turned to heavy metal, which was reflected in his 1986 album *Constrictor*. He followed that up with *Raise Your Fist and Yell* in 1987, *Trash* in 1989, *Hey Stoopid* in 1994, and *The Last Temptation* in 1994.

SUGGESTED READING: Alice Cooper, *Me, Alice: The Autobiography of Alice Cooper*, 1976.

COOPER, D. B. D. B. Cooper is the alias of the individual who hijacked a Northwest Airlines flight on November 24, 1971. A middle-aged man in a business suit boarded Northwest Flight 305 in Portland, Oregon, a Boeing 727 scheduled to land in Seattle, Washington. Once the jet was airborne, he showed a flight attendant a briefcase, in which he claimed to have a bomb, and threatened to blow up the plane unless his demands were met. He requested $200,000 in ransom money and four parachutes. The aircraft then landed in Seattle, and passengers were kept on board while Northwest Airlines officials loaded the money and the parachutes. Cooper then ordered the Boeing 727 to fly to Reno, Nevada. Somewhere between Seattle and Reno, the man parachuted from the aircraft. He was never found. Because of the success of the hijacking and the fact that he was never apprehended, D. B. Cooper became an icon of sorts, an antihero for the 1970s.

SUGGESTED READINGS: *New York Times*, November 26–30, 1971, and November 30, 1975.

COOPER-CHURCH AMENDMENT. In reaction to the invasion of Cambodia* by the Richard Nixon* administration in 1970 without consultation with Congress, Senators John Sherman Cooper (Republican, Kentucky) and Frank Church* (Democrat, Idaho) proposed an amendment that would prohibit spending funds without congressionial approval after June 1, 1970, for the purposes of keeping U.S. troops in Cambodia, for sending U.S. advisers into Cambodia, for providing combat air support for Cambodian troops, or for financing the sending of troops or advisers into Cambodia by other nations.

Supporters saw the proposed amendment as an overdue attempt by Congress to reassert its constitutional control over the power to make war. The administration and its supporters in Congress denounced the amendment as an unconstitutional intrusion into the president's power as commander in chief. After a bitter debate, the Senate adopted the Cooper-Church Amendment on June 30 by a vote of 58 to 37.

The amendment was attached to a foreign military sales bill. That bill also carried another amendment repealing the Gulf of Tonkin Resolution. The repeal was not significant because the Nixon administration cited the president's constitutional powers as commander in chief and not the Gulf of Tonkin Resolution as the basis for his war-making authority.

SUGGESTED READINGS: *Facts on File*, 1970, 343–44, 359, 461–62; Paul L. Kattenburg, *The Vietnam Trauma in American Foreign Policy, 1945–1975*, 1980.

Joseph M. Rowe, Jr.

COUNCIL OF ENERGY RESOURCE TRIBES. During the 1970s, the red power* movement gained momentum as Native American leaders tried to assert themselves in the areas of civil rights, tribal self-determination,* and tribal control of reservation resources. For centuries non-Indians had either seized Indian land or contracted to exploit reservation resources at rates far below market levels. Groups such as the National Congress of American Indians and the National Tribal Chiefs Association had long protested such exploitation, but they made little headway until the 1970s.

In 1976 the leaders of twenty-five American Indian tribes formed the Council of Energy Resource Tribes (CERT) to augment Native American economic power. Among the most prominent of these leaders was Peter MacDonald,* chairman of the Navajo tribal council. MacDonald knew, as did many other Indian leaders, that Indian reservations contained up to 40 percent of all U.S. uranium, 33 percent of its coal, and 5 percent of its oil and natural gas. CERT was made up of tribes rich in such resources. At the time of CERT's founding, the United States was in the midst of the economically disastrous energy crisis.* After the Yom Kippur War* in the Middle East in 1973, oil-producing Arab nations—upset with U.S. loyalty to Israel—imposed the oil embargo. The Organization of Petroleum Exporting Countries* (OPEC), which became the model for CERT, took advantage of oil shortages to increase prices dramatically. Energy costs skyrocketed.

Since OPEC nations were based in Asia, Africa, the Middle East, and Latin America—regions long exploited by Europeans and Americans—people of color around the world exulted at OPEC's success in humbling the West. American Indians took pleasure in it as well. Most energy-rich tribes had a history of leasing energy resources out at prices well below market levels, and the energy crisis of the 1970s only exacerbated that problem. While global oil, coal, and natural gas prices skyrocketed, many Indian tribes were locked into deleterious long-term contracts requiring tribes to sell their resources to energy users at ridiculously low levels. CERT was committed to maximizing tribal profits by renegotiating those contracts and bringing the prices paid for reservation coal, oil, and natural gas up to market levels. CERT negotiated with foreign governments to improve prices and lobbied for federal legislation to protect Indian assets. CERT also sought federal financing for training programs so Indians could learn the engineering and technical skills necessary for effective management of those resources. In its major design, CERT was part of the broader self-determination movement, since many Indian activists considered economic self-sufficiency to be the key to real freedom and independence.

Most private companies, of course, insisted that the long-term leases were valid contracts that tribes could not renegotiate. CERT filed lawsuits in state and federal courts to secure the right to renegotiate the contracts and, in the process, won some cases and lost others. When CERT lost in court and companies continued to refuse to renegotiate contracts, CERT leaders threatened economic action, strikes, protest marches, demonstrations, and global boycotts of those company products. In most cases, the companies caved in to CERT demands and then passed on their increased costs to consumers.

During the late 1970s and early 1980s, the Council of Energy Resource Tribes lobbied vigorously for federal legislation protecting Indian resources. In 1982 their efforts resulted in the Indian Mineral Development Act and the Federal Oil and Gas Royalty Management Act, both of which contained provisions allowing for the renegotiation of royalty contracts, establishment of joint ventures between mineral companies and Indian tribes, amendments to national environmental laws giving tribes clear control of resource use on their own lands, education and job training programs to develop reservation expertise, and revolving funds to improve reservation infrastructures. By the mid-1990s, CERT's membership included forty-three American Indian tribes and four Canadian tribes.

SUGGESTED READINGS: Marjane Ambler, *Breaking the Iron Bonds: Indian Control of Energy Development*, 1990; Vine Deloria, Jr., and Clifford Lytle, *The Nations Within: The Past and Future of American Indian Sovereignty*, 1984; Roxanne Dunbar Ortiz, *Indians of the Americas: Human Rights and Self-Determination*, 1984; Hurst Hannum, *Autonomy, Self-Determination and Sovereignty: The Accommodation of Conflicting Rights*, 1990; Phyllis Mauch Messenger, ed., *The Ethics of Collecting Cultural Property: Whose Culture? Whose Property?*, 1989.

COX, ARCHIBALD. Archibald Cox was born in Plainfield, New Jersey, on May 17, 1912. He graduated from Harvard in 1934 and then earned a law degree there in 1937. Blessed with a brilliant legal mind, Cox specialized in labor law, where he earned a reputation as the country's premier legal scholar. After serving with the solicitor general's office during World War II, Cox returned to Harvard, where he taught at the law school from 1946 to 1961. Among his publications during those years were *Cases on Labor Law* (1948), which subsequently went through eight editions, and *Law and the National Policy* (1960). From 1961 through 1965, Cox served as solicitor general of the United States, and he returned to Harvard in 1966 as Williston Professor of Law.

Archibald Cox became a household name in the 1970s as a result of the Watergate scandal.* He took a leave of absence from Harvard in 1973 to serve as a special prosecutor pursuing the Watergate investigation. He did so with enthusiasm and his characteristic genius, and when he learned that secret tapes of White House conversations existed, he worked to secure access to them. President Richard Nixon* grew tired of Cox's zealous prosecution of the case, and in what is known today as the Saturday Night Massacre,* he fired Cox as special prosecutor in October 1973. Cox then returned to Harvard, where he taught until he retired in 1984.

SUGGESTED READINGS: James Doyle, *Not Above the Law: The Battles of Watergate Prosecutors Cox and Jaworski*, 1977; Ken Gormley, *Archibald Cox: Conscience of a Nation*, 1997.

CRAIG V. BOREN **(1976).** One of the primary objectives of the women's movement* in the 1970s was to achieve equal protection under the law, and occasionally that goal resulted in judicial decisions that some considered to go against women. One of these was *Craig v. Boren* in 1976. It was not uncommon for state legislatures to impose laws that treated women differently from men. Several states, for example, permitted eighteen-year-old women to purchase beer with a 3.2 percent alcohol content while, at the same time, requiring men to be twenty-one years old. The U.S. Supreme Court decided the case on December 20, 1976, by a 7 to 2 vote. Justice William Brennan* wrote the majority opinion, ruling that all such gender classifications are violations of the equal protection clause of the Fourteenth Amendment unless the state can prove a substantive need for gender restrictions in order to achieve a compelling state interest. In this instance, the court concluded, the state could not prove such a need, even though it claimed that the law was necessary to achieve a stated goal of enhanced traffic safety.

SUGGESTED READING: 429 U.S. 190 (1976).

CREDIBILITY GAP. The term "credibility gap" became a buzzword in the 1960s and 1970s to describe the American public's erosion of faith in the pronouncements of political leaders. The term referred to the discrepancies between the public pronouncements and the private policies of American political leaders in the 1960s and 1970s. The idea of the credibility gap first emerged during Lyndon Johnson's presidency in general but with the Vietnam War* in particular. In February 1968 White House staffer Fred Panzer wrote a position paper explaining the psychology of the credibility gap. He blamed the phrase on "antiwar and anti-Johnson forces" who focused on the charge that Johnson lied to the American people in the election of 1964 by promising to stay out of Asian wars. The events surrounding the Gulf of Tonkin incident in August 1964 and whether or not U.S. ships had really been attacked by North Vietnamese vessels only heightened levels of distrust toward the Johnson administration.

On May 23, 1965, the term "credibility gap" first appeared in print in a *New York Herald Tribune* article written by David Wise. It was popularized by Murray Marder in a December 5, 1965, article in the *Washington Post*. Talk about the credibility gap had escalated during 1966 and 1967, and it reached a fever pitch after the Tet Offensive. All throughout 1967 the Johnson administration had promised the American public that the end of the war was in sight, and General William Westmoreland had said as much in his speech before a joint session of Congress in November. Large numbers of Americans no longer trusted the word of their political leaders, even on such important matters as war, peace, and victory.

During the years of the Richard Nixon* administration, the credibility gap escalated again, eventually reaching unprecedented levels of public distrust and alienation from politicians. Release of the Pentagon Papers provided the first episode of public distrust for the Nixon administration. The Pentagon Papers clearly revealed how a succession of presidents, from Dwight Eisenhower through John Kennedy and including Lyndon Johnson, had repeatedly misled the American people about actual events in Indochina. Then, when the *New York Times* began publishing the Pentagon Papers in 1971, the Nixon administration, on the grounds of national security, tried to force the paper to cease publication. Eventually, the Supreme Court, in the name of the First Amendment's protection of freedom of the press, allowed publication to proceed. The bombing of Cambodia* also increased public skepticism about the truthfulness of President Nixon. In March 1969, in order to attack Vietcong and North Vietnamese forces using Cambodia as a sanctuary, Nixon ordered the secret bombing of Cambodia. The bombing was dubbed "Operation Menu," but when the press asked the administration if such a bombing was occurring, Nixon repeatedly denied it. After the invasion of Cambodia in April 1970 and revelations about the bombing, Nixon's credibility diminished further.

What little credibility he had left vanished completely with the Watergate scandal.* Throughout 1973 and 1974, revelation after revelation of abuse of power and obstruction of justice in the Nixon administration rendered an already doubtful public completely jaded, and when the president fought release of the White House tapes, a presumption of his guilt became widespread. The credibility gap came to a peak in August 1974 when a White House tape demonstrated beyond a shadow of a doubt that the president had obstructed justice by ordering a cover-up of the Watergate incident. His resignation several days later was all but guaranteed.

SUGGESTED READINGS: Peter Braestrup, *Big Story: How the American Press and Television Reported and Interpreted the Crisis of Tet 1968 in Vietnam and Washington*, 1983; David Culbert, "Johnson and the Media," in *Exploring the Johnson Years*, ed. Robert Divine, 1981; Stanley Kutler, *Abuse of Power: The New Nixon Tapes*, 1997; William Shawcross, *Sideshow: Kissinger, Nixon, and the Destruction of Cambodia*, 1979; Theodore H. White, *Breach of Faith*, 1975; Robert Woodward and Carl Bernstein, *All the President's Men*, 1974.

Frances Frenzel

CREEDENCE CLEARWATER REVIVAL. Creedence Clearwater Revival, one of the most successful rock-and-roll bands of the late 1960s and 1970s, was formed by John Fogarty and Tom Fogarty in El Cerrito, California, in 1959. The group also included Stu Cook and Doug "Cosmo" Clifford. They released a number of albums in the late 1960s, including *Creedence Clearwater Revival* in 1968; *Bayou Country, Green River*, and *Willie and the Poor Boys*, all in

1969; and *Cosmo's Factory* in 1970. *Bayou Country* was the breakthrough album for Creedence. Their 1969 and 1970 albums included seven hit singles: "Bad Moon Rising," "Green River," "Fortunate Son," "Down on the Corner," "Travelin' Band," "Up Around the Bend," and "Lookin' Out My Back Door." The album *Cosmo's Factory* was their high point. John Fogarty quit the group shortly after the 1971 release of *Pendulum*. Their final album was *Mardi Gras*. The band broke up late in 1972.

SUGGESTED READING: Hank Bordowitz, *Bad Moon Rising: The Unauthorized History of Creedence Clearwater Revival*, 1998.

CREEP. The Committee for the Re-election of the President (CREEP) was formed in early 1971 by a handful of loyalists intent on running Richard Nixon's* reelection campaign outside of Republican party (and legal) control. While the committee's ostensible purpose was the reelection of Nixon, its primary duty was to sabotage political opposition by the use of illegal fund-raising and dirty tricks.* It was under the de facto leadership of Attorney General John Mitchell* that several members of the committee, including John Dean* (Nixon's legal counsellor), Jeb Magruder, and G. Gordon Liddy,* planned the committee's most infamous dirty trick, the break-in and electronic bugging (in June 1972) of the Democratic National Committee's headquarters located in Washington D.C.'s Watergate complex (*see* Watergate scandal).

By the time Nixon was reelected in November 1972, CREEP had at its disposal more than $3 million in unexpended funds, most of which were used to pay for the legal defenses of those involved in the Watergate conspiracy, and to settle (for $750,000) a lawsuit instigated by the Democratic National Party. During the Watergate controversy of 1973–1974, *Washington Post* reporters Robert Woodward and Carl Bernstein exposed CREEP's illegal activities on behalf of the president.

SUGGESTED READINGS: Stanley Kutler, *Abuse of Power: The New Nixon Tapes*, 1997; Robert Woodward and Carl Bernstein, *All the President's Men*, 1974.

Robert L. Perry

CROCE, JIM. Jim Croce was born on January 10, 1943, in Philadelphia, Pennsylvania. He attended Villanova University and began to host a local radio show; he also joined a number of bands. A singer and songwriter, Croce's first album, *Approaching Day*, was released in 1969, but it did poorly. His popularity was slow in coming. After graduating from Villanova he moved to New York City and played the club scene, but his second album was also a bust. Croce made a living doing construction work. His 1972 album, *You Don't Mess With Jim* had two hit singles: "Operator" and "You Don't Mess with Jim." His 1973 album *Life and Times* had the spectacularly successful single "Bad, Bad Leroy Brown." On September 20, 1973, at the peak of his popularity, Croce died in a plane crash in Natchitoches, Louisiana.

SUGGESTED READINGS: Linda Altman, *Jim Croce: The Feeling Lives on*, 1976; *New York Times*, September 21, 1973.

CROSBY, STILLS, NASH, AND YOUNG. Crosby, Stills, Nash, and Young, a premier rock-and-roll group of the 1970s, included David Crosby, Stephen Stills, Graham Nash, and Neil Young. The group first formed in Los Angeles, California, in 1968. Crosby had previously been with the Byrds, and Young had been with Buffalo Springfield. Nash had previously performed with the Hollies. Their first album, *Crosby, Stills, and Nash,* was released in 1969 and included such hit singles as "Marrakesh Express" and "Suite: Judy Blue Eyes." Neil Young joined the group in the summer of 1969, shortly before they performed at Woodstock. As a quartet, their first album was *Déjà Vu,* and its hit singles included "Woodstock," "Teach Your Children," and "Our House." The single "Ohio," a tribute to the four students killed at Kent State University* in 1970, was a hit, but the group disbanded soon after releasing *Four Way Street.* During the 1980s, various permutations of the group appeared as several joined together for recording and concert tours.

SUGGESTED READING: Dave Zimmer, *Crosby, Stills and Nash: The Authorized Biography,* 1982.

D

DALKON SHIELD. The Dalkon shield, a birth control device, was first introduced in the United States in 1971. Developed by A. H. Robbins Pharmaceuticals, the Dalkon shield, an interuterine device, was a plastic-covered metal coil that was placed permanently in a woman's uterus. The shield prevented a fertilized zygote from implanting itself in the uterine wall. It soon became apparent, however, that the device carried serious side effects. A number of users suffered from inflammatory pelvic disease and uterine bleeding. Miscarriage rates were significantly higher among shield users. Although A. H. Robbins denied any culpability, the company removed the product from the market in 1974. The case remains in litigation today.

SUGGESTED READING: Morton Mintz, *At Any Cost: Corporate Greed, Women, and the Dalkon Shield*, 1985.

THE DAN WHITE CASE. On November 27, 1978, Dan White shot and killed George Moscone, the mayor of San Francisco, and Harvey Milk, a member of the city's elected Board of Supervisors. Milk had been the first city politician to reveal his homosexuality. White was a political conservative who had recently resigned from the Board of Supervisors. In the subsequent murder trial, White's attorney offered up what became known as the "Twinkie defense," arguing that too much junk food had deranged White's mind. Astonishingly, the jury bought the story and convicted White of voluntary manslaughter. They sentenced him to from five to seven years in prison. The gay community in San Francisco was outraged with the verdict, claiming that White had really avoided a first-degree murder conviction because one of his victims had been gay. White was paroled before serving his full term, but he committed suicide in 1985.

SUGGESTED READINGS: Emily Mann, *Execution of Justice*, 1986; Michael Weiss, *Double Play: The San Francisco City Hall Killings*, 1984.

DARYL HALL AND JOHN OATES. Daryl Hall and John Oates was one of the most successful rock-and-roll duos in the history of popular music. The two men grew up in Philadelphia, Pennsylvania, met at Temple University, came together as a musical act in 1969, and signed a contract with Atlantic Records. Their first album, *Whole Oates* (1972), was a commercial disappointment, as were their next two: *Abandoned Luncheonnette* (1973) and *War Babies* (1974). Atlantic dropped them, and they signed with RCA. RCA then took them to the top of the rock world, with such hit albums as *Daryl Hall and John Oates* (1975), *Bigger Than Both of Us* (1976), *No Goodbyes* (1977), *Beauty on a Back Street* (1977), and *Along the Red Ledge* (1978). Their major hit singles included "She's Gone," "Kiss on My List," "Private Eyes," and the number-one hit "Rich Girl."

After a slump in 1979, Hall and Oates decided to produce their own albums, and the results were the phenomenally successful *Voices* (1980), *Private Eyes* (1981), and *H₂0* (1982). Those three albums produced a string of hit singles, including "How Does It Feel to Be Back," "Kiss on My List," "You've Lost That Loving Feeling," "I Can't Go for That (No Can Do)," "Did It in a Minute," "Family Man," and "One on One." They had several major hits in the mid-1980s before they broke up in 1985. Hall and Oates came back together in 1988, but they could not reproduce their earlier success. They did, however, return to the concert circuit with smaller bookings in 1997.

SUGGESTED READINGS: Brad Gooch, *Hall and Oates*, 1994; Nick Tosches, *Hall and Oates: Suburban Contemporary: An Authorized Biography*, 1985.

DAVIS, ANGELA. Angela Yvonne Davis was born in Birmingham, Alabama, on January 26, 1944. Both of her parents were schoolteachers and active members in the local chapter of the National Association for the Advancement of Colored People (NAACP). They taught her the importance of education and personal pride, and they also taught her never to acquiesce to Jim Crow segregation. That was not an easy stand to take in Alabama in the 1940s. The Davis family lived in the Dynamite Hill neighborhood of Birmingham, a section of the city regularly attacked by white night riders bent on preserving segregation. But her parents were people of courage and dignity who refused to back down.

A brilliant woman, Davis attended Brandeis University as an undergraduate, where she came under the influence of Herbert Marcuse, a Marxist philosopher. After graduating in 1961, she spent two years traveling and studying in Europe, where she worked closely with Marxist Theodore Adorno. Until 1963, however, Davis's radicalism was an abstract intellectual construct. The 1963 murder of the four black Sunday School girls in Birmingham transformed her radicalism into a personal crusade. She attended graduate school at the University of California at San Diego, where she earned a master's degree in philosophy in 1968 and had completed all of the requirements for her Ph.D., except the dissertation, by 1969.

An African American concerned about the plight of her people, Davis became increasingly radical in the late 1960s. She became active in the Student Non-violent Coordinating Committee and took a teaching position at the University of California at Los Angeles. In July 1968, Davis joined the Communist party. The next year she traveled to Cuba, where she decided that African Americans had something in common with all Third World peoples. Later that year, she became a national figure when Governor Ronald Reagan* of California fired her from her teaching post at UCLA on the grounds that she was a Communist. She appealed the case through the federal courts, and the Supreme Court eventually overturned her dismissal, arguing that her First Amendment right to freedom of speech had been violated.

The Supreme Court case soon became the least of her concerns. She had become deeply involved in the cause of George Jackson,* an African American and Black Panther* who was imprisoned in California for murdering a correctional officer. George Jackson was killed while trying to escape. On August 7, 1970, Jackson's younger brother, Jonathan, using weapons registered in Davis's name, seized several hostages during a trial in Marin County. In a shootout that followed, Jackson was killed by police, but he murdered Judge Harold Haley before he died himself. Because Davis owned the weapons, she was charged with conspiracy to commit murder. She went underground, and the Federal Bureau of Investigation placed her on its most wanted list. Davis was apprehended two months later, and she spent the next sixteen months in prison awaiting trial on murder and conspiracy charges. A jury acquitted her of all charges in June 1972.

Free of all legal burdens, Davis resumed her academic and political careers. She accepted a faculty position at San Francisco State University and wrote several books, including *If They Come in the Morning* (1971) and *Angela Davis: An Autobiography* (1974). In 1980 and again in 1984, Davis ran for vice president of the United States on the Communist party ticket. She wrote *Women, Race, and Class* in 1983 and *Women, Culture, and Politics* in 1989. In 1991 Davis joined the faculty of the University of California at Santa Cruz.

SUGGESTED READINGS: Angela Davis, *Angela Davis: An Autobiography*, 1971; Brian Lanker, *I Dream a World: Portraits of Black Women Who Changed America*, 1989.

DEADHEAD. The term "deadhead" emerged in the late 1960s and 1970s to describe an individual addicted to the music and the concerts of The Grateful Dead* band.

DEAN, JOHN. John Dean III was born in Akron, Ohio, on October 14, 1938. He graduated from Wooster College in 1961 and then earned a law degree from Georgetown University in 1965. Dean practiced law privately in Washington, D.C., before becoming chief minority counsel to the House Judiciary Committee in 1966. From that post he established contacts with leading Republican figures in the nation's Capital. When Richard Nixon* entered the White House in 1969, Dean was appointed deputy attorney general. Just one year later, when Dean was thirty-one-years old, he was appointed counsel to the president. He was the youngest man ever to hold that position, and he was bright, ambitious, and politically inexperienced.

When the cover-up of the Watergate break-in (*see* Watergate scandal) began to unravel early in 1973, Dean was asked to resign, which he did on April 30, 1973. It did not take long for him to realize that the administration was setting him up to be the fall guy for the Watergate crimes. To minimize the damage to his reputation and his own legal vulnerability, Dean agreed to testify before the Senate Select Committee on Presidential Campaign Activities (the Watergate Committee). There he fleshed out details of White House and CREEP* involvement in the Watergate break-in and the cover-up. Committee members, when they were later able to check transcripts of the White House conversations, were astonished at the accuracy of Dean's testimony, since he had been able to recall, word for word, extensive conversations from more than a year before. Dean's testimony proved to be extraordinarily damaging to the Nixon administration. Later witnesses, notably John Ehrlichman* and H. R. Haldeman,* testified that Dean had been the instigator and architect of both the break-in and the cover-up. Dean's five days of televised precise, even laconic, testimony made a deep impression on committee members and the viewing public. The Nixon administration essentially ended with John Dean's testimony. Dean was subsequently convicted of obstruction of justice and served a federal prison term. In 1998 and 1999, during the impeachment proceedings against President Bill Clinton, he resurfaced into the public limelight as a news commentator.

SUGGESTED READING: John Dean III, *Blind Ambition: The White House Years*, 1976.

Sean A. Kelleher

DEEP THROAT. Late in the 1960s, Americans began to conduct an intense debate about the definition of obscenity, the nature of pornography, and the merits of government censorship when such soft-core films as *I Am Curious (Yellow)* and plays like *Oh! Calcutta* attracted notoriety and then audiences. Hard-core pornography, graphic sequences of sexual acts with the camera focusing close up on the actors' genitals, had been around ever since Thomas Edison invented celluloid. But until the release of *Deep Throat* in 1972, hardcore pornography had remained confined to the sleazy, scandalous underbelly of American popular culture; it was not a subject for polite talk or civilized company. *Deep Throat* changed all of that. Premised on the notion that only fellatio can satisfy actress Linda Lovelace (née Linda Boreman), the film proceeds to demonstrate her prowess in grotesque anatomical detail.

Deep Throat inexplicably struck a responsive chord among elements of American society who previously would never have been caught dead viewing such a film. In New York City, Chicago, San Francisco, Boston, Los Angeles, and

Philadelphia, it became almost chic to tell friends that one had seen *Deep Throat*. Produced for a mere $25,000, the film grossed tens of millions of dollars and showed continuously at dozens of theaters for years in a row. Attempts to ban the movie only generated more publicity. In the end, *Deep Throat*'s infamous contribution to American culture was the fact that, by conveying to millions of people what real hard-core pornography was, it contributed a dubious legitimacy to soft-core pornography and less offensive, though equally gratuitous, sexual images in television and films.

Soon after the film's release, the name "Deep Throat" took on a different meaning. Bob Woodward and Carl Bernstein, the enterprising reporters from the *Washington Post* who uncovered the Watergate scandal* in 1972 and 1973, had a source of information in the White House about the extent of corruption in the Richard Nixon* administration. The source's code name was "Deep Throat." To this day the identity of Deep Throat has not been revealed.

SUGGESTED READING: *New York Times*, January 21, 1973.

THE DEER HUNTER. *The Deer Hunter*, which won an Oscar as Best Picture in 1979, is director Michael Cimino's epic film about America and the Vietnam War.* The movie revolves around the lives of three blue-collar Americans, all descended from Russian immigrants who live in a Pennsylvania steel town. Throughout their adolescence and teenage years, they play together, hunt together, and work together, and then they all go off to war together during the Vietnam era. The film stars Robert De Niro* as Michael, John Savage as Steven, Christopher Walken as Nick, and Meryl Streep as Linda.

In Vietnam, the three men face an Armageddon of violence, carnage, and insanity. Cimino uses a game of Russian roulette as a metaphor for everything wrong about Vietnam. Captured by the Vietcong, the three friends are forced to play Russian roulette with one another and with other American POWs. While the GIs pull the trigger, the Vietcong make book on the outcome. Michael eventually helps all three escape, but they are never the same. Nick goes insane and becomes a professional Russian roulette competitor in Saigon. Steven is wounded in action and becomes a double amputee. Michael, the leader of the three young men, emerges almost intact. In a desperate search to find Nick, who is absent without leave in the Russian roulette game rooms of Saigon, Michael returns to South Vietnam just before its final overrun in 1975 by the North Vietnamese. Nick's luck runs out, and he pulls the trigger with a bullet in the chamber. Back home, Michael, Steven, and Linda try to come to terms with the war. *The Deer Hunter* ends with them singing "God Bless America" at the corner bar.

SUGGESTED READINGS: Linda Dittmar and Gene Michaud, eds., *From Hanoi to Hollywood: The Vietnam War in American Film*, 1990; *New York Times*, December 15, 1978.

DELIVERANCE. The film *Deliverance*, based on John Dickey's novel of the same name and released in the summer of 1972, was a critical and box-office success. Starring Jon Voight and Burt Reynolds, the film revolves around four Atlanta suburbanites who embark on a back-to-nature canoe trip in the Georgia hill country. During the trip, they are ambushed by a group of in-bred southern hillbillies, who sodomize one of the men. The Atlanta suburbanites essentially return to the wild; they kill several of their oppressors, conceal the crime, and deny to local authorities any knowledge of it. Survival, they believed, demanded such behavior. Only in ritualized acts of violence could they find justice for the rape that occurred. The film was not a glorification of masculinity, nature, or violence, just a powerful exposé of modern society's discomfort with itself.

SUGGESTED READING: *New York Times*, August 20, 1972.

DE NIRO, ROBERT. Robert De Niro, who played lead roles in some of the most influential films of the 1970s, was born in New York City on August 17, 1943. He studied acting with Lee Strasberg and won bit parts in several 1969 and 1970 films. His first real break came with an important role in *Bang the Drum Slowly* (1971), the story of a dying baseball player. In 1974 De Niro was cast as the young Vito Corleone in *The Godfather, Part II*,* a role that won him an academy award as best supporting actor. Two years later, De Niro appeared in *Taxi Driver** (1976), a chilling portrait of an obsessed, demented Vietnam War* veteran turned political assassin. He also played the lead in *The Deer Hunter** (1978), a symbolic anti–Vietnam War film that won an Oscar as best picture. In 1980 De Niro won another Oscar for his extraordinary performance as a professional boxer in *Raging Bull*. Since then, De Niro has continued to expand his range and reigns today as one of America's finest actors.

SUGGESTED READING: Alberto Pezzotta, *Martin Scorsese: Taxi Driver*, 1997.

DEREGULATION. Ever since 1887, when Congress passed the Interstate Commerce Act and created the Interstate Commerce Commission to provide oversight for the railroad industry, and on into the 1970s, the federal government has steadily increased its regulatory role in the American economy. The political pressures to increase government interference came from a wide variety of sources. During the 1890s, farmers established the Populist party and called for regulation of railroads and banks. Labor unions called for government regulation of many industries, and even many businessmen viewed government regulation as a means of rationalizing various sectors of the economy. Some companies and trade associations actually used government regulation to stifle competition and sustain high profit margins. The size of the federal government steadily increased in size and then exploded in growth during the Great Depression and World War II.

During the 1960s, there was an increase in federal government regulations dealing with consumer goods and a simultaneous drive to lift some of the controls on the industries that had traditionally been regulated. Many Americans began to argue that the regulatory agencies were no longer "watchdogs" of the public interest but had actually been "captured" by the very industries that they were supposed to regulate. Many critics charged that the federal agencies once designed to prevent monopoly and price gouging of consumers had actually become impediments to real competition and the source of high prices and poor levels of service. Banking, transportation, communications, and the energy industry seemed especially entangled in the problem. Although Presidents Richard Nixon* and Gerald Ford* complained about the problem of excess regulation in the 1970s, they were not able to implement any real changes.

The banking industry was a case in point. During the Great Depression, Congress rigidly separated the functions and operations of savings and loan associations, commercial banks, and investment banks with the passage of the Banking Act of 1933. Subsequent regulations from the Federal Reserve Board and the Comptroller of the Currency placed a lid on the interest rates that those institutions could offer customers, thereby eliminating competition in the industry. In the 1970s, however, securities firms established mutual funds and offered rates of return in excess of those offered by insurance companies, banks, and thrifts. These latter financial institutions suffered serious outflows of capital. To deal with the problem, Congress decided to deregulate the banking industry by passing the Depository Institutions Deregulation and Monetary Control Act of 1980. Thrift institutions could now provide loans for more than real estate: interest rate caps were lifted, and all banks and thrifts became more involved in the securities business.

It was the administration of President Jimmy Carter* that launched the deregulation movement. The inflationary spiral of the 1970s gave Carter the opportunity to convince businesses that removing regulations would reduce their costs. He also promised that deregulation would increase competition, improve services, and reduce consumer costs. The three major pieces of deregulatory legislation in the transportation industry were the Airline Deregulation Act* of 1978,* the Rail Act of 1980, and the Motor Carrier Act of 1980. The Airline Deregulation Act ended the power of the Civil Aeronautics Board to set air fares and freight rates and to control the access of new carriers to the industry. The legislation allowed airlines to compete in fare rates and allowed new carriers to enter the market. The Rail Act and Motor Carrier Act similarly limited the authority of the Interstate Commerce Commission (ICC) to set freight rates. The ICC had permitted the trucking and railroad industries to establish regional rate bureaus that were allowed to fix prices. It was not at all uncommon for truckers to have to follow circuitous routes to comply with the law or to have to drive empty trucks on return trips. The regulations also severely restricted access to the industry by new lines. The ICC, originally designed to protect competition in the transportation industry, had actually created a situation in which little competition existed.

The results, of course, were mixed. Although new competition did drive down the prices of those goods and services, it also weakened a number of major economic institutions, particularly in the airline and banking industries, thus contributing to the problems of those industries in the 1980s and 1990s. During the 1980s the number of Americans flying at least once a year doubled and then doubled again, and airline fares dropped dramatically. The competition benefited consumers but also hurt a number of airline carriers, such as TWA and Pan-American, which were no longer competitive and went into bankruptcy. The Motor Carrier Act of 1980 made it much easier for independent truckers to enter the market, and it allowed real price competition to exist.

SUGGESTED READINGS: James Q. Wilson, ed., *The Politics of Regulation*, 1980; Mansel G. Blackford and K. Austin Kerr, *Business Enterprise in American History*, 1986; Barry Friedman, *Regulation in the Reagan-Bush Era*, 1995.

DETENTE. The term "detente" came to be used by foreign policy historians and international relations specialists to describe the diplomatic rapprochement between the United States and the Soviet Union and between the United States and the People's Republic of China. Although detente has usually been attributed to the work of Henry Kissinger* during the years of the Richard Nixon* administration, the thaw in the Cold War* actually began during the Kennedy administration and accelerated during the Nixon administration.

The first chapter in the history of detente was written late in 1962 in the wake of the Cuban missile crisis. The United States and the Soviet Union had come perilously close to nuclear war, and both sides had been frustrated by severe limits in their ability to communicate with one another. While the two nations faced off with their proverbial "fingers on the nuclear trigger," messages had to be wired into individual embassies, decoded, translated, and then carried by diplomatic pouch to the White House and the Kremlin. When the crisis ended, both sides realized that the safety of the world depended upon terribly anachronistic methods of communication. President John F. Kennedy and Soviet Premier Nikita Khrushchev decided to establish what became known as the "hot line," a simple communications link consisting of one telephone in the White House and one in the Kremlin, which would permit the leaders of the two superpowers to call one another at a moment's notice. The hot line was operational early in 1963.

Detente took another step forward later in the year when negotiations to ban the atmospheric testing of nuclear weapons reached fruition. Ever since the early 1950s, environmentalists had grown increasingly concerned about the health effects of atmospheric tests of nuclear weapons, in which the United States and the Soviet Union regularly engaged. Predictions of increased rates of cancer around the world produced demands for an atmospheric ban. On June 9, 1963, at American University in Washington, D.C., President Kennedy offered an olive branch to the Soviet Union. Rather than wallowing in Cold War rhetoric, he called for a reduction in mutual suspicions because both superpowers had an interest in peace and an end to the arms race. He also proposed negotiations to end the atmospheric testing of nuclear weapons. "We all inhabit this small planet," Kennedy proclaimed. "We all breathe the same air. We all cherish our children's future. And we are all mortal." By then, both sides were convinced that they could continue to upgrade their nuclear weapons through underground testing, which released no radiation into the atmosphere.

The Soviet Union responded quickly to Kennedy's offer. Test ban talks between the United States and the Soviet Union had been taking place since the 1950s, but neither side had ever been inclined to consider seriously the permanent elimination of atmospheric testing. On June 10, the day after the president's American University speech, the two countries announced the beginning of a new round of negotiations. On July 15, the United States, Great Britain, and the Soviet Union began trilateral talks on the issue, and on August 5, 1963, negotiators signed a preliminary agreement in Moscow. All three nuclear powers agreed to conduct no more atmospheric tests of nuclear weapons. Nor could they test such weapons in outer space or under the water, only in underground installations from which no radioactive particles could escape. During the next month, ninety-six other nations signed the agreement. The U.S. Senate ratified the treaty on September 24, 1963, and it went into effect on October 10, 1963.

Although many diplomats worried that the Vietnam War* might escalate into a superpower confrontation, both the Soviet Union and the People's Republic of China assumed careful diplomatic positions. Both countries provided billions of dollars in supplies to the North Vietnamese and the Vietcong, but neither nation had any interest in seeing the Indochinese war spread out of the region. China was in the midst of its Cultural Revolution, which badly damaged the economy and destabilized the political system, and the Soviet Union did not perceive Vietnam as critical to its own national survival. So even in the midst of the Vietnam War, the two sides were able to complete another important step in the history of detente. In 1967, with both countries engaged in a technological race to become the first country to place a human being on the moon, the issue of territoriality in outer space came to the forefront. Just as the European nations had to work out a way of dividing the world in the sixteenth and seventeenth centuries, the United States and the Soviet Union had to address the issue of political sovereignty on celestial bodies. On April 25, 1967, the two nations signed the Outer Space Treaty. The treaty underscored the need for the peaceful exploration of outer space, banned the existence of weapons of mass destruction in outer space, prohibited the establishment of military bases in outer space, and suspended all claims for sovereignty in outer space. The treaty was signed on January 1967 by sixty countries, including the United States, the Soviet Union, and Great Britain.

Similar concerns developed among the major powers over the issue of the proliferation of nuclear weapons. Most strategic observers were convinced that an increase in the number of countries possessing nuclear weapons would destabilize world politics and increase the likelihood of a nuclear exchange, if not between the superpowers then between smaller rivals, such as India and Pakistan or Israel and Syria. The United States and the Soviet Union led the way in promoting the nonproliferation treaty. The two countries signed the treaty on May 31, 1968, and the United Nations General Assembly then approved it by a vote of 95 to 4. More than fifty nations eventually signed the treaty, and it went into effect on March 5, 1970. The treaty prohibited the transfer of nuclear technology by a nuclear to a nonnuclear power, and it also prohibited the manufacture or acquisition by other means of nuclear technology on the part of nonnuclear nations. By January 1976, ninety-six countries had signed the treaty.

When Richard Nixon entered the White House in January 1969, the movement toward detente took several giant leaps forward. The fact that he began withdrawing U.S. troops from South Vietnam in the summer 1969 proved to the Soviets that he was serious about deescalation, and they even cooperated with him on a number of occasions in trying to convince the North Vietnamese to negotiate a settlement of the conflict. In 1972, for example, when Nixon announced the mining of Haiphong Harbor,* which could have led to an international incident had Soviet supply ships been sunk there, the Soviet Union took a decidedly low-profile stand and did not try to exploit the situation.

The real mastermind behind detente, however, was Henry Kissinger, the president's national security advisor and later secretary of state. Kissinger possessed a well-developed, carefully conceived approach to foreign policy, which rested on two fundamental assumptions. First, one nation, except in the most unusual circumstances, should not interfere with the internal political or social affairs of an international rival, especially when that intervention was based on a belief in moral superiority. Much of the Cold War, Kissinger believed, could be traced to Soviet communism's sense of moral superiority to U.S. capitalism, and U.S. capitalism's sense of moral superiority to Soviet communism. The U.S. refusal, since 1949, to extend diplomatic recognition to the People's Republic of China was a good example of high-minded bias that did not serve world peace. Second, world peace required a delicate balance between the superpowers. Kissinger firmly believed that absolute security for one nation automatically meant insecurity for all other nations. The nuclear arms race, he was convinced, had gotten completely out of hand and threatened the survival of humanity; it was a perfect example of superpower competition run mad.

As a result of the combined efforts of Henry Kissinger and Richard Nixon, detente achieved several notable successes in the early 1970s. First, the president conducted summit conferences in Moscow and Beijing in 1972, which heralded a new attempt at the cooperation of the superpowers. The trip to Beijing was especially dramatic, since the Chinese Communists had been cut off for so long from U.S. diplomatic communication. Some historians believe that only Richard Nixon could have pulled off such a diplomatic coup. Because of his unimpeachable anticomunist credentials, Richard Nixon enjoyed a powerful credibility and had unusual influence among right-wing Republicans, who would have been the most likely to scuttle detente with the Soviet Union and the People's Republic of China.

When the Nuclear Non-Proliferation Treaty had been signed in 1968, American and Soviet officials agreed that the next item in nuclear weapons diplomacy would revolve around the need for mutual reductions in the stockpiles of strategic nuclear weapons. Not only was the race for nuclear superiority increasing the risk of global thermonuclear war, the expense of developing increasingly sophisticated, and destructive, nuclear technologies posed financial problems to both the United States and the Soviet Union. What became known as the Strategic Arms Limitation Talks* (SALT) between the United States and the Soviet Union began in 1969.

Soviet diplomats, however, proved quite reluctant to cooperate in any serious negotiations until President Nixon proposed to Congress the need for the development of an anti-ballistic missile shield to protect the United States from a Soviet nuclear first strike. Nixon took heat from congressional Democrats, who argued that the defensive system would be too expensive, and from scientists, who doubted the feasibility of the proposal. But the president's proposal was more a diplomatic ploy than a nuclear arms issue. The nuclear arms race placed more pressure on the Soviet economy than on the American, and the Russians did not want to find themselves in an expensive race to develop an anti-ballistic missile system. The SALT negotiations began to progress.

Talks continued until early 1972 when the two sides agreed to the Anti-Ballistic Missile Treaty,* in which they mutually decided to disengage from the development of anti-ballistic missile shields. With the threat of an expensive new weapons system development removed, the two sides were then able to reach the Interim Agreement on Strategic Offensive Weapons, which froze deployment of intercontinental ballistic missiles (ICBMs) at current levels. That agreement was much less than it appeared to be because new technologies had already rendered it obsolete. Both the United States and the Soviet Union had developed multiple independent reentry vehicles (MIRVs), which enabled several nuclear warheads to be placed in one missile, each of which could be dropped on a separate target. Still, it was the first time the two superpowers had agreed to impose limits on their nuclear arsenals. These initial strategic arms limitations talks, which became known as SALT I, also included an agreement on an improved hot-line communication system. During President Nixon's summit visit to Moscow in May 1972, the SALT I treaties were signed.

In November 1972, the SALT II discussions began with the hope of developing a quantitative limit on the number of MIRV warheads possessed by each side. The Watergate scandal* in the United States stalled the SALT II talks, as did the short-term presidential administration of Gerald Ford.* When Jimmy Carter* defeated President Gerald Ford in the presidential election of 1976,* SALT II discussions were again delayed. The SALT II Treaty was finally signed in June 1979, but by that time the spirit of detente was already dissipating in the United States, and the Senate did not ratify the treaty.

During the Carter administration, the United States again began to use human rights issues as a litmus test for cooperation with the Soviet Union and the People's Republic of China. Both of those countries had preferred Kissinger's willingness to not concern himself with internal political issues in other countries unless they had a direct bearing on U.S. national security. What really ended detente in the 1970s was the Soviet Union's decision in 1979 to invade Afghanistan.* The Carter administration bitterly opposed the intervention, and Congress began to supply sophisticated weapons to the Afghan rebels fighting the Russians. In protest of the invasion, President Carter announced that the United States would boycott the 1980 Olympic Games, which were scheduled to take place in Moscow.

SUGGESTED READINGS: William Epstein, *The Last Chance*, 1976; Raymond Garthoff, *Détente and Confrontation*, 1985; Robert Litwack, *Détente and the Nixon Doctrine*, 1984; Keith Nelson, *The Making of Détente*, 1995; John Newhouse, *War and Peace in the Nuclear Age*, 1989; Mason Willrich, *The Non-Proliferation Treaty*, 1969.

THE DEVIL IN MISS JONES. Once described as a "breakthrough erotic odyssey" by a supposedly mainstream East Coast film critic, *The Devil in Miss Jones* was, like *Deep Throat*,* nothing more than sleazy, hardcore pornography that managed to titillate elements of legitimate American society early in the 1970s. Released in 1973, starring Georgina Spelvin, the film focuses on the escapades of a nymphomaniac who engages in every kind of sexual act, commits suicide in her misery, and then is confined to the eternal damnation of being in a room with an impotent, sexually disinterested man. It frequently enjoyed billing as a second feature to *Deep Throat*, and like *Deep Throat*, it helped legitimize soft-core pornography and more graphic sexual images in film and television.

SUGGESTED READING: *New York Times*, April 8, 1973.

DIGGS, CHARLES. Charles Diggs was born in Detroit, Michigan, in 1922. He attended the University of Michigan and Fisk University before joining the army during World War II. After the war, Diggs attended Wayne State University's mortuary science program and started a funeral business. Active in local Democratic politics, he won a state senate seat in 1951. Three years later, Diggs was elected to the U.S. House of Representatives. While serving in the state legislature, Diggs studied law at nights at the Detroit School of Law. He quickly earned a reputation as a friend of labor.

In 1954 Diggs set his sights on the U.S. Congress. He defeated George O'Brien, the Democratic incumbent, in the primary election and then went on to become Michigan's first African-American congressman. From his first day in Congress, he was an outspoken advocate of civil rights legislation, and he actively fought against de facto discrimination against African Americans in the U.S. military and in the federal government. On a number of occasions, he succeeded in getting the Pentagon to make policy changes designed to end discrimination against black servicemen and servicewomen.

By 1970 Diggs was the most influential of Congress's nine African-American members. He formed the Congressional Black Caucus* in 1971 and served as its first chairman. Diggs also chaired the District of Columbia Committee and the Foreign Affairs African Subcommittee. He used the first appointment to campaign for home rule for the District of Columbia, and on the African sub-committee he openly campaigned against apartheid in South Africa. President Richard Nixon* had in 1969 appointed Diggs as a member of the U.S. delegation to the United Nations, but Diggs resigned in 1971 to protest U.S. African policy, particularly the government's willingness to acquiesce in apartheid.

By 1978 Diggs was clearly the most powerful African American in Congress and, with twenty-four years of seniority, one of the most influential political figures in the United States. But at the peak of his power, he came under investigation for mail fraud and payroll kickbacks. He was convicted of the charges, which also included using money from his congressional staff budget to pay personal bills, but his constituents reelected him to a thirteenth term in Congress. He appealed the convictions, but in Congress the pressure mounted on him to resign. He was forced to resign all of his committee chairmanships, and on July 31, 1979, by a vote of 414 to 0, the House of Representatives formally censured him. When the U.S. Supreme Court refused to hear his appeal in 1980, Diggs resigned from Congress. He then served seven months in the federal prison at Maxwell Air Force in Montgomery, Alabama. After his release, he worked for a while as a special aide to the Congressional Black Caucus and then went back into the private mortuary business. Charles Diggs died on August 24, 1998.

SUGGESTED READING: *New York Times*, November 28, 1981, and August 25, 1998

DIRTY HARRY. As the 1960s gave way to the 1970s, American popular culture needed a new, younger icon to satisfy its need for the vicarious expression of frustration with the mass society created by bureaucracy and industrialization. Ever since the late 1930s, the persona of John Wayne had supplied that icon, but Wayne had been born in 1907, and he was now an aging icon at best. Also, Wayne had fought the good fight in Old West settings, while America had become an urban nation. The icon of the western hero needed to be transported from the nineteenth century to the twentieth and from the country to the city. Clint Eastwood,* in the figure of "Dirty" Harry Callaghan, became that urban cowboy.

In 1971 the lead in the film *Dirty Harry* was first offered to John Wayne, who turned it down. At the time, he felt the character of Harry Callaghan was too "sleazy," but Wayne later admitted that giving thumbs down to the part "was the stupidest thing I ever did." The role went to Clint Eastwood, who became a superstar because of it.

Harry Callaghan, a San Francisco detective, is frustrated with the notion of criminal rights and the difficulties they posed in securing convictions. Callaghan carries a Smith & Wesson Model 29 .44 magnum revolver, a gun with an extra long, 8 ⅜-inch barrel. He disdains permissive judges, police bureaucrats, liberal politicians, and gutless politicians. In *Dirty Harry*'s world, the criminals get what they deserve, even if Callaghan has to serve as judge, jury, and executioner. He is the reincarnation of John Wayne characters—the lone individual who uses violence to protect good people and punish evil people. Audiences loved seeing justice handed out the old-fashioned way. *Dirty Harry* spawned several successful sequels, including *Magnum Force* (1973), *The Enforcer* (1976), *Sudden Impact* (1983), and *The Dead Pool* (1988).

SUGGESTED READING: Richard Slotkin, *Gunfighter Nation: The Myth of the Frontier in Twentieth-Century America*, 1992.

DIRTY TRICKS. The term "dirty tricks" was a euphemism for the campaign tricks and pranks developed and pursued, in large part, by members of President Richard Nixon's* Committee to Re-Elect the President (CREEP).* While Nixon had a long history of employing such tactics in his previous political campaigns, the use of dirty tricks as part of his 1972 reelection campaign was particularly extensive and malevolent. Nixon's team had as one of its primary goals to help get the weakest Democratic candidate nominated. This was to be accomplished by undermining the campaigns of any apparent frontrunners. The standard procedure was infiltration and harassment. One of the first targets was Senator Edmund Muskie of Maine. Tactics used against Muskie ranged from such sophomoric things as stink bombs at campaign rallies to such malicious acts as fabricated stories sent to major newspapers and the theft of Muskie's campaign scheduling program. By April 1972, after poor showings in several primary elections, Muskie withdrew from the presidential race. After this success, CREEP later focused on the campaigns of Hubert Humphrey and George McGovern* and on the Democratic National Party. It was the arrest of five burglars attempting to bug the Democratic National Committee headquarters at the Watergate complex in Washington, D.C., that eventually led to the scandal known by that name, and the 1974 resignation of President Nixon (*see* Watergate scandal).

SUGGESTED READING: J. Anthony Lukas, *Nightmare: The Underside of the Nixon Years*, 1976.

Robert L. Perry

DISCO. Disco, the musical craze of the late 1970s, was popularized by John Travolta's* dancing in the 1978 film *Saturday Night Fever.** Disco became a worldwide fad. A reaction against the rock-and-roll, reformist, and protest values of the 1960s, disco music was characterized by very heavy, throbbing rhythms and sexual themes. Disco dancers, in contrast to the rebellious simplicities of 1960s fashion, highlighted fancy dresses and high heels on women and flashy suits and gold chains on men. Such artists as Laura Brannigan, the Bee Gees,* Chic, Donna Summer, and Debbie Harry sold millions of records, and New York City's Studio 54 became the heart and soul of disco culture. Disco petered out in the 1980s.

SUGGESTED READING: Randy Deats, *Dancing Disco*, 1979.

THE DOOBIE BROTHERS. The Doobie Brothers, a popular musical group of the 1970s, was formed in San Jose, California, in 1970. The group included

Tom Johnston, John Hartman, Patrick Simmons, and Dave Shogren. The group later included Cornelius Bumpus, Tiran Porter, Michael McDonald, John McFee, Keith Knudsen, and Chet McCracken. Their first album, *The Doobie Brothers*, was released in 1971 when they were still a country-boogie band. Over the years, they made the transition to popular jazz rhythms. Their name came from "doobie," which at the time in California was a slang synonym for marijuana. Their next two albums, *Toulouse Street* and *The Captain and Me*, both went platinum, and in 1975 the Doobie Brothers had their first number-one hit single, "Black Water." In 1978 their album *Minute by Minute*, which included the number-one single "What a Fool Believes," sold several million copies. The Doobie Brothers disbanded in 1982.

SUGGESTED READING: Patricia Romanowski and Holly George-Warren, eds., *The New Encyclopedia of Rock & Roll*, 1985.

DOONESBURY. *Doonesbury* is Garry Trudeau's famous comic strip. Garretson Beekman Trudeau first wrote the comic strip when he was an undergraduate student at Yale University. He created the title from the word "Doone," a Yalie expression for a friendly fool, and "Pillsbury," the surname of Trudeau's roommate in his Yale dormitory. In 1970, when Trudeau was only twenty-one years old, the comic strip went into national syndication, and it became a satire on contemporary American politics and society. In 1975 Trudeau became the first comic-strip artist to win the Pulitzer prize. By that time, more than 400 newspapers had moved *Doonesbury* from the comic pages to the editorial page.

SUGGESTED READINGS: Garry B. Trudeau, *But the Pension Fund Was Just Sitting There*, 1979, and *He's Never Heard of You Either*, 1981.

E

THE EAGLES. The Eagles, a prominent rock-and-roll group formed in Los Angeles, California in 1970, included Glenn Frey, Don Henley, Timothy Schmidt, Don Felder, and Joe Walsh. A mixture of country harmony and hard-rock guitar sounds, the Eagles became characteristic of so-called California rock. Their debut album, *Eagles*, went gold and included two hit singles, "Take It Easy" and "Witchy Woman." They released more albums in the mid-1970s, including *One of These Nights* (1975) and *Hotel California* (1977). The hit singles on these albums are "One of These Nights," "Lyin' Eyes," "Take It to the Limit," "New Kid in Town," and "Life in the Fast Lane." The Eagles disbanded in 1980 but reunited in 1994.

SUGGESTED READING: Marc Eliot, *To the Limit: The Untold Story of the Eagles*, 1997.

EARTH DAY. Throughout the 1960s, and particularly in 1962 with the publication of Rachel Carson's *Silent Spring*, concern about environmental pollution increased in the United States. On April 22, 1970, under the sponsorship of Senator Gaylord Nelson of Wisconsin, Congressman Paul McCloskey of California, and environmental activist Denis Hayes, Earth Day celebrations were held throughout the United States. Rallies, parades, and demonstrations took place in cities and towns across the country. Earth Day became the symbolic beginning in the United States of the environmental movement.*

SUGGESTED READING: *New York Times*, April 23–24, 1970.

EARTH, WIND, AND FIRE. Earth, Wind, and Fire, a rock-and-roll group formed in Chicago, Illinois, in 1969, became the leading black pop music band of the 1970s. The group included, over time, the following individuals: Larry Dunn, Ralph Johnson, Philip Bailey, Maurice White, Al McKay, Fred White, Verdine White, Johnny Graham, Donald Whitehead, Michael Beale, Chester

Washington, and Andrew Woolfolk. Maurice White, the leader and creative genius of Earth, Wind, and Fire, was able to combine Latin sounds with soul rhythms and gospel harmonies. The group's messages were wholesome and edifying. Their first album, *Earth, Wind, and Fire* (1970), was a moderate success, but they then put together a string of albums that went platinum, including *Head to the Sky* (1974), *That's the Way of the World* (1975), *Open Our Eyes* (1976), and *All 'n All* (1978). *I Am* (1979), *Raise* (1981), and *Powerlight* (1983) were still popular but less successful. Earth, Wind, and Fire's last hit single was 1983's "Fall in Love With Me."

SUGGESTED READING: J. S. Roberts, "Earth, Wind, and Fire: Mystagogic Funk," *High Fidelity and Musical America*, 29 (January 6, 1978), 103–6.

EARTHQUAKE. The special effects of *Earthquake*, one of the more popular of the natural disaster movies of the 1970s, were state of the art, with dams cracking and giving way, water levels rising precipitously, buildings collapsing, fires blazing, pavement heaving, and the earth crinkling into cracks, chasms, and crevices. The film stars Charlton Heston, Ava Gardner, George Kennedy, Genevieve Bujold, Richard Roundtree, and Marjoe Gortner as an ensemble cast of people trying to cope with a horrific earthquake in Los Angeles, California. At the time, critics considered *Earthquake* to be the best of the decade's disaster films.

SUGGESTED READING: *New York Times*, November 16, 1974.

EASTERTIDE OFFENSIVE. During the presidential election of 1968, Republican candidate Richard Nixon* hinted to voters that if he were elected, he possessed the diplomatic skills to negotiate an end to the Vietnam War,* a "peace with honor" as he called it. After he was inaugurated president in January 1969, Americans expected him to live up to his promise. With the assistance of his major advisors, Nixon developed what became known as Vietnamization,* the steady withdrawal of U.S. troops from South Vietnam and the handing of the war over to the South Vietnamese. In August 1969, Nixon began implementing Vietnamization by withdrawing 25,000 U.S. combat troops. By the end of 1970, he had reduced the U.S. troop commitment in South Vietnam from 543,000 soldiers to 334,000.

It was obvious to the North Vietnamese, however, that the Army of the Republic of South Vietnam was not ready to pick up the combat slack. Late in 1970, with Vietnamization in full gear, the North Vietnamese began planning an all-out assault on South Vietnam. Their goals were what they had been ever since the Geneva Accords of 1954 had divided the country: expulsion of the United States from South Vietnam, overthrow of the government of South Vietnam, and reunification of North and South Vietnam into one country under a Communist regime.

Le Duan, a prominent North Vietnamese leader, visited Moscow in the spring of 1971 to secure heavy weapons supplies. North Vietnam wanted to break the military stalemate in South Vietnam and, with a major victory, perhaps help defeat Nixon's reelection bid in 1972, leaving the White House open to a more moderate, even antiwar Democratic president. Throughout 1971 the Soviet Union provided heavy supplies—trucks, surface-to-air (SAM) missiles, tanks, and artillery—to prepare the North Vietnamese Army (NVA) and Vietcong for the attack.

The offensive began on March 30, 1972. Three North Vietnamese divisions, strengthened by T-54 Soviet tanks, attacked across the Demilitarized Zone and along Highway 9 out of Laos, with Hue as their objective. Three more North Vietnamese divisions attacked Binh Long Province, captured Loc Ninh, and surrounded An Loc. Other North Vietnamese troops attacked Kontum in the Central Highlands. Finally, two North Vietnamese divisions took control of several districts in Binh Dinh along the coast of the South China Sea. Quang Tri Province was lost by the end of April 1972.

But at that point the tide turned. South Vietnamese (ARVN) troops held their positions twenty-five miles north of Hue, and the NVA was unable to take Kontum and An Loc. President Nixon had already begun bombing North Vietnam again, but on May 8, 1972, he mined Haiphong Harbor* and several other North Vietnamese ports. Nixon also unleashed a merciless B-52 bombing campaign on North Vietnamese and Vietcong forces on both sides of the seventeenth parallel. Fighting continued throughout the summer, with the ARVN launching a counteroffensive that recaptured Quang Tri Province. North Vietnam had no choice but to call off the offensive.

The Eastertide Offensive had failed. North Vietnam suffered more than 100,000 killed, leaving it in no position to continue offensive operations against South Vietnam. Nixon's bombing campaign, known as Operation Linebacker, had so devastated the North Vietnamese Army that it would take them several years to regroup and prepare for another offensive. They still controlled more territory in South Vietnam than before, however, and they felt they were in a stronger bargaining position at the Paris negotiations. They also knew that it was only a matter of time. If Nixon continued withdrawing U.S. troops, and the corrupt South Vietnamese government remained in place, North Vietnam would simply have to wait a few years to rebuild its army before launching another offensive. That final offensive succeeded in overthrowing South Vietnam and reunifying Vietnam in the spring of 1975.

SUGGESTED READINGS: Ngo Quang Truong, *The Easter Offensive of 1972*, 1980; G. H. Turley, *The Easter Offensive: Vietnam 1972*, 1985.

EASTWOOD, CLINT. Clint Eastwood was born on May 31, 1930, in San Francisco, California. After high school, he worked as a lumberjack and then did a stint in the army. He played parts in a number of forgettable films during the late 1950s but secured a larger profile in the successful television western *Rawhide* during the early 1960s. At that time, John Wayne was entering his sixties, and the western genre was looking for a younger action hero to replace the Duke. Eastwood became that man because he had starred in a number of so-called Italian-made spaghetti westerns: *A Fistful of Dollars* (1964), *For a Few Dollars More* (1965), *The Good The Bad The Ugly* (1966), and *Hang 'Em High* (1968). In all four films Eastwood played the prototypical western hero: a loner willing to use violence to destroy evil.

Eastwood then transplanted the western hero to a new, modern setting—the crime-ridden American city. He first played the urban cop in *Coogan's Bluff* (1968), but Clint Eastwood became an American icon for his performances as San Francisco detective Harry Callaghan in *Dirty Harry** (1972), *Magnum Force* (1973), and *The Enforcer* (1976). He also played similarly recognizable western heroes in *High Plains Drifter* (1973) and *The Outlaw Josey Wales* (1976). Since then, both as an actor and as a director, Eastwood has broadened his range considerably, but film and pop culture history will no doubt remember him more for the cool, calculated violence he administered to bad cowboys and bad criminals. He won an Academy Award for directing *The Unforgiven* (1992), and his most recent directional effort is *Midnight in the Garden of Good and Evil* (1997).

SUGGESTED READINGS: Sondra Locke, *The Good, the Bad, and the Very Ugly*, 1997; Richard Schickel, *Clint Eastwood: A Biography*, 1996.

EHRLICHMAN, JOHN. John Ehrlichman was born in Tacoma, Washington, on March 20, 1925. He graduated from UCLA in 1948 and then earned a law degree at Stanford University in 1951. Ehrlichman practiced law privately and became active in Republican party politics in California. In 1960 he served as an advance man in Richard Nixon's* unsuccessful campaign for the presidency. Ehrlichman had a more elevated position—"tour director"—during Nixon's successful 1968 presidential campaign.

Along with H. R. Haldeman,* Ehrlichman was part of the so-called Teutonic Guard that insulated, or perhaps isolated, Richard Nixon throughout his presidency, including the period of the Watergate scandal.* He specialized in domestic affairs, which made him an intimate participant in many of the Watergate scandals. During his televised testimony before the Senate Watergate Committee, Ehrlichman blamed the entire Watergate fiasco and cover-up on White House counsel John Dean.* Ehrlichman resigned his White House post in 1973, and his "insider" role in the Watergate cover-up earned him eighteen months in federal prison. Since his parole from prison, Ehrlichman has spent his time as a communications consultant and writer. Among his many books are *The Company: A Novel* (1976) and *The Whole Truth* (1979).

SUGGESTED READING: John Ehrlichman, *Witness to Power: The Nixon Years*, 1982.

Sean A. Kelleher

ELECTION OF 1970. In 1968, Richard Nixon* became the first U.S. president since Franklin Pierce to win the White House without carrying either house of

Congress. When the dust had settled after the elections, the Democrats controlled the House of Representatives by a margin of 243 to 192; the Senate, 57 to 43. As for governorships, the Republicans had thirty-one of the fifty. President Nixon knew that he faced an uphill battle with the Democratic Congress, and he realized that antiwar movement activists* and moderate Americans alike expected him to make good on his pledge to find an honorable settlement to the Vietnam War.* When the 1970 congressional elections rolled around, the president hoped to be able to gain some ground on Capitol Hill.

It did not happen. Nixon did begin the phased withdrawal of U.S. troops from South Vietnam in the summer of 1969, but in April 1970 he had launched an invasion of Cambodia,* which had reignited the antiwar movement and subjected him to withering criticism in Congress. The elections of 1970 actually strengthened the Democrats. Although Republicans gained two seats in the Senate, the Democrats still controlled the upper chamber by 55 to 45. In the House of Representatives, Democrats actually gained nine seats, upping their majority to 252 to 183. They even managed to win eleven governorships, giving them control of twenty-nine state houses to the Republicans' twenty-one.

SUGGESTED READING: *New York Times*, November 4–7, 1970.

ELECTION OF 1972. Almost as soon as he had won the presidency in November 1968, Richard Nixon* began plotting his reelection in 1972. During the election campaign of 1968, he had been relentless in his claim that President Lyndon Johnson and the Democrats had managed the Vietnam War* badly, and that with better leadership (i.e., Richard Nixon), the war could be brought to an honorable, successful conclusion. The president realized that if he was to have any credibility in the election of 1972, he would need to have made the Vietnam War a part of the American past.

Not surprisingly, Vietnam was the obsession of Nixon's first term in office. And he did what he said he would do. Beginning in the spring of 1969, the president implemented a phased withdrawal of U.S. troops from South Vietnam. As he turned more and more of the war over to the South Vietnamese in a program he called Vietnamization,* Nixon witnessed a steady decline in the number of American troops, and casualties, in Vietnam. North Vietnam and the Vietcong were slow to compromise at the negotiating table, but as American troop levels declined, the Communists realized that they would soon have the upper hand anyway. By 1972, with the election approaching rapidly, Nixon was desperate to get a diplomatic agreement signed. He essentially conceded to all of North Vietnam's demands: the removal of all U.S. troops from Indochina, the right of North Vietnamese troops to remain in place in South Vietnam, and the right of the Vietcong to participate legally in the government in South Vietnam. In return, the United States was able to bring its prisoners of war* home. The fact that President Nixon had been willing to use B-52s so devastatingly against the North Vietnamese during the Eastertide Offensive* of 1972 helped the Communists decide to agree to peace one month before the presidential election.

While he was neutralizing Vietnam as a political issue, the president had also been careful to work on the economy as well. Richard Nixon had been around American politics long enough to understand that economics, not foreign policy, usually dictated election outcomes. His concerns were not unfounded. Prices were on the rise, boosted by Vietnam War budget deficits, declining productivity, and aging factories. The president had watched the consumer price index jump 4 percent in 1968, 5 percent in 1969, and 6.5 percent in 1970. But with the war winding down, the economy was slowing down. Unemployment leaped from 3.5 percent when Nixon took office to 6 percent in the spring of 1971. Stagflation,* an economy characterized by rising prices and slumping employment, had arrived, and Nixon needed to do something about it before the election.

The president also understood implicitly that the tired, tattered Republican rhetoric of federal spending cuts and balanced budgets would not be enough. Voters were not sophisticated enough, Nixon was convinced, to sort out the subtleties of macroeconomics; they would be quick, as they had always been, to blame the man at the top. Poor economies doomed reelection.

But none of his options was risk free. If he attacked the inflation problem by raising taxes and cutting government spending, unemployment would get worse. The president could not afford to go into the 1972 presidential campaign with unemployment moving up from 6 percent. But the downside of creating jobs through tax cuts and spending increases was more inflation.

Nixon and his advisors mulled over the problem throughout the spring of 1971. In the end, the president went with his political instincts. High unemployment was more likely than inflation to doom his reelection chances. Instead of cutting back on the federal budget, which he could have done as Vietnam War spending declined, the president inceased federal spending by pouring money into social programs. Just when the opportunity materialized to bring down federal spending, Nixon raised it to stimulate the economy.

On June 11, 1971, the president appeared before a national television audience and explained himself. In words that sent a shudder through conservative Republicans, the president announced, "I am a Keynesian." He was going to increase federal spending and the federal budget deficit. But he went after the inflation problem as well. Like a World War II Democratic bureaucrat, he imposed a ninety-day wage, price, and rent freeze across the entire economy. Three months later, in mid-September 1971, he launched phase two of his program, imposing government-regulated price, rent, and wage guidelines on the entire economy. Conveniently, the phase two controls would remain in effect until January 1, 1973, after which the economy would shift into a period of voluntary controls. By that time, he would be reelected.

While Nixon and the Republicans were taking care of every possibility, the Democrats were self-destructing. After the 1968 disaster in Chicago, Democrats had reformed their presidential nominating process to make sure voters in primary elections had more power and professional politicians in smoke-filled rooms had less. As a result, Senator George McGovern* of South Dakota, one of the most liberal congressmen in the United States, won the Democratic presidential nomination. For his vice-presidential running mate, McGovern selected Senator Thomas F. Eagleton of Missouri. The Democratic platform reflected McGovern's liberalism; he called for a unilateral U.S. withdrawal from Indochina; abolition of the draft; amnesty for all war resisters, draft dodgers, and absent-without-leave and deserted soldiers; and a guaranteed income to lift all Americans above the poverty line. The Republicans were going to have a field day with the Democratic proposals.

But a few weeks after the close of the Democratic party's national convention in Miami, enterprising reporters uncovered a salacious bit of news that threw McGovern's campaign into turmoil. Senator Thomas Eagleton had once been treated for a clinical depression, and the treatments had involved electroshock therapy. The stigma of mental illness was very powerful in 1972. Eagleton's medical history precipitated an intense debate about whether an individual who had suffered from mental illness was fit to serve as president of the United States. Instead of confronting the issue head on and standing behind Eagleton, McGovern waffled and eventually dropped him from the ticket, leaving tens of millions of Americans convinced that not only had he not done his homework before selecting Eagleton, he had no courage or loyalty either.

McGovern's replacement for Eagleton did not help much. He turned to R. Sargent Shriver, former head of the Peace Corps, and Shriver accepted the invitation. A brother-in-law to John F. Kennedy and Robert F. Kennedy, Shriver was young, energetic, and handsome, and many of the party faithful hoped he could bring some Kennedy luster to the campaign. By 1972, however, the Kennedy luster was darkening into tarnish. Senator Edward Kennedy's* escapade at Chappaquiddick in 1969, and his sleazy denials of wrongdoing, had given most Americans a healthy, new skepticism about the so-called Kennedy magic. By the time the campaign got under way full-time in September 1972, the McGovern-Shriver ticket was already aglow with an image of helpless, liberal ineptitude.

As he had been in 1968, former Alabama governor George Wallace* was the wild card. He had staged a surprisingly good showing then, taking votes away from Nixon in the Deep South and from Hubert Humphrey in the working-class suburbs of the North. In 1972 he had done well in several northern Democratic primaries, and both Democrats and Republicans speculated about how many votes his American Independent party would get. The speculation ended on May 15, 1972. While speaking at a political rally at a shopping center in Laurel, Maryland, Wallace was shot by would-be assassin Arthur Bremer. Although he survived the gunshot wounds, Wallace was paralyzed from the waist down and had to drop out of the race.

The Republican election campaign was a sure bet. Nixon called for an hon-

orable peace in Vietnam, reorganization of the federal government, welfare reform, and a strong foreign policy, and he condemned any notion of amnesty for
draft dodgers and the busing* of children to achieve racial integration. He also
subjected to national ridicule McGovern's call for a guaranteed income for
everyone and unilateral withdrawal from Vietnam. Throughout the spring, summer, and fall of 1972, Nixon's proposals resonated more clearly with voters than
McGovern's. Every poll gave the president enormous odds for victory.

Nothing more reveals the dark side of Richard Nixon—the paranoia at the
center of his identity—more than his behavior during the reelection campaign.
He created an atmosphere of fear and suspicion that inspired his underlings to
go to any lengths, even criminal lengths, to win the election. They carried out
dirty tricks* against Democratic candidates, broke into the Democratic party
headquarters at the Watergate hotel and office complex in Washington, D.C., in
order to discover campaign secrets (see Watergate scandal), and engaged in a
variety of frauds in raising a $50 million war chest for the election campaign.
Eventually, the Watergate scandal forced Nixon to resign the presidency, a first
in U.S. history.

But all that was nearly two years away. On November 7, 1972, Nixon administered a humiliating defeat to McGovern. The president won 47,169,911
votes (60.8 percent) to 29,170,383 (37.5 percent). Several splinter parties account for the rest of the votes. It was even worse in the electoral college, where
Nixon defeated McGovern by a vote of 520 to 17. Even then, however, Nixon
did not manage to turn Congress over to Republican control. Throughout his
presidency he presided over a divided government.

SUGGESTED READING: Theodore White, *The Making of the President 1972*, 1973.

ELECTION OF 1974. The congressional elections of 1974 were among the
most difficult and controversial in the history of the United States during the
twentieth century. President Richard Nixon* had won reelection in 1972, but he
still had not managed to secure control of Congress. In fact, he was the only
two-term president in American history never to gain control of at least one
house of Congress for his party. Going into the election of 1972, Democrats
controlled the House of Representatives by a margin of 252 to 183 and the
Senate by 55 to 45. Although Nixon had defeated Senator George McGovern*
by landslide proportions to win another term in the White House, Republicans
actually lost two seats in the Senate and won only nine in the House. With the
Vietnam War* no longer a divisive issue in the United States, the president
finally hoped to secure both houses of Congress for the Republican party.

His dream would never be realized. In August 1974, Nixon resigned the White
House over the Watergate scandal.* That was bad enough for the Republican
party, but the new president, Gerald Ford,* exacerbated public resentment by
granting Nixon a full pardon for any crimes he might have committed while
serving in the White House. Combined with the Arab oil boycott of 1973–1974,*
skyrocketing oil prices, and a dangerous inflationary spiral, the Nixon misad-

venture proved fatal to the Republican party in the congressional elections of 1974. The Democrats upped their majority in the House to 291 to 144, and they now controlled the Senate by a 61 to 39 margin. Not since the Great Depression had one party so thoroughly dominated Capitol Hill.

SUGGESTED READING: *Newsweek*, November 18, 1974.

ELECTION OF 1976. In the presidential election of 1976, President Gerald Ford* faced the all-but-impossible task of being elected to the White House in his own right. A longtime Republican Congressman from Michigan, Ford was the ultimate Washington insider, and he had never been elected president. In October 1973, when Vice President Spiro Agnew* had resigned from office after pleading no contest to federal charges of bribery and tax evasion, President Richard Nixon* had nominated Ford to replace him. The Senate confirmed the nomination, and Ford became vice president of the United States. Ten months later, when the president himself resigned in the shadow of the Watergate scandal,* Gerald Ford became the new president of the United States.

It was not an easy time to be a Republican. Although Ford's professional reputation was squeaky clean, Watergate and the associated Republican party scandals had left the party with a badly tarnished ethical reputation. The party faithful hoped that Ford would be able to buff up that image, but it would be an uphill battle. Ford had barely been in office before the early maneuvering for the 1976 presidential campaign started. He did not really have enough time to restore confidence in the party.

Nor did his first decision as president do him any good. Ford had barely taken the oath of office before finding himself in the middle of a political firestorm. Convinced that the Watergate scandal had to be placed permanently in the American past, Ford pardoned Nixon, rendering him immune from prosecution for any crimes he had committed while president of the United States. The press jumped on Ford for the decision, asking if Nixon should be above the law. Most Americans sided with the press, at least at the time. But Ford had decided that if the case continued through indictment, trial, conviction, appeal, and imprisonment, Watergate would be headlines for the rest of the decade, if not longer. He decided to end the controversy once and for all, but the politically expensive decision alienated millions of American voters.

The Nixon pardon was actually the least of Ford's problems. At the end of April 1975, South Vietnam fell to the North Vietnamese Army. The Vietnam War* was over, and the United States had lost. Ford, of course, bore little responsibility for that defeat, but as Harry Truman once said, "The buck stops here," and Ford was in charge when the collapse occurred. News broadcasts of jammed helicopters flying off the roof of the U.S. embassy in Saigon telecast to the world the undeniable fact that the United States was fleeing South Vietnam. American foreign policy credibility disintegrated around the world.

Ford also faced daunting economic problems. The Arab oil boycott of 1973–1974* had triggered an inflationary spiral, and subsequent increases in international oil prices by members of the Organization of Petroleum Exporting Countries* had only made it worse. The American economy was trapped in stagflation*—inflation combined with unemployment. As huge volumes of American dollars went overseas to pay for oil, consumer spending at home declined, as did production and employment. Ford faced an impossible dilemma. If he decided to work on unemployment by cutting taxes, easing interest rates, and raising government spending, he risked exacerbating the inflation problem. If, on the other hand, he tried to work on inflation by increasing taxes, cutting spending, and raising interest rates, he faced the possibility of sending the country into a depression. Although Gerald Ford had certainly not created stagflation in the 1970s, he was destined to become one of its political victims.

Finally, Ford had become, in some sense, the national laughing stock. A penchant for putting his foot in his mouth, as well as a series of widely televised falls, had made him fodder for political humorists. Lyndon Johnson, once frustrated by Ford's inability to grasp the nuances of a political situation back in the 1960s, told a friend, "Jerry Ford must have played too many football games at Yale without a helmet on." *Saturday Night Live** comedian Chevy Chase was especially good at satirizing and mimicking Ford.

The Democrats seemed a shoo-in unless some horrendous scandal or political gaff destroyed their campaign. Plenty of Democratic candidates were lusting after the nomination. Senators Hubert Humphrey of Minnesota, Walter Mondale of Minnesota, Edward Kennedy* of Massachusetts, George McGovern* of South Dakota, and Edmund Muskie of Maine all wanted the nomination, as did Governor Jimmy Carter* of Georgia. A political unknown from a state with little influence, Carter seemed the most unlikely of the bunch, but he surprised everyone, starting his campaign earliest by winning the Iowa presidential caucuses even before the New Hampshire primary, gaining enormous media attention, and then preaching ad nauseum that he was an "outsider," not part of the Washington, D.C., establishment that had brought the country to such dismal circumstances. In making that case, he was essentially arguing that people like Humphrey, Muskie, McGovern, and Kennedy were little better than the Republican scoundrels who lived their lives inside the beltway. The argument resonated well among Democrats, and Jimmy Carter won the nomination.

Under normal circumstances, Gerald Ford should have had the GOP nomination locked up. After all, he was a sitting president and the titular head of his party. But few Republicans thought he could be reelected. There was hardly an ounce of political charisma in his body; American foreign policy was in disarray; and the economy was in a shambles. Republican conservatives began touting the merits of Ronald Reagan,* the former governor of California, who had all the charisma Ford lacked. At the Republican nominating convention in the summer of 1976, conservatives even tried to talk Ford into accepting the vice-presidential spot on a Reagan ticket. Ford gave the idea serious consideration, if for no other reason than the fact that he had always been a loyal party member.

But he was also the president of the United States and a lifelong politician, and voluntarily surrendering the most powerful and prestigious political office in the world would send out a disturbing message: that even the president himself was not good enough for the office. Ford would have none of it. He accepted the Republican nomination.

The election itself was relatively uneventful. Democrats charged Republicans with presiding over the most corrupt presidential administration in U.S. history and letting the economy degenerate precipitously. Republicans tried to blame the big-spending Democratic Congress for America's plight. Still, given the problems in which the country was mired, the election proved surprisingly close. Some analysts believe that President Ford actually lost the election during a televised debate when he said, "The Soviet Union does not dominate eastern Europe." He meant to say, "The Soviet Union does not dominate the spirit of eastern Europe." The controversy cost Ford votes in the white ethnic communities of the Midwest. Jimmy Carter won by a narrow margin in the popular vote—40,828,587 (50.1 percent of the total) to Ford's 39,147,613 (48.0 percent). The Electoral College margin was somewhat broader—297 to 240.

It was a different story, however, in the congressional elections. There the voters overwhelmingly expressed their dissatisfaction with the Republican party. When Jimmy Carter entered the White House on January 20, 1977, the Democrats enjoyed a 291 to 142 margin in the House of Representatives and a 62 to 38 majority in the Senate. Not since the Great Depression had one party so thoroughly dominated the federal government.

SUGGESTED READING: *New York Times*, November 4–8, 1976.

ELECTION OF 1978. Two years after his election to the White House, President Jimmy Carter* and the Democrats were in trouble. They had been swept into power in 1976 at the height of American bitterness over Richard Nixon* and the Watergate scandal,* and many pundits wondered whether the Republican party would ever be able to recover from the scandal. Carter came into the White House with a huge Democratic majority in Congress—291 to 142 in the House of Representatives and 62 to 38 in the Senate. Democrats controlled the nation's governorships by 38 to 12. It was an auspicious beginning.

During the next two years, Carter had been able to do nothing with those majorities. The economy was bogged down in a serious case of stagflation* (simultaneous unemployment and inflation), and the federal government seemed powerless to make things right. Dissatisfied voters still left the Democrats in charge of Congress, but there could be no doubt after the congressional elections of 1978 that America was turning toward the right. Republicans gained three seats in the Senate to make the Democratic majority 59 to 41 there; they gained six governorships, narrowing the Democratic lead to 32 to 18; and they picked up fifteen seats in the House, reducing the Democratic majority there to 276 to 159. The Democratic majorities, of course, were still formidable, but the tide was turning. Just how much of a change would take place would not become evident until 1980, when Americans put Republican Ronald Reagan* in the White House.

SUGGESTED READING: *Newsweek*, November 20, 1978.

ELLSBERG, DANIEL. Daniel Ellsberg was born April 7, 1931, in Chicago, Illinois, to a well-educated, successful family. He graduated with highest honors from Harvard in 1952, where he majored in economics. Ellsberg then completed several tours of duty in the Marine Corps. After mustering out of the corps, he joined the Rand Corporation, a California think tank, where he specialized in the mathematics of nuclear warfare. In August 1964, at the height of the Gulf of Tonkin controversy, Ellsberg joined the staff of Secretary of Defense Robert McNamara. A self-confessed "company man," Ellsberg wrote speeches, memos, and policy letters supporting the Vietnam War,* even though his doubts about the controversy escalated with increasing U.S. troop levels.

In 1967, when McNamara's own doubts about the war were deepening, the secretary of defense named Ellsberg to a research team to draft a special Pentagon study—an eyes-only, in-house history of the war in Vietnam. Ellsberg eventually concluded that the Vietnam War had escalated out of control because "no American president, Republican or Democrat, wanted to be the President who lost the war." By 1968 Ellsberg was supplying antiwar material to Senator Robert Kennedy, who was running for the Democratic presidential nomination. He also advised Henry Kissinger,* soon to become President Richard Nixon's* naitonal security advisor.

Severe guilt feelings about his own role in Vietnam plagued Ellsberg, and in 1969 he began surreptitiously making xeroxed copies of the Pentagon history and taking them home with him. In an attempt to absolve himself of some of the guilt he was feeling, Ellsberg in the fall of 1969 handed the documents over to Senator J. William Fulbright, chairman of the Senate Foreign Relations Committee. Dependent upon Pentagon contracts and worried about Ellsberg's increasingly anti-Vietnam posture, Rand let him go in 1969. Ellsberg then joined the Center for International Studies at the Massachusetts Institute of Technology.

It was not long before Ellsberg decided that the Senate Foreign Relations Committee was moving too slowly on his information. The 1970 U.S. invasion of Cambodia* enraged Ellsberg, and when South Vietnamese forces invaded Laos in 1971, widening the war, Ellsberg decided to go public. He provided the so-called Pentagon Papers* to the *New York Times*. The *Times* began publishing the documents in June 1971, and when the Nixon administration managed to get an injunction against the *Times*, the *Washington Post* and the *Boston Globe* finished publishing them. At the end of June, the U.S. Supreme Court lifted the anti-publication injunction, arguing that it was an unconstitutional violation of the First Amendment.

Federal government prosecutors indicted Ellsberg for illegal possession of government documents and for exploiting government documents for personal use. At the same time, Nixon administration operatives, intent on destroying Ellsberg's reputation, ransacked the offices of Ellsberg's psychiatrist, hoping to find damaging information. On May 11, 1973, a federal judge threw out all charges against Ellsberg. The judge, Matthew Byme, greatly resented Nixon's attempt to influence his decision by offering to name him J. Edgar Hoover's successor as head of the Federal Bureau of Investigation. Ellsberg then became even more active in the antiwar movement.* Since then, Ellsberg has committed himself to the pacifist cause. He lectures widely and today is affiliated with the Nuclear Age Peace Foundation.

SUGGESTED READINGS: Daniel Ellsberg, *Papers on the War*, 1972; John Ricks, "Daniel Ellsberg," in *Historical Dictionary of the Vietnam War*, ed. James S. Olson, 1988; Peter Schrag, *Test of Loyalty*, 1981.

EMPLOYEE RETIREMENT INCOME SECURITY ACT OF 1974. Until the years after World War II, the luxury of retirement was confined to a privileged few in the United States. Even the Social Security system, launched in 1935, was designed to provide old-age pensions for the tiny number of Americans who reached the age of sixty-five. When the Social Security Act was passed, the average life span in the United States was only fifty-seven. Most people never even reached Social Security retirement age.

All that changed after World War II. The rise of antibiotics all but eliminated deadly infectious diseases, reducing mortality rates and increasing life spans. Improved nutrition had the same effect. Large numbers of Americans began to contemplate the possibility of retirement, but many in the middle class realized that Social Security benefits would not enable them to maintain their standard of living after they had stopped working.

Consequently, during the 1950s and 1960s, private pension plans in the United States proliferated dramatically. By 1970 there were more than 300,000 of those plans in operation around the country, and they constituted the life savings of millions of Americans. Corporate pensions plans were also ripe for abuse. Many companies looked longingly on the mounting volumes of cash accumulating in employee retirement accounts, and companies in financial trouble often raided those funds. Early in the 1970s, when the country slipped into recession, it became clear that many of those plans were economically vulnerable, whether to the ups and downs of the business cycle, poor management decisions, fraud, or greedy companies anxious to find new sources of revenue. Large numbers of working-class Americans, represented by labor unions, and middle-class white-collar workers began demanding federal legislation to protect retirement accounts.

The failure of a number of those plans in the early 1970s, which left retirees with nothing to live on, prompted congressional action, and in 1974 Congress passed the Employee Retirement Income Security Act. The legislation was signed into law by President Gerald Ford* on September 2, 1974. It set the date of January 1, 1976, as the deadline by which all private pension programs would have to be brought under federal control. It also provided a federal reinsurance program for failed retirement plans and set standard federal regulations for all plans.

SUGGESTED READING: D. G. Carlson, "Responding to the Pension Reform Law," *Harvard Business Review* 52 (November 1974), 133–44.

ENEMIES LIST. The "enemies list" was a term given to a plan in the Richard Nixon* administration to discredit and punish people considered to be political enemies of the president. The original list of enemies, sent in June 1972 by Charles Colson* to John Dean,* included the names of twenty people thought to be most actively opposed to the Nixon administration, including CBS news correspondent Daniel Schorr and actor Paul Newman. Subsequent lists were much longer, and it was Dean's responsibility to systematize the several lists sent to him and to categorize the names according to the level of perceived threat to the administration. These subsequent lists included politicians (such as Edward Kennedy*), federal bureaucrats, business leaders, academics, labor leaders, journalists, and individuals who had very little connection to politics: Steve McQueen, Gregory Peck, Joe Namath, and Barbra Streisand.* Many of the enemies reported that they had been subjected to phone taps, IRS audits, FBI investigations, suspension of federal funds, burglaries, mail interception, and corporate contract problems. The very existence of such a list stands as stark evidence of the paranoia that engulfed the Nixon administration, which created the poisoned atmosphere that gave rise to the Watergate scandal.*

SUGGESTED READINGS: Jonathan Schell, *The Time of Illusion*, 1976; Marvin Miller, *The Breaking of a President 1974: The Nixon Connection*, 1975.

Robert L. Perry

ENERGY CRISIS. Although there were serious concerns during the 1920s about future energy supplies in the United States, the real energy crisis of the twentieth century occurred during the 1970s and 1980s. The invention of the internal combustion engine early in the 1900s had revolutionized the domestic economy. That change and the decision to switch naval fuel from coal to petroleum just after World War I combined to make oil the single most important commodity in the world economy. Until the 1950s, domestic production had satisfied American energy needs, but cheap energy prices spawned a wasteful, consumption-oriented economy. Beginning in the 1950s, cheap oil from the Persian Gulf region gradually undermined American production. It was cheaper to produce Persian Gulf oil than domestic oil so, while American production dropped, consumption continued to climb. The crunch came after the Yom Kippur War* of 1973. Upset about the level of American support for Israel, the Arab nations instituted a boycott of oil to the United States (see Arab oil boycott of 1973–1974). Oil shortages appeared immediately, oil prices skyrocketed, and the American economy entered a decade-long period of stagflation*—high prices combined with high unemployment.

The two political parties in the United States debated how to solve the energy crisis. Democrats, because of their working-class and lower-class constituencies, wanted to make sure that oil prices stabilized, so they emphasized price controls, rationing, and energy-saving measures. Those themes epitomized the presidential administration of Jimmy Carter* (1977–1981). The Republicans were more concerned about increasing the supplies of oil, so they emphasized the need to eliminate price controls on domestic oil to encourage production. Those policies characterized the administrations of Richard Nixon* (1969–1974), Gerald Ford* (1974–1977), and Ronald Reagan* (1981–1989). In the end, however, the United States did not develop a comprehensive energy policy. Because of increases in global supplies and price-induced reductions in demand, oil prices began to fall early in the 1980s. Once again, Americans were lulled into a sense of complacency. Not until 1990, when Iraq invaded Kuwait, did the United States once again worry about the supply and price of oil. That concern led to the United States–United Nations–Iraqi War of 1991.

SUGGESTED READING: David Yergin, *The Prize*, 1991.

ENVIRONMENTAL MOVEMENT. Although the environmental movement really gained political momentum during the 1970s, particularly after the Earth Day* demonstrations in April 1970, it had its origins in the political activism of the 1960s. The godmother of the movement was Rachel Carson, a biologist whose bestselling book *Silent Spring* (1962) captured the imagination of President John F. Kennedy and millions of other Americans. An attack on the use of chemical fertilizers and pesticides by farmers, it pointed out the potentially harmful effects of these on animals and humans. *The Saturday Review* called the book "a devastating, heavily documented, relentless attack upon human carelessness, greed, and irresponsibility." Because of the debate created by this book, Kennedy ordered an investigation into the problem. In May 1963, the President's Science Advisory Committee agreed with the findings in *Silent Spring*, which this led to the banning of several dangerous chemicals, including DDT.

From that point on, the environmental movement steadily gained momentum. Special interest groups like the Environmental Defense Fund appeared to lobby for a cleaner environment through federal government industrial standards. In 1963 Congress had passed clean air legislation that provided $95 million in grants to assist local governments in developing programs to reduce air pollution. Air pollution was one of the leading environmental problems, and the primary culprit was auto emissions. Subsequent legislation (the Clean Air Act Amendments of 1965) authorized the federal government to set auto emission standards and launch research programs to reduce sulfur dioxide emissions. The Air Quality Act of 1967 greatly expanded federal control and research programs by appropriating more than $550 million. In March 1970 Senator Edmund Muskie, a Democrat from Maine, challenged the automobile industry to engage in what he called a "forced technology" and reduce harmful emissions by 90 percent. Under Muskie's sponsorship, Congress passed the Clean Air Act of 1970.* It constituted a $1.1 billion program that required 1975 automobiles to reduce carbon monoxide and hydrocarbon emissions by 90 percent. Also, 1976 automobiles had to emit 90 percent less of the nitrogen oxides.

Some environmentalists also began preaching dire macroenvironmental consequences for the world. In April 1968 a group of thirty scientists, educators, economists, humanists, industrialists, and national and international civil servants gathered in the Italian capital to consider the future of the world economy. Out of their meeting emerged the Club of Rome,* a group committed to keeping the world informed about the state of the global economy and environment. Between 1969 and 1972, the Club of Rome conducted what it called the Project on the Predicament of Mankind. Using computer models and assuming no change in population growth rates, the members of the Club of Rome predicted an ecological and economic disaster in the early decades of the twenty-first century. They warned that exponential population growth combined with continued industrialization would eventually send the world economy into a tailspin and lead to mass starvation and global suffering. The only answer, they argued, was the establishment of limits to world growth. During the late 1960s and early 1970s, when the environmental movement in the United States was especially strong, the apocalyptic predictions of the Club of Rome found a sympathetic audience.

At the height of the environmental movement in 1969, President Richard Nixon* proposed a series of laws that culminated in the Environmental Policy Act of 1969. The law required the federal government to direct each of its agencies to develop an environmental protection policy and also demanded that environmental impact studies be conducted before the implementation of any new government program. The law created a Council on Environmental Quality to serve as an advisory body on environmental concerns. Nixon staffed the Council on Environmental Quality in 1970, but since then its recommendations have had little impact on federal policy.

In 1971, responding to growing political pressure, President Nixon proposed and Congress created the Environmental Protection Agency (EPA), an independent government agency designed to promote environmental protection. The EPA was charged with coordinating federal environmental policy and activities, as well as enforcing federal regulations concerning air and water quality, use of herbicides, disposal of chemical and radioactive waste materials, and the use of pesticides. The EPA has been especially active in imposing vehicle exhaust standards on the automobile industry. By 1980, less than a decade after its creation, the Environmental Protection Agency had 10,000 employees and was on its way to becoming the federal government's largest regulatory agency.

The EPA has often been caught between the demands of business and labor for economic growth and the demands of environmentalists for protecting the environment. Because of the country's economic plight during the 1970s, the environmental movement became particularly controversial. Nuclear energy was one primary example. Because of the energy crisis* in the 1970s, the nuclear energy industry held out atomic energy power plants as the answer to petroleum shortages. Many environmentalists, on the other hand, claimed that an accident at a nuclear power plant could cause permanent, deadly radioactive pollution of an entire region. In 1979, when an accident occurred at the Three Mile Island* nuclear power plant outside Harrisburg, Pennsylvania, environmentalists received enormous free publicity for their campaign. The Alaska pipeline* was another example. The discovery of huge oil reserves at Prudhoe Bay, Alaska, promised to ease the energy crisis, but getting the oil to market required the construction of a huge pipeline across the state, a project bitterly opposed by environmentalists.

In many instances, the environmental movement made strange bedfellows out of labor unions and corporations. When environmentalists proposed limits to economic growth, corporations objected because of lost profits and labor unions protested because of lost jobs. The environmental movement confronted a powerful coalition of labor unions and large corporations who jointed hands to promote economic expansion. That issue still characterizes the relationship today among labor unions, corporations, and environmentalists.

The environmental movement was without doubt the most powerful political campaign of the 1970s. The annual celebrations of Earth Day on April 22 each year brought between 20 and 30 million Americans out to clean up their communities. Municipal governments launched recycling programs to cut down on waste, and critics charged that the United States, with 6 percent of the world's population, consumed one-third of the world's resources. Special interest groups, such as Greenpeace and the Audobon Society, exploded in membership. Their commitment was to make sure that Americans understood the environmental consequences of public and private policy decisions.

SUGGESTED READINGS: Janet Foster, *Working for Wildlife: The Beginning of Preservation in Canada*, 1978; William Leiss, *The Domination of Nature*, 1972; Alfred A. Marcus, "The EPA," in *The Politics of Regulation*, ed. James Q. Wilson, 1980; Roderick Nash, ed., *The American Environment: Readings in the History of Conservation*, 1968; Donald Worster, *Nature's Economy: A History of Ecological Ideas*, 1994.

EQUAL EMPLOYMENT OPPORTUNITY ACT OF 1972. The Equal Employment Opportunity Act of 1972 was passed in response to the demands of civil rights activists that job discrimination on the basis of race, religion, national origins, and sex be permanently eliminated. Title VII of the Civil Rights Act of 1964 had already outlawed such discrimination in the federal government and in private businesses working on government contracts and had established the Equal Employment Opportunity Commission (EEOC) to enforce the law by investigating charges of discrimination. With passage of the Equal Employment Opportunity Act of 1972, Congress expanded the reach of Title VII to include state and local governments and educational institutions.

Although the original EEOC budget anticipated 2,000 cases a year, the commission actually investigated 23,000 cases of employment discrimination in 1971, 49,000 in 1973, 71,000 in 1975, and more than 150,000 in 1980. The EEOC also played a key role in the development of affirmative action* programs designed to make up for past discrimination against certain groups. The EEOC issued employment guidelines that took on the force of law when federal courts upheld them. The defining case in sanctioning EEOC guidelines was *Griggs v. Duke Power Company** (1971), in which the Supreme Court upheld EEOC rules that companies could not require, as a standard of employment, a high school education or a certain minimum score on general intelligence tests if neither could be demonstrated as critically important to job performance. Such standards had the effect of disqualifying large numbers of black applicants.

SUGGESTED READINGS: Joan Abramson, *Old Boys, New Women*, 1979; Cornelius Peck, "The EEOC: Developments in the Administrative Process 1965–1975," *Washington Law Review* 51 (1976), 831–65.

EQUAL RIGHTS AMENDMENT. The Equal Rights Amendment (ERA) was a bellweather issue for the women's movement* in the 1970s and 1980s. Its exact language was as follows:

1. Equality of rights under the law shall not be denied or abridged by the United States or by any state on account of sex;

2. The Congress shall have the power to enforce, by appropriate legislation, the provisions of this article;

3. This amendment shall take effect two years after the date of ratification.

The ERA was a proposed amendment to the U.S. Constitution that would guarantee both sexes equal treatment under the law. The ERA's purpose was, and is, to provide equality of opportunity through the Constitution and the legal system for those women who want to realize full personal and professional expectations within mainstream America. The ERA would help women break down barriers, improve their status, and contribute to their own welfare. It originated in 1916 under the direction of women's suffragist Alice Paul and was proposed in 1923; however, it failed to pass. An Equal Rights Amendment was proposed again in 1960, but it met with the same result. Finally in 1972, forty-nine years after it had begun its torturous legislative journey, the ERA was sent to the states for ratification.

The amendment ignited a serious, often bitter debate in the United States. Changes in race relations and sexual mores, governmental actions required to implement equality in school desegregation busing,* and affirmative action* became controversial and threatening to some people. Equality may have seemed simple to proratificationists, but to others it meant sexual permissiveness, the pill, abortion, living in communes, draft dodgers, unisex men who refused to be men, and women who refused to be women. It meant women who did not believe they could or should compete with men having to do so just because some unusual women could or wanted to. It also represented fear that men would feel freer to abandon family responsibilities and nothing would be gained in exchange. These issues arose during the debates in the unratified states and recession states and had not been sufficiently debated in those that had ratified early. Thus, the Equal Rights Amendment had gone farther in the ratification process than it had in the 1920s.

However, opposition and apathy to the ERA was stronger than its support. Phyllis Schlafly,* for example, formed a group called STOP ERA, to oppose the ERA. She argued that the ERA would hurt women. Nonetheless, the ERA was ratified by thirty-five states, three states short of becoming a constitutional amendment. Therefore, when the requisite thirty-eight states failed to ratify it by June 30, 1982, the Equal Rights Amendment became the first proposed amendment in post–Civil War constitutional history to expire formally after congressional passage.

The ERA failed for several reasons. The movement was unable to devise effective, persuasive appeals that had a clear distinction in the public's mind between "political and legal equality" and "sexual sameness." The failure to ratify was additionally a failure of access to national network channels of mass media communication. Modern mass communication research strategies were not fully used because of the lack of money and political and communication expertise.

Also, the ERA movement did not focus singlemindedly on ERA until it was too late. For example, the boycott of unratified states and campaigns against insurance companies should have started sooner. Similarly, the movement became complacent after Congress had approved the amendment; the supporters failed to realize how much opposition actually existed to an Equal Rights Amendment. Furthermore, only 25 percent of female legislators in the states and 45 percent of the men supported the ERA.

Even with these failures, the ERA still remains a source of solidarity and its defeat a symbol of patriarchal control. Few attempts appear to have been made to reach out to anti-ERA women based on an understanding that sisterhood should transcend the divisions created by varied responses to gender.

Even if the ERA is never resurrected and ratified, it will remain the symbol of the second women's movement just as the suffrage amendment has been for the first women's movement. The ERA's defeat in 1982 perpetuates the condition of unequal constitutional status which generations of women have experienced because of their being omitted from the federal constitution and the Bill of Rights. The ERA would have provided, on a national basis, an unmistakable mandate of the highest order for equal rights under the law. It would have given women a clear route to seek redress against sexual bias, provided impetus for the enforcement of existing antidiscrimination laws and the completion of legislative reform, and given the courts a clear basis for dealing with gender-based discrimination.

Furthermore, the ERA was more than a mandate for changing laws and a defense weapon or legal recourse. It was a symbol, which by dramatizing a need for equality, legitimizes that need. The very act of emancipation defines one's slavery. Legal recognition of freedom makes one sensitive to violations of one's freedom previously ignored or fearfully suppressed.

In conclusion, the ERA would have united women, raised their consciousness, and increased their perception of themselves as an oppressed group at the very moment of their theoretical liberation. Liberation itself, as Herbert Marcuse has said, depends upon the consciousness of servitude. Kirsten Amundsen has defined the precondition for any liberation struggle as awareness, self-respect, and determination, which the ERA provided; it would have created awareness of discrimination, justified self-respect, and initiated determination by making legal recourse a realistic solution. Ratification of the ERA would have symbolized a public commitment to equal rights for women, but it would not by itself accomplish any of the major goals which supporters of equal rights sought for women. The ERA can be a tool for change, but it is a tool that must be used properly.

SUGGESTED READINGS: Mary Francis Berry, *Why ERA Failed: The Political Fortunes of the Equal Rights Amendment*, 1986; Joan Hoff-Wilson, *Rights of Passage: The Past and Future of the ERA*, 1986; Donald G. Mathews and Jane Sherron De Hart, *Sex, Gender, and the Politics of ERA: A State and the Nation*, 1990.

Charlotte Meadows

ERVIN, SAM. Sam J. Ervin, Jr., was born on September 27, 1896, in Morganton, North Carolina. He attended the University of North Carolina, fought and was wounded in battle during World War I, and earned a law degree from Harvard in 1922. After a brief stint in the state legislature in 1925, where he vociferously opposed legislation to ban the teaching of evolution in North Carolina public schools, Ervin returned to the practice of law. He became a county court judge in 1935 and a superior court judge in 1937. Ervin served a term in the House of Representatives before being appointed in 1948 to the North Carolina Supreme Court. He was serving as a justice there in 1954 when the governor named him to fill the U.S. Senate seat vacated by the death of Clyde Hoey.

During his tenure in the U.S. Senate, Ervin earned a reputation as an expert on the Constitution and one who interpreted it narrowly. He led the fight to censure Senator Joseph McCarthy during the Red Scare of the 1950s, and he opposed civil rights legislation in the 1960s. The Constitution, Ervin once claimed, should "be taken like mountain whisky—undiluted and untaxed."

Ervin became a household figure during the 1970s when he chaired the Senate Select Committee on Presidential Campaign Activities, known popularly as the Watergate committee (*see* Watergate Scandal). Ervin's razor-sharp mind hid behind the homespun, country lawyer demeanor. The hearings were nationally televised in 1973 and set in motion the legal process that led to the resignation in August 1974 of President Richard Nixon.* Through it all, Ervin presided with grace, wit, and integrity. He resigned his senate seat in 1974 and retired to Morganton. Sam J. Ervin, Jr., died on April 23, 1985.

SUGGESTED READINGS: Sam J. Ervin, Jr., *Preserving the Constitution*, 1985; *New York Times*, April 24, 1985.

ERVING, JULIUS. Julius Winfield Erving II was born on February 22, 1950, in East Meadow, New York. At Roosevelt High School, he earned academic and athletic honors and went to college at the University of Massachusetts. There he impressed coaches and professors with the quality of his mind and his ability to express himself. He was also an unprecedented phenomenon on the basketball court. After his junior year at Massachusetts, Erving decided to sign a professional contract, and he joined the Virginia Squires of the fledgling American Basketball Association (ABA). He made his mark on the ABA immediately, becoming rookie of the year in 1972. The next year, the Squires traded him to the New York Nets, where he lead the league in scoring. Although the ABA was considered quite inferior to the National Basketball Association (NBA), Erving was nevertheless highly regarded throughout the ranks of professional basketball. In 1974 and again in 1976, he was voted the ABA's most valuable player.

In 1976 the Nets sold Erving's contract to the NBA's Philadelphia 76ers. During his first year in the NBA, Erving was named to the NBA All-Star team. He was also voted most valuable player in the league in 1981. Erving received the nickname ''The Doctor'' because of his superlative talent. He was also the forerunner of the NBA superstars of the 1980s and 1990s, pioneering a role as the franchise player whose extraordinary skills clearly set him apart from even the best players in the rest of the league. Erving was also a man of consummate integrity. In 1986 he received his undergraduate degree from the University of Massachusetts, and he retired from the NBA in 1987, after being elected ten years in a row to the All-Star team. Since then, Erving has devoted himself to business and broadcasting pursuits.

SUGGESTED READINGS: Louis Sabin, *The Fabulous Dr. J: All Time All Star*, 1976; Josh Willken, *Julius Erving*, 1995.

EVITA. *Evita*, Andrew Lloyd Webber's hit musical of the late 1970s and 1980s, premiered in New York City on September 25, 1979, and put to music the life and career of Eva (Evita) Perón, wife of Argentina's famous political dictator Juan Domingo Perón. Perón served as president of Argentina from 1946 to his deposition in 1955. Cuban revolutionary Che Guevara narrates the musical. Although critics were initially somewhat hard on the play, it became a megahit at the box office. In 1997 Madonna, Antonio Banderas, and Jonathan Pryce starred in the film version of the play.

SUGGESTED READING: *New York Times*, September 26, 1979.

THE EXORCIST. This 1973 freakish religious horror is arguably the most upsetting movie ever made. William Peter Blatty adapted the screenplay from his own novel, which was loosely based on an allegedly real case of possession that happened in Mount Rainer, Maryland.

The film is set at Georgetown University in Washington, D.C., where actress Chris MacNeil (Ellen Burstyn) is working on a movie. Things go awry when her daughter (played by Linda Blair) interrupts her mother's party by urinating on the floor and announcing, ''You're going to die up there.'' From that point on, the film records the mother's consultations with doctors, neurosurgeons, and psychiatrists hoping to find somebody who understands what has happened to her daughter, Regan. Finally, she seeks out a skeptical Father Karras (Jason Miller) to perform an exorcism. The movie has been following him as well, and his inadequacy is highlighted when he admits to a lack of faith and blames himself for the recent loss of his mother. This sort of development lasts for more than half the film, so the actual exorcism gives the film a climactic ending. The church calls in holy man and experienced exorcist Father Merrin (Max von Sydow), and together they fight the demon, eventually prevailing at the cost of their own lives.

The violence and gore of *The Exorcist* are so intense that the film almost earned an X rating. The young Blair shouts disgusting obscenities throughout the film, throws up green vomit, turns her head around 360 degrees, stabs herself with a crucifix, and even forces her mother's head under her bloody nightgown. But the success of the film depends not on these shocking effects but more on the slow-moving scenes that develop character.

Because of this character development, which allowed Blair to horrify, Burstyn to deteriorate, and Miller to regain his faith, the film avoided the expected clichés of the horror genre. It is this aspect of the film that attracted the critics. *The Exorcist* earned ten Academy Award nominations, winning for Best Adapted Screenplay, an unprecedented event for any horror film.

SUGGESTED READING: *New York Times*, December 27, 1973.

Bradley A. Olson

F

FANTASY ISLAND. *Fantasy Island*, an ABC romantic drama of the 1970s, was patterned after *Love, American Style** and *The Love Boat.** *Fantasy Island* starring Ricardo Montalban as Mr. Roarke, the owner and mysterious guru of Fantasy Island, and Herve Villechaize as his dwarf assistant, premiered on January 28, 1978. The setting is a remote island resort where each guest can have one wish fulfilled. Two or three different stories make up each episode, and the wishes are always fulfilled: a frustrated salesman desperate to close one big deal, an over-the-hill batter wanting just one more last-inning home run, a frumpy housewife aching for romance, or a terminally ill man searching for a cure. Perhaps in the atmosphere of American life in the late 1970s, with the pains of the Watergate scandal,* stagflation,* and the Vietnam War* still resonating throughout the political system, Americans were more comfortable with fantasy than with reality. The last episode of *Fantasy Island* was broadcast on August 18, 1984.

SUGGESTED READING: Tim Brooks and Earle Marsh, *The Complete Directory to Prime Time Network and Cable TV Shows, 1946–Present*, 1995.

FEDERAL ACKNOWLEDGEMENT PROJECT. Beginning with the invasion of Alcatraz Island* by the Indians of All Tribes* in 1969, the red power* movement began to demand full civil rights for Indian people as well as the return of land fraudulently taken from the tribes during the nineteenth century. Throughout the 1970s, Indian rights activists kept up the campaign, one dimension of which was to provide increased economic, educational, and health benefits for Indian people. Large numbers of non-Indian people felt certain sympathies for Indian demands, and governments at the state and federal levels increased their levels of services.

They soon encountered, however, difficult questions. The vast majority of people claiming to be Indians are of mixed blood, with both Indian and non-

Indian ancestry. Many other people claim Indian ancestry even though they have difficulty proving that status. The federal government found itself with the challenge of determining which individuals really were eligible for government benefits as Indians.

Traditionally, the Bureau of Indian Affairs (BIA) had handled tribal petitions for official recognition on an ad hoc, case-by-case basis. Hundreds of tribes had long been recognized by congressional statutes as legal tribal entities, but many other Indian groups did not enjoy such status and the federal benefits accompanying them. In response to a congressional clamor in the 1970s for a more systematic approach to the problem, the BIA submitted its proposal to regulate the process. To receive government recognition and the accompanying benefits and responsibilities, the petitioning tribe had to meet seven criteria establishing a continuity from the past to the present through indisputable ethnic, cultural, and historical links to a particular geographical region:

1. The tribe has to be able to prove its existence as a functional entity from historical times to the present.

2. The tribe has to prove that its members inhabit a specific area as a community and have done so since historical times.

3. The tribe must prove that it has maintained political authority over its members as an autonomous entity throughout history until the present.

4. The tribe must provide a government document describing tribal membership requirements and tribal governing procedures.

5. The tribe must provide evidence that the tribal membership consists of people who have descended from historical tribal entity.

6. The tribe must show that its tribal members consist of individuals who are not simultaneously members of other tribes.

7. The tribe must show that it is not expressly terminated or forbidden by federal statute from participating in the federal-Indian relationship.

Initiated in 1978, this BIA enterprise assessed the claims of the dozens of tribes yet to be officially recognized as such by the federal government. In 1979 the BIA established the Federal Acknowledgement Project, today known as the Branch of Acknowledgement and Research, to evaluate petitions for federal recognition. At the time of the formal establishment of the Federal Acknowledgement Project, forty Indian tribes had applied to the BIA for recognition.

The process, however, proved cumbersome and controversial. Legal hassles, bureaucratic inertia, and unreasonable documentary requirements complicated and delayed the process. In addition to the forty original petitioners, another 124 petitions for recognition had been filed. By 1994, however, only ten tribes had received formal recognition: Grand Traverse Band of Ottawa and Chippewa in Minnesota (1980); the James Klallam Tribe of Washington (1981); the Tunica-Biloxi Indian Tribe of Louisiana (1981); the Death Valley Timbi-Sha Shoshone Band of California (1983); the Narragansett Indian Tribe of Rhode

Island (1983); the Poarch Band of Creeks in Alabama (1984); the Wampanoag Tribal Council of Gay Head, Massachusetts (1987); the San Juan Southern Paiute Tribe of Arizona (1990); the Snoqualmie Tribe of Washington (1993); and the Mohegan Tribe of Connecticut (1994). Frustrated with the time-consuming process, a number of other tribes have secured recognition directly through congressional statute, outside the Federal Acknowledgement Project. In 1994 the Mohegan Indians of eastern Connecticut became the 545th formally recognized American Indian tribe.

Indian activists today remain divided over the controversy. Some criticize the federal government, charging it with negligence at best or, at worst, a conspiracy to deny Indian people their legitimate rights to government benefits. Other Indians, however, especially those within already recognized tribal communities, believe that the government must maintain strict and high standards to guarantee that non-Indian peoples do not get a share of what certainly is a limited volume of available funds.

SUGGESTED READINGS: James S. Olson and Raymond Wilson, *Native Americans in the Twentieth Century*, 1984; Paul Prucha, *The Great White Father*, vol. 2, 1984; William W. Quinn, Jr., "Federal Acknowledgement of American Indian Tribes: The Historical Development of a Legal Concept," *American Journal of Legal History* 34 (October 1990), 331–64; Allogan Slagle, "Branch of Acknowledgement and Research," in *Native America in the Twentieth Century: An Encyclopedia*, ed. Mary B. Davis, 1994.

Mark Baxter

FIDDLER ON THE ROOF. *Fiddler on the Roof* is one of the most popular musicals in Broadway history. Based on the stories of Sholom Aleichem, it premiered at the Imperial Theater in New York City on September 22, 1964. Jerry Bock, Sheldon Harnick, and Joseph Stein composed the music; Harold Prince produced the musical; and Jerome Robbins directed and choreographed it. *Fiddler on the Roof* is the story of Tevye the Milkman and his family, who live in a small village in prerevolutionary Russia, where they are forced to deal with the challenges posed to their Jewish faith by heavy-handed oppression and the more benign forces of assimilation. Amidst all of the challenges, Tevye relies on tradition to anchor his life and interpret his world. *Fiddler on the Roof* continued on Broadway for more than eight years and 3,242 individual performances. Part of its stage success can be attributed to the talents of Zero Mostel, who played Tevye throughout much of the run on Broadway.

SUGGESTED READING: Kurt Ganzl, *The Encyclopedia of the Musical Theater*, 1994.

THE FISCHER-SPASSKY SHOWDOWN. In 1972 the Cold War,* for a brief time, boiled down to a chess match between American Bobby Fischer and Soviet world champion Boris Spassky. A child prodigy, Fischer had long been obsessed with bringing an end to the longtime Soviet domination of international chess.

After extended negotiations over remuneration, camera angles, and time, the match began with considerable international media attention. Fischer put together a series of stunningly brilliant games that left no doubt in anyone's mind that he was the best chess player in the world. For many American pundits, Fischer's victory was also proof of the superiority of capitalism and democracy over totalitarian communism.

SUGGESTED READING: George Steiner, *Fields of Force: Fischer and Spassky at Reykjavik*, 1972.

FISHING RIGHTS. During the 1960s and 1970s in the United States, the most conspicuous and controversial dimension of public life revolved around the issues of the civil rights movement.* Led by Martin Luther King, Jr., African Americans had launched the movement, but other minorities soon joined, including Hispanics, women, gays and lesbians, and Native Americans whose political activism became known as the red power* movement. While the civil rights demands of blacks, Hispanics, women, and homosexuals revolved around de jure and de facto discrimination, red power was a far more complicated political campaign. One of the items on the red power agenda was fishing rights. Marlon Brando first launched the movement in 1964 when he led a march on the state capitol in Olympia, Washington, to demand protection of Indian fishing rights.

During the 1970s, Native American activists engaged in a civil rights movement of their own, and like the campaigns of African Americans and Mexican Americans, they wanted to end the negative stereotyping of Indians in the media and discrimination at the ballot box and in employment. But Native American civil rights also included more unique concerns, one of which was fishing rights. Indian culture remained close to the environment in the 1970s, and during the 1800s and 1900s, when they had ceded land to the federal and state governments, many tribes had retained fishing rights on that land. Although treaties had extinguished their titles to the land, they retained fishing rights, much as non-Indian land owners can retain mineral rights when selling property. Native American activists believed that those fishing rights included fishing for sport, subsistence, and commercial purposes.

In the years after World War II, however, state governments often tried to apply local fish and game regulations to Indian tribes, subjecting Native Americans to existing prohibitions, season controls, and harvest limits. Part of the red power movement was aimed at protecting treaty-guaranteed rights to fisheries. Hank Adams, an Indian of Sioux and Assiniboine descent, formed the Survival of American Indians Association to protect fishing rights. He also engaged in civil disobedience to protest controls on Indian fishing. He focused his attention in 1968 on the Nisqually River near Franks Landing, Washington, where he protested state attempts to limit Indian net fishing. In January 1971, Adams was shot on the shore of the Puyallup River near Tacoma, where he had intentionally set an illegal fishing trap.

A number of non-Indian commercial and sports fishing lobbying groups ap-peared to make sure that Indian fishermen were subject to local regulations. Groups like S\SPAWN (Steelhead and Salmon Protection Action Now), STA (Stop Treaty Abuse), and PARR (Protect American's Rights and Resources) challenged court decisions upholding fishing rights and the Indians who exer-cised those rights. They charged that Indian overfishing was responsible for dwindling fish populations. Indians denied the charges, of course, and claimed that their fishing rights were equivalent to property rights. During the 1970s, the federal courts sided with the Indians. In *Department of Fish and Game v. Puyallup Tribe* in Washington, *Lac Courte Oreilles Band of Lake Superior Chip-pewa Indians v. Lester P. Voigt* in Wisconsin, and *United States v. Michigan* in Michigan, the courts upheld fishing rights as property rights exempt from state and local regulation. The rights had been reserved by the Indians during the treaty negotiation process and had never been granted by a state or federal government.

SUGGESTED READINGS: Fay G. Cohen, *Treaties on Trial: The Continuing Con-troversy over Northwest Indian Fishing Rights*, 1986; Robert Doherty, *Disputed Waters: Native Americans and the Great Lakes Fishery*, 1990; Anthony Gulig, "Fishing Rights," in *Encyclopedia of American Indian Civil Rights*, ed. James S. Olson, 1997; Gary D. Meyers, "Different Sides of the Same Coin: A Comparative View of Indian Hunting and Fishing Rights in the United States and Canada," *Journal of Environmental Law* 10 (1991), 67–121; Francis Paul Prucha, *American Indian Treaties: The History of a Polit-ical Anomaly*, 1994; Charles F. Wilkinson, *American Indians, Time and the Law*, 1987.

FIXX, JAMES. James Fixx, the reigning guru of physical fitness during the 1970s, was born in New York City on April 23, 1932. He graduated from Oberlin College in 1957 and went to work in the magazine business, serving in a variety of editorial posts for *The Saturday Review, McCall's, Life*, and *Hori-zon*. Although he came from a family with a history of heart disease—his father had his first heart attack at age thirty-five and died at age forty-three—Fixx was a chain-smoker and became seriously overweight. By 1967 he weighed 220 pounds. A tendon injury during a tennis match that year forced Fixx to consider rehabilitation, and he began walking and then jogging. That decision changed his life.

He ran his first race in 1970, finishing last among fifty runners, but the event exhilirated him. He continued running, quit smoking, and lost sixty-one pounds. In 1977 he wrote *The Complete Book of Running*, which became a huge hit and remained on the bestseller lists for more than a year. In the process Fixx became a sports icon, a national symbol for the virtues of physical fitness. His second book on running was entitled *Jim Fixx's Second Book of Running*.

While serving as the poster child of physical fitness, however, Fixx ignored warning signs of his own heart disease. Even though he complained to close friends of chest pains during exercise—a sure sign of angina and blocked cor-onary arteries—he continued to run, averaging from seven to ten miles per day, preaching the dogma that runners lived longer than other people. On July 21, 1984, during a long run in Vermont, Fixx suffered massive coronary and died.

SUGGESTED READINGS: Jim Fixx, *The Complete Book of Running*, 1977; *New York Times*, July 22, 1984; Randy Roberts and James S. Olson, *Winning Is the Only Thing: Sport in America Since 1945*, 1988.

FLACK, ROBERTA. Roberta Flack was born in Asheville, North Carolina, on February 10, 1939. She graduated from Howard University in 1958 and taught school for several years. Flack signed a contract with Atlantic Records in 1968, and her debut album, *First Take* (1969), was a moderate success. In 1971 she had a hit single, "You've Got a Friend," and in 1972 her single "The First Time Ever I Saw Your Face" reached number one on the pop charts. The song, which came from *First Take*, was also part of the sound track of Clint Eastwood's* film *Play Misty for Me*. The film resurrected *First Take* and propelled it to the top of the charts in 1972. She followed that success with a number-five hit single in 1972 ("Where Is the Love") and two number-one hits—"Killing Me Softly with His Song" (1973) and "Feel Like Makin' Love" (1974). She then took some time off but returned to the pop charts in 1978 with the hit "The Closer I Get to You." The success continued with such singles as "Making Love" (1982) and "Tonight I Celebrate My Love" (1983). Since then Flack has continued to record, tour, and produce.

SUGGESTED READING: Linda Altman, *Roberta Flack: Sound of Velvet Melting*, 1975.

FLEETWOOD MAC. Formed in London, England, in 1967, Fleetwood Mac was a successful rock-and-roll band of the 1970s and 1980s. Although Mick Fleetwood and John McVie were constants over the years, the personnel changed rapidly and at one time or another included Peter Green, Jeremy Spencer, Lindsey Buckingham, Christine Perfect, Danny Kirwan, Bob Welch, Stevie Nicks, Bob Weston, Billy Burnette, Rick Vito, Dave Mason, and Bekka Bramlett. At first a traditional British blues band, Fleetwood Mac continually reinvented itself, making the transition to commercially successful pop rock. They became immediately popular in Great Britain after appearing at the British Jazz and Blues Festival, and its "Black Magic Woman" was a hit single. *Fleetwood Mac in Chicago* (1971) was a moderately successful album in the United States, but with the addition of Stevie Nicks, their 1975 album *Fleetwood Mac* sold five million copies. Their next album, *Rumours* in 1977, was a spectacular success, selling more than seventeen million copies. It included the hit singles "Go Your Own Way," "Dreams," "Don't Stop," and "You Make Loving Fun." Their global concert tours were sellouts, and the band was one of the most popular of the era. They have not been so successful since then, but Fleetwood Mac continues to record and perform today.

SUGGESTED READING: Mick Fleetwood, *My Twenty-Five Years with Fleetwood Mac*, 1992.

FLOOD, CURTIS (CHARLES). Curtis "Curt" Flood was born on January 18, 1938, in Houston, Texas. The family moved to Oakland, California, in 1941, and during his youth Flood excelled as a baseball player. After graduating from high school in 1956, he signed a professional contract with the Cincinnati Reds and spent two years in the minor leagues. In 1958 the Reds sold his contract to the Saint Louis Cardinals. The Cardinals put him in center field, where he won seven Gold Glove Awards and earned a reputation as one of the best center fielders in the history of the game. He was also a fine hitter, accumulating a career batting average with Saint Louis of .293.

Flood's reputation as a player was soon overshadowed in historical significance by his role in destroying baseball's reserve clause. At the time, every professional baseball player's contract included the "reserve clause," which made him the exclusive property of one team until management decided to trade or release the individual from the contract. The reserve clause prevented players from marketing their skills to different teams. Flood likened the reserve clause to "modern-day slavery" and decided to test it in the courts.

He got his opportunity in 1969 when the Cardinals announced his trade to the Philadelphia Phillies. Flood publicly announced that he would not report to the Phillies, and he told baseball commissioner Bowie Kuhn that he would file a lawsuit accusing the National League of violating the antitrust laws by refusing to allow players to negotiate on the open market with several employers. Flood sat out the 1970 season. The case wound its way through the federal courts, and Flood lost at every stage. The Phillies traded him to the Washington Senators, and he played a few games there in the 1971 season before retiring. The Supreme Court finally heard the case and decided against Flood, arguing that professional baseball was not a form of interstate commerce and was therefore exempt from antitrust legislation. Eventually, of course, Flood's argument prevailed, and today professional baseball players, who are free to negotiate contracts with several teams, look to Flood as the forerunner of their liberation from the reserve clause. Today Curt Flood lives in Los Angeles where he manages his business interests.

SUGGESTED READINGS: Curt Flood, *The Way It Is*, 1970; David Whitford, "Curt Flood," *Sport* (December 8, 1986), 102–3.

FONDA, JANE. Jane Fonda was born on December 21, 1937, in New York City. Her father, Henry, was a well-known actor and her mother, Frances Seymour, was a socialite who, in the depths of clinical depression, committed suicide in 1950. She was the daughter of one of Hollywood's most visible and beloved actors—a man who also happened to be a somewhat distant parent—which forced upon Jane Fonda the need to carve out her own identity, one distinct from that of her family. At the same time, however, she was very interested in the film industry, and she soon found that her talents as an actress matched and even exceeded those of her father.

After attending Vassar College for two years, she appeared in her first stage role in 1954, opposite her father in a production of *The Country Girl* in Omaha, Nebraska. In 1958 she studied method acting under Lee Strasberg in the Actors' Studio. Her father, and most of the rest of Hollywood's veterans, viewed the "method" with contempt. In 1964 Fonda went to France, where she met and married director Roger Vadim, who tried to mold her into a sex symbol like his previous wife, Brigitte Bardot. He starred her in the *Circle of Love* (1964) and *Barbarella* (1968). The publicity posters for these films were popular pinups for American soldiers serving in the Vietnam War.* Fonda later regretted her nude scenes, explaining that she was "reacting against the attitude of puritanism I was brought up with."

Fonda was in Paris when the Vietnam War escalated, and there she learned about Indochina from the perspective of French history. It was quite clear to the French, who had been expelled from Indochina by Ho Chi Minh and the Vietminh, that the United States was badly confusing nationalism and communism in Vietnam, and Fonda absorbed her antiwar sentiments in Paris. During 1966 and 1967, she became disturbed at reports on French television that American planes were bombing Vietnamese villages and hospitals. Unhappy with her marriage and genuinely concerned about the war, she returned to the United States and worked with the Free Theater Association, which sponsored satirical antimilitary plays and skits in coffeehouses near bases all over America. She participated in demonstrations against the war throughout 1969 and 1970.

In late 1969 and early 1970, revelations of the My Lai massacre, which occurred in March 1968 and had resulted in the deaths of 498 Vietnamese civilians, further politicized Fonda. When groups like the Vietnam Veterans Against the War* assured her that My Lai was not an isolated incident, she decided to sponsor the Winter Soldier Investigation,* which convened in Detroit in February 1971. There a parade of more than one hundred veterans testified about war crimes they had either personally committed or witnessed in Vietnam. That same year Fonda reached the pinnacle of her profession for her performance in *Klute*, a film about a prostitute who is stalked by a serial murderer. She won an Oscar as Best Actress that year.

In the spring of 1972, when North Vietnam launched the Eastertide Offensive* against South Vietnam and President Richard Nixon* responded with massive B-52 bombings, Fonda's anger against U.S. military policy in Indochina escalated. In the summer of 1972, to protest the war more personally and more visibly, she traveled to Hanoi, visited with selected American prisoners of war,* and addressed all U.S. soldiers in Vietnam in a radio broadcast. In the speech, she conveyed her hatred of the war and her belief that it was an immoral act. She posed next to an antiaircraft gun used to shoot down American pilots, and journalists, comparing her to Tokyo Rose, dubbed her "Hanoi Jane." Her visit to North Vietnam earned her the wrath of American conservatives and visceral hatred from most Vietnam veterans, who believed that her visit to Hanoi was an act of treason.

After the end of the Vietnam War in 1975, Fonda continued her film career and her political activities. In 1978 she won her second Best Actress award from the Academy of Motion Picture Arts and Sciences, this time for her performance in *Coming Home*,* a film about the Vietnam War. Along with her husband Tom Hayden,* the founder of Students for a Democratic Society, she remained loyal to a number of liberal causes, including the civil rights movement* and the environmental movement.* During the 1980s, however, her personal interests became less political and more commercial. Her marriage to Hayden ended in divorce, and she produced and performed in *Jane Fonda's Workout Book*, a bestselling exercise book and video. In recent years, Fonda married media tycoon Ted Turner and moved to Atlanta, Georgia, and she has continued to market books and tapes on health and fitness. She also retired as an actress. In 1998, however, Fonda stirred up a political hornet's nest in Georgia when she allegedly charged that parts of Georgia were worse than Third World countries and that many of Georgia's children were starving to death.

SUGGESTED READINGS: Fred Lawrence Guiles, *Jane Fonda*, 1981; Nancy Zaroulis and Gerald Sullivan, *Who Spoke Up? American Protest Against the War in Vietnam, 1963–1975*, 1984.

FORD, BETTY (ELIZABETH). Elizabeth ''Betty'' Bloomer was born in Chicago, Illinois, on April 8, 1918. She was a dance major at Bennington College before she joined several professional dancing companies. She then worked in fashion retailing. Bloomer married Gerald Ford,* future president of the United States, in 1948. A veteran U.S. congressman from Michigan, Gerald Ford spent his formal career in Washington, D.C. When Vice President Spiro Agnew* resigned in 1973, President Richard Nixon* named Ford to replace him, and when Nixon resigned the next year, Ford became president of the United States. Betty Ford's time as First Lady was particularly memorable. While her husband was in office, she was diagnosed with breast cancer.* At the time there was a considerable stigma attached to the disease, but she was forthright about her illness and the treatment—a mastectomy. Betty Ford later let it be known that she suffered addictions to alcohol and prescription drugs. Her honesty once again reassured millions of Americans with similar illnesses. After leaving the White House in 1977, Betty Ford continued her role as a leading expert on substance abuse and became director of the Betty Ford Center—a drug treatment facility—in Rancho Mirage, California.

SUGGESTED READINGS: Betty Ford, *The Times of My Life*, 1978; Bruce Cassiday, *Betty Ford: Woman of Courage*, 1978.

FORD, GERALD. Gerald Rudolph Ford was born Leslie Lynch King, Jr., on July 14, 1913, in Omaha, Nebraska. When he was three years old, King's parents were divorced, and his mother then married Gerald Rudolph Ford. The couple adopted her son and renamed him Gerald R. Ford, Jr. He was raised in Grand Rapids, Michigan, and attended the University of Michigan on a football scholarship. Ford graduated from that university in 1935, turned down a professional football contract from the Green Bay Packers, and became an assistant football coach at Yale. He entered the Yale Law School in 1938 and graduated in 1941. Ford enlisted in the U.S. Navy in 1942. He was cited for bravery aboard the aircraft carrier USS *Monterey* in the South Pacific.

Ford left the Navy in 1946 and returned to Grand Rapids, where he joined a law practice and became active in local Republican party politics. In 1948 he was elected to Congress from Michigan's Fifth Congressional District. He served thirteen consecutive terms before resigning in October 1973 to accept President Richard Nixon's* nomination as vice president of the United States. At the time, the vice presidency was vacant because of the scandalous resignation of Vice President Spiro Agnew.* Fate soon put Gerald Ford in the White House. On August 6, 1974, President Nixon, facing impeachment as a result of the Watergate scandal,* resigned and Ford took the oath of office.

It was not an easy time to be a Republican. Although Gerald Ford's professional reputation was impeccable, the Watergate scandals had badly tarnished the Republican Party. Party members hoped Ford's own reputation for integrity would help the GOP in general, but Ford did not really have time. He had only been in office for a few months when political maneuvering for the 1976 nomination began. The fact that he had pardoned former president Richard Nixon did not help his chances, nor did North Vietnam's success in April 1975 in overrunning South Vietnam and reuniting the country under a Communist state. News broadcasts of jammed helicopters flying off the roof of the U.S. embassy in Saigon proved undeniably that the United States was fleeing South Vietnam, undermining the credibility of U.S. foreign policy. Finally, the energy crisis and Arab oil boycott* had triggered a damaging spiral of high inflation and high unemployment. Most voters were decidedly upset with the state of the nation.

When the presidential election of 1976* rolled around, Ford found himself falling behind in the polls to Democratic newcomer Jimmy Carter,* the former governor of Georgia. Carter made a great deal of the fact that he was not a Washington insider, and that the plight of America should be placed directly in the laps of the beltway's career politicians, of whom Gerald Ford was a leading example. The ploy worked. Carter won by a narrow margin in the popular vote—40,828,587 (50.1 percent of the total) to Ford's 39,147,613 (48.0 percent). The Electoral College margin was somewhat broader—297 to 240.

During his retirement, Ford has spent the last twenty years out of politics, although he flirted briefly in 1980 with the idea of serving as Ronald Reagan's* vice-presidential running mate. He serves on the boards of directors of several prominent corporations and foundations, works the lecture circuit on behalf of Republican candidates, and engages in a variety of charitable activities.

SUGGESTED READINGS: Gerald Ford, *A Time to Heal*, 1979; Robert T. Hartmann, *Palace Politics: An Insider's Account of the Ford Years*, 1980; Richard Reeves, *A Ford, Not a Lincoln*, 1975.

FOREIGNER. Foreigner, a rock-and-roll band formed in New York City in 1976, included Mick Jones, Ian Mcdonald, Al Greenwood, Lou Gramm, Ed

Gagliardi, and Dennis Elliott. A formulaic, highly commercialized heavy metal band, Foreigner sold more than 30 million records. Their 1977 debut album, *Foreigner*, was a huge success, selling more than four million copies. Its lead singles were "Feels Like the First Time," "Cold As Ice," and "Long, Long Way from Home." Foreigner's second album, entitled *Double Vision*, was an even bigger hit, with such singles as "Double Vision" and "Hot Blooded." "Dirty White Boy" and "Head Games" were hit singles in 1979. Their success continued unabated. Their 1981 album *4* sold more than six million copies, with the singles "Waiting for a Girl Like You" and "Urgent." *Agent Provocateur* (1984), with its number-one pop single "I Want to Know What Love Is" went platinum. *Inside Information* went platinum in 1987.

SUGGESTED READING: K. R. McKenna, "Foreigner: Cold As Ice," *Rolling Stone* (December 28, 1978), 124.

FRAGGING. "Fragging" is a term developed during the Vietnam War* to describe the intentional assassination of U.S. Army officers and noncommissioned officers by their own men. The term "fragging" is derived from fragmentation grenade, the weapon of choice in a fragging incident because it left no evidence. Enlisted men would throw the grenade into the tent or hooch of an unpopular officer. Pentagon officials noticed that the number of fraggings increased dramatically after 1969. In his memoir *A Soldier Reports*, General William Westmoreland concluded that fragging "increases when a sense of unit purpose breaks down and esprit de corps fails and when explosives and weapons are loosely controlled." Fragging was almost an inevitable result of a highly unpopular war.

Morale declined rapidly in 1969 when soldiers realized that President Richard Nixon's* Vietnamization* plan meant that the United States would soon be out of the war. Soldiers did not want to die in what increasingly appeared to be a losing cause and resented gung-ho commanders who were willing to risk lives in order to secure a higher rank. Racial tensions and drug use also contributed to fragging incidents. The Pentagon identified 96 fragging incidents in 1969, a number that increased to 209 in 1970 and to 333 in 1971. The vast majority of fragging incidents occurred in the army. Since then, military historians have seen fragging as an initial indicator of the disintegration of the U.S. military which accelerated during the 1970s.

SUGGESTED READINGS: Eugene Linden, "Fragging and Other Withdrawal Symptoms," *Saturday Review* (January 1972), 12–17; Richard Holmes, *Acts of War: The Behavior of Men in Battle*, 1985.

FRAMPTON, PETER. Peter Frampton was born in Beckingham, England, on April 22, 1950. He joined the band Herd when he was sixteen, and they had several hits in England. Unhappy with the Herd's teeny-bobber bubble-gum rock, Frampton left the Herd in 1969. He formed the group Humble Pie but departed in 1971 for his own recording career. He toured widely in the United States and slowly built a loyal following. His 1976 album *Frampton Comes*

Live! had three hit singles: "Show Me the Way," "Baby I Love Your Way," and "Do You Feel Like We Do." Frampton's second album, *I'm in You*, did not do as well. Depression, alcoholism, and a serious automobile wreck in 1978 took their toll on his career. By the end of the 1970s, he was back on the concert tour, but the bookings were not premier ones, and Frampton's career declined.

SUGGESTED READING: Irene Adler, *Peter Frampton*, 1979.

THE FRENCH CONNECTION. *The French Connection* (1971) was one of the most popular films of the 1970s. At a time when millions of Americans were suspicious of authority figures, soldiers, police, and politicians, *The French Connection* made a hero out of tough-as-nails New York City cop Jimmy "Popeye" Doyle, a real-life figure played by Gene Hackman* in the film. The plot twists around an attempt made by suave, sophisticated, French drug-dealer Alain Charnier (Fernando Rey) to smuggle a carload of pure heroin into New York City. Doyle smells a deal coming down, and the film is an action-packed, suspenseful hunt and crusade, with Doyle getting the heroin but Charnier getting away. Raw, earthy, and dark, *The French Connection* captured the gritty image of New York City during the hard times of the 1970s. At the 1972 Academy Awards, *The French Connection* received Oscars for Best Picture, Best Actor, and Best Director (William Friedkin).

SUGGESTED READING: *New York Times*, October 8, 1971.

FRIENDLY FIRE. "Friendly Fire" was a euphemism used during the Vietnam War* to describe air, artillery, or small arms fire from American forces mistakenly directed at American positions. The term gained national prominence as the title of C.D.B. Bryan's 1976 book *Friendly Fire*, describing the death of Michael E. Mullen in Vietnam on February 18, 1970. Mullen was killed by an accidental American artillery strike, and the telegram to his parents said he had been "at a night defensive position when artillery fire from friendly forces landed on the area." In 1983 a television movie starring Carol Burnett increased the public's awareness of the term.

SUGGESTED READING: James S. Olson, ed., *Dictionary of the Vietnam War*, 1988.

FRITZ THE CAT. For a time in the 1970s, pornographic film producers harbored fantasies of their own, the largest and most naive of which was the belief that their industry could go mainstream in American popular culture. *Fritz the Cat*, an animated film released in 1972, claimed to be America's first "pornographic cartoon," although it was more political satire and social commentary than pornography. Written and directed by Ralph Bakshi, the film follows the escapades of Fritz, a middle-class, WASP cat who drops out of New York University to find himself in the America of the late 1960s. He makes his way through Jewish synagogues, Harlem, whore houses, college drinking binges, and a variety of sexual encounters. The animated sex is graphic and the language coarse and profane. The film carried an X rating but received suprisingly good reviews. Vincent Canby of the *New York Times* called it a "low, bawdy cartoon feature that hasn't forgotten that there still can be something uniquely funny in animated films."

SUGGESTED READING: *New York Times*, April 30, 1972.

FROMME, LYNNETTE. Lynette Alice Fromme was born on October 22, 1948, in Redondo Beach, California, to a middle-class family. Her father nicknamed her "Squeaky" when she was a child. She left home when she was seventeen, spent several semesters at El Camino Junior College in Torrance, California, and then met Charles Manson two months after his release from prison and joined the so-called Manson Family. Although she was not directly linked to the Tate-LaBianca murders in 1969, she earned a reputation for notoriety by attending the seven-month 1971 murder trial of Charles Manson. She testified on Manson's behalf and then shaved her head and carved an "X" in her forehead to demonstrate her fidelity to him.

Fromme resurfaced in American consciousness four years later on September 4, 1975, when she attempted to assassinate President Gerald Ford* in Sacramento, California. She blamed President Ford for many Nixon policies and for keeping her beloved Charles Manson in prison. She was wrestled down before firing her .45 semiautomatic pistol. Fromme was also wearing a long red robe because, as she said, "We're nuns now and we wear red robes. We're waiting for our Lord and there's only one thing to do before he comes off the cross, and that's cleaning up the earth." Apparently, Fromme believed that killing Ford was part of that cleansing process. She was given a life sentence for her crime.

SUGGESTED READINGS: Jess Bravin, *Squeaky: The Life and Times of Lynette Alice Fromme*, 1997; *New York Times*, September 6, 1975.

FUNK. The term "funk" refers to an African-American musical form that emerged in the late 1960s and 1970s. Among the major funk performers were James Brown,* Sly and the Family Stone, Kool and the Gang, Ohio Players, Bary-Kays, and Parliament. Funk music is characterized by complex polyrhythmic systems, percussion instruments, horns, and vocals that emphasize liberation through having a good time. Such key phrases as "have a good time," "let yourself go," "give up the funk," and "it ain't nothing but a party" appeared repeatedly in funk. Rock musicologists see in funk one's desire to escape difficult circumstances and to express oneself in an atmosphere free from integration and white intimidation.

SUGGESTED READINGS: Trisa Rose, *Black Noise*, 1994; Eileen Southern, *The Music of Black Americans*, 1983.

FURMAN V. GEORGIA; JACKSON V. GEORGIA; BRANCH V. TEXAS **(1972).** During the late 1960s and throughout the 1970s, the constitutional and moral legitimacy of capital punishment became the subject of intense public policy debates at the state and national levels. Hundreds of court cases made their way through the federal court system, and three of them—*Furman v. Georgia, Jackson v. Georgia*, and *Branch v. Texas*—were jointly decided by the U.S. Supreme Court on June 29, 1972. By a narrow 5 to 4 vote, in which each justice filed a separate opinion, the court nullified every death penalty statute in the United States. The sentences of every man and woman on death row throughout the country were converted to life in prison. The court argued that the statutes as they existed left far too much discretion to judges and juries as to when to impose the death sentence. As a result, the laws tended to be capricious, irrational, and arbitrary, all of which deprived defendants of their Fifth Amendment right to due process of law.

SUGGESTED READING: 408 U.S. 665 (1972).

G

GARMENT, LEONARD. Born in 1924, Leonard Garment graduated from the Brooklyn Law School in Brooklyn, New York, in 1949. He went on to become special counsel and advisor on minority affairs to President Richard Nixon.* Leonard Garment was sympathetic to the needs of American Indian people, a feeling shared by President Nixon, and he used his position as special counsel to the president to support the Indians. Garment was instrumental in the drafting of President Nixon's 1970 message setting forth his American Indian policy of "self-determination[*] without termination." In this statement, drafted by Garment and his assistant, Bradley H. Patterson, Jr., Nixon told the American people, "[I]t is long past time that the Indian policies of the Federal government began to recognize and build upon the capacities and insights of the Indian people."

In addition to his drafting of this statement of support for American Indian people, Garment was the central figure in three significant events that changed forever the lives of American Indian people and the perception of Indian people by the American public at large: the 1969 occupation of Alcatraz Island,* the 1972 occupation of the Bureau of Indian Affairs (BIA) building in Washington, D.C., and the 1973 occupation of Wounded Knee* Village, South Dakota. On November 20, 1969 eighty-nine American Indians landed on Alcatraz Island in San Francisco Bay. Identifying themselves as Indians of All Tribes,* this group of young urban Indian college students claimed the island by "right of discovery." The occupiers demanded clear title to Alcatraz Island and the establishment of an American Indian University, an American Indian Cultural Center, and an American Indian Museum on Alcatraz Island. When U.S. marshals were ordered to remove the Indians from the island at gunpoint, Garment recognized the danger of the use of excessive force and the public relations problems faced by the Nixon administration if blood was shed in an attempt to remove the Indians from Alcatraz Island. Garment instructed the Washington, D.C., Government Services Administration Office (GSA) to call off the marshals, and he issued instructions for the White House to coordinate all future actions with the Indian occupiers directly with the San Francisco GSA office. Garment and his assistant, Patterson, orchestrated the government's actions, reactions, and negotiations which took place over a nineteen-month period, ending on June 11, 1971, when the few remaining occupiers were removed from the island. Garment was sympathetic to Indian issues and felt that his feelings mirrored those of President Nixon and recognized that the Alcatraz occupation was an attempt on the part of urban Indian people to focus the attention of the American people, particularly politicians in Washington, D.C., on their needs.

In the fall of 1972, Indian leaders from the American Indian Movement* (AIM) planned a civil rights march to Washington, D.C., which became known as the Trail of Broken Treaties.* The march, a cross-country caravan, started at three separate points on the West Coast, picked up Indian people from reservations as it went along, and arrived in Washington, D.C., just prior to the 1972 presidential election. Several hundred Indian people arrived in the nation's capital on November 2; however, no arrangements had been made to provide housing or meals. A few Indians were housed with the assistance of the Department of the Interior. Many, however, had no place to stay and nothing to eat. The Indian people met at the BIA building on Constitution Avenue while awaiting word on housing. When shelter could not be found, the Department of Interior offered the use of the BIA building's auditorium. The Indians accepted, but when the BIA employees left the building at the end of the work day, some young Indians were shoved out the door by guards. The Indians believed that they were being shoved outside into a waiting District of Columbia riot squad. They stopped, turned around, and then seized the BIA building. They barricaded the doors, blocked the windows, upended desks, and piled metal chairs against doors to prevent forcible removal.

On November 6, 1972 a judge ordered the forcible removal of the Indians by 6:00 P.M. that day. The situation inside the BIA building worsened as tensions grew. The Indians decided to wait until 5:45 P.M. for the government to respond to their demands, and if they had not heard anything positive, or seen any police withdrawal, they would set the building on fire. Leonard Garment, along with Office of Management and Budget (OMB) Director Frank Carlucci, Secretary of the Interior Rogers Morton, and Commissioner of Indian Affairs Louis Bruce, agreed to negotiate with the Indian people on behalf of the president. On election morning, Garment, Carlucci, and Bruce met with the Indians. A federal task force was agreed upon to review the complaints of the Indian people. It would examine wide issues in Indian country. Amnesty was promised. Negotiations were conducted under direct White House auspices with Garment in charge. A settlement was reached whereby the government would provide $66,500 in travel expenses to get the Indians home, and in return the Indian people would leave the BIA building. They left the building before a 9:00 P.M. November 8, 1972 deadline.

On the evening of February 27, 1973, some two hundred Indian people occupied the village of Wounded Knee, South Dakota, the site of the 1890 Wounded Knee massacre of 150 Lakota Indians, to protest against the corrupt tribal government headed by Richard "Dicky" Wilson and numerous uninvestigated murders of Indian people on the Pine Ridge Indian Reservation. The White House was immediately notified of the occupation, and Garment once again became the federal government's point man for the negotiations. Keenly aware of the president's views and his concerns for American Indian people, Garment established the initial policy against the use of violence to remove the Indian occupiers from the village. The Indian occupiers, however, had various weapons with them, and the three hundred federal police aligned against them had in their possession fifteen armored personnel carriers and over one hundred M-16 rifles. Soon rifle fire was exchanged, two Indian occupiers were killed, fourteen Indian occupiers were injured, and one FBI agent was wounded.

During the occupation of Wounded Knee, three hundred news people, including representatives from twelve foreign countries, converged on Wounded Knee. The attention of the nation was focused on the village. In Washington, D.C., the decision-making machinery was totally under White House direction, specifically Leonard Garment. Despite the urgency of the situation and the involvement of the assistant attorney general, Garment's decisions carried the most weight, that of the president of the United States. The occupation of Wounded Knee, which lasted seventy-one days, required patience and persistent, trying negotiations, tasks at which Leonard Garment had become a master.

SUGGESTED READING: Leonard Garment, *Crazy Rhythm: Richard Nixon and All That Jazz*, 1997.

Troy Johnson

GAY POWER. During the 1970s in the United States, the "gay power" movement emerged as the most controversial of the civil rights crusades. The origins of the movement can be traced back to the 1950s. In such cities as San Francisco and New York, beat writers like Allen Ginsberg openly admitted to their homosexuality, to which the famous Kinsey Report of 1948 had given some credibility. Alfred Kinsey, a zoologist at the University of Indiana, had long been studying the sexual behavior of American men, and in 1948 he published his book, *Sexual Behavior in the Human Male*. Kinsey's conclusions created a firestorm of political debate. He claimed that half of all American men had at least fantasized about a same-sex erotic experience, that one-third of American men, after adolescence, had had at least one homosexual experience leading to orgasm, that one in eight American men had lived as homosexuals for at least a three-year period, and that one of every twenty-five American men was exclusively gay. Congress launched an investigation of the Kinsey Report, conservatives attacked Kinsey as a Communist, and social scientists disputed Kinsey's conclusions and cited flaws in his methodology. But nobody could doubt anymore that homosexual behavior was much more widespread in the United States than previously thought.

The Kinsey Report had an electrifying effect on gays, particularly people like

Henry Hay, who were tired of living a double life. The fact that there might be millions of gay men in the United States helped create an urban gay subculture—a definable sense of group membership. They no longer felt as isolated as before. Although gay men knew they were in the minority, they took comfort from the fact that the minority was not nearly as small as many people had long assumed. The first openly gay group, the Mattachine Society, was formed in Los Angeles in 1950. Although the group had trouble attracting members, it was quite open about its purposes. Franklin Kameny, a Mattachine Society member in New York City, remarked,

I take the stand that not only is homosexuality . . . not immoral, but that homosexual acts engaged in by consenting adults are moral, in a positive and real sense, and are right, good, and desirable, both for the individual participants and for the society in which they live. . . . We owe apologies to no one—society and its official representatives owe us apologies for what they have done and are doing to us.

Lesbians organized as well, forming in 1955 the Daughters of Bilitis.

The Mattachine Society and the Daughters of Bilitis engaged in their own civil rights crusade, targeting discriminatory federal employment policies, particularly Civil Service Commission rules against hiring homosexuals, as well as military exclusion of homosexuals and government refusal to extend security clearances to homosexuals. They hounded federal officials, wrote letters to congressmen, scheduled meetings with government officials, and filed suits in the federal courts. Mattachine Society members picketed the White House in 1965 to protest discriminatory employment practices. Kameny also denounced Washington, D.C., police raids on gay bars and secured legal counsel from the American Civil Liberties Union on behalf of all gay men arrested on misdemeanor charges. When Congressman John Dowdy of Texas tried to pass legislation outlawing Mattachine Society activities, the local press condemned him, giving the society a huge volume of favorable press coverage. The Mattachine Society wrote the first chapter in the history of the gay rights movement.

The second chapter came with the so-called Stonewall Inn Riots of 1969. The Stonewall Inn was a gay bar on Christopher Street in New York City's Greenwich Village. New York City police, often at the best of headline-seeking politicians, regularly raided the bar and roughed up patrons. Until June 1969, the patrons of the Stonewall Inn and other local gay bars acquiesced passively in the treatment they received at the hands of public officials.

That all changed on the evening of June 27, 1969, when two detectives, accompanied by several uniformed officers, met at the Sixth Precinct headquarters, discussed the raid, and headed out to Christopher Street. They anticipated having a little fun—screaming epithets, nightsticking some "fags," and arresting a few drag queens. They backed a paddy wagon up to the entrance of the Stonewall Inn and then strutted in, loudly asking to see the liquor license and pushing the customers around. Police frisked each patron, ostensibly looking for drugs, and then released them one by one out the front door. Three drag queens, the bartender, and a bouncer, who loudly protested what he called "police brutality," were arrested on a variety of charges, including public lewdness, selling alcohol without a state license, and resisting arrest.

A crowd had gathered outside, across Christopher Street, as soon as the paddy wagon parked, and they waited to see what would transpire. They seemed passive enough at first, like any other group of onlookers waiting for a show. Suddenly, however, the temper of the crowd changed. They started jeering the police, shouting epithets and making catcalls and obscene gestures of their own. Two policemen then came out of the Stonewall Inn, trying to wrestle a lesbian into the paddy wagon. She was not cooperating at all—kicking, twisting, biting, and screaming—putting up a struggle every inch of the way. The police grappled and kicked back, calling her "butch" and "bitch" and "dike." What had been a police raid quickly escalated into a gay rebellion. Cobblestones, bottles, full beer cans, and coins rained down on police. Like a medieval army of old trying to storm a fortified castle, several men uprooted a parking meter and used it as a battering ram, pounding it repeatedly against the doors of the Stonewall Inn. The police retreated into the bar and called for backup after several Molotov cocktails exploded through the windows and set the Stonewall Inn ablaze. Reinforcements soon poured into Sheridan Square, but marauding groups of gay protesters attacked police cars, turning them over or setting them on fire, spooked police horses, and continued the hailstorm of rocks and bottles. The free-for-all continued into the early morning hours of June 28.

It started up again the next evening. Overnight, gay power graffiti slogans had been spray painted on walls throughout Greenwich Village and at scattered sites in Lower Manhattan. Clusters of angry gay men and lesbians dotted Christopher Street, and the police showed up 400 strong, in full riot gear, complete with helmets, plastic face masks, bullet-proof vests, shields, and nightsticks. On the corner of Greenwich Avenue and Christopher Street, several dozen drag queens, shouting "Save our sister," attacked a group of police who were clubbing a young man. Over the course of the next several hours, the rioting intensified, with police now battling a crowd of more than 2,000 people. Allen Ginsberg, a leading Beat writer and one of the founding fathers of the 1960s counterculture, showed up at Christopher Street several days later and remarked to a reporter for the *Village Voice*: "You know, the guys there were so beautiful. They've lost that wounded look that fags all had ten years ago." The days of routine gay bashing, as formal police policy in New York City, were numbered.

In the weeks following the Stonewall Riots, gays and lesbians settled into intense discussions about their political future. The Christopher Street riots on June 27 and 28, 1969, had galvanized them, raising their consciousness into a "we're not going to take it anymore" mentality. Gay leaders in New York City formed the Gay Liberation Front late in July, proclaiming their rejection of society's "attempt to impose sexual roles and definitions of our nature. We are stepping outside these roles and simplistic myths. We are going to be who we are." The Gay Activist Alliance was organized at the same time. Similar groups sprouted on college campuses and in major cities around the country. When New York City police raided several gay bars in August 1970, thousands of gay men and women staged a protest march from Times Square to Greenwich Village. When antigay articles appeared in the media, gay activists stormed the publishers' New York offices, demanding retractions and organizing boycotts against the newspapers and magazines. The Stonewall Inn riots had given birth to a new civil rights constituency.

Throughout the 1970s, the gay rights movement gained momentum. Members demanded an end to discrimination against homosexuals and worked diligently to affirm their sexual identity and sexual preference. In order to augment their political power, gay rights activists urged homosexuals to "come out of the closet" and to take pride in their sexual identity. In many regions, the strategy worked. More than 1,000 gay clubs and organizations were formed during the 1970s, and large gay communities sprouted in San Francisco, New York, Miami, Chicago, Los Angeles, and Houston. Gay men and lesbians were politically active, voting in very large numbers and demanding the attention of politicians. In San Francisco, Harvey Milk* won election to the city council after he openly avowed his homosexuality. Democrat Barney Frank of Massachusetts was later elected to Congress after openly admitting his own homosexuality and demanding gay rights. Such advocacy groups as the Gay and Lesbian Alliance and Gays United began promoting homosexuality as a positive good, and the women's movement,* led by the National Organization for Women,* endorsed the notion of complete civil rights and equal treatment before the law for gays and lesbians. In 1974 the American Psychiatric Association decided to no longer classify homosexuality as a mental disorder.

Within the Democratic party during the 1970s, gay men and lesbians crusaded for recognition as an oppressed minority. Black Panther* leader Huey Newton declared that "homosexuals might be the most oppressed people" in American society, and most other Democrats agreed. Gay rights advocates soon found a home in the Democratic party and among other civil rights constituencies. In 1980 the Democratic party formally adopted a gay rights position in its presidential election platform.

Late in the 1970s, however, just when the gay power movement was gaining national attention, physicians and epidemiologists began to grow concerned about a strange new illness appearing among gay men. It appeared to be a disease of immune deficiency, characterized by fatigue, weight loss, Kaposi's sarcoma, bizarre opportunistic infections, and inevitable death. The disease came to be known as Acquired Immune Deficiency Syndrome (AIDS), and by the early 1980s it had transformed the gay rights movement, making it far more militant, and politically successful, than it had ever been.

SUGGESTED READINGS: John D'Emilio, *Sexual Politics, Sexual Communities: The Making of a Homosexual Minority in the United States, 1940–1970*, 1984; *New York Times*, June 28–30 and July 1–2, 1969; Randy Shilts, *And the Band Played On: People, Politics, and the AIDS Epidemic*, 1987.

GAYE, MARVIN. Marvin Gaye was born Marvin Pentz Gay (he later changed the spelling) in Washington, D.C., on April 2, 1939. His father, Marvin Gay, Sr., was a Pentecostal minister, and the younger Gay early on displayed his musical talent by singing in the church choir and playing the church organ. In 1958, while performing at a high school talent contest, Gay was noticed by Harvey Fuqua, a promoter for Chess Records. Gay signed a recording contract with Chess the next year. Fuqua and Gay moved to Detroit in 1960 and associated with Berry Gordy and his fledgling Motown Records. In 1962 Motown released Marvin Gaye's first album, *The Soulful Mood of Marvin Gaye*, a collection of jazz-based ballads. In 1964 Gaye had his first hit record with Motown, "Hitch Hike." Later in the year his single "Pride and Joy" made it into the top ten on the pop charts.

Gaye was soon widely known as a Motown artist who could succeed in both the pop and rhythm-and-blues markets. He recorded a string of hits, including "Ain't That Peculiar" (1965), "It Takes Two" (1967), "Your Precious Love" (1967), "Ain't Nothing Like the Real Thing" (1968), "You're All I Need to Get By" (1968), "Heard It on the Grapevine" (1968), and the fabulously successful "What's Going On" (1971). In 1971 his album *What's Going On* included three top-ten hits: "Inner City Blues," "Mercy Mercy Me," and "What's Going On." Gaye's 1973 album *Let's Get It On* reached number one on the pop charts.

In the mid-1970s, however, Gaye's life hit the so-called skids. He divorced his wife Anna, who was the daughter of Berry Gordy, and Motown released him. Drug abuse and clinical depression afflicted him, and he fled to Europe to avoid tax problems with the Internal Revenue Service. Upon his return to the United States he revived his career, which included the hit single "Sexual Healing." On April 1, 1984, however, during a heated argument, Marvin Gay, Sr., took out a gun and killed his son.

SUGGESTED READING: David Ritz, *Divided Soul: The Life of Marvin Gaye*, 1985.

GENESIS. Formed in Godalming, England, in 1966, Genesis was a spectacularly successful rock-and-roll band in the 1970s and 1980s. Included in the group have been Peter Gabriel, Tony Banks, Michael Rutherford, Anthony Phillips, Chris Stewart, John Mayhew, Phil Collins, and Steve Hackett. At first they were known more for their outlandish costumes and elaborate sets on the concert tour than for their music. They slowly gained a cult following in the United States, with their albums steadily increasing in sales: *Nursury Cryme* (1971), *Foxtrot* (1972), *Genesis Live* (1973), *The Lamb Lies Down on Broadway* (1975), *A Trick of the Tail* (1976), and *Wind and Wuthering* (1977). Their first hit single, "Your Own Special Way," did not come until 1977. The 1978 album . . . *And Then There Were Three* included the hit single "Follow You, Follow Me," and "Misunderstanding" was a hit single from the 1980 album *Duke*. Since then Genesis has continued to perform, and several of its members, particularly Phil Collins, have had dramatically successful solo careers as well.

SUGGESTED READING: Armando Gallo, *Genesis: From One Fan to Another*, 1984.

GILMORE, GARY. On January 17, 1977, Gary Gilmore became the first individual in ten years to be executed in the United States. His pending death, and then his execution, sparked a vigorous national debate over the merits of capital punishment. At the time, there were 354 inmates on death row throughout the country, and, because of various federal court rulings, no executions had taken place since 1967. In the ten-year interval, opponents of capital punishment had hoped that a permanent end to the death penalty had been achieved.

Their hopes were hopelessly naive. Gilmore had been convicted of murdering two men who worked at a motel in Provo, Utah. Both victims were law students at Brigham Young University. A thirty-six-year-old career drifter and criminal, Gilmore had spent most of his life in jails and penitentiaries, and he decided not to contest the death penalty. In fact, he admitted his crimes and refused to appeal the verdict. He expressed utter contempt for the "do-gooders out to save my life. I deserve to die for what I did," he told a reporter. Opponents of capital punishment tried to block the execution in spite of Gilmore's repeated requests that they cease and desist, but without his cooperation, the wheels of the appeals process soon ground to a halt. As his execution date approached, Gilmore became the focus of extraordinary media attention. The end came just after 8:00 A.M. on June 17, 1977, when Gilmore died in front of a firing squad.

SUGGESTED READINGS: Norman Mailer, *The Executioner's Song*, 1979; *New York Times*, January 15–19, 1977.

GO TELL THE SPARTANS. *Go Tell the Spartans*, released in 1978, was one of the first Hollywood films to try to explain, and commercially exploit, the Vietnam War.* The film stars Burt Lancaster as an army major on duty in South Vietnam in 1964, just before the introduction of American ground troops. The major is no gung-ho careerist; he knows that the South Vietnamese government is hopelessly corrupt; that Vietcong troops are highly motivated and competent; and that the U.S. mission in Indochina is misguided. He is more concerned that the troops under his command, who are assigned to advise and train South Vietnamese soldiers, survive than win the war. *Go Tell the Spartans* portrayed the Vietnam War in a way that was pleasing to antiwar movement* activists.

SUGGESTED READINGS: Linda Dittmar and Gene Michaud, eds., *From Hanoi to Hollywood: The Vietnam War in American Film*, 1990; *New York Times*, September 23, 1978.

THE GODFATHER. Based on Mario Puzo's bestselling novel of the same name, *The Godfather* was one of the best films of the 1970s and, in the minds of many film critics, one of the best in Hollywood's history. The movie stars Marlon Brando as Vito Corleone, head of a rich and powerful Italian-American crime family. James Caan plays his hot-headed son "Sonny" Corleone; Al Pacino, Michael Corleone, the youngest son and heir apparent as the upcoming "Don" of the family; Diane Keaton, Michael's wife Kay; and Robert Duvall, Tom Hagen, the family's lawyer. *The Godfather* was directed by Francis Ford Coppola.

A dark and ominous reflection of one side of American life, the film is set in New York City and Las Vegas in the late 1940s and early 1950s. At the time, the primary Mafia families are making the transition from numbers running and union racketeering to prostitution and drugs. Vito Corleone, an old-school mobster, is willing to buy off all the police, politicians, and judges he needs to stay in business. When Michael inherits the mantle of the "Don" after the death of Vito Corleone, he strives to legitimize the family businesses by investing capital in the gambling casinos of up-and-coming Las Vegas. In the end, of course, Michael proves to be more malignant in his violence than his father had ever been. The crime and violence is ironically contrasted with Italian-American family values. Although the Italian-American Civil Rights League protested the film as a grossly stereotypical portrayal of Italian immigrants and their descendents, *The Godfather* rang true to people inside and outside the organized crime community. *The Godfather* won a string of Oscars, including Best Picture and Best Actor for Marlon Brando.

SUGGESTED READING: Peter Biskind, *The Godfather Companion: Everything You Ever Wanted to Know About All Three Godfather Films*, 1990.

THE GODFATHER, PART II. *The Godfather, Part II* was the 1974 sequel to Francis Ford Coppola's fantastically successful 1972 film *The Godfather.** Some film historians consider *Godfather II* to be the best sequel in Hollywood's history. The screenplay was written by Mario Puzo, and Coppola directed the next chapter in the history of the Corleone family. This film stars Al Pacino, once again, as Michael Corleone; Diane Keaton, his wife Kay; Robert Duvall, lawyer Tom Hagen. Robert De Niro* plays the young Vito Corleone.

The film is divided into two parts: one takes place before Vito Corleone ever became a godfather, and the second part details Michael's takeover of Las Vegas and his battle with the federal government's anticrime crusaders of the early 1950s. In the beginning, Vito Corleone is a child in Sicily whose father and brother are murdered in a mafioso revenge killing. He is spirited away to America before he is killed as well. In New York City's Little Italy early in the twentieth century, Vito grows up and rises to power in the local rackets, always loyal to a code of honor whose boundaries do not extend much beyond his own family. Eventually, he returns to Sicily and avenges his father's and brother's deaths. The film then segues ahead forty years to the 1950s when the violence and crime eventually catches up to Michael Corleone, consuming and ultimately destroying his family.

SUGGESTED READINGS: Peter Biskind, *The Godfather Companion: Everything You Ever Wanted to Know About All Three Godfather Films*, 1990; *New York Times*, December 13, 1974.

GOLD STANDARD. At the Bretton Wood Conference in 1945, the world monetary system became pegged to the value of the dollar. All of the world currencies measured their values against the dollar. By the late 1960s and early 1970s, that system had become increasingly anachronistic. Economic challenges had undermined the dollar. Serious inflation, a growing world U.S. trade deficit, declining U.S. gold reserves, and increasing unemployment had so weakened the American economy and the dollar that the Bretton Wood system no longer worked. In August 1971 President Richard Nixon* made a decision to devalue the dollar in order to increase the marketability of U.S. goods in foreign markets. He suspended all U.S. gold payments, which essentially cut the dollar's last remaining connection to hard currency. The dollar's value vis-à-vis other currencies then began to float. The gold standard was finally dead.

SUGGESTED READING: Roger Miller, *The New Economics of Richard Nixon: Freezes, Floats, and Fiscal Policy*, 1972.

THE GONG SHOW. *The Gong Show* was one of the more bizarre pop culture phenomena of the 1970s. An audience participation parody of television talent shows, *The Gong Show* featured celebrity guests, including Jamie Farr, Rex Reed, Jaye P. Morgan, Rip Taylor, and Phyllis Diller, who judged a seemingly endless parade of not-so-talented performers. The judges scored the performances and had the power to "gong" or immediately end the worst acts. Gary Owens hosted the syndicated show in 1976 and 1977, and Chuck Barris took over until 1980. Rowdy, irreverent, and occasionally raunchy, *The Gong Show* survived until 1980, by which time its antics had worn thin on its American audience.

SUGGESTED READING: Tim Brooks and Earle Marsh, *The Complete Directory to Prime Time Network and Cable TV Shows, 1946–Present*, 1995.

GOOD TIMES. *Good Times*, a situation comedy spinoff from the popular television series *Maude*, featured Esther Rolle as Florida Evans, the African-American maid on *Maude*. *Good Times* took her home to her husband James (John Amos), sons James Jr. "J.J." (Jimmie Walker) and Michael (Ralph Carter), and daughter Thelma (Bernadette Stanis). The Evans, a working-class family, live in the South Side of Chicago. John Amos left the show after one season, and Esther Rolle became disenchanted two years later, worried about the stereotypes being reinforced by James Jr.'s jive talking, woman chasing, and shady business dealings. Rolle returned to the show a year later, but the revival of her character did not boost the show's ratings back to where they had been. The legacy of *Good Times* was far more than J.J.'s famous "Dy-No-Mite" catchphrase. The show was a pioneer African-American prime-time television series.

SUGGESTED READING: Tim Brooks and Earle Marsh, *The Complete Directory to Prime Time Network and Cable TV Shows, 1946–Present*, 1995.

GRAHAM V. RICHARDSON **(1971).** During the 1950s and 1960s, the number of immigrants and resident aliens without U.S. citizenship living in the United

States increased dramatically. Many Americans were alarmed about the numbers of immigrants and the tax burdens they allegedly represented. Immigrant advocates claimed that immigrants contributed far more to the economy than they consumed, but their arguments satisfied few nativists. A number of states began passing discriminatory legislation, requiring extended periods of residency before aliens could qualify for welfare benefits. The state of Arizona imposed a fifteen-year requirement, for example, and Pennsylvania denied all welfare benefits to legal, resident aliens.

Cases involving such legislation made their way through the federal courts in the 1960s, and on June 14, 1971, the U.S. Supreme Court decided the *Graham v. Richardson* case by a unanimous vote. In essence, the court expanded the meaning of the equal protection clause of the Constitution to include all legal aliens. The Arizona and Pennsylvania laws were unconstitutional.

SUGGESTED READING: 403 U.S. 365 (1971).

GRAND FUNK RAILROAD. Formed in Flint, Michigan, in 1968, Grand Funk Railroad became the most commercially successful hard-rock band of the 1970s. The original group included Mark Farner, Mel Schachner, and Don Brewer, and Craig Frost joined in 1971. Their early act was little more than loud power chords and onstage sweating and gyrations. Their first album, entitled *On Time*, was released by Capitol Records in 1969. During the next two years, Grand Funk Railroad recorded five other albums: *Grand Funk* (1970), *Closer to Home* (1970), *Live Album* (1970), *Survival* (1971), and *E Pluribus Funk* (1971). The six albums did extraordinarily well, one going gold and five going platinum. Their concerts were sellouts. *We're an American Band* was a hit album in 1973, as was *Shinin' On* in 1974. After releasing *Caught in the Act* (1975), *Born to Die* (1975), and *Good Singin'; Good Playin'* (1976), Grand Funk Railroad disbanded.

SUGGESTED READING: E. T. Sparn, "Grand Funk—Shinin' On," *Senior Scholastic* 1.5 (September 26, 1974), 31–33.

THE GRATEFUL DEAD. The Grateful Dead enjoys the reputation of being the psychedelic rock-and-roll band with the most longevity. Formed in San Francisco in 1965, the group included Jerry Garcia, Bob Weir, Ron McKernan, Phil Lesh, and Bill Kreutzmann. Although they never really had huge commercial success on the pop charts, they created a virtual movement of deadheads*— fans who followed them from concert to concert and preserved the 1960s culture of tie-dyed clothing and hallucinogenic drug use. Their highly improvised music was a mix of country, blues, and rock.

The Grateful Dead are one of the most extraordinary phenomena in the history of modern American rock and roll and popular culture. They became a permanent time warp for America back to the 1960s, and their hippie concert following was more of a "happening" than an event. Deadheads followed the band everywhere, showing up at every concert possible, and became a sort of communal tribe drawing meaning for their lives from association with the Grateful Dead. The band kept ticket prices low, permitted fans to tape their concerts, tended to stay away from recording studios, refused to become involved with any political candidate, and performed a freestyle, jazz-style music. Throughout the 1970s, 1980s, and early 1990s, the Grateful Dead focused their energies on live performances rather than on recording, and in doing so they became one of the world's most profitable bands. Jerry Garcia's death in 1995, however, seems to have marked the end of the group's extraordinary career.

SUGGESTED READING: Sean Piccoli, *The Grateful Dead*, 1997.

GREEN, AL. Born into a family of African-American sharecroppers in Forrest City, Arkansas, on April 13, 1946, Al Green became one the most popular soul artists of the 1970s. With several of his brothers, he put together a gospel quartet that toured the southern circuit in the late 1950s, and in 1961 he formed Al Green and the Creations, a pop music group. Their first album, *Green Is Blues*, received modest success in 1970. The second album, entitled *Gets Next to You*, contained several hit singles, including "You Say It," "Right Now, Right Now," "I Can't Get Next to You," and "Tired of Being Alone." Success followed success, and over the course of the next four years, Green recorded no fewer than eight hit singles: "Let's Stay Together" (1971), "Look What You Done for Me" (1972), "I'm Still in Love with You" (1972), "You Ought to Be with Me" (1972), "Call Me (Come Back Home)" (1973), "Here I Am (Come and Take Me)" (1973), "Sha La La (Make Me Happy)" (1974), and "L-O-V-E (Love)" (1975). The suicide of Green's former girlfriend in October 1974 precipitated a spiritual crisis for the singer, and in 1976 he made the decision to go into the ministry. Since then, he has returned artistically to his gospel roots.

SUGGESTED READING: Patricia Romanowski and Holly George-Warren, eds., *The New Encyclopedia of Rock & Roll*, 1985.

GREENSPAN, ALAN. Alan Greenspan was born on March 6, 1926, in New York City. He started his educational career by studying music at Juilliard, but he switched to economics and graduated from New York University in 1948. He pursued a doctorate in economics at Columbia University, and in 1953, he formed a private consulting firm with David Townsend. Over the next two decades, Greenspan earned an outstanding reputation for economic sagacity. In terms of his politics, he was a conservative Republican, and as a young man, he had become enamored of the ideas of Ayn Rand. Although he became more pragmatic over the years, he maintained a deep faith in the power of the marketplace and the superiority of capitalism. He advised Richard Nixon* during the presidential campaign of 1968, and in 1974 Nixon named him chairman of the Council of Economic Advisors. Greenspan remained there until the end of the Gerald Ford* administration in 1977. He returned to public life in 1981 when President Ronald Reagan* named him to the President's Economic Policy Board.

Although Greenspan never liked the tag of being a supply-sider or monetarist, he was convinced that the greatest threat to the American economy was inflation. In 1987 Reagan named him to fill the shoes of Paul Volcker,* who had retired as chairman of the Federal Reserve Board. Greenspan proved to be a popular and successful leader of the Federal Reserve Board, and in 1996 Democratic President Bill Clinton reappointed him to another term. During the stock market volatility of the late 1990s, Greenspan was one of the most influential people in the world.

SUGGESTED READING: *Time*, June 15, 1987.

GREER, GERMAINE. Germaine Greer was born outside Melbourne, Australia, on January 29, 1939, and received her early education in a Roman Catholic convent school. In 1959 she received an undergraduate degree in French and English literature from the University of Melbourne. Two years later, intent on an academic career, she was awarded a master's degree in English from the University of Sydney. Greer then moved to England to work on her Ph.D., which she received from Cambridge in 1967. Her degree was in English literature with a special emphasis on Shakespeare. While working on her doctorate, Greer accepted a lectureship at the University of Warwick, where she remained until 1973.

By that time she had become an icon in the fledgling women's movement,* as a result of her bestselling book *The Female Eunuch*, which was published in 1970. The book took a fresh look at female sexuality and psychological development within the context of the historical subordination of women. Society, she argued, had effectively achieved the "castration of our true female personality," leaving women with all the "characteristics of a female eunuch: timidity, plumpness, languor, delicacy, and preciosity." The book instantly carved out a place for Greer in the pantheon of modern feminists.

It was not a role she accepted completely. Greer constantly asserted her independence from what she called "party-line feminism" because of its middle- and upper-class preoccupations. She cultivated an image of overt sexuality and celebrated orgasms and hetereosexual relations, insisting that a woman's vagina was "an organ, not a hole." Greer also refused to lay all the blame for women's modern circumstances on men, claiming that women too bore some of the responsibility for their plight. Throughout the 1970s, she lectured and wrote widely. In 1979 Greer becamed director of the Tulsa Center for the Study of Women's Literature in Tulsa, Oklahoma.

During the 1980s, she remained a controversial figure in American culture. Her 1984 book *Sex and Destiny: The Politics of Human Fertility* produced a storm of controversy when she castigated Western nations for imposing birth control programs on Third World nations. She insisted that natural forms of birth control and abstinence were preferable to artifical means of contraception. Her 1991 book *The Change* was an analysis of aging and menopause among women. Greer continues to be her iconoclastic self.

SUGGESTED READINGS: Germaine Greer, *Daddy: We Hardly Knew You*, 1989; Christine Wallace, *Germaine Greer: Untamed Shrew*, 1998.

GREGG V. GEORGIA (1976). During the 1970s, the constitutionality of the death penalty became an intense point of public debate in the United States. While many Americans argued that the death penalty was a perfectly legitimate method of punishing the perpetrators of the most heinous crimes, others argued that it was cruel and unusual punishment, that it was biased against racial minorities and the poor, and that it did not deter other violent criminals. Federal and state courts, as well as state legislatures and the U.S. Congress, struggled with the issue. In 1976 the U.S. Supreme Court had to decide whether capital punishment was "cruel and unusual punishment" as defined by the Eighth Amendment to the Constitution. A number of cases involving the issue wound their way through the federal court system, and on July 2, 1976, by a 7 to 2 vote, the court decided the *Gregg v. Georgia* case.

In its decision, the Court claimed that the death penalty was not necessarily cruel and unusual punishment or a violation of the Eighth Amendment. The court simply ordered that the Eighth Amendment requires that judges and juries consider the individual character of the defendant and the general circumstances of the case before imposing the death penalty. The Court decided that a two-stage trial procedure was necessary: one stage to determine guilt or innocence and the second stage to assess punishment. The death penalty might very well be appropriate in cases of particularly heinous crimes or in crimes committed by violence-prone individuals who had already demonstrated in earlier crimes their capacity for mayhem. The jury should decide whether the defendant posed a future threat to society.

On the same day, the U.S. Supreme Court decided the *Woodson v. North Carolina* case (428 U.S. 280), overturning a North Carolina law that imposed mandatory death penalties in cases of first-degree murder. The justices believed that such mandatory requirements did not allow juries and judges to give consideration to individual circumstances.

SUGGESTED READING: 428 U.S. 153 (1976).

GRIGGS V. DUKE POWER COMPANY (1971). In the *Griggs v. Duke Power Company* case of 1971, the U.S. Supreme Court upheld for the first time the right of Congress under the Civil Rights Act of 1964 to forbid employment discrimination on the basis of race. The Duke Power Company required a high school diploma and minimal scores on general intelligence tests before it would hire or promote an individual, but the effect of the requirements was to exclude far more blacks than whites. The U.S. Supreme Court ruled on the case on March 8, 1971, by a unanimous vote. The justices decided against the Duke Power Company and ruled that such diploma and test score requirements are unconstitutional when neither of them is related to the job skills at hand.

SUGGESTED READING: 401 U.S. 424 (1971).

H

HACKMAN, GENE. Gene Hackman was born on January 30, 1930, in San Bernardino, California. His stature as an actor grew immensely in 1967 with his performance in *Bonnie and Clyde*, for which he received an academy award nomination as best supporting actor. *Bonnie and Clyde* launched his career, which led to a string of memorable film performance during the 1970s. He won a best actor Oscar for his performance as Detective Popeye Doyle in *The French Connection** (1971), and he followed that up with successful, workmanlike performances in *Cisco Pike* (1971), *The Posiedon Adventure** (1972), *Scarecrow* (1973), *The Conversation* (1974), *Zandy's Bride* (1974), *The French Connection II* (1975), *Bite the Bullet* (1975), *Night Moves* (1975), *Lucky Lady* (1975), *A Bridge Too Far* (1977), *The Domino Principle* (1977), *March or Die* (1977), and *Superman** (1978). Hackman's career continued to prosper during the 1980s and 1990s.

SUGGESTED READING: Allan Hunter, *Gene Hackman: A Biography*, 1987.

HAIG, ALEXANDER. Alexander Meigs Haig, Jr., was born on December 2, 1924, in Philadelphia, Pennsylvania. He graduated from West Point in 1947, and for a time in 1948 he worked on General Douglas MacArthur's staff in Tokyo. There he learned a lifelong disdain for journalists and for civilian authority, attitudes that were only reinforced when President Harry Truman relieved MacArthur of his command in 1951. After the Korean War, Haig spent a decade in obscure army posts, getting his promotion tickets punched along the way. He graduated from the Naval War College in 1960, an accomplishment quite unusual for most army officers, and in 1961 he earned a master's degree in international relations at Georgetown University. The theme of his master's thesis was the role of the military man in the making of national security policy. It advocated a military czar permanently at the president's side to advise on military challenges. In the thesis, Haig also expressed a disdain for the role of politicians in making military decisions.

By the early 1960s, Haig had found himself on a fast track to political influence within the U.S. Army. In 1962 he became a staff officer within the army's office of the chief of staff for operations, and in 1963 he became a military assistant to Secretary of the Army Cyrus R. Vance. Cyrus Vance was a rising star in military and diplomatic circles, and when Vance was appointed deputy secretary of defense under Robert S. McNamara in 1964, Haig remained with Vance, becoming deputy special assistant to both the secretary and deputy secretary of defense. McNamara found Haig to be loyal, politically astute, and militarily shrewd. Within months Haig had become the secretary of defense's right-hand man, responsible for liaison between the Pentagon and the White House. Throughout 1964, McNamara and his aides, including Haig, were steadily involved in plans for covert raids against North Vietnam and in readying U.S. escalation. Haig advocated a strong military presence in South Vietnam. Haig who saw the conflict in Vietnam as another episode in the Cold War,* regarded the North Vietnamese as mere puppets of the Soviets and Red Chinese.

When the Vietnam War* escalated in 1965, Haig found himself itching for combat, or at least for the command position within the combat theater. Haig arrived in Vietnam in July 1966 as G-3, an operations planning officer for the 1st Infantry Division. There he was awarded three Distinguished Flying Crosses. As commander of the First Battalion of the 26th Infantry Regiment, he led a surprise assault on Ben Suc, a Vietcong refuge in the Iron Triangle. In June 1967 Haig came home, was promoted to colonel, and received command of a cadet regiment at West Point. Late in 1968, Henry Kissinger* asked him to join the White House staff as his military adviser on the National Security Council. Among other duties, he screened all intelligence information to the president. Although few people knew his name, insiders began to recognize Haig as one of the most important people in Washington, D.C. By 1970 he had acquired direct access to President Richard Nixon* as well as the authority to conduct presidential briefings in the absence of the national security advisor, Henry Kissinger. On September 7, 1972, in what triggered an enormous controversy within the military establishment, Nixon promoted Haig over the heads of 240 senior officers to four-star general rank. At the same time, he was designated vice chief of staff of the United States Army.

Haig played a central part in the final settlement of the Vietnam War by convincing Nixon that his survival in office was more important than how Vietnam came out, and that he should escalate the use of military force, especially bombing, in order to get a settlement from North Vietnam before the November 1972 elections, when Americans would support or reject Nixon's reelection on the basis of the president's 1968 promise to end the war honorably. In the peace negotiations of October 1972, Kissinger and Haig fought a war of telegrams over the settlement. Haig thought Kissinger was going too far and giving up too much. Haig advocated the 1972 Christmas bombings of Hanoi and Haiphong Harbor* and personally delivered the ultimatum to Nguyen Van Thieu* to accept the peace agreement.

By early 1973, with Nixon reelected and the war over, Haig had become one of the most influential individuals in the country. He was appointed vice chief of staff of the army in 1973, and in May 1973, Haig became permanent assistant to the president. His power rivaled and often exceeded that of Secretary of State Henry Kissinger in 1972 and 1973, when Nixon visited the Soviet Union and normalized relations with the People's Republic of China.

In mid-1973, when the Watergate scandal* erupted into a full-blown political crisis, Nixon adopted a siege mentality. When his close aides H. R. Haldeman* and John Ehrlichman* left the White House in disgrace because of their involvement in Watergate, Nixon appointed Haig as his chief of staff. There Haig found himself trying to maintain national security and political stability while the Nixon administration disintegrated. His power was so extensive during the Watergate crisis that Special Prosecutor Leon Jaworski* called him the country's secret president.

Haig knew that the president had been mortally wounded politically, and that his emotional condition, along with severe political problems, constituted a threat to national security. Haig decided that the resignation of President Nixon was the only answer to the country's critical situation. Some journalists speculate that Haig was the "Deep Throat"* source to *Washington Post* correspondents Robert Woodward and Carl Bernstein, whose investigation eventually forced the president's near impeachment and resignation. Journalist Jules Witcover described his actions in getting Nixon to resign as a bloodless presidential coup.

After Nixon's resignation, Haig continued for several months to serve as a national security advisor to President Gerald Ford.* He returned to active duty in the army late in 1974 when Ford appointed him commander in chief of the European Command, a post Haig held until 1979. That year he retired from the army and became president and CEO of United Technologies Corporation. When Ronald Reagan* won the presidential election of 1980, he appointed Haig his secretary of state, but Haig chaffed in the position. He had always harbored disdain for diplomats, whom he believed made the work of military officers impossibly difficult, and he left the State Department in 1982. In 1986 Haig gave serious consideration to running for the Republican presidential nomination in the election of 1988, but he had neither the charisma nor the personality for national politics on a media stage. Since then Haig has continued to write and work as a political and national security consultant.

SUGGESTED READINGS: Alexander Haig, *Realism, Reagan, and Foreign Policy*, 1984, and *Inner Circles: How America Changed the World, A Memoir*, 1992; Roger Morris, *Haig: The General's Progress*, 1982.

Frances Frenzel

HAIPHONG HARBOR. The city of Haiphong sits at the outlet of the Red River into the South China Sea. It is the third largest city in the Socialist Republic of Vietnam. Because it is linked by railroad to Hanoi, the capital of Vietnam, and to major population concentrations in the Red River Delta, Haiphong is the key to the country's economy, the point through which virtually all imports and exports flow. During the Vietnam War,* large volumes of military supplies from the Soviet Union and the People's Republic of China arrived in the Democratic Republic of Vietnam (North Vietnam) through Haiphong.

During the war in Vietnam, Haiphong became a point of intense debate among U.S. military and civilian policymakers. Conventional strategic wisdom dictated that any site so central to an enemy's logistical enterprise deserved to be neutralized. During previous wars, the United States had not hesitated to bomb and mine enemy port facilities, always in hope of denying needed supplies to enemy military forces. Between 1965 and 1968, the United States subjected Haiphong to intense strategic bombing campaigns, and in response the North Vietnamese dispersed Haiphong's population and factories out into the countryside.

Both the Lyndon Johnson and the Richard Nixon* administrations refused to mine Haiphong Harbor, in spite of intense lobbying to do so from military and logistical specialists. Lurking behind their reluctance to engage in what seemed so obvious a military tactic was a primal fear of widening the war. Throughout the Vietnam conflict, U.S. leaders worried about a repeat of the Korean War, in which the People's Republic of China entered what had been a regionally and politically limited conflict and transformed it into a major war. By mining the harbor, opponents of the tactic claimed, the United States risked injuring Soviet or Chinese civilians and military personnel. If Chinese or Soviet personnel died at the hands of the U.S. military, China and the Soviet Union might be forced to respond militarily, which might then cause the Vietnam War to spin out of control into a global conflagaration.

Nixon's Vietnamization* policy also increased the pressure to mine the harbor. Between 1969 and 1972, the president gradually withdrew the vast majority of U.S. military personnel from South Vietnam, turning the war over to the South Vietnamese. But the loss of U.S. troops, combined with the continuing inability of South Vietnam's military forces to deal successfully with North Vietnamese forces, inevitably forced the president to escalate his remaining options, which included more bombing, mining North Vietnam's harbors, and invading surrounding countries. The U.S. invasion of Cambodia* in 1970 and the U.S.-backed South Vietnamese invasion of Laos in 1971 were part of that escalation, as was Nixon's secret bombing of Cambodia and Laos. Mining Haiphong Harbor was one of Nixon's options.

In the spring of 1972, North Vietnam launched the Eastertide Offensive* in an attempt to overrun South Vietnam. In response to the offensive, President Nixon ordered massive B-52 bombings of North Vietnam, including the cities of Hanoi and Haiphong. He also ordered the mining of Haiphong Harbor, the mining of several other North Vietnamese port cities and inland waterways, and the imposition of a naval blockade of the entire coast of North Vietnam. The president made it clear to the American public that his decision was based on a desire to protect remaining U.S. personnel in South Vietnam and to stem the flow of supplies to North Vietnamese troops fighting in South Vietnam. Along with National Security Advisor Henry Kissinger,* President Nixon hoped that the mining and the bombing would convince North Vietnamese to sign a peace treaty and end the war.

Although the mining of Haiphong and the massive bombing campaign over North Vietnam helped revive temporarily the waning antiwar movement,* most Americans supported Nixon's decision, especially by the fall of 1972 when negotiations to end the war became serious. Since that time, many military analysts have argued that the mining of Haiphong let North Vietnam know that the United States was so frustrated with the war that Nixon was willing to use whatever force was necessary to bring an end to the conflict. North Vietnam, so the argument goes, signed the peace treaty out of fear of American firepower. Critics of Nixon's decision argue otherwise, claiming that the mining of Haiphong only postponed the inevitable triumph of North Vietnam over South Vietnam.

SUGGESTED READINGS: *New York Times*, May 9–12, 1972; Joseph M. Rowe, "Mining of Haiphong Harbor," in *Dictionary of the Vietnam War*, ed. James S. Olson, 1988.

HAIR. *Hair* was an extraordinarily popular tribal-rock musical of the late 1960s and 1970s. Written by Gerome Ragni and James Rado, with music by Galt MacDermot, *Hair* opened originally at the Anspacher Theater in New York City on October 17, 1967; a revised version premiered at the Biltmore Theater on April 29, 1968. *Hair* was a celebration of the values of the hippie, "make love, not war" generation of the 1960s, with members of the group a hedonistic bunch who want a life without responsibilities or rules. Sex, drugs, and doing anything one wants whenever one wants are the group's values. On-stage nudity was used to reinforce those themes. *Hair* eventually had a run of 1,742 performances and became the Broadway version of the 1960s counterculture.

By the 1970s, the musical was being performed in a completely different pop culture context. When it previewed in the late 1960s, some Americans saw it as a precursor of a new future for American values, as if the hedonism of *Hair*'s characters would lead to a new utopia. Within a few years, however, American audiences viewed *Hair* as a nostalgic look at a world that had already disappeared after being overwhelmed by the Vietnam War* and the staggering economic problems of the 1970s. *Hair* was not the harbinger of a new America but a nostalgic glimpse at a short-lived social experiment.

SUGGESTED READING: Kurt Ganzl, *The Encyclopedia of the Musical Theater*, 1994.

HALDEMAN, H. R. (HARRY ROBBINS). H. R. "Bob" Haldeman was born in Los Angeles, California, on October 27, 1926. He was raised in upper middle-class prosperity in Beverly Hills. His father owned and managed a successful plumbing and air conditioning business. H. R. Haldeman's grandfather, Harry Marston Haldeman, was a conservative Republican and an intense anti-Communist, who in the 1920s founded the Better American Federation of California, one of the country's first anti-Communist organizations. Conservative political credentials came naturally to H. R. Haldeman.

As an undergraduate at UCLA, however, Haldeman's overtly political attitudes were not readily apparent. He later remarked, "I was not only apolitical, but had gone completely the other route. I was a rah-rah college type, a homecoming chairman, no less, and a campus leader." One of his close friends at UCLA was John Ehrlichman.* Years later, Haldeman invited Ehrlichman to join the White House Staff of President Richard Nixon.*

Haldeman graduated from UCLA in 1948 and then went into public relations, rising up the corporate ladder with the J. Walter Thompson Company. Haldeman specialized in political campaigns. During those years he hired Dwight Chapin and Ron Ziegler, who also joined Nixon's staff between 1969 and 1974. Taking leave periodically from his duties at J. Walter Thompson, Haldeman was involved in Nixon's successful vice-presidential campaign in 1956, his failed bids for the presidency in 1960 and the California governorship in 1962, and his victory in the presidential election of 1968. In 1969 he became White House chief of staff to President Nixon.

As chief of staff, Haldeman jealously guarded the president's schedule. So complete was Haldeman's control of presidential access that he and UCLA classmate John Ehrlichman were dubbed the "Teutonic Guard" by the White House press corps. Haldeman's closely cropped, crew-cut hair style enhanced his image for toughness. Critics charged that he had the demeanor of a "Prussian guard" and a gaze that "would freeze Medusa."

Haldeman, an advertising executive by profession, was a pioneer in the wholesale marketing of political candidates, or at least candidate Richard Nixon to whom Haldeman was totally devoted. During his testimony before the Senate Watergate Committee, Haldeman insisted that John Dean,* who had testified earlier, had been the instigator of the Watergate break-in and cover-up (*see* Watergate scandal). Haldeman's testimony in this regard was similar to that of his former White House colleague, John Ehrlichman. For his role in the Watergate break-in and the subsequent cover-up, Haldeman served eighteen months in a federal prison. He was released in December 1978. After his release from prison, Haldeman worked in real estate development in Southern California and owned a number of Sizzler Family Steakhouse franchises. He died of abdominal cancer on November 12, 1993, at the age of sixty-seven.

SUGGESTED READINGS: H. R. Haldeman, *The Ends of Power*, 1978, and *The Haldeman Diaries*, 1994; Theodore H. White, *Breach of Faith*, 1975.

Sean A. Kelleher

HALEY, ALEX. Alex Haley was born in Ithaca, New York, on August 11, 1921. He attended the Elizabeth City Teachers' College in North Carolina from 1937 to 1939 and then enlisted in the U.S. Coast Guard. Haley made the Coast Guard his career, retiring in 1959. During long stays aboard ship, Haley took up writing, a skill at which he was quite adept. He once remarked, "I was a sailor, I was a cook and this and that, and it might be said I was bootstrapped up to being a writer." By the early 1960s his work was being published in *The Atlantic, Harper's, New York Times Magazine*, and *Reader's Digest*. In 1964 he wrote *The Autobiography of Malcolm X*, in collaboration with Black Muslim leader Malcolm X. The book, published soon after Malcolm X's assassination, became an instant bestseller, eventually selling more than six million copies.

But Haley's real impact on American culture in the 1970s came with the publication of his book *Roots: The Saga of an American Family*. First published in 1976, the book eventually sold 1.5 million copies in cloth and more than four million in paperback. Roots* tells the story of Alex Haley's ancestors, beginning with Kunta Kinte, "The African" taken from the Gambia River region of West Africa in 1750 and carried as a slave to Maryland. From there the book traces the history of Haley's family up to the death of his father in Tennessee. The book inspired the 1977 ABC television miniseries *Roots*. Broadcast in eight episodes in January 1977, *Roots* played to a huge audience of tens of millions of Americans, who for the first time got a real glimpse of what slavery must have been like.

As a result of *Roots*, Alex Haley became an icon in the African-American community and the country's leading advocate of strong families, family reunions, and family history. He spent the rest of his life writing and speaking on the lecture circuit. Haley died of a heart attack on February 10, 1992. His book *Alex Haley's Queen: The Story of an American Family* was published posthumously in 1993.

SUGGESTED READINGS: *New York Times*, February 11, 1992; David Shirley, *Alex Haley*, 1994.

HAPPY DAYS. *Happy Days*, first broadcast by ABC on January 15, 1974, is a television spinoff of George Lucas's phenomenally successful film *American Graffiti** (1973). It is set in Milwaukee, Wisconsin, late in the 1950s or early in the 1960s—before the assassination of John F. Kennedy, the urban riots, and the Vietnam War.* A situation comedy revolving around the lives of high school students Richie Cunningham (Ron Howard), Potsie Weber (Anson Williams), and the high school dropout and motorcyclist Arthur "Fonzie" Fonzarelli (Henry Winkler), *Happy Days* evoked a more innocent time in American history. Script writers played off the contrast between squeaky-clean, innocent Richie and the cooler, wiser, more worldly Fonzie. Howard left the show in 1980, and although ABC continued to broadcast *Happy Days*, its ratings and revenues began to decline. The last episode was broadcast on July 12, 1984. *Happy Days* continued for the next decade, however, to be a popular rerun on most media markets.

SUGGESTED READING: Barbara Kramer, *Ron Howard: Child Star and Hollywood Director*, 1998.

HARGIS, BILLY JAMES. Billy James Hargis was born in Texarkana, Texas, on August 3, 1925. He was converted to Christianity as a teenager, attended Ozark Bible College for two years, and in 1943 was ordained to the ministry at the Rose Hill Christian Church of the Disciples of Christ in 1943. In 1948, after several pastorates, he settled in Tulsa, Oklahoma, where he founded the Christian Echoes National Ministry, a Christian anti-Communist organization. By the mid-1950s, his group had targeted communism, socialism, liberalism, the United Nations, and the National Council of Churches as enemies of America, as well as Martin Luther King, Jr., John F. Kennedy, and Lyndon B. Johnson. He enjoyed a considerable following in Oklahoma, Arkansas, Missouri, and Texas, and he was one of the leading Cold War* anticommunists in the United States during the 1960s.

In 1966 Billy James Hargis decided to leave the Disciples of Christ. He founded an independent ministry—the Church of the Christian Crusade—in 1966 in Tulsa. He sponsored Christian Anti-Communist Crusade rallies and mass meetings throughout the South and Southwest. In 1970 Hargis established the American Christian College in Tulsa to provide an opportunity for college students to study ''anti-communist patriotic Americanism.'' After the Supreme Court's *Roe v. Wade** decision in 1973, he founded Americans for Life to oppose abortion.*

During the early 1970s, Hargis was on the cutting edge of an important phenomenon that swept through the South and much of middle America later in the decade—the rise of the Christian right as a conservative political force. Hargis held liberals responsible for the decline of the United States as a world power, abortion, divorce, illegitimate births, and crime, and he called on the ''people of God'' (primarily fundamentalist Protestants) to enter the political process and become a force to be reckoned with by mainstream politicians. In this endeavor, Hargis was a forerunner of such individuals as Pat Robertson, Jim Bakker, Jimmy Swaggert, and Jerry Falwell, who have used their ministerial credentials and pulpits as political forces.

Ironically, Hargis was also a forerunner of the sexual scandals that affected so many of the leaders of the Christian right in the 1980s. His ministry crumbled in 1974 when several students at the American Christian College accused him of sexual misconduct. Hargis denied the allegations, but the scandal destroyed his ministry. He then formed the Billy James Hargis Evangelical Association and continued to grind out books and pamphlets condemning liberalism, socialism, and communism, but he never regained the influence he possessed during the early 1970s.

SUGGESTED READINGS: Richard Durham, *Men of the Far Right*, 1962; Billy James Hargis, *My Great Mistake*, 1986; John Redekop, *The American Far Right: A Case Study of Billy James Hargis and Christian Crusade*, 1968.

HARRIS, EMMYLOU. Emmylou Harris was born in Birmingham, Alabama, on April 2, 1947 and was raised in the Virginia suburbs of Washington, D.C. After three semesters at the University of North Carolina at Greensboro, she moved to New York City and began playing in clubs there. Her soprano voice sang country songs with a rock-and-roll flavor, and her reputation grew. In 1970 her first album, *Gliding Bird*, was released to little success. She then became acquainted with Gram Parsons, formerly of the Burrito Brothers, who had a dramatic influence on her music and career. Her next four albums were successes: *Pieces of the Sky* (1975), *Elite Hotel* (1977), *Quarter-Moon in a Ten-Cent Town* (1978), and *Profile* (1978). The hit singles from those albums included "If I Could Only Win Your Love," "Together Again," "One of These Days," "Sweet Dreams," "(You Never Can Tell) C'est la Vie," "Making Believe," and "To Daddy." By 1982 Harris had put together a total of eight gold albums, and her crossover success in country as well as rock-and-roll continued in the 1980s.

SUGGESTED READING: Patricia Romanowski and Holly George-Warren, eds., *The New Encyclopedia of Rock & Roll*, 1985.

HATFIELD, MARK ODUM. Mark Hatfield was born in The Dalles, Oregon, on July 12, 1922, and he was raised there on the deserts of western Oregon, where he acquired a streak of independence that later characterized his political career. Hatfield graduated from Willamette University in 1943 and joined the U.S. Navy, where he served until the end of World War II. He took a master's degree from Stanford University in 1948. Hatfield then began what he assumed would be an academic career, teaching political science at Willamette from 1950 to 1956. He was elected to the state legislature as a Republican in 1951. Over the years, he grew bored with the banalities of academic politics and yearned to exercise his considerable political talents on a larger stage.

In 1956 he won election as the secretary of state of Oregon, and two years later he was elected governor. Because of the unique state of Oregonian politics, Hatfield was not the typical western governor who condemned the federal government at every opportunity and praised the virtues of rugged individualism. Oregonians were concerned about the environment, which forced politicians, Hatfield included, to be willing to employ the power of the state periodically to prevent abuse of the environment by cost-cutting corporations. It was possible to be liberal and Republican and survive in Oregonian politics. In 1966 Hatfield sought and won election to the U.S. Senate.

He soon found himself in a most unusual political position, one that characterized his political career during the 1960s and 1970s. While the Republican party grew more conservative, Hatfield maintained his credentials as one of the party's few viable, genuine liberals. His career in the Senate was marked by a vigorous opposition to the Vietnam War.* By 1967 he was criticizing the scale of the American military effort in Indochina, and he became a frequent critic of the Richard Nixon* administration's handling of the war. In Hatfield's opinion, Nixon and Henry Kissinger* were unnecessarily lengthening the American stay there. When Nixon authorized the invasion of Cambodia* in 1970, Hatfield spoke militantly against it and sponsored, along with Senator George McGovern,* a Senate amendment cutting off funds for the Vietnam War after December 31, 1971. The Hatfield-McGovern Amendment* never passed, but it did reveal to President Nixon just how tenuous his political position was. He had promised in 1968 to find a way out of the war, and Americans expected him to do it. Hatfield also opposed the military draft and called for the establishment of a voluntary army. When the Nixon administration implemented both proposals, Hatfield felt vindicated.

During his last term in the Senate, Hatfield established his credentials as an environmentalist and backed Nixon in the passage of the Environmental Policy Act of 1970 and the creation of the Environmental Protection Agency. He established himself as one of the Senate's experts on energy, Indian, and natural resource policy. Hatfield could also be counted on to support civil rights programs and affirmative action.* In the wake of the Vietnam War, Hatfield became a vocal advocate for the extention of legal amnesty to those who had opposed the war through desertion and draft avoidance. His 1976 book *Amnesty: The Unsettled Question of Vietnam* put the issue before the American people. President Jimmy Carter* implemented the amnesty program, and Hatfield directed the necessary legislation through Congress.

During the 1980s, Hatfield increasingly found himself out of place in the Republican party. Conservatives in the tradition of Barry Goldwater took control of the party in the late 1970s, and Ronald Reagan's* success as a president cemented conservatives as the dominant force in the party. He was a strong advocate of freezes in nuclear arms construction, which he expressed in his 1982 book *Freeze! How You Can Help Prevent Nuclear War.*

During the last stages of his career, Hatfield turned to health care issues, especially the national crusade against cancer, for which he advocated increased funding. He also remained his unpredictable self, making conservatives mad by being the only Republican to vote against the balanced budget amendment in 1996, and angering liberals by his stand against abortion.* Tired of politics by 1996, Hatfield decided not to stand for reelection and retired in 1997.

SUGGESTED READINGS: Robert Eells, *Lonely Walk: The Life of Senator Mark Hatfield*, 1979; Mark Hatfield, *Conflict and Conscience*, 1971, and *Amnesty: The Unsettled Question of Vietnam*, 1976.

HATFIELD-MCGOVERN AMENDMENT. In the presidential election of 1968, Republican candidate Richard Nixon* promised the American public that if elected he would end the Vietnam War* honorably. He won the election, and soon after his inauguration, Americans began to watch carefully to see whether the new president would be able to live up to his promise. When he announced the Vietnamization* program of turning the war gradually over to the South Vietnamese, most Americans hailed the decision as a step in the right direction, and when the president began withdrawing U.S. combat troops from South Vietnam in August 1969, most Americans concluded that he was living up to his campaign promise.

All that changed in April 1970. The president had approved a combined American–South Vietnamese invasion of Cambodia* to attack Vietcong and North Vietnamese sanctuaries there. Nixon studiously avoided use of the term "invasion," preferring the euphemism "incursion," but many Americans saw it as a dangerous escalation of the war, and widespread protest demonstrations erupted across the country. Especially violent confrontations between students and National Guard troops occurred at Kent State University* in Ohio and at Jackson State University in Mississippi. During the first week of May more than 100,000 protesters gathered in Washington, D.C., to denounce the invasion. Outraged at not being consulted about the invasion, the Senate symbolically protested by terminating the Gulf of Tonkin Resolution in June 1970. Senator George McGovern* of South Dakota and Senator Mark Hatfield* of Oregon jointly sponsored an amendment requiring a total American withdrawal from South Vietnam by the end of 1971. Although the Hatfield-McGovern Amendment failed to pass in the Senate, it was an indication of the frustration felt by large numbers of Americans about the war. It also signaled to the president that he had very little political maneuvering room concerning Vietnam.

SUGGESTED READINGS: George Herring, *America's Longest War: The United States and Vietnam, 1950–1975*, 1986; James S. Olson and Randy Roberts, *Where the Domino Fell: America and Vietnam, 1945–1995*, 1995; William Shawcross, *Sideshow: Kissinger, Nixon, and the Destruction of Cambodia*, 1979.

HAWAII FIVE-O. *Hawaii Five-O*, starring Jack Lord as Detective Steve McGarrett, James MacArthur as Detective Danny Williams, Kam Fong as Detective Chin Ho Kelly, and Zulu as Detective Kono Kolakaua, was one of the most popular and long-lived police dramas in American television history. First broadcast by CBS on September 26, 1968, *Hawaii Five-O* was prime-time viewing for tens of millions of Americans for the next twelve years. A special team of the Hawaii State Police, the group of detectives worked out of Iolani Palace in Honolulu and reported directly to the Hawaiian governor. The steely, unemotional, street-smart, and intellectually gifted McGarrett presided over the Hawaii Five-O team like a medieval lord. There were no doubts about who was in charge. They battled petty criminals, sadistic killers, and the Hawaiian underworld. At a time of rebellion and social instability in America, *Hawaii Five-*

O was a symbol of discipline, law and order, and moral clarity. The last episode of *Hawaii Five-O* aired on April 26, 1980.

SUGGESTED READING: Tim Brooks and Earle Marsh, *The Complete Directory to Prime Time Network and Cable TV Shows, 1946–Present*, 1995.

HAYDEN, TOM. Thomas Emmett Hayden was born on December 12, 1940, in Royal Oak, Michigan, the only child of Catholic parents in a conservative working-class neighborhood. In December 1961, as a University of Michigan student, Hayden helped found the Students for a Democratic Society (SDS) and drafted the Port Huron Statement: "We are the people of this generation, bred in at least modest comfort, housed now in universities, looking uncomfortably to a world we inherit." At first SDS was not much more to the left than the liberal wing of the Democratic party, but under pressure of the civil rights movement* and opposition to the Vietnam War,* Hayden's politics gradually became more and more radical. By the fall of 1965, SDS was organizing against the draft and was accused of sabotaging the war effort. In 1966 and 1967, SDS escalated its campus demonstrations and protest marches. Hayden met with North Vietnamese representatives in Czechoslovakia in 1967, where the release of American prisoners of war (POWs) was discussed. He later flew to Cambodia* and escorted three released prisoners home.

In 1968 Hayden joined Rennie Davis in planning the National Mobilization Committee's anti-Vietnam demonstrations at the Democratic National Convention in 1968. The protesters were assaulted by the Chicago police, but Hayden was later arrested and became one of the "Chicago 8" defendants charged with conspiracy. Although he was convicted, the decision was later overturned on appeal. After the trial, he joined actress Jane Fonda* on the antiwar circuit, and they were married in January 1973.

After that Hayden began to change his radical image and entered California politics. He ran a surprisingly close race against Senator John Tunney in the senatorial primary in 1976, and in 1979 he and Fonda established the Campaign for Economic Democracy, a movement designed to secure popular control over major corporations. Dubbed the "Mork and Mindy" of the left in a column by George Will, they made appearances dressed conservatively and toned down their rhetoric from the militancy of the 1960s. Hayden won a seat in the California state legislature in 1980 and explained his political evolution by saying, "The radical or reformer sets a climate. The politician inherits the constituency that the reformer created. My problem is to be both."

Throughout his career in the state legislature, Hayden's Campaign for Economic Democracy focused on community development, sustainable economic growth balanced by environmental quality, inner-city employment programs, and corporate responsibility. In 1996 he staged an unsuccessful bid to unseat Richard Riordan as mayor of Los Angeles.

SUGGESTED READINGS: John Bunzel, *New Force on the Left: Tom Hayden and the Campaign Against Corporate America*, 1983; Tom Hayden, *The American Future:*

New Visions Beyond Old Frontiers, 1980, and *Reunion*, 1988; Nancy Zaroulis and Gerald Sullivan, *Who Spoke Up? American Protest Against the Vietnam War, 1963–1975*, 1984.

Frances Frenzel

HEARST, PATRICIA. The Patricia Hearst case was one of the most controversial, and notorious, of the 1970s. Patricia Campbell Hearst was born in 1955 to Randolph and Catherine Hearst, owners of the vast Hearst newspaper and publishing empire. On February 4, 1974, members of the Symbionese Liberation Army (SLA), a mysterious Marxist terrorist group, kidnapped Patricia Hearst and held her for ransom, demanding that her family give $400 million in free food to California's poor. Cinque,* leader of the SLA, claimed that Randolph Hearst headed a fascist economic empire that oppressed millions of poor people around the world. A ransom demand ordered the Hearsts to hand over, in a four-week period, $70 in high-quality meat, dairy products, and vegetables to each of the 5.9 million Californians who were disabled veterans, welfare recipients, probated convicts, and social security recipients.

The Hearsts agreed to the demands and soon set in motion the food distribution program, hoping to win the release of their daughter. But the incident took on a bizarre twist when it appeared that Patricia Hearst had converted to the SLA cause, by willingly participating in several robberies, brandishing automatic weapons, and shouting revolutionary slogans during the holdups. Whether Hearst had been acting under her own will or performing under threat of death from her kidnappers became the hottest topic of conversation and pop psychology in America in 1973 and 1974.

Hearst split up with the SLA before the bloody shootout in Los Angeles, California, that killed Cinque and five other SLA members. But instead of going home, she went on the run, evading the Federal Bureau of Investigation for sixteen months. She was finally captured in San Francisco on September 18, 1975.

Her trial could certainly be considered the trial of the decade. The Hearsts retained famed defense attorney F. Lee Bailey to keep her out of prison, but a federal jury, in March 1976, convicted Patricia Hearst of armed bank robbery and using a firearm to commit a felony. She was later convicted on state charges of armed robbery, kidnapping, and assault with a deadly weapon and sentenced to seven years in prison. Hearst served twenty-three months of the sentence before President Jimmy Carter* commuted it. She was released from prison on February 1, 1979. Today Patricia Hearst lives a quiet life as a homemaker and mother of two children in a small Connecticut town.

SUGGESTED READINGS: Shana Alexander, *Anyone's Daughter*, 1979; Anne Taylor Fleming, "The Heiress," *Ladies Home Journal* (September 1996), 124–26; Patricia Hearst, *Every Least Thing*, 1982; *Newsweek*, February 25, 1974, and March 29, 1976.

HEARTS AND MINDS. *Hearts and Minds* was a critically acclaimed 1974 documentary film about the Vietnam War.* It won an academy award in March

1975 as the best documentary of the year. The work of Peter Davis, *Hearts and Minds* voiced the horror of the Vietnamese people over the destruction they endured from the American military machine, and it exposed the callousness with which many American soldiers and pilots administered the destruction. The movie, a series of film clips and interviews, brought together all of the most horrific images of the Vietnam War: the brutality of South Vietnamese police and soldiers toward their own people, the horror of napalm raids, the deaths of so many children, and the meaningless futility of American policy in Southeast Asia. Although the film was considered to be a masterpiece by critics (and a piece of anti-American propaganda by Vietnam War supporters), it failed to convince any major film producer to give it a general release. Studio executives wanted nothing to do with the film because of the guaranteed controversy it was certain to generate. In reviewing *Hearts and Minds*, the *New York Times* told its readers about "An Undeclared War—Now an Unseen Film."

SUGGESTED READING: *New York Times*, November 17, 1974.

HELMS, RICHARD. Richard McGarrah Helms was born in Saint Davids, Pennsylvania, on March 30, 1913. After graduating from Williams College in 1935, he became a staff correspondent for United Press International and joined the *Indianapolis Times* in 1937. He quickly proved himself to be a shrewd observer of political affairs and a gifted writer. Helms remained with the *Times* until the outbreak of World War II, when he joined the U.S. Navy. At the time, the Department of War was busy developing a new military intelligence branch, which became known as the Office of Strategic Services, or the OSS. Naval officials assigned Helms to work with the OSS, and he remained with the agency throughout the war and into the postwar years. When Congress converted the OSS into the Central Intelligence Agency* (CIA), Helms enjoyed great influence in the fledgling intelligence enterprise.

Helms was appointed deputy director of the CIA in 1965, just when President Lyndon Johnson escalated the Vietnam War* and introduced U.S. ground troops into the conflict. By the time that Helms became director of the CIA, the Vietnam War had become a political disaster, with Helms supplying the Johnson and Richard Nixon* administrations with intelligence information far more pessimistic about Vietnam than the estimates coming from the Pentagon. While General William Westmoreland, commander of U.S. forces in South Vietnam, assured the president that enemy forces in Vietnam were getting weaker, Helms correctly concluded that North Vietnam was actually growing stronger.

At the same time, however, the CIA came under siege from critics protesting clandestine CIA activities in Indochina—secret armies, assassination squads, sponsored coup d'états, and domestic surveillance. Intelligence leaks also indicated that the CIA had regularly engaged in assassinations of acutely unfriendly politicians in other countries as well. In 1973 President Nixon replaced Helms as head of the CIA. As a result of congressional hearings, new legislation required the CIA to secure presidential approval of all covert operations, surrender documents to public scrutiny as long as it did not compromise agents in the field, stop surveillance of Americans abroad unless national security required it, and cease all domestic surveillance. Helms was forced to appear before a number of House and Senate committees in the mid-1970s as the legislation was evolving. Between 1973 and 1976, he served as ambassador to Iran.* Since leaving Teheran, Helms has worked as president of Safeer Corporation and as a consultant to international business and political concerns.

SUGGESTED READING: Thomas Powers, *The Man Who Kept the Secrets: Richard Helms and the CIA*, 1979.

HOFFA, JAMES. James Riddle "Jimmy" Hoffa was born in Brazil, Indiana, on February 14, 1913. He quit school in Detroit when he was fifteen and became a stockboy in a department store. In 1930 Hoffa became a freight handler for Kroger's, and four years later he joined the International Brotherhood of Teamsters, Chauffeurs, Warehousemen, and Helpers of America. Later that year, Hoffa became a full-time Teamster organizer, and he spent the rest of his life in Teamster politics. On a number of occasions, federal agents accused him of racketeering, but he managed to escape conviction.

In 1957 Hoffa became president of the Teamsters Union. He played a key role during the next several years in expanding Teamster control throughout the trucking industry. President John F. Kennedy and Attorney General Robert F. Kennedy, committed to dealing with the problem of labor union corruption, targeted Hoffa for investigation and prosecution. In 1964 he was convicted of jury tampering, misuse of union pension funds, bribery, and conspiracy. He entered the federal penitentiary in 1967 and resigned the Teamster presidency in 1971. He was pardoned by President Richard Nixon* on the condition that he would stay out of union affairs for the next ten years. (Hoffa had usually supported the Republican party.) He disappeared under suspicious circumstances in July 1975 and was never seen again. During the 1980s, it was rumored that Hoffa had been the victim of a mob murder, and that his body was buried in the concrete foundation of the Meadowlands Stadium in New Jersey.

SUGGESTED READINGS: Steven Brill, *The Teamsters*, 1978; Walter Shendan, *The Fall and Rise of Jimmy Hoffa*, 1972.

HOFFMAN, ABBIE (ABBOTT HOWARD). Abbie Hoffman, an icon of the 1960s who eventually came to symbolize the decline of the counterculture, was born in Worcester, Massachusetts, on November 30, 1936. He received a degree in psychology from Brandeis University in 1959 and then a master's degree at the University of California at Berkeley. Hoffman returned to Worcester in 1960 where he found work as a hospital psychologist. He was soon active in the civil rights movement* and the peace movement and helped raise money in the north for the Student Nonviolent Coordinating Committee (SNCC). His commitment to civil rights for African Americans was deep and sincere, but he soon collided with the rise of the black power movement, which often held Jewish liberals like Hoffman in suspicion and contempt. In 1966 SNCC purged all of its white leaders, and Hoffman found himself temporarily without a cause.

That state did not last long. He quickly emerged as the leader of the countercultural antiwar movement,* in which he fused the peace crusades, the youth culture's contempt for the World War II generation, and the counterculture's reverance for drugs, rock and roll, and sex. Hoffman produced several antiwar street theater productions. In a sarcastic move designed to expose materialism in America, he alerted the press one day in 1967 and then threw money from a balcony on to the floor of the New York Stock Exchange. A number of newspaper photographers and television correspondents had been tipped off in advance, and the next day the press was full of pictures of stock brokers groveling for every bill they could get their hands on.

Hoffman joined with Jerry Rubin in 1968 to form the Youth International Party, or "Yippies," a loosely defined political organization opposed to the Vietnam War* and to capitalism and in favor of sex, drugs, and pranksterism. Along with other antiwar groups, they staged the demonstrations in Chicago at the Democratic National Convention in 1968 that became the famous "police riot." Hoffman was charged with conspiracy to commit violence and, during the famous "Chicago 8" trial in 1969, he was convicted on that charge as well as for contempt of court. Both charges were later overturned on appeal.

In the 1970s, a different spotlight came to focus on Hoffman's life. His advocacy of recreational drug use turned into an addiction and criminal behavior. In 1973 Hoffman was arrested for selling cocaine. He was convicted and received a ten-year sentence. Rather than serve his time, he jumped bail and went underground, living as Barry Freed. Even then, he could not keep himself out of the political limelight. In 1978, as Barry Freed, he led the Save the River campaign to keep the Hudson River from being dredged. He wrote his autobiography, *Soon to Be a Major Motion Picture*, in 1980 and came out of hiding to promote it. He resolved his legal problems, and in 1984 he led the campaign against construction of a power plant at Point Pleasant on the Delaware River. By that time, Hoffman was suffering from a serious bout with depression, an illness that had frequently plagued him during his life. He committed suicide on April 12, 1989.

SUGGESTED READINGS: Abbie Hoffman, *Soon to Be a Major Motion Picture*, 1980; Marty Jezer, *Abbie Hoffman: American Rebel*, 1992.

HOFFMAN, DUSTIN. Dustin Lee Hoffman was born August 8, 1937, in Los Angeles, California. After earning excellent reviews on the New York stage in the early 1960s, Hoffman rocketed to fame in American popular culture as the troubled, rebellious college student in the film *The Graduate* (1967). The movie made Hoffman a cult figure. He received an Academy Award best actor nomination for his brilliant performance as "Ratso" Rizzo in *Midnight Cowboy* (1969), a dark film about the underside of the American Dream. Although Hoffman did not win the Oscar (it went to John Wayne for his performance in *True*

Grit), *Midnight Cowboy* elevated Hoffman's status as one of the country's finest actors. His performance as Jack Crabbe in *Little Big Man** (1970), a veiled anti-Vietnam War* film, confirmed that status. Hoffman's other four major films of the 1970s were *Straw Dogs** (1971), *Papillon* (1973), *All the President's Men* (1976), and *Kramer vs. Kramer* (1979). Since then, Hoffman has continued to earn accolades for his performances in such films as *Tootsie* (1982), *Rain Man* (1988) for which he won an Oscar for best actor, and *Outbreak* (1995).

SUGGESTED READING: Douglas Brode, *The Films of Dustin Hoffman*, 1983.

HUNT, EVERETTE HOWARD. E. Howard Hunt, Jr., was born on October 9, 1918, in Hamburg, New York. He graduated from Brown University in 1940 and then worked as a war correspondent, editorial writer, and screenwriter during the 1940s, before embarking on a twenty-one-year career as an agent for the Central Intelligence Agency* (CIA). As an employee of the CIA, Hunt served in a wide variety of locations worldwide. During his career, Hunt wrote forty-two novels and short stories, mainly of the mystery/espionage genre. After leaving the CIA, Hunt went into the professional security business and eventually became a security consultant to Richard Nixon's* administration, which provided him with an office in the White House. He was one of the men arrested for breaking into Democratic party offices at the Watergate office complex in 1972. Hunt's White House address provided journalists and criminal investigators with the link they needed to pursue the Watergate scandal.* Hunt pleaded guilty to burglary of the Watergate headquarters of the Democratic National Committee and eventually spent eighteen months in federal prison for his role in the Watergate affair.

SUGGESTED READINGS: Stanley Kutler, *Abuse of Power: The New Nixon Tapes*, 1997; Robert Woodward and Carl Bernstein, *All the President's Men*, 1974.

1

INDIANS OF ALL TRIBES. In the early morning hours of November 20, 1969, eighty-nine American Indians landed on Alcatraz Island* in San Francisco Bay. Identifying themselves as "Indians of All Tribes," this group of young urban Indian college students claimed the island by "right of discovery" and by the terms of the 1868 Sioux Treaty of Fort Laramie, which they interpreted as giving Indians the right to claim unused federal property that previously had been Indian land. The occupiers demanded clear title to Alcatraz Island and the establishment of an American Indian University, an American Indian Cultural Center, and an American Indian Museum on Alcatraz Island.

The Indian group initially used the name of United Native Americans but recognized that the name was not representative of the large number of Indian tribes who participated in the occupation. While casting about for a name, Belvia Cottier, a Lakota Indian woman who had been instrumental in the planning of a brief 1964 occupation of Alcatraz Island as well as the 1969 occupation, suggested the name Indians of All Tribes. The name was more appropriate because Indian people from tribes all across the United States participated in planning and carrying out the occupation. The name was adopted and remained unchanged until January 15, 1970, at which time the group filed legal articles of incorporation with the State of California and became a legal entity: Indians of All Tribes, Inc. The corporation's principal office was listed as Alcatraz Island in San Francisco, California.

The specific and primary purpose of the incorporated group was to promote the welfare of all Indians on Alcatraz Island and elsewhere. The general purposes and powers were listed as: (a) to administer Alcatraz Island; (b) to promote the welfare of residents of Alcatraz Island; (c) to negotiate with the federal government for the purpose of obtaining title to Alcatraz Island and other demands; (d) to establish Indian educational and cultural centers on Alcatraz Island and elsewhere; (e) to enter into and perform contracts, agreements, and other transactions of any description; and (f) to receive, own, possess, administer, and dispose of money and property of any description, individually in its own name, as trustee, or fiduciary, jointly with others or in any other manner. The corporation was organized pursuant to the California General Nonprofit Corporation Law, and the board of directors, known as council members, were all Indian people: Stella Leach (Colville/Sioux), Alan Miller (Seminole), Judy Scraper (Shawnee), David Leach (Colville/Sioux), Denis Turner (Luiseño), Richard Oakes* (Mohawk), and Ray Spang (Northern Cheyenne).

Criteria for membership in Indians of All Tribes was set forth in the bylaws of the organization.

Every Indian on Alcatraz Island in San Francisco Bay is a member of the corporation if he or she (a) is registered with the coordinator's office as a resident, and (b) has lived continuously on Alcatraz for at least seven days. An Indian loses his membership if (a) he leaves Alcatraz for more than seventy-two hours in any calendar week, without permission from Council; or (b) a majority of the Council votes to revoke his membership for violation of the security rules. If membership was lost by leaving Alcatraz for more than seventy-two hours, it could be regained by re-registering as a resident and living continuously on Alcatraz for a least seven (7) days.

The members of the island council established by Indians of All Tribes, changed numerous times during the nineteen-month occupation of Alcatraz Island, which ended on June 11, 1971. Provisions in the bylaws called for regular elections so that the island leadership would reflect the choice of leadership of the Indian people on the island. Throughout much of the nineteen-month occupation, Indians of All Tribes provided a sound framework for the diverse groups of Indian occupiers on Alcatraz Island. The council subcommittees provided for housing, security, finance, public relations, sanitation, cooking, day care, and medical care, as well as a negotiation team to meet with federal officials during the occupation. Every resident of Alcatraz Island was assigned duties in one of these areas. Indians of All Tribes ceased to exist following the Alcatraz occupation; however, the name remains today as part of the United Indians of All Tribes Foundation in Seattle, Washington.

SUGGESTED READING: Troy R. Johnson, *The Occupation of Alcatraz Island: Indian Self-Determination and the Rise of Indian Activism*, 1996.

Troy Johnson

INDOCHINESE IMMIGRANTS. One of the most dramatic outcomes of the Vietnam War* was the series of demographic changes that occurred throughout Indochina. During the 1950s and 1960s, the American presence in Indochina stimulated monumental demographic change. In 1954 nearly one million Roman Catholics from North Vietnam relocated to South Vietnam under protocols established by the Geneva Accords. As more and more American money poured into South Vietnam, beginning in the early 1960s and especially after 1964, the country's economy changed. South Vietnamese gravitated toward Saigon looking for jobs spawned by the American war machine. Between 1960 and 1970, the population of Saigon increased from just over one million people to nearly four million people. Most of them were peasants who had lived their lives in rural villages. The sheer destructiveness of the war, as a result of the blowing up of thousands of villages, also set in motion a vast migration within South Vietnam, as did U.S. policies to resettle peasants into militarily secure areas.

Similar demographic changes came to Laos and Cambodia.* The American invasion of Cambodia in 1970 drove large numbers of Vietcong and North Vietnamese soldiers deeper into Cambodia, and it had the same effect on Cambodian peasants. The population of Phnom Penh grew dramatically in the 1960s and 1970s as peasants headed for the city where they thought they might be free from military action at the hands of American soldiers and bombers and various factions of Cambodian guerrillas. In Laos, the Central Intelligence Agency* (CIA) recruited an army among the Hmong tribe to fight the Vietcong and North Vietnamese along the Ho Chi Minh trail. The combined American— South Vietnamese invasion of Laos in 1971 also destabilized hundreds of communities throughout the country.

The war in Southeast Asia during the 1960s and 1970s, and its aftermath in the 1970s and 1980s, stimulated the exodus of more than one million people to the United States. Between 1970 and 1992, approximately 120,000 people came from Thailand, nearly 140,000 from Cambodia, approximately 190,000 from Laos, and more than 550,000 from Vietnam.

The story of the Indochinese migration to the United States is still incomplete, although historians now identify three basic stages of the immigration process. Until the early 1960s, there were very few Vietnamese, Cambodians, and Laotians in the United States, and most of them were students enrolled in scientific and engineering programs at American universities. Those numbers increased along with the American escalation of the war in the 1960s, but even then the number of permanent Indochinese immigrants living in the United States numbered only a few thousand people. Many of them were the wives of American soldiers who had completed a tour of duty in South Vietnam. By 1975 a total of only 20,038 Indochinese immigrants had settled in the United States during the previous decade. The vast majority of them were Vietnamese. The Immigration and Naturalization Service did not even keep track of the number of Laotians and Cambodians because there were so few of them.

The second wave of Indochinese immigrants began in 1975 when North Vietnam completed its conquest of South Vietnam, the Khmer Rouge* overran Phnom Penh, and the Pathet Lao assumed power in Laos. Indochina had fallen to the Communists, and those Indochinese who came to the United States consisted of the people most closely associated, politically and economically, with the anticommunist regimes of Nguyen Van Thieu* in South Vietnam, Lon Nol in Cambodia, and Souvanna Phouma in Laos. The initial wave of Indochinese immigrants after the Communist takeover totaled approximately 170,000 people, of whom 155,000 were Vietnamese, 7,500 were Cambodians, and 7,500 were Laotians. The vast majority of them were former employees of the United States or the previous regimes in power. More than 40 percent of the Vietnamese were Roman Catholics who had been born in North Vietnam, migrated south in 1954, and then worked for South Vietnam during the intervening twenty years. Most of the Laotian immigrants were Hmong tribesmen who had cooperated with the CIA in attacking the North Vietnamese during the war. By the end of 1975, the United States had received 130,000 Indochinese refugees at receiving centers in Guam and the Philippines; another 60,000 were waiting in refugee camps in Hong Kong and Thailand.

This second wave of Vietnamese immigrants tended to be well-educated and blessed with good job and professional skills. In South Vietnam they had been large landowners, physicians, dentists, attorneys, civil servants, small business-men, and employees of large U.S. corporations doing business in South Vietnam, and when they settled in the United States they brought their educations and entrepreneurial skills with them. Many of them were Roman Catholics and al-ready spoke English, or at least understood English. They were accustomed to the economic and social rhythms of modern industrial society, and they had enjoyed substantial contact with Americans during the previous ten years. Their culture shock upon arrival, though considerable, was less than what subsequent waves of Vietnamese immigrants would undergo.

The third wave of Indochinese immigrants began arriving in the United States in the late 1970s. They were political and economic refugees from the brutal and ineffective policies imposed by the Communist regimes in Vietnam, Laos, and Cambodia. North Vietnam reunited the country under the name Socialist Republic of Vietnam, and political authorities in Hanoi implemented sweeping collectivization schemes all over the economy. The economies of Vietnam and Cambodia (Kampuchea) went into tailspins. Gross national product fell dra-matically, as did labor productivity. Income levels fell precipitously as capital, and the most talented people, fled. In addition, the economies of Indochina were suffering from the rapid drop in American spending, which had fueled income and employment for the previous decade. Large numbers of Vietnamese and Cambodians suddenly found themselves living in cities but out of work.

The Communist takeover also led to a variety of ethnic discriminations throughout Indochina. In Laos, the Hmong and Mien tribesmen who had co-operated with the Americans found themselves the objects of discrimination. In Cambodia, the Vietnamese and Cham Muslims became the objects of scorn by the ruling Khmer majority. The ethnic Chinese in Saigon, as well as the ethnic Khmers in the Mekong Delta, were targeted for discrimination by the Vietnam-ese government. Also, the rural mountain peoples of Laos and Vietnam, partic-ularly those who were living in the cities, were treated as second-class citizens by the more urbane groups in Cambodia and Vietnam. Because of the ethnic discrimination, there were significant pockets of discontented people who were anxious to leave their respective countries.

In addition to severe economic and social problems imposed by Communist economic dictates and the end of U.S. military spending there, the people of Indochina were suffering from significant political problems. The government of the Socialist Republic of Vietnam began relocating large numbers of southern

Vietnamese out of Saigon back out into the countryside, and many former employees of the United States and South Vietnam who had not been able to escape in 1975 found themselves subject to political "reeducation." Politically suspect individuals were forced out into reeducation camps in rural areas where they engaged in hard manual labor, received political indoctrination, and participated in mortification programs in which they confessed their sins. When political authorities decided they were "rehabilitated," they were reassigned to new jobs, usually where their skills could be employed. International human rights authorities protested the entire business but to little avail.

But the violation of civil rights in Vietnam was nothing compared to the genocidal rage that swept through Cambodia in the late 1970s. Pol Pot* and the Khmer Rouge came to power and launched a liquidation campaign aimed at eliminating everyone who had ever held political power in Cambodia, who had worked as a professional or intellectual, who had owned a small business, or who had worked for a foreign entity—in short, everyone but the peasants. Declaring "Year Zero," Pol Pot and the Khmer Rouge virtually depopulated the cities and major towns of Cambodia and went on a killing rampage. Some scholars and American intelligence experts estimate that between 1975 and 1979, when Vietnam invaded Cambodia in order to stop the slaughter, the Khmer Rouge assassinated more than one million people, including the elite and middle class of the entire country.

It was these economic, social, and political disasters in the late 1970s and 1980s that produced the third wave of Indochinese immigration to the United States. The people tended to be less educated than the original wave of immigrants, and they were more ethnically diverse, often consisting of Vietnamese, Cambodians, Cham, Hmong, Mien, Chinese, and a variety of other tribal people from the highlands. Comparatively few of them were Roman Catholics. They were desperate to escape the political oppression and economic blight of Indochina. Many of them also had family members who had already escaped to the United States with the earlier immigrants. They came out of Vietnam, Cambodia, and Laos illegally, either crossing overland through the mountains and jungles into Thailand, where they ended up in refugee camps, or escaping by sea in boats.

By far, most of the Indochinese who got away after 1976 were boat people* who left by sea in small boats, hoping to make it to Indonesia, Thailand, Malaysia, or the Philippines. Demographers now estimate that as many as 1.3 million people fled Indochina by boat. Their voyages were beset with danger. Pirates in the South China Sea regularly victimized them, and Indonesia and Malaysia, and later Hong Kong, frequently rejected them even when they did make landfall. Most historians suspect that only half of those who left Indochina in boats survived the journey.

At first the United States welcomed the new immigrants. Congress passed the Indochinese Migration and Refugee Assistance Act of 1975, renewed in 1977, which provided unprecedented economic assistance to the immigrants. The U.S.

government took a systematic approach to the settlement of the Indochinese refugees, making sure that they were not concentrated in any single geographical location. Thousands of small and large communities throughout the United States were asked to sponsor immigrant families, and the government often employed the services of local charitable organizations and churches in settling the immigrants into apartments, jobs, and schools. Most Americans, even those who opposed the war, felt a certain responsibility toward its victims. The government paid for their air fare to the United States, extended loans to those who wanted to start businesses of their own, and provided scholarship assistance for Vietnamese children wishing to attend college. The federal government also provided funds to local school districts to assist them in teaching the Vietnamese immigrants.

But that assistance was not permanent. The third wave immigrants were not as well educated or as well off as the first immigrants. They came from rural backgrounds and did not adjust as well to economic life in America. Because they came in such large numbers, they raised nativist concerns in the United States. The country was full of American veterans who did not like the Vietnamese anyway, and economic problems in the United States created fears that the immigrants would take jobs from natives and lower the prevailing wage levels. Another problem involved the definition of a refugee. The term ''refugee'' in U.S. immigration policy refers to an individual who is fleeing his or her homeland to escape political persecution. The United States does not recognize economic suffering, at least in terms of conferring refugee status, and the Immigration and Naturalization Service began to deny entry to many Vietnamese on the grounds that they were not true political refugees.

For some of the immigrants, especially the uneducated, rural peasants and the mountain people from the Central Highlands of South Vietnam and Laos, the adjustment was particularly difficult. By 1992 there were more than 250,000 Hmong and Mien tribesmen from Laos and Montagnards from South Vietnam living in the United States. The Laotian tribesmen were concentrated in Fresno, Sacramento, and Oakland, California, while thousands of Montagnards settled in North Carolina. Because most of them were essentially a premodern people practicing an animistic religion before the Vietnam War, their arrival in California in the late 1970s was an especially wrenching experience. Many of the mountain people went into clinical depressions after their arrival in the United States, and an astonishingly large number of them died of a type of sudden-death syndrome.

In 1998 only twenty-three years had passed since the end of the Vietnam War and the beginning of the large-scale Indochinese migration to the United States. A total of more than one million people from Indochina had settled here. Like other immigrant groups, they stirred up resentment as well as admiration among native Americans, and they had also established the ethnic institutions they needed to maintain their personal identity and begin the assimilation process in the United States. At the present time, tens of thousands of Vietnamese are languishing in refugee camps in Thailand, Malaysia, Indonesia, and Hong Kong waiting for the chance to come to the United States, and hundreds of thousands more in Vietnam hope for the same opportunity.

SUGGESTED READINGS: "No More Room for Refugees," *Time*, May 10, 1982; Muriel Stanek, *We Came from Vietnam*, 1985; Darrel Montero, *Vietnamese Americans: Patterns of Resettlement and Socioeconomic Adjustment in the United States*, 1979; Bruce Grant, *The Boat People*, 1979.

INTERNATIONAL INDIAN TREATY COUNCIL. One of the most powerful protest movements of the 1970s involved American Indians, whose civil rights concerns went far beyond those of blacks and Hispanics (*see* Civil Rights Movement). Native Americans, in addition to making sure that their individual civil rights were protected, were concerned about tribal sovereignty and the return of tribal lands illegally seized by non-Indians throughout the course of U.S. history. But in achieving their political objectives, Indians encountered a sobering reality: they constituted less than 1 percent of the U.S. population and had nowhere near the political clout of other, larger minority groups.

At the same time, however, they realized that their historical experiences in the United States were often mirrored by those of other indigenous peoples. In June 1974, representatives of ninety-seven indigenous peoples from North America, Central America, and South America gathered at the Standing Rock Sioux Reservation in South Dakota for the First International Indian Treaty Conference. Organized by the American Indian Movement,* the conference was designed to protest the exploitation of indigenous peoples and to organize an international political force to stop such exploitation in the future. The conference organized the International Indian Treaty Council (ITC) to lobby for its goals of Indian independence throughout the Western Hemisphere. Three years later, the United Nations formally recognized the ITC as a nongovernmental organization on its Economic and Social Council. As a result of that recognition, the ITC sponsored the 1977 International Non-Governmental Organizations Conference on Indigenous Peoples of the Americas in Geneva, Switzerland. The conference called on the United Nations to declare Columbus Day, October 12, an International Day of Solidarity and Mourning with Indigenous Peoples of the Americas. They also recommended formation of a United Nations Working Group on Indigenous Populations, which the United Nations established in 1981. Out of the working group has come a number of recommendations to promote Indian self-determination* and protect tribal landed estates.

SUGGESTED READING: Roxanne Dunbar Ortiz, *Indians of the Americas: Human Rights and Self-Determination*, 1984.

IRAN. Since the early 1950s, the United States had maintained a very close relationship with the Shah of Iran, an anticommunist on the Persian Gulf who seemed to improve U.S. access to precious oil supplies. During the next quarter of a century, the shah brought Iran into the world economy, modernized the country's economic institutions, but maintained a political dictatorship. Although American dollars and military assistance allowed the shah to build one of the Middle East's most formidable military establishments, he soon became politically vulnerable at home. The growing Iranian middle class resented his political authoritarianism, and Muslim fundamentalists were disgusted with modernization and what they called the westernization and secularization of Iranian society. In 1979 revolutionaries drove the shah from power.

Into the political breach came the Ayatollah Ruhollah Khomeini, a Muslim religious leader who despised the United States. Anti-American rhetoric became common in Iran as the Ayatollah whipped Muslim fundamentalists into a religious frenzy. On November 4, 1979, after the Jimmy Carter* administration allowed the shah to enter the United States for cancer treatment, a mob in Teheran stormed the U.S. embassy and took sixty American hostages. They promised to release the hostages only when President Carter turned the shah over to them. The mobs then took to the streets, parading blindfolded American hostages before the world press corps, burning U.S. flags, and characterizing the United States as the ''Great Satan.''

President Jimmy Carter was helpless. The United States formally protested seizure of the embassy and threatened diplomatic and economic pressure, but the Ayatollah would not back down. The crisis dragged on and on, all but ruining whatever credibility Jimmy Carter still had with the American public. In April 1980 the president staged a rescue attempt, but it was poorly planned and plagued by mechanical difficulties. The rescue helicopters never got within hundreds of miles of the hostages.

The U.S.-Iranian crisis lasted 444 days, and the hostages were released when President Ronald Reagan* took the oath of office on January 20, 1981. U.S.-Iranian relations remained strained for the rest of the century.

SUGGESTED READING: James A. Bill. *The Eagle and the Lion: The Tragedy of American-Iranian Relations*, 1988.

IRVING SCANDAL. In 1970 McGraw-Hill gave writer Clifford Irving a $765,000 advance for his proposed autobiography of Howard Hughes. Irving ostensibly had the full cooperation of the reclusive billionaire and had conducted more than one hundred interviews with Hughes. Hughes had even read the transcripts of the interviews and had made his own handwritten notes on them, which Irving submitted to McGraw-Hill as part of his proposal. Early in 1972, two weeks before publication, Irving admitted that the book was a complete hoax. Hughes had not given him any interviews, and the transcripts and handwritten notes on the manuscript were actually Irving's own forgeries. On March 14, 1972, Irving pleaded guilty to felony conspiracy charges and served a short prison sentence.

SUGGESTED READING: *New York Times*, March 14–16, 1972.

J

JACKSON, GEORGE. George Lester Jackson was born in Chicago, Illinois, on September 23, 1941. His family moved to Los Angeles when he was fourteen. In 1956, when he was just fifteen, Jackson was convicted of attempted robbery and spent time in a California juvenile facility. Shortly after his release, he was convicted of attempted robbery and sentenced to county jail. In 1960, soon after his release from the county jail, he was convicted of stealing $71 from a gas station, and a judge sentenced him to from one year to life in prison. He was incarcerated at the Soledad State Prison in Salinas, California.

From the view of prison authorities, at least, Jackson was not the proverbial "model" prisoner, which made it impossible for him to secure parole. He began reading widely and came to agree with the political theories of Karl Marx, Mao Zedong, and Fidel Castro. Convinced that capitalism was at the root of racism and discrimination around the world, Jackson began politicizing Hispanic and black inmates at Soledad, which led prison authorites to place him repeatedly in solitary confinement. Prison officials considered him to be a dangerous militant.

Jackson came to the attention of the rest of America in 1970–1971. He was accused of murdering, on January 16, 1970, a prison guard widely considered to be a vicious killer himself, a man whom prisoners believed had murdered three black inmates. Two other inmates—John Clutchette and Fleeta Drumgo—were accused of being Jackson's accomplices in the killing. The press soon dubbed all three the "Soledad Brothers." Their case became a cause célèbre and precipitated an investigation into the abuse of black and Hispanic inmates in California prisons. In interviews with journalists, George Jackson, who appeared to be thoughtful and articulate, called for the politicization of all prison inmates and the development among them of a revolutionary consciousness. His 1970 book *Soledad Brother: The Prison Letters of George Jackson* enhanced his growing reputation. The Soledad Brothers in general and Jackson in particular became darlings of the radical left, who considered them political prisoners.

On August 7, 1970, in a desperate and foolhardy attempt to secure his older brother's freedom, Jonathan Jackson entered the Marin County Courthouse, distributed guns to several accused criminals there, and took the judge, an assistant district attorney, and three jurors hostage. He demanded the release of George Jackson from prison. A struggle ensued, during which Jonathan Jackson, the judge, and two prisoners were killed. Radical philosopher Angela Davis* was accused of providing Jonathan Jackson with the weapons used in the incident.

By that time George Jackson and the other Soledad Brothers had been transferred to San Quentin Prison, where they were scheduled to go on trial for the murder of the prison guard. On August 21, 1971, under mysterious circumstances, Jackson was killed by prison guards, who subsequently accused him of armed rebellion. Earlier in the day, a prison riot had ended in the deaths of two prisoners and three guards. Jackson immediately became a hero and even an icon to New Leftists and black power advocates. Many other Americans, of course, viewed him as nothing more than a petty criminal and violent thug. In March 1972, John Clutchette and Fleeta Drumgo were acquitted of the murder charge that had first given rise to the Soledad Brothers.

SUGGESTED READING: Jo Durden-Smith, *Who Killed George Jackson? Fantasies, Paranoia, and the Revolution*, 1976.

JACKSON, JESSE. Jesse Louis Jackson was born Jesse Burns on October 8, 1941, in Greenville, South Carolina. His mother was Helen Burns and his father was Noah Robinson. When his mother married Charles Jackson in 1943, Jesse was adopted. A gifted athlete, he received a football scholarship to the University of Illinois in 1959, but he experienced what he considered unacceptable racist treatment in Urbana. He wanted to play quarterback, and the University of Illinois coach did not believe that African Americans had the innate intelligence to play the position. Jackson transferred to North Carolina A&T College in Greensboro where he became the leader of the famous sit-ins held at the town's lunch counters. Jackson would enter the restaurant and ask to be served. When the proprietors denied him service, students set up picket lines, occupied the other seats in the establishment, and refused to leave.

After graduating from North Carolina A&T in 1964 with a degree in sociology, Jackson decided to go into the ministry. He moved back to Illinois to attend the Chicago Theological Seminary. After one year, he returned to the South, joined the Southern Christian Leadership Conference (SCLC), and soon came to the attention of Martin Luther King, Jr. In 1966 King appointed Jackson to lead the SCLC's Operation Breadbasket campaign in Chicago. The program called on black people to boycott stores and businesses that would not hire black workers. Jackson's campaign in Chicago was so successful that in 1967 King named him head of the national Operation Breadbasket campaign. Jackson was in Memphis, Tennessee, with the civil rights leader when King was assassinated.

After King's death, the SCLC experienced major political struggles over leadership, and Jackson resigned in 1971. That same year he founded Operation PUSH (People United to Save Humanity), an advocacy group dedicated to promoting black education and the hiring of black workers. Throughout the 1970s Jackson dedicated himself to PUSH activities; he also spoke out widely on a variety of issues affecting black and working-class people, and in doing so he slowly emerged as the most visible African-American leader in the country. He spoke with passion and inspiration about black pride and black responsibility and about the need for compassion for the poor and downtrodden.

In the 1980s Jackson turned to more traditional political action. He decided to run in the Democratic presidential primaries in 1984 and 1988 under the aegis of what he called the Rainbow Coalition, an alliance of minority groups. Although he did not win the nomination, he became a power broker in the Democratic party because of the support he had among African-American voters. He frequently found himself, however, at the center of intense controversies. In 1984 he told a reporter that New York City was "Hymietown." Jews consider the term "Hymie" an ethnic slur. Jackson's close relationship with Louis Farrakhan of the Nation of Islam also rattled many American Jews, as did his sympathies for the plight of the Palestinian people.

During the 1990s Jackson kept the faith, maintaining his role as spokesman for the poor and weak, even as the Democratic party, and much of the American electorate, grew more conservative. He has frequently criticized Bill Clinton and Al Gore for abandoning the traditional Democratic party commitment to minority and working-class people.

SUGGESTED READINGS: Teresa Noel Celsi, *Jesse Jackson and Political Power*, 1991; Adolph Reed, *The Jesse Jackson Phenomenon*, 1986; Arnold Gibbons, *Race, Politics, and the White Media: The Jesse Jackson Campaigns*, 1993; Barbara Reynolds, *Jesse Jackson: The Man, the Movement, the Myth*, 1975.

THE JACKSON FIVE. Early in the 1960s, Joseph Jackson of Gary, Indiana, created a singing group out of three of his sons, Tito, Jermaine, and Jackie. Known as The Jackson Family, they performed locally in northern Indiana. When younger brothers Michael and Marlon joined in 1964, the group became known as The Jackson Five. They signed a contract with Motown Records and released their first single in 1969. "I Want You Back" hit number one in January 1970. Twelve more top-twenty hits followed, including "ABC" (1970), "The Love You Save" (1970), "I'll Be There" (1970), "Mama's Pearl" (1971), "Never Can Say Goodbye" (1971), "Maybe Tomorrow" (1971), "Sugar Daddy" (1971), "Little Bitty Pretty One" (1972), "Lookin' Through the Windows" (1972), "Corner of the Sky" (1972), "Dancing Machine" (1974), and "I Am Love" (1975). By that time they were the most commercially successful singing group in the world. In 1975, however, when the family broke with Motown Records, Jermaine refused to go along, and he started his own solo career. The other brothers, known now as The Jacksons, produced several top-ten rhythm-and-blues hits in the early 1980s. Michael then split off and launched his extraordinarily successful, and controversial, solo career.

SUGGESTED READINGS: George Nelson, *The Michael Jackson Story*, 1984; Patricia Romanowski and Holly George-Warren, eds., *The New Encyclopedia of Rock & Roll*, 1985; Randy Taraborrell, *Michael Jackson: The Magic and the Madness*, 1991.

JACKSON STATE COLLEGE. In 1970 Jackson State College was a predominantly black, state-supported public college of 3,000 students located in Jackson, Mississippi. On May 14, 1970, local police and Mississippi state highway patrol members fired into a crowd of demonstrating students, killing two and wounding twelve. City and state police had been summoned to the campus to put down a riot of rock- and bottle-throwing protesters who were targeting white motorists. Jackson State officials claimed that the rioters were not students.

Tensions had been building for some time. The racist atmosphere prevailing in Mississippi politics had long generated resentments among African Americans, and the antiwar movement* protests following the U.S. invasion of Cambodia* and the killings at Kent State University* heightened tensions. The fact that the university regularly expelled students accused of civil rights activism only made matters worse. On May 7, 1970, 500 Jackson State students staged a peaceful demonstration protesting the Vietnam War.* Six days later, tensions escalated on campus when students decided to protest racial killings and disturbances that had occurred in Augusta, Georgia. On the evening of May 13, about 150 young people began hurling rocks at cars driven by white motorists. Governor John Bell Williams of Mississippi alerted the National Guard and deployed some of them to the campus.

On May 14, the rock-throwing began again. A crowd of about 100 students gathered in front of Alexander Hall, the women's dormitory, and shouted at police. A dump truck near the campus was arsoned, and crowds harassed the firefighters who arrived on the scene to put out the blaze. Some firemen claimed that they had been fired upon by snipers. When a wine bottle was thrown and exploded on the street, the melee went out of control. Police claimed to have heard two rounds of small calibre weapons fire, after which they fired 140 rounds of buckshot into the crowd. Two young men—James Green and Phillip Gibbs—were killed. Students claimed to have heard no gunfire. Coming in the wake of the Kent State killings two weeks before, the Jackson State incident further alienated student activists, even though the shooting in Mississippi was not part of a Vietnam War protest.

SUGGESTED READING: *New York Times*, May 15–16, 1970; Tim Spofford, *Lynch Street: The May 1970 Slayings at Jackson State College*, 1988.

JACKSON V. GEORGIA. See FURMAN V. GEORGIA; JACKSON V. GEORGIA; BRANCH V. TEXAS.

JAVITS, JACOB. Jacob Koppel Javits, one of the most liberal Republicans in modern U.S. history, was born in New York City on May 18, 1904. He took a law degree from New York University in 1927, practiced law privately, and served in the U.S. Army during World War II. In 1946 Javits was elected to Congress, and he won a seat in the U.S. Senate in 1956. At the time, Governor Nelson Rockefeller* and moderate to liberal Republicans controlled the party machinery in New York, and Javits's own political philosophy, which believed in the power of government activism to promote the general welfare, fit in perfectly.

During the 1960s Javits became the leading Republican critic of the Vietnam War.* He believed strongly that the moving force behind the Vietnamese conflict was nationalism, not communism, and that Vietnam was not worth the investment of so much American money or the sacrifice of so many American lives. He supported both the Cooper-Church Amendment* and the Hatfield-McGovern Amendment,* and in 1970 he sponsored legislation to restrict the ability of the president to conduct war without congressional authorization. It was passed, over Richard Nixon's* veto, in 1973 and known as the War Powers Resolution. During the Watergate scandal* of 1973–1974, Javits urged President Nixon to resign from the presidency and save the country from a constitutional and political disaster.

During the remainder of the 1970s, Javits lost political power in New York. The winds of political philosophy were shifting, and conservatism was making a resurgence. In 1980, the year in which Ronald Reagan* was elected president on a conservative Republican platform, Javits lost the Republican primary in New York. By then he was in the early stages of the amyotrophic lateralsclerosis (Lou Gehrig's disease) that killed him on March 7, 1986.

SUGGESTED READINGS: Jacob Javits, *Javits: The Autobiography of a Public Man*, 1981; *New York Times*, March 8, 1986.

JAWORSKI, LEON. Leon Jaworski was born in Waco, Texas, on September 19, 1905. He received undergraduate and law degrees from Baylor University and George Washington University. Blessed with a brilliant mind and a home-spun country demeanor, Jaworski went into private practice and eventually made his firm—Fulbright & Jaworski—one of the most successful in Texas. He served as an assistant attorney general in the Department of Justice from 1963 to 1965, and from 1965 to 1969, Jaworski was an advisor to President Lyndon B. Johnson. In 1973, when Richard Nixon* fired Archibald Cox* as special Watergate prosecutor, Jaworski replaced him (*see* Watergate scandal). Nixon believed that Jaworski's more conservative Texas connections would help the administration, but Jaworski pursued the investigation with all the tenacity of a pit bull. He eventually secured access to the secret White House tapes which implicated a number of White House officials, including the president himself, in charges of obstructing justice. Jaworski's investigation eventually led to the resignation of

Nixon and federal prison terms for many of his associates. He then returned to his law practice.

SUGGESTED READINGS: James Doyle, *Not Above the Law: The Battles of Watergate Prosecutors Cox and Jaworski*, 1977; Leon Jaworski, *The Right and the Power: The Prosecution of Watergate*, 1976.

THE JEFFERSONS. A spinoff of *All in the Family*,* *The Jeffersons* premiered on CBS television on January 18, 1975, and became one of the most popular situation comedies of the 1970s. It was also the most successful of a new genre of African-American television programs. George Jefferson (Sherman Hemsley), a black version of Archie Bunker, was a self-made millionaire who had little patience for liberals or conservatives. With his wife Louise (Isabel Sanford), his son Lionel (Mike Evans and later Damon Evans), and their sassy, outspoken maid Florence (Marla Gibbs), Jefferson lived in a luxury, high-rise apartment on the East Side of Manhattan. Snobbish and self-centered, with a sharp tongue, Jefferson could not abide liberals, racists, or fools. What America had become used to on the small screen was either the sychophantic buffoonery and exaggerated mannerisms of Amos and Andy or Redd Fox. George Jefferson was a proud, outspoken, successful black man, perhaps the first in American television history. The last episode of *The Jeffersons* was broadcast on July 23, 1985. The program remained in wide rerun distribution well into the 1990s.

SUGGESTED READING: Tim Brooks and Earle Marsh, *The Complete Directory to Prime Time Network and Cable TV Shows, 1946–Present*, 1995.

JEWISH DEFENSE LEAGUE. The Jewish Defense League (JDL) was founded in 1968 in New York City by Rabbi Meir Kahane. Militantly committed to promoting Jewish power and the state of Israel, and opposing, violently if necessary, all forms of anti-Semitism, Kahane was the Jewish equivalent of such black power activists as Stokely Carmichael and H. Rap Brown. Kahane organized "Jewish Is Beautiful" rallies, engaged in civil disobedience to protest black anti-Semitism, and called for all Jews to return to traditional religious practices and to consider emigrating to Israel. More moderate Jewish organizations opposed Kahane's militant radicalism, and JDL membership never exceeded seven thousand people. In 1971 Kahane emigrated to Israel.

SUGGESTED READING: Meir Kahane, *The Story of the Jewish Defense League*, 1975.

JOE. By the late 1960s, working-class Americans, tired of the antiwar movement* and the counterculture, began to engage in a backlash against liberalism's excesses. On the television screen, *All in the Family*'s* Archie Bunker epitomized the racism and ethnocentrism in America, but his son-in-law Michael Stivic's knee-jerk liberalism was no more admirable. In the summer of 1969, hard-hat construction workers in New York City, more than 150,000 of them, demonstrated in favor of the American flag and the Vietnam War.* On the movie screen, the 1970 film *Joe* tried to expose the central values of lower middle-class American culture and its views about the Vietnam War. The main character goes through changes in attitude that reflect the shift in conciousness many Americans underwent during the 1960s. Joe has to deal with the counterculture and antiwar activists, and he comes to face his own feelings about American involvement in the war. The film is about as subtle as an M-16; Joe has to confront personal violence as well as the violence of the war.

Joe Curran (Peter Boyle) is a blue-collar stereotype who loves guns and hates hippies, communism, and homosexuals. He crosses paths with Bill Compton, an uptown, upper middle-class executive who has just murdered his daughter's lover, a sleazy, loathesome drug pusher. The two unlikely comrades form an alliance to find the whereabouts of the daughter, cover up the murder, and avenge those who have exploited her. Their search carries them through the countercultural underground of Greenwich Village in 1970, where participants engage in demeaning, pot-smoking orgies. The film, which compares and contrasts the differences between the upper middle-class in America and the lower middle-class, exposes Joe Curran for the best and the worst that are in him.

SUGGESTED READING: *New York Times*, July 16, 1970.

JONESTOWN MASS SUICIDE. Late in November 1978, newspapers around the world headlined a mass suicide that had occurred in Jonestown, Guyana. The Reverend Jim Jones, a charismatic evangelist who had launched the People's Temple in San Francisco early in the decade, had transplanted his ministry from the United States to Guyana, where he and his followers established a religious community based on a confused mixture of Marxist ideology and apocalyptic Christianity. Followers used the paternalistic "Dad" to refer to Jones, who demanded absolute loyalty, expecting his "children" to obey his every word, including his sexual demands.

Early in 1978, political officials began to respond to complaints from friends and relatives of Jonestown residents, who claimed that Jones was running an ideological cult and perhaps kidnapping residents and keeping them there against their will. Congressman Leo J. Ryan decided to fly to Guyana and investigate the charges. Convinced that a conspiracy existed to destroy the People's Temple, Jones had Ryan killed before he returned to California. Once Ryan was dead Jones realized that his movement was doomed, and he convinced his followers to commit mass suicide. The community's physician distributed Kool-Aid laced with poison, and, on November 20, 1978, the residents obediently consumed it and fed it to their children and died. A total of 405 people, including Jim Jones, were found dead. The suicide precipitated a vigorous debate in the United States about religious freedom and the future of messianic cults.

SUGGESTED READINGS: Mary Maaga, *Hearing the Voices of Jonestown*, 1998; *New York Times*, November 27–28, 1978.

JORDAN, BARBARA. Barbara Carolina Jordan was born in Houston, Texas, on February 21, 1936. She graduated from Texas Southern University in 1956 and then received a law degree from Boston University in 1959. After a brief stint as a lawyer in private practice, she became an administrative assistant to the judge of Harris County. Jordan lost bids for the state legislature in 1962 and 1964, but in 1966 she finally succeeded, helped by the large numbers of African Americans now able to vote because of the Voting Rights Act of 1965. Seven years later, in 1972, Jordan won a seat in the House of Representatives, making her the first black woman from the South to ever serve in Congress.

Fate soon put her into the public spotlight. She received an appointment to the House Judiciary Committee, and when the impeachment hearings arising from the Watergate scandal* against President Richard Nixon* took place in 1974, Jordan found herself in the public limelight. She spoke eloquently, in a deep resonant voice, of her love for the U.S. Constitution. "I am not going to sit by," she said to a national television audience, "and be an idle spectator to the diminution, the subversion, the destruction of the Constitution." She voted for the bills of impeachment. During the rest of her three terms in Congress, Jordan crusaded against the Vietnam War* and in favor of the Equal Rights Amendment,* the environmental movement* and the civil rights movement,* and economic assistance to the elderly and the poor. Faced with health problems, Jordan decided not to run for reelection in 1978 and instead accepted a faculty position at the University of Texas in Austin. In 1982 she was appointed there to the Lyndon B. Johnson Chair in Public Policy. She remained in that position until her death on January 17, 1996.

SUGGESTED READINGS: James Haskins, *Barbara Jordan*, 1977; *New York Times*, January 18, 1996.

JORDAN, HAMILTON. William Hamilton McWhorter Jordan was born in Charlotte, North Carolina, on September 21, 1944. In 1967 he graduated from the University of Georgia with a degree in political science, and in 1970 he managed Jimmy Carter's* successful campaign for governor of Georgia. During Carter's governorship, Jordan served as his executive secretary and special assistant. Carter tabbed Jordan to run his 1976 presidential campaign, and when Jimmy Carter won the election, he named Jordan as his special assistant and later chief of staff. When Jimmy Carter left office in 1981, Jordan went into private business as a communications and political public relations consultant.

SUGGESTED READING: Hamilton Jordan, *Crisis: The Last Year of the Carter Presidency*, 1982.

JUDAS PRIEST. Judas Priest, a popular rock-and-roll band of the 1970s, was formed in Birmingham, England, in 1969. Over the years, the group included Kenneth Downing, Rob Halford, Ian Hill, Scott Travis, David Holland, and Glen Tipton. Known for their heavy-metal sound and all-leather costumes, Judas Priest released its first album in 1976. *Sad Wings of Destiny* was a commercial disappointment. So was their next album, *Sin After Sin* (1977). By that time, however, they had become quite popular in England. Their reputation in the

United States steadily increased, particularly with the release of their hit albums *Stained Class* and *British Steel*. They became huge American superstars in 1982 when their album *Screaming for Vengeance* went platinum. Their next two albums also went platinum. Judas Priest, the pioneer of heavy metal rock and roll, disbanded in 1990.

SUGGESTED READING: Steve Gett, *Judas Priest, Heavy Duty: The Official Biography*, 1984.

K

KC AND THE SUNSHINE BAND. KC and the Sunshine Band, a rock-and-roll group formed in Hialeah, Florida, in 1973, included Harry Wayne Casey, Richard Finch, Jerome Smith, Robert Johnson, Fermin Coytisolo, Denvil Liptrot, James Weaver, and Charles Williams. Pioneers of what later became known as the Miami sound, the band released its first album, *Do It Good*, in 1974. It was only a modest success, but in 1975 the band hit it big and stayed at the top of the pop music charts for several years, during which they released the following hit singles: "Rock Your Baby," "Get Down Tonight," "That's the Way (I Like It)," "(Shake, Shake, Shake) Shake Your Booty," "I'm Your Boogie Man," "Keep It Comin' Love," "Do You Wanna Go Party," "Yes, I'm Ready," and "Please Don't Go." After their last top-twenty record in 1979, the band entered a long period of decline.

SUGGESTED READING: J.S. Roberts, "KC and the Sunshine Band: Not for Teeny boppers only," *High Fidelity and Musical America* 28 (April 1978), 123–25.

KENNEDY, EDWARD. Edward Moore "Teddy" Kennedy was born on February 20, 1932, near Boston, Massachusetts, to one of America's most distinguished political families. His father, Joseph Kennedy, had amassed a fortune in the banking, liquor, real estate, and film industries, and his mother, Rose, was a Fitzgerald, one of Boston's most powerful political families. Rose Fitzgerald Kennedy was a devout Roman Catholic, but Joseph was only nominal in his religious devotions, although he identified closely with the church because of his Irish background. Edward Kennedy was their ninth and final child.

The Kennedys had extraordinary expectations for their children, and Edward, whom they affectionately called "Teddy" or "Ted," was no exception. They insisted that their children succeed in the world of Anglo-Protestants, and, for the most part, they did. Like his brothers, Edward Kennedy attended several prestigious New England preparatory schools, and in 1950, he entered Harvard, where everyone expected him to follow in the footsteps of his brothers Joseph, John, and Robert. But Ted Kennedy had a knack for getting himself into trouble. In 1951 he was expelled from Harvard for allowing another student to take a Spanish final for him. Humiliated, Kennedy imposed a personal penance upon himself and joined the U.S. Army as an enlisted man. After basic training, he spent the next sixteen months stationed in Germany as a private.

Kennedy was honorably discharged from the army in 1953, and with his personal sense of self-respect restored, he was readmitted to Harvard. He worked hard and received his undergraduate degree in the spring of 1957, but Ted Kennedy was not as intellectually gifted as his brothers, and he was not admitted to Harvard Law. Instead, he enrolled in the University of Virginia Law School and took a degree there in 1959.

By that time he had joined the Kennedy family organization that was planning and organizing John F. Kennedy's run for the 1960 Democratic presidential nomination. John F. Kennedy secured the nomination and went on to defeat Richard Nixon* in the November 1960 presidential elections. Kennedy's victory vacated his seat in the U.S. Senate, which Ted sought in 1962. The Kennedy name had become political magic in the United States, and Ted won a landslide victory to become the junior senator from Massachusetts.

Tragedy then struck the family. John F. Kennedy was assassinated on November 22, 1963, and in 1964, on the eve of his reelection bid, Ted Kennedy was almost killed in an airplane crash. He suffered multiple fractures and underwent a long convalescent period, but he managed to win reelection from a hospital bed. During the next several years, he served in the shadow of his brother Robert F. Kennedy, who had won election in 1964 as a U.S. senator from New York and had become heir to the Kennedy political legacy. During Robert's run for the presidency in 1968, a campaign based on opposition to the Vietnam War* and the need to continue and expand civil rights (see civil rights movement) and antipoverty legislation, he was assassinated.

Ted was now the only Kennedy son left. His oldest brother, Joseph, had been killed in World War II, and John and Robert had been assassinated in 1963 and 1968, respectively. The mantle of leadership now passed to him, and he was ready to assume it. In 1969 he defeated Russell Long of Louisiana for the majority whip position in the U.S. Senate, which allowed him to push his own legislative agenda. He intended to carry on for his brother Robert and see to it that the Vietnam War was brought to a rapid conclusion and that minorities and the poor received a share of the American Dream.

But all of those dreams, as well as Ted Kennedy's hope to become president of the United States, ended on July 18, 1969. He found himself in the midst of a terrible scandal from which he could never really extricate himself. The incident occurred at Chappaquiddick on the island resort of Martha's Vineyard in Massachusetts around midnight. He had been partying on the island with several political associates and young women close to his campaigns. While trying to drive off the island, Kennedy lost control of his car and plunged off a bridge.

He managed to escape, but his passenger, Mary Jo Kopechne, drowned. He neglected to report the accident but instead returned to the party the two had been attending and secured the assistance of a former U.S. attorney for the state of Massachusetts, Paul Mackham, and his cousin, Joseph Gargan. They returned to the scene of the accident, but belated attempts to rescue Kopechne failed. Kennedy reportedly swam the channel to the mainland, while his two companions returned to the party, leaving her in the water. Neither Kennedy nor the two men reported the accident to the police.

The wrecked car was spotted the following morning and reported to Edgartown Police Chief Diminich Arena. The vehicle was later identified as belonging to Kennedy. Police launched a search for him, but around 8:30 A.M. Kennedy and his two assistants reported to Edgartown police headquarters. On July 25, 1969, Kennedy pleaded guilty to leaving the scene of an accident and was given a two-month suspended sentence and a one-year probation. The apparent miscarriage of justice gave rise to a widespread belief that a massive cover-up was taking place. The incident forever tarnished Edward Kennedy's political reputation. The married Kennedy had been partying with a single woman, and after his own driving caused the accident, he had apparently been more worried about his own political career than her life. Senate Democrats unceremoniously dumped him as majority whip. Massachusetts voters, however, elected him to a third term in 1970.

The vaunted Kennedy political machine hired a legion of spin doctors to try to salvage his reputation, but Americans were unwilling to forgive. His brothers had all died heroically, but he had run away from danger and abandoned a young woman to her death, it was charged, in order to save his political skin. The reality of his destroyed national ambitions became abundantly clear in 1972, when he tested the political waters again. President Nixon appeared to be in political trouble in the spring of 1972. The North Vietnamese had launched the Eastertide Offensive* and the Vietnam War was once again in the headlines. Kennedy declared his candidacy for the Democratic presidential nomination and entered several primaries, but his campaign was stillborn. Chappaquiddick would not go away, and the Democrats had no intention of putting up a presidential candidate with a political millstone around his neck.

Inside Massachusetts, however, the Kennedy magic survived, and he won reelection in 1976. With twelve years in the U.S. Senate, he was enjoying the power and committee chairmanships that seniority brings, and he continued to strengthen his reputation as one of the Senate's most powerful liberals. He specialized in minority affairs—especially the plight of the American Indian, as well as in education and health care. Kennedy also bided his time, hoping that Chappaquiddick would drift into the past and allow him another run at the White House.

Late in 1979 he thought his opportunity had arrived. Under President Jimmy Carter,* the country seemed in disarray. The economy was in a shambles, wracked by unemployment, inflation, and the energy crisis,* and in foreign affairs the United States seemed impotent, especially after Iranian militants seized hostages at the U.S. embassy. Confident that Chappaquiddick was ancient history, he decided to challenge President Carter for the Democratic nomination. In short order, Kennedy learned that Chappaquiddick would never go away. Carter defeated him handily.

During the 1980s, Kennedy went through a divorce and battled alcoholism, but Massachusetts voters would not abandon him. He was reelected to the U.S. Senate in 1982, 1988, and 1994. Today, as a seven-term U.S. Senator, Ted Kennedy continues to speak out for a variety of liberal causes.

SUGGESTED READINGS: James E. T. Lange, *Chappaquiddick: The Real Story*, 1993; Joe McGinniss, *The Last Brother*, 1993.

Jerry Jay Inmon

KENT STATE UNIVERSITY. Throughout the Vietnam War,* the ability of Vietcong and North Vietnamese soldiers to flee to safety across the border in Cambodia* had frustrated U.S. military planners. Because of Cambodia's declared neutrality, Presidents Lyndon Johnson and Richard Nixon* had been reluctant to widen the war by staging offensive military operations there.

But all that changed in 1970. Richard Nixon had campaigned for the presidency in 1968 on a promise that he could find an honorable peace in Vietnam, and after his inauguration American voters held him to that promise. In the spring of 1969 he announced what he called Vietnamization,* the staged withdrawal of U.S. troops and the handing of the combat back to South Vietnamese soldiers. As the withdrawal of U.S. troops began in August 1969, it soon became clear that South Vietnam was not ready to assume responsibility for all of the combat. In order to keep South Vietnam from falling to the Communists, President Nixon decided to escalate U.S. bombing campaigns over Indochina and to take the war to enemy troops in Cambodia.

On April 30, 1970, he authorized a joint U.S.-South Vietnamese invasion of Cambodia in order to eliminate Vietcong base camps and sanctuaries as well as to block the infiltration of weapons, supplies, and personnel from North Vietnam. At the time, because of Nixon's withdrawals of American troops from Indochina, the antiwar movement* had almost become moribund. The invasion of Cambodia rejuvenated it. College students across the country demonstrated against the invasion.

On May 1, 1970, students at Kent State University in Ohio marched against the war and rioted, shattering windows, lighting fires, and damaging cars. The next night some of them set the campus ROTC building on fire. When firemen arrived to put out the blaze, some students seized the firehoses and turned them on the firemen. Governor James Rhodes ordered in the National Guard, declared martial law, and announced that campus violence must come to an end. Rhodes felt the rioters were part of a revolutionary group, and he ordered that students not be allowed to assemble in groups on the campus until the disturbances were over.

Around noon on May 4, 1970, antiwar protesters staged another rally. Campus police asked them a number of times to disperse, and when they refused, armed guardsmen advanced on them. A group of students began hurling chunks of concrete and rock at the guardsmen, and the guardsmen reacted with tear gas grenades. Apparently one of the guardsmen thought he had heard a sniper shot and he opened fire. Others joined him, some of them firing directly into the crowd of students. They fired a total of thirty-five rounds at students approximately sixty feet away. Four students died and fourteen were wounded. The incident triggered hundreds of college protest movements and a march on Washington, D.C., on May 9, 1970. The guardsmen were brought to trial but found not guilty. Ever since then the incident at Kent State has become a political and historical symbol of the antiwar movement.*

SUGGESTED READINGS: James Michener, *Kent State: What Happened and Why?*, 1971; Richard E. Peterson and John Bilorsky, *May 1970: The Campus Aftermath of Cambodia and Kent State*, 1971.

KEYES V. DENVER SCHOOL DISTRICT NO. 1 **(1973).** During the 1950s and early 1960s, the federal courts pursued with vigor the policy created by *Brown v. Board of Education* (1954) to desegregate all school districts where de jure segregation had been practiced. But a new controversy emerged over de facto segregation in school districts that had never been segregated by law. Were school districts obligated to desegregate schools when the segregation was a result of residential demography and not state law? The Denver, Colorado, schools, although mostly segregated, had never been segregated by law. In the case of *Keyes v. Denver School District No. 1*, the U.S. Supreme Court decided the issue.

The court rendered the decision on June 21, 1973, by a 7 to 1 vote. Justice William Brennan* wrote the majority opinion, ordering that school officials had to desegregate a school system when the segregation was a result of school board policies, whether or not those policies had the force of law. Schools officials did not have to desegregate a school system where neither the law nor school district policies had created the problem originally. Nevertheless, the burden of proof to demonstrate that such segregation had not been intentional rested on the school board. One year later, in 1974, the Supreme Court clarified that point of view in *Milliken v. Bradley*. The case involved multidistrict busing* of schoolchildren to achieve desegregation. The court ruled that districts were obligated to cooperate in such programs only when their own policies had fostered the segregation.

SUGGESTED READINGS: 413 U.S. 189 (1973); 418 U.S. 717 (1974).

KHMER ROUGE. Ever since the late nineteenth century, nationalist elements in Indochina had protested French colonialism. By the 1920s, those nationalists had added communism to their ideological repertoire because they believed Karl Marx and V. I. Lenin had provided historical explanation for the relationship between capitalism and imperialism. In Vietnam, the Communist insurgents became known as the Vietminh; in Laos, the Pathet Lao. In Cambodia,* the Communist guerrillas called themselves the Khmer Rouge, or "Red Cambodians." The strongest of those insurgent groups was the Vietminh, who played a crucial role in the creation and maintenance of the Pathet Lao and the Khmer Rouge.

Throughout the 1960s, during the height of the Vietnam War,* the Khmer Rouge staged a guerrilla war against the neutral government of Prince Norodom Sihanouk.* Until 1969 the North Vietnamese gave only tacit support to the Khmer Rouge because Sihanouk allowed them to ship military equipment and supplies across the country by truck to Communist bases along the Laotian and Cambodian borders with South Vietnam. But the North Vietnamese were angered when Prince Sihanouk agreed to Operation Menu, the secret U.S. bombing of those bases in 1969. They increased their support of the Khmer Rouge and substantially increased it in 1970 when General Lon Nol, an American supporter, deposed Sihanouk. In the spring of 1970, when President Richard Nixon* launched the combined U.S.-South Vietnamese invasion of Cambodia, the Khmer Rouge were driven deep into northern and western Cambodia, regions where they heretofore had not existed in any real sense. The U.S. invasion and massive bombing of Cambodia also led to the deaths and injuries of large numbers of Cambodian civilians, who became more inclined to support the Khmer Rouge. Between 1970 and 1975, the Khmer Rouge strengthened its position in Cambodia, isolating Lon Nol's Cambodian army to the city and forcing their surrender in 1975.

Led by Pol Pot,* formerly Saloth Sar, the Khmer Rouge decided to reinvent the social order. They had concluded that all the evils of the world came from industrialism, urbanization, education, and technology, so they systematically set out to rid Cambodia of all four. They even decided to destroy history, setting 1975—the year of the Khmer Rouge victory—as "Year Zero." Within months, the Khmer Rouge had imposed a genocidal reign of terror throughout Cambodia, depopulating the cities in the hope of creating an agrarian utopia, and murdering more than two million people in the process. Their reign of terror was later depicted in the film *The Killing Fields*.

By 1979 the Khmer Rouge had become a threat and an embarassment to the Vietnamese, who had defeated the United States and reunited their country in 1975. The Khmer Rouge threatened to destabilize politics throughout Southeast Asia, and the world community was outraged by the mass deaths. In December 1978 Vietnam invaded and then conquered most of Cambodia, forcing the Khmer Rouge to withdraw to remote jungles to resume their guerrilla activities, this time against their Vietnamese enemies.

The Vietnamese proved to be more than Pol Pot could handle. Although ethnic Cambodians had traditionally resented Vietnamese expansionism, they welcomed the 1979 invasion as a way of liberating them from Pol Pot's megalomania. Pol Pot and the Khmer Rouge continued their political and guerrilla struggle throughout the 1980s and early 1990s, even though their strength and influence were greatly diminished. Pol Pot was finally captured in 1997 and placed under house arrest, all the time denying that he had had anything to do with the holocaust in Cambodia. Although many people in the world community wanted Pol Pot put on trial for crimes against humanity, the political situation in Cambodia remains delicate and unpredictable, and Cambodian authorities are moving very slowly in any efforts to punish him. Just when political leaders around the world began demanding that Pol Pot be brought to trial on charges of genocide and crimes against humanity, he died in his sleep on April 15, 1998.

SUGGESTED READINGS: William Shawcross, *The Quality of Mercy: Cambodia and the Modern Conscience*, 1984, and *Sideshow: Kissinger, Nixon, and the Destruction of Cambodia*, 1979; François Ponchaud, *Cambodia: Year Zero*, 1978.

KISS. Kiss, a rock-and-roll band formed in New York City in 1972, included Gene Simmons, Paul Stanley, Peter Criss, and Ace Frehley. Characterized by complete anonymity because of their ghoulish, outlandish makeup, Kiss marketed an image of menacing rebellion. Their first three albums, *Kiss* (1974), *Hotter Than Hell* (1974), and *Dressed to Kill* (1975), were critical failures, but the music attracted an increasingly large following of fans known as the Kiss Army. Their next album, however, was a hit. *Alive* contained the hit single "Rock and Roll All Night." Their 1977 single "Beth" was a ballad that sold a million copies and went to number seven on *Billboard's* pop charts. Between 1975 and 1979, Kiss had six platinum albums, including *Destroyer, Kiss—The Originals, Rock and Roll Over, Love Gun, Alive II*, and *Double Platinum*. In the process, their menacing original image gradually commercialized into a comic-book, cartoonish profile. Their concerts were theatrical spectacles and sellouts in the largest venues of the world. Criss left the group in 1980, and their next album, *The Elder*, did not go gold. In 1983, however, Kiss removed its makeup and had a resurgence. They then went into decline again, only to return to the concert circuit as a nostalgia act in the late 1990s.

SUGGESTED READING: C. K. Lendt, *Kiss and Sell: The Making of a Supergroup*, 1997.

KISSINGER, HENRY. Henry Alfred Kissinger was born in Fürth, Germany, on May 27, 1923. Even as a small child, his intellectual gifts were undeniable, and his parents nurtured that intellect. As Jews, however, they became increasingly concerned about the rising tide of anti-Semitism in Germany, especially after Adolf Hitler and the Nazis came to power in 1933. They debated emigration almost until it was too late, but in 1938 they managed to secure exit visas and emigrate to the United States. With the outbreak of World War II, Henry Kissinger was drafted into the U.S. Army and returned to Europe, where he worked in military intelligence and in linguistic interpretation and translation.

After World War II, Kissinger mustered out of the army and launched his career in academe, beginning with brilliant undergraduate years at Harvard, where he graduated in 1950. His experiences in Germany and the reality of the

Holocaust convinced Kissinger that the causes of World War II lay in the failure of the major powers to conduct effective diplomacy, and he dedicated his academic career to the discipline of political science, with specialties in diplomacy and international relations. He received a Ph.D. in government from Harvard in 1954. Kissinger's dissertation was a study of the Congress of Vienna (1815), in which the major powers of Europe tried to come to terms with the impact of the Napoleonic Wars.

Kissinger came away from his analysis of the Congress of Vienna with several principles of power politics that governed much of the rest of his career. First, he believed that moralistic assumptions had no place in international power politics, especially when those assumptions involved one power's trying to impose its own value system on another. President Woodrow Wilson's moral diplomacy, for example, had undermined the Treaty of Versailles after World War I. Major powers, Kissinger argued, had to respect and tolerate their rights to govern themselves internally without ideological interference from foreign powers.

Second, Kissinger disdained the entrenched foreign policy bureaucracies that existed in all the major capitals of the world. Tradition bound and inflexible, the foreign policy establishments looked to the past, not to the future. It would require a powerful, charismatic leader to establish foreign policy objectives, develop new initiatives to achieve them, and shape public opinion in such a way to force the foreign policy establishments to enforce them. Kissinger viewed the State Department as one of those inflexible, tradition-bound establishments.

Third, Kissinger believed that effective diplomacy was a complicated, delicate affair, a balancing act among the major powers. He accepted it as a given that any major event in the life of one major power inevitably affected the lives of all the other major superpowers. Kissinger also believed in the importance of maintaining a balance of power. As one chronicler of Kissinger has written, he believed that "the achievement of absolute superiority by one power imposed absolute insecurity on every other power and destabilized international politics."

Kissinger's intellectual brilliance so impressed his professors at Harvard that they invited him to join the faculty in 1954. He soon became a leading figure in the rise of "nuclear strategy" among intellectuals who considered thermonuclear weapons a reality that must be coordinated in any realistic defense policy. Kissinger's 1957 book *Nuclear War and Foreign Policy* argued that tactical nuclear weapons could be considered a highly useful tool in defense strategy. Filmmaker Stanley Kubrick used Kissinger as the model for the deranged Dr. Strangelove in his 1964 movie of the same name. Kissinger served as a consultant to both the Kennedy and Johnson administrations in the 1960s, and he acquired a larger political profile between 1964 and 1968 as a foreign policy aide to Governor Nelson Rockefeller* of New York, who was unsuccessfully pursuing the presidency. Before his inauguration in January 1969, President Richard Nixon* appointed Kissinger special assistant for national security affairs.

From the very beginning, both Kissinger and Nixon took the middle road about the Vietnam War,* realizing that military victory was impossible but refusing to implement a unilateral withdrawal. Personally, Kissinger believed U.S. policy in Vietnam to be badly misguided. The United States should never have become involved in the war in the first place. Indochina was tangential to U.S. national security and definitely not worth such a horrific investment of dollars and dead soldiers. He also believed that a U.S. military victory there was impossible, unless the president increased troop levels to 1.3 million men and committed the United States to remain in South Vietnam for an entire generation. Since such a commitment was politically impossible, especially after the disastrous Tet offensive of 1968, disengagement from Vietnam was the only alternative.

At the same time, however, Kissinger knew that the United States could not simply pull out of Vietnam. "The commitment of 500,000 Americans," he told Nixon, "has settled the issue of the importance of Vietnam. For what is involved now is the confidence of American promises." As one of the world's superpowers, the United States needed to maintain its political credibility, and a wholesale retreat from Vietnam would only undermine it. Instead, Kissinger and Nixon developed the Vietnamization* policy, which they announced in June 1969. Simultaneous with a gradual, phased withdrawal of American troops, the United States would hand over war material to the South Vietnamese and continue to provide them with naval and air support. Kissinger realized that the government of South Vietnam was notoriously corrupt and probably incapable of defeating the Vietcong and North Vietnamese, so he intended, through the threat of military escalation and the carrot stick of U.S. economic assistance, to convince North Vietnam to settle the conflict. He did understand a fundamental reality, which he explained to President Nixon: "The United States is so powerful that Hanoi is simply unable to defeat us militarily. . . . It must negotiate about it. Unfortunately our military strength has no political corollary; we have been unable so far to create a political structure [in South Vietnam] that would survive military opposition from Hanoi."

Between 1969 and 1973, Henry Kissinger was the central figure in the diplomatic effort undertaken to restore peace in Southeast Asia. He held secret talks with officials from North Vietnam, the Vietcong, the Soviet Union, and the People's Republic of China between 1969 and 1973 while the official peace talks were going on in Paris. The negotiations were complicated by the rigidity of both sides: the North Vietnamese insisted on a complete halt of American bombing of North Vietnam, total withdrawal of U.S. troops from South Vietnam, removal of Nguyen Van Thieu* as president of South Vietnam, and participation of the National Liberation Front (NLF) in any new government in South Vietnam. The United States demanded a mutual withdrawal of American and North Vietnamese troops from South Vietnam, refused to abandon Nguyen Van Thieu, and insisted that the NLF be excluded from the political process in South Vietnam.

Progress in the peace talks did not really come until 1972. Adept at power politics, Kissinger was intent on exploiting the rivalry between the Soviet Union and the People's Republic of China, and he secretly visited Beijing in July 1971 to prepare for Nixon's famous February 1972 trip there. Similarly, Kissinger pursued a policy of detente* with the Soviet Union, which Nixon followed up on with his summit meeting in Moscow in May 1972. By that time, pressure to end the war in Vietnam was becoming overwhelming. Both Kissinger and Nixon realized that the conflict in Southeast Asia was retarding their efforts to reach an accommodation with China and the Soviet Union; and the antiwar movement* at home, particularly after the invasion of Cambodia* in 1970, was demanding an end to the conflict.

In the summer of 1972, the peace talks finally began to yield results but only because of major modifications in the U.S. negotiating position. Kissinger was dealing head to head with Le Duc Tho,* North Vietnam's negotiator, and in October 1972 they reached an agreement. The United States agreed to halt the bombing of North Vietnam, allow the NLF to participate in the political process in South Vietnam, let North Vietnamese Army (NVA) troops remain in place in South Vietnam, and withdraw all American troops. The North Vietnamese agreed to a prisoner-of-war* exchange and dropped their demand that Nguyen Van Thieu be removed from office in South Vietnam. When the North Vietnamese appeared in November 1972 to be stepping back from their October agreement, Nixon ordered massive bombing of Hanoi and Haiphong, as well as mining of Haiphong Harbor.* In January 1973, Le Duc Tho agreed to uphold the October 1972 settlement. The two nations signed a formal agreement on January 27, 1973.

In September 1973, Nixon named Kissinger the new secretary of state, but by that time the Watergate scandal* had compromised the administration's ability to pursue either its domestic or foreign policy agenda. After Nixon's resignation in August 1974, Kissinger remained in office, serving as secretary of state under President Gerald Ford* and engineering the ill-advised attack on Cambodia in 1975 after the Mayaguez* incident. Kissinger left the State Department in January 1977 when President Jimmy Carter* and the Democrats assumed the reins of power.

Since then Kissinger has lectured and written widely about American foreign policy. He has served as a foreign policy consultant to the Reagan, Bush, and Clinton administrations, although no American president has wanted in recent years to be too closely associated with Kissinger. His role in Vietnam and Indochina made him extraordinarily controversial and a virtual anathema to the American left, which held him responsible for the catastrophe that occurred in Cambodia in the 1970s.

SUGGESTED READINGS: Walter Isaacson, *Kissinger: A Biography*, 1992; Henry A. Kissinger, *White House Years: The Memoirs of Henry A. Kissinger*, 1979, and *Years of Upheaval: The Memoirs of Henry A. Kissinger*, 1982; Robert Schulzinger, *Henry Kissinger: Doctor of Diplomacy*, 1989.

KNIEVEL, EVEL. Evel Knievel, who became one of the pop culture phenomena of the 1970s, was born Robert Craig Knievel in Butte, Montana, in 1938. When he was fourteen, he was arrested for stealing hubcaps and was put in the same cell as John Knauffel. An enterprising reporter put them on the front page of the Butte newspaper the next morning with the headline, "Awful Knauffel and Evil Knievel." Knievel loved the moniker and adopted it as his own, changing the spelling from Evil to Evel.

A shameless self-promoter, Knievel began marketing himself in the late 1960s and early 1970s as a "professional risk-taker." Actually, he had become fascinated with finding out just how far a man could jump while driving a motorcycle. He began by jumping motorcycles from a ramp over a stretch of parked automobiles. With each jump, he increased the number of automobiles, from twelve at first. He also jumped over tanks loaded with sharks, trucks filled with rattlesnakes, and finally over the fountain at Ceaser's Palace in Las Vegas. On March 23, 1972, he nearly died while trying to jump thirty-six cars at the Houston Astrodome. Knievel miscalculated the distance, crashed, broke ninety-nine bones in his body, and spent more than a month in a coma. Amazingly, he recovered and, before environmentalists got wind of the stunt, talked the Department of the Interior into granting him permission to jump over the Grand Canyon. When government officials rescinded the permission, Knievel took his plans to the Snake River Canyon in Idaho, where he drove off a ramp in at canyon's edge and parachuted to safety. Knieval retired in 1978.

SUGGESTED READING: Jane Stern and Michael Stern, *Encyclopedia of Pop Culture*, 1992.

KOHOUTEK. Kohoutek was the name of a comet discovered by astronomer Louis Kohoutek on March 7, 1973. For a while in 1973, the press hyped the comet promising that it "would become the most spectacular comet of this century." *Time* magazine, in what can only be considered extraordinary hyperbole, argued that the comet "might be a messenger—of light and knowledge for all mankind." Explaining the hype is difficult. Perhaps all of the interest in 1973 and 1974 was due to the fascination of Americans with notions of natural disaster, fed by such films as *The Poseidon Adventure,** *Earthquake,** and *The Towering Inferno.** Obviously, if Kohoutek hit the earth, it would be the biggest disaster of all time. If it even came too close, the comet could unleash tidal waves, volcanic eruptions, earthquakes, and a series of political crises. In 1974, when Kohoutek became visible to the naked eye, all of the hype was transformed into a bad joke. The comet was little more than a dot in the night sky.

SUGGESTED READINGS: Joseph F. Goodavage, *The Comet Kohoutek*, 1973; Jane Stern and Michael Stern, *Encyclopedia of Pop Culture*, 1992.

KOJAK. *Kojak*, a highly popular television police drama of the 1970s was first broadcast by CBS on October 24, 1973, starring Telly Savalas as Lieutenant Theo Kojak, a Greek-American New York City detective who tried to keep the streets of Manhattan safe. Kojak, a no-nonsense cop, was willing to break the rules in order to get an arrest. Characterized by an ever-present lollipop in his mouth and his "who loves ya baby" line, Kojak was a conservative, almost traditional pop culture hero just when Americans were tiring of antiheroes. The last episode of Kojak was broadcast on April 20, 1978.

SUGGESTED READING: Tim Brooks and Earle Marsh, *The Complete Directory to Prime Time Network and Cable TV Shows, 1946–Present,* 1995.

KUNG FU. *Kung Fu* was one of the more unlikely pop culture successes of the 1970s. Starring David Carradine as Kwai Chang Caine, a young man born to Chinese and American parents in the 1800s, the series premiered on ABC on October 14, 1972. Orphaned as a child, Caine was raised by Buddhist monks in a temple, where they taught him their philosophy of mystical harmony and the martial arts. After killing a member of the Chinese royal family, Caine fled to the American West, where he engaged in a search for a lost American half-brother. In the United States, Caine engaged in a weekly battle against racists and desperadoes, always trying to teach as he fought. Some television historians explain *Kung Fu*'s success with a fascination with Asian tenacity in the early 1970s, when most Americans realized that tiny, backward Vietnam was going to outlast the United States and win the war. Not coincidentally, *Kung Fu* was canceled on June 28, 1975, just two months after the fall of South Vietnam to the Communists.

SUGGESTED READING: Tim Brooks and Earle Marsh, *The Complete Directory to Prime Time Network and Cable TV Shows, 1946–Present,* 1995.

L

LAM SON 719. Lam Son 719 was the code name for the South Vietnamese invasion of Laos in February 1971. President Richard Nixon* had won the election of 1968 after promising to find an "honorable peace" in South Vietnam, which implied bringing the war to a successful conclusion. What it really meant, of course, was bringing the Vietnam War* to an end, successfully or unsuccessfully, since political opposition to it had risen to unprecedented levels. In the spring of 1969, the president had announced his Vietnamization* program, in which he promised to launch a gradual reduction of U.S. troops from South Vietnam and a gradual handing of the war over to the South Vietnamese army.

By late 1970 both processes were well under way. U.S. intelligence sources revealed heavy infiltration of men and materiel into Laos in preparation for a major North Vietnamese offensive. To prevent such an offensive and to test the progress of Vietnamization, the Nixon administration decided to have the Army of the Republic of Vietnam (ARVN) invade Laos along Route 9 in order to cut the Ho Chi Minh Trail, over which most of the North Vietnamese Army (NVA) troops and supplies were moving.

The invasion proved to be an unmitigated disaster. Planning was confined to a few people in Washington and Saigon, and the invasion units were given minimal notice and planning time. Congressional restrictions prohibiting American ground troops in Cambodia* and Laos prevented American advisers from accompanying their units and coordinating artillery, helicopter, and tactical air support. Despite American predictions that four divisions would be necessary to secure the road from the border to Tchepone (the objective), the ARVN committed only two divisions. The NVA had four seasoned divisions in opposition. The terrain was rugged, restricting ground movement and limiting flight patterns to the NVA's advantage. The NVA's artillery had greater range, and their familiarity with the terrain gave them a fire direction advantage. Finally, the weather was unusually rainy, impeding air support and resupply.

The ARVN's best units were committed—1st Infantry, Airborne, Marines, and Rangers. But the NVA was not surprised, and they drew the ARVN away from U.S. artillery, lengthening ARVN supply lines and marshaling resources for a counterattack. Seizing the opportunity to annihilate the ARVN's best units, the NVA would have succeeded except for massive U.S. air strikes and the American helicopter pilot's ability to extract beleaguered units. Lam Son 719 proved the failure of Vietnamization. The ARVN's best units suffered 50 percent casualties. Morale plummeted. It became obvious that the ARVN was hard-pressed to stand alone.

The failure of Lam Son 719 also allowed the North Vietnamese to continue building a staging area for a massive invasion of South Vietnam. Known as the Eastertide Offensive,* that invasion took place in the spring of 1972. Once again, the ARVN failed to stem the tide and, without massive U.S. air support, would have suffered a complete defeat. North Vietnam realized that as soon as the United States was gone from South Vietnam and the ARVN had to rely completely on its own resources, victory would come in short order.

SUGGESTED READINGS: Nguyen Duy Hinh, *Lam Son 719*, 1981; Keith William Nolan, *Into Laos: The Story of Dewey Canyon III—Lam Son 719*, 1986.

Samuel Freeman

THE LAST PICTURE SHOW. Based on Larry McMurtry's novel of the same name, *The Last Picture Show* was one of the most compelling cinematic accomplishments of the 1970s. Directed by Peter Bogdonavich, it stars Ben Johnson, Cloris Leachman, Timothy Bottoms, Jeff Bridges, and Cybill Shepherd. Set in the small, West Texas town of Anarene in 1951, *The Last Picture Show* offers a disturbing portrait of a town, and perhaps a way of life, in its last death gasp, with most of the characters—the high school football coach's wife, the successful young athlete, the cowboy owner of the town's soda fountain–post office–gas station—realizing that their chances for success and fulfillment on those wind-swept prairies are nil. The film's black-and-white cinemography is superb and its performances brilliant. Critics lauded *The Last Picture Show* as one of Hollywood's most enduring achievements.

SUGGESTED READINGS: Larry McMurtry, *The Last Picture Show*, 1967; *New York Times*, October 17, 1971.

LAST TANGO IN PARIS. *Last Tango in Paris*, director Bernardo Bertolucci's controversial 1973 film, was hailed by one critic as "the most powerfully erotic movie ever made that altered the face of an art form." Others deemed it "obscene, indecent, and catering to the lowest instincts of the libido." *Last Tango in Paris* stars Marlon Brando* as a middle-aged American living in Paris and Maria Schneider as a young French woman engaged to be married. They meet while apartment hunting in Paris and enter into a torrid, though anonymous, affair that engulfs both of them in domination and degradation, ending only when she murders him. The sexual scenes were more explicit than in any previously widely released film, and film historians identify *Last Tango in Paris* as a watershed that marked the nearly ubiquitous use of explicit sexuality in dramatic films.

SUGGESTED READING: *New York Times*, January 28, 1973.

LAU V. NICHOLS (1974). The case for bilingual education for minority children whose first language was not English was made in the *Lau v. Nichols* case of 1974. It began with a class-action suit against the San Francisco Unified School District filed by Chinese school system students in 1970. It was argued that no special programs were available to meet the linguistic needs of these students. As a consequence, they were prevented from deriving benefit from instruction in English and were not receiving equal treatment under the law. The appeal was made on the basis of the Civil Rights Act of 1964, which stated, "No person in the United States shall, on the ground of race, color or national origin, be excluded from participation in, or be denied the benefits of, or be subject to discrimination under any program or actively receiving Federal financial assistance." The case was lost locally but won on appeal to the Supreme Court in 1974. *Lau v. Nichols* was a landmark because it was the first time in U.S. history that the language rights of non-English speakers were recognized as a civil right. In subsequent years, the federal government used the case to require public schools involved in the education of non-English-speaking children, including American Indians, to provide bilingual programs.

SUGGESTED READINGS: David H. DeJong, *Promises of the Past: A History of Indian Education in the United States*, 1993; Margaret Connell Szasz, *Education and the American Indian: The Road to Self-Determination Since 1928*, 1977; Judy Olson, *Whole Language Alternative Approach for English Language Acquisition Among Young Japanese Women*, 1991.

Judith E. Olson

LAVERNE & SHIRLEY. A situation comedy spinoff of *Happy Days*,* *Laverne & Shirley* was one of the decade's most popular television series. Set in Milwaukee, Wisconsin, in the late 1950s, the series starred Penny Marshall as Laverne De Fazio and Cindy Williams as Shirley Feeney, two working-class, single young women who share an apartment and collect paychecks at a local brewery. The show premiered on ABC television on January 27, 1976, and remained on the air until May 10, 1983. The comedy emerged from their weekly antics to land an eligible bachelor, even when the prospective husbands were a string of endearing losers. *Laverne & Shirley*, like *Alice*,* was one of the few television series of focus on working-class women.

SUGGESTED READING: Tim Brooks and Earle Marsh, *The Complete Directory to Prime Time Network and Cable TV Shows, 1946–Present*, 1995.

THE LAWRENCE WELK SHOW. *The Lawrence Welk Show*, a weekly musical variety program, was produced by ABC and hosted by Lawrence Welk. It was first broadcast on July 2, 1955. Welk offered an old-fashioned program to his viewers: old-fashioned music in an era of rock and roll; old-fashioned ballroom dancing, square dancing, and polkas in the age of the stomp and the twist; and old-fashioned homilies in an age of rebellion. Over the years, the audience became steadily older but they were faithful. ABC canceled the show after its last broadcast on September 4, 1971, but it continued in syndication until 1982.

SUGGESTED READING: Tim Brooks and Earle Marsh, *The Complete Directory to Prime Time Network and Cable TV Shows*, 1946–Present, 1995.

LE DUC THO. Born in 1910 in Nam Ha Province in Tonkin, Le Duc Tho was North Vietnam's principal negotiator at the Paris Peace Talks.* The son of a French functionary in the Vietnamese colonial government, Le was educated in French schools before joining the revolution. He spent years in jail and in hiding because of his revolutionary activities, and he helped found both the Indochinese Communist party and the Vietminh. During the French Indochina War he was chief commissar for southern Vietnam and maintained primary responsibility for the region after U.S. intervention ended.

The Paris Peace Talks formally began on May 13, 1968, and deadlocked immediately. Le insisted that U.S. bombing of North Vietnam stop before anything else could be negotiated. While his position was firm, Le apparently had considerable discretion in how to pursue negotiations until Ho Chi Minh's death in September 1969. After that, North Vietnamese decision making became collegial and Le reported to the collective leadership. Beginning on February 21, 1970, Le met secretly with Henry Kissinger* for two years. Seeing the military and political struggles as part of the same overall conflict, Le maintained a negotiating position throughout that any agreement must simultaneously resolve both issues. Furthermore, any armistice must include replacement of Nguyen Van Thieu's* government with a coalition that included the Vietcong.

In order to effect American withdrawal from Vietnam, Le ultimately made concessions on these points. The principal provision of the October 1972 agreement allowed Thieu to remain in power with 150,000 North Vietnamese Army troops remaining in South Vietnam. Thieu angrily rejected the agreement, and all sides sought "modifications." Renewed negotiations stalled in December. They were soon back on track, however, and an agreement almost identical to the October agreement was signed in Paris on January 27, 1973. Although the ceasefire never took place, President Richard Nixon* proclaimed "peace with honor." The settlement really provided only a face-saving "decent interval" before the Vietnamese finally settled the issue among themselves. When the agreements were roundly violated by all parties, Le Duc Tho and Kissinger attempted in June 1973 to effect better observance of them, but there were no substantive results. Both men were awarded the Nobel Peace Prize, but Tho refused to accept, contending it would be inappropriate until there was genuine peace in Vietnam. In 1975 Le Duc Tho returned to South Vietnam to oversee the final assault on Saigon. Between 1975 and 1986, he served on the politburo in Hanoi and as the Lao Dong party's chief theoretician, but he resigned his post in December 1986 because of continuing economic troubles in the Socialist Republic of Vietnam.

SUGGESTED READINGS: Stanley Karnow, *Vietnam: A History*, 1983; Joseph Buttinger, *Vietnam: A Dragon Embattled*, 1967; *Washington Post*, December 18, 1986.

Samuel Freeman

LED ZEPPELIN. Led Zeppelin, a rock-and-roll group formed in England in 1968, included Jimmy Page, Robert Plant, John Paul Jones, and John Bonham. Known for their earthshaking volume and sledgehammer rhythms, Led Zeppelin was unquestionably the most influential and successful of the early heavy-metal rock groups of the 1970s. Folk music, mythology, and the occult all influenced their music. Led Zeppelin made its first concert tour of the United States in early 1969, and their first album, *Led Zeppelin*, broke into *Billboard* magazine's top ten; so did *Led Zeppelin II*, released later in 1969, and *Led Zeppelin III* in 1971. *Physical Graffiti* sold four million copies in 1975, as did *Presence*, released in 1976. During the early 1970s, they made five platinum albums and enjoyed sold-out concert bookings in the biggest stadiums of the world. Rumors of psychic phenemona, satanism, and the occult followed them wherever they went. Led Zeppelin's 1978 album *In Through the Out Door* was their last. On September 25, 1980, the band broke up when drummer Bonham died in his sleep, drowning in his own vomit during a drunken stupor.

SUGGESTED READINGS: Stephen Davis, *Hammer of the Gods*, 1997; Dave Lewis, *Led Zeppelin: A Celebration*, 1991.

LENNON, JOHN. John Lennon was born in Liverpool, England, on October 9, 1940. During the 1960s, as one of the Beatles, Lennon became one of the most famous artists and personalities in the world, but even after the breakup of the Beatles in 1970, Lennon went on to a highly successful solo career. On March 20, 1969, just before the Beatles broke up, Lennon married Yoko Ono,* a Japanese-American artist. On their honeymoon, they held what they called their "bed-in" for peace, in which they protested the Vietnam War* by remaining in bed all day and all night at the Amsterdam Hotel in New York City, answering reporters' questions about world problems. During the bed-in, they recorded the hit single "Give Peace a Chance."

Lennon then toured and recorded with the Plastic Ono Band, a group that included Eric Clapton.* He and Yoko also continued their antiwar movement* activities, plastering "War Is Over! If You Want It" messages on billboards all over the world. Lennon and Yoko Ono recorded a variety of avant-garde music together, but Lennon's solo performances were far more popular. In 1971 Lennon's album *Imagine* rocketed to number one on the charts. *Mind Games* went to number nine in 1973, and *Walls and Bridges* was the number-one album in rock and roll in 1974. It included the number-one single "Whatever Gets You Thru the Night." When they had a baby in 1975, Lennon dropped out of the music business and devoted himself full-time to his family. After nearly five years outside a recording studio, Lennon made a comeback in 1980, recording the album *Double Fantasy*, which quickly went to number one on the basis of its hit single "(Just Like) Starting Over." But Lennon did not have much time to enjoy his musical resurrection. On December 8, 1980, as he and Yoko were returning to their apartment on the upper West Side of New York, Lennon was shot to death by Mark Chapman, an unemployed drifter and Beatles fanatic. Hundreds of millions of people around the world mourned Lennon's death.

SUGGESTED READING: Jon Weiner, *Come Together: John Lennon in His Times*, 1983.

LIDDY, G. GORDON. G. Gordon Liddy was undoubtedly the most colorful personality involved in the Watergate scandal.* When he joined the staff of the White House Domestic Council, headed by John Ehrlichman,* in 1971, the forty-two-year-old Liddy had already been an FBI agent, an assistant district attorney, and a law-and-order Republican congressional candidate. He held this White House post only briefly. In late 1971, he joined the Committee to Re-elect the President (CREEP*) and later became counsel to CREEP's financial arm.

Because of his affiliation with CREEP, Liddy was originally suspected of being the mastermind behind the ill-fated Watergate break-in and bugging attempt. Indeed, the later-released Nixon tapes revealed that Liddy had volunteered to take the fall for the entire Watergate affair, from break-in to cover-up. In this same taped conversation, H. R. Haldeman* characterized Liddy as being "a little crazy."

Although events precluded blaming Liddy for Watergate, he was convicted by a jury in federal district court of conspiracy, illegal wiretapping, and burglary. Liddy's refusal to testify before the Watergate grand jury added to his jail time, which eventually totaled more than four years—longer than any other participant in the Watergate affair.

Federal prison failed to mellow Liddy, who after his release boasted, "I am proud of the fact that I am the guy who did not talk . . . I resisted all three branches of the U.S. government in attempting to get me to be a little rat like John Dean[*]." In 1991 Liddy and others published *Silent Coup*, in which the authors claim John Dean instigated the ill-fated burglary. Liddy was promptly sued by Dean.

G. Gordon Liddy eventually became the host of his own enormously popular syndicated radio talk show, which is produced in Washington, D.C. Now in his late sixties, Liddy's Corvette sports this license plate: "H2OGATE."

SUGGESTED READINGS: G. Gordon Liddy et al., *Silent Coup*, 1991, and *Will: The Autobiography of G. Gordon Liddy*, 1997; Theodore H. White, *Breach of Faith*, 1975.

Sean A. Kelleher

LITTLE BIG MAN. *Little Big Man*, a film released in 1970, is on one level a comedy and quasi-historical film about the Cheyenne Indians and the "massacre'' at Little Big Horn. It begins with 121-year-old Jack Crabbe (Dustin Hoffman*) recounting his life to a researcher who is studying the lifestyle of Plains Indians. The film follows the life of Jack Crabbe as he is captured by the Cheyenne, lives with them, is recaptured by the whites, returns to live with the Cheyenne, and is with the Cheyenne when General George Custer's troops are annihilated at the Little Big Horn. There are obvious parallels with the Vietnam War* throughout the film. Indian villages are destroyed as "pay back," often the wrong village and the wrong tribe. Innocent women, children, and old men are brutally murdered, often because they are of a different color. Many critics saw reflections of the My Lai incident in director Arthur Penn's movie, and some compared the near genocide of the Cheyenne to U.S. treatment of "gooks" in Vietnam. The Cheyenne are shown to have a more ancient and more humane culture than the whites who show little respect for ways they do not understand. The parallels need no explanation. The film was based on a 1964 novel by Thomas Berger.

SUGGESTED READING: Linda Dittmar and Gene Michaud, eds., *From Hanoi to Hollywood: The Vietnam War in American Film*, 1990.

LITTLEFEATHER, SACHEEN. Sacheen Littlefeather had a brief moment of fame in the history of American Indian civil rights in 1973. Marlon Brando, the actor, sympathized with the plight of American Indians, and at the Academy Award ceremony in 1973 he decided to make a personal statement. When he received the Best Actor award for his portrayal of Vito Corleone in *The Godfather*,* he had Sacheen Littlefeather accept the award on his behalf. Wearing a white buckskin dress and a leather thong headdress, she shuffled down the aisle to accept Brando's award. Claiming to be an Apache and president of the National Native American Affirmative Image Committee, she denounced the stereotyping of American Indians in film and television.

Sacheen Littlefeather was actually Maria Louise Cruz, a native of Arizona who was one-quarter Yaqui, one-quarter Apache, and half-white. She had been raised by her white grandparents in Salinas, California. In 1969 she joined the Indians of All Tribes* during the occupation of Alcatraz Island* and adopted the name Sacheen Littlefeather. An aspiring actress who had worked in the radio business, she had been named Miss American Vampire in 1970. Despite her dubious credentials, Sacheen Littlefeather's performance at the 1973 Academy Awards ceremony stimulated enormous national interest in the issue of Indian civil rights.

SUGGESTED READING: Peter Manso, *Brando: The Biography*, 1994.

LITTLE HOUSE ON THE PRAIRIE. The creation of Michael Landon ("Little Joe" of *Bonanza** fame), *Little House on the Prairie*, based loosely on the "Little House" novels of Laura Ingalls Wilder, was a staple of prime-time American television from its premier on NBC on September 11, 1974, until its last episode, which aired on March 21, 1983. The program, set in the small town of Walnut Grove, somewhere out West, in the 1870s, starred Michael Landon as Charles Ingalls, Karen Grassie as his wife Caroline, and Melissa Sue Anderson and Melissa Gilbert as daughters Mary and Laura. The Ingalls were kind and hardworking, typical of the yeoman farmers that Jeffersonian democracy had idealized in early American history. They fought the elements for survival and carved out a good life for themselves.

During the 1970s, *Little House on the Prairie* possessed enduring qualities that seemed to have disappeared in 1970s America. Such problems as the energy crisis,* inflation, unemployment, and foreign policy impotence afflicted the United States, and many Americans found comfort and peace in the simple homilies and rural, small-town familiarity of *Little House*. When television critics of the 1990s called for more "family viewing," they had *Little House on the Prairie* in mind.

SUGGESTED READING: Tom Ito, *Conversations with Michael Landon*, 1992; Cheryl Landon Wilson, *I Promised My Dad*, 1993.

LOCKHEED SCANDAL. In 1976 Japanese national police arrested former Prime Minister Kakuei Tanaka and charged him with a number of felony offenses, the most serious of which involved the taking of bribes from Lockheed Corporation, a major U.S. defense contractor and manufacturer of jet aircraft. Tanaka had been forced to resign as prime minister and head of Japan's Liberal Democratic party when journalists learned of questionable practices in his own personal finances. In July 1976 Lockheed admitted paying Tanaka $12 million in kickbacks for opening up the Japanese commercial passenger service to non-Japanese companies.

In the United States, the scandal touched off a vigorous political debate over the ethics of international business. Lockheed claimed that bribery was commonplace in most of the world and that without it U.S.-based companies would not be able to compete for contracts. Corporate critics charged that Lockheed officials were just trying to rationalize illegal activities. In Japan, the scandal blew over quickly. Tanaka managed to plea bargain and negotiate his way out of trouble, although he earned the nickname "Shadow Shogun." The title served him well because he remained a behind-the-scenes power force in Japanese politics well into the 1980s.

SUGGESTED READING: *Newsweek*, March 8, 1976.

LONGEST WALK. During the course of the 1970s, American Indian activism enjoyed the most prominent profile of the civil rights movements* in the United States. Nicknamed the red power* movement, the Indian crusade was interested not only in ending political and legal discrimination against Native Americans and the stereotyping of native peoples but also in the recovery of land taken illegally by the federal and state governments in the past. One of the most spectacular of the Indian protest demonstrations of the 1970s had been the Trail of Broken Treaties* caravan, sponsored by the American Indian Movement*

(AIM), which marched on Washington, D.C., in 1972. Although the demonstration had been a comedy of errors in its planning and execution and had ended up with the occupation and trashing of the Bureau of Indian Affairs building, it nevertheless brought extraordinary media attention to the Indian cause.

In 1978, to commemorate AIM's Trail of Broken Treaties, Dennis Banks* sponsored another AIM demonstration. The walk commenced in San Francisco in February 1978 and moved east across the country. Along the way, AIM members sponsored "teach-ins" and workshops to educate the public about Indian concerns. As the journey continued across the United States, other Indians joined the march. By July 25, when they arrived at the Washington National Monument, more than eight hundred Indians were participating in the demonstration. They issued a manifesto demanding civil rights for American Indians, tribal sovereignty, and the return of alienated lands.

SUGGESTED READINGS: Ward Churchill and Jim Vander Wall, *Agents of Repression: The FBI's Secret War Against the Black Panther Party and the American Indian Movement*, 1988; Rex Weyler, *Blood of the Land: The Government and Corporate War Against the American Indian Movement*, 1982.

LOU GRANT. The hit situation comedy *The Mary Tyler Moore Show* broadcast its last episode on September 3, 1977, and less than three weeks later, Edward Asner reprised his role as newsman Lou Grant in the *Lou Grant* dramatic series. Grant had moved from WJM-TV in Minneapolis to the city editor's desk of the *Los Angeles Tribune*, and the show had changed from a situation comedy to a dramatic series. Grant often found himself butting heads with Margaret Pynchon (Nancy Marchand), the old-school, autocratic editor of the *Tribune* who often worried more about the bottom line than about journalistic standards. Mason Adams starred as managing editor Charles Hume, Robert Walden as reporter Joe Tossi, and Linda Kelsey as reporter Billie Newman. In the post–Watergate scandal* political atmosphere of the late 1970s, *Lou Grant* delivered up an image of reporters as hard-boiled crusaders whose mission was to root out evil and corruption in American society. The last episode was broadcast on September 13, 1982.

SUGGESTED READING: Jason Bonderoff, *Mary Tyler Moore*, 1995; Mary Tyler Moore, *After All*, 1996.

LOVE, AMERICAN STYLE. *Love, American Style* was one of the most unlikely television hits of the early 1970s. An ABC comedy anthology of several different stories about love and relationships each week, the program was silly, superficial, and enormously popular. Its cast read like a hit parade of Hollywood's television elite, with actors and actresses competing to do a campy bit role on at least one episode. First broadcast on September 29, 1969, *Love, American Style* survived on prime time for five years, offering a weekly respite of escapism to a country wallowing in the Vietnam War,* the Watergate scandal,* and the energy crisis.*

SUGGESTED READING: Tim Brooks and Earle Marsh, *The Complete Directory to Prime Time Network and Cable TV Shows, 1946–Present,* 1995.

THE LOVE BOAT. *The Love Boat* was a clone of *Love, American Style,** except that it had a permanent setting aboard a luxury cruise liner and a permanent cast—Gavin McLeod as Captain Merrill Stubing, Bernie Kopell as ship's doctor Adam Bricker, Fred Grandy as ship's purser Burl "Gopher" Smith, and Ted Lange as bartender Isaac Washington. It was a situation comedy with an anthology approach; several different stories were presented each week. First telecast on September 24, 1977, by ABC, the show was loosely based on Jeraldine Saunders' novel *The Love Boats.* Nobody with a serious acting reputation would be caught dead on *The Love Boat,* but the show did provide work for some up-and-comers in Hollywood and some aging stars whose best days were behind them. The last episode was broadcast on September 5, 1986.

SUGGESTED READING: Tim Brooks and Earle Marsh, *The Complete Directory to Prime Time Network and Cable TV Shows, 1946–Present,* 1995.

LOVE CANAL. Love Canal, a residential neighborhood in Niagara Falls, New York, became a symbol of the environmental movement* in the 1970s. During the 1940s and early 1950s, the Hooker Chemical Company dumped toxic chemical waste into an abandoned industrial canal. The company then filled in the canal with dirt and sold the property in 1953 to the city of Niagara Falls. The city built a school on the site and allowed its development into a residential neighborhood. Families moved in.

Over the years, however, residents complained of unusually high rates of skin rashes, headaches, liver problems, spontaneous abortions, cancer, and birth defects. In 1976 the source of the ailments became clear. When heavy rains flooded the region, chemical residues began bubbling up into people's basements. The Environmental Protection Agency (EPA) investigated and proclaimed the neighborhood a federal disaster area in August 1976. Eventually, the neighborhood had to be permanently evacuated. Environmentalists then cited Love Canal as a perfect example of corporate polluting and irresponsibility. The EPA estimated that more than 1,000 similar toxic dump sites existed around the country.

SUGGESTED READING: *New York Times,* August 11–18, 1976.

LOVE STORY. Based on Erich Segal's bestselling, if hopelessly syrupy, novel of the same name, *Love Story* was one of the most popular films of the early 1970s. The movie details the romance and marriage of Jenny Cavilleri (Ali McGraw), a brilliant but socially unknown Italian-American student at Radcliffe, and Oliver Barrett IV (Ryan O'Neal), an equally brilliant young man and scion of one of New England's most blue-blooded families. The two meet in Cambridge, Massachusetts, during Barrett's senior year at Harvard. Her parents, red-blooded, salt-of-the-earth, blue-collar people, accept Barrett immediately, but his parents reject Jenny as immigrant white trash. The two young lovers get married, and after Oliver receives his law degree from Harvard they move to Manhattan, where he begins the rat race toward a partnership in a law firm. Extremely romantic in its premise and execution, *Love Story* ends when Jenny comes down with a vague but deadly "blood disease." During the course of her illness their love only deepens. The film ends with what must be one of Hollywood's corniest lines: "Love means never having to say you're sorry." Love means nothing of the sort, of course, but tens of millions of Americans swooned at the line and exited theaters with tears in their eyes.

SUGGESTED READING: *New York Times*, December 18, 1970.

LUCAS, GEORGE. George W. Lucas, Jr., was born in Modesto, California, on May 14, 1944. He graduated from the University of Southern California in 1966 and went to work in the film industry, where he soon came to the attention of such media leaders as Francis Ford Coppola. His first big hit, *American Graffitti*, was released to critical and box office acclaim in 1973. *American Graffitti* portrayed the youth culture of small-town America on the eve of the Vietnam War.* Four years later, in 1977, he took Hollywood by storm when he wrote and directed *Star Wars*,* a megahit that solidified Lucas's place as one of the film industry's most successful young directors. *Star Wars* became a trilogy with the release of *The Empire Strikes Back* in 1980 and *Return of the Jedi* in 1983. His *Raiders of the Lost Ark* (1981) and *Indiana Jones and the Temple of Doom* (1984) made campy adventure films out of the themes of 1930s and 1940s serials.

SUGGESTED READING: Dale Pollock, *Skywalking: The Life and Films of George Lucas*, 1983.

THE LUCY SHOW. In 1962, after her unprecedented success with the *I Love Lucy* show, Lucille Ball abandoned her association with Desi Arnaz and launched *The Lucy Show*. It starred Lucille Ball as Lucy Carmichael and Vivian Vance as Vivian Carmichael, a widow and divorcee who live together, share expenses, raise their children, and try to land husbands. Like *I Love Lucy, The Lucy Show* is full of pranks, pratfalls, practical jokes, and the physical humor at which Lucille Ball was so adept. *The Lucy Show* became known as *Here's Lucy* in 1968. CBS broadcast the last episode on September 2, 1974.

SUGGESTED READING: Tim Frew, *Lucy*, 1998.

LYNYRD SKYNYRD. Lynyrd Skynyrd, a critically acclaimed, southern-style rock-and-roll band, came to prominence in the 1970s. Formed in Jacksonville, Florida, in 1966, Lynyrd Skynyrd over the years included Leon Wilkeson, Allen Collins, Ronnie Van Zant, Gary Rossington, Steve Gaines, Cassie Gaines, Artimus Pyle, Ed King, Bob Burns, and Billy Powell. They were highly influenced by the hard-rock, three-guitar music and style of the Allman Brothers Band.

Lynyrd Skynyrd's debut album in 1973, entitled *Pronounced Leh-Nerd Skin-Nerd*, earned them a devoted though small constituency, but on the concert road, as openers for The Who,* their reputation as an outstanding live act grew. Their second album, *Second Helping*, was a megahit that went double platinum and included the single "Sweet Home Alabama." Their next two albums were less successful, but *Street Survivors* in 1977 went triple platinum. A plane crash killed Ron Van Zant, Steve Gaines, and Cassie Gaines on October 20, 1977.

SUGGESTED READING: Patricia Romanowski and Holly George-Warren, eds., *The New Encyclopedia of Rock & Roll*, 1985.

M

MACDONALD, PETER. Official records cite Peter MacDonald's birthday as December 16, 1928, but the accuracy of the date is suspect because it was arbitrarily established by officials of the Bureau of Indian Affairs (BIA). Mac-Donald himself claims to have been born late in 1928 or early in 1929 at Teec Nos Pos, Arizona, to Navajo parents. He was a bright, articulate child who impressed family members and friends. As soon as he could, near the end of World War II, he joined the Marine Corps, although he was probably still under age for military service. After the war, Macdonald worked at a number of jobs before he decided to get a college degree. In 1952 he went to the University of Oklahoma, which enrolled a significant number of Indian undergraduates. He graduated there in 1957 with a degree in electrical engineering. Hughes Aircraft Company offered him a job, and he moved to California that summer.

MacDonald was not happy in California. He could succeed in the assimilated world of white people, but he missed the reservation and the presence of a Navajo community. In 1963 he decided to move back to Arizona, and that same year tribal members elected him to the Navajo Tribal Council. At the time, the termination program, which was designed to end the federal supervision and protection of Indian tribes, was well under way, and MacDonald became its bitter opponent. He viewed termination as nothing more than a bald-faced attempt by non-Indians to secure control over reservation land. When tribes lost federal protection, they became subject to state and local taxes, which often resulted in the sale of tribal lands to non-Indians. MacDonald proved to be an articulate opponent of termination, and his political profile among Navajos in particular and other Native Americans in general rose substantially.

In fighting termination, MacDonald also became one of the early leaders of the self-determination* movement among American Indians. He resented the paternalistic, self-serving methods of the BIA, whose officials, he believed, were more concerned about the perpetuation of their own jobs and careers than about the needs of Indian peoples. In 1965, to promote self-determination among the

Navajos, MacDonald founded the Office of Navajo Economic Development (ONED). Instead of allowing the BIA to control government funds going to the reservation, MacDonald wanted the ONED to control all contracting on the reservation as well as job training programs, home improvement programs, and infrastructural development. He also believed that energy corporations with contracts for coal and uranium development on the reservation were guilty of exploiting the Navajos. MacDonald's activism threatened BIA authority.

MacDonald's calls for tribal pride and tribal self-determination resonated clearly with many Navajo people, however, and in 1971 they elected him chairman of the tribal council. He remained in the post until 1982 and then served again from 1987 to 1989. During the energy crisis* of the 1970s, MacDonald played a leading role in founding and directing the Council of Energy Resource Tribes* (CERT), a pan-Indian organization designed to protect Indian uranium, coal, water, and oil resources from non-Indian exploitation. As CERT chairman, MacDonald fought to renegotiate long-term contracts and leases with private companies to ensure that reservation resources were sold at fair market values. He described CERT as a "Native American OPEC" (see Organization of Petroleum Exporting Countries*) CERT played the key role in increasing tribal revenues by tens of millions of dollars.

Inside and outside the Navajo nation, however, MacDonald's assertiveness and success earned him influential enemies. He repeatedly denounced the FBI for interfering with Navajo tribal police and for trying to investigate his personal life. He was also a bitter opponent of the 1972 congressional act to transfer 1.8 million acres of joint-use Navajo-Hopi land in Arizona to the Hopi nation, which required the relocation of thousands of Navajos. Critics then accused MacDonald of accepting bribes associated with the business affairs of the Big Boquillas Ranch. MacDonald's supporters, however, claimed that such practices fell within Navajo cultural traditions and should not be considered crimes. A federal grand jury disagreed, however, and MacDonald was eventually convicted on bribery and conspiracy charges and sentenced to fourteen years in prison. He began serving that sentence in 1993 and today is incarcerated at a federal penitentiary in Bradford, Pennsylvania. Imprisonment, however, has not ended MacDonald's influence in Navajo Nation politics. Tens of thousands of Navajos still believe in him, and Navajo politicians often court his support for their policies and candidacies.

SUGGESTED READINGS: Marjane Ambler, *Breaking the Iron Bonds: Indian Control of Energy Development*, 1990; *The Arizona Republic*, May 8, 1994; S. Carol Berg, "Peter MacDonald," in *Historical Dictionary of the 1960s*, ed. James S. Olson, 1998; R. David Edmunds, ed., *American Indian Leaders*, 1983; Peter MacDonald and Ted Schwarz, *The Last Warrior: Peter MacDonald and the Navajo Nation*, 1993; Philip Reno, *Mother Earth, Father Sky, and Economic Development: Navajo Resources and Their Use*, 1981.

MANILOW, BARRY. Barry Manilow was born in Brooklyn, New York, on June 17, 1946. He attended Julliard, and, when he was twenty years old, he wrote *The Drunkard,* a musical that enjoyed a long run off Broadway. He worked as a music arranger for CBS television late in the 1960s and then, in 1972, became Bette Midler's accompanist and music arranger. He also wrote musical jingles for a number of Madison Avenue commercials. After touring with Midler, Manilow signed his own contract with Arista Records. His first album, *Barry Manilow,* came out in 1972, but his second album, 1973's *Barry Manilow II,* included such hit singles as "Mandy," "Could It Be Magic," "It's a Miracle," "I Write the Songs," and "Tryin' to Get the Feeling Again." The album went platinum. Although critics accused Manilow of a syrupy commercialism, the public loved him, and he eventually sold more than fifty million records and had thirteen platinum albums.

SUGGESTED READING: Barry Manilow, *Sweet Life: Adventures on the Way to Paradise,* 1987.

MARCUS WELBY, M.D. Medical dramatic series have long been a staple of prime-time television, but programs like *Dr. Kildare, Ben Casey, St. Elsewhere, Chicago Hope,* and *ER* have concentrated on the daily lives of big-city medical centers. *Marcus Welby, M.D.,* an ABC product first telecast on September 23, 1969, was different in that it focused on a suburban family practice. It starred Robert Young as Dr. Marcus Welby and James Brolin as his associate, Dr. Steven Kiley. The show was soon the biggest hit in ABC television history. In an age of increasingly specialized medical science and wealthy doctors, Marcus Welby was a throwback to an earlier time when physicians made house calls, treated the whole patient, and became lifelong family friends. The last episode of *Marcus Welby, M.D.* was broadcast on May 11, 1976.

SUGGESTED READING: Tim Brooks and Earle Marsh, *The Complete Directory to Prime Time Network and Cable TV Shows, 1946-Present,* 1995.

MARINER 9. In May 1971 scientists for the National Aeronautic and Space Administration (NASA) launched *Mariner 9,* a spacecraft designed to enter into orbit around the planet Mars. At the time Earth and Mars were completing a fifteen-orbital cycle that brought the two planets into close proximity with one another. On November 14, 1971, the 2,200-pound *Mariner 9* entered into a Martian orbit and became the first craft from Earth to ever orbit another planet. The mission's eventual scientific value was quite limited because severe Martian dust storms compromised *Mariner's* photographs. Metereologists and geologists did enjoy limited opportunities to study Martian weather and erosion patterns.

SUGGESTED READING: *New York Times,* November 15–29, 1971.

MARSHALL TUCKER BAND. The Marshall Tucker Band, a rock-and-roll band formed in Spartanburg, South Carolina, in 1971, included Toy and Tommy Caldwell, George McCorkie, Doug Gray, Paul Riddle, and Jerry Eubanks. Mixing country, jazz, and pop sounds, the Marshall Tucker Band released a self-titled album in May 1973 and toured as openers for the Allman Brothers.* With the hit singles "Take the Highway," "24 Hours at a Time," and "Fire on the Mountain," the album went gold. Their next five albums also went gold, and *Carolina Dreams* (1977) earned platinum. In 1980, however, Tommy Caldwell died in an automobile accident, and the Marshall Tucker Band lost its identity.

SUGGESTED READING: Michael B. Smith, *Carolina Dreams*, 1997.

MARSHALL V. BARLOWS, INC. (1978). During the 1960s, consumer advocates and labor unions pushed forward the definition of workplace safety, and in 1970 Congress passed the Occupational Safety and Health and Act which established the Occupational Safety and Health Administration* (OSHA) to establish workplace safety standards and to investigate violations of those standards. Criminal and civil penalties could be imposed on companies found guilty of not abiding by OSHA rules. OSHA administrators developed the practice of surprise, on-site inspections to determine levels of compliance. Corporate leaders, of course, developed an adversarial relationship with OSHA, and lawsuits were filed, arguing that the surprise inspections were violations of the Fourth Amendment to the Constitution because OSHA did not bother to acquire search warrants. The case of *Marshall v. Barlows, Inc.*, reached the U.S. Supreme Court and was decided by a 5 to 3 vote on May 23, 1978. The Court agreed that the Fourth Amendment was being violated when OSHA administrators did not secure search warrants before making inspections.

SUGGESTED READING: 436 U.S. 307 (1978).

M*A*S*H (Film). *M*A*S*H*, the first film to reflect the themes of the antiwar movement* that achieved commercial success during the 1970s, was released in January 1970. This film, which stars Elliott Gould, Donald Sutherland, Tom Skerrit, Robert Duvall, and Sally Kellerman, was directed by Robert Altman. The film revolves around the antics, skills, and tragedies of a Mobile Army Surgical Hospital (MASH) during the Korean War. The film is not about Vietnam; it's about Korea. It portrays most combat officers as power-hungry incompetents and most of the killing as unnecessary. Black comedy is central to *M*A*S*H*. The plot revolves around three army surgeons drafted during the Korean War. Antimilitary, antiestablishment, and antiauthoritarian, it perhaps matched America's mood in 1970. The film so disturbed Pentagon officials that they would not allow it to be played on military bases. *M*A*S*H* reflects a growing feeling that the United States made a mistake in trying to be the global policeman. Whether one felt that the war was wrong on moral grounds or being waged badly by the administration, the mood of a large number of Americans reflected distrust. *M*A*S*H* combined humor, sarcasm, and gore in equal amounts, and when audiences left the theater in 1970, their thoughts had been brought to bear on the meaning of the war in Vietnam. The film spawned one of the most successful situation comedies in American television history.

SUGGESTED READINGS: Linda Dittmar and Gene Michaud, eds., *From Hanoi to Hollywood: The Vietnam War in American Film*, 1990; *New York Times*, January 26, 1970.

M*A*S*H. *M*A*S*H* which many pop culture historians consider the best series in American television history, was first broadcast by CBS on September 17, 1972. Based on the hit movie of the same name, *M*A*S*H*, an acronym for Mobile Army Surgical Hospital, is set in an army field hospital during the Korean War. The cast of characters, which evolved during the show's twelve-year run, included Alan Alda as surgeon Benjamin "Hawkeye" Pierce, Wayne Rogers as surgeon John "Trapper John" McIntyre, Loretta Swit as nurse Margaret "Hot Lips" Houlihan, Larry Linville as the inept surgeon Frank Burns, Gary Burghoff as Corporal Walter "Radar" O'Reilly, McLean Stevenson as Lieutenant Colonel Henry Blake, William Christopher as Chaplain Father Francis Mulcahy, Harry Morgan as Colonel Sherman Potter, Mike Farrell as surgeon B. J. Hunnicut, Jamie Farr as the cross-dressing Corporal Maxwell Klinger, and David Ogden Stiers as the arrogant, blue-blooded surgeon Charles Emerson Winchester.

M*A*S*H was antimilitary and anti–Vietnam War* without ever mentioning Vietnam. In fact, the events presented each week ostensibly took place more than a decade before most Americans had ever hard of Vietnam. But in terms of portraying senseless slaughter and the Catch-22* antics of most military officers, *M*A*S*H* made a statement each week about the tragedy and absurdity of war. Its last episode, a two-and-a-half-hour special telecast on February 28, 1983, was the most watched program in American television history.

SUGGESTED READING: James H. Wittebols, *Watching M*A*S*H, Watching America: A Social History of the 1972–1983 Television Series*, 1998.

MASTERS AND JOHNSON. The term "Masters and Johnson," which became a buzzword for the sexual revolution in the 1970s, referred to William H. Masters and Virginia E. Johnson, two biologists with the Reproductive Biology Research Foundation at Washington University in Saint Louis, Missouri, who specialized in human sexuality. In 1966 their laboratory and clinical work left the ivory towers of academia and made headlines when Masters and Johnson published the results of their research, *Human Sexual Response*. For an academic publication, it received unprecedented media attention, not just because its topic was human sexuality but because Masters and Johnson had studied, in laboratory settings, human sexual activity in an attempt to determine methods to deal with such problems as premature ejaculation and impotency in men and inability to reach orgasm in women. Not since the publication of Alfred Kinsey's research in 1949 had America been so preoccupied with the biology of sexual behavior.

During the 1970s, Masters and Johnson continued to push the envelope of social acceptance in the United States. The fact that they discussed their scientific work so candidly and matter of factly scandalized the more conservative elements of American society, who viewed them as part of the so-called sexual revolution. Their willingness to employ surrogate sexual partners to assist individuals with sexual dysfunctions also proved highly controversial. Their book *Human Sexual Inadequacy* explained the science of sexual dysfunction and explained techniques for improving sexual performance. As the gay power* movement gained momentum, Masters also tackled the issue of sexual dysfunction among homosexuals, a topic that caused the eruption of more controversy. In 1979 Masters's book *Homosexuality in Perspective* was published.

SUGGESTED READING: Paul A. Robinson, *The Modernization of Sexuality: Havelock Ellis, Alfred Kinsey, William Masters, and Virginia Johnson*, 1989.

MAYAGUEZ. The *Mayaguez*, a U.S.-registered merchant vessel, was plying the waters of the South China Sea in the spring of 1975, making its way from Hong Kong to Thailand, when North Vietnam overran South Vietnam and the Khmer Rouge* assumed power in Cambodia.* In fact, the *Mayaguez* was just off the coast of Cambodia when the Khmer Rouge expelled the pro-U.S. government of Lon Nol and changed the name of the country from Cambodia to Kampuchea. On May 12, 1975, Kampuchean gunboats boarded the *Mayaguez* and took the crew prisoner. Kampuchea claimed that the *Mayaguez* had been on an intelligence-gathering mission and had been seized within Kampuchean territorial waters.

At the time, the United States was reeling from the collapse of its foreign and military policy in Indochina and was desperate to reestablish its credibility. President Gerald Ford* charged Kampuchean with having committed ''an act of piracy'' and demanded release of the ship and crew. When Kampuchea refused, Ford sent in a company of U.S. marines to rescue the crew. It was believed that the *Mayaguez* crew was being held on Koh Tang Island, and 200 marines arrived there by helicopter on May 14, 1975. A pitched firefight took place between the marines and Kampuchean troops, but the *Mayaguez* crew had been moved from Koh Tang the day before. During the firefight, Kampuchea released the *Mayaguez* crew, but the fighting continued on Koh Tang Island. Before the marines could be extracted, fifteen were dead and fifty wounded.

During the next several years, most U.S. officials admitted that the Ford administration had probably overreacted in the *Mayaguez* incident, opting so soon for a military solution when a diplomatic efforts would have probably yielded success. At the time, however, Ford and Secretary of State Henry Kissinger* were anxious to prove that the United States had not become a ''paper tiger'' just because of the defeat in Vietnam.

SUGGESTED READING: Roy Rowan, *Four Days of Mayaguez*, 1975.

MAYFLOWER II. The term ''Mayflower II'' refers to a demonstration staged by members of the American Indian Movement* (AIM) in 1970. Led by Russell Means* and Dennis Banks,* AIM was on the leading edge of the red power* movement, which was committed to full civil rights for American Indians, an end to police brutality against Native Americans, and the return of tribal lands that had been taken illegally or under false pretenses at various times during U.S. history. Like other minority activists in the 1970s, Means and Banks knew that political success depended on attracting media attention, and they searched for the most appropriate public relations vehicle to stage a protest. They decided that Plymouth Rock near Plymouth, Massachusetts, would be the perfect place to stage a protest, and that Thanksgiving would be the perfect day.

On Thanksgiving Day, 1970, Means and Banks boarded and seized control of the *Mayflower II*, a replica of the ship that had brought the Pilgrims to the New World in 1620, as it lay at anchor off Plymouth, Massachusetts. Means used the ship as a stage to air Native American grievances, and AIM members painted Plymouth Rock red for the occasion. Banks declared Thanksgiving Day a national day of mourning to commemorate the taking of Indian lands by colonists. Critics, of course, charged AIM with political grandstanding, but that was exactly what Banks and Means had set out to do. Along with the occupation of Alcatraz Island* by the Indians of All Tribes* in 1969, the Mayflower II incident constituted one of the defining moments in the history of the red power movement.

SUGGESTED READINGS: Henry Dennis, ed., *The American Indian, 1492–1976, A Chronology and Fact Book*, 1977; Russell Means, *Where White Men Fear to Tread: The Autobiography of Russell Means*, 1995; Churchill Ward, *Agents of Repression: The FBI's Secret War Against the Black Panther Party and the American Indian Movement*, 1988.

McCARTNEY, PAUL. Paul McCartney was born in Liverpool, England, on June 18, 1942. One of the original Beatles, he went on to a successful solo career after the 1970 breakup of the famous band. His music became famous for its soft, pop styles, and with his band Wings (1971–1981), McCartney remained one of the most popular faces in rock-and-roll music. Late in 1969, just before the Beatles' breakup, he released his first solo album, *McCartney*, which contained the international hit single "Maybe I'm Amazed." His 1971 album *Ram*, a collaboration with his wife Linda, also had several hit singles, including "Uncle Albert/Admiral Halsey." McCartney released *Red Rose Speedway* in 1973 and saw it go to number one on the pop music charts. It contained the hit single ballad "My Love." Wings also recorded the single "Live and Let Die" for the soundtrack of the James Bond film of the same name, and it too went to number one.

McCartney's success continued unabated, even though he was becoming one of the older rock stars. *Band on the Run*, an album released in 1974, went platinum and included two hit singles: "Helen Wheels" and "Jet." *Venus and Mars* also went platinum, with the number-one hit single "Listen to What the Man Said." In 1977, McCartney's single releases "Mull of Kintyre" and "Maybe I'm Amazed" made it to the top ten. Since then, Paul McCartney has remained a popular entertainer. In 1997 his first classical composition was performed at Carnegie Hall in New York City.

SUGGESTED READING: Geoffrey Giuliano, *Blackbird: The Life and Times of Paul McCartney*, 1997.

McCLOUD. *McCloud*, starring Dennis Weaver as Sam McCloud, was a successful television police drama of the 1970s. NBC broadcast the first episode on September 16, 1970. Sam McCloud was a deputy marshall from Taos, New Mexico, who had chased an escaped prisoner to New York City. After catching the culprit, the New York City police, implausible as it must seem, invited McCloud to remain on special assignment at Manhattan's 27th precinct. The appeal of McCloud was that he was a western cowboy sheriff let loose in the big city. Unaccustomed to bureaucracy and rules, McCloud did things his way, almost in a frontier way, stretching the law and expanding the violence necessary to get the job done. He was the small screen's version of Clint Eastwood's* "Dirty" Harry Callahan character. Audiences loved watching criminals get justice.

SUGGESTED READING: Tim Brooks and Earle Marsh, *The Complete Directory to Prime Time Network and Cable TV Shows, 1946–Present*, 1995.

McGOVERN, GEORGE. On July 19, 1922, George Stanley McGovern was born in Avon, South Dakota. Gifted intellectually, he possessed, even as an adolescent, a sense of equality and fair play consistent with his Midwestern heritage. During World War II, McGovern served in the U.S. Army Air Corps as a pilot. After the war, he graduated from Dakota Wesleyan University with a degree in history. An academic at heart who loved history and politics, McGovern went to graduate school and earned a master's degree and Ph.D. from Northwestwern University in 1949 and 1953, respectively. While earning his Ph.D., he also taught at Dakota Wesleyan.

He soon found the academic life to be somewhat boring, at least compared to the rough and tumble of politics, and he also came to believe that his opportunities to effect real change in American society would be better in politics than in academe. Between 1953 and 1955 McGovern served as executive secretary of the South Dakota Democratic party. It was the perfect platform for launching a political career. In 1956 McGovern was elected to Congress. He served for two terms, stepping down in 1961 to accept President John F. Kennedy's appointment to head the Food for Peace program.

As a result of heading the Food for Peace program, McGovern received a great deal of political attention, which he parlayed into a seat in the U.S. Senate, taking the oath of office in 1963. As a freshman senator, he had little power, and he soon found himself at odds with President Lyndon B. Johnson. Their differences revolved around foreign policy, not domestic politics, since both men were dedicated Democratic liberals. McGovern decided that the U.S. policy in Vietnam was misguided and doomed to failure, and he tentatively expressed those feelings in 1966 and 1967. In 1968, after the assassination of Robert F. Kennedy, McGovern staged a belated run for the Democratic presidential nomination, emphasizing opposition to the Vietnam War and the need to reinforce Great Society programs. He positioned himself as the logical candidate to inherit the mantle of Robert Kennedy, but he lost the nomination to Vice President Hubert Humphrey, who had a lock on the Democratic party. Humphrey went on to lose the election to Richard Nixon.*

Between 1968 and 1972, McGovern emerged as the leading Democrat in the United States. One of President Nixon's severest critics, he accused the president of abandoning the Great Society, and with it the needs of poor and suffering people, as well as escalating the war in Vietnam. President Nixon, of course, considered himself the man who was disengaging the United States from Vietnam. McGovern also targeted the Democratic party for harsh criticism. The party, he claimed, was under the control of old white men whose rules discriminated against minorities and women. When he announced his candidacy for the 1972 Democratic presidential nomination, he proposed a series of rule changes designed to reduce the power of the old urban political machines of the North and the lily-white political organizations of the South.

McGovern won the Democratic presidential nomination in 1972, by emphasizing his antiwar views and calling for more federal economic programs for the poor. He even suggested that, if elected, he would launch an immediate and complete withdrawal of the United States from Southeast Asia. He also suggested that the federal government give each American $1,000 as a means of boosting purchasing power. Both ideas, combined with his commitment to increasing the power of the women and minorities in the Democratic party, won him votes in the presidential primaries.

But they also served as liabilities in the general election. McGovern failed to do his political homework in selecting a running mate in 1972. Senator Thomas Eagleton of Missouri got the nod, but the press soon learned that Eagleton had battled psychological depression for years and had even undergone shock therapy treatments. Instead of taking the high road and standing by Eagleton, McGovern dumped him unceremoniously, an act that many Americans equated with crass disloyalty. McGovern then picked Sargeant Shriver to replace Eagleton. Shriver was a brother-in-law of John and Robert Kennedy, and McGovern hoped he could bring some of the Kennedy charm to the campaign. Because of Senator Edward Kennedy's* behavior at Chappaquidick in 1969, however, the Kennedy charm had lost some of its luster, and Shriver could not help McGovern. Campaigning on the theme of an immediate, unilateral withdrawal from Vietnam, McGovern suffered a landslide defeat at the hands of President Nixon in the general election. He continued to serve in the Senate until his retirement in 1981, specializing in agriculture and foreign policy. Since his retirement, McGovern has continued to lecture, consult, and write. He is the author of *The Colorado Coal Strike, 1913–14* (1953), *War Against Want* (1964), *Agricultural Thought in the Twentieth Century* (1967), *A Time of War, A Time of Peace* (1968), *The Great Coalfield War* (1972), *An American Journey* (1974), and *Grassroots* (1978). Most recently, he wrote *Terry* (1996), the poignant story of his daughter's struggle with and death from alcoholism. In 1998 he accepted an appointment from President Bill Clinton to serve as U.S. ambassador to the United Nations' food and agricultural agencies, which are headquartered in Rome.

SUGGESTED READING: Normal Mailer, *St. George and the Godfather*, 1983.

McMILLAN AND WIFE. A companion series to *McCloud** and *Columbo,** *McMillan and Wife* was a police drama that first aired on NBC on September 29, 1971. The series starred Rock Hudson as San Francisco Police Commissioner Stewart McMillan and Susan Saint James as his wife Sally, who almost on a weekly basis managed to stumble upon some sinister plot and discover crimes for her husband to solve. Part police drama and part situation comedy, *McMillan and Wife* was loosely based on the *Thin Man* television series of the 1950s. The last episode of *McMillan and Wife* was telecast on August 28, 1977.

SUGGESTED READING: Tim Brooks and Earle Marsh, *The Complete Directory to Prime Time Network and Cable TV Shows, 1946–Present*, 1995.

MEANS, RUSSELL. Russell Means was born at Porcupine, South Dakota, on the Pine Ridge Reservation, in 1940 to mixed Irish, Oglala Sioux, and Yankton Sioux parents. The family moved to Oakland, California, when Means was a child, and he was raised there. Means tried his hand at accounting, rodeo riding, and teaching dance before he returned to South Dakota and took a job in the tribal offices of the Rosebud Agency. Means then moved to Cleveland, Ohio, where he became director of the Cleveland Indian Center. A powerful advocate of pan-Indianism and the rights of indigenous peoples, he was a founder of the American Indian Movement* (AIM).

Means came to national attention in February 1972 when local thugs in Gordon, Nebraska, beat and killed Raymond Yellow Thunder. Means organized a two-hundred-car caravan of AIM supporters, who traversed Nebraska to protest the killing and the unwillingness of local authorities to punish the perpetrators. The protest led to the firing of the police chief in Gordon. Less than a year later, when a local businessman killed Wesley Bad Bull Heart near Custer, South Dakota, a riot erupted. The Federal Bureau of Investigation (FBI) assigned sixty-five marshals to the Pine Ridge Reservation to protect local property, enforce security, and maintain surveillance to find possible ''radicals.'' On February 28, 1973, to protest the FBI's presence, Means led an AIM demonstration to Wounded Knee,* South Dakota, where he claimed the establishment of a sovereign nation and demanded recognition. FBI agents and federal marshals soon surrounded them and set in motion a long-term siege. When it was over, two Indians were dead and a federal marshal was permanently paralyzed. Along with Dennis Banks,* Means was tried in federal court, but the judge threw out the indictments on grounds of misconduct by federal prosecutors.

One year later, in February 1974, Means narrowly lost the election for tribal chief to Richard Wilson. In retaliation, Wilson harassed those Sioux who supported AIM and tried to expel them from the reservation. Means resisted the expulsion and was shot by a Bureau of Indian Affairs official. Between 1973 and 1980, Means continued his protests and served a year in a South Dakota prison for assault. In 1981 he laid claim to eight hundred acres of U.S. Forest Service land in the Black Hills, a claim that is still being litigated. He left AIM in 1988. More recently, Means has found a home in Hollywood. In 1992 he played Chingachgook in the film *Last of the Mohicans*, and in 1995 he had a voice role as one of the Indians in the Disney film *Pocahontas*.

SUGGESTED READING: Russell Means, *Where White Men Fear to Tread: The Autobiography of Russell Means*, 1995.

MEDICAL CENTER. *Medical Center*, a hit medical television series of the 1970s, was first telecast on CBS on September 24, 1969, starring Chad Everett as Doctor Joe Gannon and James Daly as Doctor Paul Lochnar who work at a large medical complex in the Los Angeles metropolitan area associated with an unnamed university medical school. It was not unlike the old Dr. Kildare movies, with the youth vs. experience theme running throughout the scripts. In *Medical Center*, Gannon was the young, talented, aggressive surgeon; Lochnar, the voice of prudence, caution, and experience. Each program focused on a medical condition and how it affected the lives of patients, their families and friends, and the hospital staff. The last episode was broadcast on September 6, 1976.

SUGGESTED READING: Tim Brooks and Earle Marsh, *The Complete Directory to Prime Time Network and Cable TV Shows, 1946–Present*, 1995.

MERCURY, FREDDIE. Freddie Mercury was born in 1946 as Frederick Bulsara in Zanzibar, the East African country today known as Tanzania. His father was an accountant for the government. The younger Bulsara moved to Great Britain after leaving school, and in 1971 he formed the rock band Queen.* At the same time he adopted Freddie Mercury as his stage name. Queen soon enjoyed extraordinary success. Under Mercury's leadership, the band fused rock-and-roll, disco,* heavy-metal, and cabaret styles into a unique sound. Among the group's major hits are "We Are the Champions," "Crazy Little Thing Called Love," "Killer Queen," and "Another One Bites the Dust." Their hit song "Bohemian Rhapsody" became a hit again in 1991 when it was used in the film *Wayne's World*. By that time Freddie Mercury was in the end stages of AIDS. He died of the disease on November 24, 1991.

SUGGESTED READINGS: David Bret, *The Freddie Mercury Story: Living on the Edge*, 1997; Peter Hogan, *The Complete Guide to the Music of Queen*, 1994; *New York Times*, November 25, 1991.

MIDISKIRT. In 1970 fashion designers on both sides of the Atlantic unveiled what became nicknamed the "midiskirt," a new women's skirt characterized by its length—a hemline reaching down to mid-calf. Designers touted the midiskirt as a fashion alternative to the miniskirt, which had revolutionized women's dress in the 1960s. The midiskirt, however, fell flat on the consumer market. American women had not tired yet of 1960s fashion simplicity, and the women's movement* left many women feeling unwilling to purchase a whole new wardrobe just to meet the dictates of the fashion industry. In fact, the midiskirt was one of the great marketing busts in recent fashion history.

SUGGESTED READING: Marybelle Bigelow, *Fashion in History: Western Dress, Prehistoric to the Present*, 1979.

MIDWAY. Midway, a classic, epic World War II film, was released in 1976. Boasting an all-star cast of such actors as Henry Fonda, Charlton Heston, Robert Mitchum, and Glenn Ford, *Midway* put to film the great naval battle of World War II, when U.S. aircraft carriers surprised a Japanese fleet planning to conquer Midway Island and then use the island for an assault on Hawaii. The battle itself took place during the first week of June 1942. U.S. forces destroyed the Japanese fleet. The battle was a turning point in the war; after Midway, Japan was on the defensive until surrendering in August 1945.

The film was a popular one in 1976. Those were difficult times for the United States. In the spring of 1975, North Vietnamese forces overran Saigon and all of South Vietnam, and American audiences witnessed nightly television footage of the last Americans escaping from the roof of the U.S. embassy in Saigon. The Vietnam War* had been a debacle that had called into question the reality of American power and American virtue. World War II, on the other hand, had confirmed those virtues, and when Americans watched the film *Midway*, they were nostalgically engaged in old memories of different, less complicated times.

SUGGESTED READING: *New York Times*, June 19, 1976.

MILK, HARVEY. Harvey Milk was born in New York City in 1930 to Russian-Jewish immigrant parents. He graduated from Albany State College for Teachers in 1951 and then went to Wall Street as a financial analyst. He moved to San Francisco in 1969, where he continued his career in finance. Milk, who was quite open about his homosexuality, soon became active in city politics. He ran unsuccessful campaigns in 1973 and 1975 for one of nine city supervisor posts, but he was elected in 1977 on a platform calling for expanded child-care facilities, gay rights, free municipal transportation, and low-rent housing. Milk's political profile in San Francisco soon made him a leading figure in the national gay power movement. On November 27, 1978, Milk was shot and killed by Dan White (*see* the Dan White Case), a conservative member of the San Francisco board of supervisors. Gay rights advocates considered the killing a political assassination. In the subsequent murder trial, White's attorney offered up what became known as the "Twinkie defense": too much junk food had deranged White's mind. Astonishingly, the jury bought the story and convicted White of voluntary manslaughter. They sentenced him to from five to seven years in prison. The gay community in San Francisco was outraged with the verdict, claiming that White had really avoided a first-degree murder conviction because one of his victims had been gay. Milk further endeared himself to the gay community when a close associate revealed a statement Milk had written in case he was ever assassinated:

I cannot prevent anybody from getting angry, or mad or frustrated. I can only hope they'll turn that anger and frustration and madness into something positive, so that hundreds will step forward, so that gay doctors come out, the gay lawyers, gay judges, gay bankers, gay architects. I hope that every professional gay would just say, "Enough!" Come forward and tell everybody, wear a sign, let the world know. Maybe that will help.

SUGGESTED READING: Emily Mann, *Execution of Justice*, 1986; Randy Shilts, *The Mayor of Castro Street: The Life and Times of Harvey Milk*, 1982; Michael Weiss, *Double Play: The San Francisco City Hall Killings*, 1984.

MILK PRODUCERS' SCANDAL. The dairy industry, whose profits were largely dependent upon government regulation, was one of the largest contributors to Richard Nixon's* reelection campaign. On March 23, 1971, the issue of dairy price supports was discussed in a White House meeting; on March 25, a price boost was announced. Thereafter, a steady stream of contributions from dairy co-ops were funneled to various Nixon causes. At the center of this controversy was John Connally, Nixon's Treasury secretary, who played a key role in obtaining the price supports. It was Connally who was largely responsible for arranging the March 23 meeting between Nixon and several dairy representatives, including Harold Nelson, general manager of Associated Milk Producers, Inc. (AMPI), who had previously pledged $2 million for Nixon's 1972 campaign.

White House staffers, in order to avoid publicity concerning a possible contribution-price support link, went to great lengths to set up several campaign committees in Washington, D.C., where the committees could take advantage of several supposed campaign finance law loopholes. However, by September 1971, several newspapers, including the *Washington Post* and the *Wall Street Journal*, were reporting the scandal. Embarassed by the reported wrongdoings, the White House put a halt to the milk producers' donations (which would eventually total approximately $250,000). In the end, AMPI pled guilty to making illegal campaign donations and was fined $35,000.

SUGGESTED READING: Marvin Miller, *The Breaking of a President 1974: The Nixon Connection*, 1977.

Robert L. Perry

***MILLER V. CALIFORNIA* (1973).** During the late 1960s, as hard-core pornography emerged from an illegal underworld into legitimate adult theaters and adult bookstores, the debate over the nature of obscenity and the need for censorship intensified in the United States. Many civil libertarians argued that the First Amendment's protection of freedom of speech and of the press allowed the publication and distribution of anything, regardless of how obscene it appeared to some members of the community. At the other end of the political spectrum, conservatives argued that communities should be allowed to regulate the types of books, magazines, and films distributed in it. The women's movement* then took a position on pornography: by stereotyping sexual behavior, pornography encouraged violence against women and should be censored on those grounds.

The debate has been a vigorous one since then, but in the case of *Miller v. California*, decided on June 21, 1973, the U.S. Supreme Court set the judicial guidelines for determining whether material is obscene and subject to censorship. The court ruled that state and local governments can, without violating First Amendment protections, regulate obscene material. The court defined as obscenity any material that an average person, applying local community standards, would conclude that it appeals only to "prurient interests" and lacks any "serious literary, artistic, political, or scientific value."

SUGGESTED READING: 413 U.S. 15 (1973).

MILLETT, KATHERINE. Katherine Millett, née Murray, was born in Saint Paul, Minnesota, on September 14, 1934. She graduated from the University of Minnesota in 1956, did postgraduate work at Oxford from 1956 to 1958, and then matriculated to Columbia University for a Ph.D. She received her doctorate in 1970 and took a teaching post at the University of North Carolina at Greensboro. She then tried her hand at art and sculpting before taking a faculty position in 1964 at Barnard College. Millett taught at Barnard for the next six years and left for Bryn Mawr College in 1970. That same year she published her first book, *Sexual Politics: A Surprising Examination of Society's Most Arbitary Folly*. The book, which chastises patriarchal culture for leaving women with a profound sense of inferiority, became a bestseller. The book earned Millett instant intellectual stardom among American feminists. Millett followed up *Sexual Politics* with *The Prostitution Papers* (1973).

As a leading light in American feminism, Millett felt compelled to come out of the closet and admit her lesbianism, which she did at a mass feminist rally in 1973. Her 1974 book *Flying*, a confessional, received horribly negative reviews. Millett found herself battling depression and shifted her intellectual interests away from politics to art. She remained an active feminist, however, campaigning for the Equal Rights Amendment* and visiting Iran* in 1979, where she called for female equality. The trip earned her a reprimand and deportation from the Ayatollah Khomeini. Her 1982 book *Going to Iran* described that experience. Millett's 1990 book *The Loony-Bin Trip* details her experiences with mental illness. Her most recent book is *The Politics of Cruelty* (1994).

SUGGESTED READINGS: Kate Millett, *A.D.: A Memoir*, 1995; Jeanne Perreault, *Writing Selves: Contemporary Feminist Autography*, 1995.

MINORITY SET-ASIDES. The federal government's program of minority set-asides proved to be one of the most controversial aspects of affirmative action* during the 1970s and 1980s. The U.S. government's affirmative action policies require that a certain percentage of government contract work be completed by minority-owned businesses. Throughout much of the twentieth century, federal government policies prohibited the awarding of government contracts to minority-owned businesses, especially in certain parts of the country. A black contractor, for example, was never allowed to bid for construction of a federal highway in Mississippi, nor could a Mexican-American contractor bid for a federal airport runway job in Texas or Arizona. This intentional and blatant racial discrimination certainly contributed to the fact that minority groups had faced long-term difficulty in developing their own middle classes.

Affirmative action programs in general were designed to compensate for discrimination in the past, and since minority-owned businesses had consistently been refused permission to even bid on U.S. government contract jobs, the idea of set-asides emerged in the early 1970s. African-American, Hispanic, Asian, and Native American businessmen were classified as designated groups whose businessmen were entitled to such set-asides. Soon state, county, and municipal governments followed the federal government's lead and established set-aside programs of their own. Most set-asides were used for government construction projects and procurement programs.

The program triggered bitter resistance from white businessmen, since contracts were awarded to minority businesses regardless of the bid they had presented. It was not at all uncommon for a white-owned business to submit the low bid for a proposed job, only to see the contract awarded to a minority-owned business that had submitted a higher bid. White businessmen claimed reverse discrimination—arguing that the only reason they had been denied the contract was because of race—and logically claimed that taxpayers were paying more for the job.

Advocates of affirmative action defended set-asides. They claimed that because minority-owned businesses had never even been able to bid on such jobs in the past, their companies had not been able to grow substantially. Large, profitable, white-owned businesses, they claimed, could submit lower bids because they enjoyed economies of scale that smaller minority-owned businesses could not claim. Without set-asides, advocates further charged, minority-owned businesses would never be able to reach an economic level where they could compete with white businesses.

Opponents of set-asides sued in the federal courts, claiming that their Fifth Amendment rights to private property and due process and their Fourteenth Amendment protection against racial discrimination had been violated. In 1977 Congress passed the Public Works Employment Act, which stipulated a 10 percent set-aside for minority-owned businesses. The case of *Fullilove v. Klutznick* challenged the law, but in 1980 the U.S. Supreme Court, by a 6 to 3 vote, upheld the constitutionality of set-asides.

SUGGESTED READING: Harold Orlans and June O'Neill, eds., *Affirmative Action Revisited*, 1992.

MISSING IN ACTION. During the course of the Vietnam War,* millions of American military men served in the combat theater. They fought in jungles, mountains, and lowland swamps where unprecedented volumes of firepower were expended. When the war was over, however, there were far fewer soldiers listed as missing in action than in any previous American war. After the repatriation of the prisoners of war* in 1973, 2,546 American personnel—2,505 servicemen and 41 civilians—were not accounted for, only 4 percent of the

58,152 killed. This can be compared with the 78,750 who remain unaccounted for from World War II (19.4 percent) and 8,300 (15 percent) from the Korean War.

SUGGESTED READING: Arlene Leonard, "Prisoners-of-War, Missing-In-Action," in *The Vietnam War: Handbook of the Literature and Research*, ed. James S. Olson, 1993.

MITCHELL, JOHN. John Newton Mitchell was born on September 5, 1913, in Detroit, Michigan. He grew up on Long Island. Mitchell attended Fordham University and received a law degree there in 1938. During World War II, Mitchell served in the U.S. Navy. He then joined the law firm of Caldwell & Raymond, which specialized in the financing of state and municipal bonds. City and state bond issues are the most politicized area of modern finance, and Mitchell, who became an expert at it, rose to become a partner in the firm. He practiced law in San Francisco, California, and became active in Republican party affairs. During the 1950s, Mitchell became close friends with Vice President Richard Nixon.* Their two law firms merged in 1967 to become Nixon, Mudge, Rose, Guthrie, Alexander & Mitchell.

When Nixon decided to seek the 1968 Republican presidential nomination, he convinced Mitchell to sign on as campaign manager. Mitchell later remarked, "I did it because I believed in the cause and in the individual." That cause, of course, was the restoration of stability to a country, Mitchell firmly believed, that had fallen prey to the rabble of antiwar movement* and civil rights movement* activists. Nixon won the election of 1968 and promptly announced that John Mitchell would become his attorney general.

Committed to a restoration of "law and order in America," Mitchell immediately launched a series of constitutionally questionable activities designed to weaken and disrupt the antiwar and civil rights movements. In the paranoid atmosphere of the Nixon White House, those activities soon expanded to include Washington bureaucrats leaking information to enterprising journalists and politicians critical of the administration. When Nixon sought reelection in 1972, he named Mitchell to head the Committee to Re-elect the President (CREEP*). Mitchell resigned as attorney general in February 1972. The president's paranoia and Mitchell's willingness to tamper with the constitution eventually destroyed the Nixon administration.

During the reelection campaign, Mitchell engineered a series of dirty tricks* to discredit Democratic candidates and disrupt their campaigns for the presidency. Included in the activities were illegal wiretaps, illegal searches and seizures, money laundering, break-ins, and forgery, and when Mitchell operatives were caught and arrested at the Watergate complex in Washington, D.C., in June 1972, Mitchell added perjury and obstruction of justice to his crimes (*see* Watergate scandal). After Nixon's resignation in August 1974, Mitchell found himself in a series of legal binds that eventually resulted in convictions for conspiracy, perjury, and obstruction of justice. He served nineteen months in a federal penitentiary. Mitchell was released from prison in January 1979. Refusing most interviews, he lived out his life in retirement in Washington, D.C. Mitchell died on November 9, 1988.

SUGGESTED READINGS: Elizabeth Drew, *Washington Journal*, 1974; Stanley Kutler, *Abuse of Power: The New Nixon Tapes*, 1997; Winzola McLendon, *Martha: The Life of Martha Mitchell*, 1979; *New York Times*, November 10, 1988; Theodore H. White, *Breach of Faith*, 1975; Robert Woodward and Carl Bernstein, *All the President's Men*, 1974.

Sean A. Kelleher

THE MOD SQUAD. ABC broadcast the first episode of *The Mod Squad*, a popular police drama in the late 1960s and early 1970s, on September 24, 1968, with Michael Cole as Pete Cochran, Clarence Williams III as Linc Hayes, and Peggy Lipton as Julie Barnes. In the era of hippies and the counterculture, *The Mod Squad* portrayed hippie police officers who infiltrated the youth movement to ferret out criminals. Each member of the squad had already dropped out of straight society and remained irreverent and rebellions in his or her own right. The last episode of *The Mod Squad* was broadcast on August 23, 1973.

SUGGESTED READING: Richard Deming, *The Mod Squad*, 1969.

MONDAY NIGHT FOOTBALL. The brain child of NFL Commissioner Pete Rozelle and ABC sports director Roone Arlidge, *Monday Night Football* was an instant television hit when first introduced in 1970. Arlidge assembled a team of three broadcasters: Frank Gifford, a former running back for the New York Giants; Don Meredith, a former quarterback for the Dallas Cowboys; and Howard Cosell, an ABC sports journalist. Gifford provided the play by play, Meredith the technical analysis, and Cosell the human interest and opinions. *Monday Night Football* was a runaway hit, with huge viewer ratings and unprecedented revenues for ABC television. In 1978 *TV Guide* announced that Howard Cosell was the most popular *and* the most hated broadcaster in sports. Today *Monday Night Football*, twenty-six years after its first broadcast, is as popular as ever.

SUGGESTED READING: Howard Cosell, *I Never Played the Game*, 1984.

MORRISON, JAMES. James Douglas "Jim" Morrison was born on December 8, 1943. While attending UCLA he got involved in the mass drug culture of the 1960s. In 1965 he showed former classmate Ray Manzarek some of his poems. The poetry impressed Manzarek, and he and Morrison both liked the idea of starting a rock band. Morrison would be the vocalist and write most of the songs, and Manzarek would be the organist. Jon Densmore joined as drummer and Robby Krieger as guitarist. Morrison suggested The Doors as the band's title, inspired by *The Doors of Perception* by Aldous Huxley. The Doors began playing in Los Angeles clubs and had their breakthrough at the legendary club Whiskey A Go-Go, where The Doors were introduced as a dark, mysterious rock band compared to the "flower power" Haight-Ashbury scene springing up from San Francisco. Morrison met his girlfriend, Pamela Courson, there. Though both were unfaithful, they remained together until Morrison's death.

In 1966 Elektra Records signed The Doors. Their first self-titled album, *The Doors*, which became a national success in 1967, contains the number-one hit "Light My Fire," written by Robby Krieger. The same year The Doors released their second album, *Strange Days*, in which the song "Love Me Two Times" reached the charts. Jim Morrison remained estranged from his parents, brother, and sister and eventually cut off all contact with them and withdrew further into drugs and alcohol. Meanwhile, The Doors continued playing but often had problems as a result of Morrison's extreme actions, including his arrest on obscenity charges at a concert in New Haven, Connecticut, and their ban from *The Ed Sullivan Show*. One critics described his lifestyle as one of "epic debauchery."

In 1968 The Doors were extremely popular in America and equally controversial. *Waiting for the Sun*, the third album released, was a number-one hit, as well as the song "Hello, I Love You." The band created a musical film enacting the song "Unknown Soldier" from the album. The Doors also went on a brief European tour. At a concert later that year in Miami, Morrison was arrested and charged with "lewd and lascivious" behavior and released on bail. The group released *The Soft Parade* in 1969, in which "Touch Me" was a hit. *Morrison Hotel*, released in 1970, made The Doors the first American rock group to achieve five gold albums in a row. The same year Elektra Records produced the group's first live album, *Absolutely Live*. Morrison also recorded *An American Prayer*, an album of his poetry reading. Meanwhile, the relations among the four group members worsened as Morrison fell into destructive alcoholism.

L.A. Woman was the last album recorded by the original Doors. The record, which was released in 1971, contained the successful songs "Riders on the Storm" and "Love Her Madly." The group was beginning to disintegrate, and in March 1971 Jim Morrison left with Pamela Courson for Paris. Exhausted from alcohol, drugs, and stardom, he died there on July 3, 1971. The official cause of death was listed as heart failure. He was buried in Paris's Père-chaise cemetary. The burial site soon became a shrine of sorts. Fans steadily flocked to it, leaving behind flowers, love letters, and whiskey flasks. In 1998 cemetery officials tired of the crowds and decided to relocate Morrison's grave.

SUGGESTED READINGS: James Riordan, *Break on Through: The Life and Death of Jim Morrison*, 1991; Bob Seymour, *The Death of James Morrison*, 1991.

Anne G. Woodward

MOSCOW SUMMIT CONFERENCE (1972). From May 22 to May 29, 1972, President Richard Nixon* met in Moscow with Soviet Premier Leonid Brezhnev. To outside observers, it was an extraordinary meeting. Throughout his political career, Richard Nixon had been a bitter anticommunist, but now he had become the leading figure in the movement toward detente.* Both the United States and the Soviet Union were interested in developing new security mechanisms that would make accidental confrontations—and nuclear war—less likely. During their sessions together, Nixon and Brezhnev reviewed a variety of joint concerns, including nuclear arms limitation, scientific and cultural exchanges, and economic matters. One result of the meeting was the signing of the Strategic Arms Limitation Treaty* (SALT I), which limited the deployment of defensive missiles and froze the number of offensive nuclear warheads for a period of five years.

SUGGESTED READINGS: Jacob Beam, *Multiple Exposure*, 1978; Henry Brandon, *The Retreat of American Power*, 1972; Tad Szulc, *The Illusion of Power*, 1978.

MOSCOW SUMMIT CONFERENCE (1974). At the time of the second Moscow summit conference between President Richard Nixon* and Soviet Premier Leonid Brezhnev, the Watergate scandal* was about to destroy the Nixon presidency. The two world leaders met in Moscow between June 29 and July 3, 1974, just five weeks before Nixon resigned. The 1974 summit meetings accomplished very little. The Soviets were not about to make any long-term commitments, especially since President Nixon's political position at home was so weak. They did agree to limit underground nuclear testing and also decided to reduce the number of defensive missile sites to one each. They also discussed a variety of cultural, economic, and scientific issues.

SUGGESTED READINGS: Jacob Beam, *Multiple Exposure*, 1978; Henry Brandon, *The Retreat of American Power*, 1972; Tad Szulc, *The Illusion of Power*, 1978.

MOTHER TERESA. Mother Teresa, the late twentieth-century's greatest humanitarian, was born Agnes Gonxha Bojaxhiu in Shkup, Albania, in 1910. Her birthplace is known today as the town of Skopje in the country of Macedonia. At the age of seventeen, Bojaxhiu decided to become a Roman Catholic nun, and she joined the Sisters of Loretto. After completing her novitiate, she was assigned to Calcutta, India, where she spent the next twenty years teaching upper-class Catholic girls in a convent school.

But after several years, teaching provided less and less satisfaction. Teaching upper-class children in a city full of poverty and suffering began to instill in her a sense of hypocrisy. Late in the 1940s, she received what she later called a "call within a call" from God to minister to the poorest of the poor. In 1950 she became a citizen of India and founded the Order of the Missionaries of Charity, a Catholic order dedicated to the alleviation of human suffering.

In the process of caring for the poor, the sick, and the homeless, Bojaxhiu became known as "Mother Teresa" and eventually developed into a religious icon in her own right. Her compassion seemed boundless and pure. Food kitchens, clinics, hospitals, orphanages, leprosariums, AIDS centers, and hospices for the dying became specialities of the Order of the Missionaries of Charity. In 1979, when Mother Teresa received the Nobel Peace Prize, she also acquired a global profile that allowed her to raise more money and extend her work worldwide. When a journalist once accused her of "spoiling the poor," she replied:

"I have been told I spoil the poor by my work. Well, at least one congregation is spoiling the poor, because everyone else is spoiling the rich."

During the 1980s and 1990s, Mother Teresa continued her work, although failing health, especially a chronic cardiac condition, began slowing her down. What did not change, however, was her commitment to the dignity of the those for whom she cared. When she died on September 5, 1997, the world hailed her as one of the great individuals of the modern world. Within the Catholic Church, a movement began to extend to her sainthood.

SUGGESTED READINGS: Joanna Hurley, *Mother Teresa: A Pictorial Biography*, 1997; *New York Times*, September 6–7, 1997; Anne Sebba, *Mother Teresa: Beyond the Image*, 1997.

MS. Ms. is the title of the magazine that became the ensign of the women's movement* during the 1970s. With some initial funding from *New York* magazine, a group of women led by Gloria Steinem* founded *Ms.* magazine "for the liberated female human being—not how to make jelly, but how to seize control of your life." The first issue was published in January 1972, and it sold out all 300,000 copies in eight days. Warner Communications then invested $1 million in the project, and *Ms.* began appearing monthly in July 1972. By early 1973 it had a readership of more than 500,000 people. The success of *Ms.* constituted proof that the women's movement had become a permanent part of American society.

SUGGESTED READING: Amy Erdman Farrell, *Yours in Sisterhood: Ms. Magazine and the Promise of Popular Feminism*, 1998.

MUHAMMAD, ELIJAH. Elijah Muhammad was born as Elijah Poole on October 10, 1897, in Georgia. His roots were in the American South, although he looked to the Middle East for the religious philosophy that shaped his life. His parents were poor tenant farmers who, in the mid-1920s, joined hundreds of thousands of other blacks in moving north to find decent jobs. The Poole family settled in Detroit, Michigan, where Elijah was raised.

By the time he was in his twenties, Poole was searching desperately for meaning in his life. A northern city was hardly a promised land for a young black man, and Poole needed a new identity. In 1932 he joined the Islamic Temple, which had been founded in Detroit by Farrad Muhammad. He rose quickly in the religion by exhibiting a charismatic presence that lent itself to prosletying and conversion. Within a few years he was chief minister of the Black Muslim movement and headed up his own temple in Chicago. He was committed to converting African Americans to Islam, and he took on the name of Elijah Muhammad. Black Muslims rejected their given names and their surnames as symbols of slavery and oppression. Elijah Muhammad had a number of run-ins with the law in Chicago, primarily because he insisted on taking black children out of the public schools and educating them at the temple. By the mid-1930s, he had emerged as the national leader of the Black Muslim movement.

During World War II, he refused to obey the selective service laws and served a four-year term at the federal prison in Milan, Michigan. The war, he claimed, was nothing more than an example of racist Europeans trying to assert their global dominance. When he returned to Chicago after his release, he called the movement the Nation of Islam and watched it grow steadily. In the theology of the Nation of Islam, black people were seen as direct descendents of Allah; whites were "devils." Members dropped white names in favor of Koranic names, and they frequently used the initial "X," which meant "unknown." Elijah Muhammad called on black men to work hard, obey the law, govern their families with authority and righteousness, make their devotions to Allah, avoid all but the most necessary contact with white people, and await for the prophetic redemption of black people.

During the 1960s, Elijah Muhammad gained notoriety because of the assassination of Malcolm X in 1965 and the conversion of Muhammad Ali* to the movement. Ali refused to join the army during the Vietnam War* just as Muhammad had done during World War II. Ali's conversion placed a national spotlight on the Black Muslims, whose ideas of racial separation offended mainstream whites and blacks. During the 1960s and early 1970s, Elijah Muhammad wrote several books defending his ideas: *Message to the Blackman* (1965), *How to Eat to Live* (1967), *The Fall of America* (1973), and *Our Savior Has Arrived* (1974).

By the early 1970s, however, the racial separatism and racism inherent in Elijah Muhammad's religious philosophy became a hindrance to the movement. Malcolm X's realization that Islam was a religion for all races set the stage for the change of theological direction. That change, of course, could not take place during Elijah Muhammad's lifetime. When he died on February 27, 1975, his son launched the necessary changes. At the time, the Nation of Islam enjoyed a membership of more than 100,000 people in seventy temples. Elijah Muhammad's son, Warith Deen Muhammad, assumed his father's mantle and soon abandoned the antiwhite theology and steered the National of Islam into the mainstream Sunni Muslim community.

SUGGESTED READINGS: C. Eric Lincoln, *The Black Muslims in Chicago*, 1974; *New York Times*, February 28 and March 1, 1975.

MY LAI. See CALLEY, WILLIAM (LAWS, JR.)

MY THREE SONS. My Three Sons was among the most popular situation comedies in television history. ABC produced the series—first broadcast on September 29, 1960—from 1960 to 1965, when CBS took it over. Fred MacMurray starred as Steve Douglas, the widower-patriarch of the Douglas clan. He was an aerospace engineer living first in a Midwestern town and then in a Southern California suburb, all the while trying to raise three rambunctious boys.

The family was squeaky clean, and the humor came from the typical spinoffs of an all-male household. Tim Consodine starred as Mike Douglas, Don Gradie as Robbie Douglas, and Stanley Livingston as Chip Douglas. The last episode of *My Three Sons* was broadcast on August 24, 1972.

SUGGESTED READINGS: Tim Brooks and Earle Marsh, *The Complete Directory to Prime Time Network and Cable TV Shows, 1946 to Present*, 1995.

N

NASHVILLE. Many pop culture historians consider *Nashville* one of the best films in American history. Directed and produced by Robert Altman, with a screenplay by Joan Tewkesbury, the film stars Lily Tomlin, Ned Beatty, Geraldine Chaplin, Henry Gibson, Ronee Blakley, Keith Carradine, Shelley Duvall, and Barbara Harris. An epic film that uses country music capital of the world Nashville, Tennessee, as its backdrop, *Nashville* offers a microcosm of American values. More than two dozen characters inhabit the film, each of them afflicted with greed, ambition, and hubris. For Altman, American culture is awash in hucksterism, betrayal, superficiality, and political apathy; it is a country of vapid people interested only in making a buck. He tells that story in *Nashville*, where the characters will go to any lengths to make it big in country music. Vincent Canby, film reviewer for the *New York Times*, gushed that *Nashville* is "the movie sensation that all other American movies this year will be measured against." Pauline Kael, another reviewer, proclaimed that *Nashville* "is the funniest epic vision of America ever to reach the screen."

SUGGESTED READING: *New York Times*, June 12, 1975.

NATIONAL CANCER ACT OF 1971. When Neal Armstrong stepped on the surface of the moon on July 20, 1969, Americans exulted in the triumph of their technology. They had won the space race, upstaging the vaunted Soviet program and finishing a Cold War* battle that had begun in May 1961 when President John F. Kennedy, still recovering from the disastrous American invasion of Cuba at the Bay of Pigs in April, stood before Congress and, hoping to give his fledgling administration a new beginning, challenged his countrymen: "I believe that this nation should commit itself to achieving the goal, before this decade is out, of landing a man on the moon and returning him safely to earth." Eight years and $25 billion later, Apollo 11 made good on that commitment. More astronauts soon visited the moon, driving on the dusty surface in a "moonmobile,'' collecting rock samples, and taking seismic measurements. When Alan Shepherd, whose suborbital *Mercury* flight in 1961 made him the first American to fly in space, finally got to the moon in Apollo 17, he wielded a club and drove a golf ball over the lunar horizon.

By that time, however, most Americans had grown complacent about space. Critics had long questioned the value of the investment—whether the billions of dollars spent on ''shooting the moon'' really had paid any lasting dividends. They often chastised administration officials—Democrats and Republicans—for throwing money at the moon while ignoring serious problems on earth. Politicians were anxious for a new technological sweepstakes, but any new scientific crusade had to show tangible rewards. It also needed to be free of political controversy. Curing cancer seemed the ideal goal. More than 200,000 Americans died of the disease each year, even though, according to the American Cancer Society, ''It is one of the most curable of the major diseases in the country.'' R. Lee Clark, president of the M. D. Anderson Hospital in Houston and a leading figure in American oncology, picked up the space race analogy, claiming that if Congress ''would appropriate a billion dollars a year for ten years we could lick cancer.'' Ann Landers concurred in one of her April 1971 syndicated columns, claiming that ''if the United States can place a man on the moon, surely we can find the money and technology to cure cancer.'' The column struck a responsive chord, prompting hundreds of thousands of letters and telegrams to be sent to senators and congressmen. Several congressional secretaries, responsible for answering constituent requests and buried by correspondence, placed ''Impeach Ann Landers'' placards on their walls.

President Richard Nixon* wanted a piece of the political action. The cancer crusade played into the hands of Senator Edward Kennedy,* who had long since staked out cancer and health care as his personal turf. Concerned that the Massachusetts Democrat was considering making a run for the presidency in 1972, Nixon wanted to neutralize the cancer issue by making it his own. In the State of the Union message in January 1971, he launched the war on cancer, telling his countrymen, ''The time has come when the same kind of concentrated effort that split the atom and took man to the moon should be turned toward conquering this dread disease. Let us make a total commitment to achieve this goal.'' Fighting cancer was like supporting motherhood and apple pie. Practically every American had a friend or relative who had died of cancer, and few politicians were prepared to stall or block the president's recommendation for giving the National Cancer Institute independent budgetary status and billions of dollars. Congress passed the necessary legislation later in 1971. What neither Ann Landers nor Richard Nixon realized, however, was that compared to finding a cure for cancer, the splitting of the atom and the race to the moon were child's play.

SUGGESTED READINGS: James Patterson, *The Dread Disease: Cancer and Modern American Culture*, 1987; Richard A. Rettig, *Cancer Crusade: The Story of the National Cancer Act of 1971*, 1977.

NATIONAL ORGANIZATION FOR WOMEN. The National Organization for Women (NOW) was founded in January 1967 to promote the civil rights of American women. Its agenda soon broadened out to include abortion* rights, equal pay for equal work, gay power,* and an end to sexual harassment. The women most responsible for the establishment of NOW were Dorothy Haener, Betty Friedan, Kathryn Clarenbach, and Pauli Murray. The formal purpose of NOW was ''action to bring women into full participation in the mainstream of American society now, exercising all the privileges and responsibilities thereof in truly equal partnership with men.''

For the first few years of its existence, NOW was a fledgling organization competing for attention in the charged political atmosphere of 1960s America. By the early 1970s, however, NOW had developed a political agenda that resonated with increasingly large numbers of American women, and its membership and number of local chapters began to grow. That agenda included the issues of reproductive rights, developmental child care, equal pay, limits on nuclear weapons, an end to poverty, antirape reform, and initiatives to end violence against women. NOW's leaders turned the group into one of the country's most effective lobbying organizations. They worked the halls of Congress and state legislatures and, when necessary for political effect, took to the streets in protest demonstrations.

During the 1970s, NOW campaigned especially hard on three fronts. Ratification of the Equal Rights Amendment* (ERA) consumed much of their energy. They considered approval of the ERA to be at the top of the agenda. Sufficient state legislatures had not ratified the amendment by 1977, when the mandated approval time limit expired, and NOW crusaded for and secured from Congress a five-year extension. At the state level, NOW campaigned for ratification and eventually succeeded in getting thirty-five states to approve the amendment and threatened national boycotts of cities and vacation sites in states that had not approved it. The threats did not work. Ratification required thirty-eight states, and NOW never managed to get the last three. The eventual refusal of enough states to ratify the ERA is still considered NOW's greatest failure.

NOW leaders also labored to end the stereotyping of women, which they considered a precursor to discrimination and violence. In 1972, for example, they asked Congress to refuse to allow the Federal Communications Commission to relicense WABC television in New York City for what NOW considered egregious stereotyping of women in station programming. NOW followed that up with similar protests of biased coverage of women in films, television and radio programming, and newspapers.

NOW also made reproductive rights a central issue. When the Supreme Court in *Roe v. Wade** (1973) upheld abortion rights, NOW had its greatest victory of the decade, but NOW leaders soon found themselves in pitched battles to protect a woman's right to choose as antiabortion forces began organizing. By

1980 NOW membership exceeded 210,000 women. (*See also* women's movement.)

SUGGESTED READINGS: National Organization for Women, *Women, Assert Your Self! An Instructive Handbook*, 1976; *New York Times*, January 12, 1992; Sarah Slavin, *U.S. Women's Interest Groups*, 1995.

NEUTRON BOMB. The neutron bomb was one of the most controversial weapons proposed by the Defense Department during the post–World War II era. Ever since the late 1950s, scientists working under government contract had worked on a "doosmday" nuclear weapon with an ability to kill masses of human beings without damaging buildings and other inanimate objects. The neutron bomb was a so-called clean hydrogen warhead—a small, 1-kiloton warhead that would destroy property only within a 200-yard radius but whose released neutrons could kill people for miles around. Because the explosive was so small, very little radiation poisoning would take place after detonation. Military commanders felt that such a weapon could be employed tactically to destroy enemy troops without producing widespread damage or danger to friendly soldiers and civilian populations. Its formal name was the W70 Mod 3 Lance Enhanced Radiation Warhead, and the technology had been perfected by 1976. The Pentagon proposed deploying the weapon in 1977.

At that point, critics released the news to the press, and an enormous controversy developed. They charged that radiation from such a device would have lingering, disastrous environmental effects and that it would actually encourage nuclear warfare by limiting physical destruction. Others charged that it would actually accelerate the nuclear arms race, which was already becoming prohibitively expensive for the both the United States and the Soviet Union. There was also fear that the deployment of neutron bombs would undermine continuing progress on the Strategic Arms Limitation Talks.* Late in 1977, President Jimmy Carter* made the decision not to deploy the weapon.

SUGGESTED READINGS: Betty Glad, *Jimmy Carter: In Search of the Great White House*, 1980; "Battle over the N-Bomb," *Newsweek* (July 4, 1977), 44–45; Laurence H. Shoup, *The Carter Presidency, and Beyond: Power and Politics in the 1980s*, 1980; James Wooten, *Dasher: The Roots and the Rising of Jimmy Carter*, 1978.

NEW FEDERALISM. During the presidential election campaign of 1968, Republican candidate Richard Nixon* made much of the fact that, in his opinion, the federal government, particularly the federal bureaucracy and the federal court system, had assumed too much centralized power in the United States. He proposed that state governments be reempowered within the federal system. In particular, Nixon proposed the idea of block grants in which federal agencies would provide grants of funds to state governments, which would then administer their own social programs, rather than have them administered from Washington, D.C. During his first administration, Nixon called this proposal the

"New Federalism." Although little of it was enacted during the Nixon presidency, the idea of block grants became part of the conservative political agenda of the 1980s, and during the 1990s the block grant ideas began to be implemented.

SUGGESTED READING: Richard M. Nixon, *RN: The Memoirs of Richard Nixon*, 1978.

NEW YORK CITY. During the 1970s, the financial health of New York City became a political and economic issue of national proportions. After decades of a liberal political administration that provided the most lucrative social benefits in the world, financed by year after year of annual budget deficits, New York City found itself in deep financial trouble. The city's debt, refinanced every month by the issuance of new bonds, exceeded that of most developed nations in the world. As long as interest rates remained low, as they had been in the 1950s and 1960s, the city could afford the debt payments. But in 1973, when the outbreak of the Yom Kippur War* triggered the Arab oil boycott of 1973–1974* and stagflation,* prices and interest rates skyrocketed, and city officials found themselves spending unprecedented volumes of tax revenues in debt and interest payments. In June 1975, with debt payments exceeding $1 billion a month and the payment overdue, the city informed President Gerald Ford* that default on city bonds had become a real possibility.

A bond default posed the potential for an economic crisis. Pensions, retirement funds, mutual funds, and a variety of other investors owned tens of billions of dollars in New York City bonds. A default would not only make it impossible for New York City to refinance its debt and continue current levels of services, it might also stimulate a financial meltdown on the stock and bonds markets, which were already in a highly fragile state because of the weakness in the global economy.

In an effort to stave off bankruptcy, Governor Hugh Carey of New York and investment banker Felix Rohatyn established the Municipal Assistance Corporation and the Emergency Financial Control Board. Both were designed to negotiate new repayment schedules, to force the city to become more efficient in its delivery of services, and to increase tax revenues. They also requested federal financial assistance. President Gerald Ford* threatened to veto any government bailout bill, but he eventually caved in to political pressure from Wall Street and the movers and shakers in the Republican party. On December 18, 1975, he signed legislation providing for a multibillion dollar bailout of city finances.

SUGGESTED READINGS: *New York Times*, October 29–31, and December 18–20, 1975.

NEWTON, HUEY. See BLACK PANTHERS.

NEWTON-JOHN, OLIVIA. Olivia Newton-John was born in Cambridge, England, on September 26, 1948. She grew up in Melbourne, Australia. After winning a talent contest in 1964, she quit school and moved to England. In 1971 Newton-John began touring with Cliff Richards, and her first single, "If Not For You," was a hit in the United States. Her big breakthrough, however, came with the 1973 album *Let Me Be There*. With its hit single of the same name, the album went gold. Her second album, *If You Love Me, Let Me Know*, also had a hit single of the same name and also became a gold record. It included her number-one hit single "I Honestly Love You." She followed those up with such hit singles as "Have You Never Been Mellow" and "Please, Mr. Please."

In 1978 Newton-John starred with John Travolta* in the film *Grease*, which was a huge success. Its title track included three hit singles: "You're the One That I Want," "Summer Nights," and "Hopelessly Devoted to You." Her success peaked in 1980 with her appearance in the film *Xanadu*. Although it was a commercial failure, the film had a musical track of Newton-John songs that went double platinum. Her 1981 album *Physical* included a hit song of the same name, which went to number one on the pop charts and remained there for ten weeks. Olivia Newton-John married in 1984, had a daughter in 1986, and successfully fought a battle with breast cancer later in the decade. She came out of retirement in 1997 and began performing on the concert and television circuits.

SUGGESTED READINGS: Linda Altman, *Olivia Newton-John: Sunshine Supergirl*, 1975.

NGUYEN CAO KY. Nguyen Cao Ky was born on September 8, 1930, in Son Tay, Tonkin, near Hanoi. Ky was drafted into the Vietnamese National Army in 1950, served with distinction, and rose to the rank of lieutenant. He was trained as a pilot in France and Algeria in 1953 and 1954, and during the regime of Ngo Dinh Diem he became an officer, eventually a lieutenant general in the South Vietnamese Air Force. Flamboyant and with an iron will, Ky first came to prominence in 1964 when he threatened to conduct an air strike against the headquarters of Nguyen Khanh because of all of the squabbling during the military regime. Ky finally agreed to cooperate after being dressed down by U.S. ambassador Maxwell Taylor. In 1965 he became prime minister, sharing power with General Nguyen Van Thieu.*

A dedicated elitist with decidedly Western tastes, Ky imposed brutal restrictions on the Buddhists—far more than even Ngo Dinh Diem had imposed—and invited their wrath. Throughout 1966 the Buddhists demanded Ky's ouster, but Ky continued in power. In 1967, he agreed, with considerable support from the United States, to let Thieu become the sole head of state, with Ky serving as vice president. Although Ky had promised Lyndon Johnson he would strive to bring about a "social revolution" in Vietnam, he had no intention of upsetting the status quo of corruption and power that was enriching him and his family. Between 1967 and 1971, Ky's influence was gradually eclisped as Thieu consolidated his power, and in 1971 Thieu disqualified Ky from challenging him for the presidency of South Vietnam. Ngyuen Cao Ky fled South Vietnam before the Final Offensive and opened a liquor store in Southern California.

That liquor store went bankrupt in 1984, and Ky tried his business hand again with a Vietnamese shrimping and fishing operation in Louisiana. But that venture failed as well. He moved in with a sister and her family in Westminister, California, a community today known as "Little Saigon" because of the presence of tens of thousands of Vietnamese immigrants. During the 1980s, investigative reporter Jack Anderson accused Ky of masterminding some of the Vietnamese criminal gangs in Southern California, but Ky heatedly denied the charges.

With the collapse of the Communist bloc countries between 1989 and 1991, Ky became politically active again, claiming in 1990 that with "all the changes in Eastern Europe and even in Soviet Russia, we now have more hope, more confidence that soon the Vietnamese Communists will have to accept change. I think Americans and Vietnamese can achieve today what we could not achieve during the Vietnam War[*]: a final victory over the Communists." During the 1990s, he continued to speak widely among Vietnamese audiences about his hope for the political collapse of the socialist Republic of Vietnam.

SUGGESTED READINGS: David Halberstam, *The Best and the Brightest*, 1972; Nguyen Cao Ky, *Twenty Years and Twenty Days*, 1976; George C. Herring, *America's Longest War: The United States in Vietnam, 1950–1975*, 1986; *New York Times*, April 30, 1990.

Samuel Freeman

NGUYEN VAN THIEU. Ngyuen Van Thieu was born in 1923 in Tri Thuy village in Ninh Thuan Province. Nguyen Van Thieu distinguished himself against the Vietminh after graduating from the Vietnamese Military Academy as an infantry lieutenant in 1949. Thieu also graduated from the U.S. Command and General Staff College in 1957. His major commands in the Army of the Republic of Vietnam, beginning in 1959, included the 21st Infantry Division and the 5th Infantry Division. He led a brigade of the 5th Division against Diem's presidential guard during the 1963 coup. Thieu continued to rise in power after the overthrow of Ngo Donh Diem and was instrumental, along with General Ngyuen Cao Ky,* in bringing General Nguyen Khanh to power in January 1964. By February 1965, Ky and Thieu had positioned themselves to take over the government. Suprisingly, the Ky-Thieu government was South Vietnam's longest. Although Ky originally was premier and Thieu was chief of state and commander in chief of the armed forces, Thieu outmanuvered Ky to become the presidential candidate (with Ky as vice president) in the 1967 elections.

While Thieu would have been more acceptable in 1965 to the United States than Ky, they were about equally acceptable by 1967. The primary American concern was that they not run against each other, splitting the military and raising prospects for civilian government or more coups. A Thieu-Ky ticket ensured military unity and their victory. However, Thieu managed to garner only 35 percent of the vote when a surprise peace candidate ran an unexpectedly strong second in elections marred by the double voting of military personnel and stuffed ballot boxes. When Ky attempted to run against him for president in 1971, Thieu outmanuvered him again, disqualifying his candidacy on a technicality. Eliminating Ky prompted General Duong Van "Big" Minh to withdraw, leaving Thieu to run unopposed and to head the government until just before its collapse in April 1975.

Thieu bitterly opposed the proposed 1972 peace agreement. Calling it a sellout, he delayed its signing until January 1973. To gain Thieu's assent, some minor modifications were effected. More important, President Richard Nixon* made secret promises regarding future American military support. In August 1974, Nixon resigned rather than face impeachment, and Gerald Ford* became president. Congress passed the War Powers Resolution and other legislation restricting American involvement in Southeast Asia. When Thieu asked the United States to honor Nixon's promises, President Ford had neither the authority nor the sense of obligation to provide assistance. For the first time, Thieu and South Vietnam stood alone.

The stability of Thieu's regime did not result from his establishing a popular government. Like its predecessors, it was noted for corruption, incompetance, and oppression. Stability resulted from Thieu's keeping the Vietnamese military command either unable or unwilling to mount a successful coup. This depended largely on maintaining the confidence of the United States. At bottom, it was the American military and American money that kept South Vietnam afloat, as demonstrated by its rapid disintegration as soon as the support was terminated. Some criticize the United States for not coming to Thieu's assistance in 1975; however, a strong case can be made that since South Vietnam had failed to build a viable government after a massive twenty-five-year effort, there were no meaningful prospects for ever building one.

After the collapse of the government of South Vietnam, Thieu fled to Taiwan, and from there he moved to London, England, where he lived for the next thirteen years. In London, Thieu adopted a very low political profile, refusing public interviews and rarely speaking in public. In 1989 he relocated to Boston, Massachusetts, where he became more outspoken. The collapse of the Communist bloc between 1989 and 1991 strengthened Thieu's convictions that the Communist government of Vietnam could not survive long, and he began calling for political change there. In 1990 Thieu predicted, "I would like to say that sooner or later there will be an explosion. I have no political ambition. I only want to participate, to do the best I can do to support the movement for democracy and freedom inside Vietnam."

SUGGESTED READINGS: Edward Doyle and Terrence Maitland, *The Vietnam Experience: The Aftermath, 1975–1985*, 1985; Stanley Karnow, *Vietnam: A History*, 1983;

Who's Who in the Far East and Australasia,1974–1975, 1975; *New York Times*, April 30, 1990.

Samuel Freeman

NICHOLSON, JACK. Jack Nicholson was born in Neptune, New Jersey, on April 28, 1937. He broke into acting in the late 1950s, appearing in small roles in even smaller movies, such as *Cry-Baby Killer* (1958), *Studs Lonnigan* (1960), and *Ensign Pulver* (1964). Nicholson's big break came in 1969 when he received an Academy Award nomination for his role in *Easy Rider*, a major cult film of the 1960s. In *Five Easy Pieces* (1970) and *Carnal Knowledge** (1971), Nicholson established a persona as an irreverent rebel, and in 1975, in his Academy Award–winning Best Actor performance as Randall McMurphy in *One Flew Over the Cuckoo's Nest*,* that persona was transformed into an icon. The film made Nicholson one of Hollywood's superstars—not only an extraordinary actor but a bankable property. He received subsequent Academy Award nominations for his performances in *Reds* (1981), *Terms of Endearment* (1983), *Prizzi's Honor* (1985), *Ironweed* (1987), and *A Few Good Men* (1992). Jack Nicholson continues to be one of Hollywood's most gifted performers. In 1998 he won an Oscar for his performance in *As Good As It Gets*.

SUGGESTED READING: Patrick M. Gilligan, *Jack's Life: A Biography of Jack Nicholson*, 1994.

NIXON, RICHARD. Richard Milhouse Nixon was born on January 9, 1913, in Yorba Linda, California. His father ran a small grocery store, and the younger Nixon worked there before and after school. Bright, ambitious, and capable of outworking all of his competition, he succeeded at every educational level. Nixon graduated from Whittier College in 1934 and then took a law degree at Duke in 1937. He returned to California, where he intended to live a quiet life as a prosperous, small-town attorney.

World War II changed those plans, as it did the plans of tens of millions of other Americans. A member of the U.S. Naval Reserve, he was called into active duty during the war, and when he returned to Whittier, he was given a political opportunity he could not refuse. Local Republicans were looking for a young Republican war veteran to run against Democratic Congressman Jerry Voorhis, whose impeccable liberal credentials suddenly seemed suspect in the burgeoning Red Scare years of the late 1940s. Nixon accepted the invitation, won the GOP nomination, and waged a vicious campaign, unseating Voorhis in the election of 1946. Nixon then worked in obscurity as a first-term Congressman and managed to win reelection in 1948.

His life and political fortunes then changed dramatically in 1949. Nixon was assigned to the House Un-American Activities Committee, which was active in ferreting out Communists and alleged Communists in the federal government. The Soviet Union had detonated an atomic bomb in 1949, helped by spies in the United States who shipped them top-secret nuclear weapons data, and Americans suddenly became convinced that the international Communist conspiracy was alive and well within the United States, even at the highest levels of government.

Nixon found himself leading the crusade when he charged Alger Hiss, a liberal Democrat and former upper-echelon advisor in the Franklin D. Roosevelt administration, of having once been a Communist. Hiss denied the charges and liberals assailed Nixon for taking on one of their own, but the controversy elevated Nixon to political stardom in the United States. He won a seat in the U.S. Senate in 1950 by advertising himself as an uncompromising, conservative, anticommunist Republican. In 1952 Republican presidential candidate Dwight D. Eisenhower selected Nixon to serve as his vice-presidential running mate. Nixon survived a controversy over personal use of campaign funds to become vice president of the United States.

In 1960, considering himself the heir apparent to the White House, Nixon decided to run for president, but he came up against John F. Kennedy, the charismatic Democratic. Kennedy defeated Nixon by the narrowest of margins. The former vice president then returned to the practice of law, now as a highly paid corporate attorney. He could not get politics out of his blood, however, and in 1962 he staged an ill-considered and poorly executed campaign for the governorship of California. Edmund G. "Pat" Brown, the Democratic incumbent, defeated Nixon. Most people considered Nixon's political career to be over. He even said as much to the press on the morning after the election, announcing that "you won't have Dick Nixon to kick around anymore because, gentlemen, this is my last press conference."

It was not. Nixon bided his time and watched the Vietnam War* and racial unrest destroy Lyndon B. Johnson's presidency. During the elections of 1964 and 1966, Nixon campaigned widely for Republican candidates, building up an impressive list of political IOUs. In 1968, certain that the Democrats were badly wounded, Nixon announced his own candidacy for the presidency and called in those IOUs. He won the GOP presidential nomination. By then the Democratic party was self-destructing over Vietnam, and in the general election, promising a new plan to end the war, Nixon narrowly defeated Hubert Humphrey.

Although Nixon's political career had taken a hard-line, ideological tone over the years, especially in foreign policy, he proved to be a pragmatic president willing to explore a variety of initiatives. Until 1967 he had supported the American commitment in Vietnam, but he became more critical as the election politics of 1968 heated up. By the time he took office in 1969, Nixon, along with his national security adviser, Henry Kissinger,* was convinced that the war must come to an end, but they wanted to avoid an ignominious withdrawal. Anything less than an "honorable" peace would compromise their grand design to reach an accommodation with the People's Republic of China and the Soviet Union without abandoning traditional allies.

The Nixon-Kissinger approach to peace, known as Vietnamization,* rested on several major assumptions: (1) the government of Nguyen Van Thieu* was stable and prepared to assume more responsibility for conducting the war; (2) troops of the Army of the Republic of Vietnam (ARVN) would gradually replace American troops in combat operations, and American troops would simultaneously be withdrawn; (3) the American withdrawal must not bear the slightest taint of defeat; (4) there must be no coalition government with the Vietcong in South Vietnam; (5) all prisoners of war* would have to be returned; and (6) the withdrawal of all North Vietnamese troops from South Vietnam would have to be carried out before the United States would terminate its support of the Republic of Vietnam.

In the ongoing Paris Peace Talks,* as well as the secret diplomacy of Henry Kissinger,* the North Vietnamese refused to cooperate, insisting on an unconditional withdrawal of all American troops and the creation of a coalition government, without Nguyen Van Thieu, in South Vietnam. Nixon initiated a large-scale bombing of the infiltration routes in Cambodia* and strategic targets in North Vietnam, but it had little impact on negotiations. The pace of Vietnamization quickened. Most American combat troops were removed between 1969 and 1972, and massive amounts of military equipment were handed over to South Vietnam. In 1970 Nixon launched an incursion into Cambodia by American and ARVN troops to attack Vietcong and North Vietnamese sanctuaries there, but the invasion triggered a storm of protest, as well as tragedy at Kent State University.* In 1971 Nixon ordered an invasion of Laos to sever North Vietnamese supply lines, but it too did little to stop the flow of supplies.

In March 1972, conscious of the upcoming presidential election and anxious to fulfill his promise of ending the war, Nixon was ready to make some concessions, and the North Vietnamese were equally ready to intensify their commitment to the fall of South Vietnam. They launched a massive invasion of South Vietnam; in response, Nixon unleashed intensive, widespread bombing of the Democratic Republic of Vietnam. Late in 1972, negotiations finally became serious, but only because the United States had surrendered on most major points. Nixon was anxious to finalize the agreement before the election. He agreed to a coalition government in South Vietnam, complete withdrawal of all American troops, leaving North Vietnamese troops in place, and the exchange of all prisoners of war (POWs). The treaty was concluded late in October, and Nixon won reelection in November, defeating George McGovern.* In December 1972, when North Vietnam appeared to be dragging its feet on the POW issue, Nixon ordered a new round of Christmas bombings, and North Vietnam acquiesced. In March 1973, in what will surely be remembered as the high point of the Nixon administration, the American POWs came home.

No sooner had the prisoners of war come home than Nixon found himself in a political quagmire that, within eighteen months, would destroy his presidency. During the election campaign of 1972, Nixon had established a campaign organization known as the Committee to Re-Elect the President (CREEP*). At its head was former Attorney General John Mitchell,* a Nixon loyalist willing to do whatever was required to give the president a second term in the White

House. Under Mitchell's direction, CREEP operatives engaged in a series of illegal activities to disrupt the Democratic party's campaign at the national and local levels. Those activities included wiretapping and searches and seizures without warrants, Internal Revenue Service audits of political enemies, forgery, money laundering, and other varieties of fraud. The most spectacular incident, and the one which eventually forced President Nixon's resignation, occurred at the Watergate hotel and office complex in Washington, D.C. (*see* Watergate scandal). CREEP had authorized a break-in at the Democratic party headquarters in the Watergate complex. They botched the break-in and were arrested by local police. A few days later, when Nixon learned of the arrest, he initiated a cover-up and tried to block formal investigations of the crime.

During the next two years, the president consistently denied that he had engaged in such a cover-up, but in August 1974 White House tapes revealed his complicity. By that time, the House Judiciary committee had already voted articles of impeachment against Nixon, and when Senator Barry Goldwater told the president that he could count on only twelve to fifteen votes in the Senate, which would mean removal from office, the president resigned in disgrace. Only a pardon from President Gerald Ford* kept him out of prison.

During the next ten years, Nixon went almost into hiding, giving few interviews and saying little about public policy. Most Republican politicians wanted little to do with him because of the stigma attached to his administration. But late in the 1980s, Nixon slowly reentered public life, giving more interviews, delivering selected lectures, and writing articles and books about public affairs. He died on April 21, 1994.

SUGGESTED READING: Stephen A. Ambrose, *Nixon*, 3 vols., 1987–1991.

NIXONOMICS. The term ''Nixonomics'' was used by liberal economists during the 1970s to describe the economic policies of Richard Nixon.* Although Nixon had campaigned for president in 1968 by calling for cuts in government spending and less government interference in the economy (what he called the New Economic Policy), Nixon found himself facing the expensive Vietnam War* and a growing inflation problem when he took office. In 1971, to put a lid on prices, Nixon dramatically imposed a government-mandated freeze on all wages and prices for six months. When decontrols went into effect early in 1972, prices began to rise again and so did unemployment. Nixon then declared that he was a ''Keynesian,'' meaning that he was willing to use government spending as a tool to stimulate the economy. He urged Congress to reduce taxes and the Federal Reserve Board to lower interest rates. Critics dubbed these policy gyrations ''Nixonomics.''

SUGGESTED READING: R. L. Miller, *The New Economics of Richard Nixon*, 1973.

NUCLEAR REGULATORY COMMISSION. By the 1960s, criticism of the Atomic Energy Commission (AEC) had begun to appear on the grounds that a government agency responsible for regulating the atomic energy industry and protecting public health and safety should not also be involved in promoting the industry itself. The apparent discrepancy first came to light in 1956. The AEC had approved the construction of a 100-megawatt fast-breeder reactor in Lagoona Beach, Michigan, by the Power Reactor Development Company, even though the AEC's own safety experts had serious reservations about the project. There were other examples in subsequent years, and the rise of the environmental movement* in the 1960s intensified those concerns. In 1974 Congress passed the Energy Reorganization Act. It abolished the AEC and created the Nuclear Regulatory Commission (NRC) to protect public health and safety and the Energy Research and Development Administration to promote the uses of nuclear energy.

The NRC, however, faced the same dilemmas as its predecessor had. In fact, the political and economic challenges of producing nuclear power cheaply and safely became more complicated than ever in the 1970s. The fledgling environmental movement, which had barely got under way during the 1960s, accelerated during the 1970s, and concern over the safety of nuclear power increased geometrically. Critics charged that an accident or meltdown at a nuclear power reactor could create an environmental holocaust; the accident at Three Mile Island* in 1979, along with the nearly simultaneous release of the film *The China Syndrome*,* provided environmental critics of nuclear power with enormous political ammunition.

At the same time, however, the energy crisis* was afflicting the United States. With the prices of coal, oil, and natural gas skyrocketing, the economy entered a sustained period of serious inflation and unemployment, which economists dubbed "stagflation."* Proponents of nuclear energy argued that it was a clean fuel that could provide cost-effective energy for centuries to come.

SUGGESTED READING: Fred Clements, *The Nuclear Regulatory Commission*, 1989.

O

OAKES, RICHARD. Mohawk Richard Oakes, perhaps best known for his leadership during the American Indian occupation of Alcatraz Island* from 1969 to 1971, was born in 1942 on the St. Regis Indian Reservation in New York, the son of Art Oakes of St. Regis and Albany, New York. He attended the Salmon River Central School until he was sixteen years old and quit during the eleventh grade because he felt the American school system failed to offer him anything relevant to his Indian culture and heritage. Oakes then began a brief career in the iron work industry, working both on and off reservation, including high-steel work which was common among Mohawk Indian men. The early years of his life were spent in New York, Massachusetts, and Rhode Island before he moved to California. During that time, he attended the Adirondack Community College in Glen Falls, New York, and Syracuse University. While traveling cross-country to San Francisco, Oakes visited several Indian reservations and became aware of the political and economic situations of the Indians living there. Oakes worked at several jobs in San Francisco until he had an opportunity to enroll in San Francisco State College in February 1969 under the government's new economic opportunity program. During this time, he met and married Annie Marufo, a Kashia Pomo Indian from northern California, and he adopted her five children.

Oakes was a leader in the November 1969 occupation of Alcatraz Island, an event that became the catalyst for the emerging Indian activism that continued into the 1970s. The occupation of Alcatraz Island was an attempt by Indian college students and urban Indian people to attract national attention to the failure of U.S. government policy toward American Indians. The press and many of the Indian occupiers recognized Oakes as the "Indian leader" on Alcatraz, even though Oakes never claimed that position. Oakes left Alcatraz in January 1970 following the death of his step-daughter Yvonne Oakes, who died from a head injury after falling down a stairwell in a vacant building on Alcatraz Island.

After leaving the island, Oakes remained active in Indian social issues and was particularly instrumental in the Pomo and Pit River Indian movements to regain ancestral lands in northern California. He participated in the planning of additional occupations of federal property in northern California and at key places around the country.

On September 21, 1972, Oakes was shot and killed by Michael Morgan, a YMCA camp employee in Sonoma Country, California. Oakes had gone to the camp to locate an Indian youth who was staying with the Oakes family. The camp employee was charged with involuntary manslaughter, but charges were later dropped on the grounds that Oakes had come "menacingly toward" him. Oakes was buried on his wife's reservation on September 27, 1972, with traditional religious rites. The murder of Oakes unified the various Indian protests groups and gave impetus to the Trail of Broken Treaties* march, a march planned on the Rosebud Indian Reservation and scheduled to arrive in Washington, D.C., in time for the 1972 presidential campaign.

SUGGESTED READINGS: Troy R. Johnson, *The Occupation of Alcatraz Island: Indian Self-Determination and the Rise of Indian Activism*, 1996; *New York Times*, September 22, 1972.

Troy Johnson

OCCUPATIONAL SAFETY AND HEALTH ADMINISTRATION. Concern about working conditions has been central to the American labor movement ever since the 1880s, when Samuel Gompers, head of the American Federation of Labor, first raised the issue in collective bargaining negotiations. That concern remains a key issue among American labor leaders to this day. During the 1970s, the most important legislative symbol of that preoccupation was the Occupational Safety and Health Act of 1970. The legislation had been on congressional dockets since the beginning of President Lyndon B. Johnson's Great Society, but it foundered again and again until 1969, when an explosion in Farmington, West Virginia, killed seventy-eight miners. The legislation established the Occupational Safety and Health Administration (OSHA) and empowered OSHA inspectors to enter any workplace in the United States, without a warrant or notice, to inspect it for safety violations. The law also established a National Institute for Occupational Safety and Health to conduct research.

OSHA immediately became one of the most controversial federal agencies in U.S. history. Businessmen accused OSHA of violating constitutional restraints and pushing up the costs of products by imposing expensive, unnecessary safety regulations. The fact that inflation was such a serious problem in the 1970s lent credibility to corporate criticisms. Labor leaders, on the other hand, believed that the government was not vigorous enough in going after safety violations. By the late 1970s, conservative Republicans pushing Ronald Reagan* for president had targeted OSHA as their best bet for raising the spectre of irresponsible big government bureaucracies.

SUGGESTED READING: S. T. Gluck, *OSHA and Ideology*, 1981.

THE ODD COUPLE. *The Odd Couple*, one of the most successful situation comedies in television history, was based on the hit movie of the same name, starring Walter Matthau and Jack Lemmon. *The Odd Couple* is the hilarious story of two opposites-attract roommates. Felix Unger (Tony Randall), a prim-and-proper, fastidious, anal-retentive photographer and clean-up freak, makes life miserable for his roommate, Oscar Madison (Jack Klugman), a sportswriter for the *New York Herald*. Oscar is everything Felix is not: vulgar, gross, trashy, unkempt, gruff, and sloppy. The clash of their two personalities provides the show with a seemingly endless amount of amusing material. *The Odd Couple*, a prime-time hit for thirteen years, remains today a popular rerun in most major media markets.

SUGGESTED READING: Tim Brooks and Earle Marsh, *The Complete Directory to Prime Time Network and Cable TV Shows, 1946–Present*, 1995.

OLYMPIC GAMES OF 1972. Early in the 1960s, the International Olympic Committee (IOC) agreed to hold the 1972 summer games in Munich, Germany. The IOC hoped that the decision would be an act of reconciliation to alleviate remaining World War II bitterness. For Americans in particular, however, an Olympiad in Germany hearkened back to the 1936 games, when Adolf Hitler snubbed African-American sprinter and broad jumper Jesse Owens. The Germans were intent on making sure that the 1972 Munich games would epitomize the "New Germany" as a land of equality, democracy, and tolerance.

But it was not to be. In the early hours of September 5, 1972, terrorists from the Palestinian Liberation Organization (PLO) made their way into the dormitory of the Israeli team, killed two coaches, and took nine team members hostage. The Germans surrounded Olympic Village with 12,000 policemen and began negotiating with the PLO terrorists. The terrorists demanded the release of two hundred Palestinian guerrillas held in Israeli jails, but Israeli Prime Minister Golda Meir refused. German authorities promised to fly the terrorists and hostages to Egypt, but on the tarmack at the airport, police sharpshooters opened fire, hoping to kill the terrorists. The action backfired. All of the terrorists were killed, but before they died they managed to murder all of the hostages. The International Olympic Committee allowed the games to continue.

SUGGESTED READINGS: *New York Times*, September 4–12, 1972.

THE OMEN. This 1976 religious horror film revolves around Damien (Harvey Stevens), son of Satan, Antichrist, and adopted son of the American emissary to Great Britain, Robert Thorn (Gregory Peck). The mystery unravels slowly, and much of the plot revolves around finding the actual origin of the boy. In the beginning of the film, Damien has developed into a completely normal four-year-old. But after a mysterious black rottweiler appears (later revealed to be his protector), strange and gory things begin to happen. The boy's nursemaid hangs herself from a window of the Thorn mansion in view of Damien's birthday party on the lawn in front of Damien and his parents, proclaiming happily,

"This is for you Damien, all for you." She is replaced by the cold Mrs. Baylock, and from there Damien begins to reveal his true identity in real horror fashion. A mad priest, who warns Thorn that Damien is the Antichrist, is later killed by a spire falling from a church. Thorn eventually believes him, and accompanied by a photographer played by David Warner, he travels to Italy to find out who Damien really is.

The movie, which was not taken seriously by critics, is nevertheless an important film for several reasons. First, it is part of the wave of horror films that surfaced after the Vietnam War.* The end of the war robbed America of clear villains and adversaries, and horror films created them for audiences all over the country. Second, America was awash in conspiracy theories and scandals at the highest level during the 1970s. The Watergate scandal* was going on, a credibility gap* was developing between the government and the people, and the Cold War* was reaching new heights. *The Omen* revolves around a conspiracy of cosmic proportions. Finally, the film took new risks with some of its violent scenes. The movie depicted a woman hanging herself, a priest being run through by a spire, and decapitation. The film was, in many ways, a reflection of the fears and biases of the 1970s.

SUGGESTED READINGS: *New York Times*, June 26, July 25, and October 17, 1976.

Bradley A. Olson

ONE FLEW OVER THE CUCKOO'S NEST. Many American literary historians consider Ken Kesey's 1962 novel *One Flew Over the Cuckoo's Nest* the intellectual bridge between the beat generation of the late 1940s and 1950s and the counterculture of the 1960s. A satirical critique of modern society, particularly the conformist pressures of mass culture and bureaucracy, the novel, set in an insane asylum in the Pacific Northwest during the 1950s, focuses on the efforts of one patient—Randall McMurphy—to maintain his identity and sense of self. Michael Douglas decided to produce a film based on the novel, even though many of his Hollywood contemporaries did not think the book would translate well on the big screen. He purchased the rights to the novel, commissioned Lawrence Hauben and Bo Goldman to write a screenplay, and hired Milos Forman to direct the film. Jack Nicholson plays R. P. McMurphy, and Louise Fletcher, control-freak Nurse Ratched, whose life revolves completely around her ability to manipulate the lives of her patients. The film launched the acting careers of Christopher Lloyd and Danny De Vito, who have parts as patients.

Brilliantly executed, the film is a dark comedy about a petty criminal who gets himself transfered from a county work detail to a hospital, thinking that finishing out his six-month sentence would be a lot easier in the confines of a mental ward. How wrong he was. McMurphy and Ratched confront one another in a power struggle to the death, in which the bureaucratic system finally triumphs by forcing McMurphy to submit to a personality-destroying lobotomy. Redemption in the end is provided by Chief Bromden (Will Sampson), who kills McMurphy to put him out of his misery and then escapes from the hospital. *One Flew Over the Cuckoo's Nest* won an Oscar as best picture of 1975, as did Jack Nicholson for best actor, Louise Fletcher for best actress, and Milos Foreman for best director.

SUGGESTED READING: *New York Times*, November 20, 1975.

ONO, YOKO. Yoko Ono was born in Tokyo, Japan, on February 18, 1933, to a wealthy banking family. She became the first woman to enroll at Gakushuin University in Japan, and in 1953 she came to the United States and studied at Sarah Lawrence College. Yoko Ono dropped out of Sarah Lawrence and moved to New York City, where she became involved with the avant-garde artistic community. She met John Lennon* in the late 1960s, and after his divorce they became constant companions. They recorded the album *Two Virgins* early in 1969, but the album's nude cover photos of them was quite controversial. So was their honeymoon. They were married on March 20, 1969, but instead of leaving on a honeymoon, they held a "bed-in for peace" in a suite at the Amsterdam Hilton in New York City. They protested the Vietnam War* by staying naked in bed and holding a press conference.

Their recording career soon took off. Yoko Ono and John Lennon released the hit singles "Give Peace a Chance" and "The Ballad of John and Yoko." When Lennon quit the Beatles, Beatles' fans blamed Yoko for the breakup. Although Lennon's solo career was singularly successful, most of their joint recording projects were only marginally successful until 1980, when their album *Double Fantasy* went to number one, largely on the merits of the hit single "(Just Like) Starting Over." Lennon was assassinated on December 8, 1980, and since then Yoko Ono has promoted her artistic endeavors. Late in 1997 rumors hit the Hollywood trade papers that Yoko Ono was planning to make a film based on Lennon's life, but she has denied such plans.

SUGGESTED READINGS: *The Ballad of John and Yoko*, 1982; Yoko Ono, *Yoko Ono*, 1995.

ORGANIZATION OF PETROLEUM EXPORTING COUNTRIES. Throughout the 1950s, oil-producing nations in the Middle East, South America, and Africa felt increasingly exploited by the multinational oil companies, which seemed arbitrary in their pricing decisions, unfair in their concession arrangements, and concerned exclusively with their own profitability. The Arab League began calling for collective actions on the part of oil-producing nations, and in September 1960, five nations formed the Organization of Petroleum Exporting Countries (OPEC): Iran,* Iraq, Kuwait, Saudi Arabia, and Venezuela. Since then OPEC has added Libya, Indonesia, Algeria, Nigeria, Ecuador, Gabon, and several other countries.

OPEC had little impact on global energy prices and policies in the 1960s, but as U.S. demand for oil skyrocketed and U.S. production declined, the economics of oil changed. Late in the 1960s and early in the 1970s, OPEC members were able to take advantage of market conditions by increasing production taxes and nationalizing foreign-owned oil facilities. In 1973 and 1974, OPEC became the major player in the game of international oil prices and politics. The Yom Kippur War* between Israel and the Arab states in 1973 exacerbated Arab resentments of America's pro-Israel foreign policies, and the Arab states imposed an oil embargo on exports to the United States. Because the United States had grown dependent on oil imports, OPEC was able to initiate a series of price increases that pushed the price of crude oil from approximately $3 per barrel in 1969 to nearly $36 a barrel in 1981. The decision precipitated an era of stagflation* in the United States as well as the international energy crisis* during the 1970s.

SUGGESTED READINGS: Abdul Amir Q. Kubbach, *OPEC: Past and Present*, 1974; Dankwart A. Rustow and John B. Mugno, *OPEC: Success and Prospects*, 1976; Tad Szulc, *The Illusion of Peace*, 1978; Daniel Yergin, *The Prize*, 1991.

ORR V. ORR (1979). One of the primary objectives of the women's movement* in the 1970s was to achieve equal protection under the law, and occasionally that goal resulted in judicial decisions that some considered to go against women. One example of this was *Orr v. Orr* in 1979.

During the course of the twentieth century, as divorce law evolved, it became common in many states to require men to pay alimony to their former wives. The logic of the requirement revolved around the assumption that women, who did work outside the home but remained there to nurture children, would not be able to support themselves without their husband's income. But in the unusual circumstances when the wife's assets and income exceeded those of her former husband, divorce courts did not force the female to pay alimony. The case made its way to the U.S. Supreme Court, which decided it on March 5, 1979, by a 6 to 3 vote. Justice William Brennan* wrote the majority opinion, which concluded that states violate the equal protection clause of the Fourteenth Amendment when they permit women, but not men, to receive alimony payments.

SUGGESTED READING: 440 U.S. 268 (1979).

P

PALIMONY. "Palimony," a new legal concept, evolved in the 1970s. In March 1979 Michelle Triola Marvin sued actor Lee Marvin for half of his income during the six years in which they had lived together. They had never married legally, but she had assumed his name and they had lived as man and wife. In the case of *Marvin v. Marvin*, a California court ultimately rejected her claim to half of his earnings, but the court did order Marvin to pay her $106,000 in so-called palimony. In doing so the court established the precedent that unmarried cohabitants enjoyed certain property rights and compensation in the event of estrangement.

SUGGESTED READINGS: *Los Angeles Times*, March 28–31, 1979.

PANAMA CANAL TREATIES (1977). Ever since President Theodore Roosevelt's escapades to seize in 1903 what later became the Panama Canal Zone, U.S. sovereignty there had been a cause for anger and distress for Panamanian nationalists. In 1964, after anti-American riots in Panama City had resulted in the deaths of twenty-four people, negotiations began between the two countries. Thirteen years later, on September 7, 1977, drafts of two treaties were signed in Washington, D.C. The Panama Canal Treaty, which repealed the Hay-Bunau-Varilla Treaty (1903), stated that after its expiration on December 31, 1999, the United States would transfer control of the canal and the Canal Zone to Panama. Other provisions included annual U.S. rent payment of from $60 to $70 million until the transfer and U.S. loan guarantees for Panamanian economic development.

The second treaty, entitled "Treaty Concerning the Permanent Neutrality and Operation of the Panama Canal," guaranteed the political neutrality of the canal after the 1999 transfer, absolute nondiscrimination against all users of the canal, and regulations concerning canal maintenance and efficiency. The United States promised to assist militarily in maintaining the canal's neutrality, and the treaty promised preferential treatment for naval vessels during international political emergencies. Just a month after the signing of the treaties, the people of Panama overwhelmingly approved the treaties in a national plebiscite. After a bitterly partisan debate, the U.S. Senate ratified the treaties in March and April 1978 by the narrow (a two-thirds majority is required for all treaty ratifications) margin of 68 to 32.

SUGGESTED READINGS: Walter LaFeber, *The Panama Canal: The Crisis in Historical Perspective*, 1989; David G. McCullough, *The Path Between the Seas: The Creation of the Panama Canal, 1870–1914*, 1977.

PARIS PEACE TALKS. The Paris Peace Talks refer to the extended negotiations that took place among the major combatants during the Vietnam War.* The four parties to the talks were the United States, North Vietnam, South Vietnam, and the Vietcong, or the National Liberation Front. The formal talks began in Paris, France, on May 13, 1968, but the discussions made no progress toward a negotiated settlement. North Vietnam had no intention of accepting anything less than the complete reunification of the two Vietnams under Communist control. Because of that commitment, North Vietnam refused, absolutely and completely, to agree to withdraw its troops from South Vietnam. South Vietnam, of course, realized that reunification was nothing more than a euphemism for its own demise, and they too proved recalcitrant about any compromises. Most Americans grew quickly skeptical about the merits of the negotiations, especially when it took months for the parties to agree on the size and the shape of the table at which the talks would occur once they began. All parties also realized in 1968 that a presidential election was taking place in the United States in the fall, and that no real political progress could be made until the election had taken place.

Richard Nixon* won the election, and he named Henry Kissinger* as his national security advisor. Kissinger believed that the Vietnam War had been a colossal mistake for the United States. U.S. national security was not involved in the region; therefore, the war had not been worth the cost. At the same time, Kissinger knew that the United States could not simply declare it a mistake and withdraw. Other U.S. commitments in the world would then be brought into serious question. The United States needed to get out of Vietnam with its credibility intact, something Nixon called "peace with honor." The Paris Peace Talks, Kissinger was certain, would never achieve that goal. They were too public, too exposed to media scrutiny, and too politicized.

While the discussion were taking place in Paris, Henry Kissinger began conducting secret negotiations with North Vietnam. By 1971 the United States was tired of the war and ready to compromise, and both Nixon and Kissinger believed that secret negotiations would make concessions easier. President Nixon was desperate to achieve a negotiated settlement before the November 1972 elections, since he had promised during his first presidential election campaign to get the United States out of Vietnam. Eventually, the United States agreed to North Vietnam's demands: North Vietnamese troops were allowed to remain in South Vietnam, while all U.S. troops were withdrawn; the Vietcong were permitted to participate in the government of South Vietnam; and all prisoners of war* would be returned. The initial settlement was agreed to by all parties in October 1972, but in December North Vietnam began backpedaling, which prompted Nixon to launch Operation Linebacker II, a massive B-52 bombing campaign all over the country. Under such punishment, North Vietnamese leaders decided to move ahead with the settlement, although they had no intention of abandoning their long-held goal of reunifying the country. On January 25, 1973, Kissinger and Le Duc Tho* of North Vietnam signed the Paris Peace Accords, which officially ended the Paris Peace Talks, more than four-and-a-half years after they had begun.

SUGGESTED READINGS: Allen E. Goodman, *The Lost Peace: America's Search for a Negotiated Settlement of the Vietnam War*, 1978; Walter Dillard, *Sixty Days to Peace*, 1982.

PAT GARRETT AND BILLY THE KID. *Pat Garrett and Billy the Kid* (1973) is Sam Peckinpah's awkward appraisal of the legend of William H. Bonney and the time in which he lived. Peckinpah, who also directed *The Getaway, The Wild Bunch*,* and *Straw Dogs*,* used some of the same motifs for this film, such as an obsession with death and an emphasis on children, but he also strayed from his own style by parodying the classic chivalrous masculinity in westerns.

The story begins in 1881, the final days of the Wild West, when powerful cattle barons were beginning to secure their lands, forcing civilization down the throats of outlaws like Billy the Kid (played by Kris Kristofferson). Pat Garrett (James Coburn), formerly an outlaw and Billy's best friend, is hired and given a badge by the rancher Chisum, with directions to either chase Billy out of the country or kill him. Garrett, because of his relationship with Billy, confronts him with a warning and explains, "It seems like times have changed." And Billy replies, "Times. Not me." The chase begins, each man avoiding his ultimate fate—Garrett, to kill Billy, and Billy, to accept the inevitable.

As mentioned earlier, Peckinpah's use of death and violence in nearly all his films also appears in *Pat Garrett and Billy the Kid*. However, unlike Peckinpah's work in *The Getaway*, death becomes somewhat artistic and connected to fate, losing its usual grotesque quality. This is especially clear with Billy's death in the end: he does not shed any blood from a wound in his chest.

Perhaps the most striking aspect of the film is the motivations of the leading male characters. Because of Peckinpah's direction, and perhaps because of the acting of Kristofferson and Coburn, the film loses the classic western dichotomies of good and evil and becomes an ambiguous and complex anti-western. In the end, the audience has no hero to worship. Billy is a wild, bull-headed murderer, and Garrett is a puppet of the cattle barons. Kristofferson was perfect for the role—his slow, uncharismatic style made Billy not quite worthy of sympathy. Coburn, in perhaps the best work of his career, succeeded in making Garrett uncomfortable with a fate that requires him to kill his best friend.

The film fit well into the antihero ethos of the 1960s and early 1970s. During the 1970s, when the women's movement* gained momentum, traditional values associated with masculinity were being called into question. The failure of the United States to prevail in Vietnam also helped undermine those values. Aljean Harmetz, who reviewed the movie for the *New York Times*, made this statement about the film, "In the confrontation between a man who will compromise and a man who cannot, at a time when adaptation offers the only chance of survival, lies the film's enormous and disturbing power."

SUGGESTED READINGS: *New York Times*, June 17 and September 30, 1973.

Bradley A. Olson

PELTIER, LEONARD. Leonard Peltier, a Native American of Ojibway tribal descent, was born in Grand Forks, North Dakota, in 1944. His father changed jobs frequently during Peltier's childhood, going from mining, to lumberjacking, to truck driving, all of which kept the family constantly on the move. Long periods of unemployment between jobs made raising a family difficult, and when Peltier was ten years old, his parents separated and then divorced. His mother could not raise him herself, and Peltier moved to the Wahpeton Indian School, a boarding school in North Dakota. He stayed there throughout his school years. Peltier impressed his teachers as a bright but troubled young man.

After leaving the Wahpeton Indian School, Peltier moved frequently and worked at a variety of jobs. He also became involved in the American Indian Movement* (AIM), an organization committed to ending police brutality against Indians and negative stereotyping of Indians and securing a return of lands illegally seized by the federal government. By 1970 Peltier had emerged as one of AIM's key leaders. He traveled widely with Dennis Banks,* promoting AIM'S agenda in the early 1970s, and he was a key figure in AIM's Trail of Broken Treaties* caravan to Washington, D.C., in 1972.

In June 26, 1975, Peltier's life took a dramatic turn. He was involved with several Lakota Indians at the Pine Ridge Reservation in South Dakota when a firefight erupted with Federal Bureau of Investigation (FBI) agents. Two agents—Ronald Williams and Jack Coler—had been searching for a robbery suspect on the reservation when they were gunned down from point-blank range. Peltier, along with three other suspects, was arrested and charged with first-degree murder. The evidence against the four was circumstantial at best. During the trials held in 1976, two of the men were acquitted, and the charges against a third were dropped for lack of evidence. Peltier, however, was convicted of first-degree murder and sentenced to two life sentences.

Since then, Peltier has become an icon to the red power* movement. Most Indian activists, who are represented by the Leonard Peltier Defense Committee, are convinced that Peltier is innocent and that he is being railroaded because of his high profile with the American Indian Movement. They consider Peltier to be a political prisoner. Government officials are just as convinced that he is guilty. Peltier will not come up for a full parole hearing until 2008.

SUGGESTED READINGS: Peter Matthiessen, *In the Spirit of Crazy Horse*, 1992; *New York Times*, June 27, 1996; John M. Peterson, *Aim on Target: The FBI's War on Leonard Peltier and the American Indian Movement*, 1994.

PENTAGON PAPERS. During the early 1960s, Daniel Ellsberg joined the staff of Secretary of Defense Robert McNamara, and in doing so he found himself on the ground floor of Vietnam policymaking. But as doubts about the U.S. military effort mounted in 1966, McNamara ordered a study of the history of American involvement there, and Ellsberg became a leading figure in the project. It only increased Ellsberg's doubts about the war, primarily because Presidents Eisenhower, Kennedy, and Johnson had been guilty of misleading the public and even lying outright about the war. He began secretly photocopying the study—known as "History of U.S. Decision-Making Process on Vietnam Policy"—which consisted of thousands of pages of documents and analysis. Ellsberg then handed them over to Senator J. William Fulbright, chairman of the Senate Foreign Relations Committee, who used them to build his own case against the war. In 1971, Ellsberg delivered a copy of the documents to the *New York Times* which began publishing them.

The Nixon* administration, citing national security, obtained a court order blocking publication, but the *Washington Post* then began publishing what had now become known as the "Pentagon Papers." On June 30, 1971, the U.S. Supreme Court vacated the court order and allowed publication to proceed. The Pentagon Papers became a cause célèbre throughout the country, proving the duplicitousness of the federal government and showing just how deeply and for how long the United States had been involved in Vietnam.

Daniel Ellsberg and Anthony Russo were put on trial in 1972–73 for their role in exposing the coverup. Both were charged with treason, espionage, and theft of government documents. The trial began in July 1972, but on May 11, 1973, the presiding judge dismissed all charges against the two men after learning that the Nixon administration had illegally wiretapped them and had burglarized the office of Ellsberg's psychiatrist, hoping to find incriminating evidence against the defendant. The last straw came when John Ehrlichman, one of Nixon's closest advisors, offered to bribe the judge with the top spot at the FBI.

SUGGESTED READING: Peter Schrag, *Test of Loyalty*, 1974.

PERCY, CHARLES. Charles Harting Percy was born in Pensacola, Florida, on September 27, 1919. He graduated from the University of Chicago and joined the firm of Bell & Howell, but the outbreak of World War II took Percy into the U.S. Navy. He was honorably discharged in 1945 and returned to Bell & Howell where he rose quickly through the corporate ranks and became chief executive and chairman of the board in 1955. A liberal Republican, Percy accepted appointment from President Dwight D. Eisenhower as special U.S. ambassador in 1956. He could not buck the Democratic landslide of 1964, however, and lost his bid to become governor of Illinois. He was elected to the U.S. Senate in 1966, a post he held until 1985. Over the years, as a GOP liberal, Percy found himself increasingly isolated in the party, which was growing more and more conservative. He retired to private business in 1985. He continues to work actively in Washington, D.C., as a lobbyist and member of many corporate boards.

SUGGESTED READINGS: *Chicago Tribune*, February 7, 1994; Robert Hartley, *Charles H. Percy: A Political Perspective*, 1975; David Murray, *Charles Percy of Illinois*, 1968.

PET ROCK. In 1975 and 1976, Gary Dahl decided to market what he called a "pet rock," the ultimate in pet efficiency. The pet was cheap, obedient, and clean. Dahl took a common rock found along the California coast, placed it in a handsome carrying carton, equipped it with his "Pet Rock Training Manual," and took the idea to the annual gift and toy show in San Francisco. For reasons unknown to Dahl or anybody else, the idea took off. Several major department store chains ordered the rocks, *Newsweek* magazine described the phenomenon, and Johnny Carson and the *Tonight Show* booked Dahl as a guest. In the month before Christmas 1975, Dahl was delivering more than ten thousand rocks a day, at a whopping $3.95 each. The fad died in the spring of 1976, but by that time Dahl was a multimillionaire.

SUGGESTED READING: Jane Stern and Michael Stern, *Encyclopedia of Pop Culture*, 1992.

PHAM VAN DONG. Pham Van Dong was born on March 1, 1906, in Quang Nam Province. At the time, Quang Nam Province was part of the French protectorate of Annam. Dong's family had an educated, mandarin background, and he was educated at the French Lycée academy at Hue, where two of his classmates were Vo Nguyen Giap* and Ngo Dinh Diem. As a student, Dong became active in nationalist groups and eventually defined himself as a revolutionary bent on the expulsion of the French. In 1930 French authorities arrested him for sedition, and he spent the next eight years in prison. He finally fled to China where he met Ho Chi Minh and became one of the founding fathers of the Lao Dong party. For the next four decades, along with Ho Chi Minh and Vo Nguyen Giap, Dong was one of the triumvirate that dominated North Vietnamese politics.

Pham Van Dong was active in the Vietminh during their struggle against the Japanese during World War II and the French between 1946 and 1954, and he served as the leader of the Vietnamese delegation to the Geneva Conference in 1954. Dong was Ho Chi Minh's prime minister from 1950 to Ho's death in September 1969, and after his death Dong emerged as the most public figure in North Vietnam. Between 1969 and 1975, Dong released several diplomatic initiatives, always insisting on an American withdrawal, and frequently gave interviews to the Western press. He played a key role in the Paris Peace Talks* of 1973 in which the United States agreed to withdraw from South Vietnam. After the conquest of South Vietnam in 1975, Pham Van Dong was appointed prime minister of the Socialist Republic of Vietnam. He remained at that post until December 1986, when a series of economic setbacks in the Socialist Republic of Vietnam forced his resignation.

SUGGESTED READINGS: *Who's Who in Socialist Countries*, 1978; *Washington Post*, December 18, 1986; *New York Times*, June 19, 1987.

PINK FLOYD. Pink Floyd, a highly successful rock-and-roll band of the 1970s was formed in London, England, in 1966. Pink Floyd included Sid Barrett, Richard Wright, Roger Waters, Nick Mason, and David Gilmour. Known as a pioneering acid-rock group who combined soul, country, blues, and even classical themes into their rock, Pink Floyd had several marginally successful albums in the late 1960s and early 1970s. With the release of their 1974 album *Dark Side of the Moon*, Pink Floyd rocketed to stardom and became one of the most successful acts in popular music. The album was dark indeed, a tribute to paranoia, social anomie, and angst—a sharp contrast to the reform-minded rhythms of the 1960s. *Dark Side of the Moon* remained on the *Billboard* list of the Top 200 albums for an unprecedented 741 weeks—more than sixteen years. *Wish You Were Here* (1975) and *The Wall* (1979) were also number-one albums. By that time, several members of the band were developing solo acts, and Pink Floyd disintegrated early in the 1980s.

SUGGESTED READING: Nicholas Schaffer, *Saucerful of Secrets: The Pink Floyd Odyssey*, 1991.

PIONEER 10. *Pioneer 10*, an interplanetary space probe, was launched by the National Aeronautics and Space Administration (NASA) in 1972. Its original mission was to last only twenty-one months, at which time it would pass near the planet Jupiter. *Pioneer 10* navigated the asteroid belt without incident and closely examined Jupiter, which allowed scientists to conclude that the giant planet was composed primarily of gases and liquids. As *Pioneer 10* flew past Jupiter, the planet's gravitational, sling-shot-like pull hurtled the probe into deep space. Much to its delight, NASA managed to keep *Pioneer 10's* instruments transmitting data for the next twenty-five years. *Pioneer 10's* instrumentation did not begin to break down until 1997, when the probe was more than 6.2 billion miles from Earth. Hoping that *Pioneer 10* might someday encounter intelligent life in the universe, NASA placed on the satellite an aluminum, gold-plated plaque depicting the spacecraft's directional path, the sun's approximate location in the galaxy, and drawings of a man and a woman.

SUGGESTED READING: Michael Abrams, "To Aldebaran and Beyond," *Discover* 18 (January 1998), 75.

POCKET CALCULATOR. One of the most visible symbols of new technology during the 1970s was the invention of the pocket calculator. In 1974 manufacturers began including a single large-scale integrated (LSI) circuit in calculators, which allowed instantaneous processing of large volumes of information. By the late 1970s, students, scientists, mathematicians, and engineers had at their fingertips an electronic instrument capable of performing sophisticated trigonometric and logarithmic functions. In 1975 consumers purchased more than twelve million pocket calculators, and the average price of each unit soon fell from $100 to less than $10. The calculators brought the microchip technology into nearly every household and destroyed the slide rule industry.

SUGGESTED READINGS: *Newsweek*, October 2, 1972; *Time*, October 30, 1972.

POL POT. Pol Pot was born in 1925 as Saloth Sar to a prosperous farming family in Cambodia.* A brilliant child, he was educated at an elite private school housed in the royal palace in Phnom Penh. Late in the 1940s, he traveled to Paris to continue his education, planning to study electronics, but in Paris he got caught up in revolutionary politics and joined the French Communist party (FCP). At the time the FCP was a bastion of Stalinist orthodoxy complicated by a streak of Puritan rigidity. He returned to Cambodia in 1953 and spent several years working as a teacher. At the same time he diligently worked as an organizer for the Khmer Rouge,* Cambodia's insurgent Communist movement, and he rose through the organization's ranks to become its leader. Cambodia had gained its independence from France after the Geneva Accords in 1954, but the Khmer Rouge chaffed under the monarchical leadership of Prince Norodom Sihanouk,* who, they believed, was little more than a filthy capitalist out to serve himself at the expense of the masses. By the early 1960s, Pol Pot was leading a guerrilla war against Sihanouk's government.

The Khmer Rouge slowly gained strength until the years of the Vietnam War,* when its fortunes rose. For centuries, Cambodians had also worried about Vietnamese expansionism, and when the Vietnam War erupted in the 1950s and 1960s, they found themselves walking a political tightrope, hoping to maintain their independence. Prince Norodom Sihanouk, who had become head of state in Cambodia in 1954, proclaimed neutrality in the Indochinese War, not wanting to offend either the powerful Americans or his long-time nemesis, the Vietnamese.

Under international law, however, Cambodia's claim to neutrality was undermined by the fact that the Vietcong and the North Vietnamese used the country as a sanctuary. From bases in Cambodia, they regularly staged military actions on U.S. and South Vietnamese troops, and they just as regularly fled across the border of South Vietnam into Cambodia when U.S. forces pursued them. Both the Lyndon Johnson and Richard Nixon* administrations pressured Prince Sihanouk to expel Vietcong and North Vietnamese forces from Cambodia, but Sihanouk actually feared the North Vietnamese more than he feared the Americans.

Walking that neutralist tightrope eventually proved impossible. Lon Nol, a bitter anticommunist serving as Sihanouk's prime minister, resented the willingness of Sihanouk to allow Vietcong and North Vietnamese Army (NVA) troops to occupy sanctuaries in eastern Cambodia and infiltrate supplies and personnel into South Vietnam via the Ho Chi Minh Trail. Sihanouk tolerated their presence only because he feared a North Vietnamese invasion and the triumph of the Khmer Rouge. At the same time, he had to appease the United States and anticommunists like Lon Nol. In 1969 he secretly allowed the United States to begin bombing enemy targets inside Cambodia. The bombing campaign, designated Operation Menu, really did not satisfy the Nixon administration. The president and National Security Advisor Henry Kissinger* wanted still wider U.S. military operations in Cambodia. That suddenly became possible in the spring of 1970 when Sihanouk traveled to France. While he was gone Lon Nol engineered a coup d'état. The National Assembly displaced Sihanouk, and Lon Nol became the new head of state.

One month later, President Nixon and Kissinger took advantage of the coup d'état and, with Lon Nol's active encouragement and consent, launched the infamous invasion of Cambodia. Euphemistically termed an "incursion," the invasion destroyed Cambodia politically. The massive bombing campaigns and artillery bombardment, directed at Communist forces there, accidentally killed hundreds of thousands of Cambodian civilians. The Khmer Rouge took great political advantage of those deaths and blamed Lon Nol for the widespread deaths. Lon Nol's government lost political influence, and the Khmer Rouge assumed a heroic stance among millions of Cambodians. The invasion also drove the North Vietnamese deeper into western Cambodia than they had ever been before, a political and military reality that greatly strengthened the Khmer Rouge. By the time U.S. troops were withdrawn several months later, the Khmer Rouge had become a much stronger political force in Cambodia.

In October 1970 Lon Nol abolished the monarchy and proclaimed a republic, but in effect he had become the dictator of Cambodia. His administration was marked by extraordinary corruption and ineptitude, and his 1971 stroke left him unable to maintain control of the government. Pol Pot and the Khmer Rouge made steady gains in the countryside. In the spring of 1975, the Khmer Rouge surrounded the Cambodian capital of Phnom Penh. Lon Nol fled to Hawaii early in April 1975, and the Khmer Rouge overran the capital later in the month. They then renamed the country Kampuchea, its ancient name.

Pol Pot, now Cambodia's head of state, declared "Year Zero" and launched a reign of terror that would have made Josef Stalin proud. Pol Pot had decided on nothing less than a complete redesign of Cambodian society. He insisted on deindustrializing the country and deurbanizing it. Khmer Rouge zealots forcibly depopulated Kampuchean cities, forcing everyone into rural labor camps and murdering anyone and everyone with ties to the French, Norodom Sihanouk, or Lon Nol. The killings assumed genocidal dimensions; as many as two million people died between 1975 and 1979. Astonished by the brutality of Pol Pot, worried about the political stability of the regime, and still interested in their ancient quest for dominance of the Khmer people, the Vietnamese went on the march again in 1979 when soldiers of the Socialist Republic of Vietnam invaded Kampuchea. They drove to the capital, and Pol Pot fled back into the jungles where he organized the remnants of the Khmer Rouge into a new guerrilla force to fight against the Vietnamese occupation force.

The Vietnamese proved to be more than Pol Pot could handle. Although ethnic Cambodians had traditionally resented Vietnamese expansionism, they welcomed the 1979 invasion as a way of liberating them from Pol Pot's megalomania. Pol Pot and the Khmer Rouge continued their political and guerrilla struggle throughout the 1980s and early 1990s, even though they had lost most of their former strength. Pol Pot, who was finally captured in 1997 and placed under house arrest, denied that he had anything to do with the holocaust in Cambodia. Although many people in the world community wanted Pol Pot put on trial for crimes against humanity, the political situation in Cambodia was delicate and unpredictable, and Cambodian authorities moved very slowly in making any effort to punish him. Just when political leaders around the world began to demand that Pol Pot be brought to trial on charges of genocide and crimes against humanity, he died in his sleep on April 15, 1998.

SUGGESTED READINGS: Jerry Adler and Ron Moreau, "Pol Pot's Last Days," *Newsweek* (April 27, 1998), 38–41; Ben Kiernan, *How Pol Came to Power*," Ph.D. diss., 1986; *New York Times*, April 16–17, 1998; François Ponchaud, *Cambodia: Year Zero*, 1978; William Shawcross, *Sideshow: Kissinger, Nixon, and the Destruction of Cambodia*, 1979, and *The Quality of Mercy. Cambodia, Holocaust, and the Modern Conscience*, 1984; Michael Vickery, *Cambodia, 1975–1982*, 1984.

POSEIDON ADVENTURE. During the early 1970s, Americans became enamored of the so-called disaster movies—like *Earthquake** and *The Towering Inferno**—which included an ensemble cast of superstars who demonstrated what could go wrong in modern society when a natural disaster strikes. In the case of the *Poseidon Adventure*, a December 1972 release, the disaster is a giant, open-ocean tidal wave that capsizes a luxury liner in the Atlantic Ocean. The cast includes Gene Hackman* as the jaded, cynical preacher/philosopher Frank Scott; Ernest Borgnine as Rogo; Red Buttons as Martin; Carol Lynley as Nonnie; Roddy Mcdowell as Acres; Stella Stevens as Linda; and Shelly Winters as Belle. While the rest of the crew and passengers opt to sit tight and wait to be rescued in their underwater luxury liner turned upside-down, Reverend Scott leads his cohorts in a desperate quest to stay ahead of the seawater by climbing up through the interior compartments to the bottom hull of the ship, which is exposed on the surface of the ocean. On the way, Scott, Acres, Linda, and Belle die, but the others reach safety and are rescued just before the *Poseidon* sinks. Throughout the ordeal, the filmmakers worked hard to demonstrate just how stupid, vain, self-serving, or heroic people can be under stress.

SUGGESTED READING: *New York Times*, December 13, 1972.

PRETTY BABY. This controversial 1978 film was loosely based on the life of photographer Ernest J. Bellocq. French autuer Louis Malle, who cowrote the screenplay with Polly Platt, brought the patience and artistic quality of European film to this American work.

The movie opens in Storyville, New Orleans, in 1917, where Violet (Brooke Shields) watches innocently as her mother, Hattie (Susan Sarandon), gives birth. Soon afterward, viewers are introduced to the goings-on downstairs, where Malle brings an eerie comfort to Nell's Place, one of the fancier brothels in New Orleans. Hattie is one of Nell's "best" women, and Violet, born in the same manner as her newly acquired half-brother, is destined to become Nell's premier attraction, a twelve-year-old "Pretty Baby."

Before disappearing into the dismal world of prostitution, she has a brief liaison and marriage with an obsessive photographer named Bellocq, who is the central focus of the film. In addition to chronicling the last days of Storyville, before the famous red-light district was shut down, the movie uses the classic relationship between art and life to paint a sad picture of the tortured Bellocq, who falls in love with his subject and, even more, with his portrayal of her. John Carradine gives a brilliant performance as the haunted artist whose works now have a respected place in history. In addition, the twelve-year-old Shields plays her role perfectly, no doubt a result of Malle's precision in guiding her.

As anyone might expect, the movie was extremely controversial, because the very idea of any prostitute so young is disconcerting to many. By the late 1970s, most Americans had come to realize that the "make love, not war" slogans of the 1960s sexual revolution had a dark side, and child prostitution, even if just portrayed on film, was one of them. Critics accused Brooke Shield's mother of exploiting her daughter, and some even proposed legislation preventing children from acting in such roles. Others, however, claimed that because Malle had told the story through Violet's naive and passive eyes, he had succeeded in creating a Nell's Place that transcends judgment.

SUGGESTED READING: *New York Times*, April 5, 1978.

Bradley A. Olson

PRISONERS OF WAR. During the course of the Vietnam War,* the question of what to do about U.S. military men being held as prisoners of war (POWs) became a central concern to the Lyndon Johnson and Richard Nixon* administrations. As the war became more and more unpopular in the United States, getting out of Vietnam and bringing home the POWs developed into major political issues. U.S. military personnel were held by North Vietnamese forces as well as by the Vietcong, which made the negotiations to secure their release even more difficult. Both the Vietcong and the North Vietnamese realized that getting the POWs home was a major concern of the Nixon administration, which gave the Communists more diplomatic leverage at the bargaining table.

During the course of the Paris Peace Talks* from 1968 to 1973, and throughout National Security Advisor Henry Kissinger's* secret negotiations with North

Vietnam, return of the POWs was a central demand in the American negotiating position; the Communists exploited that bargaining chip for all it was worth. Eventually, the United States compromised on its opposition to a coalition government in South Vietnam and its insistence on a withdrawal of all North Vietnamese troops from South Vietnam but continued to insist on the return of all American POWs. That was arranged in the 1973 Paris Peace Accords, and between February and April 1973, North Vietnam returned 566 American military POWs and twenty-five civilian POWs.

After the POWs had returned home and had been completely debriefed, it became clear that their treatment at the hands of the North Vietnamese and the Vietcong had not been in compliance with the 1949 Geneva Convention on treatment of prisoners of war. The American POWs had been subjected to torture, malnutrition, inadequate medical treatment, political manipulation, and generally inhumane treatment. North Vietnam denied the charges, but a number of unbiased international organizations agreed that the American POWs had been treated inhumanely.

Although the POWs had been returned home to the United States in 1973, the prisoner-of-war issue did not go away. Disgust about the conduct and outcome of the war was widespread in the United States in the late 1970s, and the fact that 2,546 U.S. military personnel were classified as missing in action fueled rumors that the Communists were still holding U.S. POWs. Those rumors fostered a cottage industry of books and films—such as *First Blood* (1982), *Uncommon Valor* (1983), *Missing in Action* (1984)—in the late 1970s and throughout the 1980s. Groups such as the National League of Families of American Prisoners and Missing in Action in Southeast Asia continued to lobby Congress in the 1990s for ongoing investigations into the issue.

SUGGESTED READINGS: Bruce Franklin, "The POW/MIA Myth," *Atlantic Monthly* (December 1997), 45–51; William Homolka, *Americans in Southeast Asia: The POW/MIA Issue*, 1986; Reader's Digest, *POW: A Definitive History of the American Prisoner of War Experience in Vietnam, 1964–1973*, 1976; Guenter Lewy, *America in Vietnam*, 1978.

PROPOSITION 13. In 1978 Howard Jarvis led a campaign in California to reduce property taxes. The state legislature had repeatedly declined to cut taxes, claiming that it would result in serious declines in state services. Jarvis decided to launch an initiative campaign which, under California law, allows voters who secure enough signatures on petitions to place a proposed law on the next general election ballot for approval or disapproval. Jarvis succeeded in getting enough signatures, and on June 6, 1978, California voters approved the measure—known as Proposition 13—by a 65 percent majority. The measure rolled back property taxes by a whopping 57 percent and produced serious cuts in education and social services budgets. Proposition 13 was a harbinger of the taxpayer rebellion that spread throughout the country in the 1980s.

SUGGESTED READINGS: *New York Times*, June 7–9, 1978.

PSYCHOPHARMACOLOGY. The new medical discipline of psychopharmacology came into being in 1970 when the Food and Drug Administration
approved the use of the drugs lithium and L-dopa. L-dopa was an effective,
though temporary, treatment for Parkinson's disease, and lithium proved to be
an effective antidepressant. The two drugs launched what became, by the 1990s,
a veritable revolution in psychiatry, providing pharmacological treatments for
disorders formerly treated, for the most part unsuccessfully, by psychoanalysis.
Subsequent years would see the approval of dozens of drugs for the treatment
of an increasing variety of mental and emotional disorders.
  SUGGESTED READING: David M. Grilly, *Drugs and Human Behavior*, 1997.

PUNK ROCK. Punk rock was a popular music fad of the late 1970s and early
1980s. At the time, mainstream rock-and-roll music seemed to have lost its
rebellious edge and had become almost establishment chic. Punk rock was a
reaction against that trend. The leading example of punk rock was the Sex
Pistols,* a band led by Sid Vicious (John Simon Ritchie) and Johnny Rotten
(John Lydon). Their sound was loud and their politics outrageous, and they were
known for heavy drug use and sexual obsessions. The Sex Pistols also popularized body-piercing jewelry and mutilated hairdos. They preached the message
that life was meaningless and the world had no future. Critics accused them of
being "sick" and "sleazy." Other prominent punk-rock bands of the era included the Clash, the Buzzcocks, and the Ramones. The Sex Pistols broke up
in October 1978 when Sid Vicious was arrested for the murder of his girlfriend,
Nancy Spungen. While out on bail in February 1978, Vicious died of a heroin
overdose.
  SUGGESTED READING: Gina Arnold, *Kiss This: Punk in the Present Tense*, 1997.

Q

QUEEN. Queen, one of the more spectacular rock-and-roll bands of the 1970s, was formed in England in 1971. With Freddie Mercury* as its lead singer, the band included Brian May on guitar, John Deacon on bass, and Roger Meddows-Taylor on drums. Their musical style became known for its multidubbing sounds and fusion of rock and roll, disco,* cabaret, and heavy metal. Their debut album, *Queen* (1973), was a major success, and they followed it up with *Queen II* (1974), *Heart Attack* (1975), *A Night at the Opera* (1976), *A Day at the Races* (1977), *News of the World* (1978), and *Jazz* (1979). Among their major single hits during the 1970s were "Killer Queen" (1975), "Bohemian Rhapsody" (1976), "You're My Best Friend," (1976), "Somebody to Love" (1976), "We Are the Champions" (1977), "Fat Bottomed Girls" (1978), and "Crazy Little Thing Called Love" (1979). Queen also had a number of popular hits in the early 1980s.

Queen was a great hit among concert-goers because of its elaborate stage designs, which reflected Mercury's college degree in illustration and design, as well as smoke bombs, fireworks, and Mercury's elaborate on-stage preening. During the 1980s, Queen steadily lost influence in the United States, although the group continued to secure major concert bookings around the world. Rumors of Mercury's physical decline as a result of AIDS circulated widely, and in 1991 Mercury released a statement acknowledging his illness. He died two days later.

In the capricious world of modern entertainment, Queen enjoyed a fantastic revival in 1992 when the film *Wayne's World* adopted "Bohemian Rhapsody" as its theme song. "Bohemian Rhapsody" rocketed to number two on the pop music charts in the United States that year.

SUGGESTED READINGS: Peter Hogan, *The Complete Guide to the Music of Queen*, 1994; David Bret, *The Freddie Mercury Story: Living on the Edge*, 1997.

R

RADNER, GILDA. Gilda Radner was born in Detroit, Michigan, on June 28, 1946. She attended the University of Michigan where she majored in drama, but before graduating she moved to Toronto, Canada, where she worked on a local production of *Godspell* and then joined Second City, a comedy-theatrical group. In 1974 Radner moved to New York City to work for the *National Lampoon Radio Hour.* She also worked in a number of CBS television productions. Producer Lorne Michaels saw her work when he was putting together his ensemble comedy cast for a new program entitled *Saturday Night Live.** In 1975 he signed Radner as the first member of the ensemble, remembering later that "she had a remarkable quality to her, a goodness which came through whatever she was doing."

Radner soon became a pop culture icon. *Saturday Night Live*, which at the time included Chevy Chase, Dan Aykroyd, Jane Curtin, Bill Murray, Garrett Morris, Laraine Newman, and John Belushi, was a runaway hit, and Radner proved to be its heart and soul. Her routines of Baba Wawa (a spoof of television journalist Barbara Walters), Rosanne Rosanneadanna, Lisa Loopner, and Emily Litella became American favorites. She left *Saturday Night Live* in 1980 for a film career. Among her best films were *Gilda Live* (1980), *Hanky Panky* (1982), *Woman in Red* (1984), and *Haunted Honeymoon* (1986). Gilda Radner died of ovarian cancer on May 20, 1989.

SUGGESTED READINGS: *New York Times*, May 21, 1989; Gilda Radner, *It's Always Something*, 1989; David Saltman, *Gilda: An Intimate Portrait*, 1992.

REAGAN, RONALD. Ronald Wilson Reagan was born in Tampico, Illinois, on February 6, 1911. Because his father was a traveling salesman and the family moved frequently, the younger Reagan could legimimately claim a number of small Illinois towns as his boyhood home. In 1932 he graduated from Eureka College with a degree in economics and sociology. Times were hard and he took the only job he could get—as a sportscaster with a small radio station in Davenport, Iowa. Five years later, while on assignment covering spring training for the Chicago Cubs on Catalina Island in Southern California, Reagan was noticed by a movie scout, who arranged a screen test for him. Warner Brothers signed him to a movie contract, and Reagan spent the next thirty years performing in films and television. He also earned the respect of other actors, if not so much for his on-screen talent than for his political skills. Reagan served as president of the Screen Actors Guild from 1947 to 1957 and then again from 1959 to 1960.

Reagan's experiences in Hollywood transformed his political opinions. During the 1930s, he was a dedicated New Deal Democrat, but during the Red Scare of the late 1940s and early 1950s, he steadily became more conservative. From 1954 to 1962, he hosted *General Electric Theater* and then *Death Valley Days* on prime-time television, and in the process Reagan became one of the country's most recognizable personalities. He also became the darling of conservative Republicans at the GOP national convention in San Francisco in 1964 when he delivered an electrifying speech endorsing Barry Goldwater for the presidency. Handsome, charismatic, and blessed with a shrewd sense of timing and audience expectations, Reagan emerged from the Republican debacle of 1964 as a candidate in his own right. At a time when most Republicans found Goldwater too conservative, Reagan was unapologetic, and he soon emerged as Goldwater's heir apparent for the GOP's right wing. When he won the California gubernatorial election of 1966, Reagan became one of the most prominent conservatives in the United States. He was reelected to a second four-year term in 1970.

Reagan's two terms as governor of California cemented his Republican credentials. He publicly condemned radicalism and antiwar movement* protesters and won rave reviews from conservatives when he slashed the budget of the University of California (UC), which he considered a bastion of liberalism. He also slowed the growth of social welfare programs in the state. Late in 1968, when he fired Angela Davis* from the UC faculty because she was a Communist, liberals vilified Reagan but conservatives hailed his courage. In 1968 he staged a feeble bid for the Republican presidential nomination and then gave his complete support to Richard Nixon,* who won the nomination and then won the presidency. Reagan was a steadfast supporter of Nixon, publicly at least, until the president's resignation in 1974.

By that time, conservative Republicans were eying Reagan as the party's nominee for the 1976 presidential nomination. The major obstacle to that choice, however, was President Gerald Ford,* who had entered the White House when Nixon resigned in August 1974. Ford was a moderate Republican wired into the Washington establishment, but he carried political baggage through his association with the Nixon administration. Conservatives wanted to dump him. At the Republican presidential convention in 1976, conservatives tried to get Ford to accept the vice-presidential spot with Reagan as the presidential candidate, but Ford refused. When Ford lost the election to Jimmy Carter,* Reagan finally emerged as the frontrunner for the 1980 presidential nomination.

In 1980 conditions were perfect for Reagan. President Carter had presided over difficult times. The economy suffered from stagflation*—high unemployment and inflation—and oil shortages hit consumers in the pocketbooks. The Vietnam War* had ended in 1975 with a complete victory for the Communists, and American foreign policy impotence was underscored by the Iran* crisis of 1979–1981, when Islamic fundamentalists seized the U.S. embassy and took the entire staff hostage. Employing his patented charisma and television presence, Reagan won the Republican presidential nomination, and during the campaign he repeatedly asked voters if four years of the Jimmy Carter administration had left them better off or worse off. Most Americans believed they were worse off, and Ronald Reagan won a decisive victory.

He proved to be one of the most popular presidents in recent history, even though most scholars panned his tenure in the White House. The economy recovered during his term in office, and he was reelected by a landslide in 1984. Reagan retired from politics at the conclusion of his second term. Today he is living outside of Los Angeles and suffering from Alzheimer's disease. Publicity about Reagan's condition has boosted interest in finding a cure.

SUGGESTED READINGS: Bill Boyarsky, *Ronald Reagan: His Life and Rise to the Presidency*, 1981; Peter Hanaford, *The Reagans: A Political Portrait*, 1983.

RED POWER. During the 1960s and 1970s in the United States, the most conspicuous and controversial dimension of public life revolved around the issues of the civil rights movement.* Led by Martin Luther King, Jr., African Americans had launched the movement, but other minorities soon joined, including Hispanics, women, gays and lesbians, and Native Americans, whose political activism became known as the red power movement. While the civil rights demands of blacks, Hispanics, women, and gays revolved around de jure and de facto discrimination, red power was a far more complicated political campaign.

At the heart of the red power movement in the late 1960s was the end of the termination program, a federal initiative widely condemned by American Indians. On August 1, 1953, Congress had inaugurated the termination program, passing resolutions removing federal authority over all Indian tribes, ending their status as wards of the United States, and granting them all the privileges of citizenship. State and local governments were to take legal jurisdiction over the reservations, and federal authority would be terminated. During the 1950s, Congress "terminated" the Alabama-Coushattas in Texas, the Utes and Paiutes in Utah, the Klamaths in Oregon, and the Menominees in Wisconsin. As a result, between 1953 and 1956 more than 1.6 million acres of reservation land fell into white hands. Without federal funds and with tribal corporate power negated, terminated Indians had no means of livelihood and sold their land to support themselves. The Klamaths and Menominees suffered especially heavy losses.

An anti-termination movement steadily gained steam during the late 1950s and 1960s, propelled by the work of such groups as the National Congress of American Indians, the Indian Rights Association, and the Association of American Indian Affairs and by such journals as the *Christian Century, Harper's*, and *The Nation*. The civil rights movement had raised the national consciousness about the problems of America's ethnic minorities, and Indian activists began demanding the restoration of tribal sovereignty. Termination was not formally reversed until 1970, when the Richard Nixon* administration successfully promoted its repeal. It was not until 1988, however, that Congress passed an omnibus measure repealing termination—the Repeal of Termination Act—which prohibited Congress from ever terminating or transferring Bureau of Indian Affairs (BIA) services without the express permission of the tribes involved.

The end of termination was red power's first victory, but it was hardly the last. By the time Nixon announced the end of termination, the red power movement was also working on such concerns as equality, self-determination,* return of alienated land, and the restoration of hunting and fishing rights. Between 1964 and 1966, activists had staged "fish-ins" to proclaim Indian independence from state fish and game laws. Such groups as the Indian Land Rights Association, the Alaska Federation of Natives, and the American Indian Civil Rights Council demanded the restoration of tribal lands, denouncing the idea of monetary compensation for the loss of the Indian estate. The pan-Indian movement, led by such people as Lehman Brightman and his United Native Americans, worked to overcome tribal differences and to construct a united, powerful Indian political constituency in the United States.

In 1969 a pan-Indian group known as the Indians of All Tribes* occupied Alcatraz Island* in San Francisco and demanded its return to native peoples. In addition to insisting on the restoration of tribal lands, groups, such as the American Indian Movement,* demanded complete Indian control over the Bureau of Indian Affairs. In 1972 activists Hank Adams of the fish-ins and Dennis Banks* of the American Indian Movement organized the Trail of Broken Treaties* caravan and traveled to Washington, D.C., to demand the complete revival of tribal sovereignty by the repeal of the 1871 ban on future treaties, restoration of treaty-making status to individual tribes, the provision of full government services to unrecognized eastern tribes, a review of all past treaty violations, restitution for those violations, and the elimination of all state court jurisdiction over American Indians. They also invaded and trashed the offices of the Bureau of Indian Affairs in Washington, D.C., to dramatize their demands.

By the early 1970s, however, the red power movement had increasingly developed into a campaign for self-determination. Although self-determination meant different things to different people, several controlling principles emerged during the debate over its merits. First, self-determination revolved around Indian control of the government agencies dealing most directly with them. Having non-Indians administer Indian health, educational, and economic programs was unacceptable to self-determinationists. Second, self-determination called for an end to assimilationist pressures and a restoration of tribal values and culture. Allotment, citizenship, compensation, relocation, and termination had all aimed at the annihilation of tribal cultures, and self-determinationists wanted to prevent the future emergence of such programs. Third, self-determinationists insisted on maintaining the trust status of the tribes with the federal government.

Although many non-Indians saw self-determination and the continuance of the trust status as contradictory—a combination of paternalism and independence—self-determinationists were convinced that Indians needed the trust status to protect them from non-Indian majorities at the state and local level. Finally, self-determinationists hoped to bring about the economic development of reservation resources so that Indians could enjoy improving standards of living without compromising their cultural integrity or tribal unity. Many of the demands of self-determinationists were achieved when Congress passed the Indian Education Act of 1972, the Indian Finance Act of 1974, the Indian Self-Determination and Education Assistance Act of 1975, and the Indian Child Welfare Act of 1978.

Finally, the red power movement committed itself to the recovery of Native American remains and the protection of Indian archaeological sites. Throughout U.S. history, economic developers and scientists plundered Indian archeological sites and burial grounds, and there was little Indian people could do to protect what they considered to be sacred. In 1960 Congress passed the Reservoir Salvage Act to require notification of the Secretary of the Interior if dam construction could lead to the loss of significant historic sites, and amendments to the law in 1974—known as the Archaeological Recovery Act—strengthened the provisions of the law concerning archaeological sites. The legislation provides money for the protection, recovery, or relocation of such sites, as well as the publication of information about such sites. The Archaeological Recovery Act was a major step in the campaign to protect Native American cultural resources. In 1979 Congress passed the Archaeological Resources Protection Act, which provides for fines and prison sentences for individuals caught removing artifacts from federal lands without permission. Subsequent amendments to the law, particularly in 1988, require all federal agencies to carry out archaeological surveys of all lands under their jurisdiction and conduct public awareness campaigns to stop the looting of archaeological sites. The law, however, does not protect Indian archaeological sites on privately owned land.

SUGGESTED READINGS: Michael M. Ames, *Cannibal Tours and Glass Boxes: The Anthropology of Museums*, 1992; Russel Lawrence Bars and James Youngblood Henderson, *The Road: Indian Tribes and Political Liberty*, 1980; Douglas Cole, *Captured Heritage: The Scramble for Northwest Coast Artifacts*, 1985; George P. Horse Capture, *The Concept of Sacred Materials and Their Place in the World*, 1989; Phyllis Mauch Messenger, ed., *The Ethics of Collecting Cultural Property: Whose Culture? Whose Property?* 1989; H. Marcus Price, *Disputing the Dead: U.S. Law on Aboriginal Remains and Grave Goods*, 1991; John R. Wander, *"Retained by The People": A History of American Indians and the Bill of Rights*, 1994; Wilcomb E. Washburn, *Red Man's Land, White Man's Law*, 1971.

***REED V. REED* (1971).** One of the primary objectives of the women's move-ment* in the 1970s was to achieve equal protection under the law, which required adjudication of a wide variety of de jure obstacles limiting legal equality among women. One of the cases was *Reed v. Reed*, which the U.S. Supreme Court decided by a unanimous vote on November 22, 1971. The case involved the Fourteenth Amendment guarantees of equal protection when state law automatically prefers fathers over mothers when called upon to serve as an executor of an estate. The court threw out the law, arguing "to give a mandatory preference to members of either sex over members of the other . . . is to make the very kind of arbitrary legislative choices forbidden by the equal protection clause." It was the first time the Supreme Court overturned a state law on the grounds that it discriminated against women.

SUGGESTED READING: 404 U.S. 71 (1971).

REVENUE SHARING. Revenue sharing, or what President Richard Nixon* called his New American Revolution, was the centerpiece of the president's domestic program. At the time, the administration wanted to cut federal spending. Revenue sharing involved distributing federal money to cities and states in bloc grants rather than in the mandated programs of the past. The policy went into effect in 1973 with the distribution of $5.4 billion. The program soon became highly controversial, however, because the governors and mayors discovered that they were actually receiving less money than before. By that time the program had become institutionalized, as so many federal programs do, but it did not set a permanent pattern for federal funding.

SUGGESTED READING: Stephen E. Ambrose, *Nixon*, 1989.

ROBINSON, FRANK. Frank Robinson was born in Beaumont, Texas, on August 31, 1935. The family relocated to Oakland, California, when he was just four years old. While growing up, he displayed considerable baseball skills in junior high school, high school, and American Legion teams. In 1952 the Cincinnati Reds signed him to a professional contract. Robinson spent the next four years playing for several of Cincinnati's minor league franchises. The Reds brought him up to the major leagues in 1956, the year in which Robinson won the National League's Rookie of the Year award. In 1961 he won the National League's Most Valuable Player award. He spent ten years in Cincinnati, where he earned a reputation as a "franchise player."

In 1966 the Reds traded Robinson to the Baltimore Orioles in the American League. During his first season in a Baltimore uniform, he won the prestigious Triple Crown, leading the league in home runs (49), batting average (.316), and runs batted in (122). He was the American League's Most Valuable Player in 1966—the only man to ever win that award in both leagues. The Orioles traded Robinson to the Los Angeles Dodgers in 1972, and in 1973 he went to the

California Angels. One year later, in 1974, he was traded to the Cleveland Indians.

By that time, with African-American players becoming so important in professional sports, civil rights movement* activists had begun to criticize professional baseball for its unwillingness to name blacks as managers of baseball teams. In 1975 the Cleveland Indians responded to the criticism by announcing that Frank Robinson would assume managerial duties over the team and continue to play. In doing so, Robinson broke the color barrier in professional baseball, becoming the first African-American manager. In 1976, with a career total of 586 home runs, Robinson retired as a player. He went on to manage the San Francisco Giants from 1981 to 1984 and the Baltimore Orioles from 1988 to 1991.

SUGGESTED READING: Frank Robinson, *My Life Is Baseball*, 1975.

ROCKEFELLER, NELSON. Nelson Aldrich Rockefeller was born in Bar Harbor, Maine, on July 8, 1908, to one of the world's richest families. His grandfather, John D. Rockefeller, had founded the Standard Oil Company of New Jersey and built it into the world's most powerful corporation, a virtual monopoly that made him a billionaire. By the time Nelson Rockefeller graduated from Dartmouth College in 1930, he was heir to a fortune that reached into the hundreds of millions of dollars.

In fact, money soon became an abstraction to him. After leaving Dartmouth, he entered the family business in New York City, managing real estate sales and development. From 1930 to 1935, he clerked at the family-owned Chase National Bank, and from 1935 to 1940, he served as chairman of the family-owned Creole Petroleum Company. Like so many other children of the fabulously wealthy, Rockefeller could not find satisfaction in working to make more money for the world's already richest family. Instead, he began to develop what became a lifelong interest in fine art and an enduring concern about world affairs, especially Latin American affairs.

During World War II, Rockefeller decided to devote his life to public service, where he thought his efforts might make a contribution to building a better world. In 1940 President Franklin D. Roosevelt appointed him coordinator of Inter-American Affairs. In 1944 he was appointed assistant secretary of state for Latin American affairs. Rockfeller returned to the family businesses in 1945 and held various volunteer posts in the Truman and Eisenhower administrations. A liberal Republican, he accepted Eisenhower's appointment as chairman of the Advisory Committee on Government Organization as well as undersecretary of Health, Education, and Welfare and special assistant on foreign policy. In 1958 Nelson Rockefeller defeated W. Averell Harriman to become governor of New York. At the same time, he became one of the leading Republicans in the United States.

He eventually served four terms as governor. His administrations were liberal ones, noted for their expansion of social welfare programs and an increase in the size of the state budgets and annual deficits. Rockefeller was also a devoted fan of higher education, and during his tenure in Albany he built the State University of New York system into one of the best in the nation.

Presidential ambitions struck Rockefeller, and many Republicans backed him, but he turned out to be a perennial also-ran for the Republican presidential nomination. In 1960 he lost to Vice President Richard Nixon,* and in 1964 Senator Barry Goldwater of Arizona edged him for the nomination. By the late 1960s, liberal Republicans were starting to become a vanishing species in the United States. They could not distinguish themselves politically or ideologically from such liberal Democrats as President Lyndon B. Johnson, whose Great Society and civil rights programs occupied center stage in American politics.

At the same time, more and more Americans were questioning the virtues of the welfare state and big government. Conservatism began a resurgence that eventually took control of the Republican party and led to the 1980 election of Ronald Reagan* as president. Rockefeller was the leading liberal Republican at a time when liberal Republicanism was heading down a dead-end street. His refusal to endorse Barry Goldwater in the general election of 1964 earned the eternal ire of Republican conservatives. Rockefeller made another bid for the presidency in 1968, but GOP conservatives vetoed him. Nixon got the nomination instead.

Rockefeller retired from public life in 1973, but in 1974 President Gerald Ford* nominated him to serve as vice president of the United States. Spiro Agnew* had resigned the vice presidency under criminal indictment in 1973, and Nixon had replaced him with Gerald Ford.* When Nixon resigned amidst the Watergate scandal* revelations of August 1974 and Ford succeeded to the presidency, the new president picked Rockefeller to replace him. Rockefeller served faithfully, but the Ford administration was plagued by serious economic and political problems. Overseas, the Vietnam War* came to an ignomanious end in 1975 with a Communist victory, and unemployment and inflation worsened steadily. Ford and Rockefeller were doomed to defeat in the election of 1976.* Jimmy Carter* and the Democrats came to power. Nelson Rockefeller was by then more than ready to retire and he left public life. He died of a heart attack on January 26, 1979.

SUGGESTED READINGS: Robert H. Connery and Gerald Benjamin, *Rockefeller of New York: Executive Power in the Statehouse*, 1979; Joseph E. Persico, *The Imperial Rockefeller: A Biography of Nelson A. Rockefeller*, 1982.

ROCKY. *Rocky* was one of the great hit films of the 1970s. Sylvestor Stallone had worked in several films during the early 1970s, but his career in Hollywood was going nowhere. He wanted to write a screenplay and star in the film, but he had little success at that until he was inspired by the Muhammad Ali*–Chuck Wepner heavyweight championship fight in 1975. At the time, Ali was widely considered the greatest fighter in boxing history, whereas Wepner was a ham-

and-egg club fighter who had long since seen his best days. Nevertheless, before the entire world, Wepner managed to go the length with Ali even though he lost the fight. It was a time when America needed an underdog hero. The Vietnam War* and the Watergate scandal* had robbed the country of hope and innocence, and millions of people were ready to find in popular culture what they could not find in the real world.

Stallone's screenplay, *Rocky*, is set in Philadelphia. Rocky Balboa (Sylvester Stallone) is an all but washed-up light heavyweight who pays his bills by working as a small-time Mafia collector. Apollo Creed (Carl Weathers), a Muhammad Ali clone who is the heavyweight champion of the world, puts together a rags-to-riches promotional stunt to give some unknown fighter a shot at the title. An African American, Creed decides he wants to face a white fighter, particularly a white ethnic, because of the promotional value of the race issue. He picks Balboa, who goes by the professional name of the "Italian Stallion." Of course, nobody gives Balboa a chance of lasting even one round with Creed, and the betting odds against him are astronomical.

Rocky has a surprise for the champion. His left-handedness catches Creed off-guard, ruining his timing, and nobody can take a punch like Rocky. Creed hits Balboa seemingly thousands of times during the fight, turning Rocky's face into hamburger, but Balboa delivers numerous body blows to Creed, wearing him down to the point of physical exhaustion. Creed wins the fight on a split decision, but Rocky captures the hearts of America by going the distance with the champ. What Rocky Balboa lacked in talent he made up for in heart, and it was a message America yearned to hear in the 1970s.

Stallone had played his financial cards correctly. He rejected a $300,000 offer for the film and signed instead to do it for $20,000 and 10 percent of the gross. *Rocky* eventually grossed more than $200 million, and Stallone became an instant multimillionaire. *Rocky II*, the 1979 sequel in which Rocky wins the heavyweight championship from Apollo Creed, was equally successful. Stallone went on to make three more *Rocky* films.

SUGGESTED READINGS: *New York Times*, November 22, 1976, and June 15, 1979.

ROE V. WADE (1973). On January 22, 1973, the U.S. Supreme Court rendered its decision, by a vote of 7 to 2, in the *Roe v. Wade* case. At the time, Texas law prohibited abortions* except in instances where the procedure was necessary to save the life of the mother. Most other states in the United States had similar statutes on the books. Upholding personal privacy as a right protected by the Fourteenth Amendment to the Constitution, the court proclaimed that during the first three months of pregnancy, the state has no "compelling" interest to limit a women's right to have an abortion for any reason. During the last six months of pregnancy, the state may "regulate the abortion procedure in ways that are reasonably related to maternal health," which included licensing and regulating abortion providers. The court allowed states to ban abortions during the last ten weeks of pregnancy because, at that point in the pregnancy process, the fetus is capable of surviving outside the womb.

The decision ignited a ferocious debate over abortion that continues today. Alan Guttmacher of Planned Parenthood hailed *Roe v. Wade* as a ''wise and courageous stroke for the right to privacy, and for the protection of a woman's physical and emotional health.'' John Cardinal Krol, the Roman Catholic archbishop of Philadelphia remarked, ''The Supreme Court's decision today is an unspeakable tragedy for this nation.'' The National Organization for Women* praised the decision as a ''great victory for individual rights and privacy.'' Supporters and opponents of abortion began organizing, and by the early 1980s abortion had become the most contentious issue in American politics.

SUGGESTED READINGS: Leonard Stevens, *The Case of Roe v. Wade*, 1996; Susan Gold, *Roe v. Wade: Abortion*, 1994; *New York Times*, January 23, 1973.

ROGERS, WILLIAM. William Pierce Rogers was born in Norfolk, New York, on June 23, 1913. He graduated from Colgate University in 1934, and in 1937 he earned a law degree at Cornell University, where he edited the law review. Rogers worked briefly with a Wall Street firm in 1937 before joining the staff of New York County District Attorney Thomas E. Dewey, who was about to launch his campaign against racketeers. While serving on Dewey's staff, Rogers gained extensive experience as a trial lawyer. He served as an officer with the U.S. Naval Reserve in the Pacific during World War II. After the war, Rogers returned to Dewey's staff briefly and then went to work as counsel to several congressional committees. During those years he came to know Congressman and later Senator Richard Nixon* and worked on the Alger Hiss case. In 1950 Rogers returned to private law practice but continued his work as a Nixon adviser. When Dwight D. Eisenhower was elected president in 1952, Rogers became deputy attorney general, and in October 1957, he became attorney general in the Eisenhower cabinet.

Between 1960 and 1968, Rogers practiced law, but when Nixon entered the White House in 1969, Rogers became secretary of state. Nixon also named Henry Kissinger* to the post of special White House assistant on foreign affairs. From the beginning, Kissinger's influence was dominant. Nixon tended to be suspicious and secretive, and he distrusted the ''Ivy League types'' at the State Department. Rogers was always upstaged by Kissinger. The making of foreign policy had definitely shifted to the White House. Thus, William Rogers was often put in the position of explaining and defending policies before Congress and the nation that had been formulated by Nixon and Kissinger with little or no input from the State Department. This was especially true in the areas of Sino-Soviet and Vietnam War* policy. Even though Rogers was often the subject of unkind chatter on the cocktail circuit, he continued to serve until 1973, when he resigned to return to his private law practice. In 1986 he was chosen by the Ronald Reagan* administration to head the investigation into the *Challenger* disaster.

SUGGESTED READINGS: *Current Biography*, 1969; William P. Rogers, *Vietnam in Perspective*, 1969; Thomas G. Paterson, *American Foreign Policy*, 1983; *U.S. News and World Report*, February 24, 1986.

Joseph M. Rowe, Jr.

RONSTADT, LINDA. Linda Ronstadt was born in Tucson, Arizona, on July 15, 1946. Of Mexican and German descent, she grew up singing country, rhythm and blues, and Mexican folk songs. After a brief stint at the University of Arizona, she moved to Los Angeles to promote her musical career, and she soon became part of the group Stone Poneys. The group had a top-twenty single in 1967, "Different Drum," but then fell on hard times. The Stone Poneys broke up, and Ronstadt went off on her own. Her next album, *Heart Like a Wheel*, which included favorite oldies and contemporary tunes, eventually topped the album charts. Its single "You're No Good" hit number one on the pop singles chart, and "I Can't Help It If I'm Still in Love with You" was a number-one hit on the country charts. *Heart Like a Wheel* was the first Ronstadt album to go platinum, and over the years she added sixteen more. Her reportoire included rhythm and blues, rock, folk, country, and even reggae. In 1977 she had two number-one albums: *Simple Dreams* and *Living in the U.S.A.* During the late 1970s and early 1980s, she attracted attention because of her relationship with Jerry Brown,* the bachelor Democratic governor of California. Early in the 1980s, Ronstadt released three more albums that went platinum or gold: *What's New* (1983), *Lush Life* (1984), and *Sentimental Reasons* (1986). In the 1990s she returned to her roots with a series of successful Mexican ballads.

SUGGESTED READING: Melissa Amdur, *Linda Ronstadt*, 1993.

ROOM 222. *Room 222*, a hit dramatic television series during the early 1970s, was first telecast on ABC on September 17, 1969. *Room 222*, starring Lloyd Haynes as history teacher Pete Dixon, Denise Nicholas as school counsellor Liz McIntyre, and Michael Consodine as high school principal Seymour Kaufman, was unique as a television dramatic series because its two stars—Haynes and Nicholas—were African Americans in roles that did not require them to be African Americans. It was one of the first television dramatic series to deal with racial and ethnic diversity in a positive light. The last episode of *Room 222* was broadcast on January 11, 1974.

SUGGESTED READING: Tim Brooks and Earle Marsh, *The Complete Directory to Prime Time Network and Cable TV Shows, 1946–Present*, 1995.

ROOTS. Broadcast on eight consecutive nights in January 1977, *Roots* was the most widely viewed dramatic series in American television history. The program was based on Alex Haley's* bestselling memoir/novel *Roots* (1976), which grew out of the stories Haley had heard his grandmother and great aunt tell and retell during his boyhood in Hemming, Tennessee. Decades later, he tracked the family's roots back to The Gambia in West Africa. Twelve years in the writing, the book tells the story of Haley's family's West African roots, the 1750 capture of ancestor Kunta Kinte and his journey to the United States as a slave, and the history of the family in Maryland and Tennessee. The book won a Pulitzer Prize and sold more than six million copies.

Independent television and film producer David Wolper bought the rights to *Roots* and convinced ABC television to turn the story into a miniseries. The program told the story of Kunta Kinte (played by LeVar Burton and John Amos) from his birth to his capture and transport to America at the age of seventeen. He remained a proud, rebellious African all of his life. The series then focused on the life of his daughter Kizzy (Leslie Uggams) and her son, Chicken George (Ben Vereen). The series ended with emancipation in 1865, when Tom (George Brown), the great-grandson of Kunta Kinte, went off on his own to make a life for himself.

Approximately 130 million Americans—more than half the country's population—watched *Roots* during its initial broadcast, and although its story of racism, exploitation, and violence was a harsh one, the series proved to be a source of black pride as well as black and white accommodation in the United States. *Roots* remains a seminal event in the lives of the African Americans who watched the program and in modern American popular culture as well.

SUGGESTED READINGS: Tim Brooks and Earle Marsh, *The Complete Directory to Prime Time Network and Cable TV Shows, 1946–Present*, 1995; David Shirley, *Alex Haley*, 1994; William Stanley, *The Impact of the TV Event "Roots,"* 1979; Sylvia Williams, *Alex Haley*, 1996.

ROTHKO SCANDAL. The 1970 suicide of Mark Rothko, one of the world's greatest abstract expressionist painters, revealed one of the most notorious art scandals in American history. Within three months of Rothko's death, his dealer, Francis Lloyd of Marlborough Galleries, purchased more than 800 paintings from the dead artist's estate. Lloyd paid prices far below market value. Rothko's daughter filed a lawsuit against Lloyd, charging him with conspiracy and fraud. After four years of litigation, including an eighteen-month trial, Lloyd was found guilty of fraud, sentenced to 200 hours of community service, and forced to reimburse the Rothko estate to the tune of $9.2 million.

SUGGESTED READING: *New York Times*, July 12, 1975.

RUSTBELT. During the 1970s, when the American economy was characterized by serious inflation and serious unemployment, the term "rustbelt" was used to describe one of the causes of the nation's economic malaise. U.S. heavy industry, so the theory went, was no longer competitive because the physical plants were so old. Many American steel factories, for example, had been constructed in the late nineteenth and early twentieth centuries, and they no longer enjoyed a technological advantage over the newer European and Asian facilities. The prices of American-produced steel were too high, which led to layoffs in heavy industry.

SUGGESTED READINGS: Barry Bluestone and Bennett Harrison, *The Deindustrialization of America*, 1982; Lorna Petersen, *Rustbelt Resurgence*, 1989.

S

SALOTH SAR. *See* POL POT.

SAN ANTONIO INDEPENDENT SCHOOL DISTRICT V. RODRIGUEZ
(1973). As the civil rights movement* gained momentum in the late 1960s and
early 1970s, activists in the African-American and Latino communities began
to question the use of local property taxes to finance public schools. They
claimed that the right to an education is guaranteed by the U.S. Constitution,
but because the local property tax base varies from school district to school
district, there are huge discrepancies in the amount of money spent per child
per year. Such disparities, civil rights advocates claimed, violated the equal
protection clause of the Fourteenth Amendment. The case of *San Antonio Independent School District v. Rodriguez* revolved around that issue. In its decision of March 21, 1973, however, the U.S. Supreme Court ruled, by a 5 to 4
vote, that the right to an education is not guaranteed by the Constitution;
therefore, the equal protection clause is not relevant. The use of property taxes
to finance public education does not deny anyone the opportunity for an education.

SUGGESTED READING: 411 U.S. 1 (1973).

SANDANISTAS. The term ''Sandanistas,'' common on front pages of newspapers and on network newscasts during the 1970s and 1980s, is the name of
a political movement that came to power in Nicaragua in July 1979. The Somoza
family, who had dominated Nicaraguan politics for two generations, had earned
reputations for political assassinations and gross corruption, all backed by hundreds of millions of dollars of aid from the United States. By the late 1970s a
left-wing guerrilla movement threatened the survival of the Somoza regime,
which had managed to alienate much of the Nicaraguan middle and lower classes. This movement, known as Sandanistas, was named after Augusto César
Sandino, a Nicaraguan revolutionary who had been murdered by the Somozas

in 1934. Somoza had given the revolutionaries a huge boost in 1972 when he pocketed $16 million of international aid intended for victims of a devastating earthquake that had destroyed the capital city of Managua. Guerilla warfare raged throughout the decade.

By 1979 the Somozas were bankrupt, financially and politically. By the early summer of 1979, troops of the Sandanista National Liberation Front were closing in on the capital. The Somoza's army fled the city early in July and the Sandinistas seized control. Anastasio Somoza made it to Miami with $20 million, but he had to relocate to Paraguay a year later, where he was assassinated. As soon as the Sandanistas came to power, destruction of the regime, which had the backing of the Soviet Union, became official U.S. policy. That policy lead to the huge Iran-contra scandal during the Ronald Reagan* and George Bush administrations.

SUGGESTED READING: Bernard Diederich, *Somoza and the Legacy of U.S. Involvement in Central America*, 1981.

SANFORD AND SON. Sanford and Son, a hit television situation comedy in the 1970s, starred Redd Foxx as Fred Sanford and Demond Wilson as his son, Lamont. The show was first broadcast on NBC on January 14, 1972. The Sanfords owned a junkyard in Los Angeles. An elderly widower with a sharp tongue, Fred was perfectly happy making a living out of the junk business, but his son Lamont was more ambitious and wanted to get out of the business and into something more interesting and lucrative. Most of the cast were African Americans, and *Sanford and Son* had some of the humor, and a few of the stereotypes, of the older Amos and Andy Show. At the same time, there was not an obsequious bone in Fred's body, and his wit was quick, sarcastic, and laced with the street-talking jive of urban ghettoes. *Sanford and Son* actually received some criticism from the black community on the grounds that it reinforced negative stereotypes, but they could never charge it with being racist, only in bad taste. The last episode was broadcast on September 2, 1977. *Sanford and Son* remained popular in reruns well into the 1990s.

SUGGESTED READING: Tim Brooks and Earle Marsh, *The Complete Directory to Prime Time Network and Cable TV Shows, 1946–Present*, 1995.

SATURDAY NIGHT FEVER. Saturday Night Fever was a hit film and part of the disco* craze of the 1970s. The film stars John Travolta* as Tony Manero, a young Bay Ridge, Brooklyn, paint store worker by day whose life comes alive on weekend evenings at the ''2001 Odyssey'' disco, where he is the best dancer in the crowd. With the Bee Gees* supplying the sound track, Manero and his friends escape the blandness of their day-to-day lives on the dance floor of the ''2001 Odyssey.'' For some critics, the film was a clear symbol in the shift of American youth culture from the counterculture, rebellious 1960s to the more staid, pessimistic 1970s.

SUGGESTED READING: *New York Times*, December 16, 1977.

SATURDAY NIGHT LIVE. *Saturday Night Live* was the comedy television hit of the 1970s. It premiered as ''Saturday Night'' on October 11, 1975, at 11:30 P.M. in the Eastern and Pacific time zones (10:30 P.M. in the Central and Mountain time zones). In 1977 the name of the program was changed to *Saturday Night Live*. The program first appeared in the wake of the Vietnam War* and the Watergate scandal,* when Americans had become cynical about their leaders and their institutions. The original cast included Bill Murray, Chevy Chase, Gilda Radner,* Dan Aykroyd, Garrett Morris, Laraine Newman, Jane Curtin, and John Belushi; they called themselves ''The Not Ready for Prime Time Players.'' Their humor was irreverent and their sarcasm pointed. Few prominent Americans—celebrities or politicians—escaped their wit and wrath. Performances were live and uncensored, and by 1978 more than 28 million Americans were tuning in every Saturday night. Murray, Chase, Radner, Aykroyd, and Belushi became superstars in their own right, and it became hip for many of those celebrities who were victims of the satire to appear as guest hosts on the program.

SUGGESTED READINGS: Eric Barnouw, *Tube of Plenty: The Evolution of American Television,* 1975; Doug Hill, *Saturday Night: A Backstage History of Saturday Night Live,* 1987; *Saturday Night Live: The First Twenty-Five Years,* 1994; Gilda Radner, *It's Always Something,* 1989.

SATURDAY NIGHT MASSACRE. Ever since the last week of October 1973, journalists and historians have used the phrase ''Saturday Night Massacre'' in relation to President Richard Nixon's* decision to fire special Watergate prosecutor Archibald Cox.* Senate investigation hearings into the Watergate scandal* during the summer of 1973 uncovered substantial new evidence, especially the existence of tapes of White House conversations. Cox pursued the new evidence actively, even while the Nixon administration refused to deliver much of it on the grounds of ''executive privilege.'' Frustrated and worried about the investigation, the president decided to fire Cox on October 20, 1973. Attorney General Elliot Richardson, a former student of Cox's at Harvard Law School, refused to carry out Nixon's order and resigned instead. William Rucklehaus, second in command at the Justice Department, also refused to fire Cox and joined Richardson in resigning. The president had to turn to Solicitor General Robert Bork, who carried out the dismissal.

The press had a journalistic field day with the events of October 20, 1973, and the American public began to realize that a political cover-up of unprecedented proportions was under way. Nixon replaced Cox with Leon Jaworski,* who proved to be just as indefatigable in pursuing the Watergate case. Eventually, Nixon resigned the presidency in August 1974.

SUGGESTED READINGS: Stephen Ambrose, *Nixon,* 1989; Elizabeth Drew, *Washington Journal,* 1974; Stanley Kutler, *Abuse of Power: The New Nixon Tapes,* 1997; Theodore H. White, *Breach of Faith,* 1975; Robert Woodward and Carl Bernstein, *All the President's Men,* 1974.

SCHLAFLY, PHYLLIS. Phyllis Schlafly was born in Saint Louis, Missouri, on August 15, 1924. She graduated from Washington University and then earned a master's degree in government at Radcliffe. After leaving Radcliffe, she found work in banking and she became active in Republican politics. In 1964 she sided with Barry Goldwater and conservatives in the Republican party. Her book, *A Choice Not an Echo* (1964), accused the Republican party of being controlled by a moderate and liberal elite. Schlafly then spent the next five years researching and writing in the field of strategic defense policy, in which she took a hard-line stance toward the Soviet Union.

In the 1970s, Phyllis Schlafly rose to public consciousness as the leading woman in the anti-feminist campaign in the United States. She outspokenly denounced divorce, abortion,* socialism, big government, welfare, and homosexuality, and she led a successful campaign to block the Equal Rights Amendment* (ERA), which she considered redundant, since existing constitutional protections and the Civil Rights Act of 1964 already outlawed gender discrimination. In fact, she was convinced that the ERA would actually hurt tens of millions of American women, since it would, in her opinion, render unconstitutional many existing legislative protections based on gender. Working-class women would be especially vulnerable. During the crusade to get the ERA ratified during the 1970s, Schlafly served as national chairman of the Stop ERA group. She also enraged feminists by claiming that men and women are fundamentally different and that women should not try to compete with men.

In recent years, Schlafly has continued her work as the leading conservative woman in the Republican party. She has been president of the Eagle Forum, a conservative advocacy group, since 1976. She has also continued to write. In addition to *A Choice Not an Echo*, her books include *Kissinger on the Couch* (1975), *Equal Pay for Unequal Work* (1984), *Pornography Victims* (1987), *Who Will Rock the Cradle* (1989), *Stronger Families or Bigger Government* (1990), and *Rethinking Family Leave* (1991).

SUGGESTED READINGS: Carol Felsenthal, *The Sweetheart of the Silent Majority: The Biography of Phyllis Schlafly*, 1981; Phyllis Schlafly, *The Power of the Positive Woman*, 1977.

SEALE, BOBBY. See BLACK PANTHERS.

SEALS AND CROFTS. Seals and Crofts was a very successful soft-rock group of the 1970s. Jim Seals and Dash Crofts formed the group in California in 1969 after having spent several years touring with the Champs and working as studio musicians. Their first three albums, *Seals and Crofts* (1970), *Down Home* (1970), and *Year of Sunday* (1971), were only marginally successful, but *Summer Breeze* in 1972 was a hit. Their next album, *Diamond Girl* (1973), a repeat success, contained two hit singles, "Diamond Girl" and "We May Never Pass This Way Again." Their 1974 album *Unborn Child*, an anti-abortion,* pro-life testament, failed critically and commercially and resulted in demonstrations by pro-choice groups at their concerts. Their last top-forty hit, entitled "Get Closer," appeared in 1976.

SUGGESTED READING: Patricia Romanowski and Holly George-Warren, eds., *The New Encyclopedia of Rock & Roll*, 1985.

SECRETARIAT. Secretariat is widely considered to be one of the greatest, if not the greatest, race horses in U.S. history. In the summer of 1973, the chestnut stallion became the first horse in twenty-five years to win the Triple Crown—first place in the Preakness, Kentucky Derby, and Belmont Stakes. Secretariat won the Belmont by an unprecedented thirty-one lengths. Secretariat's career earnings totaled a record $1.3 million. The horse was sold for $6 million in 1974 and retired to stud.

SUGGESTED READING: William Nack, *Secretariat: The Making of a Champion*, 1975.

SEGER, BOB. Bob Seger was born in Dearborn, Michigan, on May 6, 1945. Combining elements of both soul and hard rock, Seger performed for years in the vicinity of Detroit, singing and writing songs that reflected his working-class, blue-collar origins. His first hit was released in 1969; "Ramblin' Gamblin' Man" made it to number seventeen on the pop charts. Several years of commercial drought then followed, but Seger scored in 1976 with his album *Live Bullet*. It eventually sold enough copies to become a quadruple platinum record. He topped that in 1977, however, with the album *Night Moves*, which sold more than five million copies. His 1978 album *Stranger in Town*, another success, included the four hit singles "Still the Same," "Hollywood Nights," "We've Got Tonight," and "Old Time Rock & Roll." His popularity then began to decline, although Seger continued to write and perform in the 1980s and 1990s.

SUGGESTED READING: Patricia Romanowski and Holly George-Warren, eds., *The New Encyclopedia of Rock & Roll*, 1985.

SELF-DETERMINATION. The term "self-determination" refers to the central objective of the red power* movement during the 1970s. Throughout the nineteenth and twentieth centuries, U.S. government Indian policy disregarded the importance of tribal authority and tribal governance and, except for the years of the Indian New Deal during the 1930s, subjected Native Americans to powerful assimilationist pressures. The Bureau of Indian Affairs (BIA) administered federal government Indian programs and was, many Indians believed, paternalistic at best and racist at worst. The central goal of the self-determinationists was to put Indians in control of the government programs affecting their lives.

During the 1970s, Native American activists campaigned to achieve self-determination, and they succeeded in securing from Congress four pieces of legislation that came to constitute the backbone of self-determination: the Indian Education Act of 1972, the Indian Finance Act of 1974, the Indian Self-

Determination and Education Assistance Act of 1975, and the Indian Child Welfare Act of 1978.

During the 1960s, concern about the state of Indian education increased dramatically throughout the United States. Lyndon B. Johnson's Great Society programs focused their attention on civil rights and anti-poverty campaigns, and Native Americans suffered from the effects of both racism and poverty. Many Indians felt culturally alienated from public schools, had extremely high dropout rates at the middle school and high school levels, were unlikely to go on to higher education, and suffered inordinately high rates of poverty. In response, Congress passed the Indian Education Act of 1972, which mandated parental and tribal participation in all federal aid programs to public schools with Indian students; appropriated funds to assist community-run schools; allocated money to state and local education agencies, colleges, universities, and tribes to develop new Indian history, culture, and bilingual curricula; funded tribal adult education programs; provided funds for teacher training at BIA schools; and established an Office of Indian Education to administer the Indian Education Act. The Office of Indian Education was staffed completely by American Indians.

The Indian Finance Act of 1974 was another important element in the self-determination movement. As a reaction to the termination movement of the 1950s and 1960s, Congress had restored federal protection to most tribes by restoring the trust relationship, and the desire to upgrade the reservations economically was very strong. During the termination era, Congress had emphasized relocating Indians away from reservations rather than strengthening reservation economies, but the new political paradigm placed a high premium on reservation economic viability. The Indian Finance Act of 1974 provided new moneys for reservation economic development and individual entrepreneurship, creating a loan guarantee and insurance fund, partially subsidizing loan costs, and providing grants for new businesses. Although the Indian Finance Act did not transform reservation economies, it did provide new opportunities for many Indian entrepreneurs.

Self-determination was formally recognized as U.S. government policy when Congress passed the Indian Self-Determination and Education Assistance Act in 1975. Many Native Americans considered federal Indian policy to be a complete failure. Poverty stalked the reservations and life spans were scandalously low. School districts educating Native American children employed non-Indian teachers and administrators incapable of providing the necessary curricula and environment. The BIA often subcontracted reservation services to non-Indian companies, whose fees drained resources and whose policies often appeared racist and condescending to Indian people. The Indian Self-Determination and Education Assistance was Congress's way of responding to those problems. In its introductory section, the law spelled out its intentions:

The Congress hereby recognizes the obligation of the United States to respond to the strong expression of the Indian people for self-determination by assuring maximum Indian participation in the direction of educational as well as other Federal services to Indian communities so as to render such services more responsive to the needs and desires of those communities.

The Congress declares its commitment to the maintenance of the Federal Government's unique and continuing relationship with and responsibility to the Indian people through the establishment of a meaningful Indian self-determination policy which will permit an orderly transition from Federal domination of programs for and services to Indians to effective and meaningful participation by the Indian people in the planning, conduct, and administration of those programs and services.

The legislation authorized tribal governments to negotiate directly with the Bureau of Indian Affairs and the Department of Health, Education, and Welfare for the provision of social welfare services to members of the tribe. In doing so, the legislation gave tribal leaders much more control over federal programs. When tribal leaders determined that the programs were not meeting tribally established goals and priorities, they could terminate the programs. The Indian Self-Determination and Education Assistance Act also appropriated money so that tribal governments could establish programs to train tribal members in financial, personnel, and administrative management so that Indians would not have to rely on non-Indians to manage their programs, to purchase land, and to build and maintain health facilities. The law also required that all school districts receiving funds for the education of Indian children use that money exclusively for Indian children.

In 1978 Congress passed the final piece of self-determination legislation: the Indian Child Welfare Act. Throughout the nineteenth and twentieth centuries, a variety of federal, state, and private programs worked to secure the adoption of Indian children by non-Indian families. By the early 1970s, anywhere from 25 to 35 percent of Indian children in the United States were taken from their parents in adoption proceedings. The adoption programs were based on a paternalistic logic that only away from reservations, in the hands of white families, could Indian children receive good educations and escape lives of crime, abuse, alcoholism, and disease. Indian activists, in response, complained that the programs deprived Indian children of their cultural and familial moorings and made their lives worse.

In response, Congress passed the Indian Child Welfare Act. The law treated tribes as sovereign nations and awarded tribal courts, not state or federal courts, jurisdiction over the adoption or foster care placement of Indian children. The law works to achieve the following goals: Indian children in need of adoption or foster placement should be placed first with a member of his or her extended family. If such a placement proves impossible, the child should be placed with a family in his or her own tribe. If that is not possible, the child should be placed in the home of an Indian family. Finally, and only as a last resort, were Indian children to be placed in the homes of non-Indians. As a result of the law, non-tribal private and public agencies lost a great deal of their authority over Indian children.

SUGGESTED READINGS: William C. Canby, *American Indian Law in a Nutshell*, 1988; Estelle Fuchs and Robert J. Havighurst, *To Live on This Earth: American Indian Education*, 1973; Linda A. Marousek, "The Indian Child Welfare Act of 1978: Provisions and Policy," *South Dakota Law Review* 25 (Winter 1980), 98–115; Gaylene J. McCartney, "The American Indian Child-Welfare Crisis: Cultural Genocide or First Amendment Preservation," *Columbia Human Rights Law Review* 7 (Fall-Winter 1975–1976), 529–51; James S. Olson and Raymond Wilson, *Native Americans in the Twentieth Century*, 1984; Margaret Connell Szasz, *Education and the American Indian: The Road to Self-Determination Since 1928*, 1977; Charles F. Wilkinson, *American Indians, Time, and the Law*, 1987.

SEX PISTOLS. The Sex Pistols, a rock-and-roll band formed in London, England, in 1975, was one of the pioneers of punk rock.* The group included Johnny Rotten (John Lydon), Steve Jones, Glen Matlock, and Paul Cook. Sid Vicious (John Ritchie) joined the Sex Pistols in 1977. Before they broke up early in 1978, the Sex Pistols had released only two albums, *Never Mind the Bollocks Here's the Sex Pistols* (1977) and *The Great Rock-and-Roll Swindle* (1979). Intentionally offensive, vulgar by design, and critical of social conventions, the Sex Pistols were an outrageous but short-lived musical success of the 1970s.

SUGGESTED READING: David Dalton, *El Sid: Saint Vicious*, 1997.

SHAFT. In 1971 black actor Richard Roundtree starred as *Shaft*, a private investigator known for his street smarts and no-nonsense style. Gordon Parks directed the film and Isaac Hayes composed its award-winning score. *Shaft* began a new genre in the action film, dubbed blaxploitation,* because it featured an all-black cast, black slang, black fashion, black situations, and urban black settings. *Shaft* was an instant hit and had enough appeal to justify two sequels. *Shaft* also spawned what became known as blaxploitation films, such as *Superfly* and *Cleopatra Jones*, which similarly appealed to black audiences.

SUGGESTED READING: *New York Times*, July 11, 1971.

SHAMPOO. *Shampoo*, a farcical satire of sex, politics, and relationships in the 1970s, was written by Robert Towne and Warren Beatty and directed by Hal Ashby. *Shampoo* stars Warren Beatty as George, a Beverly Hills hairdresser who cannot resist the women he glamorizes. An awkward gigolo, he often mumbles and gestures inarticulately and never is in complete control of himself or his situation. He rides his motorcycle day and night, moving from one house to the next, and stops in at work occasionally. The only tangible desire he has in the film is to own his own shop, and when the bank turns him down for a loan, he goes to Lester (Jack Warden), the rich husband of one of his lovers. Before the end of the film, he has slept with Lester's wife Jackie (Julie Christie), his mistress Felicia (Lee Grant), and his daughter Lorne (Carrie Fisher); in addition, he has a girlfriend (Goldie Hawn). All his freewheeling comes to a climax one night at an election party attended by everyone. They all desperately seek his attention, and the resulting mess causes him to reconsider his lifestyle. His resolution to change has come too late, and he loses nearly everything.

Shampoo hit the screens in the immediate wake of the Watergate scandal* when the bloom was coming off the sexual revolution of the 1960s. The characters in *Shampoo* are hopelessly superficial in spite of the extraordinary self-importance they exhibit, and their concerns—both personal and political—are vacuous and trivial. *Shampoo* was a perfect symbol of the disappearance in America of the 1960s and its values.

SUGGESTED READING: *New York Times*, February 12, 1975.

Bradley A. Olson

SIHANOUK, NORODOM. Born in 1922 in Cambodia,* Norodom Sihanouk was crowned king of Cambodia by French officials in 1941. He functioned as a puppet ruler until 1954 when, after the French defeat at Dienbienphu, Cambodia was given its independence. Between 1954 and 1970, Sihanouk tried to maintain Cambodian neutrality between the People's Republic of China and the Vietnamese, and between the United States and the major Communist powers, but it proved to be an impossible task. When the American buildup in South Vietnam began in 1965, Sihanouk began to lean toward the Vietnamese, but that only lasted until North Vietnamese Army (NVA) troops began exploiting his neutrality. In 1969 Sihanouk acquiesced to American requests for the secret bombing of NVA installations in Cambodian territory, and in March 1970, while he was visiting the Soviet Union and asking them to assist him in expelling the NVA troops, he was deposed by Lon Nol. Sihanouk then moved to Beijing, hoping but failing to get Chinese support for his attempt to regain power. After the Khmer Rouge* reign of terror in the 1970s, Sihanouk returned to Cambodia as king, but his power was limited. His son, Norodom Ranariddh, became premier in the 1990s. As late as May 1996, Khmer Rouge Communists were still making attempts to assassinate Sihanouk.

SUGGESTED READINGS: William Shawcross, *Sideshow: Kissinger, Nixon, and the Destruction of Cambodia*, 1979; Norodom Sihanouk, *Sihanouk Reminiscences*, 1992.

SIMON, CARLY. Carly Simon was born in New York City on June 25, 1945. The Simon family had made a fortune in the publishing business, and Carly attended Sarah Lawrence College for several years. She quit before graduating and began singing folk songs with her sister Lucy. Her debut album, *Carly Simon*, in 1971 had a top-ten single: "That's the Way I've Always Heard It Should Be." In 1971 her second album, *Anticipation*, made it to number thirteen. Simon's real breakthrough came in 1972. Spurred by the megahit single "You're So Vain," which became a number-one hit, *No Hits* went gold. Simon had hit singles in 1973 ("The Right Thing to Do") and in 1974 ("Haven't Got

Time for the Pain''). Simon sang the theme song for the 1977 James Bond movie *The Spy Who Loved Me*, and ''Nobody Does It Better'' went to number two on the pop charts. In 1978, with *Boys in the Trees*, Simon had her first platinum album. It was also her last top-ten album.

SUGGESTED READING: S. M. Holden, ''Queen Carly Woos Her Court,'' *Rolling Stone* (July 13, 1978), 68–69.

SKYLAB. For several weeks in the summer of 1979, *Skylab* was the source of much speculation in the United States and around the world. A seventy-seven-ton laboratory launched into earth orbit in 1973, *Skylab* was the site of three scientific missions before a 1978 trajectory error by NASA engineers sent it into a misguided orbit. By early 1979 it was obvious that *Skylab* would reenter the Earth's atmosphere, but because of its size, it would not burn up completely before hitting Earth. Concerned scientists around the world worried about the consequences of a *Skylab* crash, or even a great deal of *Skylab* debris, impacting a populated region. On July 11, 1979, *Skylab* reentered the earth's atmosphere but broke up and distributed debris over the Indian Ocean and uninhabited regions of western Australia.

SUGGESTED READINGS: *New York Times*, July 1–14, 1979.

SOCIOBIOLOGY. During the mid-1970s, academic circles buzzed with talk of the new birth of a new discipline—sociobiology. Harvard entomologist E. O. Wilson coined the term in his book *Sociobiology: The New Synthesis* (1975). At a time when geneticists and social scientists were battling over the ''nature v. nurture'' issue, or whether genetics was more important than environment in determining human behavior, Wilson came clearly down on the side of genetics. His area of scientific expertise was the social behavior of insects, which Wilson knew was genetically based and targeted solely at the survival of the species. The purpose of all living things, Wilson claimed, ''is not even to reproduce other organisms; it reproduces genes and serves their carriers. The organism is only DNA's way of making more DNA.''

Few people argued with Wilson's theory as long as it was applied to insects, but when Wilson took a giant scientific leap and applied his theories to human behavior, he created a storm of controversy. Even altruistic behavior, he claimed, was genetically programmed. When an ant sacrifices its own life to defend the larger colony from invaders, it is not an act of altruism, only a genetic imperative to preserve the species. He suggested that the same might be true for human beings. Critics accused Wilson of reducing all higher human emotions to simple biochemical equations.

Actually, Wilson's theories were far more complex than his critics implied. Wilson fully accepted the role of religion and ethical human behavior, claiming that perhaps only 10 percent of human behavior was, as he called it, ''pre-wired.'' Although predictions of a new discipline were vastly premature, Wilson's theories inspired debate and new research in a variety of academic fields, including psychology, sociology, anthropology, biology, neurology, and linguistics.

SUGGESTED READING: E. O. Wilson, *Sociobiology: The New Synthesis*, 1975.

SOLDIER BLUE. *Soldier Blue* is a 1970 anti–Vietnam War* film that never mentions the word Vietnam. Unlike World War II, which spawned dozens of films throughout the conflict, Vietnam did not produce any, with the exception of John Wayne's *The Green Berets*. The Vietnam War was so controversial that few Hollywood studios were willing to risk making either prowar or antiwar films. The major studios virtually ignored the conflict, as if it were not happening at all.

Two 1970 films, however, managed to protest the war without getting into Vietnam. One of them was *Little Big Man**; the other, *Soldier Blue*. *Soldier Blue* starts Candice Bergen as Cresta Marybelle Lee and Peter Strauss as Private Honus Gant, two people whose trite frontier love story is lost in the carnage of the film. The real story of *Soldier Blue* is its indictment of the U.S. Army, which fronts for American GIs in South Vietnam. For all intents and purposes, the Indians, who appear to be an earlier version of the Vietcong, are innocent Vietnamese civilians. *Soldier Blue*'s violence is graphic and calculated, even gratuitious, in its portrayal of an orgy of military abuse of innocent Indian men, women, and children. U.S. government policies in the American West, according to *Soldier Blue*, are just as immoral as they are in Vietnam.

SUGGESTED READING: *New York Times*, August 13, 1970.

SOLEDAD BROTHERS. *See* JACKSON, GEORGE.

SOLZHENITSYN, ALEXANDR. Alexandr Solzhenitsyn, the Nobel Prize–winning Russian author, was exiled to the United States in 1974. His body of work, which includes *August 1914, The Gulag Archipelago, Cancer War*, and *A Day in the Life of Ivan Denisovich*, paints a dark, critical picture of the impact of communism on Russian life. During his life he spent more than eleven years in Soviet prisons for criticizing Soviet authorities and the Communist ideology.

Solzhenitsyn was welcomed as an anticommunist hero when he settled in rural Vermont in 1974, where he lived in isolation for twenty years. Americans soon learned, however, that Solzhenitsyn was no friend of capitalism either. A devout Russian nationalist who revered the czars and abhorred democracy, Solzhenitsyn criticized the consumer culture that seemed, to him at least, to have robbed the United States of any sense of national purpose, and the cult of individuality that had so damaged group identity. In 1990 Mikhail Gorbachev restored Solzhenitsyn's citizenship, and in 1994 the Nobel laureate returned to live in Russia.

SUGGESTED READING: Edward E. Ericson, *Solzhenitsyn and the Modern World*, 1993.

SONNY AND CHER. Salvatore Bono was born on February 16, 1935, in Detroit, Michigan, and Cherilyn Sarkasian LaPier was born on May 20, 1946, in El Centro, California. They married in 1964 and became very popular, hippie-style pop singers. After several unsuccessful releases, they recorded a number-one hit in 1965—"I Got You Babe." Bono wrote and produced the record, as well as the string of hits that followed: "Baby Don't Go," "The Beat Goes On," "Laugh at Me," "All I Really Wanna Do," and "You Better Sit Down Kids." Their career as a duo peaked then, although they made two top-ten hits in 1971–1972: "All I Ever Need Is You" and "A Cowboy's Work Is Never Done." They had a successful, if short, Las Vegas career, and their *Sonny and Cher* television variety show gave them a national profile. Sonny and Cher divorced in 1975 and they pursued individual careers. Cher went on to become a highly respected actress, and Sonny went into politics, serving as mayor of Palm Springs, California, and three terms in Congress as a Republican before his accidental death in a skiing accident on January 5, 1998.

SUGGESTED READINGS: Thomas Braun, *Sonny and Cher*, 1978; *New York Times*, January 6, 1998.

SONTAG, SUSAN. Susan Sontag was born in New York City in 1933, raised in Tucson and Los Angeles, and educated at Berkeley and Harvard. Brilliant, trendy, and intellectually fashionable, she wrote *Benefactor* (1963), *Against Interpretation* (1966), *Death Kit* (1967), *Trip to Hanoi* (1968), *Styles of Radical Will* (1969), and *Art of Revolution* (1970). A contemporary critic of American culture, she wrote that "most people in this society who aren't utterly mad are, at best, reformed or potential lunatics." After a visit to North Vietnam, she decided that that country epitomized patriotism, neighborliness, joy, and faith in the human condition. She reserved the sharpest barbs in her verbal arsenal for her own culture. There is no hope for the West, no redemption for "what this particular civilization has wrought upon the world. The white race is the cancer of human history." She was especially eloquent in her descriptions of American degradation, a decline inherent in a lack of genuine guilt over rampant consumerism, social alienation, bourgeois expectations, moral bankruptcy, psychological impotency, and the inability to communicate or sustain relationships.

Nor did intellectuals escape her wrath. In what many critics considered an anti-intellectual diatribe, she raged against the flight from feeling in modern literary criticism and the futile attempt made by scholars to interpret literature, to reduce its contents to convenient intellectual categories. All it created, she argued, was the "perennial, never consummated project of intepretation," which is inherently "reactionary, impertinent, cowardly, and stifling." She went on to argue that "the world, our world, is depleted, impoverished enough. Away with all duplicates of it, until we again experience more immediately what we have." Interpretation buries the aesthetic experience, preventing people from coming to terms emotionally with art. "The effusion of interpretation of art today poisons our sensibilities." The plague of the modern mind, Sontag reasoned, is too much thinking, not enough feeling.

In the 1970s, after a bout with breast cancer,* Sontag put her fertile mind to work examining the relationship between disease and culture. Her 1977 book *Illness as Metaphor* rests on the premise that cultures mythologize what they do not understand, producing an endless series of very potent, and potentially misleading, metaphors. Society has tried to find psychosocial etiologies for cancer as an earlier generation did for tuberculosis. Since cancer has defied understanding for so long, it has produced a particularly large and intoxicating lexicon of metaphors. So does AIDS, which Sontag wrote about in her 1989 book *AIDS and Its Metaphor*. Her 1992 historical novel *The Volcano Lover* made the bestseller lists, and her most recent effort as a playwright, *Alice in Bed*, premiered in 1996.

SUGGESTED READING: Liam Kennedy, *Susan Sontag*, 1995.

SOPHIE'S CHOICE. *Sophie's Choice*, William Styron's brilliant, haunting novel of 1979, is set in Brooklyn, New York, in 1947. It is narrated by Stingo, a writer-to-be from Tidewater, Virginia, who aspires to gain literary success in the big city. He falls in love with Sophie Zawidstowska, a Polish Catholic woman who survived incarceration at Auschwitz during World War II. She befriends him but is entangled in a messy relationship with Nathan Landau, a pathological Jewish biologist. Sophie is tortured by a choice she had to make during the war. Upon her arrival at Auschwitz, a Nazi physician forced her to sacrifice one of her two children. One of the children, he told her, would go to a youth camp and survive; the other was destined for a gas chamber. Sophie must make the choice in an instant, and she selects life for her little boy and death for her little girl. For the rest of her life she is tortured by the choice, and it fills her with a self-hatred that leads to alcoholism, abuse, and suicide. In 1982 the novel was made into a movie of the same name. *Sophie's Choice* is a monument to the dark side of human nature.

SUGGESTED READING: William Styron, *Sophie's Choice*, 1979.

SOUL CITY. Soul City, an experiment in black power, was launched in 1974 by Floyd McKissick, the national director of the Congress of Racial Equality. McKissick wanted to go beyond the rhetoric of black power and establish a black-controlled community. Late in the 1960s, he had received a Ford Foundation grant to train black politicians in cities that had or were about to have black majorities. With limited amounts of external funding, McKissick set out to do better than that. His Soul City was located in Warren County, North Carolina, just south of the Virginia border. From the ground up he intended to build a community that would be politically and economically controlled by blacks, and then, using Soul City as a prototype, he hoped to build similar communities throughout the United States.

McKissick's plans for Soul City, though heralded publicly, collided with the severe economic problems America experienced during the 1970s. He was not able to attract the investment capital he needed, nor was he able to convince enough businesses to relocate there. In June 1980 the federal government had to take over all but eighty-five acres of the Soul City project.

SUGGESTED READING: William Van Deburg, *A New Day in Babylon: The Black Power Movement and American Culture, 1965–1975*, 1992.

SOUTHERN STRATEGY. The term "southern strategy" is today used by historians and political scientists to describe the electoral strategies of the Richard Nixon* administration (1969–1974). In the election of 1964, despite his overwhelming loss nationwide, Barry Goldwater had proven that a conservative Republican could do well in the South. In fact, except for his home state of Arizona, Goldwater had done well only in the Deep South. Republican successes there had caught the Democrats off-guard; ever since the Civil War they had come to rely upon the so-called Solid South as a guaranteed set of electoral votes in presidential elections. Barry Goldwater had showed just how vulnerable Democrats were in their old stronghold. The Kennedy and Johnson administrations, with their emphasis on civil rights, had offended many southerners, who began to see in the Republican party their best chance for preserving the political status quo. When Nixon won the Republican presidential nomination in 1968, he decided to implement a "southern strategy" in order to win the South.

The southern strategy posed a real political challenge to Nixon who did not want to so pander to southern conservatives that he alienated the more moderate Republicans in the Midwest, Northeast, and border states, where he needed significant support. It would have been easy for Nixon to appeal to the South by denouncing the civil rights movement,* but he personally approved of the Civil Rights Act of 1964, and he feared that condemning the legislation would cost him more votes in the North than it would gain him in the South. Nixon also realized that a good number of Republicans supported the Civil Rights Act of 1964. He had to find a way to appeal to southerners without alienating mainstream Republicans.

The approach he took proved to be brilliant. Instead of publicly condemning civil rights legislation, Nixon decided to proclaim the virtues of law and order, condemn antiwar protestors, and denounce the busing* of children to achieve school integration, all of which conservative southerners loathed. Without even mentioning the civil rights movement,* Nixon managed to endear himself to millions of southern Democrats. Privately, he also encouraged southern political leaders, Democrats as well as Republicans, to believe that, if he won the election, he would make sure that conservative southerners were appointed to the federal bench. In both the elections of 1968 and 1972, Nixon swept the Deep South. Subsequent Republican presidential candidates, such as Ronald Reagan* and George Bush, have perpetuated the southern strategy in their own election campaigns.

SUGGESTED READING: Stephen Ambrose, *Nixon*, 3 vols., 1987–1991.

SPACE PROGRAM. When the Soviet Union launched the satellite *Sputnik*, on October 4, 1957, the United States entered a time of technological identity crisis. In 1958, in the wake of that crisis, Congress established the National Aeronautic and Space Administration (NASA). During the next two years, a number of existing military space programs were transferred to the new agency, but it was during the Kennedy administration that NASA experienced its huge growth after the president announced his intention to land an American on the moon before the end of the decade. The manned spacecraft center was placed in Houston in November 1961, and over the next decade—through the Mercury, Gemini, and Apollo programs—NASA achieved the president's goal. The first lunar landing occurred in July 1969.

The rest of the Apollo flights to the moon, except the ill-fated *Apollo 13*, seemed somewhat anticlimactic during the 1970s, and NASA had to search for a new mission. Public support for space exploration also waned, primarily because of its expense and the apparent domestic needs of the country. NASA personnel declined in number from 37,000 in 1967 to only 24,000 in 1980. Although the emphasis on manned flight declined, the improvement of satellite technology gave NASA a new mission in terms of commercial economics, scientific research, and military security. NASA satellite missions provided dramatic improvements in weather forecasting, resource exploration on earth, and telecommunications. The space shuttle, or Space Transportation System, became dominant in the 1980s. The *Challenger* disaster in 1986 compromised the program, however, and during the Bush administration, NASA found itself under increasing pressure to deemphasize its scientific research program in favor of commercially profitable programs.

SUGGESTED READING: John M. Logsdan, *The Decision to Go to the Moon: Project Apollo and the National Interest*, 1976; National Aeronautic and Space Administration, *NASA Historical Data Book*, 1988.

SPOCK, DR. BENJAMIN. Benjamin Mclane Spock was born on May 2, 1903, in New Haven, Connecticut. He graduated from Yale in 1929 and took a medical degree from Columbia in 1933. He specialized in pediatrics and psychiatry and served a tour of duty in the U.S. Navy during World War II. While on duty, he wrote *The Common Sense Book of Baby and Child Care*. It was published in 1946 and eventually became one of the most successful books in American publishing history. The timing of the book could not have been more propitious. The first infants of the post–World War II "baby boom" were just being born, and Spock offered their mothers revolutionary advice on child raising. Until his book, parents were usually advised to raise their infants on firm, strict schedules, feeding them well-defined diets and making them sleep, play, and eat on a time line. Spock's book advised mothers to relax, to understand that each child and each parent was unique, and that no firm rules could be applied to everybody. By the late 1950s, Benjamin Spock had become the authoritative voice on child care in the United States. *Baby and Child Care* eventually sold fifty million copies and was translated into forty languages. In addition to *Baby and Child*

Care, Spock wrote *A Baby's First Year* (1954), *Feeding Your Baby and Child* (1955), *Dr. Spock Talks with Mothers* (1961), and *Problems of Parents* (1962). In all of them he continued to emphasize the individuality of children and the need for parents to be flexible.

He was also became politically active. He opposed the testing of nuclear weapons because of radioactive contamination, and from 1963 to 1967 Spock served as president of the National Committee for a Sane Nuclear Policy. He was also a bitter, outspoken critic of U.S. involvement in Vietnam. He actively participated in acts of civil disobedience to protest the draft, advising young men not to register for the selective service, to burn their draft cards, and not to report for physicals. In 1968 he was convicted of conspiracy to violate draft laws, but the conviction was overturned on appeal. Critics charged that Spock was partly responsible for the youth rebellion of the 1960s and early 1970s. Parents, they claimed, had raised children without discipline, and the country was now reaping what Benjamin Spock had sown. Spock's response to such allegations was always consistent: "I didn't want to encourage permissiveness, but rather to relax rigidity."

Spock ran for president in 1972 on the People's party ticket but received only 78,000 votes. After Vietnam, he continued his activism, protesting nuclear weapons, nuclear power plants, and U.S. defense spending. He was eventually arrested twelve times for acts of civil disobedience. In 1996, at the age of ninety-three, Spock was still lecturing about politics and medicine. He completed another revision of *Baby and Child Care* in February 1998. By that time he was quite ill, and he died on March 16, 1998.

SUGGESTED READINGS: Lynn Z. Bloom, *Doctor Spock: Biography of a Conservative Radical*, 1972; *New York Times*, March 17, 1998.

STAGFLATION. The term "stagflation," which emerged in the 1970s, describes an American economy mired in unemployment and, at the same time, afflicted with rising prices. Throughout modern economic history, unemployment and inflation had rarely been companions. When fewer people were working, gross demand in the economy was down and so was spending, which tended to bring prices down as merchants competed to sell their inventories. Unemployment and deflation were companion problems, and the solution for one also solved the other. By stimulating the economy through government spending and tax cuts, the government created jobs and lifted prices. The opposite was true during World War I, World War II, and Korea. Unemployment almost ceased to exist, but prices turned upward. Policymakers could pursue restrictive monetary policies to control prices, and although such an approach tended to create more unemployment, the economy nevertheless remained at full employment.

Not surprisingly, stagflation posed painful dilemmas to policymakers. With serious unemployment and inflation coexisting, politicians had to choose their poison. By implementing expansive monetary and fiscal policies, they stimulated production and enhanced employment, but they also made inflation worse. Treating the price problem was not any easier. Restrictive monetary and fiscal policies might force prices down, but they also threw more people out of work. Richard Nixon,* Gerald Ford,* and Jimmy Carter,* the presidents who found themselves in the clutches of stagflation during the 1970s, could not make any adjustments to the economy without creating serious political problems for themselves.

The roots of stagflation were deep and complex. Long before the 1970s ever arrived, the industrial belt of the Northeast was becoming the so-called rust belt.* Aging factories were steadily losing productivity while labor union wages climbed. The only way for businesses to cover their increasing overhead was to increase prices. Inflationary pressures were already evident in the early 1960s.

President Lyndon B. Johnson's vision of the Great Society had contributed to increasing prices. In his enthusiasm for Medicare, the War Against Poverty, and educational improvements, Johnson had increased federal spending in ways the country had not seen since Franklin D. Roosevelt and the Great Depression. For the 1968 fiscal year, Johnson pushed through a federal budget of $178 billion, which included a whopping $25 billion deficit. With the Department of the Treasury competing for capital in the financial markets, interest rates inched upward and, as interest rates climbed, so did prices.

The Vietnam War* exacerbated the problem. With defense spending up and so many young men entering the military, the economy was operating at full capacity. Consumer purchasing power outpaced the economy's productive capacity. With too many dollars chasing too few goods, prices rose. Such a scenario was not unusual during wars, but President Johnson's reaction was unprecedented. During World War I, President Woodrow Wilson dramatically increased taxes to pay for the war and keep prices down. President Roosevelt, during World War II, and President Harry Truman, during the Korean War, followed the same course.

Johnson's alternatives did not appeal to him. Cutting federal spending would limit consumer purchasing power and ease prices, but unacceptable political consequences were guaranteed. He could drastically cut defense spending and withdraw U.S. troops from South Vietnam, but then he would face the consequences of watching an American ally fall to communism, an event right-wing Republicans would be anxious to exploit. He could cut federal spending by slicing into his Great Society programs, which would reduce gross demand in the economy and impose downward pressure on prices. After all of his Great Society promises, however, the president risked losing support among traditional Democratic constituencies.

Increasing taxes was another option. If history offered any lessons about wartime finance, it was that war calls for new taxes. Because the war in Vietnam grew steadily more unpopular between 1965 and 1968, the president knew that calling for tax increases to pay for such a war would lead to a difficult battle in Congress. Johnson could win the fight, but it would require the support of conservative Democrats and Republicans, and they would exact a price, most likely downsizing the antipoverty and civil rights programs. The president told one of his advisors: ''I don't know much about economics, but I do know the

Congress. . . . And I can get the Great Society through right now—this is a golden time. We've got a good Congress and I'm the right President and I can do it. But if I talk about the cost of the war, the Great Society won't go through and the tax bill won't go through.'' Johnson finally abandoned an across-the-board tax cut in favor of a much smaller income tax surcharge.

Too little too late, the surcharge did not have the power to put a brake on the economy. In 1968 unemployment remained around 3 percent, well below the full-employment level of 4 percent, but inflation jumped up to 4 percent, not enough to alarm economists but certainly enough to make them take notice. Talk about the possibilities of hyperinflation began to bounce around the Washington, D.C., cocktail party circuit.

During the presidential election of 1968, Republican candidate Richard Nixon criticized Lyndon Johnson's handling of the war and the economy. When he took office in 1969, he had to do something about both. None of the options—reductions in defense spending, cuts in social spending, or tax increases—seemed palatable to Nixon either. His Vietnamization* program, however, proved successful. The president steadily reduced the number of U.S. troops in South Vietnam, beginning in the summer of 1969, and as he did so the pressures on the defense budget fell. Nixon soon had an option that Johnson never had—the opportunity to cut the defense budget.

Nixon was a shrewd political animal and, intent on running for reelection in 1972, he worried that cutting the Pentagon budget would be unpopular in the West, where defense spending was a bastion of local economies. He also knew that cutting federal spending would increase unemployment, and he did not want to launch a reelection campaign by trying to defend joblessness. So Nixon made a fateful economic decision not unlike the one made by Johnson. When Johnson could have pushed through a tax increase, he did not. When Nixon could have reduced federal spending as Vietnam wound down, he chose not to. Defense spending as a percentage of the gross national product began to subside, from 9.5 in 1968 to 5.0 percent in 1978, but the reduction was replaced by concomitant increases in spending for Medicare, Social Security, retirement, and unemployment programs. The president ratcheted up the budget and the deficits in fiscal 1970. Inflation jumped to 6.5 percent in 1970.

By 1971 U.S. troop levels in South Vietnam had dropped to 125,000. With the war gradually ending, the economy was slowing. Millions of soldiers bailed out of the military and landed in a shrinking job market. Unemployment leaped from 3.5 percent when Nixon took office to 6 percent in the spring of 1971. Democrats were already talking about "Nixonomics"—inflation and unemployment—the worst of all possible economic worlds. Nixon understood implicitly that the tired, tattered Republican rhetoric of federal spending cuts and balanced budgets would not be enough. Voters were not sophisticated enough, Nixon was convinced, to sort out the subtleties of macroeconomics; they would be quick, as they had always been, to blame the man at the top. Poor economies doomed reelection.

Nixon and his advisors mulled over the problem throughout the spring of 1971. In the end, the president went with his political instincts. High unemployment was more likely than inflation to doom his reelection chances. Instead of cutting back on the federal budget, which he could have done as Vietnam War spending declined, the president inceased federal spending by pouring money into social programs. Just when the opportunity materialized to bring down federal spending, Nixon raised federal social spending to boost his reelection chances.

On June 11, 1971, the president appeared before a national television audience to explain his program. In words that sent a shudder through conservatives, the president announced, "I am a Keynesian." He was going to increase federal spending and increase the federal budget deficit, to do what Roosevelt, Truman, Kennedy, and Johnson had all done before—to walk the walk of the liberal Democrats. When Barry Goldwater heard the news, he was dumbfounded, shook his head, and moaned to a close friend, "This is all we need, a Republican president dancing to a Keynesian tune."

Nixon was ready, however, to pull more economic rabbits out of the proverbial hat. He was not just a Keynesian. In what can only be described as a decision to have his cake and eat it too, Nixon went after the inflation problem as well. Like a World War II Democratic bureaucrat, he imposed a ninety-day wage, price, and rent freeze across the entire economy. Three months later, in mid-September 1971, he launched phase two of his program, imposing government-regulated price, rent, and wage guidelines on the entire economy. Conveniently, the phase two controls would remain in effect until January 1, 1973, after which the economy would shift into a period of voluntary controls. By that time, he would be reelected.

Nixon won reelection in 1972, but world events soon destroyed his anti-inflation program. The jump from inflation to hyperinflation began on October 6, 1973, when the Yom Kippur War* erupted in the Middle East. The American-backed Israelis made short work of the Arab armies. The Israeli military victory, however, was instantly transformed into an American economic defeat when Saudi Arabia announced a boycott of all oil exports to the United States. To Arab leaders, American devotion to Israel was incomprehensible in light of the huge volumes of oil being imported from the Middle East. Political loyalty ought to reflect economic reality. Arab leaders wanted to find out whether they could pressure the United States into a more neutral Middle East foreign policy. Other Arab states soon joined the Saudi boycott (*see* Arab oil boycott of 1973–1974). By the spring of 1974, oil had jumped from $3 to $9 a barrel and gasoline from 25 cents to 60 cents a gallon. As the price of oil went though the roof, so did everything else. The inflation rate leaped to 7 percent a year. With hundreds of billions of dollars filling the coffers of the oil companies, the economy slowed and unemployment rose. America entered the age of staglation—a stagnant economy with rising prices. The Nixon administration found itself in a no-win economic situation as 1973 turned into 1974. Unemployment was approaching

7 percent and inflation was rocketing toward 10 percent. In April 1974, the Nixon administration quietly scuttled its anti-inflation program.

The final peace documents ending the Yom Kippur War were not signed until May 31, 1974, but the war's impact on the world economy was just beginning. Although the Arab nations had called off the boycott on March 18, 1974, the decision had little impact on prices. After years of importing cheap foreign oil, American production, which was more expensive, had declined dramatically. For the first time in its history, the United States was dependent on foreign oil producers and had to accept world market prices. The boycott ended but inflation did not. In 1974 the consumer price index went up 7 percent.

The Watergate scandal* drove Nixon from the White House in August 1974, and the new president, Gerald Ford, inherited stagflation. The problem only got worse. Soon Ford faced an unemployment rate of 7 percent and an inflation rate of 10 percent. At first, the president reacted like a traditional Republican, vetoing congressional spending bills and hiking interest rates. He also unveiled his WIN (Whip Inflation Now) public relations blitz, which established wage and price guidelines and asked Americans to comply voluntarily. Inflation dropped to 6.6 percent in 1975, but unemployment skyrocketed to 9 percent, and Ford then reversed himself, proposing a 1976 budget of $366 billion with a whopping $66 billion deficit, the largest since World War II. He also implemented a $22 billion tax cut.

Frustrated Americans replaced Republican Gerald Ford with Democrat Jimmy Carter in the election of 1976,* but Carter had no more luck with stagflation than his predecessors. Unemployment dropped because of Ford's fiscal policies, but in 1979, the revolution in Iran* all but stopped oil production there and sent the world into another inflationary spiral. The price of a barrel of crude oil reached $34 a barrel in 1979, and gasoline prices at the tank in the United States hit $1.40 a gallon. The price of everything else in the economy went up with the price of oil. When Carter left office in 1981, the prime rate for business borrowers exceeded 20 percent, and inflation was at 14 percent annually.

Republican President Ronald Reagan* entered the White House in January 1981. He promised to end stagflation by cutting federal spending, cutting federal taxes, and cutting cumbersome federal regulations on business. He did not suc-ceed in implementing his campaign economic program, but his promise that stagflation would disappear under a Reagan administration proved, ironically, to be correct. The president did manage the tax cuts, but he dramatically increased the federal budget and the annual deficits. According to traditional Keynesian economics, prices should have shot up, but they actually fell. Just as Nixon, Ford, and Carter had been victims of rising oil prices, Reagan was the benefi-ciary of falling oil prices. When Iran stabalized under the rule of the Ayatollah Khomeini, oil production increased. In 1981 Iran and Iraq went to war, and both countries pumped as much oil as they could in order to finance the conflict. World oil supplies boomed, and oil prices fell dramatically. Falling oil prices took the steam out of inflation and Americans, with more disposable income in their pockets, began purchasing the country out of its unemployment. By the mid-1980s, stagflation appeared to be a phenomenon of the past.

SUGGESTED READINGS: Barry Bluestone and Bennett Harrison, *The Deindustrialization of America*, 1982; David Calleo, *The Imperious Economy*, 1982; Chaim Herzog, *The War of Atonement, October 1973*, 1975; Hobart Rowan, *Self-Inflicted Wounds: From LBJ's Guns and Butter to Reagan's Voodoo Economics*, 1994.

STAR TREK. *Star Trek*, a modestly popular science fiction television series in the 1960s, became a pop culture phenomenon in the 1970s and 1980s. The creation of Gene Roddenberry, NBC television first broadcast *Star Trek* in the fall of 1966. Before it was canceled after the 1969 season, NBC had broadcast seventy-nine episodes. Set several centuries in the future, *Star Trek* starred William Shatner as Captain Kirk, commander of the starship *Enterprise*; Leonard Nimoy as Mr. Spock, a half-human, half-Vulcan executive officer who was no emotion and all logic; and DeForrest Kelley as Leonard "Bones" McCoy, the *Enterprise*'s physician. The programs revolved around space exploration and the confrontations between human and alien civilizations. Some critics saw *Star Trek* as a veiled criticism of the Vietnam War.* Spock's Vulcan salute was a hand raised, palm-facing forward peace sign. The *Enterprise* tried to avoid violence and the use of its massive firepower whenever possible. The crew of the *Enterprise* had a fundamental rule upon discovering a new civilization: they were not to engage in any activities designed to change the culture or values of that society.

After its 1969 cancellation, *Star Trek* took on a pop culture life of its own in the United States. The seventy-nine episodes became one of the most popular reruns in television history, playing in every media market. Devoted fans of the show became known as "Trekkies" for their obsessive interest in the program. *Star Trek* paraphernalia and *Star Trek* conventions became annual events in the 1970s, and the original *Star Trek* eventually spawned two television series in the 1980s and 1990s as well as six feature films.

SUGGESTED READING: Herbert F. Solow, *Inside Star Trek: The Real Story*, 1996.

STAR WARS. *Star Wars*, released in 1977, was the first installment of George Lucas's* science fiction, space adventure film trilogy. An amalgam of Superman comics, King Arthur tales, and the Wizard of Oz, *Star Wars* describes a futuristic death struggle between a band of rebels fighting for their survival and an evil empire headed by Darth Vader. Alec Guiness plays Ben Kenobi, an aging guru still in tune with the Force; Mark Hamill is Luke Skywalker, a young idealist determined to destroy the evil empire; Harrison Ford is Han Solo, a freelance rogue pilot who assists Skywalker in his quest; and Carrie Fisher is Princess Leia, heir to the rebel throne. An old-fashioned story of good triumphs over evil, *Star Wars* combines state-of-the-art special effects with the plot of an old-fashioned western. Lucas followed up the phenomenal success of *Star Wars* with two sequels: *The Empire Strikes Back* (1980) and *Return of the Jedi* (1983).

SUGGESTED READING: *New York Times*, May 26, 1977.

STARSKY AND HUTCH. *Starsky and Hutch*, a successful police drama television series of the late 1970s, premiered on ABC television on September 3,
1975, starring Paul Michael Glaser as Detective Dave Starsky and David Soul
as Detective Ken "Hutch" Hutchinson. They were young, plainclothes cops and
swinging bachelors, and the show's plot themes focused on their dates and their
arrests. They raced around Los Angeles in a red, souped-up 1974 Ford Torino
and made quick work of drug dealers, pimps, kidnappers, mobsters, and street
hustlers. The series lasted through the 1978–1979 season.

   SUGGESTED READING: Tim Brooks and Earle Marsh, *The Complete Directory to
Prime Time Network and Cable TV Shows, 1946–Present*, 1995.

STEINEM, GLORIA. Gloria Steinem was born in Toledo, Ohio, on March 25,
1934. She graduated from Smith College in 1956 and then lived in India for a
year as a Chester Bowles Asian Fellow. Upon her return, she wrote her first
book, *The Thousand Indias* (1957), and went to work for the India Research
Service in Cambridge, Massachusetts. In 1962 she became a contributing editor
to *Glamour* magazine—an experience that intensified her already well-
established feminism. Steinem did a stint as a *Playboy* bunny during the 1960s
to observe a culture in which women were treated exclusively as sexual objects.
In 1969 she became a contributing editor of *New York* magazine, a position she
held until 1972, when her book *Wonder Woman* was published.

   By that time, Steinem was emerging as a leading figure in the budding
women's movement.* Her experience in the publishing business, as well as her
views about sexism and politics in America, convinced her that a feminist magazine was not only needed but also could be a profitable enterprise. Skeptics
disagreed, but in January 1972, on a financial shoestring, Steinem published the
first issue of *Ms.** magazine. The first print run was 300,000 copies, which sold
out in eight days. Her success then attracted a $1 million investment from War-
ner Communications, and in July 1972 monthly editions commenced. *Ms.* magazine quickly became an icon in the women's movement.

   Since then Steinem has become the most recognized American feminist in
the world. Active in Democratic politics, she has supported the presidential
campaigns of George McGovern,* Jimmy Carter,* Walter Mondale, George
Dukakis, and Bill Clinton. Steinem's recent books include *Outrageous Acts and
Everyday Rebellions* (1983), *Norma Jean* (1986), *Revolution from Within: A
Book of Self-Esteem* (1992), and *Moving Beyond Words* (1994).

   SUGGESTED READINGS: Carolyn Heilburn, *The Education of a Woman: The Life
of Gloria Steinem*, 1995; Gloria Steinem, *Outrageous Acts and Everyday Rebellion*, 1983.

STEVENS, CAT. Cat Stevens was born Steven Demetri Georgiou on July 21,
1947, in London, England. As a teenager in London, he became fascinated with
folk music and rock and roll, and in 1967 his debut album, *Matthew and Son*,
was a hit in Great Britain. The 1968 album *New Masters* was similarly successful in Britain, but Stevens was already getting bored with the music. In 1971

he became a success in the United States with the release of *Tea for the Till-erman.* "Wild World" was the hit single on the album. Three hit singles—"Morning Has Broken," "Peace Train," and "Moon Shadow"—took his *Teaser and the Firecat* album to gold. Stevens had several more successes, but he was once again questioning the meaning of life. In 1975 he converted to Islam, changed his name to Yusef Islam, and permanently left the entertainment world.

SUGGESTED READING: Patricia Romanowski and Holly George-Warren, eds., *The New Encyclopedia of Rock & Roll*, 1985.

STEWART, ROD. Rod Stewart, one of rock and roll's most enduring perform-ers, was born in London, England, on January 10, 1945. A singer and songwriter known for his gritty voice and earthy style, Stewart yearned to be a professional soccer player until he realized that only through music was he going to earn superstardom. During the mid- and later 1960s, Stewart played guitar as a studio musician and performed with a number of bands. He recorded his solo album *The Rod Stewart Album* in 1969, which was a modest success. He then formed the band Faces, and for the next several years, he recorded albums with the band and by himself. His album *Gasoline Alley* made it into the top forty on the pop charts in 1970. His next effort, the album *Every Picture Tells a Story* (1971), went to number one and made Stewart one of rock and roll's most successful artists. His music combined soul, folk, rock, and barroom ballads. *Every Picture Tells a Story*'s primary hit single was "Maggie May." *Never a Dull Moment*, with its hit single "You Wear It Well" made it to number two on the album charts.

By that time Stewart's relationship with Faces was disintegrating, and he broke with the group. His 1975 album *Atlantic Crossing* went gold, and he recorded a double platinum, number-one megahit in 1976—*A Night on the Town*. Its single "Tonight's the Night (Gonna Be Alright)" topped the pop charts for nearly two months. Stewart closed out the 1970s with such hit singles as "The First Cut Is Deepest," "You're In My Heart," and "Da Ya Think I'm Sexy?" He continued to record platinum albums and hit singles in the 1980s and 1990s.

SUGGESTED READING: Geoffrey Giuliano, *Rod Stewart: Vagabond Heart*, 1993.

THE STING. *The Sting*, released in 1973, was one of the hit films of the 1970s. The film stars Paul Newman as Henry Gonderoff, Robert Redford as Johnny Hooker, and Robert Shaw as Doyle Lonnegan. The film is set in Chicago during the Great Depression, where Gonderoff and Hooker are out to score the "Big Con" at the expense of crime boss Doyle Lonnegan. Their scam is a simple one. They set up a phony gambling parlor where betters can come in and put down wagers on horse races throughout the country. Gonderoff and Hooker convince Lonnegan that they can get reports of winners before bets are placed in the parlor. Lonnegan believes them after a test run and makes a bet of

$500,000. Just after the bet is placed and just before the race gets under way, police raid the gambling parlor and Lonnegan's friends hustle him out of the place leaving the money behind. The raid, of course, was all part of "the sting."

SUGGESTED READING: *New York Times*, December 26, 1973.

STRAIGHT. The word "straight" had two meanings during the 1960s. Within the counterculture, "straight" was used to refer to white, middle-class culture, which youthful rebels found synonymous with materialism, stress, and anomie. In the subculture of homosexuals, "straight" was being used to describe heterosexuals; the term "gay" was being used for homosexuals.

SUGGESTED READING: Ruth Bronsteen, *The Hippy's Handbook—How to Live on Love*, 1967; Lewis Yablonsky, *The Hippie Trip*, 1968.

STRATEGIC ARMS LIMITATION TREATY (SALT). When the Nuclear Non-Proliferation Treaty was signed in 1968, American and Soviet officials agreed that the next item in nuclear weapons diplomacy would revolve around the need for mutual reductions in the stockpiles of strategic nuclear weapons. Not only was the race for nuclear superiority increasing the risk of global thermonuclear war, the expense of developing increasingly sophisticated, and destructive, nuclear technologies was posing financial problems to both the United States and the Soviet Union. What became known as the Strategic Arms Limitation Talks (SALT) between the United States and the Soviet Union began in 1969.

Soviet diplomats, however, proved quite reluctant to cooperate in any serious negotiations until President Richard Nixon* proposed to Congress the need for development of an anti-ballistic missile shield to protect the United States from a Soviet nuclear first strike. Nixon took heat from congressional Democrats, who argued that the defensive system would be too expensive, and from scientists, who doubted the feasibility of the proposal, but the president's proposal was more a diplomatic ploy than a nuclear arms issue. The nuclear arms race placed more pressure on the Soviet economy than on the American economy and the Russians did not want to find themselves in an expensive race to develop an anti-ballistic missile system. The SALT negotiations finally began to progress.

Talks continued until early 1972 when the two sides agreed to sign the Anti-Ballistic Missile Treaty,* which called for both sides to disengage from the development of anti-ballistic missile shields. With the threat of an expensive new weapons system development removed, the two sides were able to reach the Interim Agreement on Strategic Offensive Weapons, which froze deployment of intercontinental ballistic missiles (ICBMs) at current levels. That agreement was much less than it appeared to be because new technologies had already rendered it obsolete. Both the United States and the Soviet Union had developed multiple independent reentry vehicles (MIRVs), which allowed several nuclear warheads to be placed into one missile; each warhead could be dropped on a separate target. It was the first time that the two superpowers had agreed to impose limits on their nuclear arsenals. These initial strategic arms limitations talks which became known as SALT I, included an agreement on an improved "hot-line" communication system. During President Nixon's summit visit to Moscow in May 1972, the SALT I treaties were signed.

In November 1972, the SALT II discussions began with the hope of developing a quantitative limit on the number of MIRV warheads each side possessed. The Watergate scandal* in the United States stalled the SALT II talks, as did the short-term presidential administration of Gerald Ford.* When Jimmy Carter* defeated President Ford in the presidential election of 1976,* SALT II discussions were again delayed. The SALT II Treaty was finally signed in June 1979, but by that time the spirit of detente* was dissipating in the United States, and the Senate never ratified the treaty.

SUGGESTED READINGS: *SALT and American Security*, 1978; Notburg K. Goller-Calvo, *The SALT Agreements*, 1981; Strobe Talbot, *Endgame: The Inside Story of SALT II*, 1979.

STRAW DOGS. This 1971 suspense thriller was Sam Peckinpah's first non-Western and his first film after the critically acclaimed *Wild Bunch.** He adapted the screenplay from Gordon Williams's *Siege at Trenonar's Farm* and selected Dustin Hoffman* to play the leading role. The film is set in a small Cornish village, where an American mathematician and his English wife (Susan George) seek a quiet place so he can finish writing a book and live peacefully. The premise of the film is based on the proverb, "inside every coward lies a straw dog."

When David (Hoffman) is having his garage roofed, he must pit his masculinity against that of the workers. The workers sneer at him and stare at his wife, work slowly, laugh at him in a bar, and almost cause him to drive into a tractor. After he finds his cat strangled and hung up in his closet, he invites them in for beer and attempts to make amends. They invite him to hunt with them, and while he waits all day for them, two of the men sneak into his house and rape his wife. The climactic scene takes place in the final thirty minutes of the movie, when David is forced to defend his home against the five workmen.

When they show up again at the house, David shouts, "This is me! I will not allow violence against this house!" He then shoots one man in the foot, sprays two in the face with boiling oil, throws an antique man-trap over one's head, and persuades his wife to shoot the last one through the chest at close range with a shotgun. The scene ends with David smirking at his own triumph. The graphic violence of *Straw Dogs* was controversial, and many critics found David's transition from cowardly mathematician to cheery killer slightly unbelievable.

SUGGESTED READING: *New York Times*, May 7, 1971.

Bradley A. Olson

STREAKING. "Streaking," a term developed in the 1970s, describes one of the decade's most bizarre fads—racing nude through public places. Streaking first developed on college campuses around 1972 and then spread throughout the country. The object of streakers was to surprise the public and offend their sensibilities, disrupting formal occasions all in the name of a laugh. Streakers appeared at high school and college graduations, weddings, concerts, sports events, and even at the 1974 motion picture Academy Awards ceremony, where a worldwide viewing audience of perhaps 700 million people witnessed a streaker run across the stage while actor David Niven was presenting an Oscar. Some overwrought social commentators and culturologists regarded streaking as a symbol of the sexual revolution, but others simply viewed the phenomenon as the 1970s version of swallowing goldfish or packing phone booths.

SUGGESTED READING: Gary Botting, *Streaking*, 1974.

THE STREETS OF SAN FRANCISCO. *The Streets of San Francisco*, a popular television police drama of the 1970s, was first telecast on September 16, 1972. Starring Karl Malden as Detective Mike Stone and Michael Douglas as Inspector Steve Keller, the program was loosely based on Carolyn Weston's novel *Poor, Poor Ophelia*. Stone is a wizened, craggy-faced, twenty-three-year veteran of the police department, and Keller is his handsome, wet-behind-the-ears, college-educated partner. They deal in the underside of the Bay Area—its white-collar criminals, sexual predators, professional thieves, and stupid punks. The streets of San Francisco, as portrayed in the series, were a long way from the peace-and-love images of Haight-Asbury in the 1960s. The last episode of *The Streets of San Francisco* was broadcast on June 23, 1977.

SUGGESTED READING: Tim Brooks and Earle Marsh, *The Complete Directory to Prime Time Network and Cable TV Shows, 1946–Present*, 1995.

STREISAND, BARBRA. Barbra Streisand was born Barbara Streisand on April 24, 1942, in Brooklyn, New York. Her vivacity and unforgettable voice eventually established her as a leading female vocalist and actress of the 1970s and 1980s. After high school, she studied acting briefly, but she spent most of her time performing in local clubs. On April 5, 1961, she received her first national exposure when she performed on the *Jack Paar Show*. Later in the year she appeared on the television show *P.M. East*. In 1962 Streisand made her Broadway debut in the musical *I Can Get It for You Wholesale*. The following year she released a series of bestselling pop albums. During this time she also appeared on the *Ed Sullivan Show* and the *Judy Garland Show*. In 1964 Streisand achieved stardom when she landed the lead role of Fanny Brice in the Broadway musical *Funny Girl*, and in 1968 she starred in the film version of *Funny Girl* and shared the Best Actress Oscar with Katherine Hepburn. Streisand did a sequel to *Funny Girl, Hello Dolly*, in 1969.

During the 1970s, Streisand's interest in films intensified, and she displayed a unique comedic talent as well as extraordinary dramatic ability. Her films during the decade include *On a Clear Day You Can See Forever* (1970), *The Owl and the Pussycat* (1970), *What's Up Doc?* (1972), *Up the Sandbox* (1972), *The Way We Were** (1973), *For Pete's Sake* (1974), *Funny Lady* (1975), *A Star Is Born* (1976), and *The Main Event* (1979). She captured the hearts of her audiences with a unique vigor, an amazing voice, and her stunning poise.

During the 1980s, Streisand expanded her range beyond singing and acting to become an accomplished director. She made her directorial debut in 1983 when she directed and starred in *Yentl* (originally a short story by Isaac Bachevis Singer entitled "Yentl, The Yeshiva Boy"). Her more recent accomplishments include starring roles in the films *Nuts* (1987), *The Prince of Tides* (1991), and *The Mirror Has Two Faces* (1996).

SUGGESTED READINGS: Anne Edwards, *Streisand: A Biography*, 1997; James Spade, *Streisand: Her Life*, 1995.

Aimee Bobruk

STYX. Styx, a popular rock-and-roll band of the 1970s, was formed in Chicago, Illinois, in 1963. Styx included James Young, John Curulewski, Dennis De-Young, Chuck Panozzo, and John Panozzo. A hard-working band popular among teenagers during the 1970s, Styx released its first album, *Styx*, in 1972. The album did not do well, but the band toured widely, and in 1975 they released the hit single "Lady." During the next several years, each of their albums went platinum, including *The Grand Illusion* (1977), *Pieces of Eight* (1978), *Cornerstone* (1979), *Paradise Theater* (1983), and *Kilroy Was Here* (1983). Among the hit singles on those albums were "Come Sail Away," "Fooling Yourself," "Blue Collar Man," "Babe," "The Best of Times," and "Too Much on My Hands." The band broke up after 1983.

SUGGESTED READINGS: Hermann Gaul, *Styx*, 1988.

SULLIVAN PRINCIPLES. The "Sullivan Principles" were an important part of the antiapartheid movement in the United States. The civil rights movement* during the 1960s generated increasing amounts of criticism among African Americans about South Africa's rigid system of racial segregation, known as apartheid. Many African-American activists backed the "divestment" program, urging U.S. corporations to pull their resources out of South Africa until apartheid had been dismantled. Critics of divestment claimed that U.S. corporations could exert their economic clout in South Africa to end apartheid and that an end of U.S. investment in South Africa would only hurt blacks by increasing poverty and unemployment.

In 1977 Leon Sullivan, an African-American preacher and civil rights activist, worked out a voluntary code of conduct for U.S. businesses operating in South Africa. He viewed it as a compromise between advocates and opponents of divestment. The so-called Sullivan Principles called on U.S. corporations doing business in South Africa voluntarily to train and promote black South Africans, increase wages, enhance fringe benefits, and extend formal recognition to labor unions. By the early 1980s more than 135 companies had agreed to participate in the program.

SUGGESTED READING: David Hauck, *Two Decades of Debate: The Controversy over U.S. Companies in South Africa*, 1983.

SUMMER, DONNA. Donna Summer was born Donna Gaines in Boston, Massachusetts, on December 31, 1948. As a child she became a popular singer on the church gospel circuit in Massachusetts, but she made the switch to pop music in the early 1970s. Summer's first hit was the seventeen-minute disco* single "Love to Love You Baby," part of an album of the same name. In the age of disco, she proved not to be a one-hit wonder. In 1976 she released two successful albums: *A Love Trilogy* and *The Four Seasons of Love*. Her 1977 *I Remember Yesterday* includes the top-ten hit single "I Feel Love." Her first number-one hit single, "MacArthur Park," was part of the 1978 album *Once Upon a Time*. The 1979 album *Bad Girls*, with its two hit singles "Bad Girls" and "Hot Stuff," was a crossover hit with rock, pop, disco, and rhythm and blues fans. Summer's career peaked in 1979 with the hit singles "Dim All the Lights" and "Heaven Knows." She continued to perform and record in the 1980s but never regained her former prominence.

SUGGESTED READING: Patricia Romanowski and Holly George-Warren, eds., *The New Encyclopedia of Rock & Roll*, 1985.

SUNBELT. After World War II, the United States began to witness a large-scale demographic shift out of the industrial cities of the North and Northeast into the cities and towns of the South and West. The states stretching from Virginia south to Florida and then west to California were known for warm weather, cheap labor costs, and a weakly organized labor movement. Thousands of corporations relocated to the region which became known as the Sunbelt. As the liberal, Democratic Northeast lost population and the more Republican areas of the West gained in population, the political power of conservatives and Republicans was enhanced. Those Sunbelt trends were still extremely significant in the 1990s.

SUGGESTED READING: S. D. Krunz, "Sunbelt USA," *Focus* 36 (Spring 1986), 3–35.

SUPERMAN. Superman (1978) was one of the most popular and commercially successful films of the 1970s. A glossy, technically sophisticated update of the comic strip and 1950s television series, *Superman* stars Marlon Brando as Jorrel, the real father of Superman; Christopher Reeve as Clark Kent and Superman; Jackie Cooper as newspaper editor Perry White; Margot Kidder as reporter Lois Lane; Marc McClure as cub reporter Jimmy Olsen; and Gene Hackman* as Lex Luthor, the megalomaniac bent on triggering a catastrophic West Coast earthquake. The film begins with Superman's birth on the doomed planet Krypton and shows how his parents placed him on a spaceship and ensured that he would reach the safety of Earth. He grows up, moves to New York City, and finds work as a journalist. Masquerading as Clark Kent, Superman shows his skill in saving any number of people from personal catastrophes, but his great accomplishment is foiling Lux Luthor's conspiracy. Campy, cartoonish, and slick, *Superman* was a box office hit that eventually spawned three sequels.

SUGGESTED READING: *New York Times*, December 15, 1978.

SWANN V. CHARLOTTE-MECKLENBURG COUNTY BOARD OF EDU- CATION (1971). During the 1970s, one of the most controversial public policy issues in the United States involved busing* children to desegregate public schools. In 1954 the *Brown v. Board of Education* case had outlawed de jure segregation in public schools, but public schools throughout the country remained segregated because of economic, housing, and neighborhood segregation. Civil rights activists proposed busing children across school district lines in order to overcome de factor segregation. When the federal courts began to enforce such policies, a storm of protest erupted from parents who resented seeing their children being transported long distances from their neighborhoods. Lawsuits were filed by the hundreds.

On April 20, 1971, the U.S. Supreme Court decided the *Swann v. Charlotte-Mecklenburg County Board of Education* by a unanimous vote. To those parents claiming that busing was a violation of their civil rights, the court stated that busing, racial balance ratios, and gerrymandering school districts were all constitutional methods of desegregating schools as long as they were interim, not permanent, arrangements. The court acknowledged that there could be circumstances involving children's health or time traveled per day on buses that could become constitutional issues, but it refused to establish any guidelines.

SUGGESTED READING: 402 U.S. 1 (1971).

SYMBIONESE LIBERATION ARMY. *See* HEARST, PATRICIA and CINQUE.

T

TASK FORCE ON AMERICAN INDIAN RELIGIOUS FREEDOM. During the 1970s, one of the key demands of the red power* movement revolved around Indian control of the political policies affecting Indian peoples. The expression self-determination* came to symbolize those demands. Indian activists were especially concerned about the cavalier way in which Indian religious and cultural rights had been treated in the past. The skeletal remains of thousands of Indians were housed in federal, state, and local museums; Indian burial grounds were repeatedly ruined by economic development; and sacred artifacts had been repeatedly stolen by non-Indian collectors and government museums. Indian activists wanted the preservation of burial grounds, the return of all artifacts, and the return and burial of skeletal remains.

After Congress had passed the American Indian Religious Freedom Act of 1978,* President Jimmy Carter* directed the establishment of the Task Force on American Indian Religious Freedom to evaluate federal government policies in regard to the treatment of the religious rights and cultural heritage of American Indians. Its recommendations, issued in 1979, called for increased awareness, and if necessary, congressional legislation to protect Indian burial sites and to address the care of sacred artifacts and human skeletal remains in government museums. The task force also raised the issue of returning those artifacts and remains to Indian tribes requesting them. The findings of the task force eventually helped lead to the Archaeological Resources Protection Act of 1979, which provided fines and prison sentences for individuals caught removing artifacts from federal lands without permission. Subsequent amendments to the law, particularly in 1988, required all federal agencies to carry out archaeological surveys of all lands under their jurisdiction and conduct public awareness campaigns to stop the looting of archaeological sites.

SUGGESTED READINGS: Michael M. Ames, *Cannibal Tours and Glass Boxes: The Anthropology of Museums*, 1992; Douglas Cole, *Captured Heritage: The Scramble for*

Northwest Coast Artifacts, 1985; George P. Horse Capture, *The Concept of Sacred Materials and Their Place in the World*, 1989; Phyllis Mauch Messenger, ed., *The Ethics of Collecting Cultural Property: Whose Culture? Whose Property?*, 1989; H. Marcus Price, *Disputing the Dead: U.S. Law on Aboriginal Remains and Grave Goods*, 1991.

TAXI. *Taxi*, which premiered on ABC television on September 12, 1978, became a highly successful situation comedy. It starred an ensemble cast composed of Judd Hirsch, Danny DeVito, Jeff Conaway, Tony Danza, Christopher Lloyd, Andy Kaufman, and Marilu Henner. The characters, who work for New York City's Sunshine Cab Company, are all misfit, part-time cabbies. All of them are working to pay the bills while trying to make it big in another field. *Taxi* was irreverent, scatterbrained, and witty. The last episode was telecast on May 21, 1983, but it remained popular in reruns well into the 1990s.

SUGGESTED READING: Tim Brooks and Earle Marsh, *The Complete Directory to Prime Time Network and Cable TV Shows, 1946–Present*, 1995.

TAXI DRIVER. Martin Scorsese's *Taxi Driver*, a chilling 1976 film, stars Robert De Niro* as Travis Bickle, Cybill Shepherd as Betsy, and Jodie Foster as Iris, a twelve-year-old, street-smart prostitute plying her trade in New York City. Bickle, a tightly wired Vietnam War* veteran, makes his living by driving a cab. He ticks away quietly in New York City. He has no past and no future; he seems to invent both out of thin air. Although he writes to his parents, he fills his letters with lies, and one suspects that his parents are part of his fantasy life. The only reality in his life is the war that he cannot articulate but drives him toward violence as surely as he drives his taxi. As two film critics observed:

Travis Bickle is the prototypical movie vet: In ways we can only imagine, the horror of the war unhinged him. He's lost contact with other human beings, he doesn't hear them quite properly, and his speaking rhythms are off. He's edgy; he can't sleep at night, not even with the help of pills, so he takes a job as a taxi driver on the night shift.

It is a dark film about a dark city inhabited by hookers, pimps, drug pushers, confidence men, and hustlers. Afflicted by skull-splitting headaches, Bickle passes his time driving his cab, popping pills, drinking wine, and attending porno films. Vietnam turned him into a psychotic, and he symbolizes the urban alienation of modern America. In the end, Bickle tries to find redemption and lend meaning to his life by attempting to assassinate a prominent politician. In the end, he kills a pimp. He might just as easily have killed a politician or anyone else, including himself. His violence knows no reason—it is not directed toward society or politicians or any particular person. It just is. From films like *Taxi Driver*, American society worried for a time in the late 1970s and early 1980s that all Vietnam veterans were fundamentally flawed—that the horror of the war had unhinged them all.

SUGGESTED READINGS: Linda Dittmar and Gene Michaud, eds., *From Hanoi to Hollywood: The Vietnam War in American Film*, 1990; *New York Times*, February 9, 1976.

TAYLOR V. LOUISIANA **(1975).** One of the primary objectives of the women's movement* in the 1970s was to achieve equal protection under the law. Occasionally that goal resulted in judicial decisions that some considered to go against women. One example of this was *Taylor v. Louisiana* in 1975. Many states, including Louisiana, maintained legislation that excluded women from jury duty because it would interfere with their duties as wives, homemakers, and mothers. In its 1961 decision of *Hoyt v. Florida*, the Supreme Court had already upheld a similar law. By 1975, however, times had changed. *Taylor v. Louisiana* was decided on January 21, 1975, by an 8 to 1 vote. The court overturned its 1961 decision, arguing that laws excluding women from juries violated the Sixth Amendment's requirement that juries represent a cross section of the community.

SUGGESTED READING: 419 U.S. 522 (1975).

TEST-TUBE BABIES. In 1978 extrauterine human conception became a reality. When Lesley and John Brown were unable to have a child, they sought medical assistance from physicians and physiologists at Cambridge University in Great Britain. Cambridge physiologist Robert Edwards had for years been experimenting with in vitro fertilization—inducing pregnancy by removing an ovum from a woman, collecting sperm from a donor, fertilizing the egg in a laboratory, and then surgically implanting the zygote back into the woman's uterus. Edwards finally overcame the problem of keeping the zygote alive until implantation and preventing spontaneous abortion. He succeeded with the Browns, who named their healthy daughter Louise. Critics accused Brown of tampering with the powers of God, but in vitro fertilization eventually proved to be a godsend to tens of thousands of childless couples.

SUGGESTED READING: *London Times*, September 16, 1978.

THREE DAYS OF THE CONDOR. During the 1970s, because of the opposition to the Vietnam War* and America's declining position around the world, the Central Intelligence Agency* (CIA) became the target of enormous public criticism. Rumors of widespread political assassinations conducted by CIA agents around the world were confirmed in congressional investigations, and the agency came under unprecedented political scrutiny. The film *Three Days of the Condor*, based on James Grady's novel *Six Days of the Condor*, played on those suspicions. Released in the late summer of 1975, the film stars Robert Redford as Turner, a CIA "reader" whose job is to scour through contemporary novels, short stories, and journals to determine whether any existing CIA operations have been leaked or compromised. Allegedly, he is employed by the American Literary Historical Society, a CIA front located in Manhattan. Turner's CIA code name is "Condor."

During the course of his analysis, Turner stumbles upon the existence of a "super CIA" within the CIA and reports it to his superiors. Alarmed insiders decide to terminate Turner and his entire office group at the American Literary

Historical Society. When the slaughter occurs, Turner happens to be out of the office getting sandwiches and doughnuts. The only survivor, he goes into hiding. The rest of the film traces the CIA's attempt to find and kill him and Turner's attempt to penetrate the conspiracy. Given the CIA's problems during the 1970s, *Three Days of the Condor* resonated well with filmgoers.

SUGGESTED READING: *New York Times*, September 25, 1975.

THREE DOG NIGHT. Three Dog Night, a rock-and-roll band formed in Los Angeles, California, in 1967, included Danny Hutton, Chuck Negron, Cory Wells, Mike Allsup, Jimmy Greenspoon, Joe Schermie, and Floyd Sneed. Wells, Hutton, and Negron were lead singers; other band members played backup. Their songs became known for their trademark three-part vocal harmonies. Three Dog Night's first album, entitled *Three Dog Night*, debuted to modest success in 1968. They had their first top-ten single, "One," in 1969. Three Dog Night's success mounted steadily, with such albums as *Suitable for Framing* (1969), *Captured Live at the Forum* (1969), *It Ain't Easy* (1970), *Naturally* (1971), *Golden Bisquits* (1971), *Harmony* (1971), *Seven Separate Fools* (1972), and *Around the World with Three Dog Night* (1973). A rich series of hit singles came with the albums, including "One," "Easy to Be Hard," "Eli's Coming," "Lady Samantha," "Mama Told Me (Not to Come)," "Joy to the World," "The Show Must Go On," "Liar," "One Man Band," "An Old Fashioned Love Song," "Never Been to Spain," "Black and White," and "Shambala." Success in the rock-and-roll business is ephemeral, however, and in 1975 Three Dog Night's album *Coming Down Your Way* did not go gold. By then, they had sold twelve million albums and seven million singles, making them one of the most successful bands of the 1970s.

SUGGESTED READING: Jimmy Greenspoon, *One Is the Loneliest Number*, 1991.

THREE MILE ISLAND. A bitter debate between environmentalists and the nuclear power industry raged throughout the 1970s. Industry advocates claimed that, in light of the energy crisis* and America's dwindling supplies of oil and natural gas, nuclear energy was the only realistic way of keeping the country from being held ransom by oil-producing nations. Environmentalists, however, worried about the possibilities of accidents at nuclear plants and the release of deadly radioactive material into the atmosphere. Spokesmen for the industry reassured the public that America's nuclear energy plants, built in compliance with the strict company and government safety specifications, were the safest in the world. Opponents of nuclear energy were not reassured. They claimed that it would be only a matter of time before human error of some sort brought about a dangerous incident.

During the first week of April 1979, the predictions of antinuclear activists came true. At the Three Mile Island nuclear power plant located in the Susquehanna River near Harrisburg, Pennsylvania, a mechanical failure brought about the release of radioactive gases into the atmosphere. An automatic valve closed improperly, upsetting the circulation of cooling waters in the core of one of the plant's nuclear reactors. A subsequent series of unlikely but very real mechanical malfunctions led to the accumulation of highly explosive hydrogen gas in the reactor, which could have caused a horrendous explosion, and a complete melt-down threatened. The crisis lasted for twelve days, and a large-scale catastrophe was only narrowly averted.

Although public relations people from Metropolitan Edison tried to put the best spin possible on the accident, the company had difficulty finding out the source of the problem, and Pennsylvania Governor Richard Thornborough or-dered the evacuation of all pregnant women and preschool children living within a five-mile radius of the plant.

Art also imitated life. Jane Fonda's* film *The China Syndrome** had been released a few days before the accident at Three Mile Island. The film concerns a fictional accident at a California nuclear power plant and the determined efforts of industry officials to cover it up. Fonda plays an investigative television re-porter who exposes the conspiracy. The film's producers could not have imag-ined better publicity for a movie. Combined with the impact of *The China Syndrome*, the accident at Three Mile Island gave nuclear energy opponents the upper hand in a debate that continues today.

SUGGESTED READING: Daniel F. Ford, *Three Mile Island: Thirty Minutes to Melt-down*, 1982.

THREE'S COMPANY. *Three's Company*, a silly, daffy, but popular television situation comedy, premiered on ABC on March 15, 1977, starring John Ritter as Jack Tripper, Joyce DeWitt as Janet Wood, and Suzanne Somers as Chrissy Snow. Janet worked in a florist shop and Chrissy, a "dingbat" blonde, was a typist. In order to make ends meet, the two single women, who shared a Santa Monica, California, apartment, invited Jack to move in and help with the rent. He did all of the cooking, since he was studying to be a chef, and he feigned homosexuality to reassure the landlords, and the young women's parents, that the arrangement was innocent. The program's humor revolved almost exclu-sively around sexual double entendres. Its popularity peaked in 1980. When Suzanne Somers overestimated her importance to the program and demanded a huge salary increase, the producers gradually wrote her out of the show and gave Janet a new roommate, Cindy Snow (Jenilee Harrison), another clueless blonde. The last episode of *Three's Company* was broadcast on September 18, 1984.

SUGGESTED READING: Tim Brooks and Earle Marsh, *The Complete Directory to Prime Time Network and Cable TV Shows, 1946–Present*, 1995.

THRILLA IN MANILA. The term "thrilla in manila," coined by Muhammad Ali,* came to refer to his October 1, 1975, heavyweight boxing match with Joe Frazier. After being stripped of the heavyweight championship for refusing in-duction into the U.S. armed forces during the Vietnam War,* Ali had fought

Frazier in 1971 and had lost his comeback bid. In 1974, however, Ali defeated Frazier for the title, and the next year they fought a third match in Manila. The fight was a media event of unprecedented proportions. A worldwide television audience of more than 700 million people paid to watch the fight, which Ali won decisively.

SUGGESTED READINGS: *New York Times*, October 1–3, 1975.

TOWERING INFERNO. During the early 1970s, Americans became enamored of so-called disaster movies, which included an ensemble cast of superstars and a demonstration of what could go wrong in modern society when a natural disaster strikes. *Towering Inferno*, released for the Christmas 1974 box-office season, was one of the more dramatic of the disaster epics. It stars Steve McQueen as fire chief Michael O'Hallorhan, Paul Newman as architect Doug Roberts, William Holden as real estate and high-rise tycoon James Duncan, and Faye Dunaway, Fred Astaire, O. J. Simpson, and Robert Wagner in minor roles.

The film begins with the grand opening of a new glass-and-steel 138-story skyscraper in San Francisco. During construction, unknown to the builder and architect, contractors cut corners on the specifications and installed inferior electrical wiring and equipment that cannot sustain the energy load in the building. On the evening of the grand opening, while hundreds of VIPs are partying in the top-floor penthouse, a catastrophic fire breaks out below. The film deals with the death, rescue, guilt, redemption, and heroism of the occupants of the building. Most critics felt that in three hours the *Towering Inferno* told them more than they wanted to know about high-rise fires, but ticket buyers loved the film and made it a hit.

SUGGESTED READING: *New York Times*, December 20, 1974.

TRAIL OF BROKEN TREATIES. In the summer of 1972, Native American activists Hank Adams, Dennis Banks,* and Russell Means* of the American Indian Movement* met in Denver to plan the Trail of Broken Treaties caravan. Galvanized by the media attention that the Indians of all Tribes* had received when they occupied Alcatraz Island* in 1969, and conscious of the extent to which media scrutiny had strengthened Martin Luther King, Jr., and the African-American civil rights movement,* especially King's dramatic "I Have a Dream" speech in Washington, D.C., Indian activists decided to march on the nation's capital themselves. With the 1972 presidential election looming on the horizon, they believed that they would be able to secure an extra measure of political attention from Democratic and Republican leaders. Their goal was to give a boost to their demands for self-determination.*

Caravan organizers left the West Coast in the beginning of October and picked up other demonstrators at reservations all along the way. At Minneapolis, Minnesota, where many Chippewas joined them, caravan leaders issued their Twenty Points, a series of demands for a complete revival of tribal sovereignty by repeal of the 1871 ban on future treaties, restoration of treaty-making status to individual tribes, the granting of full government services to the unrecognized eastern tribes, a review of all past treaty violations, complete restitution for those violations, formal recognition of all executive order reservations, and admission of the tribal right to interpret all past treaties. They also demanded elimination of all state court jurisdiction over Native American affairs.

From Minneapolis, the Trail of Broken Treaties moved on to Washington, D.C. Immediately upon their arrival in the nation's capital, caravan leaders learned that their advance people had done a poor job of preparing for the marchers. They had not reserved enough hotel and motel rooms to house the demonstrators. Most of the caravan went over to the Bureau of Indian Affairs (BIA) building, where they staged a demonstration that went on for hours. A number of marchers entered the BIA building and remained there until 5:00 P.M., when the building was supposed to close. Without hotel accommodations, they decided to remain in the building. When federal guards in the building tried to push some of the demonstrators outside, the affair became violent. Demonstrators outside saw federal guards taking billy clubs to the Indians inside and stormed the building, blockading all the doors and windows with office furniture. For six days they occupied the building, demanding amnesty and a government pledge to recognize the Twenty Points. Demonstrators ransacked the BIA offices, destroying files and government property.

President Richard Nixon* regarded the demonstration as a political mess to be cleaned up as soon as possible. The last thing he needed on the eve of his reelection was a bloody melee at the Bureau of Indian Affairs. He insisted on moderation and compromise, and he dispatched Leonard Garment,* a presidential advisor and well-known friend of American Indians, to head up the negotiations. The government refrained from an armed attempt at dislodgment and diffused the situation by agreeing to consider the AIM's demands for reform. On November 8, federal authorities offered the Native American protesters immunity from prosecution and $66,000 for return transportation. The offer was accepted and the crisis was over.

Caravan organizers learned important lessons from the Trail of Broken Treaties. First, the federal government, as usual, could not be trusted to live up to its agreements with Indians. As soon as the threat of violence had evaporated, the federal government resorted to stonewalling tactics and eventually rejected the vast majority of AIM demands. They also learned that they had to improve their own planning efforts. Martin Luther King, Jr., and the African-American civil rights movement had succeeded in the 1960s by securing the sympathetic support of large numbers of white voters, and Indians would have to do the same. AIM leaders realized that events in the BIA building had spun out of control, and in order to achieve the most from events planned to secure media attention, such displays had to be avoided.

SUGGESTED READINGS: Vine Deloria, Jr., *Behind the Trail of Broken Treaties*, 1974; James S. Olson and Raymond Wilson, *Native Americans in the Twentieth Century*, 1984; Paul Prucha, *The Great White Father*, vol. 2, 1984.

Mark Baxter

TRANSCENDENTAL MEDITATION. Transcendental meditation was one of the most visible of the so-called new wave religious movements of the 1970s. It was launched in the United States by Maharishi Mahesh Yogi, a native of India who had spent thirteen years studying with Swami Brahmananda Saraswati Maharaj, the founder of transcendental meditation (TM). When Maharaj died in 1953, Maharishi Mahesh Yogi inherited the burden of teaching transcendental meditation to the world. In 1959 he founded the Sonorama Society, an American branch of the movement. He taught and labored in obscurity until 1967, when the Beatles decided to take lessons from Maharishi. As a result, he developed a cult following in the United States. In transcendental meditation, one chants a mantra while sitting quietly. Daily meditation and the silent repetition of the mantra were believed to generate intelligence, harmony, and health. If the people of the world could be converted to TM, advocates believe, an indefinite period of peace and harmony would descend on the earth. Although TM was the leading new age religion of the late 1960s and early 1970s, by the late 1970s, it had rapidly begun losing followers.

SUGGESTED READING: John R. Hinnells, *Who's Who of World Religions*, 1992.

TRAVOLTA, JOHN. John Travolta—actor, musician, dancer, sex symbol, comeback king, and icon of the 1970s—was born in Englewood, New Jersey, on February 8, 1954. In his early school years he developed an interest in music and theater, and at age sixteen, with very little formal training, he dropped out of high school to pursue an acting career in New York City, where he found initial success in television and advertisements. He appeared in over forty commercials during the next two years; his theatrical debut was the role of Doody in the touring performance of *Grease*. In 1974 he made his first Broadway appearance in *Over Here!*.

High school friend and manager Bob Lemond convinced Travolta to move to Los Angeles to star in his first movie, *The Devil's Rain* (1975), but it was a critical and box office disaster. It was here that he was offered the well-known television role of Vinnie Barbarino in *Welcome Back, Kotter*,* which made him a teen idol. It was also in Los Angeles during the 1980s that Travolta became involved in the Church of Scientology, with which he is still associated today.

Because of his star status and his teen appeal, Midsong Records offered Travolta a record contract. He released two albums, *John Travolta* and *Can't Let You Go*, in 1976; won *Billboard* magazine's award for best new pop male vocalist; and performed at the ceremony. That same year, he played a supporting role in Brian DePalma's *Carrie*,* based on the Stephen King novel, toured in the play *Bus Stop*, and performed the lead in the television movie *The Boy in the Plastic Bubble*, a drama about a boy without an immune system who had to live in a sealed environment.

John Travolta was launched into superstardom in 1977 when he played the lead role, Tony Manero, in the disco* flick *Saturday Night Fever*,* for which he had to lose twenty-two pounds and learn to dance through intensive training.

Saturday Night Fever was a phenomenon that caused the popularity of discos and disco music to explode and made Tony Manero's white polyester suit a fashion classic. The next year, 1978, the film *Grease* was released, in which he stars as Danny Zuko. *Grease*, which made $400 million, was the most successful movie musical of all time. After starring in two of the biggest blockbusters ever, Travolta had become the definitive icon of the 1970s.

His next movie, *Moment by Moment*, costarring Lily Tomlin, was a spectacular failure, and he was told that he would never make another movie. Nevertheless, Travolta was named most popular actor in the world at the 1979 Golden Globe awards. Because of his dissatisfaction with the script, Travolta dropped out of production of *American Gigolo*, which became a hit at the box office with Richard Gere in the starring role. After these two embarrassing misjudgments, critics hailed *Urban Cowboy* (1980) as John Travolta's comeback. *Urban Cowboy* was a success but not as big a success as *Saturday Night Fever*, and Travolta continued to make bad career choices, such as *Blow Out* in 1981 and *Staying Alive*, a sequel to *Saturday Night Fever* directed by Sylvester Stallone, in 1983. His career was further jeopardized by a *Rolling Stone* interview in which he elaborated on some of his personal relationships. The last straw and his biggest failure yet was *Perfect* (1985), costarring Jamie Lee Curtis.

Over the next few years, Travolta made several television movies, none of which rated highly. Two comeback films, *The Experts* in 1988 and *Tender* in 1989, flopped, but during this time he fell in love with actress Kelly Preston, who became his wife in 1991.

Travolta made a bit of a comeback in 1989, when he played a supporting role in *Look Who's Talking*, but he followed it up with two more disasters, *Chains of Gold* in 1990 and *Shout* in 1991. He performed in the 1990 film *Look Who's Talking Too!* At the same time he was busy fending off rumors of his homosexuality in the tabloids, which ended after his wedding on September 6. Turning down a possible *Grease 3*, he chose to make *Look Who's Talking Now!* because he felt it was the only way to stay alive in show business. This was one of his greatest mistakes yet.

After losing confidence in his career, John Travolta made his long-overdue comeback in 1993 when he was offered a lead role in Quentin Tarantino's *Pulp Fiction*. His success continued with *White Man's Burden* and *Get Shorty* in 1995, *Broken Arrow, Phenomenon*, and *Michael* in 1996, *Face-Off* in 1997, and *Primary Colors* in 1998. Not only did he make an amazing comeback, John Travolta broke the record payment for an actor by signing a three-picture deal for $20 million per picture, making him the highest-paid actor in history.

SUGGESTED READINGS: Rachel Thompson, *John Travolta*, 1997; Dave Thompson, *Travolta*, 1996.

Bradford K. Gathright

TWILIGHT'S LAST GLEAMING. Directed by Robert Altman and based on Walter Wager's novel *Viper Three*, *Twilight's Last Gleaming* was released in

1977. The film stands as one of Hollywood's first attempts to capitalize on public dissatisfaction with the Vietnam War.* It stars Burt Lancaster as Lawrence Dell, an army general railroaded into federal prison and a death sentence on trumped-up murder charges. Liberal in his politics, General Dell had become an outspoken critic of the Vietnam War, and his enemies in the White House and the Pentagon had conspired to silence him permanently.

General Dell, however, gets his day in court. He escapes from Death Row with three other men, and together they manage (somewhat implausibly, critics argued) to seize possession of a Titan missile base in Montana. Nervously fingering the button of a nuclear weapon and threatening to throw the United States into a thermonuclear war, Dell offers a deal to the federal government: he will not launch the weapon if the government gives him $10 million, free passage on Air Force One (with the president as hostage) to a country of their choosing, and a press conference in which the government reveals its real reasons for continuing the futile war in Vietnam: The war is not a noble struggle against Indochinese communism but a cynical ruse for politicians to stay in office, for the defense industry to earn money, and for career military officers to win their combat infantry badges. The film ends in a shoot-out in which Dell and the president are killed before the nuclear button is pushed.

SUGGESTED READINGS: Linda Dittmar and Gene Michaud, eds., *From Hanoi to Hollywood: The Vietnam War in American Film*, 1990; *New York Times*, February 10, 1977.

U

UNITED JEWISH ORGANIZATION OF WILLIAMSBURGH V. CAREY
(1977). Under the Voting Rights Act of 1965, the state legislature of New York had decided to redistrict its congressional districts in order to improve minority representation. By redrawing congressional districts, it was possible to provide African-American majorities and, therefore, more African Americans in Congress. In New York City, the redistribution dramatically diluted the voting strength of the Hasidic Jewish community of Brooklyn and increased the power of African Americans. The Hasidic community sued in the federal courts, claiming a constitutional violation of their own voting rights. Improving the civil rights of one group, they argued, while reducing those of another group accomplishes nothing. The case made its way to the U.S. Supreme Court, which rendered its decision on March 1, 1977, by a 7 to 1 vote. Justice Byron White wrote the majority opinion, which found in favor of the state legislature. A state government, the court argued, does not violate voting rights when, in order to comply with the Voting Rights Act, it deliberately works to create black majorities in certain districts.

SUGGESTED READING: 430 U.S. 144 (1977).

UNITED STEELWORKERS OF AMERICA V. WEBER **(1979).** During the 1960s, as the civil rights movement* worked to end the practice of de jure discrimination that had for so long characterized race relations in the United States, the idea of affirmative action* emerged. By executive order, President Lyndon Johnson had ordered federal agencies to take "affirmative action" to make sure that minorities received equal representation in education and employment. In order to achieve that goal, many employers and colleges and universities established racial quotas, allowing them to admit, hire, and promote people on racial grounds and not simply on the basis of test scores and seniority.

One of the most challenging areas of civil rights law posed by affirmative action involved union seniority rules. For decades, labor unions had made hiring, promotion, and firing decisions based on seniority. The individual with the most years of service enjoyed the most protection. The workers most vulnerable to layoffs were those most recently hired. Because racially discriminatory hiring policies had been employed for so long in American industry, civil rights activists realized that it could be decades before minority employees enjoyed the protections of seniority. Some companies, to diversify their workforce and their management, began defying union seniority rules retaining some minority workers during lean economic times and promoting some minorities when they did not have seniority. Some white workers with seniority found themselves being laid off or passed by for promotion when minorities with less seniority succeeded.

In the 1970s, hundreds of lawsuits based on "reverse discrimination" began making their journey through the federal courts. One of them was *United Steelworkers of America v. Weber*, which the U.S. Supreme Court decided by a 5 to 2 vote on June 27, 1979. Although Title VI of the Civil Rights Act of 1964 prohibits racial discrimination in employment practices, neither the law nor the Constitution can keep employers from adopting race-based affirmative action policies to promote minority workers to positions in which they traditionally have been underrepresented. The decision was a victory for civil rights advocates, but it seemed to contradict the court's decision made in *University of California Board of Regents v. Bakke* the previous year.

SUGGESTED READING: 433 U.S. 193 (1979).

UNIVERSITY OF CALIFORNIA BOARD OF REGENTS V. BAKKE (1978).

In 1978 the U.S. Supreme Court rendered its landmark decision in the *University of California Board of Regents v. Bakke*, a test of existing federal and state government affirmative action* plans. By executive order, President Lyndon Johnson had ordered federal agencies to take "affirmative action" to ensure that minorities received equal representation in education and employment. In order to achieve that goal, many employers and colleges and universities established racial quotas, which enabled them to admit, hire, and promote people on racial grounds, not simply on the basis of test scores and seniority.

Steven Bakke, a white male, had applied for admission to the medical school at the University of California at Davis. He was denied admission, even though his grade point average and test scores on the medical school admissions examinations were higher than those of several minority candidates who had been admitted. Bakke charged that his civil rights had been violated, that he had not been admitted because he was white; the University of California had violated his Fourteenth Amendment right to equal protection under the law. A lawsuit dealing with that issue eventually made its way to the U.S. Supreme Court.

The Supreme Court decided the Bakke case on June 28, 1978, by a 5 to 4 vote. The decision, in favor of Bakke, stated that his civil rights under Title VI of the Civil Rights Act of 1964 had indeed been violated. By establishing rigid racial quotas in its admission policies, the University of California had unwittingly engaged in reverse discrimination, which was unconstitutional. Affirmative action programs, the court ordered, cannot establish fixed racial quotas. Opponents of affirmative action hailed the *Bakke* decision as a legal victory.

A few advocates of affirmative action also took some comfort in the decision, since the court ruled that government agencies could still take race into account in their admissions, hiring, and promotion decisions. Benjamin Hooks, head of the National Association for the Advancement of Colored People, called *Bakke* "a clear-cut victory for voluntary affirmative action." Most minority leaders, including Supreme Court Justice Thurgood Marshall, Georgia state legislator Julian Bond, and PUSH (People United to Save Humanity) director Jesse Jackson, recognized that, with the *Bakke* decision, affirmative action had plateaued as a political movement in the United States. They were correct. *Bakke* was the first in what became a slow, steady judicial trend to ensure that affirmative action did not discriminate against white men.

SUGGESTED READINGS: Susan Banfield, *The Bakke Case: Quotas in College Admissions*, 1998; Nathan Glazer, *Affirmative Discrimination: Ethnic Inequality and Public Policy*, 1987; Katharine Greene, *Affirmative Action and Principles of Justice*, 1990; *New York Times*, June 29, 1978; Stephen L. Pevar, *The Rights of Indians and Tribes: The Basic ACLU Guide to Indian and Tribal Rights*, 1992; Bernard Schwartz, *Behind Bakke: Affirmative Action and the Supreme Court*, 1988.

V

VIDEOCASSETTE RECORDER. The videocassette recorder, or VCR, was one of the great consumer inventions of the 1970s. In 1975 Japan's SONY Corporation began to market the Betamax VCR, an electronic device that allowed consumers to watch videotapes in their own homes and to record programs directly off their television sets for later viewing. In 1976 the Victor Company of Japan, SONY's archrival, began selling its Video Home System (VHS), a similar videocassette recorder. Mitsubishi aggressively marketed the VHS system in the United States for Victor, and American consumers eventually made VHS the VCR of choice. The Betamax machines, and the number of tapes available on them, rapidly declined.

The so-called VCR revolution was just that. VCR technology gave a wide range of choices to consumers. First, it freed them of broadcasters' schedules, allowing them to tape programs and view them at a time of their own choosing. The system also challenged advertisers, because consumers viewing a program later could fast forward through the commercials, enjoying the program without having to listen to consumer advertising. Second, VCR technology undercut the market for television movies because moviegoers could watch tapes of the films of their choice when it was convenient for them. A new industry—VCR movie rentals—was born. Third, VCRs changed the pornography industry. Adult movie theaters closed throughout the country. Consumers no longer had to head downtown to sleezy theaters to watch pornographic films. They were now free to watch pornography movies in the privacy of their own homes. Fourth, the VCR virtually destroyed the 8mm home movie business. Consumers vastly preferred the quality of videotape over 8mm film, and electronic manufacturers soon developed hand-held cameras that allowed them to make their own home movies. Finally, the VCR provided an unprecedented challenge to copyright laws. Technology had empowered individuals to copy whatever they wanted from television sets in their own homes.

By the 1990s, the vast majority of American households, rich as well as poor, had VCRs attached to their television sets. Few other consumer items in American history, with the exception of radios, televisions, and telephones, have been so readily and so completely adopted by the consuming public.

SUGGESTED READING: Akio Morita, *From a $500 Company to a Global Corporation: The Growth of SONY*, 1985.

VIETNAM VETERANS AGAINST THE WAR. Vietnam Veterans Against the War (VVAW) was founded in 1967 after six veterans, who marched together in an antiwar movement* demonstration, decided veterans needed their own antiwar organization. Its membership ultimately included several thousand veterans and a few government infiltrators. The VVAW participated in most major antiwar activities, including the 1968 Democratic National Convention held in Chicago. Government officials viewed the VVAW from its inception as a special threat because Vietnam veterans had a unique credibility. Furthermore, officials feared their capacity for violence, although VVAW demonstrations were always among the most peaceful and orderly.

With Jane Fonda's* financial assistance, the VVAW conducted the Detroit Winter Soldier Investigation* (February 1971), in which numerous veterans testified about "war crimes" they had witnessed or perpetrated. Selected testimonies were published in *The Winter Soldier Investigation* (1972). Speaking at the hearings, prompted in part by VVAW outrage over the assertion that the My Lai massacre was an aberration resulting from soldiers having "gone berserk," executive secretary A1 Hubbard stated: "The crimes against humanity, the war itself, might not have occurred if we, all of us, had not been brought up in a country permeated with racism, obsessed with communism, and convinced beyond a shadow of a doubt that we are good and most other countries are inherently evil." The government and its supporters denounced the proceedings and made several attempts to discredit the testimony given.

On April 19, 1971, the VVAW began Dewey Canyon III. (Dewey Canyon I and II were military operations in Laos.) It included over 1,000 veterans, led by men in wheelchairs and mothers of men killed in combat, who held a memorial service at the Tomb of the Unknown Soldier and then were refused permission to lay wreaths on graves of fallen comrades at Arlington Cemetery (although after much haggling two hundred were permitted in to lay wreaths the next day). They camped on the Mall in defiance of a court order, which was rescinded after it was realized that it would be poor public relations to arrest peaceful combat veterans. On April 23, 1971, more than 1,000 veterans threw medals they had won in Vietnam over police barricades on the Capitol steps.

Subsequent activities included several protests in December 1971 of the heaviest bombing of North Vietnam since 1968 and at the 1972 Republican Convention in Miami, for which eight members (and two sympathizers) were tried on contrived criminal conspiracy charges. In July 1974, about 2,000 members demonstrating in Washington demanded universal amnesty for draft resisters and

deserters, implementation of the Paris Peace Treaty, ending aid to Nguyen Van
Thieu* and Lon Nol, Richard Nixon's* impeachment, and a universal discharge
with benefits for all Vietnam veterans. In all its activities, the VVAW had an
overriding goal: to make the nation realize, in the words of cofounder Jan Barry,
"the moral agony of America's Viet Nam war generation—whether to kill on
military orders and be a criminal, or to refuse to kill and be a criminal."

SUGGESTED READING: David W. Levy, *The Debate over Vietnam*, 1991; Thomas
Powers, *Vietnam: The War at Home, Vietnam and the American People, 1964–1968*,
1984; Melvin Small, *Johnson, Nixon, and the Doves*, 1988; Kathleen J. Turner, *Lyndon
Johnson's Dual War: Vietnam and the Press*, 1985; Sandy Vogelgesang, *The Long Dark
Night of the Soul: The American Intellectual Left and the Vietnam War*, 1974; Nancy
Zaroulis and Gerald Sullivan, *Who Spoke Up? American Protest Against the War in
Vietnam, 1963–1975*, 1984.

Samuel Freeman

VIETNAM WAR. Without question, the Vietnam War was the most politically
unpopular armed conflict in U.S. history. From the outset of the U.S. commitment in Vietnam in the 1950s, American policymakers had applied a Cold War*
model to the conflict, assuming that it was simply a matter of Communist aggression against non-Communist South Vietnamese. The moving force behind
the Vietnam War, however, was a fierce nationalism led by Ho Chi Minh, the
man who had defeated the French at the Battle of Dienbienphu in 1954 and
destroyed the French empire in Indochina. The Vietnamese had spent more than
2,000 years battling foreign interlopers in their country—including the Chinese,
the Japanese, and the French—and most Vietnamese simply saw the Americans
as the latest alien presence in their nation.

The United States had also vastly underestimated the determination of Ho
Chi Minh and the Vietnamese to see to the expulsion of the Americans and the
reunification of their country. By 1968 the war had cost hundreds of billions of
dollars and tens of thousands of American lives, and the antiwar movement*
had escalated into one of the most powerful political forces in the country. In
the presidential election of 1968, Republican candidate Richard Nixon* had
implied, if not outright promised, that his administration would be able to find
"peace with honor" in Vietnam. When he took the oath of office in January
1969, he had to make good on his promise. He soon announced what he called
Vietnamization,* the gradual withdrawal of American troops and the handing
of the war over to the Army of the Republic of Vietnam. During the next four
years, Nixon steadily reduced the troop level from 543,000 Americans to only
50 in 1973. In order to secure an agreement from North Vietnam, he launched
an enormous bombing campaign in December 1972, after which North Vietnam
finally agreed to the peace settlement.

Ironically, North Vietnam had dictated the terms. Ever since the beginning
of the Paris Peace Talks* in 1968, North Vietnam had insisted on the withdrawal
of all U.S. troops from Indochina, the right of the Vietcong to participate in the

government of South Vietnam, and the continuing presence of North Vietnamese soldiers in South Vietnam. For years the United States had refused to negotiate on those terms, but by 1972, with most American troops gone, all the United States wanted was to get back American prisoners of war.* The Vietnam War, arguably the most misguided political and military crusade in American history, ended in January 1973. Two years later, in March 1975, North Vietnamese troops easily conquered South Vietnam.

SUGGESTED READINGS: Stanley Karnow, *Vietnam: A History*, 1983; James S. Olson and Randy Roberts, *Where the Domino Fell: America and Vietnam, 1945–1995*, 1995.

VIETNAMIZATION. The term "Vietnamization" was coined in 1969 by Secretary of Defense Melvin Laird to describe the process by which the Richard Nixon* administration gradually withdrew U.S. forces from Vietnam and turned the war over to the Army of the Republic of Vietnam. Actually, for decades, the U.S. presence in Vietnam had ostensibly been to buy time until the South Vietnamese forces were trained and ready for successful engagement. With the antiwar movement* at its peak, and the American public expecting Nixon to fulfill his campaign pledge to resolve the Vietnam War,* the president decided it was politically necessary for the United States to disengage. Between 1969 and 1973, he reduced the number of U.S. troops from 543,000 to only 50. As the American troops withdrew, South Vietnamese troops took over the fighting. The policy did not work, at least in terms of saving South Vietnam from a Communist takeover. In the spring of 1975, North Vietnamese forces seized control of the country.

SUGGESTED READING: George Donelson Moss, *Vietnam: An American Ordeal*, 1998.

VILLAGE PEOPLE. The Village People, a rock-and-roll group formed in New York City in 1977, included Victor Willis, David Hodo, Felipe Rose, Randy Jones, Glenn Hughes, and Alex Briley. One of the pop culture phenomona of the 1970s, they sang double entendre songs with homosexual themes in a campy style. On stage, they imitated gay sytereotypes: a biker, a sailor, a construction worker, a cop, a cowboy, and an Indian chief. The Village People, who took their name from Greenwich Village in New York City, had several megahit, disco* singles, including "Macho Man" (1978), "Y.M.C.A." (1979), and "In the Navy" (1979). After selling 20 million singles and 18 million albums in the late 1970s, they all but disappeared from the rock-and-roll scene.

SUGGESTED READING: K.T. Emerson, "Village People: America's Male Ideal?" *Rolling Stone* (October 5, 1978), 26–27.

VO NGUYEN GIAP. Vo Nguyen Giap was born in 1912 in Quang Binh Province, Vietnam. While a law student at the University of Hanoi, he joined the Lao Dong Party, which happened to be the most prominent of Vietnam's many communist political organizations. He was also a devout nationalist who joined the resistance movement against the French empire. Giap became a devoted follower of Ho Chi Minh and eventually rose to the command of the Vietminh army. They inflicted a humiliating defeat on the French in the Battle of Dien Bien Phu in 1954, which effectively ended France's Indochinese empire.

Giap then turned his attention to the American soldiers, who steadily increased in number during the 1950s and 1960s. After the Tet Offensive of 1968 all but destroyed the Vietcong as a military force, Giap's North Vietnamese Army (NVA) took over virtually all of the war's fighting. Giap's reputaiton fell in 1971 when his vaunted Eastertide Offensive* collapsed under massive U.S. aerial bombardment, which killed upwards of 100,000 of his troops. In 1975 Giap regained his heroic status when he engineered the final offensive, in which the NVA overran South Vietnam and reunited the country. Giap still lives in Hanoi today.

SUGGESTED READING: Vo Nguyen Giap, *Unforgettable Months and Years*, 1975.

VOLCKER, PAUL. Paul Volcker, known to the media as ''Mr. Dollar'' during the 1980s, was born in Cape May, New Jersey, on September 5, 1927. He graduated from Princeton in 1949 and then took a master's degree in economics from Harvard in 1951. Between 1952 and 1957, he was an economic advisor to the Federal Reserve Bank of New York, and from 1957 to 1961 he performed the same service for the Chase Manhattan Bank. Volcker later served as president of both of those institutions and a stint as undersecretary of the treasury. In July 1979 President Jimmy Carter* named Volcker to be chairman of the Federal Reserve Board. At the time, the annual inflation rate was over 13 percent, and Volcker was committed to reducing that figure. His basic conviction was that the Federal Reserve Board should concentrate its efforts on controlling the money supply rather than worrying about interest rates. It was an unpopular stance, especially when unemployment had reached nearly 11 percent and the prime rate was more than 21 percent early in his tenure.

Volcker ruled the Federal Reserve Board with an iron hand. Helped by declining oil prices in the early 1980s, he managed to bring inflation under control, even though the Ronald Reagan* administration was running up the largest government deficits in American history. He refused to increase the money supply to accommodate that spending until the mid-1980s. By that time, several Reagan appointees forced him to do so. Volcker stepped down from the Federal Reserve Board in the summer of 1987. At that point, he became chairman of the Federal Reserve Board of New York, a position he held until his retirement in 1996.

SUGGESTED READINGS: William Neikirk, *Volcker: Portrait of the Money Man*, 1987; George Russell, ''The New Mr. Dollar,'' *Time*, June 15, 1987, 46–49.

VOLUNTEER ARMY. See ALL-VOLUNTEER MILITARY.

W

WALLACE, GEORGE. George Corley Wallace was born on August 25, 1919, in Clio, Alabama, where he grew up. His father was a farmer. Wallace worked his way through the University of Alabama, received a law degree there in 1942, and joined the U.S. Army for the duration of World War II. In 1946 and 1947, he served as an assistant attorney general of Alabama, and he won a seat in the state legislature in 1947. There he earned a reputation as a Populist and somewhat of a liberal for denouncing the Ku Klux Klan. Reelected three times, Wallace served there until 1953, when he accepted appointment as a state circuit judge. He lost a bid for the governorship of Alabama in 1958, largely because he offered moderate enough views on racial issues to earn the endorsement of the National Association for the Advancement of Colored People (NAACP). He vowed never to let race defeat him again. Wallace practiced law for the next four years in Clanton, Alabama. In 1963 he was elected to the state's highest office. His campaign theme was ''Segregation now! Segregation tomorrow! Segregation forever!''

Wallace entered the governor's mansion just in time to confront the federal court-ordered integration of the University of Alabama. On June 11, 1963, he personally tried to block the door to the University of Alabama so that black students could not enter. It was political posturing at its worst because federal troops were present to make sure that integration occurred. Wallace became a hero to white segregationists throughout Alabama. He also began to secure a national following by preaching states rights and an end to the ''dictatorship of federal courts.''

In 1964 Wallace declared himself a candidate for the Democratic presidential nomination. He stunned political insiders by securing 30 percent of the vote in Wisconsin and 45 percent in Maryland. When the Republican party nominated conservative Senator Barry Goldwater of Arizona, Wallace withdrew from the Democratic race. By his opposition to the social changes sweeping the country,

Wallace had managed to develop a following in the working-class neighbor-hoods of northern cities. One year later, he refused to provide state troopers to protect the civil rights march of Martin Luther King, Jr., from Selma to Mont-gomery.

Under the Alabama constitution, Wallace could not run for reelection in 1966, but his wife Lurleen Wallace did run and won by a landslide. He became the power behind the throne. When 1968 rolled around, the antiwar movement,* civil rights movement,* and black power movement had all alienated millions of white people, and Wallace was prepared to exploit their discontent. He de-clared himself a third party presidential candidate in 1968, promising a victory in the Vietnam War* and law and order at home. Tough, charismatic, and blunt to a fault, Wallace picked retired Air Force General Curtis LeMay as his running mate. The Wallace-Lemay ticket, represented by the American party, won more than nine million popular votes (13.5 percent of the total) and forty-seven elec-toral votes in the election of 1968.

In 1970 Wallace won the governorship of Alabama again, and in 1972 he declared himself a candidate for the Democratic presidential nomination. He did well in several early primaries, but during a campaign stop in Laurel, Maryland, on May 15, 1972, he was shot. Wallace survived the assassination attempt, but it left him paralyzed from the waist down and ended his run for the White House. He won a third term as governor in 1975, and a year later he flirted with running for the Democratic presidential nomination, but his health simply was not good enough for the stresses of the campaign. Wallace remained a loyal Democrat for the rest of his political career. After leaving the governor's man-sion in 1979, Wallace publicly apologized to the state's African Americans for some of the things he had said and the positions he had defended during his career. He died September 13, 1998.

SUGGESTED READINGS: Jody Carlson, *George C. Wallace and the Politics of Powerlessness: The Wallace Campaigns for the Presidency, 1964–1976*, 1981; Marshall Frady, *Wallace*, 1970.

THE WALTONS. *The Waltons*, one of the most successful dramatic series in the history of American television, was a staple of American popular culture in the 1970s. It premiered on CBS television on September 14, 1972. The setting was Walton's Mountain in the Blue Ridge range of rural Jefferson County, Virginia, during the Great Depression. *The Waltons* told the story of the Walton extended family, who lived under one roof and eked out a living in the lumber business. The family included Grandpa Zeb Walton (Will Geer), Grandma Es-ther Walton (Ellen Corby), father John Walton (Ralph Waite), mother Olivia Walton (Michael Learned), and children John Boy (Richard Thomas), Mary-Ellen (Judy Norton-Taylor), Jim-Bob (David Harper), Elizabeth (Kami Cotler), Jason (Jon Walmsley), Erin (Mary Elizabeth McDonough), and Ben (Eric Scott).

Television audiences watched the Walton family grow up and deal with the problems of life during the Great Depression. They faced poverty, illness, and death, but all of those problems took place within the context of a loving, committed family, and American viewers fell in love with the program. The 1970s was a difficult period in U.S. history. The problems of the Vietnam War,* political scandal, and economic plight had given most people a decidedly pessimistic attitude toward the country's future. *The Waltons* reminded us of another difficult time in American history and the fact that the virtues of hard work, loyalty, and love could redeem even the most trying situations. The last episode of *The Waltons* was broadcast on August 20, 1981.

SUGGESTED READING: Tim Brooks and Earle Marsh, *The Complete Directory to Prime Time Network and Cable TV Shows, 1946-Present*, 1995.

WAR. War, a rock-and-roll group formed in Long Beach, California, in 1969, included Harold Brown, Papa Dee Allen, B. B. Dickerson, Leroy "Lonnie" Jordan, Charles Miller, Erick Burdon, Lee Oskar, and Howard Scott. Mixing Latin rhythms, jazz, and funk* rock, War became famous in the world of popular music in the 1970s for its top-ten albums, including *All Day Music* (1971), *The World Is a Ghetto* (1972), *Deliver the Word* (1973), *War Live!* (1974), and *Why Can't We Be Friends* (1975). Among their hit singles during this period were "The World Is a Ghetto," "The Cisco Kid," "Gypsy Man," "Me and Baby Brother," "Low Rider," and "Why Can't We Be Friends?" Burdon left the group in 1979, and Papa Dee Allen was murdered in 1984.

SUGGESTED READING: Patricia Romanowski and Holly George-Warren, eds., *The New Encyclopedia of Rock & Roll*, 1985.

***WASHINGTON V. DAVIS* (1976).** During the 1960s, while the civil rights movement* worked to end the practice of de jure discrimination that had for so long characterized race relations in the United States, the idea of affirmative action* emerged. By executive order, President Lyndon B. Johnson had ordered federal agencies to take "affirmative action" to ensure that minorities received equal representation in education and employment. In order to achieve that goal, many employers and colleges and universities established racial quotas, allowing them to admit, hire, and promote people on racial grounds, not simply on the basis of test scores and seniority. Many social scientists upheld such practices on the grounds that most tests were racially biased in favor of white constituencies and against minorities.

In 1976 the U.S. Supreme Court had to decide whether such affirmative action practices were constitutional or whether they constituted "reverse discrimination." The case of *Washington v. Davis* was decided on June 7, 1976, by a 7 to 2 vote. In the decision, the court argued that job qualification examinations are not inherently unconstitutional just because the test outcomes had racial implications. The fact that blacks performed more poorly than whites was not prima facie evidence of bias. "Disproportionate impact," the justices ruled, "is not irrelevant, but it is not the sole touchstone of an invidious racial discrimination forbidden by the Constitution."

SUGGESTED READING: 426 U.S. 284 (1976).

WATERGATE SCANDAL. The event known as the Watergate scandal began in June 1972 with the arrest of five burglars who were attempting to plant cameras and electronic bugging devices in the Democratic National Committee headquarters located in the Watergate office and hotel complex in Washington, D.C. The five burglars were all staff members of President Richard Nixon's* Committee to Re-Elect the President (CREEP*). The Nixon administration promptly dismissed the break-in as a "third-rate burglary"; however, the case caught the attention of Federal District Court Judge John Sirica* who felt otherwise and pressured the burglars to testify. James McCord, one of the five burglars and the "security" officer for CREEP, testified that high-ranking officials in CREEP, particularly Attorney General John Mitchell* and John Dean,* Nixon's legal counsel, had approved of the break-in as well as many other illegal campaign activities. What followed in 1973 and 1974 was a series of indictments involving several other key officials in the Nixon administration, including Nixon's White House aides H. R. Haldeman* and John Ehrlichman.*

The second phase of the Watergate scandal unfolded throughout 1973 and 1974. As Nixon officials testified about the Watergate break-in and other illegal campaign activities, the question arose as to whether the administration had conspired to cover-up these activities and obstruct Department of Justice investigations. It soon became obvious that an orchestrated cover-up of illegal executive branch activities had occurred. During the course of the hearings, it was disclosed that President Nixon had tape recordings of all official conversations. The tapes (which the Supreme Court eventually ordered Nixon to release) revealed that Nixon had been involved personally in illegal activities, particularly in ordering a cover-up to impede criminal investigations. On August 8, 1974, a few weeks after a House Judiciary Committee had voted to recommend impeachment, Nixon announced his resignation. He is the only U.S. president to resign from office.

SUGGESTED READINGS: Elizabeth Drew, *Washington Journal*, 1974; Stanley Kutler, *Abuse of Power: The New Nixon Tapes*, 1997; Theodore H. White, *Breach of Faith*, 1975; Robert Woodward and Carl Bernstein, *All the President's Men*, 1974.

Robert L. Perry

THE WAY WE WERE. This nostalgic drama, set in America during the late 1930s into the 1950s, was adapted from a novel by Arthur Laurents. Directed by Sydney Pollack and released in 1973, the film brought Robert Redford and Barbra Streisand* together, creating expectations among moviegoers for a magical chemistry between the two.

The story begins in a flashback, the 1930s, where we are introduced to the separate worlds of Hubbell Gardiner (Redford), an All-American athlete and WASP who deserves the nickname "America the Beautiful," and Katie Morosky (Streisand), the dogmatic and humorless leader of the Young Communist League, a Jewish ugly duckling. They meet after Katie gives a powerful speech about the evils of the Spanish Civil War and the rise of such fascist demagogues as Adolf Hitler and Benito Mussolini. Hubbell is impressed by her convictions; she learns later about his writing talent and comes to envy and admire him.

Some years later, during World War II, Katie is an avid supporter of President Franklin D. Roosevelt and Hubbell remains his apolitical self, having joined the U.S. Navy. She accidentally runs into him at a New York night club, and they fall in love while arguing about politics. Katie remains full of passion, but Hubbell has only skepticism about such passions. They marry and she encourages him to pursue his writing, even if it means a move to Paris to finish the great American novel. Hubbell has more pecuniary interests, however, and she follows him to Hollywood, where he agrees to write screenplays. Eventually, in her opinion, he sells his soul for money and she becomes a victim of the anti-communist witch hunts of the late 1940s and early 1950s. Her left-wing politics and moral passions bring her to the defense of the Hollywood Ten, while Hubbell tries to mind his own business and continue working. Political pressures lead to an inevitable divorce just after Katie gives birth to their first child.

The film ends in New York when Katie and Hubbell accidentally meet outside a New York hotel. She is demonstrating against nuclear weapons and he is writing television scripts. Nothing has changed, not even their affection for one another.

Americans loved the film not only because of the chemistry between the two actors—Streisand and Redford—but because the film reminded people of the tension between politics and personal lives, emphasized by the Watergate scandal* of the early 1970s.

SUGGESTED READINGS: *New York Times*, October 18 and 28; November 4, and December 2, 1973.

Bradley A. Olson

WEINBERGER V. WIESENFELD (1975). During the 1970s, at the height of the women's movement* in the United States, the drive for ratification of the Equal Rights Amendment* pushed to the front of public policy debate the question of equal treatment before the law. It was a sticky question because some feminist leaders also promoted affirmative action* for women. The case of *Weinberger v. Wiesenfeld* was an early example of the debate. The case involved Social Security survivors' benefits for widowers with small children. Social Security had long paid benefits to widows with small children but denied such benefits to widowers. Feminists claimed that women who paid social security taxes, therefore, were not receiving equal benefits when, in the event of their deaths, their survivors could not collect the complete package of benefits. The U.S. Supreme Court decided the case by a unanimous vote on March 19, 1975. The justices agreed that a violation of a widower's due process guarantee occurred when the Social Security Administration denied survivor benefits to his children.

SUGGESTED READING: 420 U.S. 636 (1975).

WELCOME BACK, KOTTER. *Welcome Back, Kotter* was a successful television situation comedy that launched John Travolta's* acting career in the 1970s. The show, which premiered on ABC television on September 9, 1975, starred Gabriel Kaplan as high school teacher Gabe Kotter; Marcia Strassman as his wife Julie; and John Travolta (Vinnie Barbarino), Robert Hegyes (Juan Luis Pedro Phillipo de Huevos Epstein), and Lawrence-Hilton Jacobs (Freddie "Boom-Boom" Washington) as remedial students in Mr. Kotter's class at James Buchanan High School in Brooklyn. The students were tough and funny, and Kotter could deal with them on their own level. He was patient, funny, understanding, and eminently forgiving. The last episode of *Welcome Back, Kotter* was telecast on August 10, 1979.

SUGGESTED READING: Tim Brooks and Earle Marsh, *The Complete Directory to Prime Time Network and Cable TV Shows, 1946–Present*, 1995.

THE WHO. In 1964 three West London young men, Roger Daltry, Peter Townsend, and John Entwhistle, formed the rock group known as The Who. Daltry was lead singer, Townsend the lead guitarist and songwriter, and Entwhistle the bass guitarist. Keith Moon, a drummer, soon joined them. The Who debuted in the United States in 1967 and soon became icons in the counterculture. Their ritualized, on-stage destruction of guitars became an anarchistic trademark of The Who concerts. Among their more memorable songs was "My Generation" and its phrase—"Hope I die before I get old"—which became an anthem of the youth movement. With the production of their rock opera *Tommy* in 1969, The Who became rock and roll's greatest attraction. For the next thirteen years, The Who engaged in a worldwide, continuous concert tour. The group disbanded in 1983.

SUGGESTED READING: Gene Busnar, *Super Stars of Rock*, 1984; Sammie Miller, "The Who," in *Historical Dictionary of the 1960s*, ed. James S. Olson, 1998.

THE WILD BUNCH. *The Wild Bunch*, a popular 1970 film, directed by Sam Peckinpah, stars William Holden, Ben Johnson, Ernest Borgnine, and Robert Ryan. Set along the Mexican border of the Southwest in the early 1900s, the film focuses on the criminal activities of a gang of bank and train robbers behaving as if the Old West were still alive. While trying to stage a robbery in a small American town, they are surprised by a company of railroad security men who had advance notice of the crime. In a violent shoot-out between the railroad agents and the gang, dozens of innocent civilians are killed in the cross fire. Most critics recognized in the film a critique of the Vietnam War,* in which American military firepower caused hundreds of thousands of deaths and casualties among South Vietnamese civilians.

The gang escapes across the border into Mexico, pursued all the way by railroad agents. They enter a Mexico torn by revolution during the 1910s, where the line between self-serving bandits and true revolutionaries is exceedingly thin. Government officials are portrayed as corrupt, power-hungry sadists, revolutionaries as committed but inept idealists, and the Wild Bunch as an anachronism. In the end, the heroes, or antiheroes, are killed in a spectacular gun battle during which they finish off hundreds of Mexicans before succumbing themselves.

SUGGESTED READING: Richard Slotkin, *Gunfighter Nation: The Myth of the Frontier in Twentieth-Century America*, 1992.

WINTER SOLDIER INVESTIGATION. Throughout the course of the Vietnam War,* charges of U.S. atrocities in Southeast Asia surfaced frequently in the media, but they escalated late in 1969 when news of the My Lai massacre became public. People wondered whether My Lai, and its nearly 500 slaughtered civilians, was an ugly aberration in an otherwise typical American war, or whether the rape, wounding, and killing of Vietnamese civilians had become commonplace. Antiwar movement* groups, of course, claimed that My Lai was not an aberration but part of a large pattern of genocidal violence. In 1970 a number of Quakers, antiwar clergy, and attorneys founded the Citizens Commission of Inquiry to address the question, and the Vietnam Veterans Against the War* (VVAW), perhaps the most influential of the antiwar groups, backed them and decided to go public with the conviction that other war crimes had occurred in Vietnam.

The American public had been conditioned by the brutality of the Nazis and the Japanese during World War II, and the "brainwashing" of the North Koreans, to assume that only other countries committed war crimes. Between January 31 and February 2, 1971, the VVAW convened the Winter Soldier Investigation in Detroit, Michigan. Al Hubbard, Craig Moore, and Mike Oliver headed the steering committee. Such antiwar celebrities as Jane Fonda,* Dick Gregory, Donald Sutherland, Phil Ochs, and Barbara Dane helped sponsor the hearings. For three days 116 veterans testified about war crimes they had committed in Vietnam or had witnessed. There were also panel discussions on weaponry, medical care, prisoners, racism, ecological devastation, and the psychological effects of the war on American soldiers. The Winter Soldier Investigation lent credence to charges that the United States had committed war crimes in Southeast Asia and that the Vietnam War had been a misguided and badly mismanaged military effort.

SUGGESTED READING: Vietnam Veterans Against the War, *The Winter Soldier Investigation*, 1972.

WOLFMAN JACK. "Wolfman Jack," a radio stage name, was born Robert Weston Smith in Brooklyn, New York, on October 6, 1938. Throughout the 1950s, he bounced from radio station to radio station, changing his name with each move, trying to establish for himself a foothold in the industry. He did so in 1960, when he went to work for XERF Radio in Via Cuncio, Mexico, a town nine miles south of Del Rio, Texas. XERF had a huge 250,000-watt broadcasting unit that could be heard all around the Southwest and into the Midwest. During daytime hours, XERF broadcast a relatively standard fare of news, sports, and religious programming, but at midnight, Smith became Wolfman Jack and switched to rock and roll. Free of Federal Communications Commission regulations, Wolfman Jack sold advice, sex pills, diet pills, drugs, and outrageous iconoclasm over the air. In 1973 George Lucas* featured Wolfman Jack in his film *American Graffiti.** The film made Wolfman Jack a national figure in American pop culture. Between 1974 and 1982, he starred on a weekly television show entitled *The Midnight Special.*

SUGGESTED READING: Wolfman Jack, *Have Mercy: The Confession of the Original Party Animal,* 1995.

WOMEN'S MOVEMENT. The women's movement of the 1970s had its beginnings in 1963, when Betty Friedan's *The Feminine Mystique* was published. It quickly climbed up the bestseller lists. The book has sold over one million copies and has been translated into thirteen different languages. Its basic theme is that women have been duped by the male-dominated society into believing that they could only aspire to be great housewives and husband pleasers. The "ailment," Friedan states, has a simple cure—women should be allowed to get out of the house, have a career, and earn their own money, and husbands should lend them support. Many women, otherwise, will be left empty shells of what they once were and will end up, later in life, on the psychiatrist's couch trying to understand what was missing.

During her book promotion tours, Friedan was amazed at all the excitement that she had caused and decided that women needed a political organization of their own. The National Organization for Women* (NOW) was founded in January 1967 to promote the civil rights of American Women. Its agenda soon broadened out to include abortion* rights, equal pay for equal work, gay rights,* and an end to sexual harassment. The women most responsible for the establishment of NOW were Dorothy Haener, Betty Friedan, Kathryn Clarenbach, and Pauli Murray. The formal purpose of NOW was "action to bring women into full participation in the mainstream of American society now, exercising all the privileges and responsibilities thereof in truly equal partnership with men." Within its first few years, NOW had targeted as its concerns the issues of reproductive rights, developmental child care, equal pay, limits on nuclear weapons, an end to poverty, antirape reform, and initiatives to end violence against women. NOW became the most influential feminist group in the country.

The women's movement also benefited from a varity of important U.S. Supreme Court decisions during the 1970s. The *Reed v. Reed** decision of 1971 involved the Fourteenth Amendment guarantees of equal protection when state law automatically preferred fathers over mothers as executors of an estate. The court threw out the law, arguing "to give a mandatory preference to members of either sex over members of the other . . . is to make the very kind of arbitrary legislative choices forbidden by the equal protection clause." It was the first

time the Supreme Court had overturned a state law on the grounds that it discriminated against women. In *Weinberger v. Weisenfeld** (1975), the court
agreed that widowers, as well as widows, were entitled to Social Security survivors' benefits. Feminists claimed that women who paid social security taxes
were not receiving equal benefits when, in the event of their deaths, their survivors could not collect the complete package of benefits. In *Taylor v. Louisiana** (1975), the Supreme Court ruled that laws excluding women from juries
violated the Sixth Amendment's requirement that juries represent a cross section
of the community. The Court's decision in the 1976 case of *Craig v. Boren**
ruled that state laws requiring different minimum ages for men and women to
purchase alcohol legally violated due process. In 1979 the court ruled in *Orr v.
Orr** that alimony payments applied to whichever spouse in a divorce case had
more assets and earning power. States violate the equal protection clause of the
Fourteenth Amendment when they permit women, but not men, to receive alimony payments. Feminists also considered the 1970 California supreme court
decision in *Marvin v. Marvin* to be a victory for women's rights. The court
decision proclaimed the precedent that unmarried cohabitants enjoyed certain
property rights and compensation in the event of estrangement.

The women's movement also targeted pornography in the 1970s. It posed a
difficult legal issue for many feminists, whose own civil liberties points of view
were usually quite liberal. They had traditionally opposed censorship, but in the
1970s they began calling for the suppression of pornography on the grounds
that it encouraged violence against women. This became especially important
to feminists when hard-core pornography, in such films as *Deep Throat** and
*The Devil in Miss Jones** threatened to go mainstream in the popular culture.
Many feminists celebrated the U.S. Supreme Court decision in *Miller v. California** (1973), in which the Court established the judicial guidelines for determining whether material is obscene and subject to censorship. The Court ruled
that state and local governments can, without violating First Amendment protections, regulate obscene material. The Court defined as obscenity any material '
that an average person, applying local community standards, would conclude
appeals only to "prurient interests" and lacks any "serious literary, artistic,
political, or scientific value."

The greatest campaign waged by the women's movement during the 1970s
was the crusade for ratification of the Equal Rights Amendment* (ERA). NOW
played a critical role in convincing Congress to pass the Equal Rights Amendment, and when it still had not been approved by enough states by 1977, NOW
convinced Congress to grant a five-year extension. At the state and local levels,
NOW campaigned for ratification of the amendment. In the process, NOW membership grew rapidly to 225,000 women by 1982. By then, however, the ERA
had still not been approved by the requisite number of states, and Congress
refused to grant another extension. The ERA was dead. During the rest of the

1980s, NOW membership declined. By the mid-1990s, NOW had 750 local chapters with more than 250,000 members.

SUGGESTED READINGS: Flora Davis, *Moving the Mountain: The Women's Movement in America Since 1960*, 1991; Barbara Ryan, *The Women's Movement*, 1996; Sharon Whitney, *The Equal Rights Amendment: The History and the Movement*, 1984.

WONDER, STEVIE. Stevie Wonder was born in 1951 as Steveland Judkins Morris. Blind from birth, Morris was a gifted musical talent, and in 1962 Barry Gordy of Motown Records signed him to a contract. The subsequent album, *Little Stevie Wonder, the 12-Year-Old Genius*, was released in 1963 and became a huge hit. Wonder enjoyed an extraordinary longevity in American popular music. He started as a harmonica player and vocalist, but over the years, Wonder developed an expertise with the piano, drums, organ, and synthesizer. He also added reggae and rap to his rock-and-roll and soul repertoire. By 1996 Stevie Wonder had released fifty-six top-ten hits and twenty-three hit albums in his career.

SUGGESTED READING: John Swenson, *Stevie Wonder*, 1986.

WONDER WOMAN. In the age of the women's movement* in the United States, the television series *Wonder Woman* provided young women and adolescent girls with their own cartoonish role model, a heroine with all of the powers of Superman and the body of a beauty pageant contestant. The series, based on Charles Moulon's 1940s comic book heroine of the same name, premiered on December 18, 1976, starring Lynda Carter as Yeoman Diana Prince (''Wonder Woman''), a woman of Amazonian origins who masqueraded as a secretary in the U.S. Army during World War II. When bandits, desperadoes, or Nazi agents threatened the innocent, she whirled herself instantaneously into Wonder Woman, a superheroine bedecked in a form-fitting, red-white-and-blue outfit, who quickly dispatched the enemy. The last episode of *Wonder Woman* was telecast on September 11, 1979.

SUGGESTED READING: Tim Brooks and Earle Marsh, *The Complete Directory to Prime Time Network and Cable TV Shows, 1946–Present*, 1995.

WOODEN, JOHN. John Robert Wooden was born in Martinsville, Indiana, on October 4, 1910. He graduated from Purdue University in 1932 and later earned a master's degree at Indiana State University (1947). An All-American basketball player as an undergraduate, Wooden became the greatest collegiate basketball coach in American history. After several years of coaching at the secondary level, Wooden became athletic director and head basketball coach at Indiana State College in 1946. Two years later he was hired as head basketball coach at the University of California at Los Angeles, where he accumulated what many consider to be an unbeatable record. When Wooden retired in 1975, he enjoyed a career record of 620 wins against only 147 losses and ten NCAA championships in his last twelve years of coaching. Since 1975 Wooden has lived in retirement but he continues to lecture and consult.

SUGGESTED READINGS: Mark Heisler, *They Shoot Coaches, Don't They?: UCLA and the NCAA Since John Wooden*, 1996; John Wooden, *They Call Me Coach*, 1988.

WOUNDED KNEE (1973). After American Indian Movement* (AIM) militants seized the symbolic site of Wounded Knee, situated on the Pine Ridge Reservation in South Dakota, federal agents descended upon the scene. Thus commenced an armed stand-off that attracted international attention. The actions of the pan-Indian activists were partially motivated by claims that the duly elected tribal leader at Pine Ridge, Richard Wilson, and his Indian police force were the pliant surrogates of the Bureau of Indian Affairs. The ensuing confrontation, which lasted for more than seventy days, fueled a media blitz that did much to publicize and dramatize the sad plight of the American Indian. In the process, the militant Indians declared the sovereign independence of the Oglala Sioux Nation in accord with the boundaries established by the Fort Laramie Treaty of 1868. Having achieved a substantial propaganda victory, AIM leaders negotiated a peaceful withdrawal and vacated their stronghold at Wounded Knee.

Although the incident at Wounded Knee succeeded in making Indian grievances front-page news, AIM tactics elicited a mixed response from the Native American community. Many Indians objected to the violent actions and inflammatory rhetoric of Oglala Sioux spokesman Russell Means* and AIM. Moreover, in most instances, American Indian military had little or no effect on the direction of federal Indian policy and in some respects proved self-defeating when it alienated formerly sympathetic whites.

SUGGESTED READINGS: Robert Burnette and John Koster, *The Road to Wounded Knee*, 1974; Roxanne Dunbar Ortiz, "Wounded Knee 1890 to Wounded Knee 1973: A Study in United States Colonialism," *Journal of Ethnic Studies* 8 (Summer 1980); James S. Olson and Raymond Wilson, *Native Americans in the Twentieth Century*, 1984; Francis Paul Prucha, *The Great White Father*, vol. 2, 1994.

Mark Baxter

Y

YOM KIPPUR WAR (1973). After the Six-Day War of 1967, Egypt and Syria severed diplomatic relations with Israel, demanding that Israeli troops withdraw from their positions in the Sinai Desert and on the Golan Heights. Israel refused, and for the next six years tensions built up to a breaking point. On October 6, 1973, Egyptian and Syrian troops launched a simultaneous invasion of the Sinai Desert and the Golan Heights, both Israeli-occupied territories. Journalists dubbed the conflict the "Yom Kippur War" because the invasion had begun on Yom Kippur, a sacred Jewish holiday. Egypt claimed sovereignty over the Sinai and Syria over the Golan Heights. The Soviet Union airlifted massive supplies to the Arab armies, and the United States agreed to resupply Israel with all the military equipment it needed to survive. Bloody, armored warfare took place on Middle East battlefields, but Israel soon prevailed and laid siege to the Egyptian city of Suez, trapping the Egyptian 3rd Army in the desert, with its back to the canal.

With the Israelis threatening to annihilate an entire Egyptian army, Secretary of State Henry Kissinger* began his so-called shuttle diplomacy between Cairo, Tel Aviv, and Damascus, trying to forge a settlement. On October 22, he managed to bring about a cease-fire between Israel and Egypt, and two days later Syria joined as well. In mid-November, Israel lifted its siege of Suez and allowed the withdrawal of the Egyptian army, and the belligerents began the mutual exchange of prisoners of war. A United Nations peacekeeping force was dispatched to the Middle East to preserve the cease-fire. Late in December, peace talks were undertaken in Geneva, Switzerland, to work out a more permanent settlement. One month later, Egypt and Israel agreed to mutual troop withdrawals. The final peace documents were signed in Geneva on May 31, 1974.

The war itself may have been over, but its impact on the world economy was only beginning. Frustrated with the transparent willingness of the United States to side so consistently with Israel, oil-rich Arab nations decided to retaliate. In mid-October, eleven Arab oil-producing states announced a 5 percent reduction in oil exports and an outright boycott of crude oil to the United States and any other country friendly to Israel (see Arab oil boycott of 1973–1974).

The economic consequences were almost immediate because the boycott produced a scramble for oil in Western Europe, Japan, and the United States. The Organization of Petroleum Exporting Countries* (OPEC) took quick advantage of the boycott and jacked up crude oil prices from less than $4 a barrel in October to $12 a barrel in January 1974. Gasoline shortages soon appeared in the United States, and pump prices skyrocketed. In Houston, Texas, regular gasoline sold for $.19 a gallon on October 1; three months later, it was $.60 a gallon. Farmers, shippers, and manufacturers passed the costs on to consumers, and the retail price index ballooned.

Although the Arab nations called off the boycott on March 18, 1974, the decision had little impact on prices. After years of importing cheap foreign oil, American production, which was more expensive, had declined dramatically. For the first time in its history, the United States was dependent on foreign oil producers and had to accept world market prices. The boycott ended but inflation did not. In 1974 the consumer price index went up 7 percent. The era of stag-flation* had begun.

SUGGESTED READING: Peter Allen, *The Yom Kippur War*, 1982.

YOUNG, ANDREW. Andrew Young was born in New Orleans, Louisiana, on March 12, 1932. He graduated from Howard University in 1951 and, determined to pursue a career as a minister, received a divinity degree from the Hartford School of Theology in 1955. He was ordained a Congregational clergymen in 1955 and accepted a pastorate in Thomasville, Georgia. From 1957 to 1961, Young worked with the National Council of Churches, but by then he had become deeply involved in the civil rights movement.* In 1961 Young joined the staff of the Southern Christian Leadership Conference (SCLC), where he became closely associated with the Reverend Martin Luther King, Jr. Young became executive director of the SCLC in 1964. He was with King in Memphis in 1968 when the civil rights leader was assassinated.

Young turned his attention to the larger political arena, and he won a Democratic seat in Congress in 1970. After serving three terms, he stepped down in 1977 when President Jimmy Carter* appointed him ambassador to the United Nations—an appointment that gave Young the highest world profile of any African American. Young left the ambassadorship in 1979 and returned to private life, only to win election as mayor of Atlanta, Georgia, in 1982. He stepped down in 1989 to head Atlanta's organization for the 1996 summer Olympic Games. Andrew Young remains today one of the most influential and respected African Americans in the United States.

SUGGESTED READING: David J. Garrow, *Bearing the Cross: Martin Luther King, Jr. and the Southern Christian Leadership Conference*, 1986.

YOUNG, NEIL. Neil Young, who was born in Toronto, Canada, on November 12, 1945, was raised in Winnipeg, where he began playing in several high school rock bands. He also became a devotee of folk music. In 1964 Young moved back to Toronto. In 1966 he drove to Los Angeles where he became part of the Buffalo Springfield band, which he quit in 1968. In January 1969, his first solo album, *Neil Young*, was released. Later in the year, his second album, *Everybody Knows This Is Nowhere*, went on sale. The second album included three of Young's most famous singles: "Cinnamon Girl," "Down by the River," and "Cowgirl in the Sand." He then joined the group that became known as Crosby, Stills, Nash, and Young.*

He continued his solo career, however, and his 1970 album *After the Gold Rush* went gold. The number-one hit single "Heart of Gold" in 1972 took the album *Harvest* to number one. Young, who had become a superstar, had gained a large, enthusiastic following in the United States because of his eclectic musical talents. A talented singer and songwriter, Young was as comfortable with sweet country as he was with hard rock. During the mid-1970s, he toured and recorded for a while with Stills, but in June 1977 he went solo again and released the album *American Stars & Bars*, which went gold. Since then, Young has maintained his presence in the world of popular music by successfully making the transition to punk* and hard rock.

SUGGESTED READING: David Downing, *A Dreamer of Pictures: Neil Young, The Man and His Music*, 1995.

Z

ZIONISM. On November 10, 1975, the United Nations General Assembly adopted a declaration that labeled Zionism a "form of racism and racial discrimination." Zionism is a belief and political movement committed to the conviction that God and destiny intend there to be a Jewish state in Palestine, and that the state of Israel represents the fulfillment of Old Testament prophecy. Ethnic Palestinians, of course, disagree, because Zionism implies their own displacement from a homeland they had occupied for centuries. Although the declaration passed easily, it ignited a firestorm of political criticism in Israel and the United States. The American Jewish community has supported Israel avidly, and the wars in 1967 and 1973 between Israel and the Arab states only intensified that commitment.

At the time, Palestinians enjoyed unprecedented support around the world, much of which came from sympathies with their plight in oil-rich Arab nations. Abundant oil supplies in the Middle East and skyrocketing global energy prices endowed the Arab states with extraordinary political clout, and Arab leaders, who identified with fellow Muslims in Israel, Egypt, Syria, and Jordan, watched the vote closely in the General Assembly. More symbolic than real in its political impact, the declaration nevertheless labeled Israel a rogue nation in world affairs and cemented the relationship between the United States and Israel. Bitterness and recrimination over the declaration continued to fester until it was repealed in 1991.

SUGGESTED READINGS: *New York Times*, November 11–13, 1975.

Chronology of the 1970s

1970

January

13 Congress passes the Indian Elementary and Secondary Education Act.

20 *All in the Family* premiers on CBS Television.

26 The film *M*A*S*H** is released.

February

20 Henry Kissinger opens secret peace negotiations in Paris with North Vietnam.

March

8 Lehman Brightman leads a group of Indians in a march on the state capitol in Sacramento, California, to protest the fatal shooting of a Hoopa Indian; United Indians of All Tribes invade Fort Lawton to demand their right to take title to surplus federal lands.

14 Indian activists stage protest demonstrations at Bureau of Indian Affairs buildings throughout the country to demand fair employment practices.

16 Indian activists demonstrate at Ellis Island to claim the abandoned immigration building as an Indian commune.

18 General Lon Nol, with U.S. backing, deposes the government of Prince Norodom Sihanouk of Cambodia.

April

15   The U.S. First Infantry Division withdraws from Vietnam.

22   The first Earth Day takes place.

30   U.S. forces invade Cambodia.

May

4   National Guard troops kill four students at Kent State University in Ohio.

17   Mohawk demonstrators try to drive non-Indian campers off Loon Island in the Saint Lawrence River in New York.

June

6   Pit River Indians stage a protest demonstration to claim ownership of Lassen National Forest.

15   Oglala Sioux demonstrators seize an area on Sheep Mountain, North Dakota, and demand that the federal government return it to the tribe.

30   U.S. land-based military forces withdraw from Cambodia. The U.S. Senate adopts the Cooper-Church Amendment.

August

1   Puyallup Indians stage fish-ins in Washington State to demand their treaty fishing rights on the Puyallup River.

September

9   *Monday Night Football*, a weekly broadcast of a National Football League game, debuts on ABC television.

    A bloody uprising occurs at the Attica State Prison in New York.

18   A group of fifty Indians from various tribes occupies Mount Rushmore in South Dakota and demand its return to Native Americans.

October

11   The U.S. Third Brigade of the Ninth Infantry Division withdraws from Vietnam.

26   Garry Trudeau's newspaper comic-strip *Doonesbury* is published in national syndication.

November

21   The United States stages an unsuccessful raid on the Son Tay Prison in North Vietnam in order to rescue American prisoners of war.

22   The U.S. Supreme Court decides the *Reed v. Reed* case.

23   The American Indian Movement holds its Mayflower II demonstration.

December

7   The U.S. Fourth Infantry Division withdraws from Vietnam.

8   The U.S. Twenty-fifth Infantry Division withdraws from Vietnam.

22   Congress prohibits U.S. combat forces or advisers in Cambodia and Laos.

31   U.S. military personnel in Vietnam is reduced to 334,600.

1971

January

1   The Winter Soldier Investigation begins in Detroit.

21   Fishing rights activist Hank Adams is shot while staging a fish-in on the Puyallup River in Washington state.

30   Operation Lam Son 719—the U.S.-backed South Vietnamese invasion of Laos— begins.

March

3   The U.S. Fifth Special Forces Group leaves Vietnam.

5   The U.S. Eleventh Armored Cavalry Regiment withdraws from Vietnam.

11   Congress passes the Alaska Native Claims Settlement Act.

29   Lieutenant William Calley, Jr., is found guilty of murder for his role in the My Lai massacre.

April

6   Operation Lam Son 719 ends.

14   The U.S. Third Amphibious Force withdraws from Vietnam.

20   Tens of thousands of antiwar demonstrators in Washington, D.C., and San Francisco demand an end to the Vietnam War.

The U.S. Supreme Court decides the *Swann v. Charlotte-Mecklenburg County Board of Education* case.

29   The U.S. First Cavalry Division withdraws from Vietnam.

30   The U.S. Second Brigade of the Twenty-fifth Infantry Division withdraws from Vietnam.

May

3   The People's Coalition for Peace and Justice demonstrates against the Vietnam War in Washington, D.C.

June

11 The nineteen-month occupation of Alcatraz Island by the Indians of All Tribes comes to an end.

13 The *New York Times* begins publishing the Pentagon Papers.

14 The U.S. Supreme Court decides the *Graham v. Richardson* case.

30 The U.S. Supreme Court blocks Nixon administration attempts to prevent publication of the Pentagon Papers.

July

4   Indian activists stage a demonstration at Mount Rushmore.

August

18 Iroquois Indians protest the widening of Interstate 81 in New York State on August 18, 1971.

25 The U.S. 173d Airborne Brigade withdraws from Vietnam.

27 The U.S. Fifth Brigade of the Fifth Infantry Division withdraws from Vietnam.

31 The Royal Thai Army withdraws from Vietnam.

September

3   The Berlin Treaty is signed.

9   The Attica prison riot occurs in New York.

October

7   The film *The French Connection* is released.

16 The film *The Last Picture Show* is released.

November

12 President Richard Nixon announces that henceforth U.S. ground forces in Vietnam will be confined to defensive operations.

14 NASA's *Mariner 9* spacecraft goes into orbit around Mars.

December

26   President Nixon orders the resumption of U.S. bombing of North Vietnam.

31   U.S. military personnel in Vietnam is reduced to 156,000.

1972

January

16   The first full issue of *Ms.* magazine is published.

February

1   The American Indian Movement begins its caravan into Gordon, Nebraska.

21–28   To begin the process of achieving detente with the People's Republic of China, President Nixon makes a one-week state visit to Beijing.

March

10   The U.S. 101st Airborne Division leaves Vietnam.

23   President Nixon suspends the Paris Peace Talks until North Vietnam and the National Liberation Front agree to enter into "serious discussions."

30   North Vietnam launches the Eastertide Offensive in Vietnam.

April

15   President Nixon resumes the bombing of North Vietnam.

15–20   Widespread antiwar demonstrations are staged throughout the United States.

23   The American Indian Movement holds a protest demonstration at the Fort Totten Indian Reservation in North Dakota to highlight the problem of police brutality.

27   President Nixon resumes the Paris Peace Talks.

May

4   President Nixon suspends the Paris Peace Talks after North Vietnamese forces conquer An Loc in South Vietnam.

8   President Nixon orders the U.S. Navy to mine Haiphong Harbor in North Vietnam.

15   Governor George Wallace of Alabama, a candidate for the Democratic presidential nomination, is shot during an assassination attempt in Laurel, Maryland.

22–29   At the Moscow Summit Conference, President Nixon signs the SALT I Treaty (Strategic Arms Limitation Talks).

June

22   The Watergate break-in and arrests occur.

26   The U.S. Third Brigade of the First Cavalry Division withdraws from Vietnam.

29   The U.S. 196th Infantry Brigade withdraws from Vietnam.

July

13   The Paris Peace Talks resume after a ten-week suspension.

August

23   The U.S. Third Battalion of the Twenty-first Infantry withdraws from Vietnam.

September

26   Kissinger conducts secret peace talks in Paris with North Vietnamese diplomats.

October

19   Kissinger meets with President Nguyen Can Thieu in Saigon to secure South Vietnamese approval of the pending Paris Peace Accords.

November

2   The Trail of Broken Treaties demonstration takes place in Washington, D.C. More than 600 Indians barricade themselves in the Bureau of Indian Affairs office.

3   Nixon is elected to a second presidential term.

20–21   Kissinger and Le Duc Tho complete negotiations on the Paris Peace Accords ending the Vietnam War.

December

12   President Nixon announces the end of all draft calls. The film *Poseidon Adventure* is released.

13   The North Vietnamese express new reservations about the Paris Peace Accords.

17   The film *The Godfather* is released.

18   President Nixon authorizes the Operation Linebacker II massive bombing of North Vietnam.

19   *Apollo 17*, the last of NASA's missions to the moon, splashes down in the Pacific.

29   Operation Linebacker II ends after North Vietnam again agrees to the Paris Peace Accords.

31   U.S. military personnel in Vietnam is reduced to 24,000 people.

1973

January

15   President Nixon stops all offensive military operations against North Vietnam.

18   The film *Deep Throat* is released.

22   The U.S. Supreme Court decides the *Roe v. Wade* case.

27   The United States, North Vietnam, South Vietnam, and the National Liberation Front sign the Paris Peace Accords.

      The film *Last Tango in Paris* is released.

February

6–8   American Indian Movement protestors clash with police in Custer, South Dakota, over a local judge's decision to grant bail to a white man accused of murdering an Indian.

12   The first U.S. prisoners of war are released by North Vietnam.

27   The standoff begins in Wounded Knee, South Dakota, between American Indian Movement officials, the FBI, and Pine Ridge Reservation officials.

March

7   The comet Kohoutek is discovered.

16   The U.S. Ninth Infantry Division withdraws from Vietnam.

21   The Supreme Court decides the *San Antonio School District v. Rodriguez* case.

27   Marlon Brando refuses to accept his Best Actor Award at the Academy Award ceremony because of the industry's treatment of Indians on film and television.

29   North Vietnam releases the last of its U.S. prisoners of war.

May

8   The standoff ends in Wounded Knee, South Dakota, between American Indian Movement officials, the FBI, and Pine Ridge Reservation officials.

June

17–25   Summit conference convenes in Washington, D.C., between President Nixon and Soviet Premier Leonid Brezhnev.

21   The U.S. Supreme Court decides the *Miller v. California* case.

      The U.S. Supreme Court decides the *Keyes v. Denver School District No. 1* case.

24   Congress prohibits all bombing in Cambodia after August 15, 1973.

August

10   The film *American Graffitti* is released.

14   All direct U.S. military operations in Indochina come to an end.

September

11   President Salvador Allende of Chile is overthrown in a CIA-backed coup d'état.

22   The War Powers Resolution becomes law in spite of President Nixon's veto.

October

6   The Yom Kippur War erupts in the Middle East.

10   Vice President Spiro Agnew resigns after pleading no contest to charges of tax evasion.

15   Arab nations announce an oil boycott against the United States.

20   The "Saturday Night Massacre"—in which President Nixon fires Watergate special prosecutor Archibald Cox—occurs.

November

11   The Yom Kippur War ends.

19   The Supreme Court decides the *Puyallup Tribe, Inc. v. Department of Game* (Puyallup II) case.

December

31   U.S. military personnel in Vietnam is reduced to fifty people.

1974

February

4   The Symbionese Liberation Army kidnaps Patricia Hearst.

April

8   Henry Aaron hits career home run 715 to break Babe Ruth's record.

12   Congress passes the Indian Finance Act on April 12, 1974.

March

18   Arab nations call off their international oil boycott.

May

31   Israel and Syria sign a peace agreement brokered by Secretary of State Kissinger.

June

10   The International Indian Treaty Council is established.

29   The Second Moscow Conference between President Nixon and Soviet Premier Brezhnev begins.

August

9   Richard Nixon resigns the presidency, and Gerald Ford becomes president of the United States.

20   Congress reduces U.S. aid to South Vietnam from $1 billion annually to $700 million.

September

16   President Ford offers clemency to draft evaders and military deserters.

November

15   The film *Earthquake* is released.

December

13   The film *Godfather II* is released.

19   The film *Towering Inferno* is released.

1975

January

1   Forty-five Menominee Indians seize a Roman Catholic convent in Gresham, Wisconsin, and demand return of its 225 acres to the Indians.

4   Congress passes the Indian Self-Determination and Education Assistance Act.

8   North Vietnam decides to launch an all-out invasion of South Vietnam.

February

25   American Indian Movement activists occupy the Fairchild Camera and Instrument Corporation Electronics Plant at Shiprock, New Mexico, to protest the company's decision to lay off 140 Navajo workers.

27   Black Muslim leader Elijah Muhammad dies.

March

14   South Vietnam retreats and withdraws all military forces from the Central Highlands.

19   North Vietnam troops overrun Quang Tri Province in South Vietnam.

26   The North Vietnamese capture the city of Hue in South Vietnam.

30   The North Vietnamese capture the city of Danang in South Vietnam.

April

1   President Lon Nol of Cambodia abdicates power when Khmer Rouge forces conquer the country.

    South Vietnam abandons the entire northern half of the country to North Vietnamese forces.

11   U.S. embassy personnel in Phnom Penh, Cambodia, leave the country.

12   Nguyen Van Thieu resigns as president of South Vietnam.

17   Cambodia falls to the Khmer Rouge Communist army.

29   All U.S. diplomatic and military personnel are withdrawn from South Vietnam.

30   North Vietnamese forces conquer Saigon and all of South Vietnam. The Vietnam War ends.

May

12   Khmer Rouge forces capture the *Mayaguez* in Cambodian international waters.

June

16   The U.S. Supreme Court reaches its decision in the *Bigelow v. Virginia* case.

26   Leonard Peltier is charged with the murder of two FBI agents in Pine Ridge, South Dakota.

July

20   SONY Corporation introduces the videocassette recorder.

30   The Helsinki Conference on European Security begins.

Teamster boss Jimmy Hoffa disappears outside a restaurant in Detroit, Michigan. He is never seen again, and his body is never found.

October

1   Muhammad Ali and Joe Frazier fight the "Thrilla in Manila" heavyweight boxing championship.

November

19   The film *One Flew Over the Cuckoo's Nest* is released.

1976

June

7   The U.S. Supreme Court decides the *Washington v. Davis* case.

July

2   The U.S. Supreme Court decides the *Gregg v. Georgia* case.

4   The United States celebrates its bicentennial.

August

12   The Council of Energy Resource Tribes is formed.

September

9   Mao Zedong, leader of the People's Republic of China, dies.

October

31   Puyallup protestors occupy the Cascadia Juvenile Diagnostic Center in Tacoma, Washington.

November

2   Jimmy Carter is elected president of the United States.

21   The film *Rocky* is released.

1977

January

23–30   Alex Haley's *Roots* appears on ABC television on eight consecutive nights.

February

9   The film *Twilight's Last Gleaming* is released.

March

1   The U.S. Supreme Court decides the *United Jewish Organization of Williamsburgh v. Carey* case.

21   Menominee activists occupy the courthouse in Keshena, Wisconsin, demanding punishment of the individuals responsible for beating up two Indian women.

April

28   Leonard Peltier is convicted on two counts of first-degree murder.

May

13   Mohawk militants begin a three-year occupation of a 612-acre campsite in the Adirondack Mountains of New York.

25   The film *Star Wars* is released.

June

20   Oil begins flowing through the much heralded, highly controversial Alaska pipeline.

July

13   A power failure plunges New York City into darkness. Power is not restored for twenty-five hours.

August

16   Elvis Presley dies in Memphis, Tennessee.

September

7   The Panama Canal Treaties are signed.

November

16   The film *Close Encounters of the Third Kind* is released.

1978

February

11   The American Indian Movement begins its Longest Walk demonstration.
15   The film *Coming Home* is released.

May

23   The U.S. Supreme Court decides the *Marshall v. Barlows, Inc.*, case.

June

6   California voters approve Proposition 13, which drastically slashes property taxes.
28   The U.S. Supreme Court decides the *University of California Board of Regents v. Baake* case.

July

25   The American Indian Movement's Longest Walk demonstration reaches Washington, D.C.
27   The film *Animal House* is released.

August

11   Congress passes the American Indian Religious Freedom Act on August 11, 1978.

September

22   The film *Go Tell the Spartans* is released.

October

13   President Carter mediates the Middle East peace negotiations between Egypt and Israel which eventually produce the Camp David Accords.

November

8   Congress passes the Indian Child Welfare Act.
20   A mass suicide takes place in Jonestown, Guyana.

27   In San Francisco, Dan White murders Mayor George Moscone and Councilman
     Harvey Milk.

December

14   The film *The Deer Hunter* is released.
     The film *Superman* is released.

1979

March

5   The U.S. Supreme Court decides the *Orr v. Orr* case.

April

4   A nuclear accident occurs at the Three-Mile Island nuclear power plant outside
     Harrisburg, Pennsylvania.
15   The film *The China Syndrome* is released.

May

24   The film *Alien* is released.

June

18   President Carter and Soviet Premier Brezhnev sign the SALT II Treaty in Vienna.
27   The U.S. Supreme Court decides the *United Steelworkers of America v. Weber* case.

August

14   The film *Apocalypse Now* is released.

October

5   Two thousand Indian activists protest the decision to develop uranium mines in the
     Black Hills of South Dakota.

November

4   Muslim militants seize the U.S. embassy in Teheran, Iran, and begin the hostage
     crisis and siege.

December

26   Soviet troops invade Afghanistan.

Selected Bibliography

AFRICAN AMERICANS

Anderson, Alan B., and George W. Pickering. *Confronting the Color Line: The Broken Promise of the Civil Rights Movement in Chicago.* 1986.

Carter, Dan T. *The Politics of Rage: George Wallace, the Origins of the New Conservatism, and the Transformation of American Politics.* 1996.

David, Jay, and Elaine Crane, eds. *The Black Soldier: From the American Revolution to Vietnam.* 1971.

Dittmer, John. *Local People: The Struggle for Civil Rights in Mississippi.* 1994.

Fairclough, Adam. *"To Redeem the Soul of America": The Southern Christian Leadership Conference from King to the 1980s.* 1987.

Fisher, Randall M. *Rhetoric and American Democracy: Black Protest Through Vietnam Dissent.* 1985.

Halpern, Stephen C. *On the Limits of the Law: The Ironic Legacy of Title VI of the 1964 Civil Rights Act.* 1995.

Hill, Herbert, and James E. Jones, eds. *Race in America: The Struggle for Equality.* 1993.

Honey, Michael K. *Southern Labor and Black Civil Rights: Organizing Memphis Workers.* 1993.

Lawson, Steven D. *In Pursuit of Power: Southern Blacks and Electoral Politics, 1965–1982.* 1985.

Lincoln, C. Eric. *The Black Muslims in America.* 1973.

Marable, Manning. *Black American Politics: From the Washington Marches to Jesse Jackson.* 1985.

———. *Race, Reform, and Rebellion: The Second Reconstruction in Black America, 1945–1982.* 1991.

Peake, Thomas R. *Keeping the Dream Alive: A History of the Southern Christian Leadership Conference.* 1986.

Powledge, Fred. *Free at Last? The Civil Rights Movement and the People Who Made It.* 1991.

Stoper, Emily. *The Student Nonviolent Coordinating Committee: The Growth of Radicalism in a Civil Rights Organization.* 1989.

Terry, Wallace. *Bloods: An Oral History of the Vietnam War by Black Veterans*. 1984.

Van DeBurg, William L. *New Day in Babylon: The Black Power Movement and American Culture, 1965–1975*. 1993.

Weisbrot, Robert. *Freedom Bound: A History of America's Civil Rights Movement*. 1990.

Wilkinson, J. Harvie. *From Brown to Bakke: The Supreme Court and School Integration, 1954–1978*. 1979.

Williams, Juan. *Eyes on the Prize: America's Civil Rights Years*. 1987.

Zaroulis, Nancy, and Gerald Sullivan. *Who Spoke Up?: American Protest Against the War in Vietnam, 1963–1975*. 1984.

ANTIWAR MOVEMENT

Bannan, John, and Rosemary Bannan. *Law, Morality and the Courts: Peace Militants and the Courts*. 1975.

Baskir, Lawrence M., and William A. Strauss. *Chance and Circumstance: The Draft, the War and the Vietnam Generation*. 1978.

Berman, William C. *William Fulbright and the Vietnam War: The Dissent of a Political Realist*. 1988.

Bloom, Lynn Z. *Doctor Spock: Biography of a Conservative Radical*. 1972.

Brodie, Bernard. *Vietnam: Why We Failed in War and Politics*. 1973.

Cantor, Milton. *The Divided Left: American Radicalism, 1900–1975*. 1978.

Capps, Walter H. *The Unfinished War: Vietnam and the American Conscience*. 1982.

Carroll, Peter N. *It Seemed Like Nothing Happened: The Tragedy and Promise of America in the 1970s*. 1982.

Clecak, Peter. *Radical Paradoxes: Dilemmas of the American Left, 1945–1970*. 1974.

Coffin, William Sloane. *Once to Every Man: A Memoir*. 1977.

Cooney, Robert, and Helen Michalowski, eds. *The Power of the People: Active Nonviolence in the United States*. 1977.

Cortright, David. *Soldiers in Revolt: The American Military Today*. 1975.

DeBenedetti, Charles, and Charles Chatfield. *An American Ordeal: The Antiwar Movement of the Vietnam Era*. 1990.

Finn, James. *Protest: Pacifism and Politics*. 1968.

Fisher, Randall M. *Rhetoric and American Democracy: Black Protest Through Vietnam Dissent*. 1985.

Gausman, William F. *Red Stains on Vietnam Doves*. 1989.

Hall, Mitchell K. *Because of Their Faith: CALCAV and Religious Opposition to the Vietnam War*. 1990.

Hallen, Daniel C. *The Uncensored War: The Media & Vietnam*. 1989.

Halstead, Fred. *Out Now! A Participant's Account of the American Movement Against the Vietnam War*. 1978.

Harris, David. *Dreams Die Hard*. 1982.

Hayden, Tom. *Reunion: A Memoir*. 1988.

Heath, G. Lewis, ed. *Mutiny Does Not Happen Lightly: The Literature of the American Resistance to the Vietnam War*. 1976.

Levy, David W. *The Debate over Vietnam*. 1991.

Lewy, Guenter. *Peace and Revolution: The Moral Crisis of American Pacifism*. 1988.

Meconis, Charles. *With Clumsy Grace: The American Catholic Left, 1961–1977*. 1979.

Rothman, Stanley, and S. Robert Lichter. *Roots of Radicalism: Jews, Christians, and the New Left*. 1982.

Sale, Kirkpatrick. *SDS*. 1974.

Small, Melvin. *Johnson, Nixon, and the Doves*. 1988.

Smith, Curt. *Long Time Gone: The Years of Turmoil Remembered*. 1982.

Surrey, David S. *Choice of Conscience: Vietnam Era Military and Draft Resisters in Canada*. 1982.

Unger, Irwin. *The Movement: A History of the American New Left, 1959–1972*. 1974.

Useem, Michael. *Conscription, Protest, and Social Conflict: The Life and Death of a Draft Resistance Movement*. 1973.

Vogelgesang, Sandy. *The Long Dark Night of the Soul: The American Intellectual Left and the Vietnam War*. 1974.

Wells, Tom. *The War Within: America's Battle over Vietnam*. 1994.

Wittner, Lawrence S. *Rebels Against War: The American Peace Movement, 1933–1983*. 1984.

Zaroulis, Nancy, and Gerald Sullivan. *Who Spoke Up? American Protest Against the War in Vietnam, 1963–1975*. 1984.

ASIAN AMERICANS

Chan, Sucheng. *Asian Americans: An Intrepretive History*. 1991.

Downey, Bruce T., and Douglas P. Olney, eds. *The Hmong in the West: Observations and Reports*. 1982.

Freeman, James M. *Hearts of Sorrow: Vietnamese American Lives*. 1989.

Grant, Bruce. *The Boat People*. 1979.

Jensen, Joan. *Passage from India: Asian Indian Immigrants in North America*. 1988.

Kelly, Gail P. *From Vietnam to America: A Chronicle of the Vietnamese Immigration to the United States*. 1977.

Kim, Hyung-chan Kim. *The Korean Diaspora*. 1977.

Kim, Hyung-chan Kim, and Wayne Patterson, eds. *The Koreans in America, 1882–1974*. 1974.

Kimura, Yukiko. *The Japanese-Americans: Evolution of a Subculture*. 1976.

Pido, Antonio J. A. *The Filipinos in America*. 1986.

Rutledge, Paul. *The Vietnamese Experience in America*. 1992.

Saran, Parmatma. *The Asian Indian Experience in the United States*. 1985.

Strand, Paul, and Woodrow Jones, Jr. *Indochinese Refugees in America: Problems of Adaptation and Assimilation*. 1985.

Sung, Betty Lee. *Chinese American Intermarriage*. 1990.

Sutter, Valerie. *The Indochinese Refugee Dilemma*. 1990.

Takaki, Ronald. *Strangers from a Different Shore: A History of Asian Americans*. 1989.

Tsai Shi-shan, Henry. *The Chinese Experience in America*. 1986.

Wain, Barry. *The Refused: The Agony of the Indochinese Refugees*. 1981.

Yanagisako, Sylvia Junko. *Transforming the Past: Tradition and Kinship Among Japanese Americans*. 1985.

CARTER ADMINISTRATION

Bitzer, Lloyd F. *Carter vs. Ford: The Counterfeit Debates of 1976*. 1980.

Bourne, Peter G. *Jimmy Carter: A Comprehensive Biography from Plains to Post-Presidency*. 1997.

Brinkley, Douglas. *Jimmy Carter: The Triumph and the Turmoil*. 1996.
Brzezinski, Zbigniew K. *Power and Principle: Memoirs of the National Security Adviser, 1877–1981*. 1985.
Carter, Jimmy. *Keeping Faith: Memoirs of a President*. 1982.
———. *Turning Point: A Candidate, a State, and a Nation Come of Age*. 1992.
Dumbrell, John. *The Carter Presidency: A Reevaluation*. 1993.
Glad, Betty. *Jimmy Carter: In Search of the Great White House*. 1980.
Hargrove, Erwin C. *Jimmy Carter as President: Leadership and the Politics of the Public Good*. 1988.
Jones, Charles O. *The Trusteeship Presidency: Jimmy Carter and the United States Congress*. 1988.
Jordan, Hamilton. *Crisis: The Last Year of the Carter Presidency*. 1982.
Kaufman, Burton I. *The Presidency of James Earl Carter, Jr*. 1993.
Lance, Bert. *The Truth of the Matter: My Life in and out of Politics*. 1991.
Miller, William Lee. *Yankee from Georgia: The Emergence of Jimmy Carter*. 1978.
Morris, Kenneth Earl. *Jimmy Carter, American Moralist*. 1996.
Powell, Jody. *The Other Side of the Story*. 1984.
Rozell, Mark J. *The Press and the Carter Presidency*. 1989.
Skidmore, David. *Reversing Course: Carter's Foreign Policy, Domestic Politics, and the Failure of Reform*.
Thornton, Richard. *The Carter Years: Toward a New Global Order*. 1991.

COUNTERCULTURE

Braden, William. *The Age of Aquarius: Technology and the Cultural Revolution*. 1970.
Cox, Craig. *Storefront Revolution: Food Co-ops and the Counterculture*. 1994.
King, Richard. *The Party of Eros: Radical Social Thought and the Realm of Freedom*. 1972.
Miller, Thomas. *The Hippies and American Values*. 1991.
Perry, Charles. *The Haight-Asbury: A History*. 1984.
Roszak, Theodore. *The Making of a Counter Culture: Reflections on the Technocratic Society and Its Youthful Opposition*. 1969.
Stevens, Jay. *Storming Heaven: LSD and the American Dream*. 1987.
Urgo, Joseph R. *Novel Frames: Literature as Guide to Race, Sex, and History in America*. 1991.
Whitmer, Peter O. *Aquarius Revisited: Seven Who Created the Sixties Counterculture that Changed America*. 1987.
Wolfe, Burton H. *The Hippies*. 1968.
Yinger, Milton. *Countercultures: The Promise and the Peril of a World Turned Upside Down*. 1982.

ECONOMIC CHANGE

Bluestone, Barry, and Bennett Harrison. *The Deindustrialization of America*. 1982.
Calleo, David. *The Imperious Economy*. 1982.
Ehrenreich, Barbara. *Fear of Falling: The Inner Life of the Middle Class*. 1989.
Kidder, Tracy. *The Soul of a New Machine*. 1981.

Markusen, Ann, et al. *The Rise of the Gunbelt: The Military Remapping of Industrial America*. 1991.
Sassen, Saskia. *The Global City*. 1991.
Serrin, William. *Homestead: The Glory and Tragedy of an American Steel Town*. 1992.
Terkel, Studs. *Working*. 1972.

ENVIRONMENT

Gottlieb, Robert. *Forcing the Spring: The Transformation of the American Environmental Movement*. 1993.
Hays, Samuel. *Beauty, Health, and Permanence: Environmental Politics in the United States, 1955–1985*. 1987.
Sale, Kirkpatrick. *The Green Revolution: The American Environmental Movement, 1962–1992*. 1993.

FILM

Adair, Gilbert. *Hollywood's Vietnam: From the Green Berets to Apocalypse Now*. 1981.
Auster, Albert, and Leonard Quart. *How the War Was Remembered: Hollywood and Vietnam*. 1988.
Brownlow, Kevin. *The War, the West and the Wilderness*. 1979.
Dittmar, Linda, and Gene Michaud, eds. *From Hanoi to Hollywood: The Vietnam War in American Film*. 1990.
Henricksen, Margot. *Dr. Strangelove's America: Society and Culture in the Atomic Age*. 1997.
Jowett, Garth. *Film: The Democratic Art*. 1976.
Ray, Robert B. *A Certain Tendency of the Hollywood Cinema, 1930–1980*. 1985.
Shaheen, Jack G. *Nuclear War Films*. 1978.
Sklar, Robert. *Movie-Made America: A Cultural History of American Movies*. 1975.
Smith, Julian. *Looking Away, Hollywood and Vietnam*. 1975.
Wilson, James C. *Vietnam in Prose and Film*. 1982.
Wood, Robin. *Hollywood from Vietnam to Reagan*. 1986.

FORD ADMINISTRATION

Bravin, Jess. *Squeaky: The Life and Times of Lynette Alice Fromme*. 1997.
Cannon, James M. *Time and Chance: Gerald Ford's Appointment with History*. 1998.
Ford, Gerald R. *A Time to Heal: The Autobiography of Gerald R. Ford*. 1979.
Greene, John Robert. *The Limits of Power: The Nixon and Ford Administrations*. 1992.
———. *The Presidency of Gerald R. Ford*. 1995.
Hartmann, Robert. *Palace Politics: An Inside Account of the Ford Years*. 1980.
Hersey, John. *The President*. 1975.
Mollenhoff, Clark R. *The Man Who Pardoned Nixon*. 1976.
Reeves, Richard. *A Ford, Not a Lincoln*. 1976.
Rozell, Mark J. *The Press and the Ford Presidency*. 1992.
Schapsmeier, Edward L. *Gerald R. Ford's Date with Destiny: A Political Biography*. 1989.

FOREIGN POLICY

Bill, James A. *The Eagle and the Lion: The Tragedy of American-Iranian Relations.* 1988.

Blaufarb, D. S. *The Counterinsurgency Era: US Doctrine and Performance, 1950 to the Present.* 1977.

Buszynski, Leszet. *Soviet Foreign Policy and Southeast Asia.* 1986.

Cady, John. *The United States and Burma.* 1976.

Edmonds, Robin. *Soviet Foreign Policy, 1962–1973: The Paradox of a Superpower.* 1975.

Garthoff, Raymond. *Détente and Confrontation.* 1985.

Havens, Thomas R. *Fire Across the Sea: The Vietnam War and Japan.* 1987.

Holsti, Ole R., and James N. Rosenau. *American Leadership in World Affairs: Vietnam and the Breakdown of Consensus.* 1984.

Hsiao, Gene T., ed. *The Role of External Powers in Indochina.* 1973.

Isaacson, Walter. *Kissinger: A Biography.* 1992.

LaFeber, Walter. *The Panama Canal: The Crisis in Historical Perspective.* 1978.

Litwack, Robert. *Détente and the Nixon Doctrine.* 1984.

Kattenburg, Paul M. *The Vietnam Trauma in American Foreign Policy, 1945–1975.* 1980.

King, Peter, ed. *Australia's Vietnam.* 1983.

Kissinger, Henry A. *White House Years: The Memoirs of Henry A. Kissinger.* 1979.

———. *Years of Upheaval: The Memoirs of Henry A. Kissinger.* 1982.

Nelson, Keith. *The Making of Détente.* 1995.

Palmer, David R. *Summons of the Trumpet: US–Vietnam in Perspective.* 1978.

Papp, Daniel S. *Vietnam: The View from Moscow, Peking, Washington.* 1981.

Patti, Archimedes. *Why Vietnam? Prelude to America's Albatross.* 1981.

Pike, Douglas. *Vietnam and the Soviet Union: Anatomy of an Alliance.* 1987.

Porter, D. Gareth. *A Peace Denied: The United States, Vietnam, and the Paris Agreement.* 1976.

Quando, William B. *Camp David: Peacemaking and Politics.* 1989.

Rosenberger, Leif. *The Soviet Union and Vietnam: An Uneasy Alliance.* 1986.

Ross, Douglas A. *In the Interests of Peace: Canada and Vietnam, 1954–1973.* 1984.

Schulsinger, *Henry Kissinger: Doctor of Diplomacy.* 1989.

Shafer, D. Michael, ed. *The Legacy: The Vietnam War in the American Imagination.* 1990.

Smith, Gaddis. *Morality, Reason and Power.* 1986.

Sutter, Robert G. *Chinese Foreign Policy After the Cultural Revolution: 1966–1977.* 1978.

Talbot, Strobe. *Endgame: The Inside Story of SALT II.* 1979.

Taylor, Charles. *Snow Job: Canada, the United States and Vietnam (1954–1973).* 1974.

Zagoria, Donald S., ed. *Soviet Policy in East Asia.* 1983.

GAY POWER

Cruikshank, Margaret. *The Gay and Lesbian Liberation Movement.* 1992.

D'Emilio, John. *Sexual Politics, Sexual Communities: The Making of a Homosexual Minority in the United States, 1940–1970.* 1984.

Marcus, Eric. *Making History: The Struggle for Gay and Lesbian Equal Rights, 1945–1990, An Oral History.* 1992.
Shilts, Randy. *And the Band Played On: Politics, People, and the AIDS Epidemic.* 1987.

GENERAL BACKGROUND

Blum, John Morton. *Years of Discord: American Politics and Society, 1961–1974.* 1991.
Freeman, Jo, ed. *Social Movements of the Sixties and Seventies.* 1983.
Hodgson, Geoffrey. *America in Our Time.* 1976.
McQuaid, Kim. *The Anxious Years: America in the Vietnam-Watergate Era.* 1989.
Patterson, James T. *Grand Expectations: The United States, 1945–1974.* 1996.

HISPANIC AMERICANS

Abalos, David T. *Latinos in the United States: The Sacred and the Political.* 1987.
Balseiro, J. A., ed. *The Hispanic Presence in Florida: Yesterday and Today: 1513–1976.* 1977.
Boswell, Thomas D., and James R. Curtis. *The Cuban-American Experience: Culture, Images and Perspectives.* 1983.
Bourne, Peter G. *Fidel: A Biography of Fidel Castro.* 1986.
Cortés, Carlos E., ed. *The Cuban Exiles in the United States.* 1980.
———. *The Cuban Experience in the United States.* 1980.
———. *Cuban Refugee Programs.* 1980.
Cripps, Louise L. *The Spanish Caribbean: From Columbus to Castro.* 1979.
Domínguez, Jorge I. *Cuba: Order and Revolution.* 1978.
Fitzpatrick, Joseph P. *Puerto Rican Americans: The Meaning of Migration to the United States.* 1987.
Gallagher, Patrick Lee. *The Cuban Exile. A Socio-Political Analysis.* 1980.
Gann, L. H., and Peter J. Duignan. *The Hispanics in the United States: A History.* 1987.
Gernard, Renée. *The Cuban Americans.* 1988.
Gomez-Quinones, Juan. *Chicano Politics: Reality and Promise, 1940–1990.* 1990.
Griswold del Castillo, Richard. *La Familia: Chicano Families in the Urban Southwest, 1848 to the Present.* 1984.
Hendricks, Glenn. *The Dominican Diaspora: From the Dominican Republic to New York City, Villages in Transition.* 1974.
Horowitz, Ruth. *Honor and the American Dream: Culture and Identity in a Chicano Community.* 1983.
Llanas, José. *Cuban Americans: Masters of Survival.* 1982.
Maril, Robert Lee. *Poorest of Americans: The Mexican Americans of the Lower Rio Grande Valley of Texas.* 1989.
Masud-Piloto, Félix Roberto. *With Open Arms: Cuban Migration to the United States.* 1988.
Mormino, Gary R., and George E. Pozzetta. *The Immigrant World of Ybor City: Italians and Their Latin Neighbors in Tampa, 1885–1985.* 1987.
Padilla, Félix M. *Puerto Rican Chicago.* 1987.
Palmer, Ransford W. *In Search of a Better Life: Perspectives on Migration from the Caribbean.* 1990.

Paterson, Thomas G. *Contesting Castro: The United States and the Triumph of the Cuban Revolution.* 1994.
Pedraza-Bailey, Silvia. *Political and Economic Migrants in America: Cubans and Mexicans.* 1985.
Pérez, Louis A., Jr. *Cuba and the United States. Ties of Singular Intimacy.* 1991.
Portes, Alejandro, and Robert L. Bach. *Latin Journey: Cuban and Mexican Immigrants in the United States.* 1985.
Ridge, Martin. *The New Bilingualism: An American Dilemma.* 1981.
Rodriguez, Clara P. *Puerto Ricans: Born in the U.S.A.* 1989.
Romo, Ricardo. *East Los Angeles: History of a Barrio.* 1983.
Sanchez Jankowski, Martin. *City Bound: Urban Life and Political Attitudes Among Chicano Youth.* 1986.
Suchlicki, Jaime. *Cuba, from Columbus to Castro.* 1974.
Weyr, Thomas. *Hispanic U.S.A.: Breaking the Melting Pot.* 1988.

NATIVE AMERICANS

Barsh, Russel Lawrence, and James Youngblood Henderson. *The Road: Indian Tribes and Political Liberty.* 1980.
Berkhofer, Robert E., Jr. *The White Man's Indian: Images of the Indian from Columbus to the Present.* 1978.
Boldt, Menno. *Surviving as Indians: The Challenge of Self-Government.* 1994.
Burnette, Robert, and John Koster. *The Road to Wounded Knee.* 1974.
Burton, Lloyd. *American Indian Water Rights and the Limits of Law.* 1993.
Cadwalader, Sandra A., and Vine Deloria, Jr., eds. *The Aggressions of Civilization: Federal Indian Policy Since the 1880s.* 1984.
Churchill, Ward, and Jim Vander Wall. *Agents of Repression: The FBI's Secret Wars Against the Black Panther Party and the American Indian Movement.* 1988.
Cornell, Steven. *The Return of the Native: American Indian Political Resurgence,* 1988.
Deloria, Vine, Jr. *Behind the Trail of Broken Treaties.* 1974.
———. *Custer Died for Your Sins; An Indian Manifesto.* 1988.
———. *God Is Red.* 1973.
Dunbar Ortiz, Roxanne. *Indians of the Americas: Human Rights and Self-Determination.* 1984.
Forbes, Jack D. *Native Americans and Nixon: Presidential Politics and Minority Self-Determination, 1969–1972.* 1981.
Fortunate Eagle, Adam. *Alcatraz! Alcatraz! The Indian Occupation of 1969–1971.* 1992.
Friesen, Carol. *Disputed Jurisdiction and Recognition of Judgments Between Tribal and State Courts.* 1990.
Green, Donald E., and Thomas V. Tonnesen, eds. *American Indians: Social Justice and Public Policy.* 1991.
Greenberg, Pam, and Jody Zelio. *States and the Indian Gaming Regulatory Act.* 1992.
Gross, Emma R. *Contemporary Federal Policy Toward American Indians.* 1989.
Guillemin, Jeanne. *Urban Renegades: The Cultural Strategy of the American Indians.* 1975.
Hannum, Hurts. *Autonomy, Self-Determination and Sovereignty: The Accommodation of Conflicting Rights.* 1990.

Johnson, Troy R. *The Occupation of Alcatraz Island: Indian Self-Determination and the Rise of Indian Activism.* 1996.

Johnston, Basil H. *Indian School Days.* 1989.

Josephy, Alvin J., Jr. *Now That the Buffalo's Gone: A Study of Today's American Indians.* 1984.

———. *Red Power: The American Indians' Fight for Freedom.* 1971.

Levitan, Sar A., and William B. Johnson. *Indian Giving: Federal Programs for Native Americans.* 1979.

Lincoln, Kenneth. *Native American Renaissance.* 1983.

Lyden, Fremont J., and Lyman H. Legters, eds. *Native Americans and Public Policy.* 1992.

Mathiesson, Peter. *In the Spirit of Crazy Horse.* 1983.

McNickle, D'Arcy. *Native American Tribalism: Indian Survivals and Renewals.* 1973.

Means, Rusell. *Where White Men Fear to Tread.* 1995.

Meyer, William. *Native Americans: The New Indian Resistance.* 1971.

Nagel, Joane. *American Indian Ethnic Renewal: Red Power and the Resurgence of Identity and Culture.* 1995.

Parman, Donald L. *The Indians in the American West During the Twentieth Century.* 1994.

Pommershein, Frank. *Braid of Feathers: American Indian Law and Contemporary Tribal Life.* 1995.

Senese, Guy B. *Self-Determination and the Social Education of Native Americans.* 1977.

Stern, Kenneth S. *Loud Hawk: The United States and the American Indian Movement.* 1994.

Vizenor, Gerald. *Manifest Manners: Postindian Warriors of Survivance.* 1994.

Waddell, Jack O., and O. Michael Watson, eds. *The American Indian in Urban Society.* 1971.

Wells, Robert N., Jr., ed. *Native American Resurgence and Renewal.* 1994.

NEW LEFT

Bacciocco, Edward J. *The New Left in America: Reform to Revolution, 1956 to 1970.* 1974.

Bone, Christopher. *The Disinherited Children: A Study of the New Left and the Generation Gap.* 1977.

Buhle, Paul, ed. *History and the New Left: Madison, Wisconsin, 1950–1970.* 1989.

Gitlin, Todd. *The Whole World Is Watching: Mass Media in the Making and Unmaking of the New Left.* 1980.

Goode, Stephen. *Affluent Revolutionaries: A Portrait of the New Left.* 1974.

Lewy, Guenther. *Peace and Revolution: The Moral Crisis of American Pacifism.* 1988.

Myers, R. David, ed. *Toward a History of the New Left: Essays from Within the Movement.* 1989.

Rand, Ayn. *The New Left: The Anti-Industrial Revolution.* 1975.

Rothman, Stanley, and S. Robert Lichter. *Roots of Radicalism: Jews, Christians and the New Left.* 1982.

Sargent, Lyman Tower. *New Left Thought: An Introduction.* 1972.

Stolz, Matthew F., ed. *Politics of the New Left.* 1971.

Unger, Irwin, and Debi Unger. *The Movement: A History of the American New Left.* 1974.

Wald, Alan W. *Writing from the New Left: Essays on Radical Culture and Politics.* 1994.

Woods, James L. *New Left Ideology: Its Dimensions and Development.* 1975.

NIXON ADMINISTRATION

Ambrose, Stephen E. *Nixon: Ruin and Recovery, 1973–1990.* 1991.

Forbes, Jack D. *Native Americans and Nixon: Presidential Politics and Minority Self-Determination, 1969–1972.* 1981.

Green, John Robert. *The Limits of Power: The Nixon and Ford Administrations.* 1992.

Kissinger, Henry A. *White House Years.* 1979.

————. *Years of Upheaval.* 1979.

Nixon, Richard M. *RN: The Memoirs of Richard Nixon.* 1978.

Shawcross, William. *Sideshow: Kissinger, Nixon, and the Destruction of Cambodia.* 1979.

Szulc, Tad. *The Illusion of Peace: Foreign Policy in the Nixon Years.* 1978.

THE SOUTH

Bartley, Numan V., and Hugh D. Graham. *Southern Politics and the Second Reconstruction.* 1975.

Belknap, Michal R. *Federal Law and Southern Order: Racial Violence and Constitutional Conflict in the Post-Brown South.* 1987.

Black, Earl, and Merle Black. *Politics and Society in the South.* 1987.

Bloom, Jack. *Class, Race, and the Civil Rights Movement: The Political Economy of Southern Racism.* 1987.

Davidson, Chandler, and Bernard Grofman, eds. *Quiet Revolution in the South: The Impact of the Voting Rights Act, 1965–1990.* 1994.

Goldfield, David. *Black, White, and Southern: Race Relations and Southern Culture 1940 to the Present.* 1990.

Jacoway, Elizabeth, and David R. Colburn. *Southern Businessmen and Desegregation.* 1982.

Lawson, Stephen. *In Pursuit of Power: Southern Blacks and Electoral Politics, 1965–1982.* 1985.

————. *Running for Freedom: Civil Rights and Black Politics in America Since 1941.* 1991.

Lesher, Stephan. *George Wallace: American Populist.* 1994.

Parker, Frank. *Black Votes Count: Political Empowerment in Mississippi After 1965.* 1990.

VIETNAM WAR

Andrew, Bruce. *Public Constraint and American Policy in Vietnam.* 1976.

Appy, Christian. *Working-Class War: American Combat Soldiers and Vietnam.* 1993.

Arnett, Peter, and Michael Maclear. *The Ten Thousand Day War.* 1981.

Ball, George W. *The Past Has Another Pattern*. 1982.

Baral, Jaya. *The Pentagon and the Making of U.S. Foreign Policy*. 1978.

Baritz, Loren. *Backfire: A History of How American Culture Led Us into Vietnam and Made Us Fight the Way We Did*. 1984.

Barnet, Richard J. *Roots of War*. 1972.

Braestrup, Peter, ed. *Vietnam as History: Ten Years After the Paris Peace Accords*. 1984.

Brodie, Bernard. *War and Politics*. 1973.

Brown, MacAlister, and Joseph J. Zasloff. *Apprentice Revolutionaries: The Communist Movement in Laos, 1930–1985*. 1986.

Campagna, Anthony S. *The Economic Consequences of the Vietnam War*. 1991.

Capps, Walter H. *The Unfinished War: Vietnam and the American Conscience*. 1990.

Charlton, Michael, and Anthony Moncrief. *Many Reasons Why: The American Involvement in Vietnam*. 1978.

Davidson, Phillip B. *Vietnam at War: The History, 1945–1975*. 1988.

Dommen, Arthur J. *Conflict in Laos*. 1971.

―――. *Laos: The Keystone of Indochina*. 1985.

Donovan, John C. *The Cold Warriors: A Policy-Making Elite*. 1974.

Ellsberg, Daniel. *Papers on the War*. 1972.

Fincher, E. B. *The Vietnam War*. 1980.

FitzGerald, Francis. *Fire in the Lake: The Vietnamese and the Americans in Vietnam*. 1972.

Gelb, Lawrence, and Richard K. Betts. *The Irony of Vietnam: The System Worked*. 1979.

Graebner, Norman A. *Nationalism and Communism in Asia: The American Response*. 1977.

Grinter, Lawrence E., and Peter M. Dunne. *The American War in Vietnam: Lessons, Legacies, and Implications for Future Conflicts*. 1987.

Hartmann, Robert T. *Palace Politics: An Inside Account of the Ford Years*. 1980.

Heardon, Patrick H. *The Tragedy of Vietnam*. 1991.

Herring, George C. *America's Longest War: The United States and Vietnam, 1950–1975*. 1986.

Humphrey, Hubert H. *The Education of a Public Man: My Life and Politics*. 1976.

Isaacs, Arnold R. *Without Honor: Defeat in Vietnam and Cambodia*. 1983.

Isaacson, Walter, and Evan Thomas. *The Wise Men. Six Friends and the World They Made*. 1986.

Joes, Anthony J. *The War for South Vietnam: Nineteen Fifty-Four to Nineteen Seventy-Five*. 1989.

Karnow, Stanley. *Vietnam: A History*. 1984.

Kattenburg, Paul. *The Vietnam Trauma in American Foreign Policy, 1945–1975*. 1980.

Kendrick, Alexander. *The Wound Within: America in the Vietnam Years, 1945–1974*. 1974.

Kirk, Donald. *Wider War: The Struggle for Cambodia, Thailand, and Laos*. 1971.

Kissinger, Henry A. *White House Years*. 1979.

―――. *Years of Upheaval*. 1982.

Kolko, Gabriel. *Anatomy of a War: Vietnam, the United States, and the Modern Historical Experience*. 1985.

Krepinovich, Andrew F., Jr. *The Army and Vietnam*. 1986.

Lee, Sam. *The Perfect War*. 1990.

Lewy, Guenter. *America in Vietnam*. 1978.

Lodge, Henry Cabot. *The Storm Has Many Eyes: A Personal Narrative*. 1973.

Lomperis, Timothy J. *The War Everyone Lost—And Won: America's Intervention in Vietnam's Twin Struggles*. 1984.

Louis, William Roger. *Imperialism at Bay: The United States and the Decolonization of the British Empire*. 1978.

Manhattan, Avro. *Vietnam: Why Did We Go?* 1984.

McCloud, Bill. *What Should We Tell Our Children About Vietnam?* 1990.

McLaughlin, Martin. *Vietnam and World Revolution: A Trotskyite Analysis*. 1985.

McQuaid, Kim. *The Anxious Years: America in the Vietnam-Watergate Era*. 1989.

Millett, Allan R., ed. *A Short History of the Vietnam War*. 1978.

Morrison, Wilbur. *Vietnam: The Winnable War*. 1990.

Moss, George. *Vietnam. An American Ordeal*. 1989.

Nickelsen, Harry. *Vietnam*. 1989.

Nixon, Richard M. *1999 Victory Without War*. 1988.

————. *No More Vietnams*. 1980.

————. *The Real War*. 1980.

————. *RN: The Memoirs of Richard Nixon*. 1978.

Olson, James S., and Randy Roberts. *Where the Domino Fell: America and Vietnam, 1945–1990*. 1991.

Osborne, Milton. *Before Kampuchea: Preludes to Tragedy*. 1979.

Palmer, Bruce, Jr. *The Twenty-Five Year War: America's Military Role in Vietnam*. 1984.

Palmer, Dave. *Summons of the Trumpet: America and Vietnam in Perspective*. 1978.

Patti, Archimedes L. *Why Vietnam? Prelude to America's Albatross*. 1981.

Podhoretz, Norman. *Why We Were in Vietnam*. 1982.

Poole, Peter. *Eight Presidents and Indochina*. 1978.

Ravenal, Earl C. *Never Again: Learning from America's Foreign Policy Failures*. 1978.

Reeves, Richard. *A Ford, Not a Lincoln*. 1976.

Rose, Lisle Abbott. *Roots of Tragedy: The United States and the Struggle for Asia, 1945–1953*. 1976.

Rostow, W. W. *The Diffusion of Power, 1957–1972*. 1972.

Salisbury, Harrison, ed. *Vietnam Reconsidered: Lessons from a War*. 1984.

Schulzinger, Robert. *A Time for War: The United States and Vietnam, 1941–1975*. 1997.

Shawcross, William. *The Quality of Mercy: Cambodia, Holocaust, and Modern Conscience*. 1984.

————. *Sideshow: Kissinger, Nixon, and the Destruction of Cambodia*. 1979.

Sharp, Melvin. *The Vietnam War and Public Policy*. 1991.

Sharp, U.S.G. *Strategy for Defeat: Vietnam in Retrospect*. 1978.

Sheehan, Neil. *The Bright and Shining Lie: John Paul Vann and America in Vietnam*. 1988.

Short, Anthony. *The Origins of the Vietnam War*. 1989.

Stevenson, Charles A. *The End of Nowhere: American Policy Toward Laos Since 1954*. 1972.

Sullivan, Michael P. *The Vietnam War: A Study in the Making of American Foreign Policy*. 1985.

Summers, Harry G., Jr. *On Strategy: A Critical Analysis of the Vietnam War*. 1982.

Szulc, Tad. *The Illusion of Peace: Foreign Policy in the Nixon Years*. 1978.

Thayer, Thomas. *Vietnam: War Without Fronts*. 1985.

Turley, William S. *The Second Indochina War: A Short Political and Military History, 1945–1975*. 1986.

Young, Marilyn. *The Vietnam Wars, 1945–1990*. 1991.

VIETNAM WAR IN LITERATURE

Anisfield, Nancy, ed. *Vietnam Anthology: American War Literature*. 1985.

Baritz, Loren. *Backfire: A History of How American Culture Led Us into Vietnam and Made Us Fight the Way We Did*. 1985.

Ehrhart, W. D., ed. *Carrying the Darkness: The Poetry of the Vietnam War*. 1989.

Heath, G. Lewis, ed. *Mutiny Does Not Happen Lightly: The Literature of the American Resistance to the Vietnam War*. 1976.

Lewis, Lloyd B. *The Tainted War: Culture and Identity in Vietnam War Narratives*. 1985.

Lomperis, Timothy J., and John Clark Pratt, eds. *Reading the Wind: The Literature of the Vietnam War*. 1987.

Louvre, Alf, and Jeffrey Walsh, eds. *Tell Me Lies About Vietnam: Cultural Battles for the Meaning of the War*. 1988.

Melling, Philip H. *Vietnam in American Literature*. 1990.

Myers, Thomas. *Walking Point: American Narratives of Vietnam*. 1988.

Newman, John. *Vietnam War Literature*. 1982.

Walsh, Jeffrey, and James Aulich, eds. *Vietnam Images: War and Representation*. 1989.

Wilson, James C. *Vietnam in Prose and Film*. 1982.

WATERGATE

Ambrose, Stephen E. *Nixon: Ruin and Recovery, 1973–1990*. 1991.

Drew, Elizabeth. *Washington Journal*. 1974.

Green, John Robert. *The Limits of Power: The Nixon and Ford Administrations*. 1992.

Kutler, Stanley. *The Wars of Watergate*. 1990.

Lukas, J. Anthony. *The Breaking of a President: The Nixon Connection*. 1975.

Schell, Jonathan. *The Time of Illusion*. 1976.

Schudson, Michael. *Watergate in American Memory: How We Remember, Forget, and Reconstruct the Past*. 1992.

White, Theodore H. *Breach of Faith*. 1975.

WOMEN

Baker, Mark. *Nam: The Vietnam War in the Words of the Men and Women Who Fought There*. 1981.

Emerson, Gloria. *Winners and Losers: Battles, Retreats, Gains, Losses, and Ruins from a Long War*. 1977.

Evans, Sara. *Personal Politics: The Roots of Women's Liberation in the Civil Rights Movement and the New Left*. 1979.

Freedman, Dan, and Jacqueline Rhoads. *Nurses in Vietnam: The Forgotten Veterans*. 1987.

Freeman, Jo. *The Politics of Women's Liberation*. 1979.

Giddings, Paula. *When and Where I Enter: The Impact of Black Women on Race and Sex in America*. 1984.

Holm, Jeanne. *Women in the Military: An Unfinished Revolution*. 1982.

Jeffords, Susan. *The Remasculinization of America: Gender and the Vietnam War*. 1989.

Marshall, Kathryn. *In the Combat Zone: An Oral History of American Women in Vietnam*. 1987.

Norman, Elizabeth. *Women at War: The Story of Fifty Military Nurses Who Served in Vietnam*. 1990.

Saywell, Shelley. *Women in War*. 1985.

Skolnick, Arlene. *Embattled Paradise: The American Family in an Age of Uncertainty*. 1991.

Walker, Kieth. *A Piece of My Heart: The Stories of 26 American Women Who Served in Vietnam*. 1985.

Walsh, Patricia L. *Forever Sad the Hearts*. 1982.

Index

About the Contributors

MARK BAXTER is a doctoral candidate in the history department at the University of Colorado at Boulder.

AIMEE BOBRUK is an undergraduate student at the North Carolina School of the Arts in Winston-Salem, North Carolina.

SAMUEL FREEMAN is a political scientist at the University of Texas, Pan American, in Edinburgh, Texas.

FRANCES FRENZEL teaches history in the public schools of Madisonville, Texas.

BRADFORD K. GATHRIGHT is an undergraduate student at Rice University in Houston, Texas.

DANIEL HARRIS is a medical student at the University of Texas Medical School in Houston, Texas.

JERRY JAY INMON is a graduate student in the parks and recreation program at Texas A&M University in College Station, Texas.

TROY JOHNSON is a historian at California State University, Long Beach, in Long Beach, California.

SEAN A. KELLEHER is a political scientist at the University of Texas at the Permian Basin in Odessa, Texas.

CHARLOTTE MEADOWS manages a Publishers' Warehouse bookstore in Willis, Texas.

TIMOTHY MORGAN is a member of the history department at Christopher Newport University in Newport News, Virginia.

CAROL NGUYEN is an undergraduate student at the University of Texas at Austin.

BRADLEY A. OLSON is an undergraduate student at the University of Pennsylvania in Philadelphia, Pennsylvania.

JAMES S. OLSON is distinguished professor of history at Sam Houston State University in Huntsville, Texas.

JUDITH E. OLSON teaches in the college of education at Sam Houston State University in Huntsville, Texas.

ROBERT L. PERRY teaches political science at the University of Texas of the Permian Basin in Odessa, Texas.

DAVID RITCHEY teaches at the Spring Creek campus of Collin County Community College in Plano, Texas.

JOSEPH M. ROWE, JR., is professor of history at Sam Houston State University in Huntsville, Texas.

ANNE G. WOODWARD is an undergraduate student at Southwestern University in Georgetown, Texas.